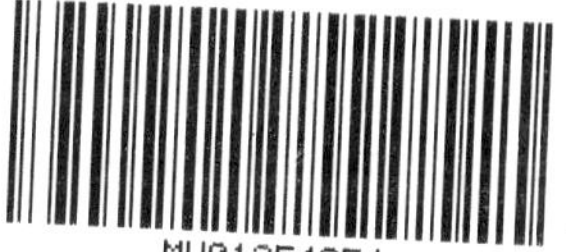

Praise for Fat Studies in Ca

"A brilliant and unapologet... field of fat studies in Canada. These skilfully curated essays expose the dynamics of fat oppression and liberation through cutting-edge research, critical theory, and the lived experiences of fat people. With a strong emphasis on intersectionality, this volume is a must-read for those looking to deepen their understanding of queer, feminist, crip, or critical race theory. The incorporation of art and poetry captures a full emotional range of fat embodiment, including anger, eroticism, and joy. Whether you're a seasoned fat activist or just starting out, this essential volume will enlighten you about what it means to be fat in Canada."

—**Margaret Robinson**, Associate Professor and Tier 2 Canada Research Chair in Reconciliation, Gender, and Identity

"These chapters weave a tapestry of theoretical, personal, and embodied responses to the provocation of what it means to be fat in Canada. Most (perhaps all) of the contributions could stand alone as articles or poems; together, they generate an intensity of thought and feeling that I've rarely observed in volumes of this kind. This volume stands to make a critical contribution across teaching and learning contexts, as well as to kickstart further theorizing around fatness, particularly situated, localized, and intersectional experiences of fatness. I find myself writing these general thoughts with mostly a round of applause running through my head as I meditate on the words so generously offered herein."

—**Andrea LaMarre**, PhD

"This powerful, path-breaking anthology brings together emerging and established leaders in the field of fat studies from across the area of Turtle Island known as 'Canada,' applying intersectional and decolonizing perspectives to fat experience, identity, and embodiment. Through accessible and engaging social and cultural analysis, innovative theoretical and methodological explorations, and compelling poetry and visual art, contributors address the structural and affective implications of fat oppression while opening and expanding possibilities for fat joy, desire, and liberation."

—**Dr. Carla Rice**, Professor and Tier 1 Canada Research Chair in Feminist Studies and Social Practice; Founding Director, Re•Vision: The Centre for Art and Social Justice, University of Guelph; Principal Investigator & Co-Director, Bodies in Translation: Activist Art, Technology and Access to Life

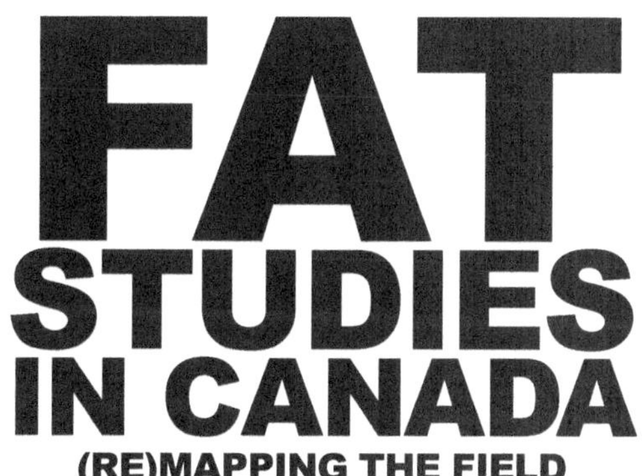
FAT
STUDIES
IN CANADA
(RE)MAPPING THE FIELD

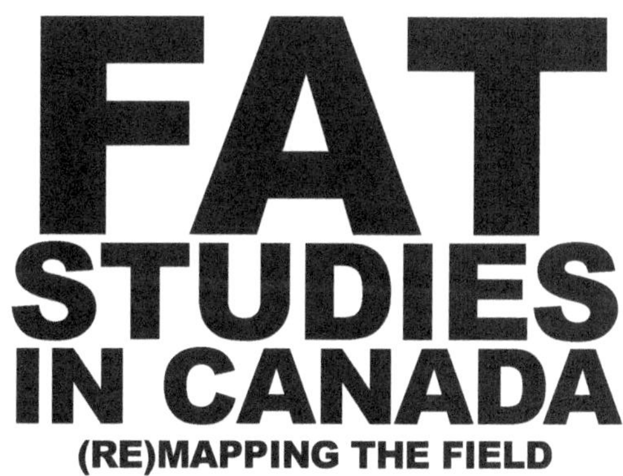

Edited by Allison Taylor, Kelsey Ioannoni,
Ramanpreet A. Bahra, Calla Evans,
Amanda Scriver, and May Friedman

INANNA
PUBLICATIONS & EDUCATION INC.
TORONTO, ONTARIO, CANADA
www.inanna.ca

Copyright © 2023 Inanna Publications & Education, Inc.

Individual copyright to their work is retained by the authors. Except for the use of short passages for review purposes, no part of this book may be reproduced, in part or in whole, or transmitted in any form or by any means, electronically or mechanically, including photocopying, recording, or any information or storage retrieval system,without prior permission in writing from the publisher or a licence from the Canadian Copyright Collective Agency (Access Copyright).

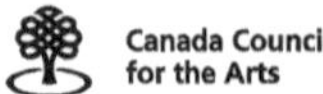

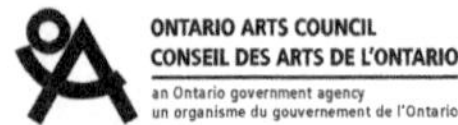

We gratefully acknowledge the support of the Canada Council for the Arts and the Ontario Arts Council for our publishing program. We also acknowledge the financial support of the Government of Canada.

Note from the publisher: Care has been taken to trace the ownership of copyright material used in this book. The author and the publisher welcome any information enabling them to rectify any references or credits in subsequent editions.

Front cover design: Val Fullard
Cover Image: Leslie Walters

Library and Archives Canada Cataloguing in Publication
Title: Fat studies in Canada : (re)mapping the field / edited by Allison Taylor, Kelsey Ioannoni, Ramanpreet Annie Bahra, Calla Evans, Amanda Scriver, and May Friedman.
Names: Taylor, Allison (Allison E.), editor. | Ioannoni, Kelsey, editor. | Bahra, Ramanpreet Annie, editor. | Evans, Calla, editor. | Scriver, Amanda, editor. | Friedman, May, 1975- editor.
Description: Includes bibliographical references.
Identifiers: Canadiana (print) 20230141870 | Canadiana (ebook) 2023014196X | ISBN 9781771339483 (softcover) | ISBN 9781771339506 (PDF) | ISBN 9781771339490 (EPUB)
Subjects: LCSH: Obesity—Social aspects—Canada. | LCSH: Overweight persons—Canada.
Classification: LCC RA645.O23 F38 2023 | DDC 362.1963/9800971—dc23

Printed and Bound in Canada.

Published in Canada by
Inanna Publications and Education Inc.
210 Founders College, York University
4700 Keele Street, Toronto, Ontario M3J 1P3
Telephone: (416) 736-5356 Fax (416) 736-5765
Email: inanna.publications@inanna.ca Website: www.inanna.ca

We dedicate this book to Drs. Crystal Kotow and Cat Pausé, who passed away during its writing.

Dr. Crystal Kotow was a leader in fat studies in Canada whose heart was as big as her brain. She modelled fat joy, kindness, and vulnerability, living life on her own terms. Crystal made this world a better place for everyone she knew, especially for fat people.

Dr. Cat Pausé was a fat studies legend. Her prolific scholarship and activism created a global fat studies community. We owe so much to Cat's brilliance, generosity, and vision for fat liberation.

May they rest in power.

CONTENTS

Mappings, Methods, and Innovations

Fattening Popular Culture

Medical Encounters

Desiring Fatness

Alternative Frameworks and Imaginings

Acknowledgments

THE EDITORIAL TEAM would like to thank Inanna Publications for making the edited collection of our dreams a reality. Thank you for the opportunity to create this book and for your support throughout the process. In particular, we would like to thank Inanna's late editor in chief, Luciana Ricciutelli, who first saw potential in our vision. We hope this collection honours her enduring legacy of fighting for social change. We would also like to extend our sincerest gratitude to the two scholars who reviewed this collection for us. Your feedback was invaluable to strengthening this anthology. We want to acknowledge, too, the time, labour, thought, and brilliance Sonia Meerai lent to this book in its early stages, especially in making sure this collection not only made space for, but centred, BIPOC engagements with fatness. Thank you also to Karen Taylor, our incredible copyeditor, for her meticulous and care-full editing of this collection. Finally, to all the contributors to this anthology, your writings, stories, and creative expressions make this book what it is. Thank you for sharing your experiences, vulnerabilities, and hopes for fat futures.

Ramanpreet would like to share her sincerest thanks to the editorial team—Allison, Kelsey, Calla, May, and Amanda—you have continued to foster tenderness, vulnerability, and community with me and the collective in this collection, making this such a memorable project to be on. Additionally, I would like to thank my dear friends who stand in solidarity with fat politics and for opening space for me to share a dialogue on fatness at the intersections. Last but not least, I would like to acknowledge and share my love for my mother, Narinder Bahra. Your strength and resiliency in this reclaiming of our fat, brown flesh has been core to our transformative fat-assemblage. For you, your love, and lessons I am forever thankful: "*door kari na dheeyan to maavan.*"

Calla would like to express her unending gratitude to the editorial team for fostering a space in which we could weather the storms and celebrate our wins together. Special thanks to May Friedman for her excellent guidance, mentorship, and tenderness. Big fat love to all of my fellow fat friends, fat activists, and those simply existing in fat bodies day to day. Thank you for imagining a different fat experience in Canada and around the world. Through radical care and community, the change will come.

May would like to thank Alli, Amanda, Kelsey, Calla, and Ramanpreet for their collective gorgeous brilliance. This has been such a labour of love and community, and I'm so grateful to share space with all of you! Special thanks in addition to Sonia Meerai for her dedication and determination. Finally, as always, my thanks to my people, big and small, for keeping me grounded. My orientation to the future is so bound up in the people I care about, and I am immensely lucky to live in networks of love and care.

Kelsey would like to thank the amazing editorial team for all its members' hard work and dedication to this collection. Collaborating with you all has been a highlight of my academic career thus far. I appreciate my friends and colleagues for their support throughout the creation of this anthology. I want to acknowledge the fat studies scholars who have come before us, paving the road for both this collection and my own personal journey to fat acceptance. Finally, to my beautiful son, being your fat mom makes me the happiest version of myself.

Ama would like to thank the entire editorial collective, including Alli, Calla, Kelsey, May, and Ramanpreet. Not only did you provide mental and emotional support through the pandemic, but you made editing a whole-ass anthology fun! You're all such wonderful individuals, and I'm so glad we had the opportunity to work together and share this space with one another. Ama would also like to thank River and Ocean, Ama's chosen family and the best friends in the whole wide world. Throughout the years, you have all played varying roles in my life: from guiding light, to cheerleader, to project manager. You've kept me strong, motivated, and most of all, humble. Without all of you, I would not be where I am today. Thank you for supporting me, day in and day out. You have all made it possible for me to chase my dreams, and pursue my passions. So today, forever, and always: I love you all, and thank you for being my number one hype squad.

Allison would like to thank her fabulous co-editors—Amanda, Calla, Kelsey, May, and Ramanpreet—for their hard work, support, and brilliance in envisioning, creating, and publishing this anthology. You've provided vital fat kinship throughout this process. During a time when fat joy and community have felt scarce and fat life has felt precarious, you have sustained me and given me hope. I would also like to thank my larger community of fat scholars, activists, artists, and friends who showed me that there was a different way to live as a fat person and who inspire me with their beautiful fat lives and commitments to fat liberation. Finally, to my chosen and blood family (you know who you are): thank you for loving, supporting, and seeing the best in me, and making spaces in this world where I can be fully myself in all of my queer, fat, femme, disabled radiance.

Foreword

Jill Andrew

Fat Studies in Canada: (Re)Mapping the Field foregrounds the voices of fat studies scholars, activists, scholar-activists, organizers, creatives, and others dismantling "eurothincentricity" who live and work in Canada as they geographically situate themselves through theories and praxis of fat and fatness. I am a Black fat queer cisgender woman living and working here in Canada and more specifically in Tkaronto, the original name of the city of "Toronto," on Indigenous land. Everyday and systemic legacies of white supremacy and colonialism, among other systems of intersecting oppression entrenched in institutions, namely health care, education, and the "justice" system, play out disproportionately on bodies made marginalized such as fat; Black; Indigenous; racialized; 2SLGBTQIA+; seniors; people experiencing poverty, mental health, and addiction; and people with disabilities.

Toronto is Ontario's most populous city and is ranked as one of the most diverse in the world. However, its diversity and zest for multiculturalism has not freed our fat bodies from dominant narratives and tropes of disease, laziness, lack of control, aggression, and the stubborn assumption of fat corporeality "eating up" economy and strained resources—this even as the truest culprits of greed and gluttony are reflective of a capitalist system that feeds on people for its own gain and quickly recycles those of us deemed unproductive or unredeemable. Documenting Canada-based voices in fat resistance and theorizing is crucial so we may trouble dangerous constructions of fat as pathology and otherness, and instead posit deeper understandings of fatness functioning as both material and socio-cultural constructs.

The fat studies and advocacy canon has predominantly told the story of fat American politics, movements, and scholarship. It has mostly centred the voices of fat white women and white scholars. It was in Brooklyn, New York, that I stumbled upon Rothblum and Solovay's *The Fat Studies Reader* while at the checkout inside Re/Dress NYC, a now permanently closed consignment shop and vintage boutique for fatshionistas. This was almost a decade after I encountered Solovay's *Tipping the Scales of Justice: Fighting Weight-Based Discrimination* and Braziel and LeBesco's *Bodies Out of Bounds: Fatness and Transgression* at the also permanently closed Toronto Women's Bookstore here in Ontario. Today, these seminal texts and others, including resources from National Association to Advance Fat Acceptance (NAAFA) such as the association's size diversity and child advocacy toolkits, reside on my bookshelf with my bourgeoning youthful fat joy scribbles in ink, highlighter, and dog-eared pages throughout (see https://naafa.org/brocheng1). In these readings, I stumbled on one aha moment after another as the texts unfolded and reimagined fatness away from binaries of good and bad. These texts, albeit heavily American, and others helped me begin to chart my intellectual journey as a young Black woman post-secondary student trying to hone my voice.

Currently, I work in politics. I am a member of provincial Parliament (MPP) in the Legislative Assembly of Ontario (Queen's Park) serving my community of Toronto—St. Paul's and the many other communities that have helped sustain me. My Blackness, fatness, and queerness are deeply personal and political identities, and they are inextricably linked to my lived experience and how people choose to see and read me or not in the legislature and in my communities as an elected official. My intersectional personhood is a politicized embodiment. As I walk into the Legislative Assembly of Ontario's Queen's Park building, which opened its physical doors on April 4, 1893, its very bones, its architecture, and the very paintings hanging on its walls are the antithesis of me. Fatness and Blackness, let alone queerness, are political and material disruptions of dominant "normalized" body ideals. They "dis-ease" whiteness, patriarchy, and heteronormativity. As Sabrina Strings demonstrates in

Fearing the Black Body: The Racial Origins of Fat Phobia, fat was initially praised in the arts and scientific literature but over time, through the Enlightenment era and beyond, fatness conflated with racial inferiority was used as a vessel to promote misogynoir and classism against fat Black women's bodies. Andrea Elizabeth Shaw's *The Embodiment of Disobedience: Fat Black Women's Unruly Political Bodies* also explores how the African diaspora has sought to resist Eurocentric erasures of Black beauty and womanhood. It is the very reason that—despite the often unsettling nature of the legislature, its obtuse language and hidden curriculum meant to confuse, frustrate, and exclude people like me, not to mention the visceral reactions chamber debates often provoke—my presence in the legislature and similarly the presence of other historically underrepresented bodies after I am long gone will be crucial. As the saying goes, if you are not at the table, you are on the menu.

Fat Studies in Canada and its Canada-based predecessors—including Ellison, McPhail, and Mitchinson's *Obesity in Canada: Critical Perspectives*; Friedman, Rice, and Rinaldi's *Thickening Fat: Fat Bodies, Intersectionality, and Social Justice*; Ellison's *Being Fat: Women, Weight, and Feminist Activism in Canada*; and more recently Andrew and Friedman's *Body Stories: In and Out and With and Through Fat*—help lay the foundation for mapping multi-dimensional fat identities and narratives across Canada as a scholarly, creative, justice-seeking act. There continues to be a significant need for more intersectional fat scholarship centring Canada-based Black, Indigenous, POC, and ethnic voices, and this is especially true as fat embodiment is shaped and reshaped against the tyranny of border politics and citizenship; heteropatriarchy; class stratification; anti-Black, anti-Indigenous, and anti-Asian racism; antisemitism; Islamophobia; food insecurity; the affordability crisis; healthism; and lack of access to the basic human right of clean drinking water, among others. Intersectional, anti-oppressive fat scholarship provides opportunity for highlighting significant differences across our fat communities while making room to explore the commonalities from which we can form alliances in solidarity to combat intersectional fat hate.

Fat Studies in Canada does not shy away from race and racism. It also transparently addresses its limitations. This is refreshing. Despite what some may call a current "global reckoning" with regards to white supremacy and colonization, as well as their and other intentional attempts to disenfranchise BIPOC folks, there are still some for whom hiding their heads in the sand like ostriches remains their happy place. As a result, *Fat Studies in Canada* creates safe(r) space for our storytelling. It creates opportunity for our fat vitality. My first private member's bill, Bill 61, which passed unanimously in the legislature, proclaimed the first week of February annually as Eating Disorders Awareness Week (EDAW). The success of my bill was deeply rooted in the support of Toronto—St. Paul's community members across party lines and of several leading organizations across Ontario and Canada, including the National Eating Disorders Information Centre (NEDIC), Sheena's Place, Body Brave, Bulimia Anorexia Nervosa Association (BANA), and the National Initiative for Eating Disorders (NIED), among others. Most important were the personal stories of survivors of eating disorders and body-based discrimination steeped in sexism in health care, racism, and fat phobia, or what I refer to as a trifecta of hate. Eating disorders have for far too long been linked exclusively to white, heterosexual, middle-class, post-secondary educated women. These assumptions are deeply rooted in heteronormative and racist assumptions that perpetuate the stereotypical image of the Strong Black Woman as impenetrable, which subsequently makes the concerns of Black women and girls largely irrelevant to eating disorders research. It is also based on eating disorders research that has largely ignored the community-based qualitative experiences of BIPOC women and girls, queer, trans, and gender nonconforming folks, as well as service providers and racialized others. Scientific research on eating disorders has also been largely void of culturally relevant questions, research methodologies, and most important, overrepresented by scientists and health care providers who are predominantly white and male in the field. My Bill 61, albeit a starting point and by no means a complete solution, builds education and awareness and recognizes that, in fact, it is Black, Indigenous, racialized, fat, and 2SLGBTQIA+

people who are developing eating disorders at alarming rates compared to our overall population. Not only are eating disorders a mental health condition with one of the highest mortality rates, but they are also developed in response to systemic oppressions such as gender-based violence, intimate partner violence, poverty, racism, homophobia, and transphobia.

This edited collection invites its contributors and arguably its readers to ponder the following questions as they consider the trajectory of fat studies as a field of research in Canada: How can we begin to map the field of fat Canadian studies in Canada? What makes the work of Canadian fat scholars in Canada unique? How does the "Canadian" fat identity define itself, and how is it constructed, reflected, and resisted in our cultural and political landscapes? And, what does the future of fat Canadian studies in Canada hold? These questions are anchored by the key themes explored, including "Structural Fat Oppression"; "Mappings, Methods, and Innovations"; "Fattening Popular Culture"; "Medical Encounters"; "Desiring Fatness"; and lastly "Alternative Frameworks and Imaginings."

Before exploring its research aims and key themes, *Fat Studies in Canada* begins by centralizing fat experience—living fat in Canada. For some, this is a radical act because most often our fat bodies are talked about. We are not often afforded the opportunity to story ourselves into fat scholarship, especially with stories of fat joy, fat sexuality, fat desire, or even fat hatred within fat communities. Our stories are not all heroic, they do not all have happy or respectable endings, and our acceptance and liberation is not one size fits all. We need to be able to tell messy, complicated, and non-linear fat stories without fear of being policed. This is how we begin to decolonize fatness and, in turn, fat studies. It is how we bring our fat selves and our fat politics in focus with the spaces, places, and policies that help shape our lives.

We cannot disaggregate our bodies from the world in which we live or vice versa, and therefore it is prudent that decision makers recognize their responsibility to support the implementation of policy that creates and invests in the social conditions necessary to support all our diverse bodies—including fat bodies. The neoliberal "boot strap" self-help ideology is painstakingly wrong. It excuses structural oppression, evades intersectionality, and places all the blame and shame of so-called "failure" on the shoulders of individuals. It is in this ideological vein that fatphobia and fat-hatred flourish. It makes the collection of voices in *Fat Studies in Canada: (Re)Mapping the Field* that much more critical at this particular juncture in world history where fat bodies have again been targeted and pathologized by many albeit hard-working health care professionals who in some cases questioned whether or not fat bodies "deserved" ventilators or life-saving interventions during the COVID-19 pandemic. Similar concerns have been raised by people with disabilities and by disability advocates who warned of a "second-class citizenship" being applied to disability community members during the pandemic who feared they would not pass the test of human value if ventilators were limited and it was them versus "able-bodied" citizens requiring medical intervention. Situating fat studies in Canada as a social and political project allows for a closer look at legislative changes that can serve to further amplify, uplift, and protect fat bodies. Instead of positioning fat and fatness as "disabling" embodiments, this anthology challenges us to remember our bodies are not the problem. We must focus attention on a problematic society that has a penchant for disabling and discrediting bodies through spatial discrimination, ableism, and archaic scientific tools based in racism and sexism, such as the body mass index (BMI).

Today in Canada, there are no laws against size, weight, or shape discrimination. There are no laws protecting us against fatphobia. While there has been some discussion of viewing "obesity" as a disability deserving of protection under the Canadian Human Rights Act, this policy proposition has not been adopted into legislation and is therefore currently moot. Without ignoring the well-documented problematics of the term "obesity" to begin with, such a proposed policy shift would depend on the further medicalizing, stigmatizing, and categorizing of fat bodies as "obese" via the discredited BMI in order to grant protective rights in situations where size is deemed a barrier to a person's performance on the job. "Uncategorized" fat and other materially subversive bodies are arguably excluded from this equation and left to the subjective treatment of fat-hating employers, doctors, landlords, and educators, for instance, leaving people without legal recourse. My partner Aisha Fairclough and I, working through our advocacy group Body Confidence Canada, which is home to the Body Confidence Canada Awards (BCCAs) and Body Confidence Awareness Week (an event recognized by two of the largest school boards in Canada), created a Change.org petition campaign #SizeismSUCKS several years ago. It garnered approximately 40,000 signatures at its peak across several provinces and joint petitions to get size and weight included in Canada's human rights legislation and, subsequently, Ontario's Human Rights Code as prohibited grounds for discrimination. We wanted to eliminate appearance-based discrimination. This remains a dream deferred but one that is still strongly supported by many who recognize what legislated protections against size, weight, shape, and fat phobia would mean for our lives. As I said in my 2014 TEDxYorkU talk "Fat Shaming & the Thin Epidemic," fat is a description and not a prescription for hate. Our fat lives are multi-dimensional, strong and weak, progressive and flawed, but above all they are absolutely worth living *and* loving. *Fat Studies in Canada: (Re)Mapping the Field* destabilizes long-held assumptions about fat. It instead provides the launch pad for unlearning and relearning fatness, reimagining the social, cultural, and political meanings of fat identities while pushing us towards theorizing and practising fatness far beyond reductive bounds.

This is an exciting collection, and it is right on time.

Introduction: Our Fat Liminal Grounds

Ramanpreet A. Bahra, Calla Evans, Kelsey Ioannoni, and Allison Taylor

The field of fat studies has grown in unimaginable ways across the globe, fattening our knowledges and exposing us to lived experiences of fatness, anti-fat narratives, and fat liberatory practices across populations and nations. As an interdisciplinary area of scholarship, its theoretical currents of fat-knowledges surrounding fat resistance and liberation allow academic and activist voices to emerge in a multitude of ways to share the realities of fatphobia and its interlocking systems of oppression while also advocating for social change. However, while working towards unfolding our fat rolls, we find some fat experiences pushed to the margins, silenced, and erased entirely. In one of the final chapters of *The Fat Studies Reader* (Rothblum and Solovay), British fat studies scholar Charlotte Cooper posits that "perhaps fat studies should be called fat American studies," due to the overwhelming influence of the United States on the field of fat studies and the seemingly well-established and well-connected networks of fat activists found in that country (327). In the years since Cooper's ringing of this geographic alarm bell, fat studies as an academic field has grown and expanded in important and necessary ways. There has been critical attention paid to diversifying the fat voices heard and the fat experiences amplified by the field. In terms of specific national experiences of fat oppression, *Fat Studies in the UK* (Tomrley and Naylor) stands alone as a key text examining discourses and experiences of fatness and fatphobia in an alternative national context. Thus, it is impossible to ignore how the academic field of fat studies remains largely focused on the fat experience in the United

States (US), and voices outside of the US are once again left out of dominant narratives of fat embodiment, including voices from Canada.

However, before we address the larger scope, themes, and questions of this collection, we first need to acknowledge the constructed, contested, and violent history of the land that many now call "Canada." As Jen Rinaldi, Carla Rice, and May Friedman remind us, we cannot present a dialogue on fatness without thinking about "the colonized landscape" and the structures of oppression that continue to play a large part in the marginalization of Indigenous nations across these lands (1). Thus, Canada, itself, is a colonial construction. We must also consider the added layers of misogynoir and anti-Blackness within larger institutions, as we see the intermingling of the regimes of racism, heterosexism, and fatphobia as fat Black flesh is read via a different lens, one not as a separate category but, as Marta Usiekniewicz and Da'Shaun L. Harrison in their individual texts argue, as a part of Blackness itself. We recognize that the marginalization of Black, Indigenous, and otherly racialized communities is not a chapter of the past as the violence and barriers of white settler colonialism remain intact and fully functioning. We also recognize that fatphobia and weight policing is one of the tools of these systems of control and suppression. With our use of the terms "Canada" and "Canadian" in this collection, we acknowledge how this contentious national identity is constantly used to mark populations and unleash violence onto those that do not fit within its exclusionary, narrow boundaries. We witness this through the policing of Indigenous women and children and the unearthing of their murdered bodies; the lack of access to systems such as food, health care, social services, and law; and the cultural and literal death of Indigenous and Black people. We also acknowledge the resilience of Indigenous nations and their critical efforts towards decolonizing cultures, languages, communities, and the body itself.

All the editors of this collection are settlers on this land, and, as such, we are compelled to remind our readers that no form of oppression can be interrogated without considering the operationalization of the systems of white supremacy

and colonization that continue to be present in Tu
Therefore, a central aim with this collection is to inv
experiences and oppressions in Canada as they are ir
and intersect with anti-Indigenous and anti-Black racism. This collection offers analyses of the ways in which dominant and oppressive conceptions of fatness in Canada are inextricably tied to settler colonialism and white supremacy, positioning fatphobia as bound up with these other violent structures of oppression (see chapters by Bonnell, Cunningham, McPhail) and, thus, opening space to reflect on Indigenous and decolonial ways of thinking about and embodying fatness. Ultimately, as editors, we wish to acknowledge the fraught project of theorizing fat studies in "Canada" and, with this collection, position the Canadian state as inherently violent and built upon the oppression of Black, Indigenous, and otherly racialized communities. Moreover, as editors, we each experience fatness at the intersections of other marginalized positions and acknowledge how difficult and emotionally taxing it can be to do fat studies work. As fat people who have experienced the tyranny of anti-fat dialectics; the denial of our lives spatially, medically, or temporally; and overall erasure, we understand that pieces in this collection can open us up to the pain of the past. Yet we also recognize the multiple ways we have found pleasure, both in utilizing fat standpoints as tools for resisting, reclaiming, and reimagining being fat and in doing fat studies in Canada and elsewhere. While others before us have already begun to unpack the complexities of fat life in this geographic realm and pursued this "geographical turn" to advance the field of fat studies, our overall intent is to push fat studies scholarship further by attending to the specificities of fat life in a nation that continues to colonize lands and bodies.

Our objective with this collection is to further our fat liminal grounds and push to the forefront the multitude of theoretical and creative interventions springing from other parts of the North of America. The scholars and activists whose work appears in this collection have been trying to fatten Canada since their initial exchange with the realm of thought. We ask the following questions to consider the mapping and departure of the field of fat studies in Canada. How can we begin to map the field of fat Canadian studies? What makes the work of Canadian fat scholars unique? How does the "Canadian" fat identity define itself, and how is it constructed, reflected, and resisted in our cultural and political landscapes? What does the future of fat studies in Canada hold? We are engaged with examining the individual and collective contextualization of how fat bodies at various intersections of gender, sexuality, racialization, disability, neurodivergence, and other axes of embodiment and experience have been understood, both historically and within contemporary Canada—a nation that has and continues to fulfill a white settler colonial agenda, while remaining in the shadows of the United States as the "Great White North."

Indeed, US influence on the political and cultural landscape of Canada has historically been a topic of conversation, concern, and division (Smith). With the burgeoning growth of Canada-specific fat studies scholarship, the academic journal *Fat Studies: An Interdisciplinary Journal of Body Weight and Society* has been the primary academic space utilized to weave an intersectional "fat Canadian standpoint" and present analyses of anti-fat narratives and fat oppression that centre the Canadian context and experience. Beyond the journal *Fat Studies*, multiple fat studies texts have developed over the years to push the Canadian fat experience to the forefront, such as *Obesity in Canada: Critical Perspectives* (Ellison et al.); *Contours of the Nation: Making Obesity and Imagining Canada, 1945–1970* (McPhail); *Fighting Fat: Canada, 1920–1980* (Mitchinson); *Thickening Fat: Fat Bodies, Intersectionality, and Social Justice* (Friedman et al.) and *Body Stories: In and Out and With and Through Fat* (Andrew and Friedman), both of which, although not entirely focused on Canada, have Canadian editors and multiple authors who theorize fatness and its intersections to present alternative frameworks; and *Being Fat: Women, Weight, and Feminist Activism in Canada* (Ellison).

Besides these foundational texts on (anti-) fatness in Canada, the research-creation projects emerging from Re•Vision: The Centre for Art and Social Justice, which is comprised of researchers, artists, and activists located at the University of Guelph, Ontario; Allyson Mitchell's writing and performance art pieces; and Mitchell's queer fat feminist performance art and activist collective *Pretty Porky and Pissed Off (PPPO'd)*, created in collaboration with Mariko Tamaki, Ruby Rowan, Lisa Ayuso, Gillian Bell, Joanne Huffa, Abi Slone, Tracy Tidgwell, and Zoe Whittall, conjoin fat activism and scholarship to map modes of fat resistance against discriminatory language, cultural and social practices, and policies in Canada. Another collective body dismantling fat stigma and fatphobia in a creative manner is the group of Canadian artists who produced *EveryBODY on Stage* (2021) across multiple social media platforms, such as YouTube, TikTok, Instagram, and Facebook. They use the digital space to share a diverse range of fat bodies that are usually made to be "out of bounds" or completely invisible in popular culture, while sharing a dialogue on reducing the harm done upon fat bodies through their performances (e.g., songs, monologues, dance, stand-up comedy). Such multi-dimensional narratives of anti-fat bias within Canadian society have always been present in the dialogues on fatness; however, they remain in the shadows of a broad-reaching geographical neighbour.

Drawing on this rich history, this collection aims to demonstrate the constitution and critiques of fat ideologies and the heterogenous, multi-dimensional experiences of fat people in Canada. Additionally, it pushes a dialogue on the question of who benefits from its micro and macro politics, which dictate how we live within our fatness (Rothblum 173). There is a wrestling with the various narratives that have labelled the fatness leaking out of our bodily container as "problematic," thus requiring actual forms of containment, removal, and/or complete erasure. Fat studies has worked towards rethinking what it means to be fat by arguing that fatness is a social construct made for the justification of fat oppressive structures that deem fat people as "pathological" and an "epidemic" to be cured, to be made thin and "healthy." The preservation of dominant anti-fat ideologies and fatphobia continues to play into the politics of the body within Canada, as we come to see how bodies have been situated historically, culturally, and socio-politically and the resulting forms of resistance and reclamation by fat Canadians. What is particularly unique about this collection is the intermingling of the academic and liminal grounds of creative projects, together pushing alternative voices to the forefront of fat scholarship in Canada. We hope truly to present the essence of fat studies and fat activism in all forms, so it is not limited to academia or inaccessible to readers across disciplines and social locations. In presenting these multiple, emergent disruptions of compulsory thinness and the achievement politics it entails, the academic and creative chapters set our intention to imprint an individual and collective fat liberatory politics. With this recognition of the continual work being done by the authors within this collection, we have organized the chapters using thematic categories: structural fat oppression; mapping, methods, and innovations; fattening popular culture; medical encounters; desiring fatness; and alternative frameworks and imaginings. In the following sections, we briefly introduce these themes and the chapters within them.

Living Fat in Canada

This collection opens with chapters on the theme of living in fat bodies in Canada, providing narratives of fat "Canadians" and their lived experiences, particularly how their experiences have been, and continue to be, shaped by a variety of oppressive structures. We open with Yolanda Bonnell's poetic piece "Soft Spaces," which brings forward the stories of Indigenous women's relationships with their bodies and the impact of colonialism on these relationships, while also reflecting on the liveliness of food, land, ancestors, and the universe in Indigenous understandings of (fat) embodiment. We continue this discussion on colonialism and fatness with the work of Deborah McPhail, as she examines the discursive shift whereby "obesity" became a category applicable to northern Indigenous peoples. Her chapter presents the linkages between white supremacy, colonialism, and fatphobia in initiating a state sanctioned system of "benevolent" colonization using the category of "obesity" to contain and oppress Indigenous bodies.

White supremacy, heteropatriarchy, and fatphobia are coexisting systems in which fat people constantly find themselves negotiating discourses of "obesity" and cultivating their fat identities as they define the parameters of living fat in Canada. In their chapter, "Fat Women's Experiences and Negotiation of Fatphobia in Canada: A Systematic Review," Bidushy Sadika and Jinwen Chen provide an important overview of how the field of fat studies has explored the experience of fatness and its intersections with age, gender, sexuality, and racialization within Canada. They discuss how Canadian cis and trans women negotiate and resist anti-fat discourses within a variety of cultural and political spaces. The gendered nature of fat identity and fat discrimination is well established; however, the ways that fatness and gender intersect with age, disability, class, and other aspects of identity are ripe areas for further study. Faith Adodo and Fardosa Warsame explore the experience of fatness and, specifically, its intersections with Blackness, gender, and migration in their chapter, "From Africa to the Diaspora, the Never-Ending Pursuit of the Standard Body." Adodo and Warsame present a dialogue on the cultural perspectives of the standard body type in their respective home countries, Nigeria and Somalia, and in the African diaspora in Canada using a duoethnographic methodology. They initiate a conversation about the negative impact colonization has on the perception of fatness for Nigerians and Somalians in their home nations and in the Canadian diaspora. These two chapters, by Sadika and Chen and by Adodo and Warsame, mark an important broadening of our understanding of how fat and fatness is a highly constructed, contested, and negotiated identity, particularly for those who bear the ongoing scars of colonial violence.

Remapping and rethinking fat studies highlights how white settler colonialism enacts an individualized notion of "health" and "thinness," leaving fat people to endure fat oppression at each turning point of their life in Canada. This makes fat discrimination an issue of social justice needing to be deeply critiqued and decolonized. This insight brings us to the next chapters of this section discussing what it means to "live fat in Canada." We continue with a poem by Indigenous writer Francine Cunningham. Her poem, "to anyone who thinks i'm ugly just because i don't look like how you think i should," shares the stories of Indigeneity and fatness as Cunningham speaks of her "survivor's body" and its temporality. For her, the fat body is "one of resilience" rooted in overcoming the weathering of crops on Turtle Island and the transgenerational experience of famine and trauma. Within this poem about the resilient fat Indigenous survivor's body emerges a narrative of bodily memory and the reclamation of Indigenous knowledge. Cunningham's poetry points to a politics of resurgence that turns focus to how Indigenous communities nourish their traditions, language, and stories, and regenerate fat-beingness beyond Western constructions and practices (Butler). In the last chapter of this section, Jacqui Gingras and John-James Stranz provide a qualitative analysis of four conceptual frames of "magical thinking" to outline the dialectics of fatphobia within medical organizations. Gingras and Stranz deploy the concept of "magical thinking" to examine the practices of Obesity Canada, a registered Canadian charity whose mission is to "improve" the lives of fat people in Canada while simultaneously pathologizing fatness. The authors find that maintaining power, privilege, and livelihood is prioritized over the "health" of fat persons or the overall elimination of fat bias from the Canadian health care system.

The chapters of our first section bring us to the conclusion that there is no such thing as "white settler innocence" or "white colonial benevolence." The colonial conquest has not been conducted on the fat lands of Turtle Island only, but also upon fat bodies (Razack 5). In retelling lived experiences of fatphobia, the chapters in this section illuminate how the structures of fat oppression operate alongside multiple systems of oppression, generating unique experiences of marginalization and resistance.

The Mappings, Methods, and Innovations of Fat Studies in Canada

In our attempt to remap fat studies in Canada, we draw on interdisciplinary ways of studying fat oppression. This next section of the collection considers the mappings, methods, and innovations from fat scholarship emerging from Canada, as the authors share "footings," "tides," "spectrums," or "fragments" from their individual projects of (re)framing and reimagining fatness. The authors use this terminology to subvert existing epistemologies and ontologies that problematize fat embodiment on the basis of the dichotomy of thinness and fatness. The aim is to expand our theorizing of the embodiment of fatness: particularly, how the way fat people embody fatness entails both a sense of pain and joy as they move within and through their fatness spatially and temporally. We open with Leslie Walters's image titled "Sure Footing," which urges us to take a step into uncertainty and the unknown, especially in a world hostile to fat people. This image has its readers enter an affective realm where we are asked to feel fat and to reclaim this ambivalent state through creative research methods. Emily Allan's creative non-fiction chapter, presented next, explores fatphobia between cities and the process of rooting herself in her own body. She speaks of this cloaking and conflation of fatphobia with notions of "wellness" while flying coast to coast in Canada. Allan concludes with affirming her fatness by no longer pushing against the tide, but being "Like the Tide" itself.

Katie Cook also addresses the theme of affective and creative mapping while reflecting on the experiences of participants in their *Feeling Fat* research project. Cook draws much needed attention toward the opportunities that arts-based research methods afford fat research participants in experiencing joy and healing in community with other fat people. The possibilities of arts-based research for reimagining and reframing the fat lived experience is also addressed by Jen Rinaldi et al. in "Fragments on Fatness: Moments from a Digital Storytelling Archive on Trans Experiences of Weight Stigma." Within their chapter, they introduce readers to their multidisciplinary project, *Transgressing Body Boundaries*, which uses a digital storytelling methodology to discuss body policing at the intersections of gender identity and body weight, shape, or size. In taking this arts-based approach, Rinaldi et al. illustrate the benefits of digital storytelling, specifically for the participants of their project. Taking this route afforded them opportunities to document creatively the ways in which participants' bodies transform, often while resisting weight and fat stigma, and the resulting emotional encounters and entanglements. j wallace skelton's zine, in the chapter "Lies Fatphobia Told Me," similarly offers an artistic rendering of lived experiences of fatphobia, as skelton explores the ways that fatphobia suffocates fat people's embodied knowledges. skelton uses the zine to (re)imagine possibilities for fat bodies, exposing the lies that fatphobia is built upon to (re)value fat embodiment. These ideas are further illustrated in Lauren Munro's research project Living Big Lives, discussed in her chapter "Coming Home to Our Bodies: (Re)framing Fatness through an Exploration of Fat Vitality." Munro explores how participants articulate pleasure, joy, resistance, love, and multiple other possibilities found in their lived experiences as fat people in Canada. With her focus groups, she explores fatness, beauty, and desirability as an embodied affective process, emphasizing the importance of finding sites of fat vitality. Fat vitality for Munro is "an unfinished map of possibilities" from which we can make space for not just fat bodies but all bodies.

While these chapters explore the possibilities for expanding our understanding of fatness through creative research methods, the piece by Mars, as well as those by Allan and Walters in this section, illustrate the power of artistic and creative work to speak back to dominant framings of fatness. In "Lines to Myself," Mars shares their experience of growing up as a fat Latinx child with the two poems titled "<snowsuit>" and "<exist>." With the two poems and images, we too breathe, blink, pause as we are invited into intimate moments of reflection. Mars illustrates the vulnerability that fat people feel when targeted by those in our interpersonal circles and medical standards. Mars invites us to "take a step" into the comfort and potentialities of fat bodies through their visual pieces. We end with the words "FAT" to remind us that we can exist in our pillowy "snowsuits" of fat. Overall, the chapters in this section weave together a transformative social justice methodology with research-creations to underscore the desire for different ways of expressing fat identity and experiences. These methodological routes of unmapping, decolonizing, and rethinking fat politics within Canada enables fat persons to build their own narratives, outside the exclusionary labels that latch onto neoliberal discourses of the so-called obesity epidemic and rehabilitation.

Fattening Popular Culture

Popular cultural products have shaped and continue to shape Canadian fat identities. In the literature of fat studies, popular culture has always been subject to critique for its role in objectifying and dehumanizing fat people. When we think of the virility of fat femininities, for example, fat women are nowhere near the "sexually beautiful," as they simply remain as fat flesh, an object of the fatphobic gaze (LeBesco). Within this theme of fattening popular culture, the contributors analyse the media and its perpetuation of iconographies that position fat people (and bodies) as "freaks" or characters for comic relief. The objective of each author in this section is to outline the multiple ways that fatness is constructed within "multicultural" media artifacts in realms of Canadian popular culture. We ask, How have fat bodies been excluded in the media? Are there positive media representations of fat bodies circulating? Are there aspects of popular culture challenging anti-fat narratives and representing intersectional experiences? We begin with Walters's second piece in this collection, "Explosive Fatness," which presents a commentary on the exclusion of fat bodies within media and popular culture overall. She suggests fat bodies are rarely included in the media and that, therefore, fat people have few places they can look to for affirming representations of themselves.

Fatness in the realm of social science has a long-rooted history in the politics of the human, and its subsequent violent discourses have been injected into the literary world too. The historical depiction of fat bodies outside the "freakshows" that have constructed racialized, gendered, and disabled bodies as spectacles needs uncovering still, particularly by considering how fatness continues to be positioned as an objectified and dehumanized cultural reference within Canadian literature and films. Emily Bruusgaard takes on the challenge of examining the Canadian cultural icon *Anne of Green Gables* in "'I'd Wish to Be Tall and Slender': L. M. Montgomery's *Anne* Series and the Regulatory Role of Slimness," exploring how the discourse of thinness/slenderness reinforces fatness as a personal and genetic failing. The fat-thin dynamics are heavily present in the series with multiple characters, according to Bruusgaard, but especially between Anne and Diana. Bruusgaard outlines how thinness has been associated with progress, imagination, intelligence, and grace, as well as with the discourse of citizenship. As a nationally acclaimed cultural artifact, the *Anne* series continues to map the futurity of thinness with "health" and progression, as the future of the nation state.

While Bruusgaard positions *Anne of Green Gables* as a cultural reproduction of fat as failure, Audrey Laurin explores the popular French-Canadian "Laura Cadieux" cultural products to bring forth fat studies in the francophone academic world. In her analysis, Laurin illustrates the shift in the experience of fatness within the novel *C't'à ton tour, Laura Cadieux* (1973) and late 1990s film adaptations of the novel. She argues that fatness is represented as the norm for the white, francophone, working-class society of Laura Cadieux in Quebec and that, within the later adaptations, fatness took on a whole new meaning with a focus on body positivity, contesting popular representations of working-class fat women as powerless. These two seemingly disparate cultural framings of fatness within *Anne* and *Laura Cadieux* serve to illustrate the complex ways in which popular representations of fatness shape fat Canadian identities. While Anne, through her relationship with Diana Barry, villainizes fatness and celebrates thinness, in the world of Laura Cadieux, fatness is seen as normal and weight loss is not considered an imperative for a better life. Although cultural depictions of fatness reinforce the idea of fat bodies as a spectacle of comical excess, adding to the depiction of fat bodies as deviant and disabling embodiments needing to be disciplined into the culturally acceptable thin and/or muscular body, there is a turn to fat resistance within popular culture through texts like the *Cadieux* series, offering new ways of thinking about fatness.

Medical Encounters: "Hello Dr. Fatphobia"

From the literary world to the medical realm, an anti-fat attitude is continuously reproducing and reinforcing the idea of the beautiful, "normal," thin body while maintaining fat as a spectacle requiring medical assistance for its excesses; these notions of "excess," "pathology," or "rehabilitation" under the dialectics of the medical industrial complex further inject fat shame and stigma into fat bodies (Bahra). As an academic field, fat studies stands in opposition to the continued pathologization of fatness by "obesity" experts through medicalized systems and institutions that weaponize "obesity" expertise and knowledge against fat people by drawing on the discourses of a so-called obesity epidemic or of fatness as "unhealthy." The chapters in this section of the collection explore the ways in which fat Canadians navigate encounters with often discriminatory and oppressive medicalized structures. We open this section of the book with another image by Walters. "Eating Scorn" initiates a critique of fat people's often-strained relationships with food due to the judgments of others or the demonization of food itself. In many ways, this piece invites the readers to consider how these judgments arise from the field of medicine and the harm endured in the process of accessing medicine.

A large component of this section is a discussion on the *Canadian Adult Obesity Clinical Practice Guidelines* developed in 2020 by Obesity Canada and the Canadian Association of Bariatric Physicians and Surgeons. Again, we must ask in what ways Obesity Canada and this key document change the way that fat experiences are theorized within medical and social research practices. Kelsey Ioannoni's chapter focuses on the 2020 Obesity Canada guidelines from a policy perspective, exploring the impact health policy has on the broader politics of fat and fatness. Throughout the guidelines, Obesity Canada employs the language "people living with obesity" to describe fat patients. Using people-first language to refer to fat patients is meant to differentiate people themselves from the disease they are affiliated with; thus, Obesity Canada further equates large(r) body size with disease. To underscore this impact, Joanna Carson offers her personal reactions to and reflections on Obesity Canada in the chapter, "A Response to the 2020 Canadian Ob*sity Guidelines." Central to the guidelines produced by Obesity Canada is an acceptance of "obesity" as a disease in need of treatment by health care professionals. Together, Ioannoni's and

Carson's chapters beg us to ask how fat bodies are medicalized to the point of being disposable under the weight of policies.

In "#NoBodyIsDisposable. Acts of Care and Preservation: Reflections on Clinical Triage Protocols during COVID-19," Tracy Tidgwell and Fady Shanouda introduce the #NoBodyIsDisposable toolkit for disabled and/or fat folks living in Ontario, Canada, during the COVID pandemic. Through disability, fat, and critical race theory, Tidgwell and Shanouda explore the eugenicist underpinnings of care rationing policies, during COVID and beyond. This intersection of fatness and disability is further explored in Derek Newman-Stille's series of poems titled "Diagnosis—Fat!" Newman-Stille's work explores how disability and fatness intersect, and it considers how fatness is seen as both a cause and result of disability. Newman-Stille speaks to their experiences with medical discrimination and the public surveillance and policing of fat and disabled bodies. Finally, both Kirthan Aujlay and Amanda Scriver explore themes of medical discrimination and fatphobic medical encounters in their chapters. While Aujlay focuses on her personal experiences of polycystic ovarian syndrome (PCOS) and medical fatphobia, Scriver weaves broader themes of fat politics into her personal reflections on navigating the Canadian mental health landscape as a fat person. Both creatively bring us to the concluding questions of this section. Are fat bodies always going to face such encounters in Canada? How can we make medical institutions in Canada more accessible for fat bodies?

Desiring Fatness: Entering the Fat Politics of Desire

In this next section, we find ourselves at the crossroads of desirability and fatness, a juncture that often remains unnamed, since fatness has been construed as an "undesirable" state of being. As Allison Taylor finds in her research with queer fat femmes across Canada, fatphobia, in tandem with femmephobia, white supremacy, and other oppressions, shapes fat people's experiences with dating and desirability in Canada. All too often, fat people in Canada—for example, fat femmes—are rejected or fetishized as sexual subjects, "generating feelings of undesirability, fear, and failure" (Taylor, "But Where Are the Dates" 1). The chapters in this section advance a fat politics of desire that could reimagine Canadian society so that fatness is no longer associated with the failing or lacking body, a society where, instead, fatness can be viewed as desirable—or as Eliza Chandler and Carla Rice state "a welcomed presence, a source of creative inspiration, and an expression of the diversity of embodiments" (238). Our hope for this discussion on desirability and fatness is to question how we shift towards a fat politics of desire and resist the cultural imperative to assign a person's worth based on that person's perceived desirability. In each chapter presented in this section, we see fat joy, play, pleasure, desire, sexuality, and vitality come alive through the authors' words.

What does it mean to desire or to reframe fatness as sexy and sensual? Walters's "Sexy Fat" is an image that speaks to the sensuality of fatness. It presents a visual commentary on the kink community and its openness to all bodies as good bodies. Next, in her series of *ghazals* (poems) titled "Punch(ing) my Paunch," Rohini Bannerjee focuses on pleasure, eroticism, and liberation as a fat Canadian woman of the Desi (South Asian) diaspora. In her stanzas, she connects alcohol, sugar, lemon, water, and tea/spices to her divine fat, gendered, and racialized experience. She concludes by inviting us to also consider our fatness as an offering of life's hors d'oeuvre. The artistic styles of both Walters and Bannerjee encourage their readers to connect to our experience of fatness beyond the limiting notions of sexy. They invite us to drink in that juicy, plump fat juice and enjoy fat kinky sex unconditionally. In "Butch Bellies, Queer Desires," Karleen Pendleton Jiménez explores fat queer butch Latinx embodiment and how fatness constructs the butch body as undesirable. Inspired by lovers, fellow butches, fat and queer scholarship, and Latinx artists, they explore how their butch belly opens possibilities for both (re)imagining fat butch embodiment and queering and fattening desire. Susie Mensah concludes this section on the theme of desire and the politics of desirability by turning focus to anti-Blackness in Canada. She states that "Let Us Taste" is a benediction for fat folks, reframing sexuality and fatness as an entity to know and a place to go (not outside ourselves). All these chapters expand our understanding of how gender, fatness, race, and sexuality intersect with desire and pleasure, and they contribute to a reimagining of what it could be like to "live fat" in Canada. Through these chapters, we come to envision fat bellies and the pleasure that can be derived from them. We come to sip the punch and taste fat queerness in all its glory. No longer is fatness distasteful. It is liberating—and oh does it feel good!

Alternative Frameworks and Imaginings: Disrupting and Finding Magic in Fat Life

This discussion of the desirability, vitality, and liberation of fatness brings us to our final section of *Fat Studies in Canada*: frameworks and imaginings that initiate alternative dialogues on fat embodiment. The alternative frameworks offered in these chapters reimagine fatness and fat as disruptive, as a processual body. These chapters disrupt dominant understandings of fat and through these disruptions may introduce new possibilities for imagining ways of knowing and being fat.

In "Fat and Mad Bodies: Out of, Under, and Beyond Control," Fady Shanouda merges the fields of fat studies and mad studies to explore how fatphobia and saneism operate together to subjugate and oppress fat and mad bodies. Attention is particularly given to the construction of different body-minds as out of control, beyond control, and, in many ways, disposable. Sookie Bardwell extends this conversation to reflect on their personal relationship with (self-)hatred and anti-fatness as violence and to explain how their experience serves as a foundation for "Body Liberation"–centred harm-reduction practice. Through this practice, Bardwell has been able to support personal and collective resistance, resilience, and healing and reimagine new ways of being fat in Canada. Ramanpreet A. Bahra reflects on similar themes in "The Affective State of Fat-Beingness within Debility Politics." Bahra considers the slippages between fat as disability, situating fat within an affective politic following an autoethnographic methodology. Bahra concludes that the personal register's systems of oppression promote debility and, subsequently, the inflicting of violence upon fat bodies that puts them onto the path of deathworlds. Bahra suggests that debility politics may offer fat bodies an alternative way to express the vitality of their fatness in this "life-in-death" status.

In this discussion on reframing and reimagining new and multi-dimensional frameworks, can fatness be understood as queerness? Fat studies in itself is troubling—or queering—normative ideologies that dictate the embodiment of fat lives even more intensely. In the turn to queer fat studies, the respective chapters of Gin Marshall, S. Bear Bergman, and Lucas Crawford present a critique of the regulatory scripts of both fatphobia (i.e., weight loss) and heteronormativity that queer fat people experience day to day, while also sharing the potential disruptive possibilities of fatness. Accounting for the intersecting experience of fatness, queerness, and transness, Gin Marshall in "Fat Trans Bodies in Motion: Hazards of Space-Taking" shares their concerns and reflections upon the fat trans experience while travelling, in seeking health care, and during the global COVID-19 pandemic. They explore the ways in which fatness queers gendered embodiment while raising concerns around the gendered nature of fat discrimination by meditating on their experiences as a fat transmasculine person. In his essay, S. Bear Bergman shares his experience tabling at a trans conference in Seattle, where he is called upon by a fellow attendee to attend a "top surgery show and tell" to represent another model of transness, a fat trans embodiment. In this moment, he found himself transgressing the positioning of his fat and trans body as a spectacle and instead came to realize he is more at home in his body now than ever. Lucas Crawford in "Slender Trouble: From Berlant's Cruel Figuring of Figure to Sedgwick's Fat Presence" argues that queer theory must address how accounts of queer affect weigh the import of fat and size, as well as how largesse lives as and within queer readings.

We end this collection with Ameema Saeed's "Fat Magic: On Fatness as a Magic Show" and an image by Leslie Walters. Saeed's creative non-fiction chapter uses magic as a metaphor for fatness and builds an ethics of care. She reminds us that fat people are "a magic show"— that fat people are resilient, we are multi-dimensional, we are beautiful, we are flawed, we are something extraordinary to behold" (487). The intention of this section is to, in the words of Kathleen LeBesco, embrace our "revolting bodies" to reclaim fatness as a social justice issue and celebrate fat lives as *lives* worth living. We conclude this theme with the image "Yummy Body Types," which considers fat bodies as shaped like ice cream cones, with fat bodies of varying shapes and sizes moving and radiating endless possibilities. Each of the authors in this section work to provide alternative frameworks that go against the grain of disposability and debility to consider the vitality in fatness. All in all, they explore the embodiment and expressions of their fatness in difference rather than in spite of it, thereby expanding fat resistance and politics. These chapters represent fat liberation as fully disruptive, creative, and playful.

A FAT Conclusion?

While fat studies has grown as an interdisciplinary field for the last two decades, with an emphasis on the United States, we now find ourselves wanting to map fat cartographies of the currents of fat scholarship in Canada. As an alternative framework, the "fat turn" reclaims the voices of fat people and creates other knowledges about fatness (Pausé 175). In this journey of theorizing fat identities within Canada across its realms (i.e., social, cultural, political), it can be said that the fattening of these multiple systems remains a work in progress. Our collection acts as a bridge that continues the critique of the individualistic model of fat "pathology" that has been established through language, culture, and the sciences. With a particular focus on the Canadian context, this collection presents the complex relationship between fat "Canadian" identities and a society that perpetuates social inequality at all intersections. Each chapter demonstrates how hegemonic structures, such heterosexism, racism, and sizeism, are experienced by fat people across gender, sexuality, race, disability, and other sites of marginalization within Canada. Gard and Wright speak of the multiple forms of resistance taking place in fat studies through academic work and fat activist movements that aim to reconfigure fatness "through performance, parody and confrontation" in the cultural imaginary (163). The merging of fat academics, activists, and community within this collection is central for fat people in Canada that have utilized these outlets as a means to build and share alternative imaginings of fatness as resistance and regeneration. Considering the global impact of the public health crisis of COVID-19 and the political climate of state-sanctioned violence against BIPOC communities, it is of the utmost importance to consider the question of how we build a fat community and map a future of fat activism in Canada, particularly when we constantly witness the bifurcation of bodies. The Canadian scholars contributing to this collection offer a wide range of fat studies perspective, and each presents a radical answer to the question of how we provide a "voice" for fat people and celebrate our differences.

The Canadian Charter of Rights and Freedoms, a Canadian constitutional document dating back to 1982, is often seen as the most important piece of legislation in Canada. The Charter guarantees our fundamental freedoms, legal rights, and equality rights, and celebrates Canada's multicultural heritage; however, various sections of this legislation itself are inapplicable for bodies that do not match the "true" Canadian identity. Canadian national identity is popularly labelled as "multicultural," but the truth of the matter is this—multiculturalism is a façade that allows a form of homonationalism to thrive. For instance, both sections 7 and 15 of the Charter outline life, liberty, security, and equality before the law for all; however, these rights and freedoms are non-existent for many fat, BIPOC, disabled, mad, queer, and otherly marginalized people, as oftentimes our bodies stand in for the "non-normative," "pathological," or even as the fat, heavy "thing" the nation is to carry. With every space that we enter, our bodies become a question of life, security, and death, most times resulting in the latter for the security of privileged communities. With every crevice our fatness folds (or unfolds) into, it is made clear that we do not have the same kind of protections or benefits as our thin, muscular, elite, non-disabled, heterosexual, white counterparts. The Charter states that we are all to be "treated with the same respect, dignity and consideration," yet you will see throughout this collection that fat oppression undermines this promise of dignity and equity (Government of Canada, "Guide to the Canadian Charter"). The social injustices experienced by these bodies in so-called "multicultural Canada" pushes bodies such as ours to the margins of its body politics. May Friedman's "Fat in Canada: Afterword" illustrates this as she beautifully grapples with the question of what it means to be "strong and free" as fat people in Canada—a land space that continues to reinforce violent structures of inequality. One thing is certain, we are far from these ideals the nation claims it stands for.

This collection attempts to bring together an extensive amount of fat scholarship springing from scholars located across Canada; however, we want to make note of the fact that many voices were left out. As much as we tried to mirror fat studies as the sibling of fat activism, by curating this collection as one composed of both academic and community pieces, there are some potholes present in this road of *Fat Studies in Canada*. While there is an intermingling of ideas between both academic and community pieces in this collection, which we truly believe allows us to grapple with our fat liminal grounds and contribute to fat activism in Canada, fat studies can also of course be critiqued for being akin to "white feminism" as it fails to bring forth the voices of those marginalized at multiple intersections of fatness, racialization, gender, sexuality, disability, and other axes of oppression. Many of the chapters here offer entry points to provide such a discussion on these missing voices. For example, the nexus of fatness and race is discussed in detail, but it is worth noting that critical Indigenous and Black perspectives on fatness, anti-Indigeneity, anti-Blackness, and (homo)nationalism need further exploration as this dialogue is limited. Another set of missing voices is that of fat trans people and those who live in superfat or infinifat bodies. Greater attention is needed on the nuanced aspects of fat oppression and how those at the larger end of the fat spectrum navigate living fat lives in Canada. For instance, we witness how compulsory thinness, heteronormativity, and racism are reproduced in the fashion industry. Although the market has opened up for fat bodies, there continues to be a privileging of straight, white, and thin embodiments, therefore pointing to the inclusionary-exclusionary body politics that remain intact even with the advancement of the body positive movement, which outlines its own version of sizeism and "shapeism" (hourglass or "sexy" curvy body vs. excessive fatness; see Taylor, "Fashioning Fat Fem(me)ininities").

As Jill Andrew argues, "much of the tensions around 'good' and 'bad' fat are played out in and around sartorial choices and the limits of a fashion industry that figuratively and literally (through its limited size availability, commitment to aesthetic quality, and marketing of 'plus' fashion) labels which consumer bodies matter to the industry, designers, advertisers, and runways and which are seen as too fat to be desirable let alone dressable." Indeed, in Calla Evans's research with infinifat and superfat people, she finds that "clothing is one of the primary ways that we indicate belonging. Without readily-available, situationally-appropriate clothing, infinifat and superfat people are limited in the subjectivities they can perform and are excluded from specific social spaces. This exclusion serves to remarginalize an already marginalized group and is felt most acutely by those who embody additional marginalized identity markers, such as those who are racialized or living in poverty" (1). The words of Andrew and Evans highlight the absence of engagement with clothing and fashion in this collection, a topic that warrants further exploration in discussions of fat embodiment in Canada.

Compulsory sizeism, racism, and heterosexism also come to police racialized fat bodies and queer fat bodies the most, as health-initiative-based policies and projects situate them as a threat to public health standards and failure overall (Rinaldi et al., "Fatness" 220–21). In the theme of popular culture, there is also a dialogue forming on what forms of archives are made of and for fat people in Canada without the language of "freakshows." In searching for positive representations of fat people on the World Wide Web, we came across a stock image bank curated by Obesity Canada centred on fat affirmation and liberation. The organization's objective is to utilize these fat-positive images to reduce disparaging representations of fat people (Obesity Canada). As much as it is a step towards fat liberation in Canadian popular culture, the terminology of *overweight*, *obesity*, or *individuals with obesity* remains problematic, so it begs us to question how we can invest into fat communities and completely abolish such medical terminology in spaces that are curated for us.

Last, our objective is to build on previous texts on the topic of being fat in Canada to highlight the rich contributions to the field from scholars and artists in Canada and in a Canadian context. In reviewing the vast knowledge produced by fat scholars, we see there has always been an underrepresentation of dialogues on the connections between fatness and anti-Blackness and anti-Indigeneity or on fatness as madness and disability; many of the chapters here act as entry points to that scholarship. Each of these chapters encapsulates the themes set out for the collection, and we hope the collection captures the multi-dimensional experiences that come with being fat in Canada—highlighting the struggle with fatphobia while also introducing new ways of celebrating our fatness. We welcome our readers to join us in the opening of a dialogue with these voices of scholars and community artists located in Northern Turtle Island. May this collection initiate your own engagement with your fatness and give you the spoons[1] to create your own version of fat activism and fat studies.

Notes

1 The concept and terminology of "spoons" is rooted in crip culture. "Spoon theory" describes the energy a disabled person may have to devote to tasks within a specific frame of time. Our use of the term in this chapter acknowledges the overlap in fat and disabled communities and in the experiences and conceptions of fatness and disability (see chapters by Bahra, Newman-Stille, and Shanouda for further discussion).

Works Cited

Andrew, Jill. "Follow Up Re: Fat Studies in Canada." Received by Kelsey Ioannoni, 6 March 2022.

Andrew, Jill, and May Friedman, editors. *Body Stories: In and Out and With and Through Fat.* Demeter Press, 2020.

Bahra, Ramanpreet A.. "'You Can Only be Happy if You're Thin!' Normalcy, Happiness, and the Lacking Body." *Fat Studies*, vol. 7, no. 2, 2018, pp. 193–202.

Butler, Stephanie. "Indigenous Resurgence." *Canadian Literature: A Quarterly of Criticism and Review*, 2020, https://canlit.ca/article/indigenous-resurgence/. Accessed 14 April 2022.

Chandler, Eliza, and Carla Rice. "Alterity In/Of Happiness: Reflecting on the Radical Possibilities of Unruly Bodies." *Health, Culture and Society*, vol. 5, no. 1, 2013, pp. 230–48.

Cooper, Charlotte. "Maybe It Should be Called Fat American Studies." *The Fat Studies Reader*, edited by Esther D. Rothblum and Sondra Solovay, New York University Press, 2009, pp. 327–33.

Ellison, Jenny. *Being Fat: Women, Weight, and Feminist Activism in Canada*. University of Toronto Press, 2020.

Ellison, Jenny, et al., editors. *Obesity in Canada: Critical Perspectives*. University of Toronto Press, 2016.

Evans, Calla. "You Aren't What You Wear: An Exploration into Infinifat Identify Construction and Performance Through Fashion." *Fashion Studies*, vol. 3, no. 1, 2020, https://www.fashionstudies.ca/you-arent-what-you-wear. Accessed 13 April 2022.

Friedman, May, et al., editors. *Thickening Fat: Fat Bodies, Intersectionality, and Social Justice*. Routledge, 2019.

Gard, Michael, and Jan Wright. *The Obesity Epidemic: Science, Morality and Ideology*. Routledge, 2005.

Government of Canada. *Guide to the Canadian Charter of Rights and Freedoms. Government of Canada*. Government of Canada, 24 March 2022, www.canada.ca/en/canadian-heritage/services/how-rights-protected/guide-canadiAn-charter-rights-freedoms.html Accessed 14 April 2022.

Harrison, Da'Shaun L. *Belly of the Beast: The Politics of Anti-Fatness as Anti-Blackness*. North Atlantic Books, 2021.

Obesity Canada. "Image Bank." *Obesity Canada*, https://obesitycanda.ca/resources/image-bank/. Accessed 14 April 2022.

LeBesco, Kathleen. *Revolting Bodies? The Struggle to Redefine Fat Identity*. University of Massachusetts Press, 2004.

McPhail, Deborah. *Contours of the Nation: Making "Obesity" and Imagining "Canada," 1945–1970*. University of Toronto Press, 2017.

Mitchinson, Wendy. *Fighting Fat: Canada, 1920–1980*. University of Toronto Press, 2018.

Pausé, Cat. "Ray of Light: Standpoint Theory, Fat Studies, and a New Fat Ethics." *Fat Studies: An Interdisciplinary Journal of Body Weight and Society*, vol. 9, no. 2, 2020, pp. 175–87.

Rinaldi, Jen, et al. "Fatness and Failing Citizenship." *Somatechnics*, vol. 7, no. 2, 2017, pp. 218–33.

Rinaldi, Jen, et al. "Introduction." *Thickening Fat: Fat Bodies, Intersectionality, and Social Justice*, edited by May Friedman, Carla Rice, and Jen Rinaldi, Routledge, 2019, pp. 1–12.

Rothblum, Esther D. "Fat Studies." *The Oxford Handbook of the Social Science of Obesity*, edited by John Cawley, Oxford University Press, 2011, pp. 173–84.

Rothblum, Esther, and Sondra Solovay, editors. *The Fat Studies Reader*. New York University Press, 2009.

Smith, Allan. *Canada—An American Nation?: Essays on Continentalism, Identity, and the Canadian Frame of Mind*. McGill-Queen's University Press, 1994.

Taylor, Allison. "'But Where Are the Dates?' Dating as a Central Site of Fat Femme Marginalisation in Queer Communities." *Psychology & Sexuality*, vol. 13, no. 1, 2022, pp. 57–68.

Taylor, Allison. "Fashioning Fat Fem(me)ininities." *Fat Studies: An Interdisciplinary Journal of Body Weight and Society*, 2021, https://doi.org/10.1080/21604851.2021.1913828. Accessed 14 April 2022.

Tomrley, Corinna, and Ann Kaloski Naylor, editors. *Fat Studies in the UK*. Raw Nerve Books, 2009.

Usiekniewicz, Marta. "Dangerous Bodies: Blackness, Fatness, and the Masculinity Dividend." *Interalia: A Journal of Queer Studies*, vol. 11, 2016), pp. 19–45, https://interalia.queerstudies.pl/wp-content/uploads/11A_2016/usiekniewicz.pdf. Accessed 14 April 2022.

STRUCTURAL FAT OPPRESSION

Soft Spaces

Yolanda Bonnell

There's something about slapping dough
You know?
When you've dusted it with flour
And it sits there
A lump
I loved patting it and slapping it and watching it jiggle
It was soft
And squishy
And I loved it
The softness
The squishiness
Of bodies
Of kwe
Was lost on me at the time
I was surrounded by mountains of women
Made of soft dough
I searched for the warmth of arms and nooks
Dark spots
Folds

ches like soft moss

Our big rolling bodies are so much like the land

Like waves and tree trunks

And earth

So much earth

You could plant flowers in our rolls and we would become gardens.

They tried to starve us out

They tried

But we became our own complicated fields

Harvested

Put in baskets

Our sweet frybread bannock bodies splashed in maple and blueberry

Sweet

Sweet

Sweet

Comfort foods and trauma and comfort foods

And sustenance

And fish on Fridays

And

Survival

See there is a reclamation that lives somewhere on or in our fat bodies

Our colonized bodies

We have to dig

And dig

And

What if for every body part you learned to love; woodland flowers grew there?

Or a constellation?

The more we unlearn, the truer it becomes—

The deeper the colour of the flowers on your thighs

And the brightness of the stars on your stomach

The louder those ancestral voices grow

Voices of Aunties and Grandmothers

And Mothers

Loud, laughing doughy mountains

Engulfed in love and comfort

It's a power

Like a Goddess

Or like earth herself

So large

Holding so much

Containing

So much

In orbit

We stretch

Out

Our bodies rooted from the deep ground up to the expanse of the universe

Taking

All of the space

Artist Statement

I am a Queer 2 Spirit Anishinaabe-Ojibwe & South Asian mixed playwright, performer, and multidisciplinary creator/educator. Although I am originally from Fort William First Nation in Thunder Bay, Ontario (Superior Robinson Treaty territory), my art practice is now based in Tkarón:to.

For this collection, I have submitted a poem titled "Soft Spaces." In this, I talk about the relationship Indigenous women have with our bodies and the colonial impact on that relationship. Through my words, I speak about the fear I had of becoming fat as a young person, due to the fat bodies I saw around me. I thought it was important to try and reclaim that narrative and think about what it would feel like if my brain wasn't colonized and to just be able to appreciate the beauty in the fatness of the Matriarchs around me, rather than fear it. I wanted to use our connection to baking to do that as a way to learn to love myself—the same way I love bannock!

"The White Man's Burden"?: Obesity and Colonialism in the Developing North[1]

Deborah McPhail

Although medical care continues to improve and once debilitating diseases are controlled, we can expect a continuing decline in cardiorespiratory fitness among the Eskimos. Whether poor cardiorespiratory function and "the white man's burden"—obesity—will ... [have] the same epidemic proportions that it has in the rest of North America depends largely on whether measures are taken to prevent the deterioration of the present high levels of fitness in ... areas in the Arctic.
– Andris Rode, 1972

THE ABOVE STATEMENT is reproduced from the master's thesis of Andris Rode, a graduate student at the University of Toronto working in Igloolik, Northwest Territories, in the late 1960s. Rode and fellow student Gaeten Godin were teamed with prominent sports scientist R. J. Shephard on a project measuring Inuit fitness for the international scientific effort organized to study both populations and landscapes said to be in danger of extinction, the "International Biological Programme" (IBP). While conflations between Indigenous people and obesity, especially as obesity relates to diabetes, are currently so ordinary as to be common sense, Rode's statement both decrying and anticipating poor cardiorespiratory health due to obesity in the Inuit was rather novel prior to 1972 ("Canada's Food Guide"; Lear et al.; Patterson; Picard, "Diabetes Putting Care System"; Picard, "Native Health Care"; Picard, "Obesity-Driven Diabetes"; Salinas; Smylie). Obesity concerns, and the diet and physical education regimes that produced and resulted from them, were generally directed at normative, white, middle-class subjects positioned as "modern." In the 1960s, however, worries about the growing girth of Canadians began to expand to a population which up to that point had been imagined as decidedly "primitive": the Indigenous peoples residing in the northern regions of the country.

This chapter traces the discursive shift whereby obesity, by 1972, became a category applicable to northern Indigenous peoples. I argue that the medical, scientific, and state application of the category of obesity helped to attempt what Mary Louise Pratt has called a type of "anti-conquest," or a system of "benevolent" colonization, achieved in part through seemingly innocent projects of scientific classification. "The main protagonist of the anti-conquest," Pratt states, is "the 'seeing-man' ... he whose imperial eyes passively look out and possess" (7). While scientists and medical practitioners in 1960s sub-Arctic and Arctic Canada were not always male, as the presence of northern nurses and women in IBP research teams demonstrate, they were certainly "seeing" (Sangster).[2] Over the course of the late 1960s, the bodies of northern Indigenous people were weighed and measured, their hands x-rayed, lung capacities determined, everyday movements filmed, and food intakes recorded. In short, the bodies of Indigenous populations became knowable to state and medical agents who were convinced that northern communities were in the midst of a transition from "primitive" (in their words) sustenance economies to "modern" (again, in their words) wage-based ones. It was believed by government officials and medical researchers that these transitions were, as Andris Rode's quotation opening this chapter attests, creating unhealthy lifestyle patterns akin to those of white populations.

Declarations that northern Indigenous populations were "in transition" were imperative to the postwar colonial project to exploit the resources of the Arctic and sub-Arctic regions. Medical, scientific, and state rhetoric claiming the modernization of the North negated Indigenous claims to a large portion of northern Canada, an expanse of land becoming increasingly important to military strategy, national sovereignty claims, and capitalist endeavour (Grant, *Sovereignty or Security*; Grant,

Polar Imperative; Zaslow). An inflection of what Daniel Francis has called the "vanishing Indian," northern communities "in transition" were to be helped along, if not pitied, in a journey toward total assimilation (58). This was a narrative greased by the discourse of anthropological "progress" that assumed all primitive populations were, in Sangster's words, "destined to be swept aside by the tides of modernity" (195). Discursive texts might express regret about the supposed expiration of a once-vibrant northern culture, but few stopped to consider the fact that the death might not in fact be predestined.

Obesity was one way in which scientists, medical practitioners, and state agents positioned northern Indigenous peoples as a "transitioning race." As a seemingly biological inflection of modern living, the accumulation of body fat on northern Indigenous bodies contributed to the notion that northern progress was only natural. In this context, the calculations of and cures for obesity were a mechanism of anti-conquest in northern lands.

Before beginning, I want to clarify that in speaking of Indigenous obesity and obesity-fighting as mechanisms of colonialism, it is neither my intent nor my place to invalidate current Indigenous concerns about the prevalence of obesity and diabetes in their communities (Assembly of First Nations, "Aboriginal Diabetes"; Assembly of First Nations, "National Chief Says"; Poudrier and Kennedy). Historians have detailed the very real health problems unleashed on Indigenous bodies during various colonial regimes, both in and outside of Canada, and I do not mean to make light of health problems that may have resulted from postwar northern colonialist practices such as the relocation of Indigenous peoples from their traditional lands, or government regulation of Indigenous peoples' hunting (Fee; Kelm; Vaughn).[3] Rather, I want to question how and why northern health problems were taken up by researchers and state agents, to interrogate the economic and political backdrop that made obesity a category of analysis for state, medical, and scientific establishments, and to explore how articulations of obesity were used to repress, oppress, and contain Indigenous bodies in order to facilitate colonialism. It is the construction of northern obesity by normative subjects that is critiqued here, not the eventual and poetically just wielding of Indigenous obesity against a negligent colonial regime (Assembly of First Nations, "National Chief Says").

Theoretical Context: Abjection and the Anti-Conquest

Feminist theorists of the body have noted the propensity for racialized and colonized bodies to be imaginatively categorized as Cartesian by dominant Western subjects, a discursive technique that has philosophically justified both white supremacy and the hyper-control and regulation of racialized people in Western nation-states and other colonized spaces (Bordo; Mohanram; Stoler). Anti-racist scholars of disease have shown, both implicitly and explicitly, that these Cartesian conflations of the body with racialized people are particularly salient in discourses of disease, as their Cartesian embodiments—and by extension their leaky abject bodies—often help to over-attach bodies of colour with certain diseases that are generally contagious. These writers further demonstrate how categories of disease and race are co-constituted.

For example, studying such diverse health issues as smallpox in San Francisco's late-nineteenth century Chinatown, AIDS in late-twentieth-century Africa and North America, and COVID-19 in current North American contexts, theorists show how conflations between racialized Cartesian bodies and a barrage of illnesses have facilitated racist discrimination and white supremacy (Devakumar et al.; Shah; Patton). In "Multiculturalism, Racism and Infectious Disease in the Global City," for instance, Roger Keil and Harris Ali show how Chinese bodies in Toronto's three Chinatowns were regulated by racialized discourses of disease during the city's 2003 SARS outbreak. Billed as a "Chinese disease" by media and public health agents alike, the SARS epidemic (or lack thereof), Keil and Ali argue, spatially segregated the Chinese community and recoded the three Chinatowns as what Anne McClintock would call "abject zones"; regulated the movement of Chinese people at local, national, and international scales; and exposed the racism of a city that supposedly celebrates its multiculturalism (163–73).

A small literature also exists critiquing the current and almost ubiquitous racialized partnering of Indigenous bodies with obesity and diabetes in Canada. For example, in her analysis of the "thrifty gene," which is said to cause the more efficient store of fat and calories and to be the result of a recent hunter/gatherer past in which times of famine were inevitable, Jennifer Poudrier argues that the questionable science that positions Indigenous peoples as genetically "thrifty" and as therefore racially distinct dangerously downplays the complex social etiology of diabetes and obesity. Thrifty gene discourse, Poudrier argues, also serves as a "powerful [form] of regulatory surveillance, which [is] based on the representation and reiteration of Aboriginal peoples as sick, disorganized and dependent, and which [legitimizes] paternalistic and regulatory management over Aboriginal health in communities" ("Geneticization" 256). Like Poudrier, Margery Fee maintains that the thrifty gene narrative racializes Indigenous bodies as "different, even willfully deviant," and as closer to their "primitive" pasts than white Canadians who are correspondingly positioned as more "civilized" (2993–94). In her analysis of discourses of Indigenous obesity and diabetes, similar to Poudrier's work, Fee argues that "[w]hat is most striking about 'the thrifty genotype' is how a rather unscientific hypothesis was transformed into a clear-cut racializing account that is now a popular and free-floating 'explanation' for the high incidence of diabetes among Aboriginal people" (2990).

Historians of various colonial periods of the past make corresponding claims to those of anti-racist scholars of disease, and argue that colonialist regimes have deployed the categories of health and illness to reify white supremacy. For example, in *Curing Their Ills*, her study of African colonial medicine in the nineteenth and twentieth centuries, Meaghan Vaughn uses the Foucauldian concept of biopower to argue that "medicine and its associated disciplines played an important part in constructing 'the African' as an object of knowledge, and elaborated classification systems and practices which have to be seen as intrinsic to the operation of [the] ... colonial power/knowledge regime" (8). Articulating "the African" as susceptible to maladies, such as leprosy, syphilis, and mental illness, and white British doctors as men who could locate, prevent, and (potentially) cure such diseases, colonial medicine not only articulated "the African" as naturally diseased but positioned the white, British man as a messianic and highly intelligent figure obligated to save dying "Africans" from their own abject embodiments (Vaughn 12–13). Medical discourse thus allowed British colonialism to appear as if it were a benevolent, rather than a devastatingly violent, project.

Speaking in the Canadian context, Mary Ellen Kelm makes similar arguments, maintaining that early- to mid-twentieth-century colonial medicine, provided both by church and state, produced European dominance by articulating Indigenous bodies as perpetually diseased.[4] Kelm notes: "Euro-Canadian medicine, as practiced among the First Nations, served [the] colonial agenda" (xix). Kelm demonstrates that racialized and essentialist conflations of Indigeneity with such diseases as tuberculosis (TB) and venereal disease conveniently side-stepped government and medical responsibility for the health of Indigenous peoples. Discourses positioning colonized bodies as "*by nature* unclean and diseased" obscured the fact that colonial processes, by debasing Indigenous medicinal practices, spreading European diseases, and stripping Indigenous communities of their traditional land, livelihoods, and food sources, were creating more disease than Euro-Canadian medicine could possibly cure (15–6, 57, 99, 177). Like Vaughn and Kelm, Kathryn McPherson and Hugh Shewell both interpret medical practices as colonial projects, and argue that state health and hygiene programs also justified such egregious colonial projects as the residential school system and the "sixties scoop," the mass removal of children from their Aboriginal homes by provincial child welfare agencies, since such projects reiterated Aboriginal peoples as unclean, unhealthy, diseased and, in short, as poor parents.

While the historians discussed above are quick to distinguish between the intent of individual state and medical agents and the intent of government policy *in general*, they also show that, overall, colonialist health practices reflected the culture of white supremacy from which they arose. Colonialist medicine furthered racist ideology and aided colonial-capitalist expansion. In positioning Indigenous bodies as ontologically diseased and unhealthy—as abject—practices undertaken in the name of Indigenous health were far from benign, and often undermined subsistence lifestyles and attachments to lands in a way that benefited the Canadian government and non-Indigenous Canadians.

As seemingly magnanimous yet inevitably injurious systems of knowledge, colonialist medicine and medical science can therefore be understood to have facilitated the anti-conquest of Indigenous lands and peoples. Analysing various sub-genres of European travel writing from the eighteenth century, Pratt describes anti-conquest as an ostensibly power-neutral process whereby the "planet's life forms were ... drawn out of the tangled threads of their life surrounds and rewoven into European-based patterns of global unity and order ... [by the] ... lettered, male, European ... eye" (31). While Pratt critiques a variety of travel narratives, it is her analysis of European scientific classification systems and naturalists' logs of the eighteenth century that is most applicable to my analysis of postwar obesity. Pratt argues that European classifications of humans, plants, and animals into scientific groupings represented a "planetary consciousness" that ideologically and materially facilitated European colonial projects. Spawned by the work of Carl Linnaeus, whose taxonomic system became the standard for botanists, an army of naturalists and scientists set out to name, divide, and classify the world's human and non-human nature for the purposes of European and scientific consumption.

The taxonomic work of Linnaeus and his followers did more than scientifically and "benevolently" classify plants and animals, though this in itself was a violent act that could not but be helpful for European capitalists or traders wishing to know what riches an unknown land might hold (Pratt 34). Linnaeus also devised a taxonomic classification for humans that was based entirely upon racist and colonialist imaginings of Europeans and their "Others." While the European was "gentle, acute, inventive" and "[g]overned by laws," for instance, peoples from Africa were "phlegmatic, ... crafty, indolent, negligent ... [and] [g]overned by caprice" (Pratt 32). Thus, human taxonomy was one epistemology upon which white supremacy and colonial-capitalism rested.[5]

In *Imperial Leather*, Anne McClintock traces connections among Victorian science, the classification of race, and colonial capitalism, arguing that the "planetary consciousness" described by Pratt did not achieve a coherent universality until the latter half of the nineteenth century, when the science of Linnaeus was popularized by Darwin's theory of evolution. Social Darwinists, armed with the idea of natural selection, applied Darwin's theories of nature to human societies in a distinctly white supremacist fashion, advocating a racial classification system now known as "scientific racism," "the most authoritative attempt to place social ranking and social disability on a biological and 'scientific' footing" (McClintock). Practitioners of scientific racism categorized races via the powerful metaphor of the "family of man," often represented as a racial family tree. Growing as the tree's lowest branches, social Darwinists purported, were the most de-evolved people, the African or the "primitive," while the white, Western European man inhabited the top branch, that of the wise and mature patriarch. Races were assigned "branches," or categories, on the basis of biological characteristics such as lips, skin colour, genitals, noses, foreheads, and buttocks (McClintock 36–44). Importantly, Amy Erdmann Farrell argues in *Fat Shame* that one such characteristic during this time was "excess" body fat, which, through Cartesian logic, equated fatness with women's reproductive processes and, related, femininity. At the same time, fat was inherently racialized and associated with the "primitive" body. As such, she argues, "the fat body ... was a primitive body, lower on the scale of civilization and highly sexual" (68).

McClintock shows that disease was also an important category that classified bodies, as scientific racism "proved" correspondence between the "lower order" of humans and greater rates of disease, much as it equated large lips and flat noses with racialized populations. The imaginative cordoning off of the races into different and distinct branches helped assuage anxieties of white colonists, whose continued worry about disease functioned as a proxy for and as a denial of the racial degeneration or, more accurately, the racial contamination that was imagined to result from Europeans' inevitable contact (both physical and non-physical) with their colonized Others.

In McClintock's words, anxieties about disease were, in part, a "[p]anic about blood contiguity, ambiguity and *metissage* [and the] ... fallibility of white male and imperial potency" (47).

While mid-twentieth-century sub-Arctic and Arctic Canada are of course very different from eighteenth- and nineteenth-century Europe and Victorian Britain, not the least because the colonization of the North in the 1960s occurred during and directly following a period of ostensible worldwide decolonization, I argue that echoes of previous European colonialist knowledge systems described by Pratt and McClintock are evident in the medical and scientific projects that helped define obesity as a burgeoning northern embodiment (Escobar; Thobani 147). Taking my cue from theorists of disease construction and historians of colonial medicine, I show how state and medical discourse regarding northern obesity worked, once again, to position colonized peoples as Cartesian bodies that were perpetually diseased. Unlike the contagious diseases described by Vaughn and Kelm, because obesity was considered a pathology of modernity, obesity discourse did not primitivize Indigenous bodies, as "obesity" was not *associated with* "primitive" bodies, but rather this discourse imbued them with an abject characteristic otherwise attributed to "civilized" Euro-Canadians.

In this way, my analysis of fat and colonialization is different from that of Erdman Farrell's in that her work demonstrates (along with Gilman's) how fat became part of the ideological schema through which certain body parts came to "primitivize" both white fat people and Indigenous peoples during the period of colonization she describes. Some of this disparateness results, in part, from the fact that excess fat in postwar Canada was transitioning from a racialized body characteristic (like large lips, buttocks, and so on) to a racialized *disease* or, at least, a condition that accompanied or caused chronic disease. As such, obesity took on the discourses, and the "risk populations," that accompanied discussions of chronic illnesses generally. In addition, discourses of body fat and obesity must be understood contextually according to the time and place in which they emerge. A careful analysis of fat in colonial projects therefore lends further credence to postcolonial theorists' well-established contention that colonialism is itself contingent, and must be understood as a collection of heterogeneous projects that were and are sometimes deployed even within *the same* time and place (Agathangelou and Ling 839–40).

Obesity in the postwar North is an example of this heterogeneity. Western scientific narratives claiming the so-called "thrifty gene" first emerged in 1962 (Poudrier; Fee 2990). Discussions of northern Indigenous obesity in 1960s Canada could therefore have very well cordoned off "genetically and biologically determined boundaries" that would have collapsed people in the North with "primitiveness" (Abonyi qtd. in Poudrier 256). Yet a study of state and medical documents suggests that in the North the opposite was also true. While thrifty gene theory laid the groundwork for the "primitivism" of obesity, obesity research also reflected the paradigm of assimilation that had for years been employed by Canadian colonial medicine and the state (Kelm 314; Lawrence; Shewell). In the documents I studied, discourses of northern obesity relied upon and were grounded in the general contention that northern Indigenous peoples and their cultures were becoming less racially distinct, which supposedly indicated both the success of state modernizing and development projects that had been occurring since the 1950s and the "racial admixture" of formerly isolated northern people with white settler Canadians (MacAlpine et al. 138). In a way, though, this inflection of the narrative is not that far removed from the thrifty gene story, according to which Indigenous peoples' genetic inheritance "kicked in" during a time of feast in order to store as much fat as possible to prepare for a time of "famine." During the postwar period, northern peoples were imaged to be in a time of "feast" due to their inevitable march up the ladder of "progress," thus creating a problem of excess fat as yet unseen—or at least unimagined—in northern Indigenous peoples.

The potential presence of excess body fat on northern Indigenous people in the 1960s, and instances of other "diseases of civilization" such as cardiovascular disease, contributed to the notion that traditional northern culture was in transition, or dying, at the very time that the state was attempting to kill Indigenous sovereignty through policy. I argue, then, that obesity discourse imaginatively altered the bodies of colonized Others in order to help assert dominant power regimes founded in the capitalist accumulation and exploitation of northern lands and people. Links among obesity, other chronic illnesses like heart disease, and northern peoples' bodies were not, however, always so easily forged. In the postwar period to the middle of the 1960s, obesity remained an embodiment primarily for white, middle-class people that Aboriginal people were imagined too primitive to develop. Indeed, a study of Canadian disease in the early postwar period demonstrates that First Nations and Inuit populations were far more associated with instances of contagious, not chronic, illness. While a few individuals may have expressed concern about chronic illness in relation to Indigenous people of this period, as demonstrated by the 1957–1958 Nutrition Division and Indian and Northern Health Services joint study into the heart disease and cholesterol levels in Inuit peoples detailed below, connections between Indigenous peoples and chronic illnesses such as obesity did not gain popularity until the mid- to late 1960s. The exclusion of Indigenous people from the category of chronic illness was in large part due to the strong partnership of colonized Cartesian embodiments with contagious illness that positioned Aboriginal peoples as "primitive" until well into the 1960s.

From Contagious to Chronic: Racialization and Disease Patterns in Canada

In the early years of the postwar era, and in a moment of unabashed hubris considering the current emergence of COVID-19, Canadian medical and public health agents took credit for the virtual elimination of contagious disease (Doughy 273–78; Farquharson 1–9; Mather, "Health and Welfare" 455–59; Mather "Need for a Truly Generalized" 143–50). Many commentators argued that the invention and widespread dissemination of antibiotics, including penicillin, and better sanitation practices were bringing an end to many diseases that had once plagued the nation. In 1952, for example, C. D. Farquharson bragged in the *Canadian Journal of Public Health*: "Now, with the ability to cure, we can confidently expect that most of the infections that have plagued the human race will become things of the past. Already the mortality from pneumonia, scarlet fever, tuberculosis, syphilis, whooping cough and wound infections has been brought to an all-time low" (1).

While an overwhelming sense of optimism is evident in many medical texts, some people were more cautious than others. As the 1950s wore on, writers noted with increasing frequency that though whooping cough and TB deaths were dropping, high numbers of the population with chronic diseases indicated that not all was completely well with Canadians (Charron, "Chronic Diseases"; Charron, "Economic and Social Consequences"; Feeder; Howie; Page; Philips, "What it Means"; Roth). As Elisabeth C. Phillips declared in a 1956 issue of *Canadian Nurse*, "Chronic illness is perhaps the most important, urgent and complex problem that society faces today"("Impact of Chronic Illness" 524). While chronic illness was one of the seemingly endless arrays of "urgent" and "most important" national health issues already discussed, this particular disease category was especially exigent in that it incorporated a range of conditions such as mental illness, heart disease, and obesity.

Much of the discourse concerned with the increase of chronic illness was related to the gradual release of data from the Canadian Sickness Survey (Acker 128–33; Canada, *Canadian Sickness Survey*; Canada, *Injuries—Frequency*; Dominion Bureau of Statistics; Elliott, "Administration and Methods"; Hatcher; Kennedy; Kohn; MacDonald; Martin; Peart, "Canada's Sickness Survey"). The Canadian Sickness Survey was an offshoot of the federal health grants program of 1948 and, though federally funded, was jointly administered by the Department of Health and Welfare, the Dominion Bureau of Statistics, and provincial departments of health (*Disability among the Gainfully Employed*). Anticipating a universal Medicare scheme, the study was designed to assess the nation's health care needs and expenses (Martin 323–29; Peart, "Canada's Sickness Survey"). The Sickness Survey lasted one year, from 1950 to 1951, and was carried out in the ten provinces and in 10,000 households, a household being defined in patriarchal terms as "all persons living in one dwelling" whose members consisted of the "head of the household," "his wife," and "his unmarried children"

(Canada, *Canadian Sickness Survey 1950* 17–18; Canada, *Injuries—Frequency*). Results were released throughout the 1950s and early 1960s. While the Sickness Survey was concerned with contagious disease, encouraging informants to report on, for example, "cough and other chest trouble," of specific interest to those writing in the medical and popular presses were the numbers of chronic conditions like "digestive," "heart," and "nerve trouble" asked about by enumerators (Canada, *Canadian Sickness Survey 1950*). Levels of Canadian chronic illness were particularly shocking to *Maclean's* writer Doris McCubbin, who waxed sensationally about Sickness Survey results in her 1955 article "Are We Breeding a Nation of Invalids?" The survey had found that 957,000 participants had some sort of permanent illness (Canada, *Canadian Sickness Survey 1950–1951* 14). Applying this figure to the nation as a whole, McCubbin was appalled that "[i]n an antiseptic age of medical miracles, when vaccines, vitamins, and penicillin have become house-hold words ... probably more than two millions [*sic*] are chronically ill and disabled"(14). Even though the Sickness Survey had found the top two chronic illnesses to be arthritis and heart disease. McCubbin warned that the increasing diabetes and mental illness reflected in Sickness Survey results would "run wild" if measures were not implemented to curtail them (Canada, *Canadian Sickness Survey 1950–1951* 14; McCubbin 15). The writer advocated sterilization laws to prevent diabetes and mental "defections" in new generations of Canadians (McCubbin 93–94).

McCubbin's eugenic solution to chronic illness was certainly not advocated by all, though other writers shared her conviction that something had to be done. For federal government representatives like Gordon E. Write from the Department of National Health and Welfare, the solution to chronic illness was more and better health care for all Canadians, regardless of income (Write 15–23). Others advocated the rather nebulous project of "prevention," the harbinger of modern health promotion, particularly for heart ailments, which were linked to sedentary lifestyles and over-nutrition. Despite disagreement regarding how to cure chronic illness, however, all agreed as to what caused it: modern living (Elliott, "Presidential Address"; Farquharson; Roemer).

Ironically, and reflecting the "suspicious ambivalence" about modernization identified by Gard and Wright, medical advances like penicillin, better health care and sanitation, and the subsequent lack of contagious diseases were said to be causing chronic illnesses. As F. B. Roth, Saskatchewan's Minister of Public Health, noted, "One of the most interesting yet most difficult challenges of modern civilization is that as we solve problems of relative simplicity, we create new problems of increasing complexity" (371). Because contagious disease no longer claimed the lives of young Canadians, the nation's population was growing older. As Canadians aged, they became susceptible to chronic illness, due to the simple fact that they were living long enough to develop heart problems, suffer strokes, or put on "excess" weight. In the words of McCubbin, "We've licked the childhood diseases, all right, but as a nation we're getting older and sicker, simply because we've become more and more skilful at keeping ourselves alive" (15).[6]

Through the trope of disease, then, whereby contagious diseases were imagined to have been conquered by modern innovation, those who continued to have tuberculosis, measles, parasites, and leprosy belonged to the terrible, really not-so-distant past where epidemics ran rampant and most people died well before old age. While "modern" Canadians were suffering from greater numbers of chronic diseases due to medical and public health advances, Indigenous peoples were, apparently, not. First Nations and Inuit people were generally regarded as throwbacks to an age previous to modern advances in pharmacology and civil engineering. In this way, Indigenous bodies were performatively positioned as *ontologically* abject (as opposed to modern bodies who could *develop* abject embodiments such as obesity).

Ostensibly due to a lack of sanitation and poor hygiene, the First Nations and Inuit were said to be suffering from such atavistic communicable diseases as TB, pneumonia, and measles, diseases that had been "licked" in so-called modern Canadians (Best et al. 412–14; Copp; Hildes et al.; Moddy 12–13, 34–38; Moore, "Medical Care"; Moore, "Puvalluttuq"; "Parasitic Diseases"; Peart, "Measles"; Ward). This was particularly true for Inuit peoples, who, as Sangster has argued, were imagined to reside in, or to have emerged only recently from, the Stone Age (194–95;

Wilkinson 28–30, 103–09). In the postwar era until the middle 1960s, medical literature almost always articulated Indigenous health problems in terms of contagious illness. As Kenneth A. Ward noted in the *Canadian Medical Association Journal* (*CMAJ*), following an Arctic ministration to tubercular Inuit peoples, “The native due to his primitive living conditions very easily develops complications such as broncho-pneumonia, otitis media and of course exacerbation of a smouldering tuberculosis” (296; Hildes 1255).

First Nations and Inuit were not the only populations positioned as abject contagions. Immigrants were also suspect (“Canada”; Cheung 330–31; Hacker; Lenczner and Owen; “Parasitic Diseases”; Rutta and Wrong 19–21). In *Gatekeepers,* Franca Iacovetta describes the medical screening program for postwar refugees to Canada, noting that such testing was part of an overall campaign to contain the supposedly contagious bodies of immigrant populations (330). Within such screening programs, TB was a major concern, as were other “tropic diseases,” which at times did now show up upon screening tests (particularly in the case of leprosy). Immigrants were therefore constructed not only as a threat to the national body but also as “non-Canadian”; even though a patient may appear “normal” and might therefore seem not to require tests, contact with immigrants could prove fateful to “real” Canadians at any moment (Rutta and Wrong 19).

Thus, studying perceptions of contagious illness in postwar Canada to the early 1960s reveals that contagious and congenital illnesses were racialized concepts and that Indigenous and immigrant bodies became racialized through what Foucault calls the “power/knowledge regimes” of the Canadian medical establishment. Specifically, and most important to this chapter, conflations of “primitive” or “less-developed” populations with contagious illness demonstrates that both contagious and chronic illnesses were forged in, through, and partially because of Canadian colonial-capitalist projects. In the era of postwar Canada under study, in addition to Canada’s continued pilfering of more southern Indigenous lands, colonial-capitalism took the form of a vigorous push north to the sub-Arctic and Arctic regions of the nation, in a complex process of sometimes-disparate practices known as "northern development." It was through discourses that allowed northern development to become tenable, and those which eventually declared developmental projects a success, that Indigenous bodies were eventually attached to the category of obesity.

Health, Northern Development, and National Identity

Canada's northern shores were crucially situated in case of all-out war with Russia, and its soil held rich deposits of uranium, facts that bestowed Canada with not only considerable clout in relation to its Western allies but also a profound sense of vulnerability. As Grant argues, "The possibility of Soviet aggression, combined with the uranium fields on the shores of Great Bear Lake and the advances in aviation technology firmly entrenched the wartime significance of the region" (Grant, *Sovereignty or Security?* 240; see also Grant, *Polar Imperative*). As a result, the government allowed the American military, which had established a presence in Canada's North in World War II, to remain in the Arctic regions. Even though such an alliance meant "being dependent upon a traditional adversary to defend against a potential one," the Canadian government permitted the United States military to erect the Distant Early Warning (DEW) line and weather stations throughout the Arctic, which would detect enemy bombers and help coordinate the American air defence (Grant, *Sovereignty or Security?*).

The Canadian public, and indeed state officials, were ambivalent about American soldiers lumbering about "their" North, and worried about a possible US takeover of the area (Grant, *Polar Imperative*; Grant, *Sovereignty or Security?* 195, 244, 245–46). In part a result of such anxieties, and in part to exploit the Cold War need for uranium, the federal government launched a scheme called "northern development." Northern development increased the presence of Canadians in the North, thus fortifying Canadian sovereignty, while it also opened the North to intense industrial exploitation. To facilitate resource extraction and assert Canada's claim to northern areas, the federal state instituted policy to assimilate Inuit and northern Indigenous peoples into what was imagined as mainstream (white) Canadian society (Grant, "Case of Compounded Error"). This was done under the auspices of the state's general policy of assimilation, which was to culminate in 1969 with the release of the federal government's *White Paper on Indian Policy*. While Inuit people were not part of the Indian Act, it is important to recognize the overall tone of federal government policy with regard to Indigenous people of this time—a tone that is captured generally by the Indian Act.

Finkel and Conrad have called the *White Paper on Indian Policy*, colloquially known as the *White Paper*, "a policy of cultural genocide" (Finkel and Conrad 403). The *White Paper* proposed that Ottawa "remove Indians' special status, dismantle the Department of Indian Affairs, and [allow] the provinces [to] assume responsibilities for Native [*sic*] people." The *White Paper* thus counteracted the federally funded *Hawthorn Report* released only three years earlier in 1966, which recommended the cessation of all federal assimilation policy and encouraged the state to regard Indigenous peoples as Canadians with special status, or as "citizens plus" (Canada *Report of Royal Commission*; Shewell 298).

Devised by Jean Chretien, then the federal minister responsible for Indigenous and northern affairs, and Prime Minister Pierre Trudeau who, Finkel argues, possessed an "insensitivity, and indeed hostility, to ethnic nationalism," the *White Paper* used the rhetoric of equality to insist that Indigenous peoples were ordinary citizens (48). As citizens, Indigenous people were eligible for the same rights as any other Canadian, no less and certainly no more. As expressed in the 1969 document,

> For many Indian [*sic*] people, one road does exist, the only road that has existed since confederation and before, the road of different status, a road which has led to a blind alley of deprivation and frustration. This road, because it is a separate road, cannot lead to full participation, to equality in practice as well as in theory. ... [T]he Government has outlined a number of measures and a policy which it is convinced will offer another road for Indians, a road that will lead gradually away from

> different status to full social, economic and political participation in Canadian life. This is the choice. (Canada, *Statement of the Government*)

Strong Indigenous dissent and organized resistance eventually led the government to scrap the *White Paper* (Finkel 250). The *White Paper* is important, however, to understanding northern development, inasmuch as development programs were moving in the overall direction of the complete assimilation proposed by the document.

Social welfare projects in general, which included and affected health and health care programming, were part of the federal government's overall agenda of northern development and assimilation. As Shewell argues, a number of social welfare programs were mobilized to draw Northerners into development schemes, some of which were implemented only after the displacement of Indigenous families from their lands to more centralized and easily managed towns and villages (Canada, *Report of Royal Commission*; Tester and Kulchyski). Within the context of economic development and social welfare projects, wherein Indigenous communities were relocated near sites of mining, military, and administrative activity so that Indigenous men could find manual work, the health of northern First Nations and Inuit families took on new meaning. Again demonstrating the metonymic relationship between the fear of contact with the abject Other and disease concerns, contagious illnesses among Indigenous populations now had the perceived potential to affect military and administrative settlements that housed non-Indigenous Canadians (Canada, *Report of Royal Commission*).[7] Further and more practically, ill Indigenous men could not perform taxing physical labour.

At the same time that health concerns reified the abjectness and degeneracy of Indigenous peoples, however, the establishment and expansion of health care bureaucracy in the North also had assimilative effects (Jasen 394–95). As the postwar northern health bureaucracy intensified, especially with the transfer of the northern health portfolio from Indian Affairs to the Department of Health and Welfare in 1945, so did the notion that northern peoples had a right to health care, just like any other Canadian in an era preparing for the imminent federally funded Medicare plan (Canada, *Report of Royal Commission* 440; Tester and Kulchyski 58). For example, the final report of the Royal Commission on Health Services clearly positioned northern peoples as rights-bearing citizens in relation to health care and, therefore, as the same as other Canadians: "Health services for those people [in the North] and the area they inhabit must become part and parcel of Canada's future health services. Our task is completed only when we have recommended such measures as we believe will ensure that the best possible health care is available to *all* Canadians" (Canada, *Royal Commission on Health*). In an ironic twist to the federal government's pre-war assertion that the Inuit, like other Canadians, had no claim to health care, the federal state of the postwar era assumed once again that northern peoples were ordinary citizens, though this time with a right to government health services. Incorporating northern Indigenous peoples into the health bureaucracy, while preferable to the complete neglect of northern health and illness in previous decades, discursively articulated northern peoples as ordinary Canadian citizens, thus helping to set the stage for the total assimilation advocated by the *White Paper*.

Anti-Obesity Regimes, Research, and "Transitioning" Indigenous Peoples

In the mid-1960s, a conflicting discourse began to surface in texts that dispelled the belief that northern peoples remained undeveloped and highly susceptible to contagious illness. During this time, some government agents, medical practitioners, and medical researchers began to argue that northern First Nations and Inuit bodies were progressing, and although contagious diseases were still a problem, Indigenous bodies were said to be more vulnerable to modern chronic illnesses such as hypertension, heart disease, and obesity. This was a result, in part, of the fact that numbers of contagious illnesses were dropping in the North due partly to the intensification of health programming there, so medical practitioners and researchers could shift their attention from contagious to chronic disease (Canada, *Report of Royal Commission* 119, 138–39). Less obviously, the notion that northern Indigenous bodies were becoming modern reflected an overall belief that the accelerated processes of northern development were annihilating northern First Nations and Inuit cultures. While some were critical of development schemes and regretted the potential loss of northern Indigenous ways of life, many agreed that traditional northern communities were quickly becoming modern and adopting southern practices, behaviours, and even genetics (Sangster 293). Belief in the ultimate end of distinct northern cultures and peoples persisted despite, or perhaps because of, the fact that northern Indigenous people had organized community councils in the 1960s and were beginning collectively to resist southern exploitation, bureaucratization, and assimilation, a movement that came to full flower in the 1970s (Grant, *Polar Imperative*; Tester and Kulchyski 43, 204).

Accompanying the notion that northern First Nations and Inuit were progressing, chronic illnesses, including obesity, became important markers of modernity for northern peoples. The idea that obesity could become a problem among the Inuit and First Nations was a significant discursive shift, given that government and medical sources had previously believed northern Indigenous peoples to be relatively free of chronic problems like heart disease, diabetes, and the obesity associated with them. Nevertheless, anti-obesity regimes and studies employed in the North did begin to collapse obesity with northern First Nations and Inuit bodies, a collapse that was possible, I argue, because of the climate of hyper-assimilation in this period.

A Shifting Discourse: The Onset of Obesity and Other Chronic Illnesses

Nutrition Surveys

In the documents studied, the earliest reference to a study of obesity in northern Indigenous populations was made in 1964, relating to a small preliminary survey carried out by Otto Schaefer, a medical researcher, physician, and federal government employee. In that year, Schaefer boarded the Eastern Arctic Patrol to measure the effects of "nutritional factors," "changing patterns of physical activity," and "civilization stresses" on Inuit groups (Schaefer to Matas). In his preliminary report, Schaefer seemed surprised by higher than expected levels of hypertension, but he was most alarmed by his findings on obesity. "It has always been my contention that obesity is rare in Eskimos [*sic*]," Schaefer noted, but the results of his survey had proved him wrong (Schaefer to Matas). In particular, Schaefer found that skinfold values (a measurement for the amount of fat on the body) in more "modern" areas of the Arctic were well above average. He noted in his report that "[i]t appears remarkable that in districts where less hunting and more handicraft and wage employment prevails as in the Hudson Strait and Ungava Bay, skinfold thickness increases, while in districts where practically all males are exclusively hunters no excess subcutaneous fat is found and minimal values prevail" (Schaefer to Matas). As an offshoot of this study, Schaefer proposed yet another one: a nutrition survey of Inuit peoples developed in concert with the federal government Nutrition Division.

Comprised primarily of self-administered food diaries that were distributed to the Inuit, the year-long study was designed to track relationships among northern development, changes in diet, and the proliferation of concomitant chronic illnesses. The federal government had expressed an interest in Inuit nutrition before, as is evident by the 1963 Medical Services publication, *Good Food—Good Health*, which was intended to guide Inuit peoples in their transition from a "traditional" to a "modern" diet (Canada, *Good Food*).[8] The 1957–1958 cholesterol study carried out by the Nutrition Division and Indian and Northern Health Services also indicated the federal state's interest in the nutrition of Inuit people in relation to potential heart problems (Moore to Armstrong; Pett to Anonymous; Pett to Blake; Pett to Moore; Pett and Lupien; Schaefer "Medical Observations"). It was not until Schaefer's 1964–1965 survey, however, that a federal government agency expressed an active interest in Inuit nutrition as it related specifically to obesity, which, Schaefer argued, had progressed from a possibility to a reality by 1964.

Schaefer made clear his intent to study obesity in his letter to Indigenous "households" introducing the survey to participants: "Since the white man came the food for many Eskimos [*sic*] has been changing. You can now buy many different foods in the stores. In some places people still live on seal, fish and caribou. When this food was scarce, flour, sugar and lard helped keep people from starving. This was a good thing. Eskimos sometimes like to eat something different" ("Letter to All Eskimo Households"). Even as people might sometimes like variety, Schaefer noted that change from a subsistence-based diet and new activity patterns could precipitate health problems, including under-nutrition but also obesity: "When you eat and how much you eat has a lot to do with your health. When people don't get enough to eat they may get sick and weak or if they eat too much and don't move around they can get fat" ("Letter to All Eskimo Households").

As reported in Schaefer's article in a 1971 edition of *Nutrition Today*, entitled "When the Eskimo Comes to Town," the nutrition survey found that Inuit diets were becoming more like those attributed to normative Canadians, particularly in relation to the consumption of sugar. Given that the increased use of sugar was "causally related to a number of phenomena intimately associated with the health of Western peoples in modern times," including obesity, it was no surprise to Schaefer that the Inuit were supposedly becoming increasingly fat (Schaefer, "When Eskimos Come" 11). Using the language of the gendered division of labour to compare the pre-contact Inuit family with the family of the post-northern development era living in settlements, Schaefer painted a dire picture of the nutrition survey findings:

> Now it is the mid-1960's. Our family has moved to the construction site of a defence installation and airstrip. The husband and son have found work there. They eat three meals a day in the cafeteria. The richness of those meals shows in their bulging paunches. ... The women while away their idle hours chewing chocolates instead of animal skins, attending movie shows, and drinking Cokes

> and other sugared soft drinks. There is little else for them to do. They no longer need to sew and make clothes or scourge for food. (Schaefer, "When Eskimos Come" 10)

In addition to obesity, Schaefer wondered if diabetes might someday affect the Inuit, though the disease had yet to obtain great significance, in his opinion, in Indigenous populations.

Mosby argues that such an argument, that "modern foodways" were unhealthy for northern Indigenous people, had been made by federal nutrition agents and others since at least the 1930s (Mosby 154–55). Thus, the urgency with which Schaefer (and others, as I explore below) spoke of the "discovery" of the changing foodways of northern Indigenous peoples seems at first blush to be somewhat odd, given that concerns of this nature had existed for quite some time. Within this earlier rhetoric, however, the concern was that "store foods" or foods bought at the store and imported from the South were malnourishing for Indigenous bodies, not *over* nourishing, suggesting that obesity discourse perhaps in part fuelled this "new" crisis. This reinvigoration of a nutritional crisis in northern Indigenous peoples was also perhaps yet another inflection of supposedly "benevolent" colonization, as settlers can claim to "help" supposedly "dying" or sick Indigenous peoples (by implementing nutritional surveys, for example), while denying colonizers' culpability in Indigenous people's ill health.

International Biological Programme

Schaefer's work was echoed by the International Biological Programme (IBP), a large scientific study occurring in the Arctic between 1968 and 1973. In this project, a cohort of international medical scientists and anthropologists dedicated themselves to tracking the transition of the Inuit from "primitive" to "modern" before it was too late for such a study. Like Schaefer's nutrition survey, the IBP tied obesity and other chronic illnesses to northern development and specifically to the arrangement of Inuit societies into nuclear families whose subsistence lifestyles were a thing of the past.

The IBP was conceived in the 1950s by a group of European scientists who were part of the International Council of Scientific Unions, and it officially began in 1961 (Kwa 415). Spread over fifty-eight countries and thirteen years, IBP scientists studied the co-evolution of humans and ecosystems, especially those populations and landscapes that were threatened or endangered by environmental degradation and economic development (IBP, "International Council"; Weiner 1; Worthington 18–19).

The IBP was organized by an international umbrella committee, which in turn spawned subcommittees in participating countries to oversee individual national projects. The Canadian Committee for the IBP was primarily funded by the National Research Council of Canada, with a contribution by the Department of Indian Affairs and Northern Development, which provided transportation, a laboratory, and living space to Arctic researchers of the IBP, at least until the laboratory, which housed most of the researchers' equipment and the researchers themselves, mysteriously burned down in 1969 (Hughes, "Director's Summary" 2). The Canada Council, the National Museum of Canada, and various universities also made smaller contributions (Hughes, "Director's Summary" 2; Hughes, "Human Adaptability" 10). The Canadian Committee for the IBP (1971) coordinated research on topics such as the "productivity" of terrestrial, freshwater, and marine communities; the conservation of ecologically sensitive areas; and human adaptability, the last of which was part of a larger IBP study of Indigenous peoples in such places as the Amazon, Africa, New Guinea, the Pacific Islands, New Zealand, India, and the Canadian Arctic (Canadian Committee for the IBP; Weiner 16, 19).

Geographically, the Canadian IBP study of the Arctic was located in Igloolik, Northwest Territories. Discursively, the project took place in the context of a veritable explosion of anthropological, geographical, sociological, scientific, and medical research on the North, which was part of the overall expansion of northern programming in the 1950s and 1960s. As Morris Zaslow notes, the northern Aboriginal peoples of this time "became one of the most heavily assisted, administered, and studied groups on earth" (Zaslow 269). Indeed, by the time the IBP was initiated in the Eastern Arctic, the Inuit there were expressing what researchers called "subject fatigue," and community members often refused to participate in the IBP or did so only half-heartedly (Chiarelli 239; De Pena "Igloolik Project" 7–8; Hughes, "Report on Status" 86). The IBP was also preceded by a larger postwar interest in molecular genetics present in the scientific and anthropological communities, spurred by what IBP participants Collins and Weiner called "the spectacular unravelling of the genetic code" (Weiner 1). In Canada, genetic research was sometimes undertaken to explain and predict the racial origins and physiological characteristics of Indigenous peoples, as in the case of the thrifty gene ("Anthropological Record"; Chown and Lewis 17; Partington and Roberts 502–09; Reid 548–49).

The IBP Human Adaptability project extended such research but was particularly interested in the introduction of white genetic material into Indigenous populations. Researchers were to study how life in the jungle, the desert, or the Arctic had affected the genetic development of the Aboriginal people, and how shifts in genetic make-up were, in turn, affecting life in these "extreme" climates. In very basic terms, the IBP project aimed to determine what was nature and what was nurture of the behavioural and physical characteristics of Indigenous peoples, and how progress and development projects were changing both (Hughes "Human Adaptability" 10; Weiner 1, 3). Such a study was important, researchers determined, for two reasons. First, it was imperative that the genetic and physiological characteristics of "dying" cultures be recorded for the sake of the anthropological record before it was too late. Characterized as what McClintock would call "anachronistic space," where the modern subject can "journey back in time to [a] ... moment of prehistory," and linking the majority world to the Canadian North, the three field sites of the jungle, the desert, and the Arctic housed peoples who provided a last glimpse at "modern man's" evolutionary past (McClintock 40; Chiarelli 236; De Pena, "Igloolik Project" 2; Weiner 1, 3). Additionally, the Human Adaptability studies were considered useful in that they scientifically quantified the effects of development projects on Indigenous peoples who were, it was imagined, becoming increasingly modernized ("A Proposal for Human Adaptability").

Almost without exception, the IBP reports on the residents of Igloolik, particularly those concerned with diet, activity, and body composition, positioned the Inuit as "almost Western" or "becoming white" and argued that urbanization and non-traditional lifestyles were changing the very morphology of "the Inuit body." Joan T. Mayhall's report on dental hygiene and dentistry, for example, found "rapidly" escalating incidence of dental caries (cavities) and periodontal disease in the "more acculturated" people of Igloolik (52). Mayhall's work was augmented by Milne's study of nutrition, which discussed escalating sugar consumption rates among the Inuit. While a food co-operative offering traditionally hunted foods had been established by Igloolik residents,[9] Milne argued that a growing number of Inuit purchased "more complex" foods at the Hudson's Bay Company store and that the "pattern of non-refusal to the child has meant that soft drink and sweet consumption has increased" (Milne 5). Krog and Wika's study of the "peripheral circulation" of Inuit hands, meanwhile, found that "the introduction of modern equipment for transport like skidoos" was modifying the flow of blood in the bodies of their subjects (174). MacAlpine et al., in their study of the genetic markers of "racial admixture" in the Igloolik Inuit, found a surprisingly high incidence of chromosomal mutation, or "alleles," for such an "isolated population" (MacAlpine et al. 138). The researchers attributed genetic changes to the recent "introduction of new alleles into the original Eskimo gene pool by Caucasian admixture," which accompanied the migration of military, government, resource extraction, and other non-Native workers to the developing North (MacAlpine et al. 138).

Joan De Pena gathered a plethora of measurements on "Igloolik Eskimos." Resonating with previous colonialist scientific practices described by McClintock, who argues that measurements of foreheads, skulls, noses, and ears helped to organize seemingly biological races on the "family tree of man," De Pena photographed and filmed the bodies of Igloolik residents, paying specific attention to such details as eye obliquity, forehead slope, nasal tip inclination, chin prominence, ear slant, eyebrow thickness, hair form and texture, lips, tongue roll, and body hair quantity (McClintock 29, 33–441; Gilman, *Making the Body Beautiful*; De Pena, "Addendum 2"). De Pena also studied the overall stature of bodies at different ages, including the body fat content and weight of individual adults and children.

The results of De Pena's study showed that Igloolik children were larger than they had previously been and exhibited a "greater and faster growth trend" (De Pena, "Igloolik Project" 29). Igloolik adults were also changing stature, depending upon age. Those adults between the ages of forty and fifty, De Pena noted, showed the "lowest sitting height," the men were more muscular in their upper arm, while the women had "the lowest triceps skinfold means" (De Pena, "Igloolik Project" 41). Younger subjects, meanwhile, were taller and had higher skinfolds. De Pena suggested that such data could be due to northern development, which was increasingly shaping the lives—and bodies—of younger adults while many of their elders remained traditional: "the current 40–50 year old age group are currently—or most recently—the most active hunters and their wives who accompany their husbands to camp ... and are thus less active partakers of the 'amenities' of community patterns (e.g., access to store foods, cash wages, care of minor illnesses)"(42). De Pena suggested that the shorter, more muscular bodies of forty- to fifty-year-old Igloolik peoples with "blocky trunks" and a "tendency toward leanness rather than fat" might represent "physical evidence of a body build positively correlated with and selective for the traditional Inuit hunting pattern" (42).

The notion that the traditionally lean, muscular "hunting body" of the Igloolik peoples was rapidly disappearing, leaving a bloated, soft, and distinctly more modern body in its wake, was repeated in R. J. Shephard's IBP study of the physical fitness of Igloolik residents. As Shephard's study noted, "the supposed unusual body build [of the Inuit], with short stature, large trunk/leg-length ratio and a low centre of gravity seems a rapidly receding phenomenon" (Godin and Shephard 185). Accompanied by graduate students Godin and Rode, a portion of whose report opens this chapter, Shephard administered physical work capacity (PWC) and energy expenditure tests on Igloolik residents. Using white Canadians as the norm against which the Inuit were measured, Shephard collected data that concurred with all other studies and showed that the population of Igloolik was a society "in transition." While maximal tests, in which participants ascended and descended an eighteen-inch step, and sub-maximal tests, in which subjects pedalled an exercise bike, showed that even though many Igloolik residents maintained the fitness levels of "athletic 'Caucasians'" and "total body fat was lower than values reported for a comparable 'white' population," northern bodies were in the process of changing (Rode 1–2). As Rode argued, cardiovascular disease and obesity were certain to increase as a "segment of the population," or the "urban group" of Igloolik people who had given up traditional hunting practices, was "already showing the effects of adopting the Southern patterns of life" (Rode 1–2).

Noting that between 1959 and 1968 "the ratio of families living at [hunting] camp to families living in settlement changed from 77% camp, 23% village to 11% camp and 80% settlement," Godin attempted to quantify the "Southernization" of the Inuit in terms of energy expenditure (33). In the study, Godin used measurements of heart rate and respiratory efficiency, accompanied by questionnaires and diaries completed by observers, to compare the energy expenditure of traditional men who hunted for food with more modern men who worked for wages. Though women also hunted, performing tasks such as skinning and tanning that were generally and euphemistically regarded as "helpful" to male hunters, Godin assumed that women's hunting activities would expend the same energy as housewifery tasks, and therefore no study of women's subsistence labour was attempted (39). Attaching such banality to Indigenous women's subsistence labour was not unusual; as Sangster notes, the labour of Aboriginal women within their subsistence economies has been unacknowledged or downplayed by colonial agents since the beginning of the fur trade, as this often-essential labour upset the patriarchal order of things (203; McClintock). Godin did measure the activity levels of "modern" Inuit women, however. Articulating his study of women in the well-worn terms of the nuclear family, Godin hired a "trained Eskimo girl [who] went into 14 different homes in the settlement" to "[monitor] the activities of the wife of the family head" (137).

Accompanying hunters on their expeditions, Godin recorded the activities performed during hunting, such as checking on fishing nets, repairing boats, making knives and handles, driving and running alongside a dog team, and digging an ice hole. Village workers' tasks, including labouring as a store clerk or in construction, were also recorded and measured in terms of calories expended. Caloric values were attached to women's modern domestic labour, which was connoted as washing the floor, making bannock, sewing, washing dishes, and general housework. Godin found that village workers expended less energy than hunters and that hunters were generally more fit due to a "variable intensity of activity" (292–93; Godin and Shephard 192). Godin, with Shephard, noted that "[t]he settlement work, be it painting, electrical wiring, or garbage collection, moves at an even tempo, whereas during the hunt, periods of intense and even maximum activity are interspersed with periods of rest" (192). As far as women went, Godin and Shephard noted that the Arctic's lack of "home convenience" rendered "[f]emale domestic tasks ... similar to those of the 'white' housewife some 30 years ago," though of course no comparison between "primitive" and "modern" Inuit women could be made (184).

While Shephard, Rode, and Godin found small evidence of a marked growth of body fat, changing activity levels, however, raised obesity concerns for these researchers. Shephard argued, "the diseases of affluence—atherosclerosis, hypertension, obesity and diabetes are rare. The trend towards adoption of the 'white' life style may, unhappily, soon reveal the extent of the protection that such peoples currently enjoy by virtue of their high level of physical activity" (Shephard 251). Anticipating a problem in the near future, Rode went so far as to suggest the institution of anti-obesity regimes in Inuit populations, including "diet education [about] sugar, soft drinks and other foods high in calories but low in nutritional value" and the "introduction of cross-country skiing to Igloolik" (333).

Thus, all IBP evidence pointed to the fact that Igloolik residents were either already developing an excess of body fat or were on the precipice of doing so. Of course, the IBP results on Igloolik were about more than the health of the people in that tiny village, as publications derived from the Human Adaptability project spoke to the "evolution" of northern Indigenous populations as a whole. Indeed, if IBP studies were correct, and racial "admixture" was on the rise, then the 1960s was witness to an entire race of peoples on the very edge of extinction. IBP reports therefore suggested that the demise of traditional culture was moulded into the very flesh of the northern Aboriginal peoples. Northern embodiments, touted to be the genetic result of thousands of years of subsistence lifestyle patterns and hunting economies, were, in Shephard's words, "rapidly receding."

Obesity and the Anti-Conquest of Northern Lands

Anti-obesity rhetoric and research in the North allied with the general health policies of the postwar era through the 1960s to assimilate northern Indigenous peoples and bodies into normative white, middle-class Canadian society. Though I tie federal nutrition programming and the IBP project to assimilative state policy, I do not argue that individual researchers or practitioners were consciously complicit in the federal state's general desire, to borrow Vanast's words, to "hasten the day of extinction" for the northern people. Indeed, IBP research engendered in some a suspicion of northern development and a conviction that the North would have been better off without southern interference (Hochbaum; Kallen; Lotz). Schaefer himself mourned the loss of tradition he perceived to have witnessed in his northern sojourns (Schaefer, "Luttamiut" 8–11; Schaefer, "When Eskimos Come"). Medical scientists and researchers, however, were working within a particular "paradigm," to use Kuhn's term, in which they could stake their claims to truth and knowledge about northern embodiment and Indigenous cultures.

In the period under study, one major paradigm through which medical practitioners, scientists, and researchers could "claim" their "truths" about the North was one of northern development that positioned Indigenous people, to coin a phrase from the *White Paper on Indian Policy*, on a "new road" toward becoming more like normative Canadians (Canada, *Statement of the Government*). Thus, as historians of colonial medicine have argued of Canada from 1945 to 1970 and of other periods, medical and scientific research was generally caught up in and made sense because of an explicit and general discourse of assimilation, the tone of which was often set by the federal state and its Indigenous policy (Kelm; Lux; Shewell).

In continuously and performatively reiterating a northern peoples who had taken up the gendered division of labour in the colonial-capitalist economy, who had organized into nuclear family forms seemingly by choice and not by government coercion, and who were living in villages, eating modern foods, and becoming sedentary and fat, federal state nutrition programming and the IBP Igloolik project pronounced the inevitable and complete decline of traditional northern cultures through the re-calculation and re-imagination of Aboriginal bodies as "almost modern." Government and IBP projects therefore provided a powerful scientific and medical discursive justification for assimilative policies and processes. Federal nutrition programming and IBP research, in their seemingly benign propensity to calculate and classify Indigenous bodies in the North, can thus be thought of as a type of anti-conquest, to use Pratt's term. Depictions of an encroaching or established obesity problem in northern bodies had discursive reverberations, through which "seeing" and "learned" northern experts positioned and repositioned the categories of the North and its people in terms that facilitated assimilative policy. Diet and exercise surveys and measurements of foreheads, lips, eyes, and body fat by federal programming and the IBP furthered racist assimilation projects, and can be understood as a form of scientific racism, albeit in reverse. Unlike the scientific racism described by McClintock, the various calculations made by government officials and researchers did not "prove" how Indigenous peoples were biologically different from white people but how they were similar to them. By positioning northern bodies as those that possessed, or were soon to develop, "excess" body fat, medical, scientific, and state documents reiterated northern Canadians as almost normative or, in other words, rather ordinary. As ordinary Canadians, with decidedly ordinary Canadian bodies, Inuit and northern First Nations peoples had no special title to traditional lands or privileges.

Conclusion

In the postwar era until 1970, obesity was wielded by government and medical agents as a modernizing category, and was part of the discursive drive to assimilate northern Aboriginal peoples into normative Canadian society. The application of anti-obesity regimes and programming to Aboriginal bodies was not even, however, and strategies overlapped chronologically and differed over time and across the Canadian state. Throughout the era, medical, government, and popular literature generally assumed that Indigenous peoples' "primitivism" precluded the presence of chronic illness in northern communities. In the middle to late 1960s, asserting the notion that such assimilative techniques were nearing completion, another discourse emerged in federal state and IBP research that depicted northern Aboriginal peoples as on the verge of developing or as already having developed an obesity problem. This discourse of northern obesity helped to characterize Inuit and northern First Nations populations as "almost-modern," ordinary citizens whose claims to "special status" would be null and void.

Obesity, then, was a physical characteristic that could position a population within the racial hierarchies of the postwar period until 1970. Through this, Inuit people were imagined to be (almost) like the dominant subject who required the abjection of fat embodiment, and racial inequities were partially furthered through the scientific and medical classification of obesity. In addition to forming and reforming categories of Indigeneity, federal state and IBP surveys and reports also rearticulated the category of obesity. The conflations between whiteness, the middle class, modernity, and obesity were strengthened by discourses of northern obesity. Edward Said has famously argued that constructions of the "Other" say less about the colonized than they do about the colonizer. That is, it is through the Other that the identity of the colonizer is produced, despite colonialists' denials of "intersubjectivity."[10] In the recitation of obesity as a modernizing type of embodiment that threatened northern Indigenous people, those identified as "problem populations" by anti-obesity rhetoric, namely white middle-class men and women, were reified as civilized and modern kinds of people. Dominant notions of white supremacy—founding Canada's identity as a white, Western European settler nation—were therefore secured.

Notes

1 This chapter first appeared as Deborah McPhail, "The White Man's Burden"? Obesity and Colonialism in the Developing North," in *Contours of the Nation* (Toronto: University of Toronto Press, 2018), 101–33 and has been reprinted with permission of the publisher.

2 For a discussion of women's participation in northern anti-conquest, see Joan Sangster's description of the travel narratives of Hudson's Bay Company wives in Joan Sangster, "*The Beaver* as Ideology: Constructing Images of Inuit and Native Life in Postwar Canada," *Anthropologica* 49, no. 2 (2007): 191–200.

3 For a discussion of the colonial state's regulation of Aboriginal hunting, see John Sandlos, *Hunters at the Margin: Native People and Wildlife Conservation in the Northwest Territories* (Vancouver: University of British Columbia Press, 2007).

4 For a similar argument, see Maureen K. Lux, *Medicine That Walks: Disease, Medicine, and Canadian Plains Native People, 1880–1940* (Toronto: University of Toronto Press, 2001).

5 For a discussion of how current epistemologies of race, gender, and nation inform and found the empirical projects of the United States, as well as organize global(ized) subjectivities, see Anna M. Agathangelou and Kyle D. Killian, "Epistemologies of Peace: Poetics, Globalization, and the Social Justice Movement," *Globalizations* 3, no. 4 (2006): 459–83.

6 See also G. R. F. Elliot, "Teaching of Preventive Medicine in Canada"; J. A. Lewis, "Hypertension— A Problem of Growing Importance"; F. B. Roth, "Chronic Disease"; A.H. Sellers, "Public Health and Medical Aspects of an Aging Population."

7 See also Grant, *Polar Imperative*, for a discussion of contagious disease contraction between the Inuit and American soldiers.

8 In discussing a similar federal government publication intended to teach Aboriginal and Inuit about conservation, John Sandlos

describes such booklets as "remarkable for [their] patronizing tone, as if the intended audience were children rather than adult[s]." *Good Food—Good Health*, written in half sentences illustrated by numerous pictures, certainly fits Sandlos's description. Sandlos, *Hunters at the Margin,* 211.

9 Dr. De Pena noted that the food co-operative offered non-traditional foods as well, including a chocolate meal-replacement "shake" marketed to combat obesity. In our interview, Dr. Pena joked that she bought several cans of it because it was "quite good." Interview with Dr. Joan De Pena (professor of Anthropology, University of Manitoba, retired), Winnipeg, Manitoba, 18 August 2008.

10 For a discussion of "intersubjectivity," see Agathangelou and Ling, "Power and Play through Poisies," 847.

Works Cited

"A Proposal for Human Adaptability Studies of Igloolik Eskimos: The Canadian Aspects of the International Study of Eskimos." c. 1964. *Medical Services—Preventive Program and Research.* Part 3, file 850–1-16, volume 2840, RG 29. Medical Services series. Department of National Health and Welfare fonds, Library and Archives Canada.

Acker, M. S. "Administration and Methods of Enumeration of the Sickness Survey in Saskatchewan." *Canadian Journal of Public Health,* vol. 44, no. 4, 1953, pp 128–33.

Agathangelou, Anna M., and Kyle D. Killian. "Epistemologies of Peace: Poetics, Globalization, and the Social Justice Movement." *Globalizations,* vol. 3, no. 4, 2006, pp. 459–83.

Agathangelou, Anna M., and L. H. M. Ling. "Power and Play through Poisies: Reconstructing Self and Other in the 9/11 Commission Report." *Millennium: Journal of International Studies,* vol. 33, no. 3, 2005, pp. 827–53.

"Anthropological Record—Coppermine Area—1958," Folder 3, *Doctor Bruce Chown Collection* Box 11, MSS 17, University of Manitoba Archives.

Assembly of First Nations. "Aboriginals Diabetes Report Card." *Assembly of Aboriginals*, June 2006, www.afn.ca/misc/diabetes-rc.pdf. Accessed 11 September 2008.

———. "National Chief Says Poverty and Lack of Access to Affordable, Healthy Foods the Main Reason for Aboriginals' Childhood Obesity Epidemic." *Assembly of First Nations*, 29 March 2007, http://www.afn.ca/article.asp?id=3486. Accessed 11 September 2008.

Best, S. C., J. W. Gerrard, and I. C. Irin. "The Pine House (Saskatchewan) Nutrition Project: II." *Canadian Medical Association* Journal, vol. 85, no. 8, 1961, pp 412–14.

Bordo, Susan. *Unbearable Weight: Feminism, Western Culture, and the Body.* University of California, 1993.

Canada. *Canadian Sickness Survey 1950: Instructions for Enumerators.* Provincial Departments of Health, Dominion Bureau of Statistics and the Department of National Health and Welfare, 1950.

———. *Canadian Sickness Survey 1950–1951: No. 6, Permanent Physical Disabilities (National Estimates).* Queen's Printer, 1955.

———. *Good Food—Good Health.* Queen's Printer, 1963.

———. *Injuries—Frequency—Severity—Health Care—National Estimates: Canadian Sickness Survey 1950–1951.* Queen's Printer, 1961.

———. *Report of the Royal Commission on Aboriginal Peoples: Volume 1—Looking Forward, Looking Back*, Queen's Printer, 1996.

———. *Report of the Royal Commission on Aboriginal People: Volume 3—Gathering Strength.* Queen's Printer, 1996.

———. *Royal Commission on Health Services: Final Report.* Vol. 2, Queen's Printer, 1965.

———. *Statement of the Government of Canada on Indian Policy.* Department of Indian Affairs and Northern Development, 1969.

"Canada: News Notes." *Canadian Journal of Public Health*, vol. 60, no. 3, 1969, p. 135.

"Canada Food Guide Adapted for Native Needs." Editorial. *Globe and Mail* [Toronto, Canada], 12 April 2007, p. A8.

Canadian Committee for the International Biological Programme. *Summary Annual Reports from Projects for 1970.* Canadian Committee for the International Biological Programme, 1971.

Charron, K. C. "Chronic Diseases in the Canadian Hospital Program." *Canadian Journal of Public Health,* vol. 48, no. 10, 1957, pp. 405–12.

———. "Economic and Social Consequences of Ill Health and Disability on a National Scale." *Canadian Medical Association Journal,* vol. 73, no. 7, 1955, pp. 542–45.

Cheung, O. T. "Tuberculosis in Recent Immigrants." *Canadian Medical Association Journal*, vol. 68, no. 4, 1953, pp. 330–31.

Chown, Bruce, and Marion Lewis. "The Blood Group Genes of the Copper Eskimo." *American Journal of Physical Anthropology*, vol. 17, no. 1, 1959, pp. 13–18.

Chiarelli, B. "The Chromosomes of the Igloolik Eskimo." *International Biological Programme, Human Adaptability Project (Igloolik, NWT): Reports for 1971–1972,* University of Toronto, 1972.

Copp, Stanley S. "Public Health Engineering in Northern Canada." *Canadian Journal of Public Health*, vol. 51, no. 60, 1960, pp. 187–93.

De Pena, Joan. "Addendum 2: Report on Activities in Study of Growth and Constitution Carried out at Igloolik, NWT May 17–July, 1968." *International Biological Programme, Human Adaptability Project (Igloolik, NWT): Reports for 1971–1972,* University of Toronto, 1972.

———. "Igloolik Project: Growth and Development Studies Progress Report 1972." *International Biological Programme, Human Adaptability Project (Igloolik, NWT): Reports for 1971–1972,* University of Toronto, 1972.

———. Personal interview. 18 August 2008.

Devakumar, Delan, Geordan Shannon, Sunil S. Bhopal, and Ibrahim Abubakar. "Racism and Discrimination in COVID-19 Reponses." *The Lancet,* vol. 395, 11 April 2020, p. 1194.

Dominion Bureau of Statistics. *Disability among the Gainfully Employed: Canadian Sickness Survey 1950–1951*, Queen's Printer, 1961.

Doughy, J. H. "Mortality in Terms of Lost Years of Life." *Canadian Journal of Public Health,* vol. 42, no. 4, 1951, pp. 134–41.

Elliot, G. R. F. "Teaching of Preventive Medicine in Canada." *Canadian Medical Association Journal*, vol. 74, no. 6. 1956, pp. 457–61.

Elliott, M. R. "Administration and Methods of Enumeration of the Sickness Survey in Manitoba." *Canadian Journal of Public* Health, vol. 44, no. 4. 1953, pp. 84–89.

———. "Presidential Address." *Canadian Journal of Public Health,* vol. 43, no. 7, 1952, pp. 273–78.

Escobar, Arturo. *Encountering Development: The Making and Unmaking of the Third World.* Princeton University Press, 1995.

Farquharson, C. D. "Antibiotics in Public Health." *Canadian Journal of Public Health,* vol. 43, no. 1, 1952, pp. 1–9.

Farrell, Amy Erdman. *Fat Shame: Stigma and the Fat Body in American Culture.* NYU Press, 2011.

Fee, Marjorie. "Racializing Narratives: Obesity, Diabetes and the 'Aboriginal' Thrifty Genotype." *Social Science and Medicine,* vol. 62, no. 12, 2006, pp. 2988–97.

Feeder, C. P. "Institutional and Medical-Care Aspects of an Aging Population." *Canadian Journal of Public Health,* vol. 44, no. 6, 1953, pp. 542–45.

Finkel, Alvin. *Our Lives: Canada after 1945.* James Lorimer, 1997.

Finkel, Alvin, and Margaret Conrad. *History of the Canadian People: 1967 to the Present.* Addison, Wesley and Longman, 2002.

Foucault, Michel. *Discipline and Punish: The Birth of the Prison.* Translated by A. Sheridan, 1977. Vintage, 1995.

Francis, Daniel. *The Imaginary Indian: The Image of the Indian in Canadian Culture.* Arsenal Pulp Press, 1992.

Gard, Michael, and Jan Wright. *The Obesity Epidemic: Science, Morality and Ideology.* Routledge, 2005.

Gilman, Sander L. *Making the Body Beautiful: A Cultural History of Aesthetic Surgery.* Princeton University Press, 1999.

Godin, Gaetan J. "A Study of the Energy Expenditure of a Small Eskimo Population." *International Biological Programme, Human Adaptability Project (Igloolik, NWT): Reports for 1971–1972,* University of Toronto, 1972.

Godin, G., and Roy J. Shephard. "Activity Patterns in the Canadian Eskimo." *International Biological Programme, Human Adaptability Project (Igloolik, NWT): Reports for 1971–1972,* University of Toronto, 1972.

Grant, Shelagh. "A Case of Compounded Error: The Inuit Resettlement Project, 1953, and the Government Response, 1990." *Northern* Perspectives, vol. 19, no. 1, 1991, pp. 3–29.

———. *Polar Imperative: A History of Arctic Sovereignty in North America.* Douglas and McIntyre, 2010.

———. *Sovereignty or Security? Government Policy in the Canadian North, 1936–1950.* University of British Columbia Press, 1988.

Hacker, Carlotta. "Aku-Aku and the Medicine Men." *Canadian Nurse,* vol. 61, no. 8, 1965, pp. 636–40.

Hatcher, G. H. "Symposium on the Canadian Sickness Survey Summary and Implications." *Canadian Journal of Public Health,* vol. 47, no. 9, 1956, pp. 378–82.

Hildes, J. A. "Health Problems in the Arctic." *Canadian Medical Association Journal,* vol. 83, no. 24, 1960, pp. 1255–57.

Hildes, J. A., J. C. Wilt, and F. J. Stanfield. "Antibodies to Adenovirus and Psittacosis in Eastern Arctic Eskimos." *Canadian Journal of Public Health,* vol. 46, no. 9, 1958, pp. 230–31.

Hochbaum, H. A. "Churchill—A Pattern for the Future?" *Productivity and Conservation in Northern Circumpolar Lands: Proceedings of a Conference Sponsored by the International Biological Program, Canadian Committee for IBP, Canada Dept of Indian Affairs and Northern Development, International Union for Conservation of Nature and Natural Resources, Commission on Ecology of IUCN, and the University of Alberta,* edited by W. A. Fuller and P. G. Kevan, International Union for Conservation of Nature and Natural Resources, 1970.

Howie, J. "The Unfinished Business of Public Health." *Canadian Journal of Public Health,* vol. 44, no. 10, 1953, pp. 349–53.

Hughes, David R. "Director's Summary, Fourth Year, 1971–1972." *International Biological Programme, Human Adaptability Project (Igloolik, NWT): Reports for 1971–1972*, University of Toronto, 1972.

———. "Human Adaptability in Eskimos," *International Biological Programme, Human Adaptability Project (Igloolik, NWT): Reports for 1971–1972,* University of Toronto, 1972.

———. "Report on the Status of Genetic Marker Inquiries." *International Biological Programme, Human Adaptability Project (Igloolik, NWT): Reports for 1971–1972,* University of Toronto, 1972.

Iacovetta, Franca. *Gatekeepers: Reshaping Immigrant Lives in Cold War Canada.* Between the Lines, 2006.

"International Council of Scientific Unions, Special Committee for the International Biological Program." *Directory of National Participation in IBP,* IBP Central Office, 1972.

Jasen, Patricia. "Race, Culture, and the Colonization of Childbirth in Northern Canada." *Social History of Medicine*, vol. 10, no. 3, 1997, pp. 394–95.

Kallen, Evelyn. "Social Change, Stress and Marginality among Inuit Youth." *International Biological Programme, Human Adaptability Project (Igloolik, NWT): Reports for 1971–1972*, University of Toronto, 1972.

Keil, Roger, and Harris Ali. "Multiculturalism, Racism and Infectious Disease in the Global City: The Experience of the 2003 SARS Outbreak in Toronto." *TOPIA Canadian Journal of Cultural Studies*, vol. 16, Fall 2006, pp. 23–49.

Kelm, Mary Ellen. *Colonizing Bodies: Aboriginal Health and Healing in British Columbia, 1900–1950.* University of British Columbia Press, 1998.

Kennedy, M. Eileen. "Administration and Methods of Enumeration of the Sickness Survey in Alberta." *Canadian Journal of Public Health*, vol 44, no. 5, 1953, pp. 177–79.

Kohn, Robert. "Volume of Illness." *Canadian Journal of Public Health*, vol. 47, no. 8, 1956, pp. 332–42.

Krog, J., and M. Wika. "Studies of the Peripheral Circulation in the Hand of the Igloolik Eskimo, Running Title: Peripheral Circulation in Eskimo." *International Biological Programme, Human Adaptability Project (Igloolik, NWT): Reports for 1971–1972*, University of Toronto, 1972.

Kuhn, Thomas S. *The Structure of Scientific Revolutions.* University of Chicago Press, 1962.

Kwa, Chunglin. "Representations of Nature Mediating between Ecology and Science Policy: The Case of the International Biological Programme." *Social Studies of Sciences*, vol. 17, no. 3, 1987, pp. 413–42.

Lawrence, Bonita. *"Real" Indians and Others; Mixed-Blood Urban Native Peoples and Indigenous Nationhood.* University of British Columbia Press, 2004.

Lear, Scott A., Karin H. Humphries, Jiri J. Fhrolich, and C. Laird Birmingham. "Appropriateness of Current Thresholds for Obesity-Related Measures among Indigenous People." *Canadian Medical Association Journal,* vol. 177, no. 12, 2007, pp. 1499–1505.

Lenczner, Michael, and Trevor Owen. "The Impact of Tropical and Parasitic Diseases in a Non-endemic Area." *Canadian Medical Association Journal*, vol. 82, no. 16, 1960, pp. 805–12.

"Letter to all Eskimo Households to Introduce and Explain the Use of the Family Food Habits Book." c. 1964. *Medical Services—Preventive Program and Research.* Part 2, file 850–1-16, volume 2840, RG 29. Medical Services series. Department of Health and Welfare fonds, Library and Archives Canada.

Lewis, J. A. "Hypertension—A Problem of Growing Importance." *Canadian Medical Association* Journal, vol. 64, no. 1, 1951, pp. 26–29.

Lotz, Jim. "Land Problems and People Problems—the Eskimo as Conservationist." *Productivity and Conservation in Northern Circumpolar Lands: Proceedings of a Conference, Edmonton, Alberta, 15–17 October 1969*, edited by Fuller and Kevan, IUCN, 1970, pp. 276–82.

Lux, Maureen K. *Medicine That Walks: Disease, Medicine, and Canadian Plains Native People, 1880–1940.* University of Toronto Press, 2001.

Mather, James M. "Health and Welfare in Rural Ontario." *Canadian Journal of Public Health,* vol. 42, no. 11, 1951, pp. 455–59.

———. "The Need for a Truly Generalized Public Health Nursing Program." *Canadian Journal of Public Health,* vol. 43, no. 4, 1952, pp. 143–50.

MacAlpine, P. J., S. H. Chen, D. W. Cox, et al. "Genetic Markers in Blood in a Canadian Eskimo Population with a Comparison of Allele Frequencies in Circumpolar Populations." *International Biological Programme, Human Adaptability Project (Igloolik, NWT): Reports for 1972–1973.* Canadian Committee of the International Biological Programme.

MacDonald, David. "How Sick (or Healthy) are Canadians?" *Maclean's*, 27 October 1956.

Martin, Paul. "Canada's Record Progress in Public Health." *Canadian Journal of Public* Health, vol. 43, no. 8. 1952, pp. 323–29.

Mayhall, Joan T. "Dental Studies: Progress Report." *International Biological Programme, Human Adaptability Project (Igloolik, NWT): Reports for 1971–1972,* University of Toronto, 1972.

McClintock, Anne. *Imperial Leather: Race, Gender, and Sexuality in the Colonial Contest.* Routledge, 1995.

McCubbin, Doris. "Are We Breeding a Nation of Invalids?" *Maclean's,* 2 April 1955, pp. 14–15, 93–94.

McPherson, Kathryn. "Nursing and Colonization: The Work of Indian Health Service Nurses in Manitoba, 1945–1970." *Women, Health, and Nation: Canada and the United States since 1945,* edited by Georgina Feldberg, Molly Ladd-Taylor, Alison Li, and Kathryn McPherson, McGill-Queen's University Press, 2003, pp. 223–46.

Milne, H. "Report of Nutrition Project Feasibility Study in Igloolik, NWT, June 7th to June 28, 1968." *International Biological Programme, Human Adaptability Project (Igloolik, NWT): Reports for 1971–1972,* University of Toronto, 1972.

Moddy, Joseph P. "How We Fought Polio in the Arctic." *Maclean's,* with W. de Groot, 1 January 1954, pp. 12–13, 34–38.

Mohanram, Radhika. *Black Body: Women, Colonialism, and Space.* University of Minnesota Press, 1999.

Moore, P. E. "Medical Care of Canada's Indians and Eskimos." *Canadian Journal of Public Health,* vol. 47, no. 6, 1956, pp. 227–33.

———. "Puvalluttuq: An Epidemic of Tuberculosis at Eskimo Point, Northwest Territories." *Canadian Medical Association Journal,* vol. 90, no. 22, 1964, pp. 1193–1202.

Moore, P. E. to A. R. Armstrong. 24 January 1957. *Nutrition Services Eskimo Research.* File 386–1-6(1), volume 925, RG 29. Department of National Health and Welfare fonds, Library and Archives Canada.

Mosby, Ian. "Administering Colonial Science: Nutrition Research and Human Biomedical Experimentation in Aboriginal Communities and Residential Schools, 1942–1952." *Histoire sociale / Social History,* vol. 46, no. 91, 2013, pp. 145–72.

Page, H. G. "The Changing Pattern of a Canadian Population." *Canadian Journal of Public Health,* vol 44, no. 6, 1953, pp. 187–95.

"Parasitic Diseases in Canada." Editorial. *Canadian Medical Association Journal,* vol. 91, no. 9, 1964, pp. 446–48.

Partington, M. W., and Norma Roberts. "The Heights and Weights of Indians and Eskimo School Children on James Bay and Hudson Bay." *Canadian Medical Association Journal,* vol. 100, no. 11, 1969, pp. 502–9.

Patterson, Kevin. "Southern Exposure: How Bad Is the Global Obesity Epidemic?" *Globe and Mail,* 7 October 2006.

Patton, Cindy. *Inventing AIDS*. Routledge, 1990.

Peart, A. F. W. "Canada's Sickness Survey: Review of Methods." *Canadian Journal of Public* Health, vol. 43, no. 10, 1952, pp. 401–14.

———. "Measles in the Canadian Arctic." *Canadian Journal of Public Health,* vol. 44, no. 4, 1954, pp. 146–56.

Pett, L. B., to Anonymous. 23 September 1957. *Nutrition Services Eskimo Research*. File 386–1-6(1), volume 925, RG 29. Nutrition Division series. Department of National Health and Welfare fonds, Library and Archives Canada.

Pett, L. B., to J. D. Blake. 23 January 1957. *Nutrition Services Eskimo Research*. File 386–1-6(1), volume 925, RG 29. Nutrition Division series. Department of National Health and Welfare fonds, Library and Archives Canada.

Pett, L. B., to P. E. Moore. 27 November 1957. *Nutrition Services Eskimo Research*. File 386–1-6(1), volume 925, RG 29. Nutrition Division series. Department of National Health and Welfare fonds, Library and Archives Canada.

Pett, L. B., and P. J. Lupien. "Cholesterol Levels of Canadian Eskimos." c. 1958. *Nutrition Services Eskimo Research*. File 386–1-6(1), volume 925, RG 29. Nutrition Division series. Department of National Health and Welfare fonds, Library and Archives Canada.

Philips, Elisabeth. "Impact of Chronic Illness." *Canadian Nurse*, vol. 52, no. 7, 1956, pp. 524–29.

———. "What It Means to Be Old." *Canadian Nurse,* vol. 52, no. 8, 1956, pp. 611–16.

Picard, Andre. "Diabetes Putting Care System in Dire Straits: Sedentary Lifestyle, Poor Eating Habits Cited as Almost Three Million Canadians Now Have Disease." *Globe and Mail,* 2 March 2007.

———. "Native Health Care Is a Sickening Disgrace." *Globe and Mail,* 3 November 2005.

———. "Obesity-Driven Diabetes Skyrocketing among Kids, Teens." *Globe and Mail*, 11 May 2005.

Poudrier, Jennifer. "The Geneticization of Aboriginal Diabetes and Obesity: Adding Another Scene to the Story of the Thrifty Gene." *Canadian Review of Sociology*, vol. 44, no. 2, 2007, pp. 237–61.

Poudrier, Jennifer, and Janice Kennedy. "Embodiment and the Meaning of the 'Healthy Body': An Exploration of Indigenous Women's Perspectives of Healthy Body Weight and Body Image." *Journal of Indigenous Health* vol. 4, no. 1, 2007, pp. 15–24.

Pratt, Mary Louise. *Imperial Eyes: Travel Writing and Transculturation.* Routledge, 1992.

Reid, Helen Evans. "Physical Development and Health of Easter Island Children." *Canadian Medical Association Journal*, vol. 98, 1968, pp 584–89.

Rode, Andris. "Some Factors Influencing the Fitness of a Small Eskimo Community." *International Biological Programme Human Adaptability Project: Physiology Section Report*, University of Toronto, 1972.

Roemer, Milton I. "The Future of Healthcare in Canada: A Symposium." *Canadian Journal of Public Health* vol. 48, no. 6, 1957, pp. 229–38.

Roth, F. B. "Chronic Disease." *Canadian Journal of Public* Health, vol. 48, no. 9, 1957, pp. 366–71.

Rutta, H. R., and Norman M. Wrong. "The Leprosy Problem in Canada: With Report of a Case." *Canadian Medical Association Journal*, vol. 78, no. 1, 1958, pp. 19–21.

Said, Edward. *Orientalism*. Vintage Books, 1979.

Salinas, Eve. "Report on Heart and Stroke Research: Obesity." *Globe and Mail,* 28 October 2006.

Sandlos, John. *Hunters at the Margin: Native People and Wildlife Conservation in the Northwest Territories*. University of British Columbia Press, 2007.

Sangster, Joan. "*The Beaver* as Ideology: Constructing Images of Inuit and Native Life in Postwar Canada." *Anthropologica,* vol. 49, no. 2, 2007, pp. 191–200.

Schaefer, Otto. "Luttamiut (Doctor's People) and 'Old Wives' Tales'—Their Unrecognized Value in Medicine." *Circumpolar Health 90: Proceedings of the Eighth International Congress on Circumpolar Health Whitehorse, Yukon, May 20–25, 1990*, edited by Brian D. Postl et al., University of Manitoba Press, 1991, pp. 8–13.

———. "Medical Observations and Problems in the Canadian Arctic, Part II." *Canadian Medical Association Journal*, vol. 81, no. 5, 1959, pp. 386–93.

———. "When the Eskimos Come to Town." *Nutrition Today*, November/December, 1971.

Schaefer, Otto to Dr. M. Matas. 6 October 1964. "Preliminary Trip Report—Eastern Arctic Patrol, 1964." *Medical Services—Preventive Program and Research*. Part 1, file 850–1-16, volume 2840, RG 29. Medical Services series. Department of National Health and Welfare fonds, Library and Archives Canada.

Sellers, A. H. "Public Health and Medical Aspects of an Aging Population." *Canadian Nurse,* vol. 47, no. 2. 1951, pp. 101–11.

Shah, Nayan. *Contagious Divides: Epidemics and Race in San Francisco's Chinatown*. University of California, 2001.

Shephard, Roy J. "Adaptations to a Lifetime of Vigorous Activity Observations on the Canadian Eskimo." *International Biological Programme, Human Adaptability Project (Igloolik, NWT): Reports for 1971–1972*, University of Toronto, 1972.

Shewell, Hugh. *Enough to Keep Them Alive: Indian Welfare in Canada, 1873–1965*. University of Toronto Press, 2004.

Smylie, Janet, and Marcia Anderson. "Understanding the Health of Indigenous Peoples in Canada: Key Methodological and Conceptual Challenges." *Canadian Medical Association Journal*, vol. 175, no. 6, 2006, p. 602.

Stoler, Ann Laura. *Race and the Education of Desire: Foucault's History of Sexuality and the Colonial Order of Things*. Duke University Press, 1995.

Tester, Frank James, and Peter Kulchyski. *Tammarniit (Mistakes): Inuit Relocation in the Eastern Arctic, 1939–1963*. University of British Columbia Press, 1994.

Thobani, Sunera. *Exalted Subjects: Studies in the Making of Race and Nation in Canada*. University of Toronto Press, 2007.

Vaughn, Meghan. *Curing Their Ills: Colonial Power and African Illness*. Stanford University Press, 1991.

Ward, Kenneth A. "Arctic Interlude." *Canadian Medical Association Journal*, vol. 67, no. 4, 1952, pp. 292–98.

Weiner, J. S. "The History of the Human Adaptability Section." *Human Adaptability: A History and Compendium of Research in the International Biological Programme*, edited by K. J. Collins and J. S. Weiner, Taylor and Francis, 1977, pp. 1–23.

Wilkinson, Doug. "How I Became an Eskimo." *Maclean's*, 15 November 1954, pp. 28–30, 103–109.

Worthington, E. B. "Substance of the Programme." *The Evolution of IBP*, edited by E. B. Worthington, Cambridge University, 1975, pp. 17–50.

Write, Gordon E. "Unmet Needs of Healthcare in Canada." *Canadian Journal of Public Health*, vol. 47, no. 1, 1956, pp. 15–23.

Zaslow, Morris. *The Northward Expansion of Canada, 1914–1967*. McClelland and Stewart, 1988.

Fat Women's Experiences and Negotiation of Fatphobia in Canada: A Systematic Review

Bidushy Sadika and Jinwen Chen

Introduction

In this chapter, we consider what it means to be "fat" in Canada through the experiences and negotiations of self-identified fat women with intersectionally marginalized identities. The interdisciplinary field of fat studies advocates recognizing fatness as a human rights issue by 1) considering weight as a human characteristic and a form of human diversity; 2) countering dominant narratives that societally stigmatize fat bodies under the health-based frameworks of "obesity" or the "obesity epidemic"; and 3) arguing to incorporate fatness as a legitimate ground of discrimination that individuals should be protected against in legislation and policies concerning human rights ("*Fat Studies*: Aims and Scope"; Schorb 168). Specifically, fat bodies are deemed as sick, unattractive, unfit, greedy, uncontrollable, fragile, and belonging to a lower social class (Rice, "Becoming 'the Fat Girl'" 158; Rice, "How Big Girls" 105). Anti-fat discrimination comes through *fatphobia,* an irrational fear of, aversion to, and/or discomfort around individuals who identify or are seen by others as fat or obese because of their deviance from body ideals (Fahs 246). Research on body and fatness suggests fatness as a gendered process, with cisgender and trans women being more likely than men to bear the unfavourable consequences of fatphobia from the patriarchal gaze on women's bodies (Daniels and Gillen 407).

In the introduction to *Thickening Fat*, Rinaldi et al. emphasize that "the normative subject of [fat studies] still tends to be a young(ish), white, cisgender woman," and "fat activist spaces ...

tend to materialize as white, middle-class spaces" ("Introduction" 2). Only recently have several researchers addressed this lack of diverse perspectives of fatness in fat studies scholarship by exploring intersections of fatness with power relations based on social categories, e.g., gender, sexuality, race, and disability (Bahra and Overboe 201; Farrell 31; Jiménez 41; Robinson 15). Similarly, Rinaldi et al. embrace an intersectionality lens, "considering fat in dynamic and unstable yet indivisible and intricate dialogue with other identity markers" and with the forces underlying those markers, such as colonialism, neoliberalism, and geopolitics ("Introduction" 1; Solovay and Rothblum 2–3). Kimberlé Crenshaw proposed intersectionality theory to explain Black women's experiences based on an intersection of racism and sexism ("Demarginalizing" 152, 166; "Mapping the Margins" 1244). Over time, scholars and activists employ this framework to describe individuals' experiences and worldviews because of their social identities such as age, race, ethnicity, gender, disability, and so on (Carbado et al. 304; Rinaldi et al. "Introduction" 3). Intersectionality lens explains how fatness intertwines with various social hierarchies (e.g., age, gender, sexuality, socioeconomic status, and ability) and, in so doing, examines fat marginalization and resistance at an institutional level and disrupts normative ways of being and embodiment.

Due to the limited intersectional focus on how fatness is considered and experienced, fat studies is predominantly centred in the United States (Cooper 330; Rinaldi et al. "Introduction" 2). No systematic review on fat women's experiences of fatness within a Canadian context exists. It is essential to explore this topic using a Canadian framework to 1) avoid both an overreliance on American data and ignoring the influence of borders as a "colonial construct" and 2) acknowledge fat studies as an emerging field in Canada that is an "imagined space with real, material impacts on marginalized lives" (Taylor et al.).

Hence, we systematically review the literature on the fatphobic discourses and social meanings experienced by self-identified fat women with intersecting marginalized identities in Canada.

We use the terms "women" and "female" to highlight fatphobic experiences of both cisgender and trans women. We do not focus on the literature on the fatphobic experiences of nonbinary individuals because we want to 1) uphold the uniqueness of nonbinary experiences and not conflate their experiences with those of female- and woman-identifying individuals and 2) limit this chapter's scope and underscore the distinct experiences pertinent to fatness for self-identified fat women in Canada. Nevertheless, we included one study that had nonbinary and gender nonconforming participants, as the study explored their experiences alongside those of cis women under the broader category of queer fat femmes (Taylor 57).

Methodology

We conducted a systematic review broadly according to the Preferred Reporting Items for Systematic Reviews and Meta-Analyses (PRISMA) guidelines (Moher et al. 336). We searched six databases on October 16, 2020: Academic Search Complete, PsycINFO, PsycArticles, Proquest, Scopus, and Web of Science. Following our review aims, we crafted a search syntax combining our four keywords: "Women," "Fatphobia" or "Body Image," and "Canada." "Body image" was used as a keyword to identify research pieces discussing experiences related to fatness without the term "fatphobia." We did not set year limits so as to capture all relevant research across time. We limited our search results to English, peer-reviewed journal articles or book chapters to streamline the number of studies and highlight the themes and gaps in published fat studies scholarship. We excluded chapters that did not have full texts available or that could not be downloaded online due to copyright issues. These exclusions have their limitations, and this chapter therefore cannot be taken to represent all work on fat studies and intersectional women's experiences in Canada.

Figure 3.1 Search Strategy

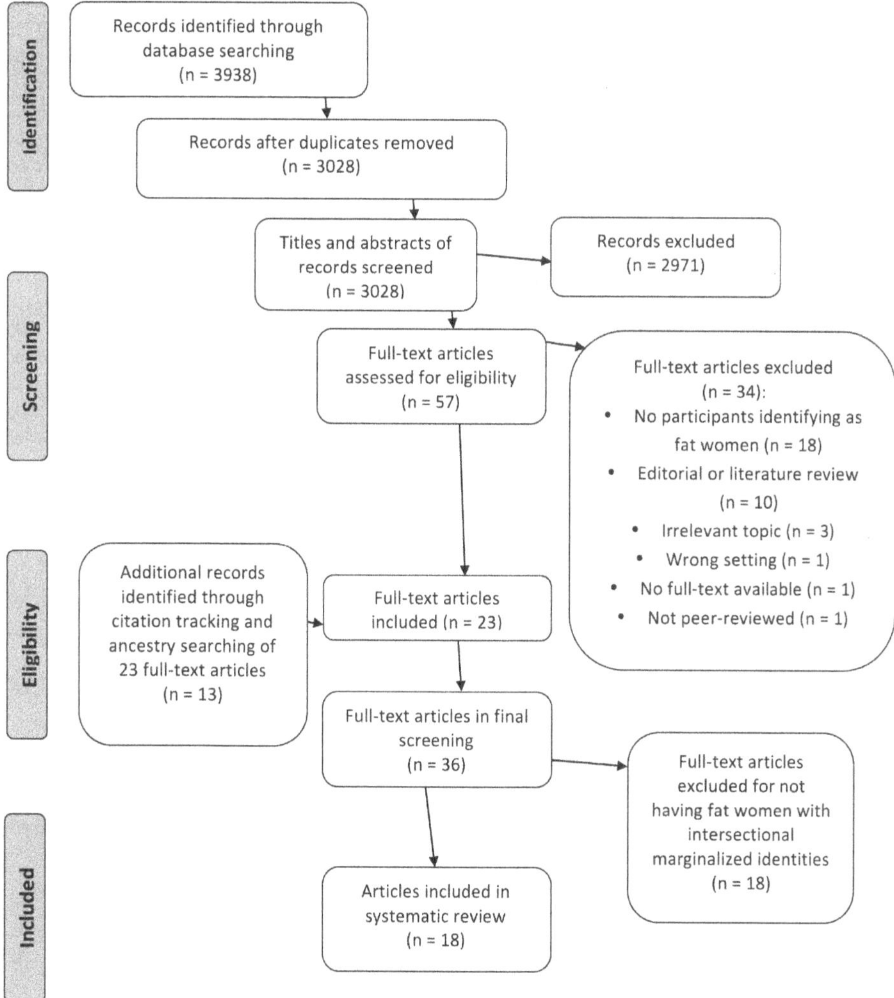

Figure 3.1 maps out the review process from identification, screening, considering eligible pieces, and finally including them.

Our database search yielded 3,938 references. After removing 910 duplicates through Covidence, we separately screened the references in three stages. First, we screened their titles and abstracts and resolved differences in reference exclusion through discussion. References were included if they discussed the experiences of (self-identified) fat women in Canada with fatness, fatphobia, and/or body positivity. After excluding 2,971 references, we reviewed the full texts of the remaining fifty-seven references to arrive at twenty-three pieces. Next, we used Google Scholar for citation tracking and ancestry searching of these twenty-three to obtain thirteen additional references. Finally, we collaboratively reviewed these thirty-six references and included eighteen that focused on the experiences of fat women with intersectional marginalized identities (e.g., age, sexuality, disability, race, and socioeconomic status). Studies were included if most or all of their participants had intersectional marginalized identities (e.g., Taylor's study on queer fat femmes) or if they fleshed out the experiences of such participants (e.g., Ristovski-Slijepcevic et al.'s study, which featured Black fat women's experiences alongside white fat women's ones). Because we did not have access to the first-hand accounts of participants, we had to rely on how well or poorly the authors disclosed and identified their participant samples and on the identity categories authors used. This is a key limitation of our systematic review and relates to the lack of intersectional analysis within fat studies (Cooper 330, Rinaldi et al. "Introduction" 2–3). For example, in references that used only "women," we were not able to ascertain if participants were cisgender or transgender. Hence, in our analysis, the identity categories we use are taken directly from the references.

Of the eighteen references, thirteen were peer-reviewed journal articles and five were open-source book chapters. The references consisted of fourteen research studies adopting qualitative research methodologies, such as interviews, focus groups, art-based methods, auto- and duoethnography, reflexivity, and discourse analyses.

Author(s)	Study Purpose	Participants	Key Findings
Bahra, Ramanpreet A.	Investigate the role of racializing assemblages in categorizing and disciplining bodies	A self-identified racialized ("Brown," South Asian) fat woman and a fat studies scholar	• Did not feel fully human due to the problematization of fatness and promotion of thin body ideologies in social institutions such as health care • Temporality as coping ○ Experienced and produced through language, narratives, myth, and many other ingredients of human traditions • Actions toward self-affirmation ○ End the cycle of internalized racism and sizeism by discontinuing to use skin lightening products and dieting programs ○ Locate desire and happiness within fat embodiment
Bahra, Ramanpreet A., and Overboe, James	Share a dialogue on how difference is experienced under personal and impersonal registers through "affect" and "exposure"	A self-identified Canadian-based, racialized ("Brown," South Asian) fat woman and a fat studies scholar (Bahra) A self-identified older, white, intersex, fat, and disabled man (Overboe)	• Encountered the personal register's colonialist, racist, and sizeist discourses in ○ Interactions with family members ○ Medicalization of fatness in health care with emphasis on "normalizing" self • Negotiation strategies: ○ Sense of devaluation ○ Strived to attain thinness and whiteness ○ Adopted makeup practices to "pass" as normal through camouflaging fatness and brownness • Affirmed intersections of fatness and brownness through makeup practices • Process of doing fatness and brownness by engaging and having a relation with the environment and being involved in body affirmation movements, fat studies scholarship, and critical disability and race studies
Bombak, Andrea E. et al. McPhail, Deborah et al. "Wombs at Risk"	Explore the reproductive care experiences of "obese" or "overweight" women in relation to the prevalent obesity stigma	Twenty-four self-identified overweight/obese women • A majority as white, middle-class, able-bodied, and straight • Few as Metis, working-class, living with a disability, and LGBTQ+ • Age = 28–57, with most falling in the category of 30–40 years old	• Anti-fat derogatory language (e.g., "obese patient," "menace to the government," and "the need for special machine to move the fat people") used by health care practitioners • Dismissal of fertility and reproductive care concerns and emphasis on fat women's weight without considering their medical histories/symptoms • Risk discourses—pregnancy in a fat body constituted as health risk (e.g., infertility, gestational diabetes, difficult births and C-sections, and cardiovascular complications) • Fat women perceived themselves as wrong and disgusting, felt hurt and haunted, and experienced serious trauma; felt less human, adopted unhealthy weight loss and maintenance practices; negotiated with moralities and expectations regarding what a "good mother" should weigh; were traumatized by "high risk" label; and internalized mother-blame narratives • Fat women resisted medical fatphobia by pushing back against the narratives of being "bad mothers"; shifting the blame discourse from weight to other types of social marginality, such as race; and citing their lack of control over the outcome of a foetus

Table 3.1 Study Summaries

Dean, Jennifer	Contextualize the social construction of body weight and acknowledge an alternative reading of childhood fatness that emphasizes the recursive nature of young bodies as well as other dimensions of people's lived experience over time and in place	Thirty-one adolescents living in low-income "obesogenic" neighbourhoods in southern Ontario, Canada; a majority self-identified as females aged 13–19 years old and had various body sizes with 29 being unhappy with their body and 25 stating that they were not at an ideal weight	• Contradictory beliefs—healthy bodies could be fat but fat bodies were risky and deadly, and certainly not desirable • Temporality as a coping strategy—temporarily paused time and erased fatness by creating an alternative reality in video games, books, creative writing/journaling, and playing with props • Perceived body fat as fluid that changed over the life course • Avoided accessing certain neighbourhood places due to fears of bodily outcomes • Spaces of bodily dis/comfort—polarized responses and dependent on past experiences of "being fat" in place • Unwanted attention and feelings of discomfort in place due to an intersection of gender and age, which had future impacts on physical being in/out of place
LaMarre, Andrea et al.	Explore the embodied experiences of individuals with intersecting identities (i.e., sexuality, gender, race, class, age, etc.) in relation to weight stigma, expectations around eating and exercise, and pathologization	Nineteen participants with a history of distressed eating but without a diagnosis; described themselves using terms such as "fat," "big girl," "thick," "chubby," "superfat," "considered big in Asia," etc.	• Encountered a lack of understanding in health care about the impact of fatphobia • Expressed feeling concern that their eating was disordered, but did not share this with loved ones or medical professionals • Knowledge of the definition of an eating disorder informed their reactions to and interpretations of their own behaviours or the ways their eating deviated from the norm, but they hesitated to label these experiences • Feared that their eating would be called out as disordered despite not feeling this was so • Disordered/distressed eating intersected with other aspects of people's lives allowing for a deeper understanding of the bodily experiences in society that induce stress
Larkin, June, and Rice, Carla	Explore connections between body-based harassment and body modification practices amongst grade 7 and 8 girls.	Forty-five girls from grades 7 and 8; primarily from working class backgrounds and identifying as Canadian born and Caucasian, with some identifying as Eastern European or girls of colour	• Healthy eating/weight curriculum discourses sent contradictory messages (e.g., body positivity vs. thin/health discourse), increased anxieties about body weight, ignored multiple causes of eating problems, marginalized issues most relevant to racialized girls, and ignored the dilemmas associated with physical development What should be done? • Address forms of racist body-based harassment in prevention programs to provide students the space to discuss skin bleaching and other body regulation practices that may have serious health outcomes for girls of colour • Expand the focus beyond weight and include various socio-cultural factors that influenced the range of body monitoring practices taken up by diverse girls

McPhail, Deborah, and Mazur, Lindsey	Explore the experiences of fat cisgender women and trans people in reproductive care	Twenty-five self-identified fat women in Winnipeg, Canada, who experienced reproductive care and encountered reproductive health care professionals	• Experienced medicalization of maternal obesity during pregnancy, birth, and while seeking contraception care, some of which were internalized by participants ○ Resisted medicalization by referring to self-intuitions and by distancing from "super fat" people who weighed more OR ○ Did not confront health care practitioners' fatphobia due to power imbalance • Complicated resistance against medicalization for Indigenous fat women—accepted medical discourse of fatness but critiqued the requirement of midwives transferring high-risk pregnancies
McPhail, Deborah et al. "Exposed Social Flesh"	Explore how the body constitutes and is constituted by the teaching and learning of critical weight and fat studies by looking at the outcomes of this process for the authors' bodies and emotional lives	A parent, professor, queer, fat/obese/morbidly obese Canadian-based researcher (McPhail)	• Not putting body on display due to a historical trauma wherein her body was singled out as "different," "wrong," and "worthless" • Used generalities or discussed other authors' work on topics related to fat studies; relied on guest speakers and fat activists to talk about their experiences of embodiment and fatphobia • To imagine the removal of body from the classroom ○ Lack of focus on the embodied effects of learning about fat and fat oppression, and allows normative identities (e.g., thinness) to go unnamed and thus uninterrogated
Meerai, Sonia	Explore the intersection of racism and fatphobia through the author's racialized fat body's experience in the health care system	A self-identified racialized fat woman and a fat studies scholar	• Flesh as a problematic site and weight loss as the "only" solution at the intersection of fatness/sizeism, race/ism, and other intersecting identities within social institutions (e.g., wedding event, health care) • No direct evidence to indicate that weight loss diminished health conditions and/or protected an individual from the intersecting impact of fatphobia and racism • Reimagined embodied realities at the intersection of race and fat by uncovering, through autoethnography, the operation of the medical discourse of fatness and its intersection with racism.

Rice, Carla. "Becoming 'the Fat Girl'"; "How Big Girls Become Fat Girls"; Imagining the Other?"; and "Rethinking Fat"	• Analyse the body histories of women who recount their experiences of becoming "fat girls" within a Canadian context • Theorize "body becoming pedagogies" that open possibilities (and therefore ontologies) for what fat bodies can be and become • Critically consider the significance of the author's body history during the research project	• Eighteen to twenty-one women who formed a fat identity by the end of childhood and/or who witnessed effects of anti-fat attitudes on others; part of a larger study on 81 women's diverse experiences of their bodies across the lifespan • Carla Rice, a "former fat girl" and a queer woman	Study Findings • Acquired an unfit identity because of the prevalence of fatphobia in personal and social contexts (e.g., family, schools, etc.) • Fatness as a marker of disqualifying and positioning women, especially racialized fat women, as Other • Surveillance and violence (e.g., unhealthy eating practices) to impose compliance with culturally feminine bodies • Found strategies to contest fatphobia, such as using humour/comedy; developing intellectual or artistic identities; using aggression, masculinity, and violence; and preserving a positive sense of self Author's Reflexivity and Theorization • Felt anxious in environments built for average bodies, even if gained privileges associated with attaining a gendered size norm by adopting strict disciplinary practices of eating and exercise • Concealing about embodied differences during research allowed her to escape the pain of being seen as Other but enabled avoidance of analysing passing within sustained oppressive ideals • Acknowledged own positions and privileges (either to interviewees or self) while prioritizing being open to and relating to participants' perspectives—led to discovery of new knowledges about bodily selves • Focused on unique aspects of each woman's story while drawing from own and participants' similarities and differences in formulating follow-up questions • Argued for "body equity" and "body-becoming" approaches to foster acceptance of diverse bodies as well as to examine the impact of physical, psychical, environmental, and cultural forces on possibilities for what bodies could become and the creativity and beauty that were missed while controlling body diversity
Rinaldi, Jen et al. "Through Thick and Thin"	Examine how discourses of obesity and eating disorders reinforce cissexist and heteronormative body standards	Sixteen queer women in Canada	• Exposed to varied levels of external control, expectations of internal control, and efforts to take control of their narrative arcs, which were resisted by reaching for strategies that facilitate self-acceptance • Experienced fat shame and eating disorder treatment • Considered how their bodies have been positioned as the stuff of "before" pictures, defied strict categorization, and shifted throughout their lives, while challenging dominant discourses • Reflected on shifts in their own beliefs and work toward self-acceptance, advocacy, and celebration

Ristovski-Slijepcevic, Svetlana et al.	Examine the perspectives on fatness and food choice amongst Black and white women and men living in Vancouver and Halifax, Canada	Black participants = 26 (19 female, 7 male) White Haligonians = 20 (13 female, 7 male) White Vancouverites = 25 (17 female, 8 males)	Women's talk • Black women experienced the risk-based discourses of fatness in health care that involved their own or family members' weight ○ Far more likely to express resistance toward obesity discourse and the thin/healthy equation ○ Believed that the ideal weight portrayed in Western culture was too thin, unhealthy, and unrealistic, and aimed to be "not obese but 'nice and thick'" ○ Still emphasized "shape," suggesting a distinct but less rigidly defined body ideal that they strove towards • White women in the study were far more likely to invoke risk and aesthetic discourses in discussing their weight concerns, but expressed criticisms of the dominant cultural beauty ideals • For Black women, resisting the thin beauty ideal through food can lead to a body that is likely to get approval from the community • For white women from Vancouver, resisting the thin body ideal through food can lead to a body that makes one different from the majority (under "the capitalist economy")
Taylor, Alison	Explore how femmephobia, fatphobia, and other oppressions operate in the context of queer fat femme women's and gender nonconforming individuals' experiences of dating	Fifteen queer fat femme women and gender nonconforming individuals living in Canada; 12 participants identified as white (80%), 1 as Black (6.6%), 1 as Latinx and white (6.6%), and 1 as East Indian and white (6.6%); 10 of the fifteen participants identified as disabled (67%)	• Dating as a space of oppression/exclusion/discrimination based on an intersection of queerness, fatness, and fem(me)ininity • Felt that they were often ignored as sexual subjects and, therefore, overlooked or rejected as viable dating or sex partners • Sexual racism—the way intersections of racism, femmephobia, and fatphobia reproduced Black, queer, fat, and fem(me)inine bodies as undesirable in relation to those of white queer fat femmes • Narratives of fetishization—queer fat femmes not seen as subjects worthy of dating, respect, or love, but rather as objects to be sexualised and dehumanised • Negative impacts of marginalization in dating— feeling hopeless and alone, questioning their desirability, fearing dating, and ultimately being let down by their own communities • Superficial queer engagements with fat politics and uninterrogated, underlying fatphobia circulating in queer communities that reproduces the exclusion of queer fat femmes in dating contexts • Intersection of femmephobia and fatphobia that produced fraught experiences of in/visibility and feelings of undesirability • Strategically used and negotiated the labels "queer fat femme" and "lady bear" to create less oppressive dating environments and spaces for themselves

Ward, Pamela et al.	Examine the embodied experiences of children enrolled in an "obesity" treatment program in a Canadian hospital	Two girls and four boys enrolled in an 11-week child "obesity" treatment program in an Atlantic Canadian hospital that used a non-weight focus and promoted self-esteem and positive body image	• Reflected a white, middle-class, gendered, and heterosexual approach to define "health," as someone fit/not fat • Defined fitness in relation to how a body looks, which could be derived from personal effort • Health equated to not eating "too much" junk food, perceiving that junk food contributed to poor health, guilt, and fatness • Fatness as unhealthy, dangerous, uncontrollable, life threatening, and a symbol of laziness and lack of care toward the corporeal self • Experiences of girls pertinent to social struggle and pressure due to the constructions of health as achieving the thin ideal: ○ Emergence of complex relationships between food, intervening social pressures, and the body ○ Forced to navigate social (peer) dynamics in striving toward a balanced sense of self ○ Resistance by accepting self and highlighting positive aspects of their identity not tied to their appearance

Note: The table summarizes 14 studies discussed in 18 research articles and book chapters that were included in this systematic review.

We took an inductive data analysis approach to derive themes from the findings. Using NVivo 12, we separately coded the articles thematically before convening to discuss the codes and to group and reorganize them. We paid attention to how fatness and gender intersected with other identities in the references. Our initial coding schemes centred on the commonalities across fat women with different intersectional marginalized identities, as well as how particular axes of oppression (e.g., race or sexuality) intersected with fatphobia. Another line of coding mapping experiences to particular spaces was added due to one author's (Chen's) geographical background. By integrating and reorganizing our coding schemes and incorporating feedback from a peer reviewer, we derived two broad themes (figure 3.2): 1) fat women's experiences and the negotiation of fatphobia across spaces within the Canadian landscape and 2) their resistance against fatphobia. Our approach intentionally investigated how access to power at different ages intersects with fatness and space to explain what it means to be "fat" in Canada, as fat bodies exist in a "world designed with smaller bodies in mind" (Owen 290), and, thus, are "often thought to take up too much space ... [and to experience] attempts to delimit and confine [them]" (Longhurst 254).

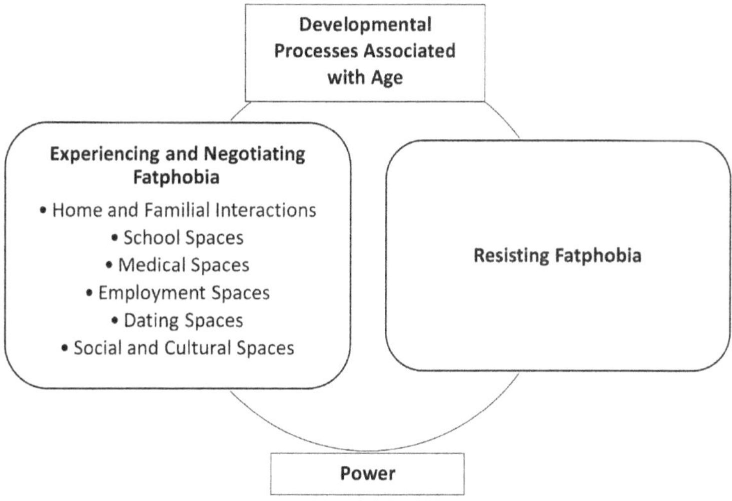

Figure 3.2 Spaces of Fatphobia

Experiencing and Negotiating Fatphobia

Fat women experience discrimination, control, abuse, and the shaming of their bodies as they move through different spaces in a Canadian context. Experiences and the negotiation of fatphobia are prominent at home and school for fat girls, and at dating, employment (academic), and medical spaces for fat women.

Fat Girls

Home and Familial Interactions

Fat-shaming and fatphobia operate within heteropatriarchal family environments in Canada; socialization of fatphobic discourses starts at a young age through home spaces. For fat girls in heteronormative families, home is where the exchange of social discourses aligned with thinness, femininity, normalcy, and the body begins. Fatphobia in home spaces is perpetuated primarily by male family members (e.g., brothers and fathers) and negatively informs fat girls' perceptions of themselves, their bodies, and their embodied being, which leads to their "unfit" fat identity as women (Dean 210; Rice, "How Big Girls" 101). While some are comfortable at their homes with non-judgmental families (Dean 210), others are constantly pressured to lose weight and conform to thin body ideals. Ramanpreet Bahra assumed that she could not be happy as a fat Brown girl because of growing up in a "thin-centric" family (197; Owen 294). As fat girls interact within the heteropatriarchal family, they feel discomfort, internalize fatphobic ideas, and continuously associate the fat-identity with "abnormalcy."

School Spaces

Fat girls in Canada experience school spaces as regulatory spaces that continuously enforce body standards, deem young fat girls as fat or "overweight," and exclude them for their body nonconformity (Bahra 197; Larkin and Rice 225; Rice, "Becoming 'the Fat Girl'" 164; "How Big Girls" 102; "Rethinking" 391;

Ward et al. 263). Through school practices, such as the dress code, and physical and health education programmes, fat girls learn the ideal body standards of thinness and the reading of fatness as deviance. With school environments being characterized by peer pressure and the need to fit in, fat or bigger girls whose bodies stood out ostensibly are bullied and fat-shamed (Larkin and Rice 223; Ward et al. 263). This bullying is frequently gendered, with beatings and physical abuse coming from boys (Rice "Becoming 'the Fat Girl'" 167). These acts make the school and its surroundings particularly dangerous and traumatic places for the girls.

Gender and ability also intersect in girls' fatphobic experiences within school spaces. In Carla Rice's "Becoming 'the Fat Girl,'" one woman recounted how her high school officials perceived fat girls with disabilities as incapable of controlling their eating behaviours and body weight. Thus, the officials segregated all "fat kids with disabilities," including her, from other children, adversely impacting the girls' development (167). Within sport and physical activities at school, being fit and able is equated with thinness and a "healthy" body weight. Fat girls are deemed "unfit," passively feminine, and incapable, and they are excluded from or considered a last choice for team sport (Rice, "Becoming 'the Fat Girl'" 164; "How Big Girls" 103). The medical model that conflates thinness with "health" and ability and fatness with disability undergirds the biopedagogical practices of physical education classes that categorize students as "healthy" thin and "unhealthy" fat bodies (Rice, "How Big Girls" 103). In these classes, teachers and peers presume that young fat girls are limited by strength, coordination, athletic skills, and agility simply because of their bodies (Rice, "Becoming 'the Fat Girl'" 164; "How Big Girls" 102). Teachers group students in accordance with their physical bodies, heightening the students' experience of fatphobia and the feeling of something being "wrong" with their bodies.

Being trapped in school spaces, fat girls are compelled to navigate fatphobic social dynamics to strive toward a balanced sense of self. Although fat girls enjoy participating in athletics, their physical agency and confidence are disrupted by fatphobia in physical education classes at school. They avoid changing in gym changing rooms and wear track pants to hide their thighs in physical education classes. They also feel stressed to participate in state-sponsored physical education curricula that implicitly use gender and size biases, e.g., favour boys and children with long legs and upper-body strength (Rice, "Becoming 'the Fat Girl'" 165). Fatphobia becomes self-fulfilling in the girls' exclusion or voluntary withdrawal from physical activities to safeguard themselves from fat shaming (166). Similarly, body-based harassment in schools leads fat adolescent girls to have a distorted body image, be anxious, and to feel coerced to sustain a fit body weight by "watch[ing] what they eat" (Larkin and Rice 224). They perceive themselves as "fat" even when they are within the normalized weight range. In this process, they are likely to develop a lifelong preoccupation with body size and eating that ironically prohibits them from incorporating "healthier" lifestyle practices. Consequently, fat girls internalize their bodies being less valued and develop a complex and often negative relationship between their bodies, food, and the social pressures to be thin. Through the discourses and policing of thinness, health, and ability in school spaces, they become increasingly cognizant of conforming to body norms and vulnerable to objectifying their own growing body and self-image.

Social and Cultural Spaces

For fat girls, fatphobia in broader social and cultural spaces in Canada manifests at the intersections of gender identity and size. In Rice's "Becoming 'the Fat Girl,'" one girl reminisced that showing any signs of femininity made her feel like an "improper female" because of the stigma associated with her fatness (168). Fat girls who "fail" at being feminine are viewed as "other-gendered," "odd," and "not-girl." They can embrace an in-between status of "tomboy" and embody attributes not typically allowed or valued in "feminine" girls such as athleticism, curiosity, and strength. However, defying heteropatriarchal norms of strength results in fat girls' experiences of violence by boys and exclusion from tomboy pursuits (Rice, "Becoming 'the Fat Girl'" 168; "How

Big Girls" 101). This judgment of and violence towards fat girls reflects and preserves the power matrix of patriarchy, male superiority, and sizeism in Canadian society.

Race and migration play aggravating roles in fat girls' anxieties about body weight. In settler-colonial Canada, whiteness and thinness are seen as ideal markers of femininity and body desirability. Fat girls who migrated to Canada attempted to conform to the white beauty ideals in order to fit into the Canadian culture; however, being fat, Brown, and/or migrant meant the impossibility of fully fitting in (Larkin and Rice 226–27). The girls with visible markers of non-normativity (e.g., skin colour) experienced race-based teasing (e.g., being exposed to comments such as "all Orientals are anorexic") about their bodies (Larkin and Rice 226). They did not know whether they were bullied for their race or size (Rice, "Becoming 'the Fat Girl'" 103).

Finally, fatness and class intersect for fat girls living in low-income neighbourhoods, who avoid certain "obesogenic" routes that tempt them to eat and hamper their goal to sustain their desired future body size (Dean 209). They escape these routes either permanently or in certain temporal periods, such as during mealtime (210). Fat girls in low-income neighbourhoods also momentarily pause time to remove their fatness, creating an alternative reality through video games, books, creative writing/journaling, and playing with props (208). While these negotiations of fatphobia reflect fat girls' internalization of fatphobic discourses, they attempt at carving out alternative temporalities and spatialities within fatphobic environments. With the omnipresence of sizeist-normative language, narratives, and practices that perpetuate the linearity of human bodies and pathologize fatness (Bahra 202), these alternative time-spaces provide a break and a refuge for fat girls at home or when moving through their neighbourhood spaces.

Fat Women

Turning from fat girls to fat (adult) women, we examine the spaces where they experience and negotiate fatphobia.

Medical Spaces

Fat trans and cisgender women's experiences of fatphobia feature overwhelmingly in Canadian spaces where medical norms of "health" and weight dominate. Using measures such as the body mass index (BMI), blood pressure, and skinfold measurement, fat, "overweight" bodies are claimed as "unhealthy," disease prone, and deviant, whereas thinner, "ideal" weight bodies are considered "healthy," "normal," and desirable (Bahra 196; Rice "How Big Girls" 102). The medical model utilizes the "obesity epidemic" banner to enforce fatphobic practices in health care spaces such as clinics and hospitals. When fat women attend medical appointments, they feel they are being measured against medical standards of "healthism" and derogatorily labelled by clinicians as fat or "obese" (Bombak et al. 95; LaMarre et al. 68). Often, their fatness is the first thing pointed out to them by clinicians. Fat women experience medical professionals' attempts at policing, controlling, and disciplining their bodies. They are denied conception support, pap smear screenings, or other treatment based on the recommendation to exercise more and lose weight before treatment (Bahra 196; Bombak et al. 98; LaMarre et al. 69; McPhail and Mazur 122, 126; Meerai 91; Rice, "Becoming 'the Fat Girl'" 169). Bahra's appointments with her family doctor subjected her to endless monitoring, weighing in, and moralizing comments about weight loss, even if her medical issues were not necessarily weight related (197). Fat pregnant women are also labelled as at a "high risk" of labour complications and were monitored closely and more strictly until they gave birth, when compared to their thinner counterparts (Bombak et al. 99; McPhail and Mazur 126–27; McPhail et al., "Wombs at Risk" 107).

The hypervisibility and medicalization of fatness and fatphobic practices in health care spaces frame fat women in terms of the risk and danger they have inflicted upon themselves (Meerai 91) and/or their foetuses if the women are pregnant (McPhail and Mazur 126; McPhail et al., "Wombs at Risk" 106). Doctors ignore fat women's personal exercise and eating habits or overall "health," immediately equating fatness with ill-health, citing statistics linking higher weight with disease, and exerting acts of discipline on fat female bodies (Bombak et al. 99; McPhail et al., "Wombs at Risk" 105). In doing so, doctors assume greater knowledge about fat women's bodies than the women have themselves. This focus on fat bodies rather than on the actual symptoms and/or illnesses women experience reduces fat women to their fatness and signifies the failure of health care practitioners and medical spaces to provide adequate care. It also reflects the patriarchal structure of medical spaces—where (male) rational, disembodied discourses of health and body weight dominate and discipline fat, female, and "out-of-control" bodies.

Race and settler-colonial mechanisms negatively impact racialized fat women's experiences of weight-based discrimination, positioning them in an even more precarious state in medical spaces. Analysing her health care experiences, Sonia Meerai concluded that brownness and fatness were both viewed as risk factors in health care narratives (91). Her body became problematized "within medical discourse as it is read through a racist lens in connection with other intersecting identities" such as fatness (92). Further, Meerai felt that her doctor did not acknowledge her body's ever-changing emotional and physical states, especially those attributable to her wedding, which is more extravagant in Brown cultures and can be exhausting due to the inclusion of traditional events and family gatherings (91–92). For Black fat women, their medical encounters are filled with risk-based narratives stereotypically associated with obesity within Black families and ethnic communities (i.e., heart disease, cancer, and high blood pressure). They worry about being obese even after losing weight throughout their lives (Ristovski-Slijepcevic et al. 323). Further, Indigenous women in reproductive health care are told by doctors that they can "'pass on diabetes due to multiple risks of fatness and their 'bloodlines'" (McPhail and Mazur 129). Indigenous fat pregnant women living in rural areas and labelled as "high risk" are shifted to urban (white) centres to give birth because of a lack of health care funding in rural Indigenous communities. Arguably, the white settler colonialism that impacts Indigenous communities' access to medical resources forces these women to give birth in isolation, away from their family, friends, and communities (127). The white settler colonialism in medical discourse also constructs Indigeneity, brownness and Blackness—alongside fatness and femininity—as risks, dangers, and threats to fat racialized women and their future children.

Fat women negotiate with fatphobia in health care spaces in adverse ways. Queer fat women rigorously exercise, adopt restrictive eating practices, and hyper-vigilantly control their bodies to escape the clinical gaze of fatness (Rinaldi et al., "Thick and Thin" 13). Although they defy viewing their body, eating choices, and health as either "normal" or "disordered," they feel alienated from their own bodies and eating habits (LaMarre et al. 70). As well, fat women who access reproductive care find it daunting to reject the doctors' medicalization of fatness overtly and hide their dissatisfaction because of the power imbalance between patients and specialists in medical spaces (McPhail and Mazur 132). Some women internalize mother-blame discourses, e.g., that they did not care about their foetuses (Bombak et al. 98–99). They feel punished by the "high-risk" label and struggle with the judgment of "failing" as a good mother (McPhail et al., "Wombs at Risk" 107–09). They fear becoming mothers because of the potential risks attached to their bodies, including birth defects, miscarriages, and gestational diabetes. Wanting to conceive and being refused reproductive care due to their weight, fat pregnant women implement unhealthy weight loss and maintenance practices, e.g., starvation diets with periods of binge eating, excessive exercise, and sweating off "water weight" (McPhail et al., "Wombs at Risk" 108). Some agree to lose weight before becoming pregnant to meet the standards of the "good" thin mother and avoid their doctors' negative perspectives about "obesity" (McPhail and Mazur 128, 130). Others attempt to mitigate mother-blame discourses in health care by discriminating against, and distancing themselves from, racialized and working-class women stereotyped to deploy poor health behaviours, e.g., not consuming sufficient nutrition (Bombak et al. 99). Those who "fail" to lose weight prior to conception experience high anxiety pregnancies and the fear of giving birth in a high-risk ward (McPhail et al., "Wombs at Risk" 106). Conclusively, the stigmatization of fatness as an illness leads to self-identified fat women experiencing fatphobia in medical spaces (e.g., doctors rejecting the provision of reproductive care) that they negotiate with by being anxious, engaging in problematic eating behaviours, and internalizing mother-blame discourses. Racialized and queer women's fatphobic experiences intensify within medical contexts in Canada because of the intersections between fatphobia, racism, and discrimination against queer individuals.

Employment Spaces

In the literature we found, only the reflexive autoethnography by Deborah McPhail and colleagues emphasized self-identified fat women dealing with fatphobia as teachers in Canadian academic settings. McPhail narrated that she viewed academia as a safe space to explore fatness and fat politics, as well as to heal past bodily traumas, which contributed to her deciding to teach fat studies courses at a university (McPhail et al., "Exposed Social Flesh" 21). Also, McPhail felt that her experiences of fatphobia in classrooms are mitigated due to privileges linked to her self-identification as white, able-bodied, and middle-class and to being categorized as heterosexual unless she mentions otherwise. Simultaneously, McPhail became self-conscious about teaching in a traditional health discipline. Teaching in a traditional health discipline, she wondered if her students perceived her as a "good fattie" (i.e., someone who exercises, does not eat fast food, and does not belong to one of the racialized and lower-class social groups who are imaged as "at risk" for "obesity") as opposed to a "bad" one (22). To negotiate with fatphobia in the classroom, McPhail reflected on how she could help her students unlearn fatphobia without centring herself and her body in the conversation (23). Regardless, she chose to separate her body from self, objectifying her body so it could be hidden and disappeared, to cope with her history of fatphobia (26). She employed generalities, focused on other authors' research, and invited guest speakers and fat activists to talk about their embodiment and fatphobic experiences so she could avoid discussing her own fatness in the fat studies classroom (27).

Dating Spaces

Of the sampled studies, only Allison Taylor's discussed fat women's experiences and the negotiation of fatphobia in dating spaces in Canada. Interviewing queer fat femme women and gender nonconforming persons, Taylor found that they face rejection in dating within the queer communities. These communities view queer fat femmes' fatness and femininity as "undesirable," "unattractive," or non-sexual (Taylor 59), limiting their options to seek romance in an already small social network. Queer fat femmes and gender nonconforming individuals also experience fetishization by others in the queer community. They are conscious of others objectifying and sexualizing their fat bodies and being interested in them out of curiosity, fascination, and to self-portray as open-minded (62). They also are stripped of subjectivity and agency, becoming bodies to be gazed upon by more privileged others in queer spaces (62). Racialized queer fat femmes feel being desired both for their "deviation" from white skin colour and thin body size. To negotiate with fatphobia, queer fat femmes doubt their own sexuality and avoid dating for fears of being hurt, fetishized, or treated as a joke. They experience loneliness and stress about flirting in a queer space because of the prevalence of fatphobia in queer community (62). Indeed, they consider fat acceptance in queer communities as "lip service" and "tokenisation," as Canadian queer spaces lack an intersectional focus and are dominated by individuals who are white, skinny, and body based and who are unaware of the fact that "desire is political" (62–63).

Social and Cultural Spaces

Fat women in Canada experience the fatphobic gaze as they move in and through thin-centric social spaces that pathologize fatness and idealize white, cisgender, abled, and thin bodies. They feel anxious, self-conscious, and uncomfortable because of the gaze, and in some instances, avoid social interactions and places with high visibility (Rice, "Becoming 'the Fat Girl'" 164; "How Big Girls" 102;). Carla Rice, a self-identified former fat woman, shared the experience of similar psychological outcomes despite having the privileges associated with a "normal" body size ("Imagining the Other?" 251). This mirrors other fat women's experience of hypervisibility. They are angered by thin others, or people in general, who cannot see past the fatness and unfairly label them as fat (Rice, "Rethinking Fat" 391).

To negotiate fatphobia within Canadian social and cultural spaces, fat women use humour, develop intellectual or artistic identities, and/or highlight their physical abilities. Some fat women resort to aggression and violence to counter the intersection of thin body ideals and heteropatriarchy, defying the lower status of fat women in society and exhibiting the power of fat female bodies (Rice, "Becoming 'the Fat Girl'" 170). However, several fat women succumb to fatphobia by policing their eating habits to meet the objective of weight loss that was pushed onto them by their families, teachers, peers, doctors, and others. They develop lifelong struggles with food and compulsive, binge, secretive, or disordered eating practices to escape the "deviant" label associated with fatness (Rice, "Becoming 'the Fat Girl'" 169; "How Big Girls" 105, 106; "Rethinking Fat" 390, 391).

Particularly race and sexuality intersect with gender in fat women's experiences and their negotiation of fatphobia. Black and other racialized women do not have a community space to aid them in creating a critical consciousness of racist beauty ideals and in imagining an alternative body aesthetic (Rice, "How Big Girls" 104). In particular, Black fat women are socially positioned as neither masculine nor feminine because of stereotypes about Black femininity as being aggressive and masculine. Therefore, their fatness is demeaned as less active and less able than that of their white fat counterparts (104). To counter the intersecting discourses of sizeism and racism, Black women vocalize how colonial heteropatriarchal systems contribute to this body politics by using anti-fatness rhetoric. They challenge the conflation of "health" and "thinness" by consuming food, underscoring the presence of individual varieties in a "healthy" and an active body shape and size, and believing that the natural diversities of bodies evolve in a space between thin and "obese" body weight (Ristovski-Slijepcevic et al. 324). Hence, they focus on achieving a "nice and thick" body, one that is likely to get approval and acceptance from Black communities (324–25). In contrast, white women mostly accept medicalized narratives of obesity and aesthetically prefer thinness (325). For Bahra, a Brown fat woman, negotiating fatphobia meant endeavouring to "pass" as "fully human." She used skin-lightening products, controlled her eating habits, exercised excessively, and/or participated in weight-loss programs like Weight Watchers. She believed that masking her otherness in size and skin colour would give her the privileges associated with a beautiful, thin, white body (198). Subsequently, she employed makeup and the techniques of contouring to camouflage her fatness and brownness and pass as "normal" (Bahra and Overboe 201).

Queer fat women struggle with eating and exercise because of intersectional stigma and discrimination (LaMarre et al. 64). They reflect on their body, desires, and desirability while perceiving their embodied subjectivities as a process (Rinaldi et al., "Thick and Thin" 19). Without seeking advice or help from their loved ones or health care practitioners, queer fat women interpret their own eating behaviours by using social or cultural understandings of eating disorders that "exemplify distress around food," a distress "that consumes day-to-day tasks of living and identity formation and calls for hospitalization or intensive attention and treatment" (LaMarre et al. 71). They do not overtly label their eating behaviours as disordered, although they are disturbed, fearful, or simply aware of these behaviours as deviant (71–72). To negotiate the marginalizing discourses of fatness and resolve ambivalence toward their own bodies, queer fat women construct an alternative understanding of self, such as affirming butch identity or queer aging femininity (Rinaldi et al., "Thick and Thin" 18).

Overall, fat girls and women in Canada are exposed to the medicalization of fatness and to thin body ideals. As well, they are discriminated against for their fat bodies both in their homes and schools as adolescents and in medical, employment or academic, and dating spaces as adults. They negotiate with fatphobia through strategies, such as adopting problematic eating practices or internalizing blame discourses.

Resisting Fatphobia

In a white settler society like Canada's, the medicalization of fat bodies both imposes and sustains white supremacy ("*Fat Studies*: Aims and Scope"). We see fat resistance being mapped out through the works of Bahra, a Brown fat woman, as she described her assemblages of negotiation, resistance, and affirmation. Bahra challenged her internalized racism and sizeism by refusing either to use skin-lightening products or to participate in dieting programs (199). Gradually, she used makeup that let her fatness and brownness become fluid, spontaneous, and creative assemblages, thus flourishing as expressions of life without a sense of resentment, a cycle that is often found in negative coping strategies to pass as "normal" (Bahra and Overboe 200). For her, the vagueness of these expressions of life becomes ever-changing moments of impotentiality located in her fatness and brownness. These practices constituted a process of "doing" that helped her to form relationships with her environment through her fatness and brownness (204). Bahra's makeup practices resulted in her process of self-affirmation, a strategy utilized to liberate oneself from fatness-related insecurities and shame, and weave a celebratory counternarrative of fat subjectivity (Bahra 198; Bahra and Overboe 206). Indeed, Bahra "g[ave] a presence" to fat bodies, acknowledging and allowing them to be expressed through affirmation and joy (Bahra and Overboe 205). She found "life" in becoming not just fatter but also more impaired, Brown, queer, and feminine.

As fatness intersects with sexuality, fat resistance manifests in Rinaldi et al.'s work entitled "Through Thick and Thin." Here, queer fat women celebrate and advocate for themselves and their bodies by "resist[ing] framings of their bodies as revolting—objects of disgust or disdain—by embracing their bodies as revolting," meaning as a rebellious force (20–21). Thus, they reclaim the term "revolt," used to express disgust toward fat bodies, to engage in fat resistance. Queer fat women also refuse the stereotyping of fatness as "disgusting" and collectively portray fat bodies as rebellious. Similar to reclaiming the term "revolt," queer fat women embrace identity labels such as "queer fat femme" to proudly present their fat bodies in dating spaces. They describe themselves as fat and cuddly or post their full-body photographs to create a less oppressive and more open dating environment for themselves (Taylor 65). Further, queer fat femmes self-identify with the term "lady bear" to challenge the perception of the bear culture as a masculine space for queer men's fat, hairy bodies (65). For Black queer fat femmes, self-identification as a racialized queer woman alleviates fatphobic experiences in dating spaces by narrowing the pool of interested individuals (61).

Fat women seeking health care in Canada engage in fat resistance by confronting the Canadian (Western) narratives that medicalize fatness by calculating "healthy" weight in accordance with the body mass index, or BMI (McPhail et al., "Wombs at Risk" 107). Those who attempt to access conception care oppose mother-blame discourses in medical spaces; that is, they contest the idea that they lack control over their body weight. They deny viewing themselves as "bad mothers" for being pregnant while embodying a bigger body (109). They challenge health care professionals' medicalization of fatness by using their own knowledge, awareness, and intuitions about their bodies; working on their bodies to conceive without seeking medical assistance; and vocalizing individual differences amongst women's bodies (McPhail and Mazur 131). Finally, fat women seeking reproductive care believe that health care professionals should understand the fatphobic experiences and medical needs of fat women and treat them like any other women (109).

In sum, fat women engage in fat resistance by confronting the white supremacist idealization of thinness and the medicalization of fat bodies. Those who also identify as queer or racialized engage in self-affirmation and redefine fatness as a site of revolt or rebellion against anti-fat narratives.

Conclusion

This chapter presents a systematic review of the literature on how self-identified fat women in Canada, who embody marginalized intersectional identities, experience and negotiate fatphobia.

By documenting the experience, negotiation, and liberation of fatness, we engage in fat resistance as advocated in the Canadian scholarship of *Fat Studies* and *Thickening Fat*. We found that fat girls and women experience and negotiate with fatphobia across various spatialities, such as home, academia, dating sites, and medical spaces, and contexts, both social and cultural. Spatialities of fatphobia vary by age: fat girls are first exposed to fatphobia in their primary spaces of socialization, such as within their familial and school environments, whereas fat women are likely to experience anti-fat attitudes and behaviours within the medical and dating spaces they navigate as they grow older. These discourses of fatphobia and thin body ideals are rooted in the medical model and "normalcy," stemming from the history of white settler colonialism, and they are maintained to strengthen white supremacy (Ristovski-Slijepcevic et al. 325; Taylor et al.).

Our intersectional approach reveals how racialized, queer, and young fat women's encounters with fatphobic discrimination and stigma are impacted by additional power imbalances of racism, sexism, and anti-queerness. Racialized fat women found their bodies doubly pathologized by medical institutions whereby settler-colonial medical discourses equated Indigenous, "coloured," and fat female bodies with risk and disease. For queer fat femmes, their exclusion by thin queer people reveals an additional layer of marginalization by and within already marginalized communities. This demonstrates the complex nature and interdependency of these oppressive systems.

Power and young age contribute to how fat women negotiate with fatphobia in the Canadian context. For instance, fat girls who hold relatively little social power over peers and teachers in schools respond to fatphobia by disciplining their bodies, becoming self-conscious, and internalizing negative perceptions of themselves while also avoiding thin-centric spaces (e.g., gyms and physical education classes). Similarly, fat women wanting reproductive care had to do the same within medical institutions (e.g., avoiding a confrontation with their doctors who endorse fatphobia). They are subjected to the "expert" pathologizing views of medical staff; thus, they internalize the mother-blame and fatphobic discourses and focus on weight loss to receive the treatment they seek from health care authorities. Whereas fat girls create alternative spatialities and temporalities to escape fatphobia, fat women resist fatphobia altogether by constructing alternative and affirmative fat identities within the normative sizeist time-spaces. They resist the dominant framing of fatness as deficiency and a state to be overcome; instead, they engage with an "unapologetic body politic" through the self-affirmation of fatness (Bahra 198; Rinaldi et al., "Thick and Thin" 13).

Our examination of how Canadian fat women experience and negotiate fatphobia underscores the importance of analysing weight and fatness through an intersectional lens. It emphasizes the usefulness of weight and fatness as a common axis of analysis across other marginalizations. While the current literature is rich, certain gaps remain. Race, (young) age, gender, and sexuality are the most prevalent identity categories represented; however, missing or underrepresented are the experiences of fat women who also embody other marginalized identities, such as older, disabled, working-class and trans women. The literature in our systematic review is qualitative, which provides in-depth insight into fat women's experiences and negotiation of fatphobia. Future researchers would benefit from quantitatively exploring the generalizability of findings to fat women within diverse Canadian communities. Finally, we included only peer-reviewed studies in our review to limit the number of studies, which unintentionally removed the work of non-academic fat activists from fat studies scholarship. Thus, exploring the unpublished and non-academic work on fatness and fatphobia is of crucial significance. Overall, the value of the current Canadian literature lies in locating fatphobia firmly within a white settler colonialist, heteropatriarchal, and pathologizing framework—and in its concurrent offering of alternative ways of conceptualizing body, weight, and fatness.

Works Cited

Bahra, Ramanpreet A. "'You Can Only Be Happy if You're Thin!' Normalcy, Happiness, and the Lacking Body." *Fat Studies*, vol. 7, no. 2, 2018, pp. 193–202.

Bahra, Ramanpreet A., and James Overboe. "Working Towards the Affirmation of Fatness and Impairment." *Thickening Fat: Fat Bodies, Intersectionality, and Social Justice*, edited by May Friedman, et al., Routledge, 2019, pp. 197–207.

Bombak, Andrea E., et al. "Reproducing Stigma: Interpreting 'Overweight' and 'Obese' Women's Experiences of Weight-Based Discrimination in Reproductive Healthcare." *Social Science & Medicine*, vol. 166, 2016, pp. 94–101.

Carbado, Devon W., et al. "Intersectionality: Mapping the Movements of a Theory." *Du Bois Review*, vol. 10, no. 2, 2013, pp. 303–12.

Cooper, Charlotte. "Maybe It Should be Called Fat American Studies." *The Fat Studies Reader*, edited by Sondra Solovay and Esther D. Rothblum, NYU Press, 2009, pp. 327–33.

Crenshaw, Kimberlé. "Demarginalizing the Intersection of Race and Sex: A Black Feminist Critique of Antidiscrimination Doctrine, Feminist Theory, and Antiracist Politics." *University of Chicago Legal Forum*, vol. 4, no. 1, 1989, pp. 139–47.

———. "Mapping the Margins: Intersectionality, Identity Politics, and Violence against Women of Color." *Stanford Law Review*, vol. 43, no. 6, 1991, pp. 1241–1300.

Daniels, Elizabeth A., and Meghan M. Gillen. "Body Image and Identity: A Call for New Research." *The Oxford Handbook of Identity Development*, edited by Kate C. McLean and Moin Syed, Oxford University Press, 2015, pp. 406–22.

Dean, Jennifer. "Imagining Body Size Over Time: Adolescents' Relational Perspectives on Body Weight and Place." *Fat Studies*, vol. 7, no. 2, 2018, pp. 203–15.

Fahs, Breanne. "Fat and Furious: Interrogating Fat Phobia and Nurturing Resistance in Medical Framings of Fat Bodies." *Women's Reproductive Health*, vol. 6, no. 4, 2019, pp. 245–51.

Farrell, Amy E. "Origin Stories: Thickening Fat and the Problem of Historiography." *Thickening Fat: Fat Bodies, Intersectionality, and Social Justice*, edited by May Friedman, et al., Routledge, 2019, pp. 29–39.

"*Fat Studies*: Aims and Scopes." *Taylor & Francis Online*, 2021, https://www.tandfonline.com/action/journalInformation?show=aims Scope&journalCode=ufts20. Accessed 1 October 2022.

Jiménez, Karleen P. "Fat Pedagogy for Queers: Chicana Body Becoming in Four Acts." *Thickening Fat: Fat Bodies, Intersectionality, and Social Justice*, edited by May Friedman, et al., Routledge, 2019, pp. 40–50.

LaMarre, Andrea, et al. "Tracing Fatness Through the Eating Disorder Assemblage." *Thickening Fat: Fat Bodies, Intersectionality, and Social Justice*, edited by May Friedman, et al., Routledge, 2019, pp. 64–76.

Larkin, June, and Carla Rice. "Beyond 'Healthy Eating' and 'Healthy Weights': Harassment and the Health Curriculum in Middle Schools." *Body Image*, vol. 2, no. 3, 2005, pp. 219–32.

Longhurst, Robyn. "Fat Bodies: Developing Geographical Research Agendas." *Progress in Human Geography*, vol. 29, no. 3, 2005, pp. 247–59.

McPhail, Deborah, and Lindsey Mazur. "Medicalization, Maternity, and the Materiality of Resistance: 'Maternal Obesity' and Experiences of Reproductive Care." *Thickening Fat: Fat Bodies, Intersectionality, and Social Justice*, edited by May Friedman, et al., Routledge, 2019, pp. 122–36.

McPhail, Deborah, et al. "Exposed Social Flesh: Toward an Embodied Fat Pedagogy." *Fat Studies*, vol. 6, no. 1, 2017, pp. 17–37.

———. "Wombs at Risk, Wombs as Risk: Fat Women's Experiences of Reproductive Care." *Fat Studies*, vol. 5, no. 2, 2016, pp. 98–115.

Meerai, Sonia. "Taking up Space in the Doctor's Office: How my Racialized Fat Body Confronts Medical Discourse." *Thickening Fat: Fat Bodies, Intersectionality, and Social Justice*, edited by May Friedman, et al., Routledge, 2019, pp. 90–96.

Moher, David, et al. "Preferred Reporting Items for Systematic Reviews and Meta-Analyses: The PRISMA Statement." *International Journal of Surgery*, vol. 8, no. 5, 2010, pp. 336–41.

Owen, Lesleigh. "Living Fat in a Thin-Centric World: Effects of Spatial Discrimination on Fat Bodies and Selves." *Feminism & Psychology*, vol. 22, no. 3, 2012, pp. 290–306.

Rice, Carla. "Becoming 'the Fat Girl': Acquisition of an Unfit Identity." *Women's Studies International Forum*, vol. 30. no. 2. 2007, pp. 158–74.

———. "How Big Girls Become Fat Girls: The Cultural Production of Problem Eating and Physical Inactivity." *Critical Feminist Approaches to Eating Dis/orders*, edited by Helen Malson and Maree Burns, Routledge, 2009, pp. 97–109.

———. "Imagining the Other? Ethical Challenges of Researching and Writing Women's Embodied Lives." *Feminism & Psychology*, vol. 19, no. 2, 2009, pp. 245–66.

———. "Rethinking Fat: From Bio- to Body-Becoming Pedagogies." *Cultural Studies ↔ Critical Methodologies*, vol. 15, no. 5, 2015, pp. 387–97.

Rinaldi, Jen, et al. "Through Thick and Thin: Storying Queer Women's Experiences of Idealised Body Images and Expected Body Management Practices." *The British Psychological Society*, 2016. *The Atrium* [University of Guelph]: http://hdl.handle.net/10214/17626.

Rinaldi, Jen, et al. "Introduction." *Thickening Fat: Fat Bodies, Intersectionality, and Social Justice*, edited by May Friedman, et al., Routledge, 2019, pp. 1–11.

Ristovski-Slijepcevic, Svetlana, et al. "Being 'Thick' Indicates You are Eating, You are Healthy and You Have an Attractive Body Shape: Perspectives on Fatness and Food Choice amongst Black and White Men and Women in Canada." *Health Sociology Review*, vol. 19, no. 3, 2010, pp. 317–29.

Robinson, Margaret. "The Big Colonial Bones of Indigenous North America's 'Obesity Epidemic'" *Thickening Fat: Fat Bodies, Intersectionality, and Social Justice*, edited by May Friedman, et al., Routledge, 2019, pp. 15–28.

Schorb, Friedrich. "Crossroad between the Right to Health and the Right to be Fat." *Fat Studies*, vol. 10, no. 2, 2021, pp. 160–71.

Solovay, Sondra, and Esther D. Rothblum. "Introduction." *The Fat Studies Reader*, edited by Esther D. Rothblum, and Sondra Solovay, NYU Press, 2009, pp. 1–7.

Taylor, Allison. "'But Where are the Dates?' Dating as a Central Site of Fat Femme Marginalisation in Queer Communities." *Psychology & Sexuality*, vol. 13, no. 1, 2022, pp. 57–68.

Taylor, Allison, et al. "Call for Papers." *Fat Studies in Canada: (Re) Mapping the Field.*

Ward, Pamela, et al. "Confusing Constructions: Exploring the Meaning of Health with Children in 'Obesity' Treatment." *Fat Studies*, vol. 6, no. 3, 2017, pp. 255–67.

frica to the Diaspora, the Never-ng Pursuit of the Standard Body

Faith Adodo and Fardosa Warsame

IN THE FIELD OF FAT STUDIES, it is evident that we have very inadequate resources for creating a conversation about "curvy" or fat bodies within the African context. Fatness is often theorized as being acceptable within African nations, and a problem of the West only. In doing so, fat studies scholars fail to consider the impact of colonialism and the ways in which colonial narratives continue to erase fat Black experiences. For this reason, we are hoping to inspire readers by providing an entry point to dialogue with and critically analyse how dominant Western perspectives construct what Black fat African bodies should look like. Society pathologizes fatness and utilizes this discourse of pathology to construct the fat body as one needing to be fixed. This discourse is shaped and strengthened through social, economic, and political norms, as well as through anti-fat ideologies that continue to function under the banner of "the obesity epidemic" (Cooper 1020). Our intention is to affirm fat bodies without the constructed dualities of "normalcy" and "abnormality"—to define and reclaim all fat bodies as diverse and beautiful and capable of being healthy. As a theoretical lens, fat studies enables us to view fatness from multiple perspectives, thus generating a more inclusive and liberatory approach to understanding different body types and/or shapes. It is crucial to contextualize the social signifiers attached to fatness and how people view their fatness. It can be said, overall, that the language, culture, and historical influences flowing between the West and African nations generate different constructions of fatness and of what it means to be fat. For this chapter, we specifically examine the cultural understandings of fatness in Nigeria and Somalia and how they influence cisgender women of the African diaspora in Canada.

Methodology

Our methodological practices for this chapter are influenced by ethnographic studies that enable us to explain cultures and the knowledge gained from them through participant observations. Feminist ethnographers found cultural explanations lacking in dialogue on social inequality and the social transformation required for social change. The aim of feminist ethnography is to give a voice to those who are marginalized by creating a source of knowledge about the community. Similarly, both of us participate in a form of feminist ethnography every day of our lives as we engage with questions of the body and its intersections of fatness, gender, racialization, and migration. This chapter presents a duoethnographic conversation between the two of us as we approach our own life stories and theoretical frameworks to better understand how our individual experiences demonstrate different, yet similar, experiences of both fatphobia and resistance. The authors in this chapter will be identified as F.A (Adodo) and F.W (Warsame). Our stories are presented for readers to consider the negative impact colonization has had on the perception of fatness for Nigerians and Somalis in their respective nations and in the Canadian diaspora.

Language and Representation in the Western Creation of Fat Bodies

Body discourses are products of the West that have continuously attempted to examine the prevalence of "obesity" in modern societies. The body, particularly the fat and Black body, has a complex history. Its colonial roots changed the way racialized people themselves understand bodies, and, as John R. Speakman suggests, theorizing fatness is thus a complex process rooted in systemic racism and heterosexism. Western discourses on the body construct the thin white female body as attractive and desirable, and anything other as problematic. In examining fatness within an

African context, many African people view their bodies in ways that differ from Western norms and utilize different languages or terminologies to define and describe fatness (Popenoe 5). Fatness as "obesity" in the West is heavily associated with biomedical practices, which makes it easier to stigmatize fat bodies (5). The disapproval of fat bodies and the general experience of fatphobia are not common in many African nations. Countries such as Nigeria, Uganda, and Tanzania appreciate female fatness and view it as desirable. In comparison to America, where the ideology of thinness maintains a stronghold, in these African nations, "various subgroups of the population do not share the dominant white value placed on thinness in women" (Popenoe 5). Within many Black African communities in Canada there exists an inclusive approach to body types and the view that all bodies, including fat bodies, are "normal" and attractive. Knowing this, we must ask, what role does language have in constructing this concept of fatness among African citizens and migrants?

According to Stuart Hall, language functions as a "representational system" (xvii) through which we create meaning and learn of processual bodies. For instance, Hall suggests that "sounds, written words, electronically produced images, musical notes, even objects ... *carry meaning* because they operate as *symbols*, which stand for or represent ... the meanings we wish to communicate" through the process of language representation (1, 5). Within Western languages (i.e., English), representations of thinness promote an unrealistic ideal of the "perfect body," resulting in the stigmatization of fat bodies through the structures of media, medicine, and interpersonal relations. In African nations, the representational system for fatness is affirming rather than limiting. Due to limited research on representations of fatness in African nations, we have chosen to map our own narratives here.

The truth is there are different perceptions of fat bodies across the continent of Africa, and we cannot truly understand the ways in which Africans, both living in the nations and the diaspora in Canada, constitute and view both thinness and fatness without discussing the effects of colonization and civil war. Colonization introduced Eurocentric beauty standards to many parts of Africa, including the admiration of the slender body.

F.A: As I reflect on my lived experience of fatness, I come to realize how female bodies are constantly viewed as something that needs fixing to meet the ideological construct of the standard body type in society. I make this assertion based on my positionality as a Black immigrant woman who has the dual experience of being skinny in the nation-space of Nigeria and later fat in Canada. I see both of my experiences as being stuck in between the walls of a prescriptive world that is made for us as women. As a Black immigrant woman, the multiple oppressive layers make it even more difficult to move between this stuckness that has been attached to my body.

F.W: As a second-generation immigrant born in Canada into a Somali family, I have experienced fatphobic attitudes being imbued onto my body throughout my life journey. They acted as constant reminders that I am not good enough because I am fat or that I made the choice to be fat. The older generation who immigrated to the West carry a conflicting perspective on the ideal body that has been projected on the younger generation due to continuous colonization through media and other outlets. Fat bodies were once celebrated in Somalia, but because of the influences of Eurocentric beauty standards, we now see many women in Somalia pressured to be thin.

The Somali diaspora in Canada has been heavily impacted by the ways in which fatness is interpreted, and, over time, the role of the medical industrial complex has created a dramatic shift in the perception of the body. It is important to acknowledge that many Somalis seeking medical attention in the West are usually met with questions and sometimes mockery by medical professionals about the Somali diet; these medical professionals correlate health with needing to avoid the Somali diet. This is also prevalent in the West where we see older generation Somalis (mostly women) constantly criticizing our bodies and trying to put our bodies in check. For them, I am forever the fat Somali.

There has always been some form of language attached to the fat body, whether in cultural, scientific, or medical practices. Accordingly, the use and interpretations of such language and representations of the body influence how we see our bodies and others'. When negative language is used to describe fatness, it can cause mental and physical harm to fat people. As a result, it is crucial to be mindful of how we use words that define fat people as "sick," "lacking," and needing to be cured of a disease.

While both ideologies and cultural practices manifest social power, Michel Foucault suggests that dominant practices have more power over people than beliefs within the context of the general population (136). In connection to fat racialized bodies, this phenomenon of the primacy of practice over belief, which occurs through the organization and regulation of time, space, and movements, creates a situation wherein our fat racialized bodies come under the social control of authorities (136). Foucault further argues that human bodies are trained, shaped, and impressed with the stamps of the prevailing historical forms of selfhood, desire, masculinity, and femininity, and their binaries are rooted in thinness and fatness (136). This training subsequently shapes individual and collective identities.

Bordo asserts that pervasive and powerful societal influences create bodies "whose forces and energies are habituated to external regulation, subjection, transformation, and improvement" (123). At the heart of it all, there is this pursuit for the ever-changing, homogenizing, exclusive ideal of femininity that requires women to constantly respond to small and often frivolous changes in fashion, rendering female bodies into "docile bodies" (123). What we experience is constant monitoring and surveying, both explicitly and subtly; that experience ensures conformity with what dominant social standards have rendered "normal," "healthy," and beautiful bodies. For fat Black people in both Africa and the diaspora, the power-knowledge relations of fatness, gender, and Blackness take multiple forms.

> *F.A.:* My story begins in Western Africa, in my home country of Nigeria. I was the "sick," "pathological" skinny girl that needed to be fat. In my adolescent years,

> I was very skinny and grew to hate my thin body so much that I constantly prayed to God to be fat one day. Each day, I would pray for fatness, and I would drink a Maltina—a multivitamin-enriched malt drink—mixed with milk and eggs to help me gain weight and to retain fat. I did all this because of the way I was viewed by my grandparents, my peers, and men. I was called different names, such as ostrich neck and hanger shoulders and many more derogatory names to describe my skinniness, to the point that my body was perceived as the sick body. Being skinny in that context was pathologized. It caused me pain; the pressure of being too thin resulted in me losing weight rapidly, allowing the bullying to continue. Consequently, my own distaste for my body in that context gave me anxiety, which later led to depression because I did not meet the African standard of beauty—the plump woman.

So many Black fat women in the diaspora become "docile bodies" as they constantly try to modify or transform their bodies to meet Western social standards of the beautiful woman. In the Global North, contemporary media representations have a large role in propagating societal views of the "normal" body type. Constant media pressure influences young people and adults, particularly women, to view themselves through the eyes of the Western male gaze. Of course, immigrant women arriving in Canada also experience strong pressure to conform to the expectations of this Eurocentric male gaze. When we analyse the intersections of gender, racialization, and fatness within Canada, Somali women of the diaspora experience ever-growing confusion trying to understand what constitutes the "perfect body." In the Western world, only thin or lean bodies are appreciated and accorded a "normal," "healthy," and beautiful status. African nations that are more strongly influenced by European norms due to the painful history of colonization also tend to have rigid views that stigmatize and pathologize fat bodies as "abnormal":

> *F.W:* Growing up in Canada, I was always the chubby little kid, resulting in a lifelong journey of discipline through

> acts of policing my food intake and clothing choices to hide away my fatness. I was always left feeling ashamed and "abnormal" as I walked through my neighbourhood on my way to school. As I grew older, the policing did not stop as now I was the one disciplining my body rather than my parents and/or family members. Throughout adolescence, I forced hard-core fad diets on myself to achieve the perfect thin body that is celebrated so highly in the diaspora and in Canada in general. This impacted my self-esteem, mental health, and overall relationship with my body in unimaginable ways as I continued to abide by this notion of normalcy that is attached to the thin body. I never questioned the acts of judgment or my position as the fat Black spectacle being policed; instead, I internalized these fatphobic narratives and did whatever I could to ensure I was accepted in my community.

In both of our experiences, what is made apparent is the constant societal pressure to meet dominant norms for female bodies, which concludes in the never-ending pursuit of the socially approved body; in this case, the fat body for Adodo and the thin, muscular body for Warsame. Unfortunately, the pursuit of these acceptable bodies creates an obsession with a desperate need to conform to dominant societal norms.

"Obesity" in the West, "*Madam*" in Africa: The Cultural Perspectives of the Fat Body

In exploring the interactions of language, biomedicine, culture, and media with the constitution of fatness, it is of utmost importance to consider the role of culture in the process of creating fat identities. Geert Hofstede, a social psychologist and pioneer in cross-cultural research, defines culture "as the collective programming of the mind that distinguishes the members of one group or category of people from others" (3). Culture influences how we view the lives of people living in different groups and nations. In inspecting this connection in the context of culture, fatness, and body size, Bordo reminds us that the body in itself is a "medium of culture" within and through which we not only see bodies but come to inscribe and reinforce cultural notions of fatness, gender, race, and migration (Bordo 124). This brings us to a question: How does culture institutionalize the fat body or the slender build in both Africa and Canada?

African Narratives on Fatness

Our analysis of the experience of fatness among African women located in Nigeria and Somalia is an attempt to demonstrate how ideas of beauty, femininity, class, and gender have circulated across nation-space. Both nations have distinct cultures based on tribes and geographic location, but they also share common ideologies and viewpoints. In both Nigerian and Somali cultures, fatness is generally highly celebrated. A common cultural perspective on fatness is that being fat is an indication of beauty for women and a sign of wealth for men. For example, in Nigeria, the practice of "*mbobo*" is a rite of passage taken up in the father's compounds, very much secluded from the routines of the households. Pamela J. Brink points out that "*mbobo*" means "fattening room girl" and is a term used exclusively to denote an adolescent girl who is in a fattening room to get fat (132). Within these spaces, a girl has a great deal of privacy so that she can avoid chance encounters with family members, visitors, or outsiders, particularly men (132). In this space of the fattening room, the girl can then use that privacy to get fat. A fat Nigerian woman has either experienced *mbobo* or is wealthy enough to eat all she wants and does not need to work very hard. This cultural experience is naturalized within Nigerian culture, so all Annang girls would like to be *mbobo* and view "obesity" as something very special to be sought after. Overall, for Annang girls, to be fat is beautiful and for the fat women, then come to be known as "*madame*" (136). Annang girls are known to be hard-working girls, and they live a difficult lifestyle. They are mostly known as fish eaters because they live very close to the river area. The fish they eat are mostly dried because they lack preservatives. So, for many Annang girls, it is difficult to add weight unless their family plans it (136–38).

The Diasporic Narratives on Fatness

We now ask, does this cultural sentiment that sees fat women as beautiful and desirable remain preserved within the diaspora? Or does the process of assimilation to Western culture push the pursuit of thinness onto African immigrants as they reshape their cultural identity in Canada? Somali immigrants and refugees living in the Somali diaspora in Canada can experience a conflict of personal and cultural identity when it comes to body size and shape. With Somalia having witnessed almost 30 years of civil unrest, many Somali people have decided to relocate to achieve a brighter future. For many of these people, coming to a new country means conforming to Western norms, including unrealistic expectations of body image. Personal identity involves the beliefs, values, and goals that shape the individual. Cultural identity, on the other hand, "refers to a sense of solidarity with the ideals of a given cultural group and to the attitudes, beliefs, and behaviours manifested toward one's own (and other) cultural groups as a result of this solidarity" (Schwartz, Montgomery, and Briones 6). Clearly, cultural identities can have a strong influence on personal identities, which would appear to make conversations about the issue of identity vitally important, especially in considering the intersections of immigration, gender, and fatness.

In considering personal and cultural identities, we now approach fat racialized identities and the intersections of migration. The conflict over personal and cultural identity is unavoidable in the African diaspora because communities and governments increasingly spread the view that "obesity" is "unhealthy" and unattractive, which, in turn, creates negative stereotypes of the fat body (Gardner et al. 9; Cooper 1022). In the West, women face constant pressure to have a small waist, to avoid "overeating" and "obesity," and to improve bodily "health" through physical exercise, dieting, and medical procedures. This creates a one-dimensional understanding of what constitutes a healthy woman's body. It skews societal standards of beauty and beauty practices in ways that exclude and stigmatize fat women (Yerima 648). Many women from Africa and elsewhere who are now located in the Global North experience personal identity conflict over the issue of their fatness. A study conducted in the United Kingdom found that many Somali women are tormented by conflicting views of what constitutes the "perfect body" (Gardner et al. 2, 5). This can be found to be a reality in Canada as well. As a result, fat people are stigmatized and excluded in the cultural and social landscape, thus, leaving immigrants feeling stuck between the two cultures, two nations.

> *F.W:* Somalis living in the diaspora are caught between two cultures: one encourages them to conform to Western norms of thinness, while the other tells them to eat voraciously since "obesity" is a sign of "health" and beauty (Gardner et al. 6). It is important to note that the traditional Somali notion of a healthy woman's body shifts when Somali women move to the West, where they encounter very different beauty standards. When I speak on this issue with other Somali women living in Canada, they too share the constant pressure to maintain a body image that is foreign to the ideals of their home cultures. Much of this experience forces them into situations of painful internal identity conflict, as they come to learn of various Western studies that reject the traditional foods consumed by Somalis and suggest that Somalis should avoid consuming foods that are high in sugars and carbohydrates (Persson et al. 4). In the discussion on fatness within the Somali community, there is a shift in ideology from first-generation to second-generation migrants. For the older generation, fatness is viewed as "healthy"; however, younger generations that have been heavily influenced by Western norms of beauty see fatness as unattractive and grotesque.

> *F.A:* My understanding of fatness changed when I immigrated to Canada. I realized that the body that I hated so much in Nigeria is celebrated as the beautiful body type in Canada. My thin body was no longer the "sick" body; the fat bodies were "pathological" here. As a new immigrant, I was shocked and confused by this

> dual experience as I tried to understand how racialized female bodies were viewed in these two very different nations, even though both nations are deeply influenced by colonial structures. Even with this feeling of being stuck between two national narratives of beauty and the body, I continued my goal to eat and gain weight—to be fat! After my first pregnancy, I started to gain weight deliberately and was so happy with the outcome as the weight on the scale continued to increase and my prayers were finally coming true. However, my fatness came to be interpreted by others in a different manner. After my third child I gained over 70 pounds, and community members began to refer to me as the fat mother and urged me to lose weight to look good again. I found myself in the position of being stuck between the two cultural narratives I have learnt my entire life: both were telling me what my body is to look like to be accepted by those surrounding me. Upon reflection, this dual experience illustrates the ways in which my previously thin body was required to gain weight and now my fat body is told to shed it. This takes me to a question—what is *my* body? What expectations have dictated the ways my body moves in these various spaces? What I have learnt is that my body was always a public body as society's prescriptions would be imprinted onto me. The label of "pathological" associated in the two contexts defined how I should feel and whether I am to be invited into the realm of the beautiful woman.

In their homeland, Somalis have always associated fatness with health and wealth, but this perspective changes with migration (Gardner 2). When they leave their home to escape horror and bloodshed and arrive in Canada, they experience a radically different view of fatness and its linkages to the discourse of health and beauty. Their understanding of beauty is turned upside down. Many first-generation Somali women experience internal body image conflict that affects their relationships with their bodies and with the food they consume. But it also impacts their self-esteem. The stigmatization of fatness in the West is extremely problematic for Somali women because fatness comes to be re-established as a sign of "self-indulgence, moral failing, and laziness," which goes against the Somali cultural definition of fatness that has celebrated experiences like *mbobo*; consequently, "fat bodies face stigma, assault, prejudice, and oppression," especially the bodies of fat racialized women (Fahs 223). It has been found that some Somalis living in the diaspora are less active than they would like to be because of various barriers that result in "unhealthy" habits and "obesity" (Gardner et al 2; Persson 2). However, in the West, it is simply assumed that a fat woman is lazy, lacks self-esteem, and is unwilling to take initiatives to improve her health and well-being. Reflecting on the impact of colonization, both authors see that our bodies have constantly been scrutinized and monitored. As a result, we have internalized this, which has affected our mental health. 

Structural Oppression Experienced by the Diaspora

We have so far attempted to map out the narratives associated with fatness and how it has transpired in our home nations and our current place of living. The oppressive structures of racism, xenophobia, and sizeism continue to define the contours of the fat body in one-dimensional terms as being "unhealthy" and "abnormal" (Burgard). Health care sustains this one-dimensional conflated view of "health" and thinness, which is extremely troubling. Researchers such as Wang et al. perpetuate the idea that fatness occurs due to unhealthy eating and living habits, instead of considering the ways in which society has created fatphobic, racist, ableist, classist, nationalist structures that come to oppress marginalized communities. Wang et al. accept that societal understandings of beauty and attraction are complex and multi-dimensional, but they explicitly state that "individuals carrying larger fat stores may have poor health and lower fertility in non-famine conditions" (1). This notion is problematic because it disseminates misinformation and over-simplified views regarding the linkages between body type and health status. When one considers migration status and racialization, this narrow perspective on fatness continues to take hold, failing to address the impacts of broader societal conflicts, barriers, and discrimination on women's health. We would suggest that fatphobia tends to inform the work of Western researchers, especially those who reflect Western cultural biases that rely on thinness and fail to offer liberating and inclusive views of the diversity of healthy bodies.

Moreover, typical medical studies of the connections between fatness and "health" fail to account for the multiple, intersecting social determinants of health, including the ideological, cultural, and socio-economic factors that construct health. It is not an exaggeration to say that medical and media discourses function to instil a fear of becoming fat in people, especially women (Fahs 222, 223, 225). If we consider Black communities, including Somali and Nigerian communities in Canada, without doubt, the Western health care systems identify "obesity" as a major health problem. However, these discussions on "obesity" do not focus on the multiple barriers that Somali women face that impact their health, including post-traumatic stress, running single-parent households, and the struggle to integrate into "Canadian" culture and society. Also, there is no acknowledgment of the ways in which, in addition to these stressors, they are bombarded with reminders from popular culture and societal and health care systems that only thin white women are attractive and "healthy." In neglecting a multi-dimensional perspective on these interacting forces and the social inequality experienced, medical studies continue to position racialized immigrant women in precarious situations.

A study conducted by Persson et al. examines the physical activity levels of Somali women in Sweden. The study begins by indicating that Somali immigrant women exhibit "increased rates of overweightness and obesity, low fitness levels and low levels of cardiorespiratory fitness compared to non-immigrant women" (Persson et al. 2). This gender difference may stem from the fact that, in Western cultures and societies, it is the female body in particular that is so closely policed by a society that is structured through a patriarchal viewpoint.

F.W: It is important to acknowledge that medical journals and various studies have fixated on the "obesity" rates within the Somali community in the West. Many of these studies suggest there is a high rate of "obese" bodies in accordance with the body mass index (BMI) but fail to acknowledge the ways in which the BMI is, in fact, a colonial biopedagogical tool utilized to continue framing Black immigrant bodies as not good enough or less human. The truth is these studies also fail to acknowledge that the Somali community felt comfortable with their body sizes, especially while living in their homeland. It was, in fact, their migration process and attempt at cultural assimilation that changed their perception for the worse. As for many Somalis in the diaspora, specifically young girls and women, there is a conflicting notion of what is acceptable and what is not acceptable regarding body types. Many feel the need to police their fatness and Blackness to be considered a member of society.

Affirming Our Fatness

With the policing of fatness, Blackness, and Africanness, there also emerges a liberatory politic that affirms multi-dimensional bodies across shape, size, and weight. For the Nigerian people, this liberatory politic continues to embrace all body types, regardless of shape, and to associate the word *fatness* with "health," wealth, and beauty, contrary to the negative connotations assigned to the word in the West. In forming counter-narratives to affirm fatness, different words and language are used to generate various meanings, depending on the social and cultural contexts in which they are used. To remedy unnecessary identity confusion often experienced by immigrant women in the Global North, dominant Western social and media constructions regarding the normal, "healthy," and desirable female body must be criticized, deconstructed, and replaced with more inclusive norms that embrace a diversity of body types.

F.A.: As I moved between the social and national spaces of Nigeria and Canada, my perspectives on fatness and its intersections with migration, Blackness, and gender have been shaped quite deeply by the standard body type—one that has had a virulence of its own through the acts of colonization to present day. In unpacking these fatphobic moments of how my body was received by not only others but myself as well, I realized I needed to make a conscious decision to affirm my fatness and claim it with authenticity, without fear of repercussion. The constant struggle of moving between the cultural spaces of Nigeria and Canada and the implications this struggle had for my mental health (i.e., anxiety, trauma, depression) led me to unlearn and reframe what fatness means to me. As a migrant, I still feel stuck in between, but this journey of affirming my fatness has awakened within me a different kind of knowledge. Black women hold so much knowledge in their bellies, thighs, arms—in their bodies—that it is time we embrace our authentic selves by loving ourselves and pushing for a conversation about the experience of fatness and the body in general in the diaspora. We must no longer play the role of the public body and become victim to the trauma of anti-fat narratives. Instead, we must build a fat politics that envisions our fat bodies as our own bodies, our own temples, no longer a spectacle of the colonial lens.

F.W: My perspective on fatness has always been, for the most part, very negative. Growing up in Toronto, I always felt that because of my size, I was not welcomed in many spaces. The stares and glances I would get at such a young age from members of my community clearly indicated that I was "different" from other folks because of my weight. It took me some time to accept who I am and to disregard the judgments of those in my community. It has been and continues to be a very long road; however, I have come to realize that this is my body and that I should appreciate and love my body no matter what. Throughout the years, I have come to realize that you must live your life for yourself. There is no room or space in my life to care about what others think about me. Taking the step of co-writing this paper has also been a way of affirming my fatness. In some ways, this journey has been therapeutic in that it has helped me situate myself in understanding and appreciating myself.

Conclusion

Fat studies represents a way to resist the systemic ideological, cultural, and health care system biases against fat people. As Fahs states, fat studies "is situated as a field that works towards explicit and unequivocal resistance, defiant rejection of contemporary body norms, and deep-seated unworking and unpacking of thin-centric ideologies" (225). We acknowledge the complexity of fatness, which is evident from the many complicated questions that can be asked about fatness, "health," desire, and the beautiful body. As we have seen, African perspectives on fatness tend to differ significantly from, or even outright oppose, the Western rejection and stigmatization of fatness, especially in relation to fat women. The omnipresent policing of women's bodies causes women to experience conflicting and problematic relationships with their bodies. For Somali women living in the diaspora, different views of fatness can lead to conflict between older and younger generations as they struggle to navigate cultures that collide in many ways.

In navigating the temporal and spatial aspects of migration and fatness, those living in Canada tend to not only abide these social discourses rooted in the ideal "healthy," thin body but also carry them to their nation of origin if they return there. For instance, many Somalis and Nigerians who have lived in the diaspora import Western beauty standards back into their home countries when they return. The rise of the global beauty market has introduced new views of beauty to the Somali and Nigerian people and propagated Western understandings of beauty, particularly Western views of the beautiful woman. Though many older generation Somali and Nigerian women continue to associate fatness with health and desirability, the younger generations are increasingly steering toward Western ideals of beauty due to the technological advancements of contemporary society. Perhaps the notion of self-expression can help to resolve the conflict? Yerima argues that "the identity of a postcolonial woman revolves around self-expression" (649). Many people experience their bodies as a major form of self-expression. Self-expression can include self-acceptance and self-affirmation. For Black women, self-expression occurs when they embrace their sexuality and affirm the beauty of their hair, skin, and body shapes (Yerima 649). That said, the fatphobic rhetoric deeply embedded in our society makes it difficult for many fat women to feel confident and content in their bodies.

Eurocentric beauty standards, including body-type standards, are deconstructed by Ibrahim and Jegede who assert that social narratives constructing hierarchies of body types are seemingly non-existent among the Yorùbá (236). The authors appear to suggest that the Yorùbá appreciate different body types because idolizing a particular body type tends to denigrate other body types. Certainly, relying upon Western beauty standards limits the appreciation that is accorded to curvy or fat women's bodies. It is important to note that the Western ideology of the perfect body incorporates more than just a specific body type, it also incorporates whiteness. Akinro indicates that whiteness includes "body shape, nose shape, eye shape, lips, and hair type" (Akinro and Mbunyuza-Memani 310). Whiteness has become incorporated into the Somali community through the ways in which women do their hair and makeup and, more recently, how women strive to obtain slimmer bodies that exemplify Western ideals of health and beauty. The rise of global beauty markets has standardized Western ideals of beauty despite the diverse ways in which beauty is represented in various parts of the world (Liebelt 12, 14). Unfortunately, in our view, Somali and Nigerian women in Canada and other parts of the Western world have embraced a narrow and exclusionary understanding of beauty that promotes problematic and unhealthy habits in women who may become obsessed with achieving the perfect body. Savell's work emphasizes the interconnections between social institutions, such as those between the legal system and the medical community. If the human body is viewed from a medicalized perspective, then human health tends to be understood narrowly in terms of strict medical norms of the healthy mind and the healthy body. These norms can discriminate against those who do not conform to dominant concepts of normality, such as individuals with fat or curvy bodies, and they can function to exclude large numbers of people from full participation in society. However, Savell's discussion also suggests that the human body can be viewed in terms of diversity, which can create more open and accepting social concepts of normality. From this viewpoint, we cannot simply assume that fat people must be struggling with physical or mental health issues. Like many other physical and mental conditions, fatness can be associated with health challenges, but we argue that norms of human health should be understood broadly to incorporate many different versions of the functioning body. Many fat bodies function very well, and if fat bodies are embraced as normal then fat people can be made exemplars of healthy and beautiful bodies. The inclusion of fat bodies within societal norms of health and beauty, without discrimination, would help to liberate many women who obsess about their bodies and empower them to embrace their uniqueness.

Works Cited

Akinro, Ngozi, and Lindani Mbunyuza-Memani. "Black Is Not Beautiful: Persistent Messages and the Globalization of 'White' Beauty in African Women's Magazines." *Journal of International and Intercultural Communication*, vol. 12, no. 4, 2019, pp. 308–24.

Amlund, Dina. "Everyone Should Be Fatactivists or Fat-Allies." *Conjunctions*, vol. 7, no. 1, 2020, pp. 3–14.

Bordo, Susan. "The Body and the Reproduction of Femininity." *The Gendered Society Reader*, edited by M S Kimmel, et al., Oxford University Press, 2015, pp. 122–32.

Brink, Pamela J. "The Fattening Room among the Annang of Nigeria." *Medical Anthropology: Cross-Cultural in Health and Illness*, vol. 12, no. 1, 1989, pp. 131–43.

Burgard, Deb. "What Is 'Health at Every Size'?" *The Fat Studies Reader*, edited by Esther D. Rothblum and Sondra Solovay, New York University Press, 2009, pp. 41–54.

Cooper, Charlotte. "Fat Studies: Mapping the Field." *Sociology Compass*, vol. 4, no. 12, 2010, pp. 1020–34.

Fahs, Breanne. "Twenty-Two: A Tale of Three Classrooms: Fat Studies and Its Intellectual Allies." *The Fat Pedagogy Reader: Challenging Weight-Based Oppression through Critical Education*, edited by Erin Cameron and Constance Russell, vol. 467, Peter Lang Inc, 2016, pp. 221–29.

Foucault, Michel. *Discipline and Punish: The Birth of the Prison*. Pantheon Books, 1977.

Gardner, Katy et al. "'The Perfect Size': Perceptions of and Influences on Body Image and Body Size in Young Somali Women Living in Liverpool—A Qualitative Study." *Diversity in Health and Care*, vol. 7, 2010, pp. 1–12.

Hall, Stuart, Jessica Evans, and Sean Nixon. *Representation: Cultural Representations and Signifying Practices*, second edition. SAGE, 2013.

Hofstede, Geert. "Dimensionalizing Cultures: The Hofstede Model in Context." *Online Readings in Psychology and Culture*, vol. 2, no. 1, 2011.

Ibrahim, Fausat Motunrayo, and Ayodele Samuel Jegede. "Tradition and Limits: Polemical Construction of Body Size among the Yoruba of Southwestern Nigeria." *Journal of African American Studies*, vol 21, 2017, pp.236–55.

Liebelt, Claudia. "Manufacturing Beauty, Grooming Selves: The Creation of Femininities in the Global Economy—An Introduction." *Sociologus*, vol. 66, no. 1, 2016, pp. 9–24.

Persson, Gerthi, et al. "Somali Women's View of Physical Activity—A Focus Group Study." *BMC Women's Health*, vol. 14, no. 129, 2014, pp. 1–11.

Popenoe, Rebecca. *Feeding Desire: Fatness, Beauty, and Sexuality Among a Saharan People*. Routledge, 2004.

Speakman, John R. "Evolutionary Perspectives on the Obesity Epidemic: Adaptive, Maladaptive, and Neutral Viewpoints." *Annual Review of Nutrition*, vol. 33, 2013, pp. 289–317.

Schwartz, Seth J., Marilyn J. Montgomery, and Ervin Briones. "The Role of Identity in Acculturation among Immigrant People: Theoretical Propositions, Empirical Questions, and Applied Recommendations." *Human Development*, vol. 49, no. 1, 2006, pp. 1–30.

Wang, Guanlin, et al. "The Relationship of Female Physical Attractiveness to Body Fatness." *Peer J*, 2015, pp. 1–29.

Yerima, Dina. "Regimentation or Hybridity? Western Beauty Practices by Black Women in Adichie's Americanah." *Journal of Black Studies*, vol. 48, no. 7, 2017, pp. 639–50.

to anyone who thinks i'm ugly just because i don't look like how you think i should

Francine Cunningham

do you think i don't know?
that i don't look like what you think i should

i realized something recently,
this body that carries my soul
has survived
—is a survivor's body
this body is made to withstand meagre winters
starvation
rations handed out by Indian agents

this body that people hate so much
will live longer
in the new future
filled with heat and change and dried up crops and drops of
stagnant water
like it lived longer in the past future

this body is one of resilience
and tells the stories of my ancestors
of their sacrifice
of every season they made it through

so while you judge my body
and tell me i am unhealthy
that i will die
that i am fill in the blank
just know that i would take this survivor's body in every
reincarnation i might one day have

Artist Statement

My poetry always speaks from my own experiences moving through this world and from where my heart is sitting at the moment that I write. For me, this poem is really about celebrating the strength of my ancestors and the strength of my body to overcome famine and desperate conditions in the past—and how my body holds on to that memory to keep me safe today.

The Magical Thinking That Permits Anti-Fat Experts to Fight Fat Stigma While Also Fighting Fat

Jacqui Gingras and John-James Stranz

... obesity discrimination should not be tolerated in education, health care, and public policy sectors; obesity should be recognized and treated as a chronic disease in health care and policy sectors; and in the education sector, weight and health need to be decoupled ...
– Sharma and Ramos Salas 89

Introduction

In the quotation from Sharma and Ramos Salas (89) above, contradictory demands about how to address fat discrimination are placed in full view. According to the authors, "obesity" discrimination is wrong, "obesity" should be classified as a chronic disease, and weight and health should be considered as unrelated. Simply put, how can these three dictates exist simultaneously? What is to be gained by holding firm to these seemingly untenable contradictions? What is required for one not only to hold these paradoxes to be true but also to share them as the guiding principles of a national organization? How is it possible that Canadian anti-fat experts fight fat stigma while also fighting fat? As social justice activists, we are seized with these questions as a means for destigmatizing the care that Canadians receive in relation to "their obesity."

Few would disagree that discrimination in any form should not be tolerated, yet there exists flourishing debate in Canada regarding how fat stigma should be addressed. On one hand, there are grassroots activist groups that insist fatness is valid on its own terms and fat people have every right to take up as much space as they wish: that fatness is a human right (O'Hara and Gregg). These groups and individuals position themselves as weight inclusive, which means they work to " a) eradicate weight-based iatrogenic practices within health care ... [and] b) end the stigmatization of health problems (i.e., healthism)" (Tylka et al. 6). Gard charmingly describes this group of "obesity sceptics [as] feminists, queer theorists, libertarians, far right-wing conspiracy types and new ageists" (38). In the mushy, depoliticized middle, there are public health professionals that have come a long way to acknowledge fatness as not necessarily unhealthy as long as other "lifestyle factors" are in play, such as regular exercise and a healthy diet. These health care professionals (really a splinter group of the more hegemonic medical community) have carved out a place on the margins of the debate and would be known as performing "weight-neutral" practice; public health nurses, dietitians, and even occupational therapists claim to practice weight-neutral health care. In this case, the term *weight neutral* denotes an attempt to depoliticize health by not focusing on a patient's weight, even if said patient wants to lose weight as a health goal. They simply choose to find value in health behaviour outside of weight loss and will not weigh patients as an affirmation of that stance (Parsons 21).

Often, weight neutrality is conflated with Health at Every Size, which has been accused of being healthist in its aims (Brady et al. 346; O'Hara and Taylor 277). Yet, weight-neutral practitioners may find a weight-inclusive approach too risky, and they might risk professional censure if they were to push the weight-inclusive approach too ardently given the dominant and often dismissive medical community that believes fat is unhealthy and will generally go to great lengths to manage it, as the "Key Principles" from Obesity Canada (1) denote. This third grouping are the "anti-obesity" experts who have diligently fought to have "obesity" classified as a chronic disease and who work tirelessly to absolve people of their "bad" fat. And, more recently, these experts have taken the somewhat surprising additional stance that fat stigma is harmful (surprising since it seems incongruous to denigrate fat and fat stigma simultaneously). Obesity experts have addressed the dichotomy previously (Ramos Salas 1) in a curiously titled post, "Highlighting How the Fat Acceptance Movement Isn't Always All That Accepting." Obesity Canada has recently doubled down on its commitment to fight fat stigma by offering an online snitch form for those who wish to "Report Weight Bias." There are multiple axes of contention with such a reporting form, including invasion of privacy and the increasing effort to promote the emphasis on individualism and responsibilization (Orsini 353).

Notwithstanding Obesity Canada holding firm to its ideological position, we contest that position through an intersectional critique. What are the ontological framings of the contradictions we have highlighted? What social positions frame the question of truth and reality for those who claim it possible to fight fat and fat stigma simultaneously? The social framings, of course, add more complexity to this question given that the continuum ranging from grassroots to public health to anti-fat experts is also gendered, raced, and classed, with the grassroots fat activists being mostly women of colour in less privileged economic positions while the medical anti-fat experts are privileged professional white men, which Liquori articulates in her work on nutrition professionals (235). What are the implications of this gendered dimension, and how does it reinforce the contradictions that emerge when anti-fat experts fight fat stigma while also fighting fat? These are questions that our chapter addresses with a view to further explicating how fatness is medicalized by anti-fat organizations in Canada.

Why turn our gaze to this wrought body politic? The implications are not insignificant. The alluring anti-fat discourse advanced by those associated with Obesity Canada reifies and reinforces power. Even though the anti-fat proponents have ample privilege and authority, they appear to crave more. Why seek to establish Obesity Canada as the centre for "obesity" prevention and treatment? Through its "Mission and Guiding Principles," Obesity Canada states that "becoming a member ... is the first step in developing a link to Canada's obesity community." There is power associated with being able to grant access to the national obesity community. For example, a member "has a chance to influence the obesity field in Canada ... has access to receive awards and grants to travel or start up a SNP [Student and New Professional] chapter [or to] receive letters of support for grant applications." One might ask for what purpose is this anti-fat position held so strenuously given the precarity of the positivist science that upholds a view that fat is relatively benign? This is a question that is surely at the heart of the exploration because it speaks to the values that we, the authors of this chapter and other social justice activists in health and community care, hold dear: truth, collective experience, and equity. We challenge the suggestion that the medicalization of fatness, which is illustrated by Obesity Canada lobbying for "obesity" to be considered a chronic disease, can be pursued without stigmatizing fat, a professed claim of Obesity Canada proponents. The medicalization of fatness does indeed stigmatize fat bodies. We need to unravel how these positions are justified within a registered national charity to begin to learn what might be required to shift the fierce hold anti-fat experts have on maintaining fat discrimination; by offering a view into this stigmatizing dilemma, we may find a way out.

Conceptual Frames

Before venturing further, we appreciate the need to expand on some terminology, which reflects our first conceptual frame—contesting the medical model. As with our contemporaries in this volume, we hold the word "obesity" in critical disregard, acknowledging that it is used by those who view the fat body as Other and who have been trained in the holy grail of the medical model, which assumes that bodies can be quantified, biological variables are infinitely tractable, a broken body can be fixed, and a medical solution exists for every medical problem (disease). It is obvious that the medicalization and the subsequent pathologizing of the fat body form the predicates for fat stigma (Goldberg 117; Pearl 146; Tomiyama et al.). Without the medical model, the fat body would be subject to far less hostility (although that is a very low bar to strive for in life). However, the medical model remains the dominant way of viewing and assessing all bodies and asserts its domination over fat bodies in particular. Therefore, we clearly signal our repudiation of this unsavoury reality by placing the word "obesity" in quotes.

Second, we contest the moral imperative that anti-fat experts should be deciding what counts as "health." We consider the anti-fat experts as those who take the position that fatness is unhealthy and who assume professional roles and livelihoods that are congruent with that view, e.g., as bariatric surgeons, weight-loss promoters, anti-fat pharmaceutical distributors, as well as nutrition and fitness experts intent on idealizing a slim and fit body shape. Many, if not all, of the people who find themselves classified as such are well-intentioned and might even heartily reject the claims that they are anti-fat or even anti-obesity, despite the obvious markers. They will uphold mantras that signal any and all efforts to "help" people lose weight are really about promoting health. They will vigorously defend "good health" as a laudable end goal for individuals and populations and will be wholly unfamiliar with literature that surfaces important and critical views on "health" (Metzl and Kirkland 4). They will also show disregard for the enormous body of literature that demonstrates the fragile association between people's weight and their health (Bacon and Aphramor). They will relish the moral stranglehold they possess (even though it is built on faulty logic) because they wish to demonstrate their unabashed commitment to people's health, which is an accepted moral good (LeBesco 75). Fundamentally, anti-fat experts hold the pernicious yet medically sanctioned position that they are doing good by doing war on fat. How does one hold such opposing views and continue to soldier on?

The answer reveals itself in the concept of magical thinking, which describes our third conceptual frame. Made popular by Didion (2006), magical thinking was what she relied on to get through the devastating grief that followed the death of her husband. Didion described the necessary mental permutations when she began acting in ways that defied rationality, namely, stoking the powerful desire that if she wished it hard enough, her husband would come back. In a more theoretical sense, magical thinking is a highly fallacious way of viewing the world that enables one to hold two (or more) competing thoughts simultaneously (Hutson 7). According to Vedantam and Mesler, magical thinking may reflect the self-delusions required to make sense of a particular reality, a self-perceived truth, which, in turn, "means you miss the truth, but it gets you to the real goal: Your brain has been designed to help you survive ... to get along with mates ... to raise offspring to adulthood, and to avoid feelings of existential despair" (xxi). And, in this way, magical thinking is a type of self-delusion that may give function to Obesity Canada since the truth would cause a fracturing in the girds of the system that keeps the organization ideologically viable.

Contradictions that may seem overt to some completely vanish among others because to acknowledge the contradictions would destabilize. This ideological "vanishing act" is ironic among a group that places a certain importance on reducing fat without much regard to the political imperatives that implies. Why would such a privileged group perceive the contradiction regarding anti-fat and anti-stigma as a danger? Likely, the danger exists in having to surrender control of compulsory professional power. This perceived danger is not insignificant among those whose professional subject position is indelibly constituted on this basis. Magical thinking permits opposing views to be true and the status quo to be maintained. At the same time, health care professionals' status and power are consolidated. We name this response as "magical" since it is what is used to restore a sense of control and familiarity over circumstances that appear unflaggingly and unrepentantly chaotic to colleagues holding the anti-obesity line; for them, the critical weight science is in plain view, the effects of iatrogenic stigma are prevalent, and only very few are served by classifying fatness as a chronic disease.

Finally, the fourth frame is about fat stigma itself. Fat stigma is coincident with a moral panic towards "obesity" and is defined as the discrediting of the fat body. Individuals who are the targets of fat stigma often experience consequences to their individual well-being (Hicken et al. 157; Hunger et al. 255; Kwan 153; Phelan et al. 320; Strings 112) More recently, it was found that fat stigma contributes to cortisol reactivity, which is a stress response (Hicken et al. 158; Hunger 267; Phelan et al.

321; Tomiyama et al. 3). Emerging stigma research reveals that it may be the stigma towards fatness that is a fundamental cause of poor health and chronic disease, not the fat itself (Hicken et al. 158; Hunger et al. 267; Phelan et al. 320; Tomiyama et al. 3). In this way, an otherwise "healthy" fat person may experience stigma in the context of an encounter with a medical expert such that the (fat) stigma has negative health implications that didn't exist previously. This would mean that the medical experts themselves are contributing to their patients' poor health through their stigmatizing beliefs; a phenomenon called iatrogenesis. In expanding upon these conceptual frames, we offer a view through which we engaged with our data, which were collected as described by the following methods.

Methods

What has long preoccupied the first author are the contradictions held between theory and practice initially in dietetics and now in health care more broadly. The study of these contradictions has centred weight science as a primary source given her recognition that research published in the late 1990s was indicating fatness was not clearly associated with poor health outcomes, yet professional groups such as dietitians and physicians were continuing to promote weight loss for health reasons. The conflation of these professions and their anti-fat practice is captured by the organization Obesity Canada (formerly the Canadian Obesity Network).

As stated on the organization's home page, "Obesity Canada is Canada's leading obesity charity, made up of healthcare professionals, researchers, policy makers, and people with an interest in obesity" (Obesity Canada). The focus of that interest includes a mission "to improve the lives of Canadians through obesity research, education, and advocacy" by "addressing the social stigma associated with obesity; changing the way policy makers and health professionals approach obesity; and improving access to evidence-based prevention and treatment resources" (Obesity Canada, "About"). Based on this stated mission, Obesity Canada represents a prominent national charity that takes as its aims what many consider conflicting goals: to be against fat stigma and to be against fat. It may argue that it is not "against" fat, but when your mandate is to prevent and treat obesity, you are certainly not fat accepting. This organization is worthy of study because it is overt about seeking these two competing claims at the same time. There are many fat activists, including scholars like ourselves, that believe in nonmaleficence, i.e., that our actions should never cause harm. These same individuals believe that by focusing education and research resources towards the goal of "obesity prevention and treatment," Obesity Canada does harm by medicalizing the fat body and thus stigmatizing the fat body (Tomiyama et al. 3); thus it has become necessary to explore how it is possible that the medical professionals who uphold the ethics of nonmaleficence in their oath of practice would be enabled to pursue a path of maleficence without repercussion.

Our data were collected through a variety of qualitative methods. For the preliminary portion of this research, we compiled literature reviews of journal articles from various perspectives, including critical feminist, sociological, and medical, which we categorized ideologically based on the authors' use of terms. Our search terms included *fat stigma*, *weight stigma*, *size discrimination*, and *"obesity" stigma*. If authors referenced words such as *fatness*, *critical*, *gender*, and *social justice*, we noted those perspectives aligned with feminist and/or sociological ideologies. When the authors used words such as *obesity* (without the quotes), *health*, *mortality*, and *morbidity*, we categorized those as medical ideologies. These papers formed the basis for our delineation of perspectives on the fat body and whether there was any intersection between "anti-obesity" or "anti-fat" ideologies.

We then examined the evidence that underpinned the operational principles of a well-known national organization, Obesity Canada, that holds as its primary vision to reach "[a] day when people affected by the disease of obesity are understood, respected, and living healthy lives" through the following three strategic goals: (1) addressing the social stigma associated with obesity; (2) changing the way policy makers and health professionals approach obesity; and (3) improving access to evidence-based prevention and treatment resources (Obesity Canada, "About").

By means of a thorough textual examination, it was determined that Obesity Canada is an anti-obesity organization governed by the sort of magical thinking we aimed to interrogate. This was evident in the three contradictory strategic goals and the use of the word *obesity* without quotes throughout. These are red flags for those who critique the medical model and its moral imperatives to promote health, and they are also markers of the self-delusions that give rise to magical thinking.

Following this determination, we proceeded to examine critically Obesity Canada's entire online representation including its website and social media presence (YouTube and Facebook). This engagement permitted us to become familiar with the organization's ideological constructions and discursive themes as they were represented online, and with how they were potentially perceived through those online interactions. This portion of our research revealed the focus of the organization and helped explain the standpoint of its researchers while defining health and "obesity." Our preliminary research was integral for the design of our interview questions, which needed to be relevant to the concepts being conveyed between the many faculties and perspectives and relate to how Obesity Canada is situated within the anti-fat paradigm that takes as its aim a national and institutionalized project to define fatness in Canada.

After our preliminary findings, we began conducting qualitative semi-structured interviews with members of Obesity Canada. We emailed all potential participants (n = 27) from their contact pages listed on the Obesity Canada website, sending them the respective documents to begin interviews (study description and informed consent). The interviews were standardized, open-ended interviews during which all participants were asked the same questions and could respond with as much detail as they chose. This approach to interviewing also allows for the interviewer to ask follow-up questions (Turner). Interview questions included, but were not limited to, the following:

> How does fat stigma look in health care? Why is obesity stigma still an issue in the health care field and beyond? Can an obese person be healthy? Is the word *obesity*

> stigmatizing? Do you think it is possible to believe obesity stigma is unhelpful and still hold the view that obesity is a disease?

It is worth noting that our interview questions do not include quotes around the word *obesity*, and this was done quite deliberately in order not to undermine the respondents' own views on fatness. We decided not to critique the norms of the participants before or during our interviews. Our role was to observe the anti-fat language and practices of others so as to understand how seemingly contradictory views could be held simultaneously. In our recruitment materials, we deliberately left out the quotes around the word *obesity*, so we could appeal to Obesity Canada's accepted norms. Some folks indicated alarm that the first author, JG, was doing a non-critical study of fatness, which required further explanation to reassure select people that we indeed had not adopted an anti-obesity stance. We took any questioning from critical fat studies scholars as ample evidence that those who asked pointedly about how that word appeared in our recruitment materials would not be considered potential anti-fat research participants.

Participant Responses

Findings and Discussion

We conducted only three interviews with Obesity Canada representatives (all women), after multiple invitations were emailed several times to over 25 individuals identified on the Obesity Canada website. We recognized that it would be difficult to recruit people to this project, in part because of JG's long-standing position against the ethics of "obesity management" and her role in literally debating Dr. Arya Sharma on the question "Is Obesity a Disease?" Nonetheless, we persisted while acknowledging that by having more respondents, our research would have inevitably been strengthened.

These interviews were hosted online, on the phone, or in person (pre-pandemic), and the interviews were recorded and transcribed for analysis. Because the sample was so small, the likelihood of being able to identify participants was high, even though they requested their identities remain confidential. Thus, participants' identifying features (position within the organization, length of time involved with Obesity Canada, and educational background) were omitted from this chapter. In general, participants were involved with various aspects of the organization and possessed varied years of service along with diverse educational backgrounds.

Although we submitted our research protocol to the Toronto Metropolitan University Research Ethics Board and our study received ethics approval (REB 2019–027), we encountered some challenges between the drafting of this paper and the preparation of the final manuscript. Participants were invited to review the initial draft prior to final completion. Typically, participants would be asked to review only their interview transcripts to ensure that what they said accurately reflected what they intended to share. However, because JG wanted to be fully transparent, she shared the chapter draft with all participants. It is relevant to note that, as a result of their review, two participants withdrew their consent to have any of their comments included in this chapter. This left only one participant from which we could infer conclusions. Accordingly, comments in this section lack the perspective that might be achieved through broader participation.

While it is highly anomalous to proceed with a single participant, we wish to do so given what this reveals about the contentiousness of these claims. We anticipate that further exploration will be conducted, especially since there are clearly several people involved with Obesity Canada that do not want to have these tensions revealed. This speaks to the importance of the work, even though we would consider that our efforts to excavate those tensions were less than satisfactory. We have opted to persist with an outline of our findings with only one participant so as to support those who come after us in seeking to explore these tensions further and more robustly.

We decided for this volume on *Fat Studies in Canada* that we would centre responses from Canadians and that we would focus on insights that would illuminate our central question: How do

Canadian anti-fat experts fight fat stigma while also fighting fat? To begin with, we asked participants to describe how fat stigma looks in health care. The remaining participant responded with the following examples: waiting rooms having inappropriate seating (arms on all chairs), small gowns, small blood pressure cuffs, and health care professionals themselves having implicit anti-fat biases. The participant identified that the hospital administrators could make the work of the doctors so much easier if they purchased equipment with larger people in mind. This participant, who identified as an "obesity researcher," described her own stigmatization, being a large woman. She shared that people attending research talks where she was a presenter had said to her, "Oh, you really have a horse in this race," even though she described herself as being objective. She perceived that people thought she was still looking for "her own *magical* cure" [emphasis added]. Based on her responses to this question, we can conclude that the respondent witnessed and personally experienced fat stigma.

The participant spoke of the shame associated with weight stigma and how she learned and became sensitized to the negative impacts of fat people's experiences of being stigmatized through Obesity Canada's Public Engagement Committee (PEC) where fat, lay people (non-medical professionals) actively teach physicians, "obesity" researchers, and medical students about their experiences of being "a person living with obesity." A note on person-first language (describing a large person as someone who lives with "obesity"): although it is employed to avoid personal shaming, working to disconnect people from "their obesity," it can simultaneously fracture and amplify one's subjective truth. It is a signal that marks someone as being subject to the medical gaze. You are not just a person; you are a person living with a scarlet letter ("obesity"). And one can't help but hear the lament in the phrasing; a person living with obesity perhaps would prefer not to be. As soon as the word "obesity" is applied as a descriptor, the medicalization of that body is equally applied. The only need for person-first language exists in the medical context of which Obesity Canada is a proponent.

With respect to Obesity Canada's PEC, its members are often targets of ridicule and stigma at conferences or public seminars or even online. Person-first language does not prevent such harm. Participation on this committee is voluntary. Wins for this committee include the Positive Image Bank, which was created by the PEC so people could use images that are more reflective of positive and less stigmatizing and less stereotypical views of fat people. The participant described that the images were shared by those associated with Obesity Canada when requested by people wanting to do a story or interview with the media or professors in medical school. The participant said, "If people are going to talk about people living with obesity, these are the images that should be used." While the images are certainly size positive and disruptive in their own right, without the critical stance to back them up, they work only superficially to promote inclusivity.

When asked how weight stigma is maintained, the participant stated that this is done by not incorporating stigma in conversations about "obesity" in medical school or in continuing education programs for practicing health care professionals. She elaborated that if governments would acknowledge "obesity" as a disease, as the Canadian Medical Association has, then it would be easier to advocate for an end to weight stigma. This was the first indication in our interview that there was a direct connection being made between naming "obesity" as a chronic disease and reducing weight stigma, but it has been described previously by the founder and scientific director of Obesity Canada, Dr. Arya Sharma. Dr. Arya Sharma has spoken extensively and publicly about Obesity Canada's stated aim to lobby federal and provincial governments to designate "obesity" as a chronic disease. In one of the Obesity Canada YouTube videos Sharma states,

> ... we've got to approach obesity like every other chronic disease, and here's the good news: we know how to do chronic disease because we do it for every other chronic disease. So we've got to talk to our politicians, we've got to talk to our medical professionals, we have to talk to our patients living with obesity. You need to understand what the science of obesity actually teaches us about obesity and what ... the problem is that we're up against, and that's when we can start finding solutions. And that is

> exactly what Obesity Canada is trying to do ... look at all the work that Obesity Canada is doing across the country educating health professionals, advocating for better access for treatment, advocating for teaching obesity to medical students and nursing students and dietitian students so that when they become health professionals they actually understand what these issues are, advocating for better coverage for medications for obesity. (Sharma, "Obesity as a Chronic Disease")

This admission of the desire to nominate "obesity" as a chronic disease speaks to the intractable efforts that Obesity Canada is going to in order to socialize medical professionals to connect the nature of "obesity" treatment to the expertise of the medical profession. As stated above, the medical profession "knows how to do chronic disease," and as soon as its experts convey that simple fact to Canadian legislators, they can enable fat Canadians to receive access to the medications necessary to relieve themselves of their chronic disease, "obesity." There are multiple assumptions underwritten into this soliloquy. The first is that only medicine knows what to do to address chronic disease appropriately. Given the increasing rates of type 2 diabetes and heart disease among Indigenous people and newcomers to Canada, this assumption derived from the medical model is worth contesting. The second assumption is that science teaches "us" all that we need to know about fatness. Given the limited scope of positivist science and the reality that body weight and shape are determined by many factors outside the realm of reductionism, Sharma's claim is a half measure. Finally, after insisting in an earlier portion of the video that there are very few treatment options for "obesity" and then stating here that the answer lies in "better coverage for medications for obesity," Sharma reveals the true intention: that by naming fatness a chronic disease, the government will indelibly bind fat patients to their Obesity Canada–informed physicians through prescriptions to pharmaceutical approaches and, of course, bariatric surgery. These approaches have been known to have high recidivism, which means the connection between a fat person and a physician could be forever.

What are the implications of such a bond? The financial benefits to physicians are significant, and if the drugs are covered by pharmacare, then Canadian citizens will be subsidizing this lifelong dependent relationship between these physicians and their patients. The logic is this: obesity has very few treatment options, and even with those options, people may lose weight but generally regain it in a few years. To avoid weight regain, you must continue with the treatment even though it is ineffective. If the government declares that people living with obesity are living with a chronic disease, it may expand access to the medications over a longer period of time, which, again, do not actually cure the disease. If physicians can hook into this perpetual cycle, they can surely benefit. But at what cost to the patient? While this rationale is shaky, the question still remains: Why has Obesity Canada added a focus on reducing weight stigma to its overall organizational aims? This may reveal itself as an essential feature of magical thinking in that there has been so much published on the perils of weight stigma by Rebecca Puhl and colleagues (Puhl and Brownell; Puhl and Heuer; Puhl and Suh) that to ignore their work would be unacceptable (non-collegial, even), yet to include it and to not critique the indelible and fundamental connection between weight stigma and poor health (Hatzenbuehler et al. 813) requires a complete break with this specific truth; fighting fat is in conflict with fighting fat stigma.

When asked why Obesity Canada adopted a focus on eliminating weight stigma, the participant described how certain physicians involved in the organization have brought the view forward that stigma is harmful. It was clear that stigmatizing physicians needed to hear this message from other non-stigmatizing physicians before changing their approaches, given the power imbalance in play and the sensitivity that addressing new approaches among physicians would elicit. Efforts have been made in this regard with the creation of BalancedView (https://balancedviewbc.ca/), an online educational resource that was developed to reduce fat bias among health care professionals.[1]

The participant answered "yes" when asked if "obese" people could also be healthy, noting that it is stigmatizing simply to look at someone and make claims about that person's health based on their weight. However, when asked if she thought the word *obesity* was stigmatizing, she responded "yes" again and said she actually preferred to use the word *fat*. She said she would usually use the term *excess weight* when writing in journals and presenting at conferences. The phrase *skinny fat* was described as a weight status assigned to thin people assumed to be healthy who actually were not.

The participant described the recidivism with bariatric surgery and weight-loss diets in general and how people can be healthy at a range of sizes. Additionally, from analysis of the interview, it was clear that the respondent believed that weight loss was not a panacea for health problems. Reference was made to Obesity Canada's Edmonton Obesity Staging System (EOSS) during the interview in order for the participant to delineate between appropriate and inappropriate approaches to fatness. EOSS is a measure of the mental, metabolic, and physical impact that "obesity" has had on a patient's health and uses these factors to determine an individual's stage of obesity (from stage 0 to 4).

As a follow up to the question about whether the participant thought the word *obesity* was stigmatizing, the interviewer asked, "Has Obesity Canada ever thought to change its name given that the word *obesity* is present right there?" The participant replied, "They just did!" (Recently the Canadian Obesity Network became Obesity Canada). She admitted, "Longer-term members of the organization would say 'no' and consider it [obesity] a medical term while the newer generation perceives that word differently." This response speaks to a type of generational divide within the organization and suggests that the intra-organizational conversation about the name may be ongoing. Notwithstanding, this issue about the name of the organization provides a useful segue to the very next and final interview question.

The final interview question elicited the most revealing response: Do you think it is possible to hold the view that "obesity" stigma is unhelpful and also hold the view that "obesity" is a disease. The participant responded with a long, thoughtful pause before saying, "That's a hard question. Unfortunately, the way the health care system works, you can't get care unless you have a diagnosis. Obesity should not be treated the same way as diabetes, but more like a stage zero cancer. It's there, but do we know if it will do something bad, and we might cause more harm if we treat it. With weight loss, we assume that is the treatment, it is not successful [recidivism], so a movement towards weight maintenance instead of weight loss. And, others will say, we don't have effective treatment, so we must focus on prevention."

The response to this final question offers some understanding of how problematic and challenging it can be to hold two opposing views, and further research is needed to explore the nuances of this duality. It is also worth noting that the interview conversation was fast-paced, and the participant responded to every question quickly and with assurance given her obvious expertise. However, her response to this last question was measured, halting, and somewhat contradictory. It seemed to the authors that her answers to all the previous questions were considered—that she had been asked these questions previously. The final question was not one that had been given much previous thought and thus was considered "a hard question." This gives some insight into what it is like to perform magical thinking: it takes time to craft answers to hard questions, and the responses to those questions can begin to unravel and disrupt the house of cards upon which the ideological contradictions are built. The conversation with this member of Obesity Canada, in addition to critical analysis of Obesity Canada's supporting video and text-based materials, demonstrates that the contradictions are not only present but appear palpable to those who have revealed them as such.

Finding Meaning in Magical Thinking

Our efforts to explore how two seemingly contradictory standpoints are held simultaneously has led us to consider the role of magical thinking. To reiterate, magical thinking is a form of cognitive dissonance that enables Obesity Canada, through the process of self-delusion, to maintain, as they are, the structures and processes of the organization. As Vedantam and Mesler state, "there are excellent reasons to prioritize functionality over reality in every domain ... yes, you miss the truth, but it gets you to the real goal: ... [it] helps you survive, forage for opportunities, ... and avoid feelings of existential despair" (xxi). The "excellent reasons" reflect the ongoing viability of Obesity Canada and its members' ability to carry on without having to contest the evidence on which its pillars (key principles) are planted. Some may be wondering at this point what the purpose is for us to rattle those pillars; why are we so intent on disrupting Obesity Canada's version of the truth? The answer is that when considering fat studies in Canada and the work to politicize the field, we must grapple with the overt likelihood that those holding the views that both fat and fat stigma are unacceptable are exacerbating the harm that comes from such intolerance. By not challenging this contradiction, we must acknowledge our own complicity in delaying a move to body sovereignty—a worldview that promotes a person's ability to "equitable rights of access for all bodies especially marginalized bodies" (Gillon 213). Body sovereignty resists medical corporatization, pharmaceutical profit mongering, and neo-liberal imperatives on individualism that condemn medical and public health practice to healthist predilections. What might be worth considering is that neo-liberalism itself is rife with contradiction and cognitive dissonance and is a necessary element of the position taken by "anti-obesity" practitioners to maintain their own visibility and relevance, but also their own oppression. If the goals of Obesity Canada were health equity, would there be any requirement for medicalizing fat bodies by calling for "obesity" to be categorized as a chronic disease? Of course, the answer is no. If Obesity Canada was interested in eliminating anti-Black and anti-Indigenous racism in the medical community, given how racism is a predicate for poor health outcomes, the organization would need to radically reconstitute itself. We imagine that if this were to occur, Obesity Canada would begin a campaign to promote a national housing program, universal pharmacare and dental care, a universal basic income, an end to boil water advisories on First Nation reserves, equal funding for the education of First Nations' children, a call to action on the 94 recommendations of the Truth and Reconciliation Commission, abolition of the police, and a wealth tax to redress rampant wealth inequality, all of which have been linked to poor health and social outcomes

(Hatzenbuehler et al. 819; Wilkinson and Pickett 6). Since none of these liberatory actions are the stated aims of Obesity Canada, perhaps it is our own magical thinking that leads us to continue to believe that the transformation of this organization is even possible.

Conclusion

The purpose of this project was to examine the seemingly contradictory coterminous perceptions among "anti-obesity" health care professionals who position "obesity" as unhealthy and "obesity stigma" as harmful. More research is required to understand the reasons that health care professionals ignore the empirical evidence supporting the existence of health among a wide diversity of body shapes, as well as the evidence suggesting that promoting weight loss in the name of health actually perpetuates weight stigma. The research question that underpinned this project was how health care practitioners who proclaim themselves to be "anti-obesity" hold simultaneous views that "obesity stigma" is harmful yet contend that "obesity" is a chronic disease that must be treated.

This chapter detailed the findings of our qualitative research project that engaged a key informant interview in addition to an analysis of Obesity Canada's text-based content and videos. The findings demonstrate that ideological perspectives on fatness concretize institutional fat stigma and reveal a type of magical thinking, which permeates medical culture and practices. The data reveal that Obesity Canada is convinced that to end the stigmatization of fatness, excessive fatness must be constructed as a chronic illness. However, this maintains the debate within dominant oppressive medical frameworks and thereby continues to utilize the same discursive functions of control and power over the body, functions which create the idealized environments enabling stigmatization to flourish. These ideological impediments embedded in medicalized and institutionalized health culture have implications for health care professionals within and outside these institutions, implications that register among health care practitioners in Canada and well beyond.

Additionally, by upholding contradicting views, physicians and other health care professionals also buttress the view that fatness, as associated with poor health, can be resolved but only through means that are expensive and individually attained, such as bariatric surgery and pharmaceuticals. This message coming from high-profile doctors and other health care professionals who are associated with Obesity Canada helps to maintain the stigmatizing view that fatness is wrong within a healthist context, a view that unhelpfully and inappropriately positions *individuals* as needing to resolve that which is a collective, social dilemma: the stigma itself. Such a path forward only perpetuates neoliberal health policies that are not truly about health but about maintaining power, privilege, and livelihoods (Orsini 353). This is the magical thinking that is deeply infused into our medical system, and this delusion is what needs to be named and rejected if people ever hope to eliminate fat stigma from Canadian health care.

Acknowledgments

The authors express their gratitude to the two anonymous reviewers for their enthusiastic response to our chapter and their constructive comments. We would like to acknowledge the thoughtful feedback from Kathy Porter, Calla Evans, and Dr. Michael Orsini, who niftily invited us to consider the notion of "vanishing acts" in relation to the work anti-obesity groups do in promoting weight loss.

Notes

1 In the spirit of full disclosure, one of the co-authors of this chapter (JG) was involved in writing the content for BalancedView.

Works Cited

Bacon, Lindo, and Lucy Aphramor. "Weight Science: Evaluating the Evidence for a Paradigm Shift." *Nutrition Journal*, 24 Jan. 2011. *BioMed Central*: https://doi.org/10.1186/1475-2891-10-9.

Brady, Jennifer, et al. "Theorizing Health at Every Size as a Relational-Cultural Endeavour." *Critical Public Health*, vol. 23, no. 3, 2013, pp. 345–55.

Didion, Joan. *The Year of Magical Thinking*. Penguin Random House, 2006.

Gard, Michael. "Truth, Belief and the Cultural Politics of Obesity Scholarship and Public Health Policy." *Critical Public Health*, vol. 21, no. 1, 2011, pp. 37–48.

Gillon (Ngāti Awa), Ashlea. "Fat Indigenous Bodies and Body Sovereignty: An Exploration of Re-Presentations." *Journal of Sociology*, vol. 56, no. 2, June 2020, pp. 213–28. *SAGE Journals*: https://doi.org/10.1177/1440783319893506.

Goldberg, Daniel S. "Fatness, Medicalization, and Stigma: On the Need to Do Better." *Narrative Inquiry in Bioethics*, vol. 4, no. 2, 2014, pp. 117–23. *PubMed*: https://doi.org/10.1353/nib.2014.0053. Accessed 8 May 2021.

Hatzenbuehler, Mark L., et al. "Stigma as a Fundamental Cause of Population Health Inequalities." *American Journal of Public Health*, vol. 103, no. 5, 2013, pp. 813–21.

Hicken, Margaret T., Hedwig Lee, and Anna K. Hing. "The Weight of Racism: Vigilance and Racial Inequalities in Weight-Related Measures." *Social Science & Medicine*, vol. 199, 2018, pp. 157–66.

Hunger, Jeffrey M., et al. "Weighed Down by Stigma: How Weight-Based Social Identity Threat Contributes to Weight Gain and Poor Health." *Social and Personality Psychology Compass* vol. 9, no. 6, 2015, pp. 255–68.

Hutson, Matthew. *The 7 Laws of Magical Thinking: How Irrationality Makes Us Happy, Healthy, and Sane*. Simon and Schuster, 2012.

"Is Obesity a Disease." *YouTube*, Uploaded by Travis Saunders, 26 June 2012, https://www.youtube.com/watch?v=fFnxjd8jMDg. Accessed 15 May 2021.

Kwan, Samantha. "Navigating Public Spaces: Gender, Race, and Body Privilege in Everyday Life." *Feminist Formations*, vol 22, no. 2, 2010, pp. 144–66.

LeBesco, Kathleen. "Fat Panic and the New Morality." *Against Health: How Health Became the New Morality*, edited by Jonathan M. Metzl and Anna Kirkland, New York University Press, 2010, pp. 72–82.

Liquori, Toni. "Food Matters: Changing Dimensions of Science and Practice in the Nutrition Profession." *Journal of Nutrition Education*, vol. 33 no. 4, 2001, 234–46. *National Library of Medicine*: https://doi.org/10.1016/s1499–4046(06)60036–5. Accessed 8 May 2021.

Metzl, Jonathan M., and Anna Kirkland, eds. *Against Health: How Health Became the New Morality*. New York University Press, 2010.

O'Hara, Lily, and Jane Gregg. "Human Rights Casualties from the 'War on Obesity': Why Focusing on Body Weight is Inconsistent with a Human Rights Approach to Health." *Fat Studies* vol. 1, no. 1, 2012, pp. 32–46.

O'Hara, Lily, and Jane Taylor. "Health at Every Size: A Weight-Neutral Approach for Empowerment, Resilience and Peace." *International Journal of Social Work and Human Services Practice*, vol. 2, no. 6, 2014, pp. 272–82.

Obesity Canada. "About Us." *Obesity Canada*, https://obesitycanada.ca/about/. Accessed 8 May 2021.

Obesity Canada. "Key Principles." *Obesity Canada*, https://obesitycanada.ca/managing-obesity/. Accessed 8 May 2021.

Obesity Canada. "Obesity Canada Homepage." *Obesity Canada*, https://obesitycanada.ca/. Accessed 8 May 2021.

Obesity Canada. "Report Weight Bias." *Obesity Canada*, https://obesitycanada.ca/report-weight-bias/. Access 8 May 2021.

Orsini, Michael. "Engendering Fatness and 'Obesity': Affect, Emotions, and the Governance of Weight in a Neoliberal Age." *Turbulent Times, Transformational Possibilities?: Gender and Politics Today and Tomorrow*, by Fiona MacDonald and Alexandra Dobrowolsky. University of Toronto Press, 2020, pp. 349–67.

Parsons, Devyn E. "Moving towards a Weight-Neutral Approach to Obesity Management." *UBC Medical Journal*, vol. 7, no. 1, 2016, pp. 21–23.

Pearl, Rebecca L. "Weight Bias and Stigma: Public Health Implications and Structural Solutions." *Social Issues and Policy Review* vol. 12, no. 1, 2018, pp. 146–82.

Phelan, Sean M., et al. "Impact of Weight Bias and Stigma on Quality of Care and Outcomes for Patients with Obesity." *Obesity Reviews*, vol. 16, no. 4, 2015, pp. 319–26.

Puhl, Rebecca M., and Kelly D. Brownell. "Confronting and Coping with Weight Stigma: An Investigation of Overweight and Obese Adults." *Obesity*, vol. 14, no. 1, 2006, pp. 1802–15.

Puhl, Rebecca M., and Chelsea A. Heuer. "Obesity Stigma: Important Considerations for Public Health." *American Journal of Public Health*, vol. 100, no. 6, 2010, pp. 1019–28.

Puhl, Rebecca M., and Young Suh. "Health Consequences of Weight Stigma: Implications for Obesity Prevention and Treatment." *Current Obesity Reports*, vol. 4, 2015, pp. 182–90.

Ramos-Salas, Ximena. "Guest Post Highlighting How the Fat Acceptance Movement Isn't Always All That Accepting." *Weighty Matters*, 5 July 2018, http://www.weightymatters.ca/2018/07/guest-post-highlighting-how-fat.html. Accessed 14 May 2021.

Sharma, Arya. "Obesity as a Chronic Disease." *Obesity Canada YouTube Channel*, https://www.youtube.com/watch?v=ruWsvfP2flQ. Accessed 8 May 2021.

Sharma, Arya M., and Ximena Ramos-Salas. "Obesity Prevention and Management Strategies in Canada: Shifting Paradigms and Putting People First." *Current Obesity Reports*, vol. 7, no. 2, 2018, pp. 89–96.

Strings, Sabrina. "Obese Black Women as 'Social Dead Weight': Reinventing the 'Diseased Black Woman.'" *Signs: Journal of Women in Culture and Society*, vo. 41, no. 1, 2015, pp. 107–30.

Tomiyama, A. Janet, et al. "How and Why Weight Stigma Drives the Obesity 'Epidemic' and Harms Health." *BMC Medicine*, vol. 16, no. 1, 2018, pp. 1–6. *Springer Nature*: https://doi.org/10.1186/s12916-018-1116-5. Accessed 8 May 2021.

Turner III, Daniel W. "Qualitative Interview Design: A Practical Guide for Novice Investigators." *The Qualitative Report* vol. 15, no. 3, 2010, p. 754.

Tylka, Tracy L., et al. "The Weight-Inclusive versus Weight-Normative Approach to Health: Evaluating the Evidence for Prioritizing Well-Being over Weight Loss." *Journal of Obesity*, vol. 2014, Article ID 983495, 18 pages, 2014. *Hindawi*: https://doi.org/10.1155/2014/983495.

Vedantam, Shankar, and Bill Mesler. *Useful Delusions: The Power and Paradox of the Self-Deceiving Brain.* W. W. Norton and Company, 2021.

Wilkinson, Richard, and Kate Pickett. *The Spirit Level: Why Equality Is Better for Everyone.* Bloomsbury Press, 2009.

MAPPINGS, METHODS, AND INNOVATIONS

Sure Footing

Leslie Walters

THIS IMAGE IS ABOUT UNCERTAINTY and the importance of stepping into the unknown, especially in a world hostile to fat people. On a personal level, I can't find sandals to fit my orthotics. I think about my feet a lot: what they endure, the path that I am on, and how it's uniquely my own.

Like the Tide

Emily Allan

I NOTICED IT THE FIRST TIME I came back west, walking down streets I knew so well, I didn't have to watch my feet. Along the sandy seawall in English Bay; on sidewalks beside vacant lots that once held the guts of Main Street; lined up outside the hip new fried chicken spot on the Drive. No matter the neighbourhood, eyes flitted up and down my body, resting for a second in the middle—just long enough to betray silent judgments made in the flutter of an eyelash. On my last visit, I stepped off the Skytrain with my belly exposed, plum lipstick vibrant, and curly hair wild. The glances I was expecting had extended into stares. *Has it always been like this?*

I grew up on a small island off of Vancouver and spent my young adult life in the city, where my family has been for four generations. In high school, I hatched plans for bootlegged coolers from the Ambleside liquor store that stood right where my great-grandfather's chicken coop used to be. In my twenties, I lived beside the East Van school where my Papa was principal. I'd picture him striding across the field in his tartan polyester suit, barking orders at kids with feathered haircuts. Whenever I visit my parents on Bowen Island, where my grandparents met, I wait at a downtown bus stop on the corner where another great grandfather ran his bookshop, Ireland & Allan. I'm the only person in my entire family to have left the West Coast with any sense of permanence.

I moved to Toronto in the winter of 2018, swapping temperate rainforest for concrete jungle, and endless sea for a series of lakes that never quite satiate. Every time I visit home, it dawns a little more on me. The glances and stares—this gaze—has been cycling through me since I was little, in and out like the tide. Quiet, so you don't always notice.

In Toronto, even without the permanent exhibition of mountain-meeting-ocean to distract the eye, I don't feel like so much of a spectacle. It's not that I've made myself less visible: the opposite, actually. I moved here at a point in my life when my relationship with my body was finally starting to heal. I gained weight as I became more comfortable taking up space. I sought out friendship and found community with other fat people for the first time. I studied a new politic that articulated my own experiences to me, and in turn helped me express them. I moved into a stage of growth that had always been stunted by constantly trying to shrink myself.

In this big new city, I felt free of the spectre of my earlier self. I didn't have to fit into any moulds of who people expected me to be, how they expected me to look. Here, I walk down the street with the crescent-moon of my belly clear against its denim sky. I let my fleshy ribcage spill over waistbands into tight, bright turtlenecks, or out from under crop tops into the muggy summer air. I should feel bigger in Toronto's narrow streets, squeezed between the crowded sidewalks and sandwiched brick buildings. But even without the cleaner, greener air and everywhere-space of back home, it feels easier to breathe. Passersby seem to mind their business, rather than my body. Maybe they're too busy to care. Or maybe it's just that in a denser and more diverse sea of people, there are more types of bodies on any given sidewalk or streetcar. The gaze exists here, of course, but it doesn't seem to single me out so much. With less of a constant external reminder that the world hates my body, it's been easier to identify and unlearn the internalized messages trying to convince me I'm at fault.

The West Coast likes to tactfully cloak its fatphobia in Lycra and call it "wellness." Every time I come home, I hear about someone's new juice cleanse or intermittent fast—with a stronger insistence as body positivity comes into fashion that each diet is just a "lifestyle change" or a "much-needed reset." Like a well-intentioned mother, Vancouver insists that she "just wants you to be healthy," as though health is both universally attainable and a measure of goodness. But even that insistence simply isn't true. As a person who spent years drinking the kale smoothies and jogging the seawall and sweating through the hot yoga classes and still being fat, I can tell you that my body, as "healthy" as it was, never earned her approval.

This rejection of my body was an ever-present mist that never quite turned to rain. Vancouver's polite and passive ethos meant that a feeling so palpable to me was almost never validated. I knew people were seeing and treating me differently, but no one would look me in the eye with it. When I was 22 and the local billionaire who founded Lululemon publicly stated that his clothes shouldn't be worn by women without thigh gaps, the city clutched its collective pearls. People expressed their shock and outrage to me in ways that I'm sure were meant to comfort but only confused me. Where had this solidarity been my whole life? Did it actually extend to this body that could barely squeeze between those stretchy seams at all? What about the bodies bigger than mine that bear the brunt of anti-fatness in all its structures and its stigmas? Did solidarity extend there too? At what point do we size out of it?

It never quite felt like I fit into Vancouver, even though I can feel the scaffolding of my parents' and grandparents' lives there in my bones. Of course, I know my family history is fraught. As deep as my roots run on the West Coast, their soil is layered with violently stolen centuries. My ancestors made homes on land that wasn't theirs, and that truth lives in my body, too. But when I stand out on the top deck of the ferry boat making its way into the mouth of my hometown, right when the smells of the sea line and the cedars collide, something clicks into a place deep inside my belly. It feels like the cove knows me back. There is no substitute for that feeling, though I've found knockoffs of it on different shores. If I think about it for too long, I start to ache.

But that scrutinizing gaze that I hardly used to notice is no longer quiet for me when I'm back west. It crashes, loud; and now that I can hear it, I can't help but feel it everywhere. The eyes of strangers on the street now echo into the forests, which look me up and down. It's even leaked into the ocean, polluting the one place where my weight has always been irrelevant. It's absurd to feel too big in a body of water that floats freighters and makes pods of orcas look like tadpoles by scale. I hate this projection, and yet I can't shake it. Home feels tainted.

I sat in my childhood bedroom at my parents' house just before moving to Toronto. Surrounded by dusty notebooks unearthed from the secret closet where I used to wedge myself while playing hide-and-seek, I found to-do lists scribbled by every version of my younger self.

Each of them placed some version of "*Get healthy!*" (never without exclamation mark) at the top. In that room, I often dreamt of a story I had read in *Seventeen*, about a chubby girl who got into running. She went for a run one day with her mom, and then she just kept running. She ran every day, and before she knew it, she became a model and got a boyfriend, and her life was perfect. I really thought one day, that would be me. I'd finally "*get healthy*" (thin) like her and cross it off my to-do list, simple as that.

I think about moving back to the West Coast someday, and I know that if I do there will be a reckoning. How will I make my home there again? How can I ever eclipse that spectre of my former, smaller self? Will there still be room in old friendships, or will we have outgrown each other? How would that little girl sitting in her room feel about my not-perfect, not-thin life?

Maybe by then things will have changed, and the gaze will soften. Maybe people will finally learn from the landscape, letting our obsession with containment go in honour of coastlines so unruly and trees so tall and ocean so incomprehensibly deep. Maybe I'll become so at home in this bigger and bolder version of myself that I'll let my body take its space among them. Maybe we'll all freely take deep, belly-swelling breaths of that clean offshore breeze. Maybe, one day, even the green juice shops and the yoga studios and the beach volleyball bros will have no choice but to welcome me home.

The Full Spectrum of Living: Body Mapping as Affective Community

Katie Cook

I'm just scared that I'm not going to be able to communicate the full spectrum of what living in this body has been. I want it to feel joyful and hopeful, because I feel joyful and hopeful all the time.
– Purple

THIS CHAPTER PRESENTS a theorized analysis of the affective space that can be created through the use of an arts-based body mapping methodology in Canadian fat studies research. I will argue that arts-based research, specifically body mapping, can provide vital opportunities for fat people to gather outside of the confines of the weight-loss industry. Typically, the opportunities that fat people have in building a community of support centre around a shared goal of weight loss and/or management. Often, in such spaces, there is a celebrated thin orientation linked to the promise of joy and success, an orientation that maintains this move away from fatness and its associated shame, fear, and disgust. Arts-based research is an opportunity for Canadian fat studies scholars to create affective communities that allow for the full spectrum of fat life and emotion, creating space for joy and healing. This chapter reports on the arts-based process of a Canadian research project titled "Feeling Fat: Theorizing Intergenerational Body Narratives through Affect." This study used interviews alongside arts-based body mapping to explore the intergenerational movement of weight-based stigma with attention to the historical and socio-political situatedness of participants' experiences growing up in the 1980s and 1990s.

Theoretical Grounding: Intersectionality and Feminist Affect Theory

Intersectionality, initially developed by Black feminists (for example, Combahee River Collective; Crenshaw; Hill Collins) to describe the unique experience of multiple oppressions, has been applied as both theory and a methodological framework across disciplines (Carastathis 308). Intersectionality has been successful in fostering deeper understandings of oppression and the ways in which complex marginalization manifests in social structures, as well as in our day-to-day interactions. The Feeling Fat study engaged with intersectionality in an embodied manner that allowed for complexity and movement within lived experiences and participant narratives. As a theoretical framework, intersectionality calls upon fat studies scholars to engage deeper analyses that speak to not only harmful mechanisms of weight stigma but also intersecting systems such as anti-Black racism, colonization, ableism, and classism. In the Feeling Fat study, intersectionality was incorporated through each step of the research process. These steps included a critical analysis of the studies and frameworks cited and of their methodological development, an assessment of the historical uses and misuses of the chosen methodology, an evaluation of each study's intentional recruitment of participants, and the tracking and integrating of aspects of embodied difference, including gender, sexuality, race, Indigeneity, (dis)ability, and size. The study's engagement with an intersectional approach is central to the integrity and purpose of this work.

Feminist affect theory provides fat studies scholars with an opportunity to theorize narratives related to fatness, moving beyond social and cultural discourse to understand the messages and affects that may be unarticulated. In her formulation of affect, Sara Ahmed notes that affect does not originate within one body and move outwards (or vice versa), but rather affect circulates in the in-between (between one body and others, between society and the body), and these affective flows define and shape the very boundaries between bodies ("The Organisation of Hate" 347). Ahmed's analysis of unequal power dynamics and how these come to shape and formulate affective flows between bodies and society makes her approach to affect theory particularly apt for fat studies scholars. Fat bodies are so often positioned as in-between—that is, in-between thinness and fatness, in-between "health" and illness, in-between life and death. Ahmed's work provides an opportunity to theorize the role of affect in the movement of stigmatizing messages about fat bodies.

Messages about bodies and the management of body size/shape have a unique quality that is felt—it is a visceral, concentrated interaction that is both expressed, absorbed, and/or rejected verbally, emotionally, behaviourally, overtly, and covertly. Affect theory can help to create a link between social discourse and the subjective, embodied experience (Fraser). The schools of thought emerging from affect studies have been taken up by fat studies scholars to date in limited, but significant, ways that contribute to transforming fat-beingness outside the "obesity epidemic" discourse that is rooted in negative affects like hate, fear, disgust, and shame. This chapter works to advance fat studies scholarship looking into the nexus of fatness and affect by providing an even richer and complex analysis of the lived experience of fatness and its potentialities within Canadian fat studies.

Diet Culture and Its Affective Flows

At a societal level, fat is constructed as ugly, unruly, greedy, lazy, risky, deadly, incompetent, and abject, and these constructions of fatness have material implications for fat people. The implications have an even greater effect on the opportunities that fat people have to gather and the futures that fat people may imagine. If a person's very embodiment is framed as inherently risky and deadly, that person's future is subsequently marked by illness and limited by early death (Murray 220). The mental and emotional weight of this takes its toll on fat people, and the pressures to become thin can be all-consuming. While this chapter will not delve into the fraught relationship between body size and "health," it is worth noting that constructions of fatness and their resulting pressures to engage in weight loss limit the very potentialities for the life of a fat person. Life becomes oriented toward weight-loss attempts through sometimes extreme food restriction and exercise to avoid death by one's own fatness. Even social interactions become consumed by talk of weight management activities. In this way, the social construction of fatness becomes woven into every aspect of a fat person's life, including the very material reality of one's movements and affective interactions with the social world.

Historically, the opportunities that fat people have to gather are nearly always tied to a shared goal of weight loss/management. In particular, one conjures images of the Weight Watchers meeting, whereby fat people assemble to share their "weight loss success" stories under the guise of self-betterment and care (Heyes 141). In these affectively charged spaces, eradicating fat(ness) is the ultimate goal—the move toward thinness offers the promise of success, moral superiority, and ultimately happiness (Bahra 194). In her exploration of the *stickiness* of particular affects, Ahmed notes, "hate becomes attached or 'stuck' to particular bodies, often through violence, force and harm" ("The Organisation of Hate" 345). One of the ways in which hate becomes stuck to fat bodies is through shared spaces that allow for limited affective flows. The very nature of these weight-loss-oriented spaces is such that membership presupposes a level of fat hatred and shame. Speaking of "wellness"-focused weight management programs, Kjaer comments, "they produce collectivities that depend on a disassociation with a non-dieting Other, who is fat, unhealthy, unhappy and unproductive. These collectives, in turn, connect healthiness to dieting, dieting with happiness, and happiness with a productive working on the self" (703). This proximity of dieting and weight loss to happiness is integral to the narrative of weight-loss programs and their money-earning potential. However, this narrative is also dependent on the proximity of fat to shame and disgust, connecting the very composition of one's body with moral judgments through affective flows of self-hatred and shame.

What might happen then, if fat people are afforded opportunities to gather in spaces that are oriented towards fat joy instead of fat hate? In these spaces, might fat people witness both the trauma of fat hate and the healing of fat joy simultaneously in both the self and others? How might these alternative affective spaces orient around difference-attuned empathy to foster community healing? In her critique of intersectionality as it has been taken up in academic spaces, Black feminist Jennifer Nash puts forth the concept of *love politics* as a turn away from the oft-conjured wounded Black female self and toward, instead, a radical embrace of difference and vulnerability, oriented toward love and healing (3). Taking up Nash's idea of love politics, along with a dialogue on difference-attuned witnessing (Rice et al. 360), offers a framework for thinking and working across difference that is rooted in affect and seeks to avoid collapsing difference. Difference-attuned witnessing as a concept asks arts-based researchers to consider the affective flows within the research apparatus, including between participants as they experience the risks and potentialities of vulnerability and the inherent power dynamics in the research space (Rice et al. 360–62). The bonds that are forged through difference-attuned witnessing, while often temporary in nature, can help to explain the deep impact of arts-based methodologies for participants and researchers alike. Within the intentional, liminal community of an arts-based research project, participants are often asked to reflect upon extremely vulnerable and personal experiences, and to create and share art that embodies these experiences. This chapter explores the opportunities for creating affective spaces for fat people to witness across difference, specifically in the context of arts-based research space, which holds great opportunity for fat healing and liberation.

Weight-Based Messaging: The Canadian Context

Biopedagogical lessons about how to have a (thin) body are one way that the so-called "war on obesity" is written on the fat body by way of measurements—from weighing and BMI calculations to skin fold measurements, waist circumference assessments, and fitness trackers worn on the body—all of which serve to make the body a political and moral space (Butler-Wall 239). As biopedagogies, prescriptive weight-cycling regimes such as Weight Watchers have been storied as weapons in the "war on obesity" that, consequently, also become weapons in the war on fat people (Rail 228). Biopedagogy is a relational and cultural practice that serves to produce knowledge through both public and private spaces, including schools and within family practices (Wright and Harwood). "Obesity" discourse in Canada has historically shown up in schools and recreational spaces via biopedagogical lessons and practices such as fitness testing, dress codes, furniture, and student placement in class pictures (Rice 165). For example, Canada Fitness—a program aimed at increasing the fitness of Canadian school children—ran from 1970 to 1992 and involved several fitness-based competitions whereby school children could earn gold, silver, and bronze medals for their achievements in various physical activities (Rice 166). The move to monitor and control fat children's bodies has intensified over the last 10 to 15 years, with efforts such as Michelle Obama's "Let's Move!" initiative in the United States in 2010, the advent of the National Child Measurement Program in the United Kingdom in 2006 (Evans and Colls 1052), and the relaunch of the "ParticipACTION" campaign in Canada in 2007. Originally launched in Canada in 1971, ParticipACTION was reformulated and relaunched in an effort to increase physical activity and fitness among the Canadian populous and included specific efforts geared toward addressing "obesity" in children and youth (Ellison 56). These public health campaigns are examples of biopedagogical tools that aim to teach lessons about how to have a (thin) body. In doing so, they serve to reinforce weight stigma at both a population and an individual level beginning in childhood. Weight control practices then continue into adulthood through various diet programs.

Affective Analysis of the Weight Watchers Meeting

The Weight Watchers meeting was established as a group therapy component of the popular weight-loss program in 1968, with the ultimate goal of behaviour modification (Parr 343). This weight-loss program operates globally. The ways in which joy and success are attached to one's proximity to thinness within the space of the Weight Watchers meeting makes it a particularly poignant example of an affective community—that is, a community forged through intangible affective flows. At a Weight Watchers meeting, participants are weighed in—usually in a semi-private manner by a volunteer—and then participants have an opportunity to share with the group leader and other members their struggles or successes, for example how much weight they lost in the previous week (Parr 345). Participants can shout out—for example, "I lost 4 pounds!" or "I lost 0.2 pounds!"—and they are met with congratulatory cheers and sometimes stickers or other small tokens from the group leader. The affective nature of this public weight-loss "success" sharing must be underscored. Participants who have lost weight in the previous week are ecstatic about their proximity to their predetermined weight loss goal. The "progress" that is represented by these changes in weight are the main purpose of this space. Participants cheer and clap for one another as their peers share their success at obtaining a smaller, and therefore more acceptable, body. After this public sharing, the group leader (who must be a Weight Watchers member who has reached their "goal weight") then gives a short lecture on a specific topic related to weight loss, for example, how to have self-control over the holidays. This affective community is centred on moving away from the various negative affects that fat people are limited by—hate, shame, and a desire to reach for thinness at all costs. The Weight Watchers meeting encourages members towards the promise of thinness and happiness through the various mechanisms of group- and self-surveillance discussed above (semi-private weigh-ins, sharing weight-loss "success," and tracking food and exercise activities).

While Weight Watchers (now WW) underwent rebranding in 2017, with celebrity experiential expert endorsement from Oprah Winfrey and a supposed focus on wellness over weight loss, it is essential to note the ways in which the affective energies of the weekly weight-loss meeting space are now distributed into the daily lives of its members. For members who opt for an online membership, the WW space exists within a phone app, and the opportunities for tracking weight-loss "success" and its associated affect are always in the pocket of the member, distributed across and integrated within all moments of the user's life, rather than in a concentrated two-hour, in-person session each week. This electronic alternative may hold diluted affective flows; however, this remains a space that is oriented around fat shame and hate, with the ultimate goal of obtaining happiness via a smaller body. In the Feeling Fat study described in this chapter, participants had direct and long-standing interactions with Weight Watchers. In fact, nearly all of the 19 interview participants discussed either being on Weight Watchers themselves or interacting with the program through a dieting parent. Participants' experiences with Weight Watchers began in childhood. For example, Tabitha (fat, Black, bisexual cis woman) described being sent to her first Weight Watchers meeting as a child and her impressions of the experience:

> I know that I was the only kid there in those meetings, and I hated how the people talked about themselves, like, I hated the fact that they were spending this time and energy on hating themselves, even as a ten-year-old I could see this clearly, like, "You all hate yourselves and you're paying people to let you hate yourselves, you're all fucking stupid!" (laughs).

Weight Watchers was a permanent fixture in many families and in the lives of many participants. This created an intergenerational component of Weight Watchers, where parents brought their children into the fold of the weight cycling program, either informally or formally. Because of its strategic model, Weight Watchers retained participants in this study (as well as their parents) for many years. At the time of the interview, some participants shared that their mothers had been on Weight Watchers for more than 15 years.

Creating Space for Fat Joy through Arts-Based Methods

Body mapping is an arts-based method of identity expression and embodied storytelling used to centralize the experiences of bodies that are most marginalized and under- or misrepresented in mainstream systems (Skop 30). Body mapping is used to encourage embodied reflections, for example, where and how affect is felt within the body (Jager et al. 15), and to provide participants with an opportunity to express marginalized or complicated aspects of their embodied experiences (Skop 29). In addition, body mapping is a helpful tool for encouraging intergenerational dialogue (Gestaldo et al.), offering an alternative means by which to access participants' embodied experiences and to help elicit reflections that interviews alone may overlook (Jager et al. 6). Canadian artist Allyson Mitchell writes about the importance of queer fat art and its ability to allow for different ways of seeing and representing fatness (Mitchell 148). Mitchell goes on to discuss how the temporality of queer fat artmaking echoes the time it takes to create a politicized fat body (157), therefore highlighting the importance of fat artmaking. This array of uses and benefits of body mapping makes it an extraordinarily suitable tool for connecting art, affect, and activism in the context of Canadian fat studies research.

The Study: "Feeling Fat: Theorizing Intergenerational Body Narratives through Affect"

The Feeling Fat study took place between June 2018 and December 2019. In total, 19 participants were interviewed, all of whom were born in Canada and the US between 1955 and 1991. Six of these participants were related mother-child dyads (three dyads total). In total, eight participants identified as straight, and the remaining 11 participants identified as queer, pansexual, bisexual, or questioning. Twelve participants identified as white, one participant was white and Indigenous, one participant identified as South Asian (East Indian), three identified as Black, one as African American, and one participant identified as a person of colour. Finally, six participants were parents, and the remaining 13 participants did not have children. Interviews were anywhere from one to two hours in length and covered various topics, including bodily descriptions (e.g., "How do you describe your body?"), messages received about the body (e.g., "What messages did you receive about your body growing up?"), family dynamics and parental relationships, food messaging, and food practices. At the end of each interview, participants who were located in geographic proximity to Waterloo, Ontario (that is, those in Toronto, Guelph, Kitchener, Waterloo, and Hamilton, Ontario), were invited to participate in the arts-based body mapping portion of the study. In total five participants expressed interest in taking part in body mapping. Four of these participants (Purple, Margaret, Aisha, and Casey—all pseudonyms chosen by participants) took part in body mapping as a group process, and one participant completed body mapping independently due to scheduling and transportation issues. Throughout all body mapping sessions, all group conversations were audio recorded with participant consent, transcribed, and analysed. All participants were given a pseudonym for use within the study—some participants chose their own pseudonyms while others preferred to have the researcher choose their pseudonyms. While the overarching purpose of the Feeling Fat study was to better understand the affective nature of intergenerational body messaging related to both weight stigma and fat liberation, the remainder of this chapter focuses on the methodological potentialities of body mapping.

The group body mapping process was completed over three sessions during the autumn of 2019. Each session was between three and four hours in duration. In the first session, participants did the following: set ground rules, got to know one another, discussed the purpose of the study and their overall goals for their body maps, reviewed the process of body mapping, and worked in pairs to create their body outlines on large rolls of paper. In the second session, participants used various art modalities—mainly paint—to design and fill in their body maps. Participants used various visual techniques in their maps, for example using colour to depict the affective flows that influence both the contours of their bodies and their relationships with the world around them. Purple used black to represent despair, red for anger, and purple for healing and self-love in her body map. Aisha used a mosaic of colourful squares surrounding her body outline to depict her memories, events, and social location that influence the person she has become and the ways she views herself. Finally, Casey used glitter to represent feelings on their body map—on the head to represent anxiety and on the belly to represent the complex feelings they have related to this politicized part of their body.

During the second session, participants engaged in both formal (guided) and informal conversation. These conversations were about the methodology, the content of their maps, and the topic of the study, as well as about living in a fat body more broadly. In the third session, participants completed their body maps, followed by a guided group discussion during which each participant presented and explained their body map to the group. This guided discussion covered various topics including both the content of the body maps and participants' reflections on the methodology.

In this chapter, I present the body mapping data relevant to the use of this methodology to create affective communities for fat people within arts-based research. Group conversations were analysed using a two-pronged approach that blended thematic analysis (Braun and Clarke 77) and the application of theory directly to the data. This latter process, known in post-qualitative inquiry as *plugging in*, allowed participants' storied accounts to remain intact. Specific stories or excerpts of text were held alongside theory, whereby theory and data were plugged into one another in an ongoing, iterative manner (Jackson and Mazzei 269). This approach does not treat data and theory as separate or separable but rather acknowledges the assemblage of factors that coalesce within the research process to create new realities—including participant subjectivity, data, researcher, methodology, literature, theory, et cetera (Jackson and Mazzei 264). This multi-pronged approach created a rigorous theoretical analysis that accounts for the complex relational aspects of the project. As well, my own positionality as a fat white (gender)queer researcher with lived experiences of weight-based stigma, including direct experience with Weight Watchers, was an important factor that influenced my theorized analysis and subsequent findings.

Affective Analysis of the Body Mapping Process

Three core aspects of the data coalesced around the co-creation of affective community within the body mapping space. These core aspects include the (co)-construction of fat identity, fat affinity, and witnessing fat joy and trauma. While these three concepts are interconnected, they are each presented here to outline a clear picture of the potentialities of the body mapping methodology with regards to accessing places that hold space for the complexity of affective flows, including an orientation toward fat joy and healing. In this section, the first time a participant is introduced, I have included descriptors of body size/type, race, sexuality, and gender. These descriptors are included for the purposes of adding context to the relational dynamics of the space and to give the reader more information about participants. Notably, the body size/shape descriptors are the specific ones used by participants themselves.

(Co)-construction of Fat Identity

Participants in the body mapping sessions varied in their fat identity, with some participants identifying as fat activists and others who had only recently begun to use the word fat as a neutral descriptor for their body shape/size. This is important because the body mapping space became a site of co-construction of fat identity, where participants discussed the terms they use to describe themselves and the meaning of their fat identity along a spectrum of body size alongside other aspects of their identities. Participants also co-constructed the very meaning of the body mapping space through these discussions, for example, in talking about what the space meant to them and who they are as fat people, and how this differs within the body mapping space versus "out there" in their daily lives. Aisha (a curvy South Asian straight cisgender woman) reflected:

> In some rooms, in certain spaces, I'm skinny, and in some rooms, in certain spaces, I am so chronically obese ... it depends on what room that I go to ... as I'm talking, I realize that I haven't adjusted my shapewear while I've been in here, I'm noticing that I haven't pulled down my shirt while I've been in here. It's weird because for the rest of the day that's all I've been doing, making certain that my shapewear wasn't showing, making certain that the rolls of my belly weren't showing.

For Aisha, her comfort and safety in the space is inextricably tied to the composition of bodies in the space. The safety that Aisha describes is inherently tied to how she holds and interacts with her very flesh—she notes not having adjusted her shapewear in order to appear thinner/smoother since entering the space. In this way, Aisha's relation to the space is tied to how her body is perceived ("skinny" vs. "chronically obese"), which in turn influences her feelings of safety in the space and in her body. Of note, in Aisha's quotation above, she uses the word *obese* without having indicated air quotes. In sharing this quotation, I have intentionally not included quotation marks around this word to honour the fraught complexity of Aisha's embodied experiences. Aisha further reflected on her access to language and to community via identity. She reflected on at first not being sure how "fat" was being defined, and whether she was "fat enough" to be in the study:

> Let me have, like let me have something, give me something, because I'm not Canadian, but I'm not Indian, and I'm not this, I'm not that, like just give me something. ... I feel accepted [here] and I feel like I can live my truth in here, I can feel and I can be all of these things that I am because out there I can't, like I can't be because I have to fit and I'm moulding in some way, but in here I'm just able to be.

Here, Aisha is expressing the intersections of her identity in terms of being Canadian, Indian, skinny, and fat. Aisha expressed feeling like she was in an in-between space, where others controlled her membership to various groups. She expressed that when she visits India, she is seen as Canadian, but in Canada, she experiences racism because she is not white and is therefore not seen as Canadian. Simultaneously, Aisha expressed that, in some spaces, she is viewed as skinny while in others (for example, doctors' offices) she is viewed as "chronically obese." This in-betweenness that Aisha expressed is a culmination of racism and fatphobia that does not allow Aisha to "just be." On the contrary, in the body mapping space, Aisha expresses feeling like she can "live her truth" because she feels that she fits as a direct result of the connection and safety within the space. Importantly, in the body mapping space, Aisha notes, "I can feel and I can be all of these things." In this way, the orientation of the space towards fat joy and away from fat shame also provided an opportunity for Aisha to feel and, in turn, to firmly belong. While the temporary existence of this affective community certainly does not resolve Aisha's ongoing experiences at the nexus of racism and fatphobia, it does provide a short, comfortable reprieve and the opportunity to co-create art and knowledge.

Related to this, participants reflected on the common ground that the group created, including a shared use of language. Margaret (a fat, white, pansexual/questioning, cisgender woman) noted, "I trust you guys [laughter]. It's not a huge, well it is a huge thing, but it's not a huge thing, I like that we can use the word fat and I didn't have to explain it." This co-creation of fat identity through use of common language contributed to the development of a safe(r) space where participants expressed feeling safe and trusting.

Fat Affinity

Largely related to the (co)-construction of fat identity were the moments of connection participants had, whether through the sharing of a common experience, the use of common language, or simply the act of making art together. These moments were most often found in conversations unrelated to the research questions, when participants were working on their body maps and engaging in informal conversation. As a researcher, I made the decision early in the body mapping process not to over-facilitate the conversation, as it was clear to me that the participants were creating community through body mapping and that casual conversation was an integral part of this process. Not only this, but as a fat researcher, I was also a participant in these conversations and in the community that emerged from the methodology. While I was not making a body map alongside the participants, and at times I was facilitating the conversation, I was often simultaneously a participant in the conversation. These casual conversations related to day-to-day life as a fat person, including both the minutiae of daily life and major life events. Participants discussed the difficulties they experienced with navigating the medical system and finding care providers that were trustworthy and respectful of fat bodies, shared resources and fashion advice, listened to fat-positive music together, shared food, and gave one another advice on the art-making process. Through these conversations, participants developed common ground, and moments of fat affinity emerged. Margaret, Aisha, and Casey describe their feelings of fat affinity below:

> It was really nice to be able to come and talk, it was kind of like when you don't realize something's really important until you sit down and start talking to other people that it affects and you're like oh, I'm not alone and you start to like really see it (Margaret)

> It started when I walked in this room and it was something about, it was some fat related something, I was like "yeah, yeah, yeah!" Like "me too! Me too!" That was the only thing that was going through my mind and I was like I fit, like I fit (Aisha)

> I was driving home [after the first session] and just felt really like connected and that we shared some difficult things and that makes me feel good for some reason [laughs] it's the, I don't know the bonding and the sharing of humanity and similar experiences (Casey, fat, white, pansexual/questioning)

This connection that Margaret, Aisha, and Casey describe developed in both tangible and intangible ways, through moments of fat affinity. These moments were felt in the room and cannot be fully captured through words on a page. Aisha's description of one such moment—"It started when I walked in this room"—captures the electric nature of fat affinity. When Aisha entered the first session, she did not know any other participants, and she and I had only met over the phone before the body mapping process started. During the casual conversation before the session started, Aisha almost immediately felt affinity with other participants: as she states, "I fit, ... I fit." This feeling is not just about what was being discussed when Aisha entered the room (as she noted above, she doesn't remember what specifically was being discussed), but rather is a result of the affective flows in the space that serve to shape the very nature of the interactions and perceptions of self and other.

Witnessing Fat Joy and Trauma

The body mapping space opened opportunities for participants to witness one another's stories and co-create a narrative. The witnessing of fat joy and trauma was influenced by the co-creation of fat identity and the fat affinity that also emerged from the process. The body mapping process became a space in which participants shared and witnessed stories of both trauma and joy that were oftentimes interwoven and inextricable. The stories of fat life were not either/or but rather both/and. Participants exhibited an ability and willingness to hold a great deal for and with one another and to witness across difference without collapsing that difference. Stories of pain and trauma were held alongside stories of joy and vitality, and this very complexity of affect contributed to the co-creation of this space. Participants noted feeling safe in the space and expressed a willingness to be and feel vulnerable. The affective flows of the space shaped the very nature of the stories that were told, the moments that were shared, and the common ground that emerged. Importantly, Purple commented on the need to highlight the dynamic, complex nature of fat life, not just the trauma:

> What I'm terrified of is that only the shitty stuff is going to boil out of me and I don't want to honour that as being the only part of the experience that I have because that just isn't fucking true, but some of the poignant things are some of the most awful, and I feel like they're really important to sort of landmark what my journey to body acceptance and body embracing has come to. ... I'm just scared that I'm not going to be able to communicate the

> full spectrum of what sort of living in this body has been. I want it to feel joyful and hopeful, because I feel joyful and hopeful all the time, but I have also experienced some absolutely fucking horrifying things as a direct result of having a fat, a visibly fat body. (Purple, a superfat, white, bisexual cisgender woman)

Aisha reflects further:

> I think this sense of community that we've built here where we've been able to be vulnerable and we've been able to share parts of our truths and these like big T Traumas that have happened to us and things we wouldn't normally share and I think there is a sense of comfort there. (Aisha)

Purple's description of feeling emotion "boil out" of her at times in the process was agreed upon by all participants in the space, myself included. This phrasing conjures for the reader the image of affective flows flying, moving, and shaping the space. The goal of body mapping was not to create exclusively positive space but rather to hold space for this very complexity of emotion, from "capital T Traumas" to affinity, safety, and connection. While participants held very different embodied experience along the lines of body size, shape, sexuality, and race, they were able to create common ground and witness joy and trauma without collapsing difference.

A Word of Caution

While the body mapping methodology had many benefits and contributed to the creation of an affective community for fat people, it is important to note the potential difficulties of this methodology. All four participants who took part in the group process noted that relaying their experiences of trauma and fat hatred was incredibly difficult and at times nearly unbearable. More than one participant noted a need to debrief after each session, whether that was in a formal way with a therapist or significant other or more informally, for example, by processing individually on the drive home after each session. There was agreement that the body mapping methodology needs to be undertaken with a great deal of care and intentionality, and that participants need to be well-supported throughout. During our third session, Purple described the nature of body mapping:

> It was, it was an interesting experience, it was very positive in a lot of ways because I felt like I was in a very safe and understanding space, but it still pulled up a lot of really negative and traumatizing memories for me, that I was actually kind of surprised at. It was a mixed bag ... like it wasn't distressing, it was just there were parts of it that were difficult because you know living in a stigmatized body is difficult, but there was also something so amazing once the outlines were drawn and wow, like this is, okay! (Purple)

During the study, there were many processes in place to intentionally foster safety for participants. This included setting ground rules at the beginning of the first session, which served to create common language and establish boundaries for safe and respectful interactions. We also extended the time allotment for each session, at the request of participants. This allowed for a slower pace with ample time during which participants could just sit together, process, share stories, and simply "be." In addition, the body mapping process took place in a large room with space to move around, a wide selection of armless chairs and couches, and full privacy. Finally, each session had food available that met all participants' dietary needs. Food was one important aspect of fostering a fat-centred space that was oriented toward liberation and healing, in contrast to the biopedagogical weight-cycling spaces that normalize food and body shame. In the body mapping space, food was celebrated as a point of connection and nourishment, where enjoyment of food could be reclaimed.

Conclusion

The body mapping space became an affective community that was oriented toward fat joy while holding space for the complexity of vast affective flows. Participants' interactions were shaped by the affective flows of the co-created body mapping space. For some participants, these interactions continued in various capacities after the Feeling Fat project concluded. For example, a number of participants began attending a fat activist social group hosted by one of the participants, and all participants intended to plan a fat swimming event. In fact, at the end of the final session, the following exchange took place:

> Aisha: Is this the last time that we're going to see each other?
> Purple: Why can't we just like be fat and hang out?
> Aisha: I would love that.
> Margaret: Well, and we have to plan our pool party.

The comfort and familiarity expressed in this final conversation points to the community and connection that developed over the course of the body mapping process. This connection was a result of witnessing one another's pain and joy and creating a safe space where participants could share their complex experiences knowing that while others may not have the same experience, there was a degree of affinity in these shared experiences of fat life. This exemplifies the practice of difference-attuned witnessing within the body mapping process.

Arts-based research—particularly body mapping—is one modality through which Canadian fat studies scholars and activists may co-create difference-attuned affective communities that prioritize fat affinity, joy, and healing as objects of happiness. Spaces such as the one cultivated in this study provide an alternative to the opportunities to gather that fat people have historically had—those that are focused on weight loss/management and oriented toward thinness as an object of happiness (Ahmed, *Promise of Happiness* 248). Body mapping and other arts-based methodologies are ripe with potential for co-creating critical, affective space for the exploration of fat affinity, joy, and liberation within fat studies scholarship and activism in Canada.

The use of body mapping led to the co-creation of community and the practice of difference-attuned witnessing, in which the researcher and participants were co-witnesses to one another's intersectional, embodied realities through art and storytelling (Rice et al. 360–62). The liminal, affective community created through body mapping stimulated affective flows that decentred body shame and allowed space for participants to express the full spectrum of emotion oriented toward fat joy and healing.

Works Cited

Ahmed, Sara. "The Organisation of Hate." *Law and Critique*, vol. 12, 2001, pp. 345–65.

Ahmed, Sara. *The Promise of Happiness*. Duke University Press, 2010.

Bahra, Ramanpreet A. "'You Can Only Be Happy If You're Thin!' Normalcy, Happiness, and the Lacking Body." *Fat Studies*, vol. 7, no. 2, 2018, pp. 193–202. *Taylor & Francis:* https://doi.org/10.1080/21604851.2017.1374696.

Braun, Virginia, and Victoria Clarke. "Using Thematic Analysis in Psychology." *Qualitative Research in Psychology*, vol. 3, 2006, pp. 77–101.

Butler-Wall, Karisa. "Risky Measures: Digital Technologies and the Governance of Child Obesity." *Women's Studies Quarterly*, vol. 43, 2015, pp. 228–45. *Project Muse*: https://doi.org/10.1353/wsq.2015.0015.

Carastathis, Anna. "The Concept of Intersectionality in Feminist Theory." *Philosophy Compass*, vol. 9, no. 2, 2014, pp. 304–14. *One Compass, Many Directions*: https://doi.org/10.1111/phc3.12129.

Combahee River Collective. "The Combahee River Collective Statement." *Circuitous* [personal site of bec.white@gmail.com], http://circuitous.org/scraps/combahee.html. Accessed 15 Jan. 2021.

Crenshaw, Kimberlee. "Demarginalizing the Intersection of Race and Sex: A Black Feminist Critique of Theory and Antiracist Politics." *The University of Chicago Legal Forum,* vol. 1, no. 8, 1989, pp. 139–70.

Ellison, Jenny. "Weighing In: The 'Evidence of Experience' and Canadian Fat Women's Activism." *Canadian Bulletin of Medical History*, vol. 30, no.1, 2013, pp. 55–75.

Evans, Bethan, and Rachel Colls. "Measuring Fatness, Governing Bodies: The Spatialities of the Body Mass Index (BMI) in Anti-Obesity Politics." *Antipode*, vol. 41, no. 5, 2009, pp. 1051–83.

Fraser, Laura. "The Inner Corset: A Brief History of Fat in The United States." *The Fat Studies Reader*, edited by Esther Rothblum and Sondra Solovay, New York University Press, 2009, pp. 11–14.

Gestaldo, Denise, et al. "Body Map Storytelling as Research: Methodological Considerations for Telling the Stories of Undocumented Workers Through Body Mapping." *KT Pathways*, 2012. ktpathways.ca/resources/body-map-storytelling-research-methodological-considerations-telling-stories-undocumented. Accessed 15 Jan. 2021.

Heyes, Cressida J. "Foucault Goes to Weight Watchers." *Hypatia,* vol. 21, no. 2, 2006, pp. 126–49. *JSTOR*: https://www.jstor.org/stable/3810995.

Hill Collins, Patricia. "Gender, Black Feminism, and Black Political Economy." *Annals of the American Academy,* vol. 568, 2000, pp. 41–53. *SSAGE Journals*: https://doi.org/10.1177/000271620056800105.

Jackson, Alecia Youngblood, and Lisa Mazzei. "Plugging One Text into Another: Thinking with Theory in Qualitative Research." *Qualitative Inquiry*, vol. 19, no. 4, pp. 261–71. *SAGE Journals*: https://doi.org/10.1177/1077800412471510.

Jager, Adele de, et al. "Embodied Ways of Storying the Self: A Systemic Review of Body-Mapping." *Forum: Qualitative Social Research*, vol. 17, no. 2, 2016, pp. 1–31. *FQS*: https://doi.org/10.17169/fqs-17.2.2526.

Kjaer, Katrine Meldgaard. "Detoxing Feels Good: Dieting and Affect in 22Days Nutrition and Goop Detoxes." *Feminist Media Studies,* vol. 19, no. 5, 2019, pp. 702–16. *Taylor & Francis Online*: https://doi.org/10.1080/14680777.2018.1508050.

Mitchell, Allyson. "Sedentary Lifestyle: Fat Queer Craft." *Fat Studies*, vol. 7, no. 2, 2018, pp. 147–58. *Taylor & Francis Online*: https://doi.org/10.1080/21604851.2017.1373515.

Murray, Samantha. "Normative Imperatives vs. Pathological Bodies: Constructing 'the Fat' Woman." *Australian Feminist Studies*, vol. 23, no. 56, 2008, pp. 213–25. *Taylor & Francis Online*: https://doi.org/10.1080/08164640802004752.

Nash, Jennifer. "Practicing Love: Black Feminism, Love-Politics, and Post-Intersectionality." *Meridians,* vol. 11, no. 2, 2013, pp. 1–24.

Parr, Jessica. "'Act Thin, Stay Thin': Commercialization, Behaviour Modification, and Group Weight Control." *Journal of the History of the Behaviour Sciences,* vol. 55, no. 4, 2019, pp. 342–57. *Wiley Online Library*: https://doi.org/10.1002/jhbs.21993.

Rail, Geneviève. "The Birth of the Obesity Clinic: Confessions of the Flesh, Biopedagogies and Physical Culture." *Sociology of Sport Jour-*

nal, no. 29, 2012, pp. 227–53. *Human Kinetics Journals*: https://doi.org/10.1123/ssj.29.2.227.

Rice, Carla. "Becoming 'the Fat Girl': Acquisition of an Unfit Identity." *Women's Studies International Forum*, vol. 30, 2007, pp. 158–74.

Rice, Carla, Katie Cook, and K. Alysse Bailey. "Difference-Attuned Witnessing: Risks and Potentialities of Arts-Based Research." *Feminism & Psychology*, vol. 31, no. 3, August 2021, pp. 341–65. *SAGE Journals*: https://doi.org/10.1177/0959353520955142. First published online 5 October 2020.

Skop, Michelle. "The Art of Body Mapping: A Methodological Guide for Social Work Researchers." *Aotearoa New Zealand Social Work*, vol. 28, no. 4, 2016, pp. 29–43 *ANZSWJ*: https://doi.org/10.11157/anzswj-vol28iss4id295.

Wright, Jan, and Valerie Harwood, editors. *Biopolitics and the "Obesity Epidemic."* Routledge, 2008.

Fragments on Fatness: Moments from a Digital Storytelling Archive on Trans Experiences of Weight Stigma

Jen Rinaldi, Karleen Pendleton Jiménez, Jake Pyne, and May Friedman

The Transgressing Body Boundaries Research Project

In this chapter we present work from our research project "Transgressing Body Boundaries." This project was an extension of "Bodies in Translation: Activist Art, Technology, and Access to Life," a multidisciplinary mega-project (funded with a Social Sciences and Humanities Research Council Partnership Grant) that took as its objective cultivating activist art. Our research team recruited ten trans people from around southwestern Ontario. We asked them to confront the body policing that they experience at the intersection of their gender identity and their body weight, shape, or size. Our recruitment screening questions enabled potential participants to choose their own gender identifiers, and their choices included trans, trans man, trans woman, two-spirit, genderqueer, gender nonconforming, nonbinary, gender-fluid, and gender-floral. The participants whose artistic work is presented in this chapter were among those who chose the following identifiers in relation to body weight, shape, or size: fat, plus size, overweight, obese, weight issues, weight stigma experience, chubby, soft, and fluffy. While these were the two key screening questions, given the project's aims, we also made a commitment to ensure diverse representation when selecting participants by asking additional questions about Indigeneity, race or ethnicity, disability, and age. Our intention was to open fields of representation or to facilitate the telling of stories from varied marginalized vantage points. This kind of work has the power to unsettle long-established, over-arching narratives about gender and body weight/shape/size.

Each selected participant created their own digital story. Digital stories are short videos that pair autobiographical scripts with curated visuals—which for this project included video, animation, drawing, stock and childhood photography, and photography of plasticine sculpture and body paint. Participants developed their digital story scripts and visual aesthetics in collaboration with artists who were affiliated with our research team, first in a workshop setting and then through remote one-on-one communication. Participants adept at video editing used software on their own computers or were provided with software they could download; other participants provided detailed directions and raw material, so artists could put together videos on their behalf. The stories they created communicate meanings on emotional registers that connect with audiences, with the expectation that empathy makes transformational justice possible.

The project produced an archive of ten digital stories, each providing a uniquely trans perspective on weight stigma. Each story also grapples with other identity markers, illustrating how weight stigma can be deeply complex, and contingent on embodiment and emplacement. Each participant decided whether their video would be credited to them or to a pseudonym, and some videos were created anonymously. They also controlled visual content, so some videos starkly feature the storyteller themselves while others obscure faces or use more oblique or abstract imagery. In this chapter, we present excerpts from these digital stories, with the storytellers' consent. Each excerpt is a still photograph paired with the script line that the storyteller delivers while that image appears in their video. We describe each image in the caption. Our intention is to show the range of participants' lived experiences at the intersection of anti-fat and anti-trans discrimination in order to develop a deeper collective understanding of how body-based oppressions operate in Canada.

"Shapeshifters": The Films

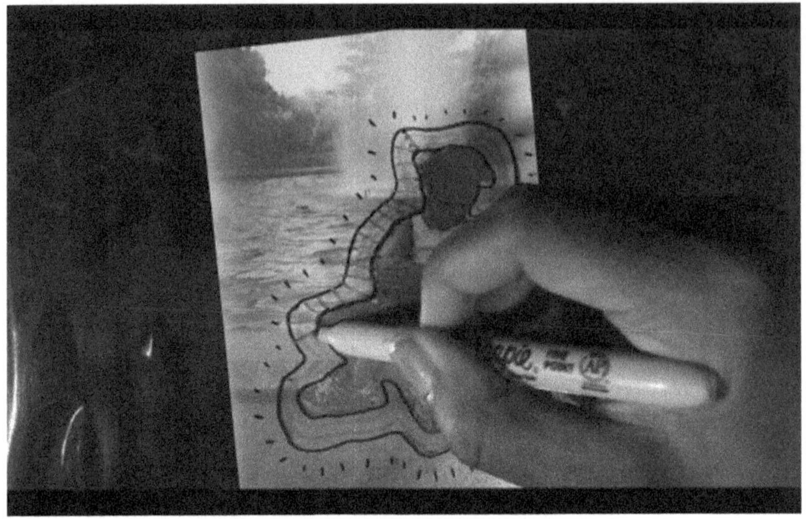

Figure 10.1 Untitled video

This untitled video features one consistent visual throughout: a hand holding a Sharpie, drawing lines around the figure in an old, sepia-toned photograph. That photograph captures a child wearing a tank top and sports shorts, sitting at a waterside, holding their left knee. The hand in the video has outlined the figure using markers of different colours. Some lines radiate outward, as if the child is pulsating. While this image is on screen the storyteller narrates: "I loathe my beating heart, for its every contraction carries the condition that I be constrained to this contraption that is my fat nonbinary body, and it hurts. And it hurts, and it hurts, and it hurts" (2:17–2:34).

Figure 10.2 *The e-girl Shapeshifter*

The e-girl Shapeshifter video uses pictures of clay figures against a black backdrop to explore how the storyteller plays with gender in virtual spaces. This excerpt includes orange clay moulded in the shape of a standing human with outstretched arms. Surrounding the figure are more abstractly moulded, much smaller characters rendered in lavender plasticine—built to look like tiny snowmen with a head ball atop a body ball. They are scattered around the orange figure as though they are Lilliputian friends or fans. According to the voice-over narration, "They never really knew who I was. That's the thing about clay and fire. It is constantly creating and shifting" (1:09–1:20).

Figure 10.3 *Acquiesce*

Acquiesce presents footage of the storyteller engaging in bodily routines (a haircut, chest binding), paired with images of their garden- and yardwork. This excerpt features woodworking, on a dirt driveway at the threshold of a garage. A left hand firmly holds a block of wood. The knuckles of a right hand are just in frame, operating a large mechanical saw—a tool that needs to be handled cautiously. In the storyteller's words, "Will the surgeons treat my body with care? Will they see my mixed complexion and treat me as less than? Will they see my BMI on their charts and be less careful with the placement of my incisions?" (1:08–1:20).

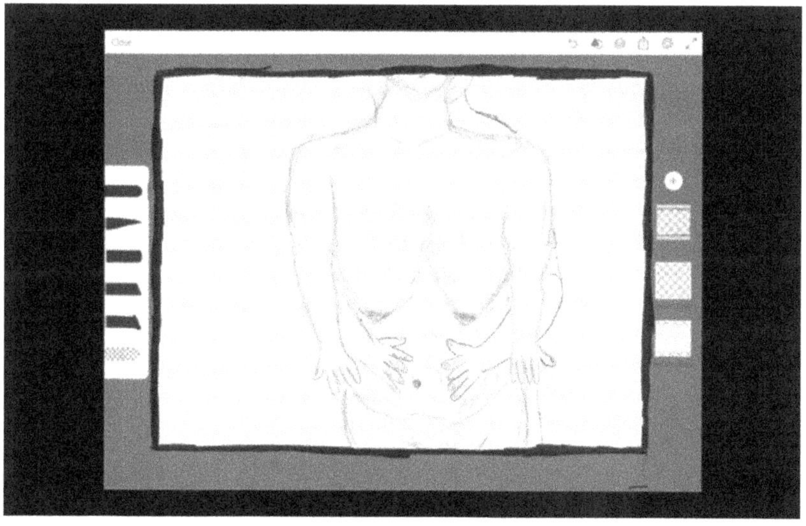

Figure 10.4 *Take Your Shirt Off*

Take Your Shirt Off screen-captures layers of drawings that the storyteller generates in a computer paint program (the tools for which are visible along the excerpt's frame). Centred in this image is a sketch depicting a nude figure from chin to pelvis, their breasts heavy and arms at their sides. Behind this body is another person whose hands reach around to cradle the central figure's soft, dimpled tummy. The storyteller reflects, "My mind is adept at losing information about feelings, my writing adept at retrieving it. Your hand wraps around the stretch marks on my belly. 'They're so beautiful'" (0:37–0:51).

Figure 10.5 *Over the Wait*

Over the Wait displays video footage and a series of "selfie" photographs. This excerpt is a screenshot from a video taken in a dark room with a stage and exposed brick walls. The storyteller is centred, midstride, while pacing the room and singing into a microphone. A dancing audience surrounds the storyteller in the background. From the voice-over: "Tits spilling over my back brace, blue light pooling over my sweat, green pigtails storming the stage, I am sweat-washed and baptized. A chameleon and Mystique-like, all queer, Black and belly rolling over Trans-Atlantic shorelines. I am singing" (0:01–0:24).

"Clay and Fire": Embracing Change

This chapter showcased artistic contributions, specifically still shots from digital stories on trans, fat persons' experiences of their bodies and on their reactions to the intersecting oppressions they encounter in their Canadian settings. The images presented speak to notions of bodily change, and to the conditions that enact these changes, for better or worse. The first untitled video creates a visual representation of the tensions of bodily change. There are multiple and expanding coloured lines drawn around the body, suggesting its presence beyond the boundaries of flesh and bone. However, the spoken words speak to the pain of the limits of the physical body. In *The e-girl Shapeshifter*, the clay character is surrounded by small figures, and the voice-over explains how the clay character was never really known. In this case, the unknowability is not presented as a painful experience but one related to the Shapeshifter's creative capacity for change. In *Acquiesce*, the image of a strong hand sawing into the wood is coupled with the spoken fear of how a surgeon might cut into the storyteller's "unacceptable" body. The storyteller's intention to transform their body comes with concern that under a surgeon's gaze, that body could lose its humanity. In *Take Off Your Shirt*, the mind is disconnected from the feelings of the body until retrieved through writing and the soft caress of a belly by a lover. The body emerges through touch and the written memory of that touch. And finally, the storyteller in *Over the Wait* struts the stage with an abundance of body spilling over clothing, sweat pouring, pigtails glowing, inspiring and reacting to a cheering audience. This moment is celebrated through the body's capacity for change within itself, and through its movement across geographic location.

While the research project was named long before the films were produced, "Transgressing Body Boundaries" aptly describes two central questions that these videos raise: 1) Are we contained by the boundary of our bodies? and 2) Is it possible to change our bodies? Trans, fat people have a particular and significant perspective for broader considerations of body transformation. On the one hand, they have most likely faced a policing of bodies, the imperative to lose weight (Rice), to change their bodies by making them smaller, more acceptable in the Canadian colonial state (Lind), as well as criticism for not having done so. On the other, they have most likely faced discrimination in Canada for conceiving of their body's gender as something other than what is listed on a birth certificate (Shraya). They face social consequences for moving beyond the constraints of the expectations of their bodies, for conceptualizing them differently and/or taking actions to change them. In other words, they are criticized simultaneously for *not changing* the fatness of their bodies and *for changing* their bodies to affirm their genders.

The "Transgressing Body Boundaries" storytellers document changes in body or perceptions of body that result in a range of emotions, from the fear of a surgeon's hand to the pleasure of a lover's touch and the creativity and power of the art of changing oneself before an audience. In each case, moments of corporeal transformation are made possible through interactions with others. These artistic works convey that we are all bodies that transgress in relation. We are "clay and fire ... constantly shifting and creating."

Works Cited

Lind, Emma. "Queering Fat Activism: A Study in Whiteness." *Thickening Fat: Fat Bodies, Intersectionality, and Social Justice*, edited by May Friedman, Carla Rice, and Jen Rinaldi, Routledge, 2019, pp. 183–93.

Rice, Carla. *Becoming Women: The Embodied Self in Image Culture.* University of Toronto Press, 2014.

Shraya, Vivek. *I'm Afraid of Men.* Penguin Canada, 2018.

Lies Fatphobia Told Me

j wallace skelton

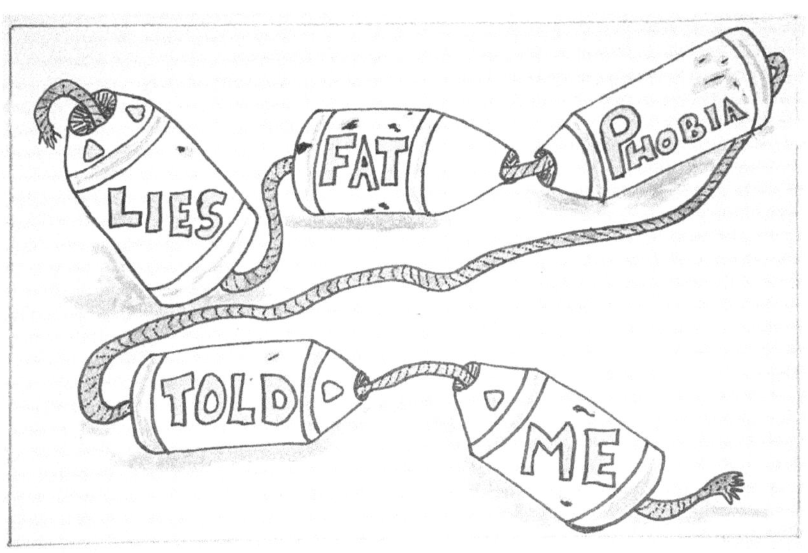

Fatphobia is a tool of racism (see Sabrina Strings Fearing the Black Body). It claims virtue for thin white bodies and claims greed, immorality and sin for Black fat bodies.

Which means there can be no swimming in it.
Help!
Help!
Help
Help!
Help?
Help
no gills
I am a fat merman. I do not have gills.
Fatphobia is suffocating.

failure
Like sand in your underpants
BAD
SHAME
It gets into the most intimate places.
It's not asthma. You are too fat....
to breath
Fatphobia tells me lies.

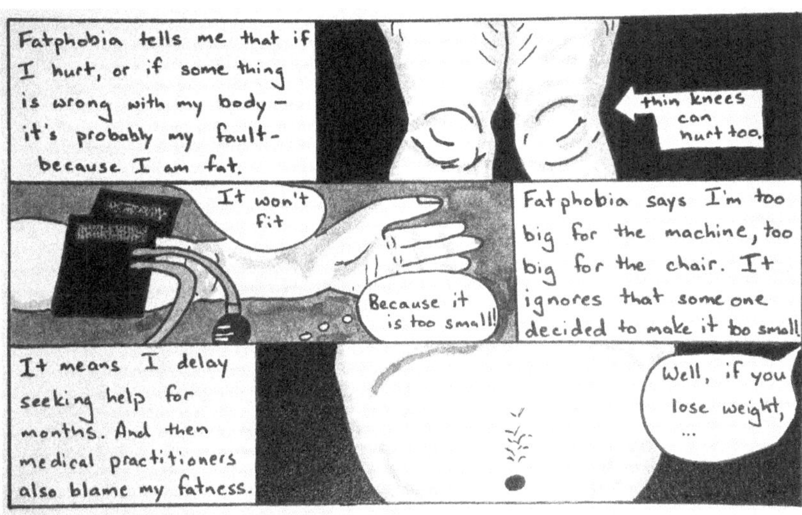
Fatphobia tells me that if I hurt, or if some thing is wrong with my body - it's probably my fault - because I am fat.
thin knees can hurt too.
It won't fit
Because it is too small!
Fat phobia says I'm too big for the machine, too big for the chair. It ignores that some one decided to make it too small
It means I delay seeking help for months. And then medical practitioners also blame my fatness.
Well, if you lose weight, ...

At the fertility clinic, the specialist said "at my size" I would have great difficulty getting pregnant. I got pregnant the very first time.
FANCY
NO

Time and time again when I stop
blaming fatness, I can
Identify real problems
and real solutions.

Fatphobia is a net of lies. Even if we don't get tangled in the whole net, even a few strands are dangerous enough.
Everything gets dragged in.

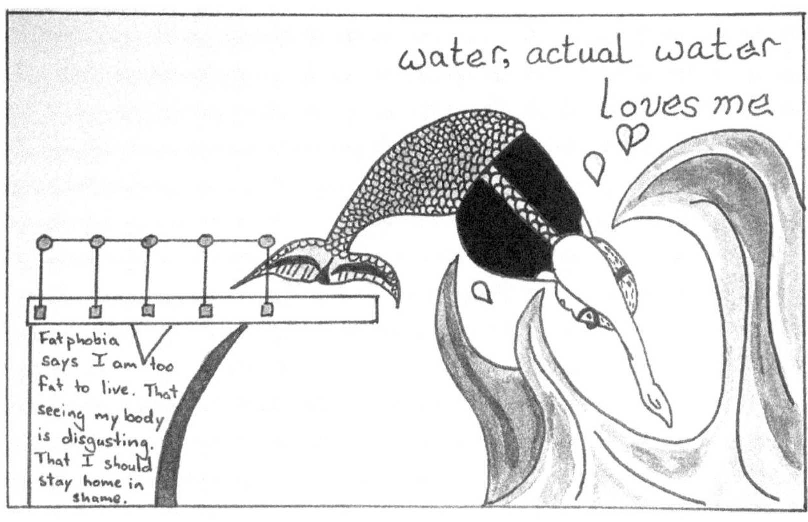
water, actual water
loves me
Fatphobia says I am too fat to live. That seeing my body is disgusting. That I should stay home in shame.

In water, my body is not too big. I float. Fat is buoyant. Fat warms and is protective. I remember that many other fat mammals call the water home. I come home to me.

Fatphobia says I don't have a "beach body. That's a lie.
All bodies are beach bodies.
I also have an ocean body. The beach is a thin strip of dead, ground-up sea creatures - and the ocean is deep, vast, and wonderous.

Coming Home to Our Bodies: (Re)framing Fatness through an Exploration of Fat Vitality

Lauren Munro

"She exists because she was meant to."

THIS SIMPLE, BUT POWERFUL, statement from a fat woman who participated in the Living Big Lives project offers fat bodies a meaningful place as part of a spectrum of body diversity. She asserts her right to exist, to take up space. The suggestion that she is perhaps part of some divine plan is at odds with the dominant discourses that aim to eradicate bodies like hers. And yet, here she is.

Introduction

Fat bodies are rarely represented as joyful, valuable, or as sites of pleasure beyond fetishization. Instead, they are often the subjects of a hostile gaze (Hladki 23), with visual representations of fatness in mainstream media tending to reflect negative stereotypes (Abel 7), perpetuating the idea of fatness as failure (Rinaldi et al., "Fatness" 224). Moss E. Norman and colleagues document a pernicious iteration of this messaging within the Canadian reality television show *Village on a Diet*, which brings together "obesity epidemic" rhetoric and healthism in an attempt to literally shrink the citizens of Taylor, British Columbia, through, arguably unsafe, diet and exercise (363). This kind of negative framing of fatness upholds and reinforces a biopedagogy of body size that sets parameters of public life for fat people, who can become bounded by shame and an endless striving for thinness.

It is in this context that people "come to believe they are nothing (and are frequently treated as nothing) unless they are trim, tight, lineless, bulgeless, and sagless" (Bordo 32). The reach of this ideology is expansive and is part of the broader neoliberal project that encourages individuals to govern themselves and each other, which, in this case, involves normalizing aspirations to thinness, diet talk, and weight-loss endeavours.

It is against this backdrop that the Living Big Lives project works towards Kathleen LeBesco's goal of "transforming fatness from a spoiled, uninhabitable, invisible identity to a stronger subject position" (*Revolting* 3) by providing other ways of knowing and being fat. The Living Big Lives project is a Canadian phenomenological photovoice project that explores fat women's experiences of and responses to body-based judgments. In this project, 15 participants generated 37 photographs and accompanying written narratives documenting the daily realities of navigating the world as fat women and then came together in focus groups in Toronto, Ontario, in 2019 to share and discuss their photographs and experiences. This chapter focuses on the ways participants subverted fat erasure; challenged stereotypical visual depictions of fat bodies; explored pleasure, love, and desirability; and celebrated and held space for their bodies.

My interest in situating fatness as a generative site of inquiry stems from my own personal experiences of non-normative embodiment. As a mad, queer, fat woman who is also cisgender and a white settler, my various points of privilege and marginality inform the kinds of body-related judgments I experience. Navigating street harassment, microaggressions, and academic contexts where fatness is maligned is exhausting, but it is not the totality of my experience. Like my queerness and my madness, my fatness has also been a source of joy and a point of connection. The findings presented herein offer a framework for thinking about, with, and through fat vitality and contribute to a body-becoming pedagogy, which Carla Rice describes as moving "away from enforcing norms toward more creative ways of expanding possibilities for what bodies could become" ("Rethinking" 387).

Thinking with Theory: Moving from Major Themes to Major Moments

From Participants to Photographs: Procedure

Participants were recruited through online advertisements and physical posters located in downtown Toronto and via word of mouth through the primary researcher's networks. The advertisements focused on the recruitment of women (inclusive of cisgender, trans, and gender nonconforming women) who were 18 years of age or older and identified as fat, plus size, thick, or curvy and had been made to feel different as a result of their body size (e.g., negatively labelled as fat, "overweight," "obese," etc.). Participation involved a phone call to determine eligibility, an online orientation to project activities, a consent form process, the collection of demographics, photo taking, and focus group components.

In the project materials and orientation, participants were offered flexibility in terms of what they photographed, with an overall guiding prompt of taking "photos that represent your experiences with and responses to body-related judgments"—several additional prompts were provided (e.g., what is it like to live in your body? How is your body treated by others? When/where do you experience body-related judgments?). For each photograph they took/selected (as some participants opted to include photos taken prior to the project), participants answered a series of questions derived from Wang's SHOWeD method to explain what was really going on in the image and how it could be used to educate people (188). Participants submitted their photos and narratives prior to attending a focus group. The images were then used in the group they attended to prompt discussion. Participants were provided with a CA$25 honorarium and printed copies of their photographs.

Embodying a Range of Identities: Participant Information

Situating the body as the point at which multiple discourses converge, LeBesco asserts, "the body is never just a material reality but also the site of contested discourses about power, health, beauty, nature, race, class, and a bevy of other possibilities" ("Epistemologies" 99). While fatness and the experience of or identification with womanhood were core recruitment criteria for the project, participants embodied a range of identities and experiences that cannot be disconnected from their experiences of gender and size (Rice et al. 180). Recognizing that some participants might feel more comfortable among others who share another salient identity category, three focus group options were made available to participants: one for LGBTQ2S participants (n = 5), one for Indigenous and Black women and women of colour (n = 4), and one general group open to anyone (n = 6). Participants self-selected their group based on identity and preference (or lack of preference). Four participants identified as racialized, with two identifying as East Asian, one as Black Caribbean, and one as Black Caribbean and Indo-Caribbean. The remaining eleven participants identified as white North American, white European, or a combination thereof. Of those eleven, one also identified as Middle Eastern, and another also identified as Jewish. The age of participants ranged from 25 to 54. Participants identified their approximate income as follows: less than $15,000 (n = 1), between $15,000 and $24,999 (n = 4), between $25,000 and $34,999 (n = 4), between $35,000 and $44,000 (n = 1), between $45,000 and $54,999 (n = 1), between $75,000 and $84,999 (n = 2), between $85,000 and $94,999 (n = 1), and $95,000 or higher (n = 1). Living in Toronto was not a requirement; however, since project activities took place in the city, all participants did end up being Toronto residents.

Though the project was not specifically focused on queer experiences, only four participants identified as heterosexual, and, of those, one had indicated in her project eligibility call that she was "straight-ish." While scholars have theorized about the queerness of fat (e.g., LeBesco "Queering"; Pausé et al.) as a characteristic that disrupts normative embodiments, the demographics of the Living Big Lives project revealed a more tangible kinship in that so many participants claimed queer identities. Bisexual and/or pansexual identities were listed by eight participants, with two more identifying as queer and one as "heteroflexible / not entirely straight." Additionally, four participants identified as gender nonconforming. All but three participants described some identification with disability, chronic health challenges, mental health issues, or learning disabilities. This provides the opportunity to consider the co-constitution of fatness with disability in ways that offer insight into what April Herndon described as the ongoing need to explore the "nuances of tying fatness and disability together and its possible consequences" (88), and it looks toward the generative entanglements between fatness and disability—entanglements that Zoë Meleo-Erwin suggests are in need of "queering."

Methodological Approach

In the spirit of exploring emancipatory alternatives to theorizing fatness, I contend that we must "transgress the boundaries of traditional research and scholarship" in the spirit of Leslie Brown and Susan Strega's approach to research as resistance (1). The methods of this project offered insight into participant reflections about their bodies across various timepoints and interactions, through images, written narratives, and group conversation. Participants used the photography process to reflect on their own relationships with their bodies—engaging with the image/experience as they took/selected each photo, as they wrote a narrative to go with each photo, and as each image came up in the focus group they attended. As such, images and experiences were taken up at both individual and collective levels. This lends itself well to a queered reading of the data that resists easy categorization. As Noreen Giffney suggests, "queer theory seeks to allow for complexity and the holding of uncertainties by encouraging the experiencing of states without necessarily trying to understand, dissect, or categorise them" (8). In line with Jen Rinaldi, Carla Rice, and May Friedman, I engage in a thickened analysis that considers "the multiple, dynamic, and complex ways fat may be layered into and muddled with other markers and materialities of identity and difference" ("Introduction" 4). Rather than simply attending to major themes, yielded through processes such as thematic analysis, I attend to what I am calling major moments, when participants collectively explored tensions and possibilities while grappling with concepts, such as beauty and desire, that are typically denied of them. This approach responds to Alecia Jackson's and Lisa Mazzei's criticisms of the ways that traditional data analysis methods that involve coding tend to merely organize data according to core themes rather than spurring in-depth reflection and analysis. Instead, I invoke Jackson's and Mazzei's "willingness to borrow and reconfigure concepts, invent approaches, and create new assemblages that demonstrate a range of analytic practices of thought, creativity, and intervention" (717). This diffractive reading of the data allows for multiple, and at times conflicting, entanglements of theory and meaning making to reveal new lines of inquiry and insight.

Theoretical Framework

It is with queer and crip theories, which have a rich history of valuing non-normative embodiments, that I set out to elucidate a framework for forwarding fat vitality. Crip theory, as described by Robert McRuer, centres disabled experiences and ways of knowing while integrating a queered perspective, aiming to disrupt—as a starting point—both compulsory able-bodiedness and heteronormativity, positioning crip theory as useful in our efforts to challenge the conditions that perpetuate oppression against non-normative embodiments, such as fatness, and thereby to "access alternative ways of being" (42). Scholars such as Zoë Melo-Erwin have drawn on McRuer's work to position fat bodies and disabled bodies within this theoretical landscape. In a virtual round table, McRuer and Merri Lisa Johnson brought together a range of scholars to theorize "cripistemologies" as ways of knowing that bring together queer, trans, critical race, and feminist perspectives. Lisa Duggan articulates this epistemological positioning as

> not a call to *add* disability to an intersectional matrix of race, gender, class, sexuality, nationality, religion ... [but] a call to step aside, provisionally, to imagine theory and politics from the capacious "standpoint" of disability. This

> is a moment in the formulation of new ways of thinking and acting politically, not an endpoint. Disability is not to be separated from other social formations; indeed it cannot be. ... It is a call to intellectual, political, and affective creativity. (McRuer and Johnson 166)

Using queer and crip theories, I follow Donna Haraway's assertion that "perhaps cracking open possibilities for belief in more livable worlds would be the most incisive kind of theory, indeed, even the most scientific kind of undertaking" (63).

(Seeking and) Findings

Engaging in a reading of the data that thickens queer and crip theory to explore fat vitality, I present findings herein that focus on how participants held space for and made sense of the ways their bodies are (de)valued. They navigated topics of beauty, neutrality, desire and desirability, fetishization, and the healing potential of recognition and affirmation.

Coming Home to Our Bodies: Moving toward and away from Beauty

Situating beauty as "an embodied affective process" Rebecca Coleman and Mónica Moreno Figueroa repudiate the ways that the concept is always out of reach, a hopeful aspiration—displaced to the past or deferred to the future—rather than a fixed state (1–2). Certainly, the proximity of fatness to beauty has been similarly temporally bound, in the shame of "before" and the possibility of "after." Participants explored the complexities of both wanting beauty and rejecting the very premise of it—a tension that is characteristic of ongoing debates, both within and outside of academia, about beauty's value. Situating the problem in patriarchy, one participant reflected on how moving away from the need for external validation has been part of their path to healing from being raised in an environment that assigns value based on physical attractiveness:

> Having the experience of being raised in a lookist environment where, especially as a feminine person living in patriarchy, I've been taught that where my value lies is in my physical appearance ... [I'm] trying to do the work of interrogating for myself what the relevance of that is and the role of healing from patriarchy ... [and] moving away from feeling the need to have outside validation of my physical appearance.

As another participant was grappling with their desire for beauty and framing it as a "little problem" (i.e., insignificant) in relation to the obstacles that their disabled children were facing, another participant interjected to say, "both are allowed to exist at the same time. You can hold space for your hurts and for their challenges. ... These are folks who are also wanting to feel beautiful and magnificent in their bodies and are not being given space to." This moment between participants offered a break from binary thinking about bodies, beauty, and pain, making room for both suffering and striving; it is reminiscent of Eliza Chandler and Carla Rice's theorizing about the ways fat and disabled people create "alterities of happiness" wherein "we find beauty, pleasure, and satiation in non-normality while at the same time, hang[ing] on to dull rage and pain within this alterity" (231).

Aware that beauty is supposedly off limits to women with bodies like theirs, some participants were firm in their assertion that they have a claim to it. Participants talked about being given partial access to beauty through backhanded compliments such as "you have such a pretty face." One participant submitted a photograph featuring her body from the neck down with those words scrawled across it and explained,

> This is a definite way of saying, the rest of you doesn't count ... we have to hide all of that. All photos should be from [the neck] up, 'cause no one wants to see the rest of that, but no! The rest of me is part of me. This is all attached. This is how I come. ... I'm more than a pretty face and I think I have a pretty body even if it doesn't conform to what people generally think of as pretty.

Situating fat bodies as worthy of artistic representation, one participant included a photo of a soft sculpture of their naked body that they made for a fat-focused art show. They expressed a desire to "take up space artistically to subvert fat-erasure and challenge the idea that fat bodies are repulsive and ought to be hidden away" and explained that their artwork could be used to educate the general public "by representing fatness as a worthy subject of contemporary artistic representation ... and attractive to the viewers' gaze and touch." Their art affirms Allyson Mitchell's suggestion that fat vitality can be crafted (149), contributing to Rice's articulation of fat aesthetics in which "fat women (and all those decreed to be unbeautiful) might begin to reclaim sensory pleasure and bodily self-celebration in their lives" ("Revisioning" 433).

One participant described the process of coming home to her body, after a day of fat microaggressions, and feeling okay, saying, "when I took this photo [figure 12.1], I was like 'okay, I might not think I'm the most beautiful or have the best body shape but I'm going to take a picture that looks pretty cool... I feel strong and powerful ... I can be okay with myself.'" She articulated the importance of loving and accepting her body and highlighted the need to "take time to get to know our bodies, care for them, and enjoy them." Though she skirted the language of beauty, other participants were quite taken with the image, with some seeing their own bodies reflected in it and others drawing parallels to bodies as landscapes.

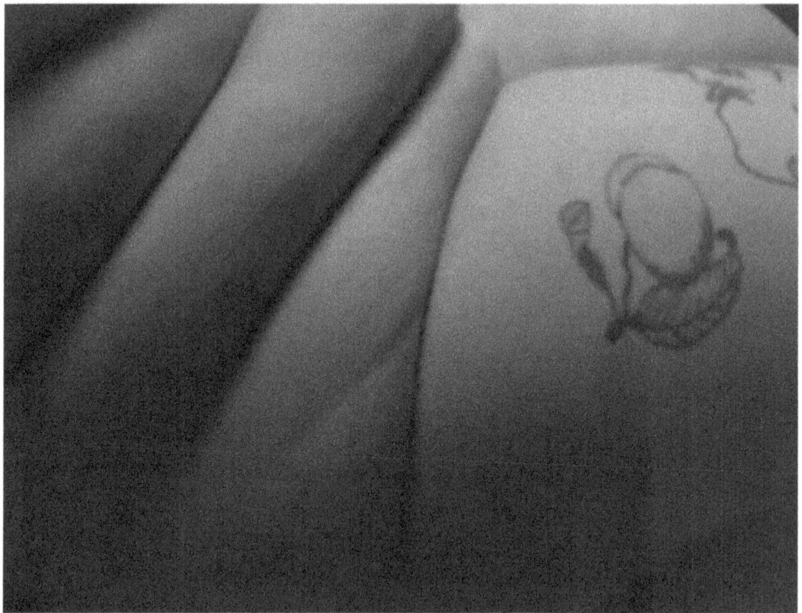

Figure 12.1

Source: Printed with permission; © C. McLeod2019/Living Big Lives Project

Contextualizing their picture (figure 12.2), another participant shared that, as part of their process of radical self-acceptance, they make regular trips to the clothing optional beach, saying

> I feel liberated, free, and beautiful when I'm there. And in that quiet moment, early in the morning, I wanted to see myself. So, with shaking hands, greasy from tanning oil, I lifted my phone over my shoulder and took a picture. And when I looked at the screen, I was in love. I loved everything about this picture. The golden, brown sugar colour of my skin, the full roundness of my ass, the look of the tanning oil, slick and shiny, and even the rolls of fat at the sides of my stomach. I loved all of it. I loved myself totally in that moment, and whenever that self-love wavers, I have this picture to look at and remind myself of my beauty.

Figure 12.2
Source: Printed with permission;
© TheXennialUnicorn2019/Living Big Lives Project

Queerying Fat Desire: Navigation, Fetishization, and Recognition

Referring to a range of non-normative embodiments, including fat, queer, disabled, racialized, and trans bodies, Tomasz Sikora and Dominika Ferens outline the threat that such bodies pose to the established order, noting, "in order to 'stay where their place is' rather than spread uncontrollably like an epidemic, they must remain undesiring and undesirable bodies" (iii). There is power in asserting desirability, evident in the image (figure 12.3) and its accompanying quotation provided by one participant, SpiritDancing, whose words opened this chapter:

> This is an "everyday image." This is She, the who and how she carries herself and demonstrates the power of her being. Taking up her rightful space, authentic and holding her boundaries firm, she exists because she was meant to. This is not an image that is historical, however. This is years of time wearing on and whispering, at times shouting to the spirit within. Nor is it fetishized.

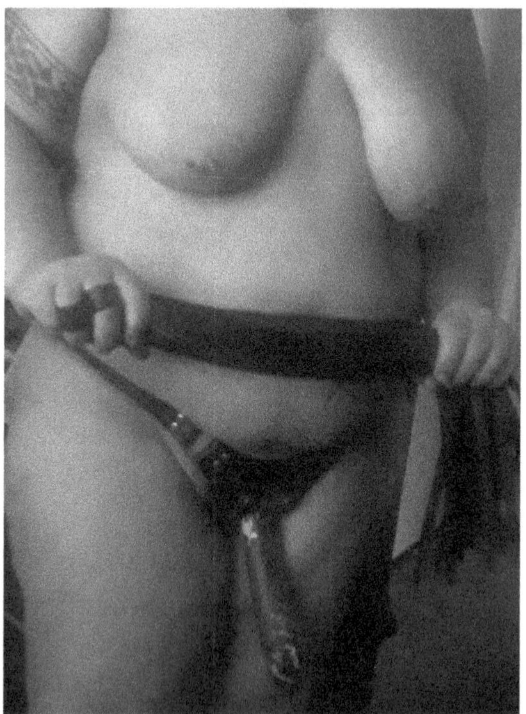

Figure 12.3

Source: Printed with permission; © SpiritDancing2019/Living Big Lives Project

In the focus group she attended, this participant reflected on her conflicted relationship with this photograph, saying "I still don't know if I can stand this picture. I wrote the description in the third person. This is obviously me but isn't me?" She went on to say that, despite her reservations, it was important that this photo be used because of its accuracy—it captures a gender nonconforming woman in her 50s standing resolute in her desirability even if, outside of that moment, she wavers:

> I'm keeping this picture and I'm saying that it can be used because it is accurate. It is a moment of time. It wasn't staged, shall we say, and frankly, I mean, I have someone who says they go weak in the knees when they see this. And I'm looking at it and thinking hmm okay, but I'm slowly ... well it's bigger up there [on the projector screen] isn't it?! Yeah, so this is a picture that is me and it didn't take me much to take the picture but sitting here now, it's taking me a lot to sit with that picture.

Alison Kafer describes a kind of compulsory nostalgia that is ascribed to both fat people and disabled people, as neither are "permitted to exist as part of a desired present or desirable future" (43); rather, they are expected to aspire to thin, able-bodied existence. The image in figure 12.3 offers an affirmation of desire/desiring that is fixed in time, despite the hesitancy of the photographer outside of that moment. Tensions around desirability were not uncommon, as one participant provided context for the ideas they feel are communicated about fat people and desire, which they named as "this feeling like you're not allowed to feel desire for others or to be desired." In the focus group specifically for LGBTQ2S people, one participant took the opportunity to reflect on their attraction to "big women" with the caveat that, despite this desire, they feel awkward in their own fat body, asking others in the group if that made sense. Many in the group affirmed these contradictory feelings and shared that their feelings and assumptions about how their bodies are perceived by other women affects their ability to act on their desires or to accept themselves as subjects of desire. One woman described how being intimate with another fat woman helped her to understand her own desirability:

> She's laying on top of me ... I have my legs kind of wrapped around her ... and I have this big beautiful soft round body on top of me and we weren't even really intimately touching but I had an orgasm just from having her on top of me because it felt so fucking phenomenal but I needed that moment to really go "this is what everyone

> else feels when they're with me" and I couldn't relate to it because even as far as I've come—I love my body even when there are times when I don't like parts of it. I love my body and I'm a slutty little goddess and I have sex all the time—I couldn't truly understand all the way why would someone want to be with me, what was it about my body, when I had that moment with her on top of me I went "oh yeah okay now I understand."

This harkens to what Kafer and Leah Lakshmi Piepzna-Samarasinha have separately named as the lust of recognition in relation to crip and queer desire. Piepzna-Samarasinha in conversation with E.T. Russian describes the connection and healing that come when you recognize an aspect of yourself—be it race, disability, or shared trauma—in a sexual partner and experience heightened desire in relation to having that part of yourself understood (117). Here, we see the potential in extending this concept to fatness. Another participant explained that they had to come to value their own fat body as desirable before they could fully understand and solidify their own multi-gender attractions. They explained how this process is intertwined with their own internalized fat oppression:

> My multi-gender attraction was real and it didn't solidify for me until I started to value my own fat body as desirable and attractive. ... I wasn't able to recognize my attraction to specifically feminine people until I recognized that I'm predominantly attracted to Fat Femmes. ... with regard to my identity as a queer person in regards to relationships, it similarly has taken a really long time to like actually understand myself as desirable and something that I still—even though I would definitely categorize myself as an angry rad fatty—I still have a lot of trouble actually conceptualizing for myself ... it's been this really weird kind of like disconnect between my political ideology and my strong assertion and belief that bodies are beautiful and desirable and then like how I still have all this fat oppression, and stigma still lives within me.

The rejection of fetishization was strong across participants, with several commenting that they were not interested in pursuing relationships with people who were only interested in them for their bodies. This was described by one participant as "a balance between the people who fetishize you and the people who fucking adore you." This adoration, or appreciation of the body, was described as healing: "having like a partner now who just like loves my body and will compliment how my belly looks, or who will want to touch my belly when we're cuddling and do those sort of things is so amazing and healing." The healing nature of this kind of affirmation was noted by another participant, who described how it felt to be with a partner who embraced every part of them:

> I was queer and fat before I was disabled. So, I found that I had more space for that piece of identity and then like as soon as disability played into it there was like no space for all of that to exist together so I kind of had to start like picking and choosing what part of me would be in the room ... that was the first time I ever fucked in my wheelchair. And I felt so seen after that experience because that was the first person who had seen me like fully and engaged with my whole personhood and nobody tells you [that] you can do that. That was so amazing ... making our own spaces as queer crips, as fat queer crips, is so healing.

Participants described the ins and outs of navigating desirability within the cultures and communities they were a part of. Reflecting on the queer dating scene, some described it as more inclusive and less judgmental of body size, while others named a disconnect between politics and actual dating practices with some fat women describing being excluded. At the intersection of race, culture, and desirability, one participant talked about how she feels more comfortable dating men who share her racial and cultural background because she views them as more accepting of her size, but she noted that they would say things like "you're not fat, you're thick!" or "you've got fat in the right places!" She explained this, saying, "in Caribbean culture there's an obsession with thick women but they have to be small in the right places, and they're not supposed to have rolls." Picking up on that notion, another participant, who described herself as a multi-island person, highlighted gender differences in how fatness is received, echoing Caribbean men's appreciation of fat in particular places and contrasting it with being fat shamed by the women in her family: "they say you're getting too fat but then it's like, you should be fat and thick. I think that's a bit of colonialism filtering through there, being ashamed of our bodies, being ashamed of our hair, it went down the line." E-K Daufin cautions us to "consider intersectional, internalized oppression and social context" in taking up Black women's experiences of weight stigma, and to not treat their experience as monolith (162). While experiences vary depending on how fat individuals are situated, Hunter A. Shackelford contends that "any and everyone who navigates and exists within fatness as a spectrum is by proxy experiencing the violence of anti-Blackness (the hunt to kill Blackness/abundance) ... the difference in non-Black people being fat means that there is still a humanization and legibility that comes with that embodiment" (255).

The intersection of race, culture, and context is apparent in the shifting ways that women's body sizes are read and reacted to depending on their geopolitical location and on what frameworks and discourses are being drawn on by those that are viewing them. One participant expressed frustration with her experiences of North American men who fetishize her by saying, "ohh an Asian woman with curves!" while another agreed, saying "we exist!" and contrasted this kind of fetishization with her family's focus on the thin ideal as exemplified in Chinese media and pageant culture and the resulting ways her body is disparaged.

Discussion: Reclamation, Rejection, and Recognition

Taken together, what do these images and accounts offer us? Moments fixed in time but also brimming with present and future possibilities. The Living Big Lives project not only opened up space for participants to reflect on their experiences of body-related judgments but also offered opportunities for joy and connection.

Throughout the project, several participants commented on how rare it was for them to gather with other fat people. In *Body Outlaws*, Nomy Lamm asserts, "I truly believe that redefining the terms of beauty, sexuality, and attractiveness is a simple and vastly rewarding act, and I feel sorry for people who have so little imagination that they just do what they're told" (80), though she points out that this attitude is easier to maintain when she is safely within the boundaries of a community of other "freaks" like her. While most participants were meeting each other for the first time, there was an openness to being vulnerable with one another that yielded rich discussions on beauty, desirability, and recognition.

In their research on fat women's experiences of beauty, Lauren Gurrieri and Hélène Cherrier called for the "opening up [of] spaces that embrace the fat body as one of multiple possibilities for beauty. This embracement of bodies should ... aid the visibility of manifold bodies that disrupt and challenge the 'straight' ideal" (292). Participants in the Living Big Lives project approached the idea of beauty from a variety of perspectives, ranging from tentative consideration to outright rejection or reclamation. At times, they challenged each other's approach to (de)valuing the concept, as was evident in the exchange between two participants detailed above where one situated beauty as trivial in relation to the challenges her disabled children face and another countered that both her and her children deserve access to the space to feel magnificent and beautiful. Another participant positioned the validation of their physical appearance as mired in patriarchal expectations and expressed a desire to move away from it.

This aligns with Hurst's caution against interventions that "represent fatness as worthy by aligning fat bodies with prevailing ideals of beauty, ability, whiteness, class, heteronormativity, and femininity" (172). Connecting to disability justice scholarship, I am reminded of Mia Mingus's call to move away from beauty and desirability and embrace the ugly and magnificent instead. So how do we reconcile these tensions? Is there value to beauty? To desirability? Or, as Coleman and Moreno Figueroa query, is there "a way of thinking differently—more hopefully—about the experience of beauty?" (20). Bringing fatness into the frame in conversations about beauty and attractiveness is, indeed, a way of thinking differently about these concepts. Fatness does not, cannot, "fit in" to beauty ideals as they are currently upheld. Rather than fitting in, a more hopeful approach could involve breaking open the category altogether. In attempting to forward an articulation of disability aesthetics that is grounded in interdependence, Jacqueline White calls on us to do away with the binary between ugly and beautiful and work collectively to "dismantle the systems that maintain the ranks of the privileged and open up space for vital connected crip futures" (140). This relational approach to aesthetics and beauty makes room for the mess of contradictions and solidarities that emerged among participants.

On the point of desirability, McRuer and Wilkinson call on us to engage in "practices that would work to realize a world of multiple (desiring and desirable) corporealities interacting in nonexploitative ways ... [offering] a recognition that another world can exist in which an incredible variety of bodies and minds are valued" (14). Recognition was central to desire/desiring in this project—participants described the importance of recognition in their intimate relationships and seized the opportunity to learn more about and find affirmation of their own desires through conversations with each other.

As Rachel Hurst points out, "there is a radical kernel of intersectional possibility to disrupt normativity in photographing fatness, precisely because this practice fixes fat in time and does not aspire to a thin future" (171). While participants themselves may have wavered in their certainty about their desire/desirability, the photographs they took serve as temporal anchors and are useful for not only the subjects of the photographs but also fellow participants and broader audiences engaging with this project. It is noteworthy that, in many cases, participants made the aesthetic decision to frame their photos from the neck down. This visual strategy, when used to promote moral panic around the "obesity epidemic" is described by Charlotte Cooper as the "headless fatty effect" and serves to dehumanize fat people. Here, participants appeared to use this framing to look upon their own bodies or to capture and hold the gaze of the viewer and to insist upon a reading of their bodies on their own terms.

The atmosphere of each focus group was one of connection and a collective sigh of relief. This echoes findings from fellow Canadian scholar Katie Cook (this volume), who identifies the power and potential in fat people both bearing witness to each other's trauma and orienting toward fat joy and liberation. I contend that the act of bringing together these groups was/is integral to the actualization of fat vitality. What I describe in the final section is an attempt to capture the essence of what was felt, experienced, and made possible in these spaces.

Fat Vitality: An Unfinished Map of Possibilities

In their edited collection, *Thickening Fat*, Rinaldi, Rice, and Friedman call for "a distinctly cultural, material, and intersectional approach to fatness—one that affirms fat's agency and vitality, and also acknowledges the pains and perils of embodying fatness at this historical and cultural moment" ("Introduction" 4). Aiming not only to document the lived experiences of fat women but to carve out space for the development of fat culture and community, the Living Big Lives project revealed the power and potential of co-creating fat vitality, offering both a theorization of and step toward its actualization. Rather than a set, prescribed path, fat vitality is an unfinished map of possibilities, ripe for play and exploration.

Fat vitality evades fixedness—it does not demand positivity or insist upon consensus. It recognizes the danger in recreating a new normal and essentializing experience. As Charlotte Cooper and Samantha Murray point out "our experiences—as they are imagined, perceived and lived—are multiple, contingent, contextual and ambiguous ... enabling the multiple voices and narratives that constitute fat lived experience has critical, political value" (132). As we map the possibilities fat vitality offers, we must be mindful of the limitations of considering fatness in isolation. Shackelford highlights the potential in mobilizing an "afrofuturistic" lens to address anti-Blackness "in the cartographies ... of abundance" whereby "freeing fatness is freeing Blackness is freeing abundance" (254–56). Fat vitality resists endpoints; instead, fat vitality is part of the ever-evolving project of a body becoming pedagogy, which, as Rice remarked is not "instrumental and outcomes driven ... [but rather] presence and process oriented, interested in body-affirming images and spaces and in expanding possibilities for bodily becoming" ("Revisioning" 432). Perhaps fat vitality could offer what beauty has withheld —the opportunity to be valued, desired, and to belong.

Ramanpreet Bahra pointed out that "the life of the fat body is always examined and re-evaluated based on what a 'normal,' 'healthy' body is within the normalizing society we live in" (194). Fat vitality pushes back against these constant comparisons. Instead, a fat vitality perspective looks to the fullness in fatness and the ways we carve out a space, not just for fat bodies but for all, that is free from aspirational ideals that harm more than they heal. Drawing on Meleo-Erwin's conception of "an ethos of bodily difference and interdependence [that] is important not just to fat people but for all people," I contend that fat vitality contributes to the project of "dismantling ... the social, cultural, and political-economic conditions and structures that create inequality and oppression in the first place" (109). In tandem with following Meleo-Erwin's call to embrace a range of contradictory experiences, we can

> make space in our scholarship and our movements for a broad range of experiences that need not be seen as necessarily contradictory: the suffering involved in embodying an outsider status, the seductive pull of normal, the pleasure involved in a moment of transgression, the sadness that results from being excluded, the pain and the messiness of our bodies, the ambivalence and fear we sometimes feel about them, the rage we feel at being denied our humanity, the strength of our desires, and the pleasures our bodies bring to ourselves and others. (Meleo-Erwin 109)

Conclusion

The Living Big Lives project contributes to the rich tapestry that is fat studies in Canada, engaging with and building upon the theorizing of interdisciplinary scholars who are thickening fat. In closing, I offer further lines of inquiry, raising questions to explore. Here are some of the questions opened up in the Living Big Lives project. How can fat vitality facilitate access to various ways of knowing, being, and moving through the world where one body is not privileged over another? How do we expand the erotic imagination to be more inclusive of and excited about body diversity generally, and fatness specifically? What role do images play in widening the gaze? How does the gathering together of fat and other non-normative bodies contribute to the actualization of fat vitality? Additionally, I echo questions raised by Le'a Kent, which is to say, what are the effects of fat women claiming beauty, and how does resisting abjection enable fat women to "begin to have a body thought valuable in the present" (131)?

Situating this work within the broader struggle for disability justice, the images and stories brought together through the Living Big Lives project offer a vital contribution toward the imagining and creation of "a world where all bodies and minds are recognized and treated as valuable and beautiful" (Sins Invalid 68). To be clear, this project is not about a yearning for normalcy; it is about imagining and exploring new, liveable worlds. It is about widening the lens we use to look at ourselves and each other. It is about the flesh and the figurative. It is about beauty and monstrosity, pleasure and pain, desire and desiring, and the infinite possibilities that can open up when we step outside of the systems that denigrate us and deny us access to vitality.

Works Cited

Abel, Samantha. *Fat Chat: An Exploration of Obesity Discourses in Canadian Media and Their Impacts on Social Work*. 2012. Toronto Metropolitan University. Major research paper in partial fulfilment of MSW.

Bordo, Susan. *Unbearable Weight: Feminism, Western Culture, and the Body*. University of California Press, 2003.

Bahra, Ramanpreet A. "'You Can Only Be Happy If You're Thin!' Normalcy, Happiness, and the Lacking Body." *Fat Studies*, vol. 7, no. 2, 2018, pp. 193–202.

Brown, Leslie Allison, and Susan Strega. *Research as Resistance: Critical, Indigenous and Anti-Oppressive Approaches*. Canadian Scholars' Press, 2005.

Chandler, Eliza, and Carla Rice. "Alterity In/Of Happiness: Reflecting on the Radical Possibilities of Unruly Bodies." *Health, Culture and Society*, vol. 5, no. 1, 2013, pp. 230–48.

Coleman, Rebecca, and Mónica Moreno Figueroa. "Past and Future Perfect? Beauty, Affect and Hope." *Journal for Cultural Research*, vol. 14, no. 4, 2010, pp. 357–73.

Cooper, Charlotte. "Headless Fatties." 2007. *Dr Charlotte Cooper*, http://charlottecooper.net/fat/headless-fatties-01–07/. Accessed 16 April 2021.

Cooper, Charlotte, and Samantha Murray. "Fat Activist Community: A Conversation Piece." *Somatechnics*, vol. 2, no. 1, 2012, pp. 127–38.

Daufin, E-K. "Thick Sistahs and Heavy Disprivilege: Black Women, Intersectionality, and Weight Stigma." *Thickening Fat: Fat Bodies, Intersectionality, and Social Justice*, edited by May Friedman, Carla Rice, and Jen Rinaldi, Routledge, 2019, pp. 160–70.

Giffney, Noreen. "Introduction: The 'Q' Word." *The Ashgate Research Companion to Queer Theory*, edited by Noreen Giffney and Michael O'Rourke, Ashgate Publishing, 2009, pp. 1–13.

Gurrieri, Lauren, and Hélène Cherrier. "Queering Beauty: Fatshionistas in the Fatosphere." *Qualitative Market Research: An International Journal*, vol. 16, no. 3, 2013, pp. 276–295.

Haraway, Donna J. "A Game of Cat's Cradle: Science Studies, Feminist Theory, Cultural Studies." *Configurations*, vol. 2, no. 1, 1994, pp. 59–71.

Herndon, April. "Fatness and Disability: Law, Identity, Co-Constructions, and Future Directions." *Routledge International Handbook of Fat Studies*, edited by Cat Pausé and Sonya Renee Taylor, Routledge, 2021, pp. 88–100.

Hladki, Janice. "Fat Politics Photography: The Stareable Body and 'Openings' for Social Justice." *InTensions,* vol. 8, 2016, pp. 1–30.

Hurst, Rachel A. J. "Photographing Fatness: Resisting Assimilation through Fat Activist Calendars." *Thickening Fat: Fat Bodies, Intersectionality, and Social Justice,* edited by May Friedman, Carla Rice, and Jen Rinaldi, Routledge, 2019, pp. 171–82.

Jackson, Alecia Y., and Lisa A. Mazzei. "Thinking with Theory: A New Analytic for Qualitative Inquiry." *The SAGE Handbook of Qualitative Research*, edited by Norman K. Denzin and Yvonna Lincoln, SAGE Publishing, 2017, pp. 717–37.

Kafer, Alison. *Feminist, Queer, Crip*. Indiana University Press, 2013.

Kent, Le'a. "Fighting Abjection: Representing Fat Women." *Bodies Out of Bounds: Fatness and Transgression,* edited by Jana Evans Braziel and Kathleen LeBesco, University of California Press, 2001, pp. 130–50.

Lamm, Nomy. "Fishnets, Feather Boas, and Fat." *Body Outlaws: Young Women Write about Body Image and Identity*, edited by Ophira Edut, Seal Press, 2000, pp. 78–87.

LeBesco, Kathleen. "Epistemologies of Fatness: The Political Contours of Embodiment in Fat Studies." *Corpus: An Interdisciplinary Reader on Bodies and Knowledge*, edited by Monica J. Casper and Paisely Currah, Palgrave, 2011, pp. 95–108.

———. "Queering Fat Bodies/Politics." *Bodies Out of Bounds: Fatness and Transgression*, edited by Jana Evans Braziel and Kathleen LeBesco, University of California Press, 2001, pp. 74–87.

———. *Revolting Bodies?: The Struggle to Redefine Fat Identity*. University of Massachusetts Press, 2004.

McRuer, Robert. *Crip Theory: Cultural Signs of Queerness and Disability.* NYU press, 2006.

McRuer, Robert, and Merri Lisa Johnson. "Proliferating Cripistemologies: A Virtual Roundtable." *Journal of Literary & Cultural Disability Studies,* vol. 8, no. 2, 2014, pp. 149–69.

McRuer, Robert, and Abby L. Wilferson. "Introduction." *GLQ: A Journal of Lesbian and Gay Studies*, vol. 9. no. 1–2, 2003, pp. 1–23.

Meleo-Erwin, Zoë. "Queering the Linkages and Divergences: The Relationship between Fatness and Disability and the Hope for a Livable World." *Queering Fat Embodiment,* edited by Cat Pausé, Jackie Wykes, and Samantha Murray, Routledge, 2014, pp. 97–114.

Mingus, Mia. "Moving Toward the Ugly: A Politic Beyond Desirability." *Leaving Evidence*, 22 Aug. 2011, https://leavingevidence.wordpress.com/2011/08/22/moving-toward-the-ugly-a-politic-beyond-desirability/. Accessed 20 January 2021.

Mitchell, Allyson. "Sedentary Lifestyle: Fat Queer Craft." *Fat Studies*, vol. 7, no. 2, 2018, pp. 147–58.

Norman, Moss E., Genevieve Rail, and Shannon Jette. "Screening The Un-Scene: Deconstructing The (Bio) Politics of Story Telling in a Canadian Reality Makeover Weight Loss Series." *Obesity in Canada*. University of Toronto Press, 2018, pp. 342–72.

Pausé, Cat, Jackie Wykes, and Samantha Murray. *Queering Fat Embodiment*. Routledge, 2016.

Piepzna-Samarasinha, Leah Lakshmi. *Care Work: Dreaming Disability Justice*. Arsenal Pulp Press, 2018.

Rice, Carla. "Rethinking Fat: From Bio- to Body-Becoming Pedagogies." *Cultural Studies? Critical Methodologies,* vol. 15, no. 5, 2015, pp. 387–97.

———. "Revisioning Fat: From Enforcing Norms to Exploring Possibilities Unique to Different Bodies." *Obesity in Canada: Critical Perspectives*, edited by Jenny Ellison, Deborah McPhail, and Wendy Mitchinson, University of Toronto Press, 2016, pp. 419–39.

Rice, Carla, et al. "Bodies at the Intersections: Refiguring Intersectionality through Queer Women's Complex Embodiments." *Signs: Journal of Women in Culture and Society,* vol. 46, no. 1, 2020, pp. 177–200.

Rinaldi, Jen, et al. "Fatness and Failing Citizenship." *Somatechnics,* vol. 7, no. 2, 2017, pp. 218–33.

Rinaldi, Jen, et al. "Introduction." *Thickening Fat: Fat Bodies, Intersectionality, and Social Justice*, edited by May Friedman, Carla Rice, and Jen Rinaldi, Routledge, 2019, pp. 1–12.

Shackelford, Hunter Ashleigh. "When You Are Already Dead: Black Fat Being as Afrofuturism." *Routledge International Handbook of Fat Studies*, edited by Cat Pausé and Sonya Renee Taylor, Routledge, 2021, pp. 253–57.

Sikora, Tomasz, and Dominika Ferens. "Introduction: Let's Talk about (Crip) Sex." *InterAlia: A Journal of Queer Studies,* vol. 10, no. a, 2015, pp. i–ix.

Sins Invalid. *Skin, Tooth, and Bone—The Basis of Movement Is Our People: A Disability Justice Primer*. Sins Invalid, 2019.

Wang, Caroline C. "Photovoice: A Participatory Action Research Strategy Applied to Women's Health." *Journal of Women's Health*, vol. 8, no. 2, 1999, pp. 185–92.

White, Jacqueline. "Towards a Relational Aesthetic in Disability Art: Interdependence and Crip Futurity." *Knots: An Undergraduate Journal of Disability Studies*, vol. 3, 2017, pp.133–43.

Lines to Myself

Mars

<snowsuit>

recess
Always wanted to love winter
But it mostly meant
Discomfort and
shame

"That's a heavy suit"
they mean body

It fits snug —
my favourite colours yet
betray me
Squeak *unwelcome*
The snow-pants
Laughter *mocking me*
Every
Step
outside
I would push myself to
wear less layers
start exposing hands
Or face *freezing*

                                        to keep from
looking like *I was*
                                                            over   heating

Struggling with **fat**
                                                          I was told   "Use it to insulate"

                                                          from?
Frost, and the sting of ridicule
                                                          teasing
Forcing myself to
Form snowballs
                                        Bare   handed

Unthrown fists full
Snow melting   hands red,
                    eyes biting—

                                        remember
I was chubby first
                    a child second

always   wanted   to
find the feeling of
                                                          loving winter
Snow *crunched* under boots,
                    crystal sheets in the sunset

just imagine
                                                                                        comfort *in my body*
                    wear the same layers
Squeak   only *welcome*
                                                                                        Laughter from we
As any other
                    — as any child

"snowsuit"

<exist>

What weight harder to carry
Than guilt and shame existing
Solely getting through to the next
Stage of living performance
Anxiety
                    Remember my lines
                    no hesitating

Climbing steps, anticipating
Desperate to hasten crossing the boundary, lest

Everywhere I am I think
What space will I fill
So much I'll draw
Disgust and derision tangible
          Assumptions I've spilled into
          Most spaces, grossly palpable
Should I dare sit between people
Be seen, felt, perceived

From strangers, at least—
Usually,   it's just
In my mind but occasionally
They too let it out
Rage their detest or
          concern over my body

Like they owe me their opinions

My body
That trembles and transforms
Restless for peace to exist whole—

Whichever way I end
Up dialling, fatter or thinner
The rules will change
To confine me to a body
That they still get to dictate
Distaste grows whilst
                    My appetite *slipped away*

Tragically ages gone, forsaken

There's no forgetting
Of family with their love
Demanding my being smaller:
          Consume less but achieve more
Cinched between the table, wall,
a number
          goal and failure

Spurned perfection
Had a voice higher than expected
Growing louder than convention allows while
          Unable to ask for love

My breath held gut   Contorted
My thighs and stomach   become too much
My legs soft, sturdy   *yet*
                    Perhaps it was just   fear
                    I would grow too large—
                    Felt my body want to shoot
                    Up higher than I
                    Could—sustain your
                    Disappointment
Throat remains constricted   Not enough,
space disappears as does
The jury observing my dissonance
Crowded subway, family Gathering
 To a vision   *clearly*

They're despondent while
I'm disengaging from   each
Moment, connection, *acceptance* of my fatness
Where no beauty or strength or love could be allowed or seen
                                        Foot hits the ground

Realize I'm left   stranded
In a trial of my own by standing   still
Can't wait to feel time passing

Waste of time, food, will, way
Waist down to empty, nothing, hollow
Wasted away

and they were happy to see

Darting eyes hurriedly
Desperate to decide
                What space can I fill...?

Jutted forward
                Mind needs to escape
                        a riddle

Theft of my footing
                        left falling

Can I ask now

How do you love what's left me
more than what's left of me?

Take a step —

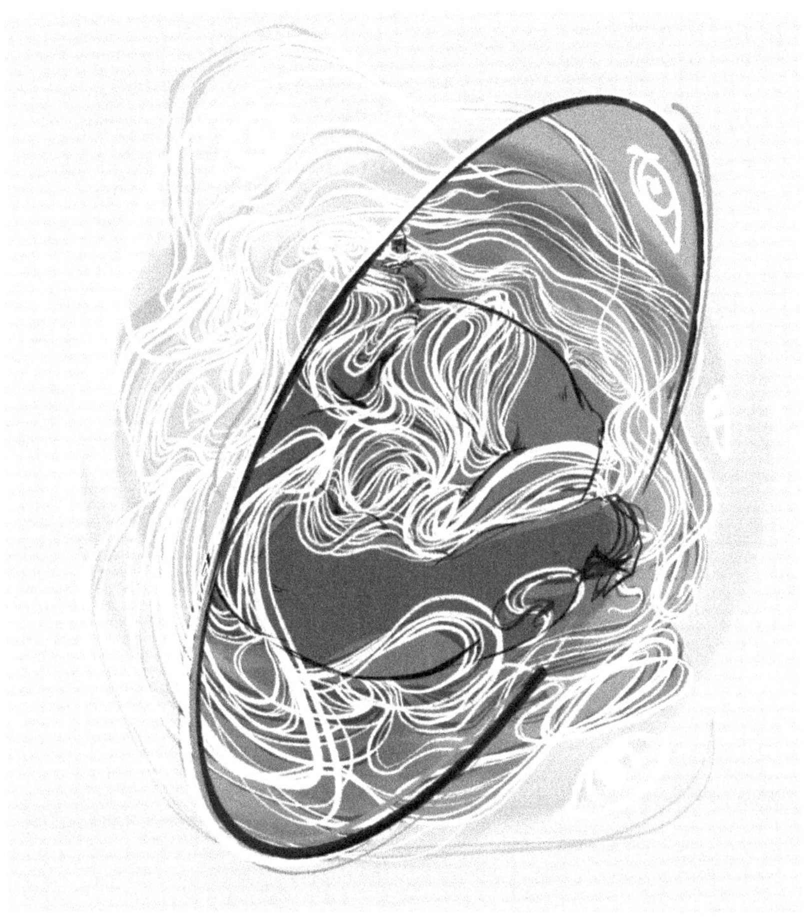

"exist"

FATTENING POPULAR CULTURE

Explosive Fatness

Leslie Walters

FAT BODIES ARE RARELY INCLUDED in the media. When 95 per cent of the people in the images we see daily have body types that less than 2 per cent of the population have, it creates a destructive dissonance. This image is about the distortion that occurs when we try to see our bodies as they are and the resulting fury and frustration with both the world and the self.

"I'd Wish to Be Tall and Slender": L. M. Montgomery's Anne Series and the Regulatory Role of Slimness

Emily Bruusgaard

Anne of Green Gables and Anti-Fatness

Anne of Green Gables has been a Canadian cultural icon almost from its first appearance in print in 1908 (Gerson 18). In the introduction to her biography of Lucy Maud Montgomery, Mary Henley Rubio argues that the novel was not written solely for children but aimed more generally at an audience of male and female readers of all ages, and that it appealed to "famous statesmen as much as to ordinary people" (2). Because of the popularity of *Anne*, aggressive marketing and branding by L. C. Page, and the intense public demand for more of her, Montgomery eventually published seven books in the series between 1909 and 1939 (Gerson 20). By the time of her death in 1942, Montgomery was a celebrity at home and abroad: she was the most well-known and beloved author in Canada, and her books were read all over the English-speaking world, as well as translated and distributed in many more languages. As Rita Bode and Jean Mitchell point out, critical studies of Montgomery in the last forty years have established her importance as a subject for scholarly pursuit, not just for her depictions of Canadian girlhood and womanhood but also for her role in the development of Canada's national culture (12–13).

The enduring popular image of the passionate, faithful friendship between Anne Shirley and Diana Barry in *Anne of Green Gables* might make it surprising to some readers that almost every interaction between Anne and Diana in the first and subsequent novels is bookended by discussions of weight.

In *Anne of Avonlea* (1909), when asked for her ultimate wish, teenaged Diana wishes to be "tall and slender" like Anne (122). On a picnic in *Anne of Ingleside* (1939), chronologically the sixth book but published last, a fatter, older Diana repeatedly envies Anne's continuing slimness after six pregnancies, while simultaneously eating a second and third piece of chocolate cake (12–13). In each of these interactions, Diana expresses her envy of Anne's figure and natural grace, her fear of becoming fat like the women of her father's family, and her desire for approval from Anne.

Despite the increasing visibility of fat studies in Canada, the historical depiction and construction of fat in Canadian literature remain underexamined. Yet anti-fatness as a contemporary cultural construct comes from *somewhere*. Why do we assume that "compulsory slimness is a modern imposition" (Rogers 19)? Elise Paradis argues that health and illness are "actively and socially constructed," and a disease does not officially exist until it is legitimated and categorized as "real" by the cultural authority of medicine (57). Joyce L. Huff argues likewise that although the fat body generally became a locus of moral panic and medical intervention, and was often stigmatized in the mid-Victorian era, fat was not yet defined by one hegemonic voice the way that it is today (Huff 42). Somewhere between a mid-nineteenth century disgust with fatness and the late twentieth-century "war on obesity," public social and medical discourses conspired to medicalize the diversity of the human body. Wendy Mitchinson argues that this change—to a medical model of "obesity"—emerged in Canada in the 1920s, around the same time that slenderness became the dominant image of a modern, young, healthy body (119). Fat became evidence for, and proof of, genetic and personal failure.

The Construction of the White, Female Canadian Citizen

I argue that Montgomery's concern with fatness in the *Anne of Green Gables* series is not accidental and that the popularity of her novels aided in entrenching and normalizing the idealization of slimness while at the same time valorizing a particularly

Canadian white imperial feminism. Through the course of the novels, slimness and idealized femininity become inextricably intertwined. As Elena-Levy Navarro has demonstrated, a cultural obsession with fat has a long and complex history: it is intertwined with the problems of modernity, the rise of consumer capitalism, the growth of empire and nation-state, and the nexuses of race, gender, and class in the outgrowths of industrialization. She insists that critical fat studies must look back to the ways that history "plays a strong, regulatory role in making fat a failed identity, mired in an antiquated past, and thin a normative one, placed in an elusive, utopian future" (Navarro 5). Literature also has a role in both anticipating these cultural shifts and reiterating the beliefs that underlay them. As Jessica Murray insists, fat is still widely regarded as the physical manifestation of a "shamefully failed" femininity, and anti-fatness works to shape the reality of all women in ways that are "profoundly gendered" (100). Minimizing or ignoring early Canadian literary depictions of anti-fatness glosses over the ways that slimness is enfolded into the privileges of citizenship in the modern Canadian nation-state.

In post-Confederation Canada, Mariana Valverde insists, femininity was white, middle class, and inextricable from the idea of national "character." A "golden future" for Canada rested on social and moral self-control, in which "some women were given the possibility of acquiring a relatively powerful identity as rescuers, reformers, and even experts, while other women were reduced to being objects of philanthropic concern" (Valverde 29). Social and moral self-control became inextricable from physical self-mastery; and physical and sexual hygiene were the "microcosmic foundation of the larger project of building a 'clean' nation" (Valverde 28). It should not be surprising, then, that a concern for physical hygiene also begins to include the policing and regulation of body size through nutrition and exercise in the twentieth century. As Mitchinson argues, while "obesity" increasingly became a medical subject, studied in medical journals and marketed in the form of weight-loss equipment and remedies, popular media also began using the slim, white, middle-class body to attract consumers (51–54). Anne and Diana's bodies are positioned at a turning point in white, Canadian, female identity, one where the right to an education and career is both pitted against motherhood and subsumed into narratives of maternal feminism and eugenics and where women's suffrage is aligned into the future of empire and the Canadian nation-state. As young, white, Anglo women, they have to prove their worthiness in Canada's future.

Cecily Devereux has argued that the *Anne* series, like Nellie McClung's *Sowing Seeds in Danny* (1908), reiterates tropes of progress, civilization, and racial dominance that propelled maternal feminism and were inextricably tied to colonialist and imperial expansion in Canada in the early part of the twentieth century. As a white woman, Anne's regulatory role as the "mother of the race," Devereux insists, is to reproduce and promote imperial white motherhood, whereby raising children (first as a teacher, then as a mother) is both destiny and reward. Her marriage to Gilbert Blythe, the doctor, an occupation "always invested with especial value in expansionist fiction as an arbiter of social and moral as well as physical hygiene," ensures a union in which both partners work together towards both race regeneration and instruction (263). In this sense, Anne's slender figure becomes Valverde's normative white female body, aligned with wholesomeness, progress, and the dream of a "Canadian" tomorrow.

But what about Diana? If Anne is the "mother of the race" whose value is in reproducing and instructing the nation, what are we to make of Diana Barry? As both Devereux and Mitchinson insist, much of the blame for childhood malnutrition and, by extension, the "racial degeneracy" of heart conditions, weak lungs, and other physical impairments resulting from undernourishment, particularly following the Boer and First World War, was placed on mothers (Devereux 260; Mitchinson 38). Kind-hearted, generous Diana also becomes a mother, with two sons and a daughter, Anne Cordelia, who closely resembles her friend (*Anne of Ingleside* 6). Diana also comes from "good stock," and her marriage to Fred Wright solidifies her position in the community. Diana and Anne give every appearance of having the kind of lasting female friendship Temma F. Berg has suggested most women long for (39). Yet Diana never leads; she is always

Anne's devoted follower and faithful lieutenant. By the end of *Anne of Green Gables* and in all the subsequent novels, Diana's weight is a constant source of discussion.

Diana's ever-fatter presence does more than simply foreground Anne's slimness. Anne goes to school when Diana does not. Anne has a creative spark, imagination, and foresight, that Diana also does not possess. Anne is a problem solver, with a "real knacky" way with babies, as Devereux points out (264). Underneath Anne and Diana's friendship is a dynamic that presages contemporary narratives about fat, failure, and individual responsibility. Anne's imagination and creativity become aligned with self-regulation. Diana's greed and lack of self-control, the stories suggest, both contribute to her weight gain and are the underlying conditions of her moral inferiority. Anne's slimness becomes intertwined with all the virtues that make Anne "special." Diana remains provincial as Anne becomes more outward looking, and yet it is Anne who espouses the Protestant valorization of early poverty, rural living, and diligent work. Diana, who is merry, round, and hyper-feminized, becomes associated with an outmoded Victorian womanhood; Anne's "slim girlishness" and "starry eyes," with a new, more outward-looking, ostensibly "Canadian" womanhood, which at the same time remains innocent and uncorrupted by all of the travails of modernity. Anne becomes the impossible, ideal, future white Canadian: svelte, attractive, maternal, capable, as well as educated, imaginative, and clever. She has a modern outlook on parenting while at the same time is committed to rural living and a rural identity. Diana becomes a relic of the Victorian past who fails to meet the challenges of the modern nation-state, and her fat body is portrayed as an obstacle to the future. As she fails to control her own body, the logic goes, she will also fail to control her children's.

Fat Bodies, Thin Bodies in *Anne of Green Gables*

Montgomery's concern with fatness in many ways anticipates medical consternation over "obesity." Mitchinson argues that, starting in the early twentieth century but particularly after World War I, Canadian physicians were consumed with familial nutrition and how to ensure that infants and children were well nourished (27). By the 1920s, maternal mortality counted four deaths a day, with many caused by malnutrition (Mitchinson 37). It was around this time, she insists, that the medical establishment turned to the issue of fat as an issue of health and "overnutrition." From the beginning of *Anne of Green Gables*, while 11-year-old Anne also understands "skinny" as negative, fat is already normalized as undesirable and unattractive in Avonlea society. In her consideration of hair in Montgomery's fiction, Juliet McMaster insists that Anne's sensitivity about her hair colour comes from the ways she has absorbed societal signals embedded in dress and appearance (58). Those social codes clearly include complex and contradictory ideas about fat. Anne fully understands the hard currency of weight and the line between "plump" and "fat." She confides to Matthew that she is "dreadful thin" and that she likes to imagine herself "nice and plump, with dimples in my elbows" (*Anne of Green Gables* 16). For her culture and her time, those are the markers of feminine health. Even so, after Rachel "twits" her for her red hair and homeliness, Anne's self-defence is to yoke Rachel Lynde's body size to maladroitness: "'How would you like to be told that you are fat and clumsy and probably hadn't a spark of imagination in you? I don't care if I do hurt your feelings by saying so!'" (76). Marilla is horrified by Anne's show of temper, but she is also amused by Rachel's "dumbfounded countenance" (81). The narrator adds that "Mrs. Rachel swept out and away—if a fat woman who always waddled could be said to sweep away" (78). Anne's hair is her "Achilles heel," certainly, but hair is only one of the markers of female beauty and intellect Anne has internalized. The narrator, Marilla, and Anne share the same codified reading of Rachel Lynde's body. Accomplished and kind she might be, but her fat is constituent with her lack of creativity, imagination, and sensitivity. Rachel's body is fair game for mockery, and she will "waddle" away from Anne again in a later novel, wondering at Anne's "queer" imagination (*Anne of Ingleside* 4).

The indexation of fat and thin bodies is repeated throughout *Anne of Green Gables*. It is important to note that it is often Anne who does this categorization. When Anne meets Diana for the first time, and they swear their oath of friendship, Anne later tells Marilla, "I'm an inch taller than Diana, but she is ever so much fatter; she says she'd like to be thin because it's so much more graceful, but I'm afraid she only said it to soothe my feelings" (*Anne of Green Gables* 103). While Anne here delineates her "bosom friend" as plump rather than fat, Diana is already mindful of how she is perceived by others. As Anne also made abundantly clear to Rachel, in this culture, fat and graceful cannot coexist. When Anne is allowed to participate in the school performance, she is excited to participate in a dialogue about fairies. "'Josie Pye is sulky because she didn't get the part she wanted in the dialogue,'" Anne tells Marilla. "'She wanted to be the fairy queen. That would have been ridiculous, for whoever heard of a fairy queen as fat as Josie? Fairy queens must be slender.'" (227). Where "fat" appears in other parts of the novel as simply a descriptor, here it is definitely an epithet. Anne's rivalry with Josie aside, Anne understands, as Diana does, that slimness is evidence of both moral and physical superiority, and it becomes its own reward. Anne justifies Jane Andrews as the queen not because she is talented but because she fulfils Anne's (and her culture's) vision of beauty. Anne's conversation with Marilla also suggests that Anne *tells* Josie so: "'Josie says she thinks a red-haired fairy is just as ridiculous as a fat one, but I do not let myself mind what Josie says'" (228). Anne's sensitivity about her hair clearly does not translate to empathy with Josie for her dress size even as she absolves Diana of the same thing. Yet these interactions taken together suggest two related ideas: Anne's "skinny" can be rectified by good parenting, good food, and love; "fat" is a gross failure of femininity and proof of moral and intellectual shortcoming.

Anne's Slimness as Evidence of Moral Superiority

Though as a girl Anne gets into trouble frequently because of her imagination and passions, her innate nature is portrayed as spontaneous, generous, and capable. She saves Minnie May from croup "with a skill and presence of mind perfectly wonderful in a child her age" (*Anne of Green Gables* 171). She is bright, disciplined in her schoolwork, and as her open confessions of wrongdoing (made variously to Marilla, Rachel, and Josephine Barry) show, she has a fundamental ethical and moral compass. In the relative health and safety of Green Gables, Anne blooms into adulthood, and her maturation is accompanied by increasing imagery of her body as "slim" rather than "skinny," as if all that is needed to correct her path is love and healthy nourishment. As Laura M. Robinson and others have pointed out, much of the narrative line of *Anne of Green Gables* is dedicated to Anne learning her "role" as an adult woman. She stops making mistakes, learns to "think more" and "talk less" (*Anne of Green Gables* 300), and her imagination is curbed, at least in public. As Robinson says, Anne's surface conformity "conceals but does not erase her 'improper' thoughts and desires" (Robinson 216). I believe the opposite: those thoughts and desires are supposed to mark her out as morally superior and more attractive than the other girls, even though the people who care for her most do not at first understand why. Marilla's impetus to make Anne a "model little girl of demure manners and prim deportment" is bound to fail, for that "disposition" is "as impossible and alien to her as to a dancing sunbeam in one of the brook shallows," and Marilla unconsciously prefers Anne's intensity of spirit (*Anne of Green Gables* 212). Matthew, in search of Anne's difference from the others, notes her "brighter face, and bigger, starrier eyes, and more delicate features" (230). Anne's "fresh enthusiasms, her transparent emotions, her little winning ways, and the sweetness of her eyes and lips" win over that "rather selfish old lady," Diana's wealthy great-aunt Josephine Barry (278–79). Even Rachel, whose own preference is for Diana's and Ruby's more showy looks, notices that when Anne is next to the other girls, "she makes them look kind of common and overdone—something like them white June lilies she calls narcissus alongside of the big, red peonies, that's what" (294). Each of these observations is accompanied by an image, impression, or metaphor of Anne's slimness as part of her appeal: she is alternately "delicate," "starry," "dainty," and "lily-like."

The Contradictions of Diana's Fatness

As Navarro has pointed out, embedded in this narrative is the normalization that the body reveals an essential attribute of the person's character (8–9). Anne's "special" and rare quality is revealed through her slim gracefulness, while fat betrays some kind of failing. If Rachel is "clumsy," Josie mean-spirited, then Diana's essential fault is her greed, much of which is initially laid at her mother's door. When Anne first meets Diana, she is a "very pretty little girl, with her mother's black eyes and hair, and rosy cheeks, and the merry expression which was her inheritance from her father" (*Anne of Green Gables* 101). Her looks play "havoc with the hearts of Avonlea schoolboys" so that her name is frequently written up on the school wall (129). Diana always laughs (102), and she is perfect to Anne in every way but imagination (108). She reads incessantly, though it becomes clear that most of her reading (or at least what she loans Anne) is romance. Together with Ruby Gillis, Diana is rural Avonlea's embodiment of beauty, with what Rachel Lynde calls "snap and colour" (294). At the same time, Diana's greediness becomes a recurrent theme. When she brings raspberry tarts to school, she mentally calculates how much she will get if she has to share with the other girls, rather than be branded "awful mean" (124). In the raspberry cordial episode, Anne is blamed for getting Diana drunk, but Marilla responds that Mrs. Barry would "better punish Diana for being so greedy as to drink three glassfuls of anything" (152). Diana, says the subtext, has not learned self-regulation, and that lesson should have come from her mother. When Anne goes to apologize, Mrs. Barry, a woman of "strong prejudices and dislikes," whose intolerance makes her "anxious to preserve her daughter from the contamination of further intimacy with such a child," refuses to accept it (153). As Mitchinson insists, "mothers were supposed to ensure that their children were neither overfed nor underfed" (38). Mrs. Barry fails in her maternal duty by not controlling Diana's greediness, and Diana's greed leads to her plumpness.

As she matures, Diana's "greed" extends to gossip and the yearning for romance. Diana's love of gossip is not singular: it is representative of "the prejudice and provinciality of Avonlea"

(Santelmann 67). Almost all of Anne's information about the town, its inhabitants, their histories, and their desires is interpreted through, and by, Diana. As they get older, that includes the romantic goings-on of Avonlea's younger set, such as who has walked home with whom. On the night of their school concert, Diana tells Anne that Gilbert picked up one of her roses from the fairy dialogue (*Anne of Green Gables* 240), and it is Diana who tells Anne the stories of Hester Gray's romance (*Anne of Avonlea* 123) and Nelson Atkins's proposal to Ruby out of "The Complete Guide to Etiquette" (273). While much of Diana's gossip appears relatively innocent, Jennie Rubio insists that gossip, particularly in *Anne of Ingleside*, functions as a kind of alternate discourse of unexpressed feminine anger. The public decorum used to share gossip is the "necessary means of keeping their private lives inside public personae: the more these women may be privately frustrated or angry, the more they are driven to construct their public personae according to an accepted cultural script" (173). Yet Anne never participates in gossip. As Rubio herself says, "as the model of more appropriate women's behaviour," Anne must be absent (173). Montgomery instead makes Diana the sacrifice to maintain Anne's moral and physical superiority.

Gilbert's feelings for Anne reinforce this distance between Anne and Diana morally. While on the one hand, he admires Anne's "big, limpid grey eyes, and a face as fine and delicate as a flower," her influence over Gilbert is one of "ideals, high and pure," and she guides his own moral compass, for "he had made up his mind, also, that his future must be worthy of its goddess" (*Anne of Avonlea* 195). "Fine" and "delicate," of course, allude as much to Anne's body as to her face, both of which are yoked to her innate maternalism. Moreover Anne's "greatest charm" is that she "never stooped to the petty practices of so many of the Avonlea girls—the small jealousies, the little deceits and rivalries, the palpable bids for favour," because doing so is "utterly foreign to her transparent, impulsive nature" (*Anne of Avonlea* 195). Anne holds herself apart from other girls, but she also inspires them to be more like her. As Devereux argues, Anne's role is as "reproductive and moral agent" doing the work of instructing other women for the good of the race (270).

Fat as Social Disease

There is a more subtle narrative at work here. On one level, Diana's body would hardly seem a threat to a Canadian future. Nonetheless, as Valverde has argued, much of the foundation of what was considered a "Canadian" social order at the turn of the century, built through "consensus, and genuine, internalized respect for authority, and only exceptionally through coercion and force," was conscious self-control (105). As Katherine Byrne argues in her account of tuberculosis and Victorian literature, from the late-Victorian era, spirituality, sexual purity, and thinness were thought to be related. Refusing food allowed a woman to control, confine, and escape her body and its more carnal desires (Byrne 81–82). Diana's excesses and faults, as small as they are, become defects when they are positioned against Anne's merits, and the more "insidious" effects of Diana's love of food, gossip, and romance show up as moral flaws with serious consequences in some of the lesser characters.

The first person who offers a mirror to Diana is Ruby Gillis. Ruby and Diana are often paired in the first two books as the prettiest girls in Avonlea. Diana and Ruby share a love of romance novels and are usually the sources for Anne's reading material. By early adulthood, however, Ruby is obsessed with boys and romance, and Anne, in particular, feels an emotional distance from her. Diana tells her that it is genetic and that Ruby cannot help it: "'She talks about nothing but boys and what compliments they pay her, and how crazy they all are about her at Carmody. And the strange thing is, they *are*, too...' Diana admitted this somewhat resentfully" (*Anne of Avonlea* 274). That Diana is jealous of Ruby's popularity with the boys becomes significant after Ruby is diagnosed with tuberculosis. From the late Victorian era, consumption was associated with sensuality and unregulated sexuality, and illness and death from the disease was seen as the logical consequences of uncontained and/or unbridled passion (Byrne 79–81). Diana's assertion that Ruby's desire for male attention is inborn to the Gillis women suggests a weakness in the Gillis line Ruby's mother has failed to suppress (not unlike Diana's own greed), a weakness that becomes dangerous to the future of the Canadian nation state. If Anne's role as "mother of the race" is to teach by example, Ruby is beyond Anne's ability to regulate until the very end of her life, when Ruby is thin (like Anne) and her "hectic flush" has disappeared, leaving her "pale and childlike" (*Anne of the Island* 125). Only at the moment of death do Ruby's character and spirituality become elevated to the level of Anne's, when her wasted body has become visual proof of internal purity and self-control: "Ruby had always been beautiful; but her beauty had been of the earth, earthy; it had a certain insolent quality to it, as if it flaunted itself in the beholder's eye; spirit had never shone through it, intellect had never refined it. But death had touched it and consecrated it, bringing out delicate modelings and purity of outline never seen before—doing what life and love and great sorrow and deep womanhood joys might have done for Ruby" (*Anne of the Island* 130–31). Ruby's suffering and death are the extreme outcomes of what Diana and Ruby share: a love of unadulterated romance, unmoderated by intellectual pursuits or self-control.

The second mirror to Diana is Anne's university rival, Christine Stuart. Both Devereux and Rubio point out that in *Anne of Ingleside* Christine has become "hard," "commonplace," and coldly unmaternal (354–57). Neither draws attention to the fact that she is also fat, a kind of predestined fate (rather like Diana's), since even as a young woman she was "in the stately style destined to become rather massive in midlife" (*Anne of the Island* 206). Christine also lives the fulfilment of Diana's childhood fantasies. On their visit to Charlottetown to stay with Miss Barry as young teens, and after eating ice cream at eleven at night, Diana suggests that she is "born for city life," while Anne argues in favour of "kind of knowing even in my sleep that the stars were shining outside and that the wind was blowing in the firs across the brook" (*Anne of Green Gables* 278). Though Diana settles for rural married life in Avonlea, Christine marries "well," moves to Winnipeg, and at the moment of this dinner, has been widowed for four years. Christine is well-dressed, fashionable, sophisticated, and, like Diana, has a love of indulgent pleasure underlined and evidenced by her tendency to fat.

Christine needles Anne throughout the dinner and openly flirts with Gilbert. Christine asks if Anne wanted a "broader life," remembering that Anne used to be "quite ambitious" (*Anne of Ingleside* 357). Anne has been at odds with Gilbert, and unhappy at home. As Jennie Rubio points out, the last few pages reinstate a normalized, heterosexual relationship, and Anne is left "apparently happy and satisfied" (171). Both Gilbert and Anne, however, link Christine's meanness of spirit and narrowness of mind to her body size. As Gilbert insists to Anne, "'That laugh of hers got on my nerves a bit. And she's got fat. Thank goodness, you haven't got fat, Anne-girl'" (367). On one level, Gilbert's comparison of Anne's slimness to Christine's fat simply reiterates Anne's fitness as "mother of the race," but it is also important to note that Christine seems to become what Diana might have been if she had lived an urban life of pleasure and self-indulgence instead of a "wholesome" one in the country. Both paths leave Diana's fat body firmly in the past, as an obstacle to maternal fitness and a Canadian future.

Diana's Internalization of Anti-Fatness

Diana's appetites for bodily pleasure in gossip and food do not dissipate with physical and emotional maturation, even as her own opinion of her appearance becomes more enmeshed in her perceived lack of slimness. As teens, on the day that Mrs. Morgan is supposed to visit, Anne admires how "neat and pretty and rosy" Diana is. Diana's response is a sigh: "'But I've had to let out every one of my dresses *again*. I weigh four pounds more than I did in July. Anne, *where* will this end? Mrs. Morgan's heroines are all tall and slender'" (*Anne of Avonlea* 160). By the time of their picnic in *Anne of Ingleside*, Diana, who has just "tipped the scales at one hundred and fifty-five" (10), eats three pieces of chocolate cake, at the same time lamenting to Anne that she fears becoming like her great-aunt Sarah, "so fat she always had to be pulled up when she had sat down," all while simultaneously regaling Anne with an account of the wedding she just attended (12). Though Diana's weight hardly qualifies her as a "small fat" by twenty-first century standards, Diana's tentative suggestions that her tendency to fatness is genetic are undercut by the second narrative, that of her overindulgence in food *and* gossip and romance.

Again, it is Anne who reinforces here what is "fat" and what is acceptably plump, and Anne's conversations with Diana consistently follow a familiar fat-thin dynamic. With Diana's every comment about her body, Anne reassures Diana that she has not yet crossed the invisible line, even as the narrator appears to disagree: "But the moonlight could not hide that she was something stouter than in years agone...and Diana had never been what Avonlea folks called 'skinny'" (*Anne of Ingleside* 5). While Anne calls Diana "a bit matronish of course, but you've escaped the middle-aged spread so far" (*Anne of Ingleside* 5), Anne also separately boasts to Mrs. Lynde that "I've never a hint of a second chin yet" (3). At the end of their picnic, as Diana packs up to go, her lack of self-control becomes a narrative object of mockery: "She [Diana] picked up the plate which held the remainder of the chocolate cake...looked at it longingly...shook her head and packed it in the basket with an expression of great nobility and self-denial on her face" (17). The undercurrent of their exchange is that Anne is proud to have retained her slim figure, a pride reinforced by popular opinion and the praise of the people closest to her, while Diana's backsliding into both fatness and provinciality stems from her lack of "character" and intelligence. Just as on the night of the Carmody concert of their girlhood, when Diana feels she must "resign herself" to her dumpling figure and Anne responds, "'But you have such dimples,'" Anne's answer to Diana's lament is a familiar one to twenty-first century fat folks. Anne essentially tells Diana that she is pretty, not fat (*Anne of Green Gables* 316).

Diana cannot be a heroine even in her own imagination. Anne, in her body, looks, and intelligence, becomes an unattainable standard of femininity that Diana can never possibly achieve. Montgomery aligns Anne with a promise of future "perfection" that becomes the marker by which Diana judges herself. While Diana appears "unenvious" of Anne's slimness at first, she does not resign herself to her own body. Her repeated wish throughout the series is to be different than what she is. On the day of the picnic in Hester Gray's garden, when Anne, Priscilla, Jane, and Diana think on their fairy wishes, Diana wishes to be "tall and slender" (*Anne of Avonlea* 122). When Anne and Diana speculate on Miss Lavendar's romantic history, Diana laments, "When I'm forty-five I'll be horribly fat. And while there might be some romance about a thin old maid, there couldn't possibly be any about a fat one" (*Anne of Avonlea* 272). Diana, the avid and rapacious reader of romance fiction, does not see herself as the heroine of her own story; she sees that person as Anne.

Conclusions

Literature both reflects and helps to create social and cultural attitudes: the hold of *Anne of Green Gables* over the Canadian imagination remains unabated. I was one of generations of children who grew up with the novels, who longed to be "like Anne." What I realize now is that I also unconsciously internalized the desire to be slim like Anne as well. Anne represented imagination, intelligence, rarefied femininity—none of which felt truly achievable or worthwhile without slenderness. Like Diana, I despaired of ever living up to Anne's example.

Anti-fatness in Canada is not new. As Mitchinson insists, underlying much of the contemporary social and medical discussion of fat is a "sense of unease with the society in which we live, a belief in an earlier time when Canadians were fit and slender, a time that gets rosier the farther we are removed from it" (265–66). The relationship between Anne and Diana in *Anne of Green Gables* suggests otherwise: fat bodies have always existed, and it is popular depictions of fat bodies that have served to normalize the privilege of slimness and enfold it in discourses of ideal femininity. The placement of Diana's body against Anne's as Canada is emerging into the twentieth century reinforces eugenic justifications for "healthy" mothers who produce healthy children to do the work of expansion and settlement. Together with race, class, and gender, body size becomes a normative category through which to determine maternal fitness and, by extension, fitness for citizenship. Anne's intelligent and imaginative "slim girlishness" becomes the future of the nation state, while Diana's body fails to conform to this modern, "civilized" femininity. There is still much more work to be done in unpacking the historical antecedents of fat stigma in Canada.

Works Cited

Berg, Temma F. "Sisterhood is Fearful: Female Friendship in L. M. Montgomery." *Harvesting Thistles: The Textual Garden of L. M. Montgomery*," edited by Mary Henley Rubio, Canadian Children's Press, 1994, pp. 36–49.

Bode, Rita, and Jean Mitchell, editors. *L. M. Montgomery and the Matter of Nature(s)*. McGill-Queen's UP, 2018.

Byrne, Katherine. *Tuberculosis and the Victorian Literary Imagination*. Cambridge UP, 2011.

Devereux, Cecily. "Writing with a 'Definite Purpose': L. M. Montgomery, Nellie L. McClung and the Politics of Imperial Motherhood in Fiction for Children." *The L. M. Montgomery Reader, Volume 2: A Critical Heritage*, edited by Benjamin Lefebvre, University of Toronto Press, 2014, pp. 259–76. *Scholars Portal Books*: books.scholarsportal.info/en/read?id=/ebooks/ebooks3/utpress/2015-12-22/1/9781442668607. Accessed 12 Dec. 2020.

Gerson, Carole. "Seven Milestones: How *Anne of Green Gables* Became a Canadian Icon." *Anne's World: A New Century of Anne of Green Gables*, edited by Irene Gammel and Benjamin Lefebvre, University of Toronto Press, 2010, pp. 17–34.

Huff, Joyce L. "A 'Horror of Corpulence': Interrogating Bantingism and Mid-Nineteenth-Century Fat-Phobia." *Bodies Out of Bounds: Fatness and Transgression*, edited by Jana Evans Braziel and Kathleen LeBesco, University of California Press, 2001, pp. 39–59.

McMaster, Juliet. "Taking Control: Hair Red, Black, Gold, and Nut-Brown." *Making Avonlea: L. M. Montgomery and Popular Culture*, edited by Irene Gammel, University of Toronto Press, 2002, pp. 58–71.

Mitchinson, Wendy. *Fighting Fat: Canada, 1920–1980*. University of Toronto Press, 2018.

Montgomery, Lucy Maude. *Anne of Avonlea*. 1909. Tundra, 2014.
—. *Anne of Green Gables*. 1908. Tundra, 2014.
—. *Anne of Ingleside*. 1939. Tundra, 2014.
—. *Anne of the Island*. 1915. Tundra, 2014.
Murray, Jessica. "Representing Fat Female Bodies: A Fat Studies Analysis of Selected Literary Texts." *Journal of Literary Studies*, vol. 36, no. 2, 2020, pp. 99–111.
Navarro, Elena-Levy. "Changing Conceptions of the Fat Body in Western History." *Historicizing Fat in Anglo-American Culture*, edited by Elena-Levy Navarro, Ohio State UP, 2010, pp. 1–16.
Paradis, Elise. "'Obesity' as Process: The Medicalization of Fatness by Canadian Researchers, 1971–2010." *Obesity in Canada: Critical Perspectives*, edited by Jenny Ellison, Deborah MacPhail, and Wendy Mitchinson, University of Toronto Press, 2016, pp. 56–88.
Robinson, Laura. "Pruned Down and Branched Out: Embracing Contradiction in *Anne of Green Gables*." *The L. M. Montgomery Reader, Volume 2: A Critical Heritage*," edited by Benjamin Lefevbre, Toronto UP, pp. 212–22. *Scholars Portal*: books.scholarsportal.info/en/read?id=/ebooks/ebooks3/utpress/2015-12-22/1/9781442668607. Accessed 12 Dec. 2020.
Rogers, Pat. "Fat Is a Fictional Issue: The Novel and the Rise of Weight-Watching." *Historicizing Fat in Anglo-American Culture*, edited by Elena-Levy Navarro, Ohio State UP, 2010, pp. 19–39.
Rubio, Mary Henley. *Lucy Maud Montgomery: The Gift of Wings*. Random House, 2008.
Rubio, Jennie. "Strewn with Dead Bodies": Women and Gossip in *Anne of Ingleside*." *Harvesting Thistles: The Textual Garden of L. M. Montgomery*, edited by Mary Henly Rubio, Canadian Children's Press, 1994, pp. 167–77.
Santelmann, Patricia Kelly. "Written as Women Write: *Anne of Gables* within the Female Literary Tradition." *Harvesting Thistles: The Textual Garden of L. M. Montgomery*, edited by Mary Henley Rubio, Canadian Children's Press, 1994, pp. 64–73.
Valverde, Mariana. *The Age of Light, Soap, and Water: Moral Reform in English Canada, 1885–1925*, with a new introduction, University of Toronto Press, 2008.

The Lives of Laura Cadieux: Fatness and Social Class in Québec

Audrey Laurin

WITH THE NOVEL *C't'à ton tour, Laura Cadieux* (*It's Your Turn, Laura Cadieux*) published in 1973, Michel Tremblay gives voice to the character Laura Cadieux, a fat, working-class woman living in the Hochelaga-Maisonneuve neighbourhood of Montréal who gossips with her friends while waiting for her weekly weight-loss injection. Laura Cadieux is depicted as a hateful shrew stuck in her unhappy life. Since then, Tremblay's novel has been adapted for numerous media—theatre, cinema, and television—and has reached a wide audience. It first became a theatre monologue in 1985, and then came two movies— *C't'à ton tour, Laura Cadieux* (1998) and *Laura Cadieux... la suite* (1999), both directed by Denise Filiatrault and with Ginette Reno in the title role. The first movie stays true to the novel, but the second one significantly departs from its social commentaries. The comedic tone is exacerbated and the scenario sprinkles body positive messages throughout the film that are noticeably absent from the novel. Denise Filiatrault wrote and directed the three seasons of the television series *Le petit monde de Laura Cadieux*, broadcast in 2003, 2005, and 2007. Laura Cadieux is played by famous comedian Lise Dion. The movies and television series constitute a rare occurrence: most of the protagonists are fat and—from the second movie on—their weight is not the focus of attention. In the movie *Laura Cadieux... la suite* and the television series *Le petit monde de Laura Cadieux* none of the protagonists, Laura Cadieux included, is depicted as actively trying to lose weight. Fatness is shown as the norm in this white, francophone, working-class universe. Spanning more than 30 years, this fictional world gives us the opportunity to examine the transformations of fat tropes and stereotypes embodied by Laura Cadieux and the people that surround her, and to explore the historical connections between fatness and social class in white Franco-Québécois identity.

Even though the original novel was written in 1973, each new iteration of Laura Cadieux and her friends is set in the present. This enables Denise Filiatrault to adapt their struggles to cater to the contemporary viewer, but it also has the effect of being at times out of touch with the rest of society. This is especially true in the television series: the protagonists seem to live in a vacuum, and the Hochelaga-Maisonneuve neighbourhood is shown as still being a white-only, working-class environment with stay-at-home wives and widows who attend church every Sunday. In this chapter, I want to first establish how Michel Tremblay contributed to the cultural definition of Québécois identity since the end of the sixties. *C't'à ton tour, Laura Cadieux* needs to be understood in the context of Tremblay's play *Les Belles-sœurs* and the controversies it provoked regarding its use of *joual* and the feminine world it depicts. If Tremblay is now considered an ambassador for Franco-Québécois culture throughout the world, it was not always the case. Then, I will highlight how fatness is depicted in the novel, the movies, and the series. I explore which depictions fall in the category of harmful stereotypes and which ones try to put forward a body positive discourse. Finally, I will demonstrate that by showing fatness as an inherently white working-class trait in an old-fashioned Franco-Québécois environment, Laura Cadieux's fictional universe unwillingly inscribes its body positivity in a form of working-class respectability where there are good and bad fat feminine embodiments.

Before I dive into Laura Cadieux's universe, it is important to point out that the fat studies field is still at a very early stage of its development in the francophone academic world. To my knowledge, there are no studies published on the specificity of fat representations in the Québec context. But, in the last few years, there has been a growing activist movement aiming to make fat bias and fat discrimination known to the francophone public through blogs, social media, and more traditional mainstream media. Gabrielle Lisa Collard started the *Dix Octobre* blog in 2016 to talk about fat fashion, fat yoga, and her experiences as a fat woman. A collection of her blog posts was edited and published along with new short essays under the title *Corps rebelle. Réflexion sur la grossophobie* in 2021. Edith Bernier founded the bilingual blog *The Plus-Size Backpacker/La Backpackeuse taille plus* in 2013 before concentrating her efforts on fighting fat bias and discrimination with the grossophobie.ca website in 2019 and the publication of *Grosse, et puis? Connaître et combattre la grossophobie* in 2020. In her book, Bernier does the important work of translating and explaining numerous fat studies publications for the general public in order to demystify fatphobia and fat discrimination and why they need to be stopped. Mickaël Bergeron, journalist and columnist for various newspapers and magazines, published *La vie en gros* in 2019, in which he shares personal reflections in the shape of short chronicles on a wide variety of subjects concerning fat stigmas. In his book, he mentions two public figures as examples of popular targets of fat hatred in Québec: Safia Nolin, a popular fat lesbian singer-songwriter, and Gaétan Barrette, a provincial MP under the Québec Liberal Party banner who was the minister of Health and Social Services from 2014 until 2018. The photographer Julie Artacho, and Safia Nolin, Gabrielle Lisa Collard, Edith Bernier, and Mickaël Bergeron are the most visible fat activists in francophone mainstream media and are invited periodically on a wide variety of platforms to discuss body diversity and fatphobia. In the academic field, Geneviève Rail, professor emerita at the Simone de Beauvoir Institute's women's studies program at Concordia University, published "Femmes, 'obésité' et confessions de la chair : regard critique sur la Clinique de l'obésité" (2014) in *Labrys, études féministes*. In this article, Rail exposes the arguments used to justify the fight against obesity to debunk its rhetoric and to show how it affects women specifically. In 2016, Audrey Rousseau published "L'institutionnalisation des *fat studies* : l'impensé des 'corps gros' comme mode de subjectivation politique et scientifique" in *Recherches féministes* in which she traces the history of the fat liberation movement and the creation of the field of fat studies, mostly in the United States. She cites Geneviève Rail as the only francophone scholar working in this field in the province, and there is no mention of any fat liberation activism in Québec. This article is nonetheless a valuable introduction to fat studies for francophone students and scholars. This short overview stresses how specific Franco-Québécois fat-centred analysis is long overdue, but it also indicates that fat studies might take off in the francophone academic field in the near future. Nevertheless, all of these studies appeared long after both the first edition of *C't'à ton tour, Laura Cadieux* in 1973 and its subsequent iterations that ended with the third season of *Le petit monde de Laura Cadieux* in 2007.

There are a few studies published on fat characters in literature, cinema, and television in the Anglo-Saxon cultural sphere (Cameron; Contois; Ganz; Norman et al.; Raisborough), but cultural productions stemming from a Franco-Québécois point of view need to be analysed through its specific sociohistorical context. It is important to keep in mind how Franco-Québécois culture developed itself against the white Anglo-protestant majority of the rest of Canada and the United States. Because of this development, it would be inappropriate to base our analysis of fat representation solely on the Anglo-Saxon model overwhelmingly used in the fat studies field. While perceptions of fat bodies in Québec are influenced by American cultural production and the global medical discourse that calls on the "war against obesity," some cultural specificities need to be taken into account and analysed.

C't'à ton tour, Laura Cadieux in Its Sociohistorical Context

Even though *C't'à ton tour, Laura Cadieux*, written by Michel Tremblay in 1973, didn't get as much coverage as his famous play *Les Belles-sœurs*, shown a few years before, their cultural meaning is undoubtedly comparable. In the play *Les Belles-sœurs*, Michel Tremblay gives voice to a group of working-class women. In the kitchen of Germaine Lauzon, without any men in sight, they can freely express their hardships as wives and mothers stuck in their routines. Presented for the first time in 1968 at the Théâtre du Rideau-Vert[1] in Montréal, *Les Belles-sœurs* sent shock waves through the French-Canadian cultural landscape. Not only were there only women on stage, but they were speaking in *joual*, the slang commonly spoken amongst the francophone lower classes in Québec. Tremblay first decided to use *joual* for the sake of realism, not in the hope of advancing a nationalist agenda.[2] Nevertheless, his theatre breakthrough became the catalyst of a larger social debate between the traditional cultural elite for whom *joual* endangered the nation and a younger generation of artists and thinkers eager to redefine Québécois identity (Jubinville 67–68). *Les Belles-sœurs* thus contributed to making working-class identity a defining part of Québécois identity—and worthy of high-culture representation. Although *joual* is unique to the province of Québec and thus significant to the francophone identity, it still signals a lack of education and a lack of propriety.[3] The fact that the women in *Les Belles-sœurs* and *C't'à ton tour, Laura Cadieux* speak solely in *joual* communicates their working-class status as well as their social stagnation.

If the fact that working-class women are at the centre of many of Tremblay's plays and novels was revolutionary at the time, the tone of his writing acts more as a testimony to the plight of working-class women than as a call for change. In *Les Belles-sœurs,* each woman has her particular reason to complain. No matter their ordeal, they, at least, can find some comfort in the fact that they are together in their misery. When Germaine Lauzon tries to better her situation, she is promptly stopped and punished for believing herself better than the others. *Les Belles-sœurs* is a cautionary tale; it is a powerful illustration of the popular Québécois saying "être né pour un petit pain."[4] There is no redemption in sight for those women, no solution to their continuous struggles. Still, it is difficult not to understand this play as social criticism. Tremblay's intentions in writing *Les Belles-sœurs* are not clear. As Michèle Martin explains,

> Tremblay consistently claimed that the world he described in *Les Belles-sœurs* was the only world he

> knew. The play, however, was clearly social criticism. Tremblay often asserted he wanted to show the misery of the majority of Québécois caused by the English and French establishment, which exploited and oppressed them, especially the clergy. Yet, his account of his own intentions was ambiguous. They seemed to be a mixture of personal feelings, critical views of society, and efforts to manipulate press releases. (119–20)

Even if it is clear who the oppressors are, none of the protagonists rebels against them. Their misery is accepted as a fact of life, something the clergy told them they have to endure to gain access to paradise.

The same applies to *C't'à ton tour, Laura Cadieux*. At the time Tremblay wrote the novel in 1973, there was no fat liberation movement in Québec. The tone of the novel doesn't denounce the injustice of fat discrimination in Québec society but offers acute observation on the reality of being fat. Laura expresses a lot of irritation. She is tired of being constantly reminded that she is fat, but she doesn't know what to do about it. She unleashes her frustration on the powerless around her while she shows compassion and respect to the doctor, the only authority figure that appears in the book. There is no silver lining, no moment of realization for Laura, and at the end, her life continues as it always has. The tone of the film and television adaptations is very different. The acerbic observations characteristic of Tremblay's writing completely disappear to show a more positive view of working-class womanhood. When Denise Filiatrault decided to adapt *C't'à ton tour, Laura Cadieux* in 1998, the political and social context had changed. The Quiet Revolution in the 1960s as well as the social movements of the 1970s led to a deep transformation of Québécois society. The francophone working class was not oppressed as it once was. In transposing the novel in the present, Filiatrault had to take a different approach.

The Endless Complaint of Tremblay's Laura Cadieux

The novel consists of one day in the life of Laura Cadieux. It starts at the Beaudry metro station where two young men insult her because of her fatness. She tries to ignore their snarky remarks with her young son by her side:

> J'leu s'ai même pas répond. J'avais assez honte! ... Le p'tit, y'a commencé par rire, mais y'a arrêté tout d'un coup, pis y m'a demandé : « Pourquoi qu'y the disent des affaires de même, moman? » Ça fait que j'y ai crié : « Parce que chus grosse, tabarnac, parce que chus grosse! » (Tremblay 18)
>
> I didn't answer. I was so ashamed! ... My son first laughed then suddenly stopped, and he asked me, "Why do they say such things, mommy?" So I yelled back: "Because I'm fat, goddamn, because I'm fat!"[5]

Laura then reflects on her fatness and the self-hatred she feels. She says that everything and everyone constantly reminds her she's fat. She finishes her diatribe:

> Si j's'rais tu-seule, j's'rais moins sur les narfs, pis j'arais peut-être moins envie de manger sans arrêter, j'engraisserais peut-être pus, aussi. J'engraisse parce que chus pas tu-seule, justement. J'engraisse parce que Pit est là pour me dire que chus grosse, pis que Madeleine est là pour me dire que chus grosse, pis que Raymond est là pour me dire que chus grosse. ... Plus y me l'disent, plus j'mange! (21–22)
>
> If I was alone, I would be less stressed out and I would maybe not feel like eating all the time, and I would maybe stop putting on weight too. I get fatter precisely because I'm not alone. I get fatter because Pit is there to tell me I'm fat, and Madeleine is there to tell me I'm fat, and Raymond is there to tell me I'm fat. ... The more they say it, the more I eat.

She thinks she is stress eating because everyone in her family constantly reminds her she is too fat. These remarks echo more recent findings that fat shaming is an important source of stress and trauma for fat people and that shaming fat people doesn't improve their will to lose weight, contrary to popular belief (Greenhalgh).

Afterward, she goes on the bus that will bring her to the doctor's office where she goes to receive her weekly injection to help her lose weight. During the ride, she projects hateful stereotypes on the immigrants she sees. Then, at the doctor's office, Laura comments on the lives of other patients she sees regularly in the doctor's office, passing judgment on their lives. She gossips with her friends and they complain about the presence in the waiting room of two nuns and two women whom they assume are Greek. All seems well until Mr. Blanchette, the only man present, comments on Laura's fatness when she complains about the heat, prompting another internal monologue:

> Y faut toujours que quequ'un finisse par me le dire... Toujours! J'peux pas l'oublier une heure ou deux, ah, non, y'a toujours quequ'épais pour v'nir me le rappeler. (65)
>
> There's always someone to say it... Always! I can't forget it for an hour or two. Oh, no, there's always some moron there to remind me.

C't'à ton tour, Laura Cadieux highlights the everyday reminder faced by fat people that their body is abnormal. Contrary to more recent depictions of fat shaming, health is never mentioned in regard to fatness in Tremblay's novel. Being fat for Laura means that she is ugly and that she does not have the willpower to follow a strict diet to lose weight. In the book, there is no hint of fat acceptance from Laura's perspective. She hates her fatness. Since she is unable to lose weight, the only solution she sees is for other people to let her be and leave her alone. This won't make her accept her body as it is, but, if she were not being constantly reminded of her size by others, it would be easier for her to forget her curse and live her life.

Denise Filiatrault's Conflicting Film Adaptation of Tremblay's Novel

In the 1998 movie directed by Denise Filiatrault, Ginette Reno, who plays Laura, recites word for word Laura's complaints against her body, exactly as these are written in the novel. Her attitude is nevertheless much more lighthearted, and the movie offers a positive ending: Laura, with the help of Mme. Therrien (played by Pierrette Robitaille), faces her fear of the moving sidewalk in the Beaudry metro station. Also, contrary to the book, there are two scenes added to show a more fat-positive stance. In the first scene, Vovonne (Danièle Lorrain), a character that is not mentioned in the book, goes to a plus-size fashion show. The models smile with pride as they show off the clothes while walking down a massive marble stairway. A fat opera singer provides the musical background, adding to the sophistication the decor already conveys. Vovonne watches in awe. She later arrives at the doctor's office wearing the light blue suit she saw during the show, and all the women compliment her clothes. The fat positive stance in the second scene is more ambiguous. Alice Thibodeau (Sonia Vachon) and her niece go to the butcher. The niece mentions to the butcher, who happens to be Vovonne's husband, that they are both on their way to the doctor to receive their weekly injection to lose weight. The butcher then suggestively eyes Alice from head to toe and tells her, "Ah...faites pas ça, c'est tellement beau des femmes qui ont l'air en santé (Ah...Don't do that, women who look healthy are so beautiful)." In this context, saying that Alice looks healthy is a common euphemism to compliment a woman's plumpness as beautiful. Alice sends her niece away, and she proceeds to have sex with the butcher. The sex scene is filmed in a comical tone with fruits falling and then the couple falling and then, once upright again, having difficulties finding a working position while standing in the freezer surrounded by huge pieces of meat. Alice embodies the trope of the lustful fat women who cannot control her sexual desire. Jana Evans Braziel characterizes these types of representations as showing "the fat female body as a site of sexual masquerade—conveying both an excessive salaciousness and a hyperbolic derision of that prurience" (233). Braziel argues that fat women's desirability is almost always shown in a carnivalesque or grotesque setting to further signal their decadence (235). Alice's high libido is also depicted as immoral since we learn later in the movie that Vovonne is her very good friend. In her quest for pleasure, Alice didn't think twice before betraying her friend by sleeping with her friend's husband.

In the novel, in contrast to the scene above from the movie, Alice is shown to enjoy sex in a very different manner. While her sex talk is meant to be funny, she only speaks about the intercourse she has with her husband. She says that because of their fatness it complicates things a bit and they have to be creative:

> On a essayé tu-sortes de positions...on a même fini par acheter le livre des positions, là, mais c'est deux maigres sèches qui font les démonstrations, ça fait qu'y ont pas d'misère, eux autres. Y devrait avoir un livre de conseils pour les gros. (Tremblay 122)

> We tried all kinds of positions...we even ended up buying the positions book, but the demonstrations are made by a wiry, thin couple. They don't have any difficulties achieving the positions. There should be an advice book for the fatties.

In her words, being fat, and her husband becoming fat, did not alleviate their desire for one another nor did it impact the quality of their sex life. She mentions that their love of sex makes it hard to lose weight because their intense sessions work up their appetite. Alice appears to be a loud hedonist who enjoys all kinds of earthly pleasures, usually referred to as "bon vivant." Her only complaint is about the lack of fat representation in her sexual positions book, which renders it unusable. This hints to the fact that fat people are not seen as sexual beings (Braziel 231), but she does not dwell on it. Denise Filiatrault transforms this character to add comedic effect; instead of saying funny things about sex, Alice is shown as a clumsy, overeager sex partner. In the end, this portrayal contributes to the accentuation of fat bias because the spectator can only laugh about the ridiculousness of the sex acts portrayed. Furthermore, Alice is shown as selfish as she gets rid of her niece, whom she is supposed to look after, and has sex with her friend's husband.

Alice is not the only character whose fatness is the butt of the joke in the 1998 movie. In one scene, Mlle. Bolduc (Adèle Reinhardt), the only thin women in Laura's circle of friends, shows off her elliptical training device to the other women in the doctor's office. She tells her friends that she's thin because she exercises, and because she does not eat any sugary or fatty snacks. When Laura tries the device, she gets very excited, but the frame of the device breaks under her weight. The camera cuts to some of the other women waiting in the office, and they snort. Laura is angry and humiliated, but she soon recovers. While the novel always makes the reader empathize with Laura's plight, the movie undermines its own few fat-acceptance messages by still making the spectators laugh at Laura and Alice's fatness.

Fat Acceptance and Working-Class Respectability in *Laura Cadieux... la suite* and *Le petit monde de Laura Cadieux*

Laura Cadieux... la suite, which came out in 1999, just one year after the first film, has the same cast, but the storyline has nothing to do with Michel Tremblay's novel. While the first movie shows several of the characters complaining about their weight and their inability to lose some, *Laura Cadieux... la suite* gives a lot of agency to the different female characters. Throughout the movie, these middle-aged women are seen as glowing and confident; for example, they strut around half naked in a massage parlour or in bathing suits around a swimming pool. They have fun, and they laugh a lot. In the end, no one is left behind, and everyone gets what she wanted. This movie is meant to be a feel-good movie, and it succeeds. After the women first voice their complaints, fat is never mentioned again as an issue for Laura Cadieux and her friends.

The television series, in which comedian Lise Dion replaces Ginette Reno in the leading role, mostly keeps the fat-positive message from *Laura Cadieux... la suite* while adding dramatic elements. The characters have different struggles, and, in the end, they always overcome them, and the viewers are invited to learn from the women's experiences. Interestingly, none of their struggle is because of their weight but a few are related to their working-class status. For instance, in the first episode, Laura learns that her son is considered gifted based on his intelligence and that he could have a scholarship to attend a private boarding school. Laura and her husband Pit (Jean-Guy Bouchard) hesitate to send him there because they feel that people like them don't belong in such a school. Pit is especially worried, and we discover it is because he is ashamed that he never learned how to read. The episode ends with Pit saying to his son that he inspired him to join an evening class to learn how to read. This episode sets the tone of the series, which places the viewer in a working-class environment where the "né pour un petit pain" state of mind is still very much alive, but the characters have the ability to change their situation.

This sets *Le petit monde de Laura Cadieux* apart from Tremblay's novel in a fundamental way. Throughout the series, the characters want to better their lives, but this bettering is social and psychological, never physical, which means that they don't try to lose weight. However, the characters and the problems they face seem oftentimes old-fashion or even backwards. The television series is geared toward an older audience, which makes it appear quite conservative and out of touch in some of the themes explored. For instance, in the fourth episode of the first season, Alice is met with reproach and shame by her friends when they learn she has contracted a non-fatal sexually transmissible disease. The tone of the series indicates that she was rightfully punished for what is constructed as her irresponsible behaviour. Another story arc, this time in the third season, involves Mme. Therrien, who is widowed and is becoming a nun in the hope of expelling her sexual lust. It fails, and she falls in love with the nunnery chaplain. They both quit the nunnery to be together. Mme. Therrien is then portrayed as utterly ridiculous, as she changes her appearance to what she thinks her new partner desires—platinum blond hair, heavy makeup, short skirts, and tops that display deep cleavage. Her friends pass judgment on her makeover, and her partner leaves her because he is ashamed to be seen in public with her.

This example is not to say that having sexual desire and being desired are absolutely frowned upon by these women in all instances. Instead, a clear moral hierarchy is instituted, demonstrating what is expected of a respectable woman. In the first episode of the series, Laura can be heard having sexual intercourse behind closed doors with her long-time husband Pit. They are both shown deeply in love and as having desire for one another. Throughout the series, all the women often compliment each other's appearance, and they are always shown as being comfortable in their own skin. Nevertheless, they never wear revealing clothing, and their wardrobe is conservative and could be characterized as "age appropriate." Even Alice, who is always shown seeking men's attention, never reveals more skin than the others. The only thing that signals her attention-seeking attitude is the fact that she mostly wears bright pink clothes, which also highlight her bubbly personality. Her friends often harshly judge her actions, but never speak against the way she looks.

In the second episode of the second season, the group of friends agrees to pose nude to make a calendar that will help raise money for the poor families living in the neighbourhood. This idea is brought forth by Mme. Gladu, who tries to convince them by saying it will be done in good taste and they will look like Botero's women.[6] Alice is, of course, the most enthusiastic, and she helps the others gain the confidence necessary to appear in front of the camera. Drama ensues when Laura and Angela's husbands refuse to let their wives pose naked. Laura and Angela are the only married women in their friend group. The crisis is averted when it is decided that both husbands will be in charge of taking the pictures of their wives. The episode ends with Laura and Pit at the grocery store where they stumble upon several copies of the calendar. Laura is proud of all the money they raised thanks to their effort while Pit panics when he understands how popular the calendar is and buys all the remaining copies. It is only then that we are finally afforded a peak at the cover of the calendar, which shows Laura, Angela, Alice, Mme. Gladu, and Mme. Therrien nude with musical instruments hiding most of their breasts, bellies, and thighs. This episode frames the women as being beautiful and worthy of being shown nude, but in a respectable and proper setting. They don't do it for their own gain, and the photographer and his assistant are each in a committed relationship with one of the models.

These few remarks show how the series builds an image of the good working-class fat women. As Layla Cameron argues, a body positive message in television is afforded to fat people only if they prove their "goodness" (260). In the American context, this means that someone is a "good fatty" if they can prove they are fat despite being active and healthy or because of a medical condition (Bias). This is not the case in *Le petit monde de Laura Cadieux*. Instead, to be a "good fatty," the women need to prove their feminine respectability. They don't have to control their fat, but they have to control how it appears. This phenomenon is characteristic of how working-class women negotiate feminine norms to alleviate the negative stereotypes associated with the working class. In *Formations of Class and Gender: Becoming Respectable*, Beverley Skegg analyses how working-class women have to cope with their continual exclusion from normative middle-class femininity:

> Historically this is because working-class women (Black and White) have been positioned against femininity with the sexual. They were precisely what femininity was not. However, to claim respectability, disavowal of the sexual is necessary and constructions, displays and performances of feminine appearance and conduct are seen as necessary. (115)

Le petit monde de Laura Cadieux celebrates fat as worthy of love only insofar as the women make the "right" choice. Incidentally, the series finishes with a happy ending: Laura and Pit renew their wedding vows in front of all their friends and family. While it is refreshing to watch a television series in which women get to live their lives as fat and proud women, fat acceptance still ends up being conditional on having behaviours deemed acceptable.

Conclusion

In Michel Tremblay's *C't'à ton tour, Laura Cadieux*, fatness was something that aggravated Laura Cadieux's powerlessness as a working-class woman living in a society without any hope of betterment. When Denise Filiatrault took over Tremblay's novel, she created a whole new meaning and put forward a body-positive message. In the process, the characters were given a new personality, and the feeling of hopelessness that pervades the novel was thrown out the window. In Filiatrault's version of Laura Cadieux's universe, fat doesn't hinder the lives of the characters. While they stay true to their working-class culture, they can still reach feminine respectability and live a happy life. Thus, while the novel bore witness to the specific oppression Laura Cadieux faced because of her fatness, *Laura Cadieux... la suite* and *Le petit monde de Laura Cadieux* offer absolutely no hint of the existence of fat oppression. This oversight is surprising given how the series tackles different working-class and feminist issues. In this regard, despite all the good sentiments, we are left feeling that Filiatrault's version is a missed opportunity. However, in the last few years, there have been several fictional characters in Québec cinema and television that picked up where Laura Cadieux and her friends left off. Series such as *Unité 9* (2012–2019) and *M'entends-tu?* (2018–2021) or movies such as Myriam Verreault's *Kuessipan* (2019) and Anne Émond's *Jeune Juliette* (2019), among others, offer interesting depictions of fat embodiment that intersect with class, gender, race, and sexuality. The Franco-Québécois cultural landscape constitutes a fertile ground for the analysis of fat representation in Canada.

Notes

1 Incidentally, Denise Filiatrault, who was much more famous at the time thanks to the success of the television series *Moi et l'autre* (1966–1971) on Radio-Canada, was instrumental in bringing the play to the

Rideau-Vert stage. She also played the character of Rose Ouimet in the play (Martin 118). Filiatrault had a working relationship with Michel Tremblay that started long before her adaption of the novel *C't'à ton tour, Laura Cadieux* into a movie in 1998.

2 Michel Tremblay, who was forcefully critiqued for his use of *joual* declared during an interview, "Je dénonce le joual qui non seulement est une langue pauvre, ou de pauvres, mais aussi l'indice d'une paresse d'esprit et d'une carence dans le sang. Le théâtre que j'écris présentement en est un de 'claque sur la gueule' qui vise à provoquer une prise de conscience chez le spectateur (I condemn *joual*, which is not only a poor language, or the poor people's language, but also a symptom of a laziness of mind. The theatre I'm writing is a punch in the face to bring about the spectator's awareness)" (Michel Tremblay quoted in Gauvin 85–86).

3 On the many debates concerning the use of *joual* in cultural productions and the inherent contradictions contained in every side of this debate, see Gérard Bouchard (2012), Lise Gauvin (1976), and Michèle Martin (2003).

4 Translated literally as "being born for a small bread," in other words, being a small breadwinner, this Franco-Québécois expression is used to described someone who is resigned, who accepts that their situation will never get better.

5 All passages in French were translated to English by the author.

6 Fernando Botero is a Colombian artist known for his sculptures and paintings of fat people.

Works Cited

Bergeron, Mickaël. *La vie en gros. Regard sur la société et le poids.* Somme toute, 2019.

Bernier, Edith. *Grosse et puis? Connaître et combattre la grossophobie.* Trécarré, 2020.

Bias, Stacy. "12 Good Fatty Archetypes." *Stacy Bias* [blog], 4 June 2014, http://stacybias.net/2014/06/12-good-fatty-archetypes/.

Bouchard, Gérard. "Collective Destigmatization and Emancipation through Language in 1960s Québec: An Unfinished Business." *Du Bois Review*, vol. 9, no. 1, 2012, pp. 51–66.

Braziel, Jana Evans. "Sex and Fat Chics: Deterritorializing the Fat Female Body." *Bodies Out of Bound: Fatness and Transgression*, edited by Jana Evans Braziel and Kathleen LeBesco, University of California Press, pp. 231–54.

Cameron, Layla. "The 'Good Fatty' Is a Dancing Fatty: Fat Archetypes in Reality Television." *Fat Studies*, vol. 8, no. 3, 2019, pp. 259–78.

Collard, Gabrielle Lisa. *Corps rebelle. Réflexions sur la grossophobie.* Québec Amérique, 2021.

Contois, Emily J. H. "Food and Fashion: Exploring Fat Female Identity in *Drop Dead Diva.*" *Fat Studies*, vol. 2, no. 2, 2013, pp. 183–96.

Filiatrault, Denise, director. *C't'a ton tour, Laura Cadieux.* Cinémaginaire, 1998.

Filiatrault, Denise, director. *Laura Cadieux... la suite.* Cinémaginaire, 1999.

Filiatrault, Denise, creator. *Le petit monde de Laura Cadieux.* Cinémaginaire, 2003–2007.

Ganz, Johanna J. "'The Bigger, the Better': Challenges in Portraying a Positive Fat Character in *Weeds.*" *Fat Studies*, vol. 1, no. 2, 2012, pp. 208–21.

Gauvin, Lise. "Problématique de la langue d'écriture au Québec, de 1960 à 1975." *Langue Française*, no. 31, 1976, pp. 74–90.

Greenhalgh, Susan. *Fat-Talk Nation: The Human Costs of America's War on Fat.* Cornell University Press, 2015.

Jubinville, Yves. "*Les Belles-Sœurs* au présent : prolégomènes à l'étude d'un lieu de mémoire québécois. " *L'annuaire théâtral*, no. 53–54, Spring–Fall 2013, pp. 63–72.

Martin, Michèle. "Modulating Popular Culture: Cultural Critics on Tremblay's *Les Belles-Sœurs.*" *Labour/Le Travail*, no. 52, 2003, pp. 109–35.

Norman, Moss E., Geneviève Rail, and Shannon Jette. "Moving Subjects, Feeling Bodies: Emotion and the Materialization of Fat Feminine Subjectivities in *Village on a Diet.*" *Fat Studies*, vol. 3, no. 1, 2014, pp. 17–31.

Rail, Geneviève. "Femmes, 'obésité' et confessions de la chair : regard critique sur la Clinique de l'obésité." *Labrys*, no. 25, 2014, https://www.labrys.net.br/labrys25/corps/rail.htm. Accessed 10 Jan. 2021.

Raisborough, Jayne. "Why We Should be Watching More Trash TV: Exploring the Value of an Analysis of the Makeover Show to Fat Studies Scholars." *Fat Studies*, vol. 3, no. 2, 2014, pp. 155–65.

Rousseau, Audrey. "L'institutionnalisation des *fat studies* : l'impensé des 'corps gros' comme mode de subjectivation politique et scientifique." *Recherches féministes*, vol. 29, no. 1, 2016, pp. 9–32.

Skegg, Beverley. *Formations of Class and Gender: Becoming Respectable.* Sage Publications, 2002.

Tremblay, Michel. *C't'à ton tour, Laura Cadieux.* 1973. Bibliothèque québécoise. 2016.

MEDICAL ENCOUNTERS

Eating Scorn

Leslie Walters

This image is about fat people's often-strained relationships with food due to the judgments of others or the demonization of food itself.

Weighing In: A Critical Analysis of the 2020 Obesity Canada Guidelines

Kelsey Ioannoni

I feel that in Canada because it's socialized, there's this idea that fat people are a burden on the health care system. I do think part of me feeling [like] a good citizen is not using the socialized health care that we're so proud of and patriotic about because I got it in my head that I'm going to cost the whatever health care system millions of dollars when I'm older, so I need to save the money now. Even when I broke my toe, I taped it up, I never went and got an X-ray ... I definitely think there was a part of it that was, "I didn't want to have to go to a doctor for a foot issue as a fat person." I also don't want to be a sad—I don't want to add the statistic of, "Fat people need our care all the time. Look, all she did was break her toe and she cost us X, Y, and Z amount of money," where that would have been the amount of money for anybody in that situation. I definitely think I purposely—Part of me being a good Canadian citizen and intersectionality with being a good fat woman means I don't use our health care system.
– Xia, Interview participant

Introduction

In 2020, Obesity Canada released an updated version of the *Canadian Adult Obesity Clinical Practice Guidelines* (CPGs), a follow-up to the *2006 Canadian Clinical Practice Guidelines on the Management and Prevention of Obesity in Adults and Children*, both of which were published in conjunction with the *Canadian Medical Association Journal* (*CMAJ*). According to Obesity Canada, this guide was "developed by Obesity Canada and the Canadian Association of Bariatric Physicians and

Surgeons ... [and] authored by more than 60 Canadian health care professionals, researchers and individuals living with obesity" (Obesity Canada, *Canadian Adult*). Together, these entities put forward 80 "key recommendations" for practitioners dealing with "people living with obesity." These recommendations were published as a guideline in the *CMAJ*, while the other 19 chapters are housed on the Obesity Canada website (obesitycanada.ca/guidelines).

My analysis of the newest version of the *Canadian Adult Obesity Clinical Practice Guidelines* in this chapter is rooted in the findings from my doctoral research. For my dissertation, I interviewed 35 women in the Greater Toronto Area (GTA) to examine ways in which fatness can act as a barrier to accessing health care services for Canadian women. These participants ranged in age from 18 to 55 years old, and almost all would be characterized as obese, based on the BMI. In this chapter, I critically analyse the recommendations put forward in the CPG guidelines for health care professionals, and I ground this analysis in the experiences of my research participants. While there are 20 total chapters put out by Obesity Canada, I focus on the first chapter, "Obesity in Adults: A Clinical Practical Guideline," which is a summary guideline designed for widespread distribution, and its key recommendations for health care providers (Wharton et al.). Drawing on fat studies literatures, a Health at Every Size (HAES) perspective, and data from my interview participants, I argue that the categorization of obesity as a disease in this guideline encourages health care practitioners to pathologize their fat patients and to view their treatment through the lens of weight loss and weight management. Based on my participants' experiences, I would argue that this practice is harmful to fat folks. Further, I contend that the recommendations for practitioners on how to interact with obese patients perpetuate fatphobia and maintain the weight-based discrimination that occurs in health care settings. The guidelines acknowledge bias against obese patients; however, they do little to improve on this inequity.

Diagnosis: Diseased!

Obesity, then, is less a biological infection of the tissue and cells, than one of moral standards of Western bodily aesthetics
– Murray 16

The Obesity Canada guidelines open by explicitly defining "obesity" as a disease. In the very first sentence and the first "key point" of the guideline, obesity is described as "a complex chronic disease in which abnormal or excess body fat (adiposity) impairs health, increases the risk of long-term medical complications and reduces lifespan" (Wharton et al. E875). Categorizing obesity as disease at the onset of the document establishes the lens in which subsequent discussions of weight will be framed and the recommendations for practitioners that follow. This lens pathologizes fat people and positions them as a major public health issue.

Throughout the guide, fat patients are described as "people living with obesity," a "people-first" perspective embraced by Obesity Canada (an approach meant to differentiate the persons themselves from the "disease" they are afflicted with). There have been calls by some scholars to use "people-first" language with respect to obesity, arguing that this language would result in a decrease in anti-fat bias and stigma against fat patients (Dietz et al. 917; Kyle and Puhl 1). Theodore Kyle and Rebecca Puhl argue that by "addressing the disease separately from the person—and doing it consistently—we can pursue this disease while fully respecting the people affected" (1). However, adopting a "people-first" approach to describe fat patients has the opposite effect; this approach further entangles fatness and disease. Meadows and Daníelsdóttir note that person-first language is "mired in the medicalization of body state" (2), and instead of resulting in fat people being treated with more respect (one of the intentions behind person-first language), using the term "people living with obesity" further entrenches anti-fat attitudes among health care providers.

The act of designating obesity as disease highlights the power of science and medicine to act as a form of social control, whereby medicine as an institution formalizes a specific classification of people as problematic (Jutel). The categorization of obesity as a disease relies on the process of medicalization, whereby something that is not inherently medical comes to be viewed through a medical lens (Boero; Paradis). This process of medicalization influences the way in which body size comes to bear disease status (Boero; Meadows and Daníelsdóttir; Murray; Paradis). Jutel argues that the power to classify a condition or person as disease is fluid. Classifying obesity as disease is influenced by societal norms; this classification then validates the anxieties of the general public about an "obesity epidemic" (Jutel).

In classifying obesity as a disease, the Obesity Canada guidelines feed on anxieties associated with the "obesity epidemic." They highlight the increase in the prevalence of obesity globally and in Canada and position this increase as a "major public health issue that increases health care costs and negatively affects physical and psychological health" (Wharton et al. E875). The impact of designating a specific body size as "disease" has manifested itself in the rhetoric of the "obesity epidemic." Boero describes the "obesity epidemic" as a type of postmodern epidemic, as obesity is not contagious. Instead, as noted previously, obesity gains disease status through the process of medicalization (Boero; Murray; Paradis). The term "epidemic" functions to scare people into acting responsibly, drawing on and employing medical discourses to do so (Murray).

The idea that health care providers see fat folks as a drain on the health care system was not lost on my participants. Many of my interview participants expressed fear or anxiety over how their health care provider would view and treat them at an appointment. Several participants shared how they felt in anticipation of seeing their doctor. For example, Demi shared these feelings:

> It's just nerve-racking. I wonder if everybody has that feeling. Just to me even just when you ask the question, in the pit of my stomach, I feel this like queasiness. It always feels like I'm going in on the defensive. I'm always like, "What's going to happen? Like, what are you going to say to me? What am I going to be dealing with? What am

> I going to have to steel myself for?" It's just embarrassing for some reason. Not for some reason. It's clear what the reasons are.

When I talked to my participants about the obesity "epidemic," many brought up the problematic way doctors interpret this "epidemic" and how it influences their practice. Participants expressed feeling frustrated with the reliance on the "obesity epidemic" narrative by their health care professionals and questioned the practical impact of dealing with body size through this lens. This classification of obesity as a disease and the guidelines' multiple references to fat folks as "people living with obesity" embody the critiques and concerns that fat folks have with the health care system.

Interview participant Danielle expressed her frustration with the way in which the "obesity epidemic" narrative dominates health care:

> I think this "obesity epidemic" that, yes, I just think that that's really infiltrated the medical system. It's still normalized in the medical system that people don't even question it. Doctors don't question it. I'm like, "What the hell are they doing in medical schools that they're not questioning this?" They must be aware of pharmaceutical companies funding studies, come on. They're smart people there in medical school. I just wish the doctors thought more critically about the information that they're being fed, that there was more of instruction on bedside manner and that kind of thing, treating your patients like people.

Similarly, Megan talked to me about the moralistic component of "war on obesity":

> The moralistic aspect of it always drives me nuts. Well, one, this treatment that like I'm some sort of burden on society and the health care system to begin with, when I can certainly point to other groups that are going to be worse that we don't criticize. Obviously, because you're entitled to health care, no matter what you choose to do.

Other research participants found the use of "epidemic" to describe increases in body size problematic. Participant Victoria reasoned that body size changes over time, and that does not constitute an epidemic:

> I do think—I don't want to say it's an epidemic because an epidemic is a pretty severe word to use. Yes, I think more people are larger than they ever were in history, but I don't think it's an epidemic. I just think that they're spinning things in a different way to make it sound worse than it is. I also feel we change over time. If people are larger, then change to make things better for them instead of just thinking of it the same way it always was. Change can be good.

Victoria's perspective is consistent with that of many fat studies and critical obesity scholars. While not explored in this chapter, scholars like Gard and Wright, Klein, LeBesco, and Oliver have all highlighted how, at particular historical junctures, different threads of thinking about weight converge to produce new understandings of the value of weight. Obesity science, according to Gard and Wright, is then trapped in its primary interest of understanding body weight through the medical lens: one that represents a large body as a diseased body.

Ultimately, describing an increase in body size as a disease highlights the immense power and impact of the medicalization of body size on people in fat bodies. This framework for viewing the fat body itself can deter fat folks from accessing care, and yet the Obesity Canada guidelines have fully embraced this perspective.

Treatment? Constant Intervention and Surveillance

I don't feel that my weight defines how healthy or unhealthy I am, but I definitely feel that when I go to the doctor's, I definitely feel like what I think I'm healthy, they throw in my face, "Yes, you're not that healthy. You're probably going to die at 50." That was a very recent conversation. That is with all blood work coming back that I'm like, "I'm good. I'm within normal ranges of everything." They're like, "Yes, but the stress that you're putting on your body by having the fat, you

are probably going to die at 50." I'm like, "Oh, well, better live my life in the next 18 years real good then."
—Ariel, Interview participant

The automatic assumption that fat people live unhealthy lives and are in need of saving is a common theme that emerged in my interview data. For example, in the passage above, Ariel recalls a recent experience with her health care provider and the frustration it led to. Instead of trusting the results that came back from her blood work, indicating no health concerns, Ariel's doctor relies instead on fatphobic tropes of early mortality and stresses that her health is at risk by virtue of her fatness. The Obesity Canada guidelines, with their focus on obesity as "chronic disease," similarly reject the idea that fat people can lead healthy lives and instead focus on ways in which health care providers should be intervening in the lives of fat folks to treat and cure their fatness. Obesity Canada outlines a five-step process to "guide a health care provider in the care of people living with obesity" (Wharton et al. E878). Taken directly from the organization's guide for practitioners, this five-step process is as follows:

1. Recognition of obesity as a chronic disease by health care providers, who should ask the patient permission to offer advice and help treat this disease in an unbiased manner.
2. Assessment of an individual living with obesity, using appropriate measurements, and identifying the root causes, complications and barriers to obesity treatment.
3. Discussion of the core treatment options (medical nutrition therapy and physical activity) and adjunctive therapies that may be required, including psychological, pharmacologic and surgical interventions.
4. Agreement with the person living with obesity regarding goals of therapy, focusing mainly on the value that the person derives from health-based interventions.
5. Engagement by health care providers with the person with obesity in continued follow-up and reassessments, and encouragement of advocacy to improve care for this chronic disease. (E878)

The process outlined above embodies the biomedical understanding of fatness as disease. It asserts that the first thing a health care provider needs to do in dealing with a fat patient is to recognize that the patient's body is diseased and in need of treatment. However, basing an appointment with a fat patient on the idea of weight loss is often unproductive and is certainly not a novel suggestion. Many of the participants in my research project expressed how, when visiting their doctor, they receive weight-loss advice despite being there for a different reason, and often the primary reason for their visit is neglected or not addressed at all. These appointments were often described to me as a waste of time. As Kristin told me,

> We regularly ignore health things because we don't want to know or because it's an inconvenience but it's just another factor on top of that is I don't want my doctor to just ignore something very serious because well, "It's just your weight." Why even bother? Why waste my time? Why would I waste my time just to be told that it's because you're fat.

Many research participants in my study often encountered this very discussion with their health care providers, repeatedly. Not only is a focus on weight loss preventing folks from receiving the care they originally went to the doctor for, it is also creating harm. As Brenda explains,

> It's always baffled me that the first rule is to do no harm in the doctors' oath and when you do that to people— They see it as being for your own good, but it totally is not. Any fat person who's being honest will tell you that, "No, it is not to my benefit for you to tell me what society and the media tells me a hundred times a day, which is that I'm too fat, I need to lose weight. I know that and it's not like..." That's the thing. They're always like, "Have you ever tried to lose weight? Have you ever thought of weight loss?" Are you fucking kidding? Of course I've tried and of course, I've thought about it. How can you not? Five-year-old children who are skinny, think about it. Everyone thinks about it. "Could I be thinner?"

The anxiety, fear, and harm caused by a focus on weight and weight loss was shared by many of my participants. Wendy describes a similar feeling of anxiety when visiting the doctor:

> I feel anxiety. It's not a good feeling. I don't enjoy going. Not even just because...I don't know that anybody particularly enjoys going to the doctor, but I dread it, because I know that I'm going to have to be prepared or potentially brace myself for some comments said about my fatness or my body. I know that my body's perceived in a certain way. I'm worried that, at some point, what's actually going on with me? Is it going to be recognized? Like you read all of these stories about women who have had like 50-pound tumours and their doctors don't recognize that, they're like, "Eat salad," and then they die. I'm like, "Oh, my god. Is that going to happen to me one day? I don't know." I feel I just don't trust or get the health care system at this point. My interactions with my own doctors have not really been any more confidence inspiring. It feels really anxiety [inducing] and unpleasant, and I need to mentally prepare myself before.

The medicalization of fatness has resulted in fat bodies being conceptualized as "obese" and in need of intervention. The five-step process of Obesity Canada outlined above neglects aspects of a fat person's health that are not weight based. The guide suggests practitioners focus on core treatment options for obesity, such as nutrition therapy, and on additional therapeutic interventions, such as bariatric surgery. The focus on "initial intervention and continued assessment" in order to improve this "chronic disease" assumes that fat folks live a specific, unhealthy lifestyle that needs to be modified through intervention. Fat people already internalize understandings of their bodies as overindulgent, as representing a lack of self-control, and as evidence of individual failure. These messages, as Gard and Wright argue, are difficult to resist. There exists an assumption that body size is indicative of individual nature, and this assumption further contributes to the pathologization of weight (Gard and Wright; Jutel). These assumptions are embodied in the five-step process outlined by the Obesity Canada guidelines.

Obesity Canada could have chosen to embrace alternative approaches to health and body size, such as the social determinants of health approach, methods that recognize factors of health outside of a biomedical model, or a Health at Every Size (HAES) perspective. Lindo Bacon[1] and Lucy Aphramor call for a reimagining of health by embracing a Health at Every Size (HAES) perspective. In their article "Weight Science: Evaluating the Evidence for a Paradigm Shift," they call for a perspective on health that focuses on intuitive eating and relies on internal body cues, instead of focusing on body size, diet, or weight loss. Key to the HAES perspective is the disentanglement of weight from health; it instead calls for a focus on creating healthy behaviours (Bacon and Aphramor). HAES allows for a focus on health that is not about becoming thin but rather about focusing on health promotion. As Deb Burgard notes, this approach differs from conventional treatment "in its emphasis on self-acceptance and healthy day-to-day practices, regardless of whether a person's weight changes" (42). In their 2016 study, Frederick, Saguy, and Gruys found that exposure to fat rights and an HAES perspective on health resulted in a decrease in the perceived risk of fatness, supporting the argument that an HAES perspective helps to combat weight stigma.

Acknowledging Bias: Does It Work?

It was really always that I really didn't want to do it. It would end up through the whole thing of getting told that I needed to lose weight because it was honestly a gamble of whether—not whether I would get told that, but whether if they would actually do anything or just say, "That's the problem, bye." It was because I got so tired of hearing that and not having anything done that I went through this [period of] two years where I just didn't see a doctor.

– Natalie, Interview participant

As previously stated, the guideline document is just one chapter in a series of 20 chapters. However, the guideline chapter contains a table of 80 key recommendations (E879) that are made as a result of the analysis in the subsequent 19 chapters. These recommendations focus primarily on assessment and intervention by health care providers, as well as on the maintenance of treatment plans.

The recommendations set out in the guidelines are solely from a biomedical perspective and neglect to incorporate other approaches to health, such as a Health at Every Size perspective (Bacon and Aphramor). For example, the four key recommendations emerging from "Chapter 2: Reducing Weight Bias in Obesity Management, Practice, and Policy" (Kirk et al.) focus on how health care providers need to recognize and assess their biases, avoid using judgmental words, and not make assumptions that an issue is related to weight (1–2). This is also the only chapter and set of recommendations that focus on understanding the potential impact of the doctor on the care of fat patients.

My dissertation research suggests that doctor biases and, more important, the discriminatory mistreatment of fat folks by their doctors due to perceptions about body size constitute a significant issue in Canadian health care. As Yasmin shared with me,

> I think, overall, the word that comes to mind is *dismissed*. I think in a way it's because if I'm not going to deal with the issue of my weight, then why are we actually helping you because until you'd address that issue, we can't help you because everything is attached to that issue. When I went to the hospital for pain, I was dismissed because of my weight. The intake with my doctor, I really had a sense of, "Well, you need to deal with this issue." I feel like the Canadian health system, that they don't really care [about you] if you're overweight, that they don't—You become second tier, in a way. I feel like it's not—I feel judged and blamed for it. Like, "If you were to do this, then you would be valued and we would make the effort to take care of you." I think that's one of the reasons why I don't regularly go to the doctor even though something might be wrong, because I'm like, "What's the point?"

Fat studies scholars critique the medical gaze and note how the subjectivity of doctors is based on their own perceptions. Since the perceptions of doctors are subjective, the dominant understanding of medicine as objective must be questioned (Murray). With respect to fatness, the fat body is always visible when it comes into contact with doctors, and this visibility and the accompanying perception of the doctor are believed to correlate to knowledge about fatness (Murray). Because fatness is hyper visible (Gailey, Murray), a fat patient is "outed" prior to any discussion of the reason for the visit. This means that a doctor will view the patient through the medicalized lens as a "person living with obesity" prior to any verbal interaction. This "confession" of fatness results in the pathologization of fat bodies (Murray) and influences the diagnostic and medical process (Jutel). The pathologization of fat bodies is not lost on the patients themselves. For example, Brenda describes her fear of visiting the doctor.

> It's multi-fold, but just as a fat person, just not being able to go...look, having to worry about, "Is this doctor going to discriminate against me," because probably 85 per cent of them do and have and will. Just the work of finding it out...it's hard enough to find a doctor for a normal person but to have to research and ask friends and I still don't have a family doctor. I've been in Toronto for 17 years. It's really just a lack of confidence. It's just the lack of any doctors giving a shit about what's wrong with you. They just see you as a fat case that needs to go lose weight.

"Health at Every Size, Please"

Interviewer: If you had a say or if you could advise or influence doctor training, what would you suggest as strategies for dealing with fat patients?

Madison: Oh my god. Health at Every Size, please [chuckles].

Interviewer: Do you want to explain what Health at Every Size is to you?

Madison: To me, Health at Every Size means you don't treat weight, you treat a person. There's lots of things that you can recommend to a patient that have nothing to do with weight. Who gives a shit about weight loss?

—Madison, Interview participant

During my interviews with fat women, I asked them what they thought doctors needed to do when working with fat patients. Overwhelmingly, participants wanted doctors to treat them with humanity and to recognize that *fat* does not necessarily mean *unhealthy*. Many participants expressed how doctors would automatically assume that they have an unhealthy diet or do not engage in exercise or movement. Yet, for many participants, this assumption is not an accurate representation of their lifestyles. Danielle states that she wants doctors "not to work from an assumption that fat is unhealthy and needs to be eradicated. I really would like doctors to have access to fair information and that is not influenced by pharmaceutical companies and diet industries, that kind of thing." Similarly, Hannah advocates

> for doctors to look at the whole picture and to understand that there are other things that need to be worked on. And also they know that this doesn't work, don't they? They're always like, "We know it's really hard. Weight loss is not really successful." They know it's not working but they're still suggesting it. What can we be suggesting instead?

The Obesity Canada guidelines do acknowledge the value of improving health and well-being:

> there is a recognition that obesity management should be about improved health and well-being, and not just weight loss. Because the existing literature is based mainly on weight-loss outcomes, several recommendations in this guideline are weight-loss centred. However, more research is needed to shift the focus of obesity management toward improving patient-centred health outcomes, rather than weight loss alone. (Wharton et al. E876)

What is frustrating about this assertion is that there has been a lot of research done and scholarship produced on the ineffectiveness of a weight-loss approach, both in terms of the negative impact this approach has on fat patients and alternatives to a weight-loss approach, such as the HAES approach. (See, for example, Bacon and Aphramor, Burgard, Campos, Gard and Wright, and Murray, to name a few.) Many participants in my research brought up HAES, even directly referencing Lindo Bacon's work on this issue. Gina describes how she uses HAES as a strategy in navigating weight-based discussions with new doctors:

> When I'm going to see new doctors, I usually pull up an article on how to deal with weight discrimination. There's a little note card with research-based evidence for Health at Every Size that I bring in case they give me a hard time. I can be like, "Look at this research."

Other participants, like Demi and Karen, explain how they try to incorporate an HAES perspective into their own understanding of their weight and health. Demi shares how, instead of rejecting dieting, which has been harmful to her in the past, she is trying to take up an HAES approach

> Now, I'm just trying to do an awareness type thing, but it's not a diet. I'm trying to move more intentionally and trying to think about food more intentionally and think about how I feel when I eat something and just being more mindful. This is kind of Lindo Bacon, right?

Karen, who similarly takes up the HAES approach to understanding her body, talks about how, in rejecting traditional diet and exercise regimes, she is learning how to live in the reality of her fat body through knowing more about how fat bodies move through and navigate daily life.

> I'm trying to move around a 400-pound body. Of course I'm going to breathe hard. I'm going to have legs that are very muscular because this is a big body to carry around every day. I think that was one of the most revolutionary

> things a friend said to me once ... "Of course you're going to breathe hard. You're moving around a lot of weight. There's nothing to be feel ashamed about that." Then Lindo Bacon's book, *Health at Every Size*, talked about like. ... Or I think it was an article that they wrote, Lindo Bacon and Lucy Aphramor, I think. They talk about how like, "Okay, maybe fat people have a higher blood pressure, but also maybe it just takes more to pump blood through a bigger body." We don't get that from the health. ... Articles and stuff like that don't study that. They just say, "It's bad that your blood pressure is that high," or whatever.

Conclusion

I feel like it's like the war on drugs. It's probably not going anywhere anytime soon, so let's learn how to deal with it. Let's learn how to deal with people where they are. It's ridiculous to say, "Go lose weight before we can do this surgery on you," because a lot of times, you don't have that option. I also think that we need size discrimination laws because this just is going to keep happening. It's not illegal. You can be like "No, you're fat, I'm not doing XYZ thing for you," and that's okay, but it's absolutely not okay.
– Brenda, Interview participant

In this chapter, I argued that the categorization of obesity as a disease in Obesity Canada's *Canadian Adult Obesity Clinical Practice Guidelines* (CPGs) is problematic and that these guidelines may in fact encourage health care practitioners to pathologize their fat patients. This practice is harmful to fat patients and further medicalizes their bodies. The guidelines set out by Obesity Canada may acknowledge the existence of bias against patients categorized as obese, but they do little to improve on this inequity. They also do not engage with any critical scholarship that works to dismantle harmful assumptions on body size.

Ultimately, the Obesity Canada guidelines and their key recommendations fail the very group of people they are supposed to be helping. Instead of working to combat weight stigma and bias or to make health care more accessible for fat folks, the guidelines further pathologize fat patients as "diseased" and categorize them as "people living with obesity" who are in need of intervention and treatment. This is not an uncommon public health strategy. Public health often portrays obesity as resulting from individual behavioural failures, yet also argues that obesity is an "epidemic" (Boero). This represents what Boero calls the normative-pathological duality. Similarly, Murray argues that when "obesity" is represented as disease and framed from a medical perspective, the "cure" is for individuals to adopt "health" behaviours and to change their lifestyles. This is the primary focus of the guidelines by Obesity Canada; they are most interested in instructing health care practitioners on how to assess their patients as "diseased" with obesity and on how to intervene to encourage the ultimate outcome—weight loss. While there is a nod to understanding weight bias and stigma, these guidelines fail to actually take up the issue of weight-based discrimination in any meaningful or productive way, and instead encourage the continuing marginalization of people based on the size of their bodies.

Notes

1 Lindo Bacon is formerly Linda Bacon. See https://lindobacon.com/lindo-linda/ for a detailed explanation of their name and pronoun change.

Works Cited

Bacon, Lindo, and Lucy Aphramor. "Weight Science: Evaluating the Evidence for a Paradigm Shift." *Nutrition Journal*, vol. 10, no. 9, 2011, pp. 1–14.

Boero, Natalie. *Killer Fat: Media, Medicine, and Morals in the American "Obesity Epidemic."* Rutgers University Press, 2012.

Burgard, Deb. "What Is Health at Every Size?" *The Fat Studies Reader*, edited by Esther Rothblum and Sondra Solovay, New York University Press, 2009, pp. 41–53.

Campos, Paul. *The Obesity Myth: Why America's Obsession with Weight is Hazardous to Your Health*. Gotham, 2004.

CMAJ. 2006 Canadian Clinical Practice Guidelines on the Management and Prevention of Obesity in Adults and Children, www.cmaj.ca/cgi/content/full/176/8/S1/DC1.

Dietz, William H., Eric Ravussin, and Donna Ryan. "The Need for People-First Language in Our Obesity Journal / Response to 'The Need for People-First Language in Our Obesity Journal.'" *Obesity*, vol. 23, no. 5, 2015, p. 917.

Frederick, David A., Abigail C. Saguy, and Kjerstin Gruys. "Culture, Health, and Bigotry: How Exposure to Cultural Accounts of Fatness Shape Attitudes about Health Risk, Health Policies, and Weight-Based Prejudice." *Social Science & Medicine*, vol. 165, 2016, pp. 271–79.

Gailey, Jeannine. *The Hyper(in)visible Fat Woman*. Palgrave Macmillan, 2014.

Gard, Michael, and Jan Wright. *The Obesity Epidemic: Science, Morality and Ideology*. Taylor & Francis Inc., 2005.

Jutel, Annemarie. "Doctor's Orders: Diagnosis, Medical Authority and the Exploitation of the Fat Body." *Biopolitics and the "Obesity Epidemic": Governing Bodies*, edited by Jan Wright and Valerie Harwood, Routledge, 2009, pp. 60–77.

Kirk, Sara, Ximena Ramos Salas, Angela S. Alberga, and Shelly Russell-Mayhew. "Reducing Weight Bias in Obesity Management, Practice and Policy." *Canadian Adult Obesity Clinical Practice Guidelines* [Chapter 2], Obesity Canada, 4 August 2020, https://obesitycanada.ca/guidelines/weightbias/. Accessed 9 October 9, 2022.

Klein, Richard. "Fat Beauty." *Bodies Out of Bounds: Fatness and Transgression*, edited by Jana Evans Braziel and Kathleen LeBesco, University of California Press, 2001, pp. 19–38.

Kyle, Theodore K., and Rebecca M. Puhl. "Putting People First in Obesity." *Obesity*, vol. 22, no. 5, 2014, p. 1211.

LeBesco, Kathleen. *Revolting Bodies? The Struggle to Redefine Fat Identity*. University of Massachusetts Press, 2004.

Meadows, A., and S. Daníelsdóttir. "What's in a Word? On Weight Stigma and Terminology." *Frontiers in Psychology*, vol. 7, 2016, p. 1527.

Murray, Samantha. *The "Fat" Female Body*. Springer, 2008.

Obesity Canada. *Canadian Adult Obesity Clinical Practice Guidelines*, Obesity Canada, 2022, https://obesitycanada.ca/guidelines/.

Oliver, Eric. *Fat Politics: The Real Story Behind America's Obesity Epidemic*. Oxford University Press, 2005.

Paradis, Elise. "'Obesity' as Process: The Medicalization of Fatness by Canadian Researchers, 1971–2010." *Obesity in Canada: Critical Perspectives*, edited by Jenny Ellison, Deborah McPhail, and Wendy Mitchinson, University of Toronto Press, 2016, pp. 56–88.

Wharton, Sean, et al. "Obesity in Adults: A Clinical Practice Guideline." *CMAJ*, vol. 192, no. 31, 4 August 2020, pp. E875-E891,

A Response to the 2020 Canadian Ob*sity Guidelines

Joanna Carson

A body is not a disease.
The way it folds won't tell you a time of death
like a fortune teller staring deep into the etchings of your palm

but it can tell you how many times you've swung your hips to the beat
in the middle of a crowded bar, or smacked your thighs together like cymbals
naked in your room, dancing only to the sound of rush hour traffic.

The doctors fail to ask the important questions
like which part of your chest houses the sound of a white pine's needles
clinking against each other like tiny glasses of champagne

and how many deep breaths does it take to quiet the meteor shower
that fills your head every time you close your eyes.

They weigh you in pounds instead of thunderclouds and act surprised
when bolts of lightning come spilling out of your mouth.

When they paint your portrait from memory, hang it next to the other subject
they also refused to look in the eye, you are not obligated to forgive them.

Just remember:
if they tell you your house is haunted, check for an errant branch
tapping lightly against the upstairs window
before letting them tear the whole thing down.

Artist Statement

This poem is the product of years and years of being subjected to fatphobia within the Canadian medical system. The release of the new *Canadian Adult Obesity Clinical Practice Guidelines* coincided with my doctor of several years recommending weight loss when I came in for a sprained ankle. For myself and every other fat person in Canada, that is not an isolated incident. The guidelines aren't all bad: I appreciate the recommendation that doctors stop bringing up weight loss without a patient's permission, and I think it's important for doctors to recognize that being fat isn't a choice. But I can't shake the feeling that within these guidelines, my body is still viewed as a burden and a curse. I wrote this poem to explore how I want so much more from the medical system. If I feel good in my body, why isn't that enough?

NoBodyIsDisposable: Acts of Care and Preservation—Reflections on Clinical Triage Protocols during COVID-19

Tracy Tidgwell and Fady Shanouda

Introduction

#NoBodyIsDisposable

It was spreading everywhere and fast. The World Health Organization declared the coronavirus disease (COVID-19) a global pandemic in early 2020 and with that the world changed. Nearly everything shut down. In Canada, we were witness to images and videos of hospitals jammed with sick and dying people, mass graves, cold storage truck morgues, and stacked body bags. The reality at the beginning of the pandemic was terrifying, traumatic, and unbelievably sad. Those of us on the margins—disabled, fat, aging, and ill people—feared the coming shortages of medical supplies and spare beds that would see our care deprioritized. Acting quickly, the #NoBodyIsDisposable Coalition, a group of fat and disabled activists and human rights lawyers across the United States and Canada, came together and created the mutual aid toolkit, "Know Your Rights Guide to Surviving COVID-19 Triage Protocols."[1]

The expression "No Body Is Disposable" was coined by Patty Berne of Sins Invalid in 2017 (Berne and Milbern). Sins Invalid is an American disability justice-based performance project led by disabled people of colour "that incubates and celebrates artists with disabilities" (Sins Invalid) and centralizes artists of colour and LGBTQ2SIA artists. Previously, the #NoBodyIsDisposable hashtag has been mobilized by a coalition of fat and disabled activists in the San Francisco Bay area in 2019 in protest of the US government's detention of immigrants in prisons and concentration camps. Later in 2019, it was reactivated to oppose the impact of the climate crisis on disposability culture when profit-driven utility company PG&E's solution to the California wildfires was to shut off the power to whole sections of the state, putting many people's lives at risk by removing access to life-sustaining medical equipment (Haney et al.). When the #NoBodyIsDisposable Coalition came together again in 2020, its work centred on resisting unjust COVID-19 triage protocols. The coalition's "Know Your Rights Guide to Surviving COVID-19 Triage Protocols" toolkit explains to fat, disabled, and/or ill people our rights and outlines strategies for survival if we get COVID-19, require hospitalization, and are faced with ration-based triage protocols that use eugenics practices to decide who will receive life-saving treatment. The toolkit and the hashtag spread widely: a search for #NoBodyIsDisposable on social media platforms returns thousands of tagged images. Fat and disabled people hold up signs that assert their lives are valuable and add their own calls for survival and care. Hashtags such as #NoICUgenics also grew in popularity as disabled and fat communities saw the triage protocols for the eugenics policies they really are. The hashtags became rallying calls to communicate our desire to live (see figures 20.1 and 20.2).

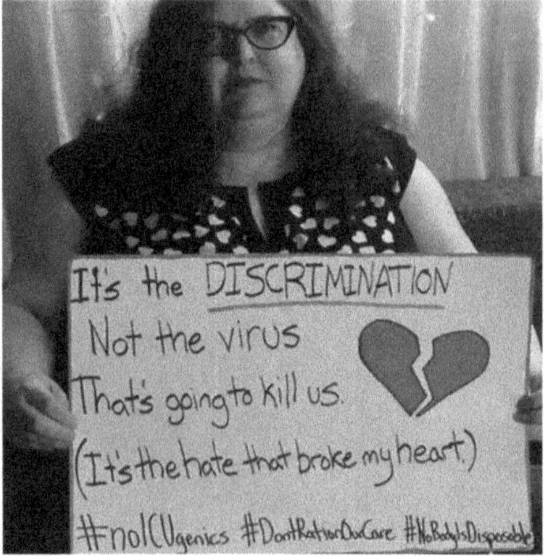

Figure 20.1
Alt-Text: A fat femme with long, dark, curly hair, and cat-eye glasses sits in front of colourful lights holding a sign that reads, "It's the discrimination not the virus that's going to kill us. (It's the hate that broke my heart) #noICUgenics #NoBodyIsDisposable #DontRationOurCare #NoBodyIsDisposable." The sign includes a drawing of a broken, red heart.

Source: #NoBodyIsDisposable

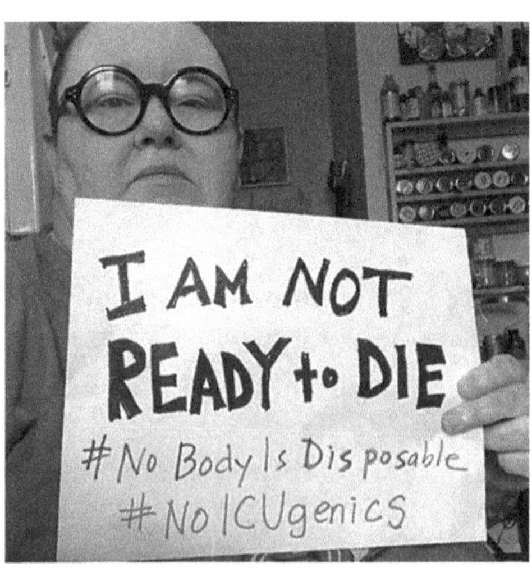

Figure 20.2
Alt-Text: A fat, white adult with round glasses, very short dark hair, and a red shirt holds a white paper sign with a handwritten message that reads "I am not ready to die. #NoBodyIsDisposable #NoICUgenics."

Source: #NoBodyIsDisposable

We Are Not Ready to Die

In Ontario, I, Tracy, became increasingly vigilant as collective fears of shortages became real with the introduction of new provincial triage protocols. The first model for COVID-19 triage was published on March 28, 2020 (Ontario Health), and embodied discriminatory protocols. Fat, disabled, and ill people's lives were at serious risk for care rationing, and systemic anti-Black and anti-Indigenous racism in medicine meant that fat, disabled, and ill Black and Indigenous people and people of colour were in even greater danger (Block and Galabuzi; Harrison, "We Are Witnessing"; Schmidt et al.; Wong, "I'm Disabled").[2] I reached out to a handful of human rights lawyers and scholars I knew to be working in disability justice and law. I wanted help adapting the "Know Your Rights Guide to Surviving COVID-19 Triage Protocols" for a Canadian context. Nobody responded.

I gathered that they were swamped with human rights abuses—both those enduring from pre-COVID times and those emerging in the wake of the pandemic. I gathered they were, like so many others, adjusting to the new reality and pressures of working from home while supporting parents, children, friends, or extended family. I wondered, too, whether they were unable to grasp fat lives as vibrant and sacred: does fatness extend too far beyond their understanding of who deserves life-saving medical care or legal protections? Is it still too radical to claim that fatness and fat life are valuable? In the "Organisation of Hate," Sara Ahmed suggests that hatred is an affective collection of emotional perspectives that move "sideways, forwards and backwards." She goes on to say that "hate is not contained within the contours of a subject, but moves across or between subjects, objects, signs and others" (348). The early stages of the pandemic encompassed so much terror and vulnerability and revealed just how disdained and disposable fat, disabled, and ill people are understood to be.

In addition to the pressures of the pandemic, the agony of the murders of many Black and Indigenous people in the United States and Canada at the hands of police in the spring of 2020 was also a catalyst for change. Massive civil unrest lasted months, and calls for both reform and abolition were forceful (#DefundThePolice,

#AbolishThePolice) and echoed across both mainstream and social media. Often absent from these conversations is fatness (Harrison, "Fatphobia"). Like Eric Garner before George Floyd, Barbara Dawson before Breonna Taylor, and Michael Brown before Ma'Khia Bryant, fat Black people, both adults and children, are derided and murdered by police. In her fat black disability framework, Anna Mollow contends that fat black lives are in effect unvictimizable—simultaneously innately disabled and superhumanly invulnerable because of their fatness and Blackness. The state, in both policing and medicine, uses this perspective to hyper-police fat Black lives as they are perceived as threatening and, at the same time, inviolable and undeserving of care. Fat bodies are understood as being closer to death, and Black fat bodies are perhaps already dead (Shackelford). Fat, disabled, and Black, Indigenous, and people of colour (BIPOC) have always known that these systems claiming to protect us are the same ones threatening to kill us.

The absence of fatness in the coverage of COVID-19 and Black Lives Matter, as well as the dearth of awareness of how fat liberation, disability justice, and other liberation movements intersect, might explain the radio silence when I reached out for solidarity around Ontario's triage protocols. Creating a toolkit for our communities during this time seemed not just necessary, but inevitable.

Creating a Toolkit for Ontario, Canada

We, Fady and Tracy, connected on these ideas and decided to work together on adapting the American toolkit for the Canadian context. We found this task overwhelming and scary, but our lived experience and our shared commitment to fat, disabled, and ill people made it clear that we want and need to protect ourselves and each other from and within the medical system. So, in the moment, we decide to get together to talk. We talk about what it means to ask fat, disabled, and ill people to spend time and money on preparing ourselves for (more) medical discrimination and lack of care in a critical, life or death, situation. We discuss what it means for white versus BIPOC community members and for supersize versus mid-size fat people to be doing this work. We talk about what is at stake for Black and Indigenous people and people of colour to beg for their/our lives. We know that it is beyond onerous for us to plead with a racist, ageist, ableist, fatphobic, heteronormative system that already denies us care, induces immense stress and feelings of self-hatred, and reduces the causes of all our illnesses and injuries to our weight. But we want to live.

We rationalize these strategies not under the banner of self-care or resiliency, but as activism. To know and practice our rights is activism. It has both an individual and collective purpose and reminds us that when we ask for what we want and need, we make space for others to ask for and get what they need too. We know, as Audre Lorde affirms, that we will not dismantle the "master's house" with the "master's tools," but surely, learning to use them at this catastrophic moment may help us take care of each other and survive.[3] The existence of fat, disabled, ill, and aging people in the past, present, and future is in itself activism against the ongoing categorization of our bodies and beings as disposable. Our approach with the "Know Your Rights Guide" intends to support both our day-to-day lives and disrupt social and cultural systems of violence and oppression. This follows Charlotte Cooper's (2021) description of the importance of both micro and macro approaches to activism and connects us to the long line of fat (and disabled) activist histories that make visible our capacities and desires for life.

Ontario Triage Protocol and the Clinical Frailty Scale

Ontario's COVID-19 triage protocols are developed by the Bioethics Table, an advisory committee that provides ethical guidance on decision-making for Ontario's Ministry of Health. One of several assessment tools the ministry proposes to help determine who gets access to treatment is the Clinical Frailty Scale (CFS). The CFS was developed by researchers at Dalhousie University for the Canadian Study of Health and Aging, an epidemiological study of dementia in Canada. Its original purpose was to "summarize the overall level of fitness or frailty of an older adult"; however, it has recently become a COVID-19 triage tool meant to help emergency care providers predict survivability and either prioritize or deprioritize people they deem most or least likely to benefit from treatment when heath care resources are scarce (Ontario Health). The second version of the CFS, version 2.0 (2020), is a written and illustrated document that outlines nine levels of vulnerability ranging from "very fit" to "terminally ill."[4]

The illustrations lack any detail, the bodies are blacked-out block images with soft edges. Level 1, "very fit," depicts a thin, masculine-presenting person dressed in shorts, a T-shirt, baseball hat, and sneakers; one foot takes a running step, the other foot slightly in the air, to show that this body is on the move. Level 2 is "fit." The person depicted is also thin and masculine presenting in form and is also in an active stride. These bodies, heralded by medical practitioners and researchers for their ideal health and form, have a cultural eminence too. Younger, smaller, fit, able-bodied people are understood to have good, beautiful, fulfilled lives (LeBesco 21). In the medical context, these supposed quality-of-life markers translate to survivability. From here, the CFS illustrations depict bodies that shift towards fatter and more disabled. By Level 4, "vulnerable," we see a fat person hunched over a cane. This person "complains" of being "slowed up" and "tired during the day." In some versions of the CFS, the fat person at Level 4 is depicted carrying a large, burdensome bag. Levels 5 and 6 are thin disabled people described as "slow" and "frail." They are shown hunched over their walkers. The person at Level 6, "moderately frail," is accompanied by another person because "they might need minimal assistance." People at Levels 8 and 9 are "approaching the end of life." Level 8, "very severely frail," is a small adult body shown resting in bed. This body is described as "completely dependent." Level 9 is "terminally ill" and described as having less than six months to live but "not otherwise evidently frail." This person is depicted as thin and sits slightly hunched forward in a chair. It's as though they could have been an exception to illness and death as they lack visible signs of sickness, disability, and fatness that are otherwise pictured at other levels on the scale. Levels 3 through 8 are presented as increasingly old, fat, ill, and disabled, leading to a predictable, inevitable death.

These prescriptive levels of medical frailty and survivability are bound up with the social and cultural understandings of what kinds of lives are worth living and what kinds of bodies are worth living with. However, fat, disabled, ill, and elderly people tell different stories about our own lives. We continually express a broad complexity of human experience, meaning, and connection. We lead immersive and full lives (Lind et al.; Tidgwell et al.; Wong, *Disability Visibility*). False and oversimplified valuations of the young, fit, white, able-bodied person puts elders and aging, racialized, fat, ill, and disabled people at severe risk for the denial or removal of life-saving treatment in situations of triaged critical care, like the one Ontario faced in April 2021.

Ontario's use of the Clinical Frailty Scale is contested by many, especially in relation to COVID-19 care rationing policies and practices (ARCH). The United Kingdom's National Institute for Health and Care Excellence changed its position on the CFS on March 25, 2020, remarking that it has limitations and should not be used for certain members of the population, including young people and many individuals with both physical and neurodiverse disabilities (National Institute for Health and Care Excellence). The widespread and sanctioned use of the CFS ignores these and other potentially harmful limitations and reinforces for us how frailty, fatness, disability, and old age become medically analogous for disposable.

A revised triage protocol has been on Ontario's horizon since the March 28, 2020, protocol was rescinded after immense community response and push back from the Ontario Human Rights Commission, the ARCH Disability Law Centre, and other social, cultural, and medical organizations and activists in the spring of 2020. The new protocol is supposed to be released to the public in April 2021, as we finalize our reflections for this chapter and face "the third wave" of COVID in Ontario, the third province-wide "lockdown," and provincial infection rates and ICU numbers that are reaching record highs (CBC).[5]

Continuing Concerns

We continue to be concerned that the forthcoming revised protocol, like the March 28, 2020, proposal, will include discriminatory frameworks despite criticisms from disabled, fat, ill, BIPOC, and aging communities, and despite the existence of the Canadian Charter of Rights and Freedoms and the Canadian and Ontario Human Rights Codes. We continue to be concerned that fat, disabled, ill, aging, and BIPOC people face direct discrimination based on weight and disability through triage protocols, as well as indirect discrimination based on weight and disability because of other diagnoses, perceived quality of life, and other stereotypes associated with higher weight. Such discrimination has a disproportionate impact on many Black and Indigenous people and people of colour, namely, on those who already experience systemic inequalities and bias within the health care system.

Our concerns are not overreactions, nor are they new. The medical system has failed us time and again. We and members of our community have been mistreated and misdiagnosed, had care withheld and denied. The "Know Your Rights Guide to Surviving COVID-19 Triage Protocols for Fat Disabled People: Ontario" may be painful for some to use, but it is an offering of mutual aid rooted in our passion for community, care, and justice. We care about our lives and yours. We refuse to be disposable.

What follows is the "Know Your Rights Guide" that we adapted for Ontarians from the US version and published online at NoBodyIsDisposable.org in January 2021 (Tidgwell and Shanouda). We've included some reflections on collecting these materials, as well as notes on what has happened since creating the guide to provide further context. These interjections are in shaded boxes throughout the guide.

Know Your Rights Guide to Surviving COVID-19 Triage Protocols for Fat Disabled People: Ontario, Canada

If you need to access this information in a different format, contact us at nobodyisdisposable@gmail.com

Overview

This is a "Know Your Rights" toolkit for people facing potential triage discrimination based on size or disability during the COVID-19 pandemic in Ontario, Canada.

We focus on Ontario because that's where we live but also because Ontario has specific rights, laws, and compliance regulations that are more stringent than other provincial or sometimes national regulations.

However, this toolkit covers survival and advocacy strategies that apply to fat and disabled people in other provinces, territories, and countries.

You can share the Ontario, Canada, toolkit using this link: https://nobodyisdisposable.org/know-your-rights/on-ca

***Important Notice:* This toolkit is not legal or medical advice. The information included below has been sourced from research and is for general information purposes only. Laws, practices, and requirements vary by province and territory, so it's best to look for what is required where you are or consult with a lawyer to make sure you have the right information for your location and situation. The COVID-19 pandemic is a changing situation. This information may not be up to date. The info in this toolkit may change as things progress, so check back. It's up to you to be sure the information is correct and applicable to you.

Background

As of January 2021, Ontario is experiencing a COVID-19 crisis. Many long-term care facilities are facing caregiver and medical-resource shortages, and hospitals are at a tipping point: acute care wards of many major hospitals are running at maximum capacity and will begin to send patients to other regions across the province for care.

> We are writing this chapter in April 2021, when the case count in Ontario is at its highest ever and emergency orders allow hospitals to transfer patients to ICUs outside of their geographical region without their consent (CBC). In Toronto and other COVID-19 "hot zones" in the province, field hospitals and pop-up clinics have been constructed in parking lots and other spaces. There is a strong collective feeling about and expression of anger at and disappointment with the government's response. There is an air of fear and worry over when the virus and its variants will infect close family, as the number of people in ICU and the death toll rise. Demographics of severely ill people are shifting towards younger people. Essential workers, disproportionately Black and Brown people are currently most affected (Canada, Statistics Canada; Cheung; Warner).

Ontario Health has rescinded its discriminatory triage protocols that excluded certain patients—disabled, ill, older, fat, and people perceived to have lower activity levels—from treatments that offer the best chance of survival, even when a sick person is likely to benefit from that treatment or will die without it. However, it has not yet proposed a revised protocol.

We are extremely concerned for our lives.

> We continue to be concerned for our lives as we anticipate the release of the new triage protocol: "Adult Critical Care Clinical Emergency Standard of Care for Major Surge" (Casey). This new protocol, already criticized by the Ontario Human Rights Commission (Chadha), the ARCH Disability Law Centre, the AODA Alliance, and others (Hauen) will supersede and ultimately violate human rights laws. Measures in the new protocol that are particularly concerning include both new guidelines that ask doctors to rank patients on their likelihood to survive a year after

the onset of critical illness and a "risk calculator" that uses age, gender, socio-demographics, and health status to determine the likelihood of mortality (Casey).

The calculator was developed by Johns Hopkins University. Its algorithm uses existing data from large health studies to determine a person's risk of death (Johns Hopkins Bloomberg School of Public Health). If we've learned anything from more recent examinations of algorithmic data, it is that they are biased and reflect the racist, ableist, and fatphobic world we live in (Noble). Fat, disabled, ill, and aging BIPOC people will not fare better with a quantitative judge; the bias is built in.

A revised protocol is coming too late to deal with the current surge in COVID-19 cases in the province. And we are concerned that a revised protocol, like the March 28, 2020, proposal, will include discriminatory frameworks despite criticisms from disabled, fat, and aging communities, and despite the existence of the Charter and the Canadian and Ontario Human Rights Codes.

We share the concern that fat and higher weight people are facing direct discrimination based on weight and disability via triage protocols, as well as indirect discrimination based on weight and disability because of other diagnoses, perceived quality of life, and other stereotypes associated with higher weight. Such discrimination has a disproportionate impact on many Black, Indigenous, people of colour, and LGBTQ2SIA people who already experience systemic inequalities and bias within the health care system.

We offer this toolkit as a way to help take care of each other. Remember that there are hundreds of thousands of fat, disabled people and allies who are rooting for you!

What to Do Before You Need to Go to the Hospital

If you can, it's a good idea to get these four critical legal documents ready before you get sick. In Ontario, you can prepare some of these documents on your own or use a kit.

Documents 1 & 2: Power of Attorney for Personal Care and Power of Attorney for Property

Power of Attorney for Personal Care, sometimes called Medical Power of Attorney, is a document giving power to a person you trust to make medical decisions and advocate for you while you are unable to do so. Power of Attorney for Property, sometimes called Financial Power of Attorney, is a document giving power to a person you trust to make financial decisions for you while you are unable to do so. In Ontario, you can create your own power of attorney forms or use a kit, but the paperwork must be signed by two adult people, in person. (See the resources at the end of this toolkit for more info and a link to a kit).

- Choose your representatives carefully. The person must be trustworthy, able to understand and communicate what you want, capable of making decisions for you if you are not able, and ready to fight for you if necessary.
- Make sure your representatives keep a signed copy of the power of attorney documents on them at all times.
- Bring a copy of your Medical Power of Attorney with you to the hospital so care workers know whom you have chosen. Otherwise, a substitute decision maker will be appointed to you by the hospital; most often this will be your closest family member.
- Discuss what you want to happen, including end-of-life decisions, with your chosen person before you go to the hospital.
- Disabled fat folks or anyone who may have more complex health directives may want to consult a lawyer.
- If care providers don't know you have an assigned decision maker or person with power of attorney, they will make other arrangements and are not liable for decisions made on your behalf.

Example:

Pilar needed a ventilator and was placed on one. She was sedated during the process and is now unable to speak. Pilar chose Ari to be her attorney for medical decisions (Medical Power of Attorney), and they talked about her wishes in advance. When a hospital worker tells Ari they want to reallocate the ventilator that is keeping Pilar alive because a non-disabled patient needs it, Ari is able to speak for Pilar and explain that Pilar does NOT consent to the removal of the ventilator, since removal is not needed for her own health and safety. Ari does not want the hospital worker to get into trouble, so Ari reminds the hospital worker that touching Pilar's body to remove the ventilator without consent might be a crime and that employees may not be covered by malpractice insurance or immunity when committing crimes. Ari tells the hospital worker that they should check with a lawyer that represents them personally (not just their boss or lawyers for the hospital) to figure out whether they could be personally liable in civil or criminal court for the harm they would cause Pilar by removing the ventilator without her consent.

Document 3: Advance Directive

An Advance Directive gives instructions about what medical decisions you want made, or it outlines the values and beliefs that will guide your decision maker in giving consent and making decisions for you if you are unable.

In Ontario, health care professionals must get consent from you or your decision maker at the time of treatment. An Advance Directive communicates your wishes clearly in writing.

In Ontario, you can create your own Advance Directive or use a kit (see the resources at the end of this toolkit).

Each province and territory has rules about what requirements must be followed in making a health care directive, so look for what is required where you are.

- Keep a copy of your Advance Directive at home, give one to your attorney (with Power of Attorney for Personal Care), and bring a copy to the hospital with you.
- Discuss what you want to happen, including end-of-life decisions, with your chosen person *before* you go to the hospital.

- Pack a copy of your Advance Directive in your go-bag.
- You may want to keep a copy of your Advance Directive, a clear instruction to not repurpose your ventilator, and info on the location of your go-bag on your refrigerator, marked clearly and boldly. (If paramedics take you to the hospital, they may look there for important documents).

Document 4: Will or Trust

Wills and trusts are end-of-life documents that provide instructions about your wishes and where you want your property to go. There are many resources online to help you create these documents. An alternative is to hire a lawyer to prepare these documents for you. If you die without these documents, the people making decisions might not be the people you want.

Access to legal protection—much like medical care—is fraught with many entrenched and systemic barriers. It was difficult for us to attain this information and to summarize it clearly. We worry that this information is not complete and that there exist additional documents and steps necessary to protect oneself. We researched this information on the internet and discovered that there is no clear, comprehensive list of what is needed and no information on how the various documents differ or on which document is necessary for which emergency care scenario. As we've outlined, you can create these documents yourself, but it's a challenging process that requires a lot of legal comprehension and navigation. If you can afford a lawyer, we agree it's best to leave the process to them. If you can't, we have provided this (incomplete) guide to creating the documents yourself.

Create a Connection Kit

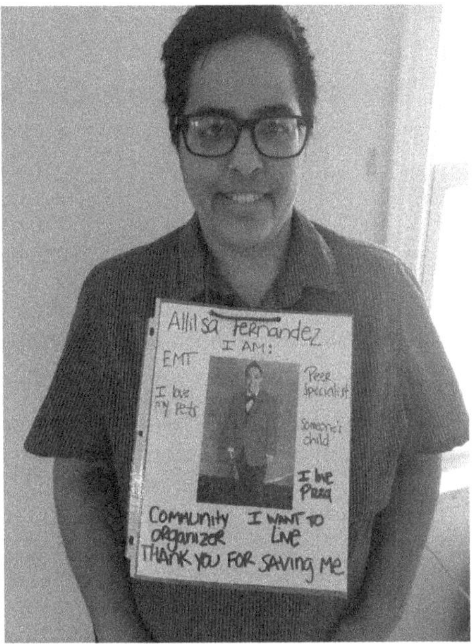

Figure 20.3

Alt-Text: A person of colour wears a Connection Kit. Around their neck is a sheet protector on a string with a piece of paper inside that includes a photo of themself dressed up in red jacket and large handwritten message that reads "Allilsa Fernandez. I am: EMT, Peer Specialist, I love my pets, Someone's child, I love pizza, Community organizer, I want to live, Thank you for saving me."

Source: #NoBodyIsDisposable

Create a Connection Kit to help you stay connected and to help providers connect with you as a human being worthy of life-saving treatment (see figure 20.3).

Make multiple copies of this because it can get lost in hospital transfers—have one attached to you / your bed / your door, one or more copies in your go-bag, and a copy that a friend can bring. Your Connection Kit can be tied to your gurney or looped around your wrist or neck where you and your care team can see it. Tie a string through the corner of a plastic paper protector or clear zip-lock bag and attach it.

Include in your Connection Kit

- A printout of phone numbers of family and friends
- A photo of family or loved ones, facing out
- A humanizing photo of yourself in your normal life with friends or at work, facing out so medical staff can view it
- A mini summary introducing yourself, facing out

In the introduction to this chapter, we mentioned briefly our conversations about what is at stake when we ask Black and Indigenous people and people of colour to beg for their/our lives. We believe that there are both tangible and intangible stakes here. To ask BIPOC folks to beg is to ask them/us to ignore their/our past experiences with these systems, to imagine a different outcome from all those before, and to put their/our lives in the hands of those who so many times have treated them/us as disposable. What is tangibly at stake is their/our lives, their/our access to care and life-saving treatment. One intangible effect of asking BIPOC folks to participate in some of the toolkit's strategies for survival are painful losses to dignity and self-worth. What does it feel like to ask or beg for what comes to others as a right, as commonplace, assumed, and expected? What are the emotional, physical, psychological, and spiritual impacts of begging to be understood as worthy of care, or worthy of life?

What's at stake is once again being ignored and having your life be devalued. What's at stake is preventing more injury, access to care, and life-saving treatment. And maybe most important, begging for what comes to others as a right—a promise, an oath to protect—is a loss of dignity. It's a total feeling of worthlessness.

What to Take to the Hospital

If you are going to the ER, you will want to bring as much support as you can. Many medical facilities have stricter limits on visitors or advocacy accompaniment right now, so bring what you want and need with you in a go-bag.

For fat intellectually disabled people, the risk of being triaged out of care or survival is especially high given the triage protocol, the risk calculator, and the inherent bias in the medical system—hence the importance of advocacy work and having a friend, guardian, or parent present at all times. We've heard from friends and colleagues that they have had to fight and argue with medical staff to ensure the right of access to an advocate. Don't back down.

A hospital go-bag is a pre-packed bag of essential items that you, your loved ones, or paramedics can grab and take to the hospital if you need to go in an emergency.

Pack the following items in your go-bag:

- A Sharpie or surgical marker (bring a colour that shows up well on your skin).
- Advocacy supports:
  - Phone
  - Phone charger
  - Charged phone batteries—as many as you can bring
  - "Know Your Rights" Toolkit printout
  - Printouts of advocacy documents/letters to providers (described below)
- Your Connection Kit
- A copy of your signed Medical Power of Attorney.
- Communication tools:
  - Paper, pens, tablet or any device you can use easily
  - Assistive communication devices
  - Extra hearing aid batteries
  - Spare eyeglasses or contacts

Consider bringing the following:

- Masks, gloves, tape, and whatever other medical supplies you need
- Medications (hospitals may not normally allow you to take your own medicine; however, some people may feel more comfortable having their medicines with them, for example,

to show a provider exactly what they are taking or because there may be policy exceptions made due to medication shortages.)

- Notes on your medical history. It's a personal decision to disclose your medical history as this may impact your access to triage-based care.
- Breathing-support equipment, such as a CPAP / BiPAP / APAP or oxygen concentrator, if you have it. Considerations:
    - If there is a shortage, the hospital may not be able to supply you with needed equipment, so having your own could make a life-or-death difference.
    - Is equipment being "reallocated"? If so, are you risking your equipment being taken from you physically if you bring it?
    - The hospital may have policies preventing the use of personal equipment or may lack the personnel to test it.
    - Make sure your name is securely on whatever equipment you bring.

Strategies for Advocacy

- Be an advocate; bring an advocate. An advocate is a friend, family member, or any person you trust to fight for you and your wishes.
- Bring an advocate by phone if they can't come in person. Many ERs and hospitals have policies prohibiting cell phone use, but you can try telling them that you want to have your advocate present via phone because they are not allowing non-patients into COVID treatment areas. If you need to have a person available by cell due to your disability, you can tell them you need them to make an accommodation in their policy. NOTE: You have the right to a reasonable accommodation for accessibility-related matters.
- If you are disabled, you have a right to communication assistance. D/deaf people can get ASL interpreting or CART. Blind or vision impaired people have a right to papers in Braille or large print or in a computer file.

- NOTE: There are no laws against weight discrimination in Ontario (or anywhere in Canada); however, you have the right to a reasonable accommodation for matters related to disability/accessibility. What "reasonable" means for the hospital or government may seem unreasonable in other sectors or situations. Remember to ask for what you need (not want) and know that it is most likely reasonable.
- You can get information in another language, or you can have an interpreter.
- If you don't have an advocate, bring someone to act as a witness; ask that person to get names and take notes about what treatment you are offered and why. Again, you can ask to have someone witness over the phone on audio or video.
- Attach your Connection Kit to your body/your bed, and/or your door. You can write your desire for care and the phone number of your advocate/decision maker on your body using a Sharpie.

Potential Survival Strategies to Consider If You Face Discrimination

Warning:

We hope that these strategies won't be necessary to use. We also know that some of us will be in life-or-death situations, so it's worth considering many options. We know that it will be exponentially harder for Black and Indigenous people, people of colour, trans/nonbinary people, and other marginalized people. We acknowledge that some of these strategies may cause the user harm and may be futile. For some people, it may be better to resist right away; for others, trying to be nice may be the best approach. Use what works for you; discard what does not.

If health care providers make you feel less deserving of the best chance to live, remember that there are hundreds of thousands of fat, disabled people and allies who know you deserve to live, and we are rooting for you! You deserve to live!!!

Build Connection with Health Care Providers

- Try to connect with your providers. Remember they are under intense stress. Ask how they are doing.
- Empathize with the challenges and pressure providers are under.
- Humanize yourself. Show pictures of your family. Share something unique about yourself. Do your best to connect and be seen as a person.
- With regard to rationing, tell them you want the treatment options that provide the best chance to recover, just like non-disabled/younger/thinner patients receive.
    - You can use your Sharpie to write your instructions directly on your arms or chest in case you become unable to communicate. Be sure that you do not accidentally write anything that conflicts with your choices in your Advance Directive

You may communicate your thoughts or desires (speak, write, gesture, sign, or point to pre-written notes). Practice saying these phrases out loud now, *before* you need to advocate for yourself or a loved one.

- I know that you became a provider to help people heal. I am asking you to help me.
- I am protected by the Constitution.
- I am protected as a disabled person under
    - The Ontario Human Rights Code
    - Bill C-81: The Accessible Canada Act, S.C. 2019, c. 10.
- What you are doing is WRONG.
- What you are being told to do is WRONG.
- This is against your oath as a provider.
- I do not consent to withdrawal of treatment.
- This is not triage; this is discrimination. I want treatment. (Examples: "I want to be resuscitated" or "I want high-flow oxygen and BiPAP if no ventilator is available.")
- I have questions. What alternative treatments are available? What treatments would be available if I were thin, not older, or not disabled?
- I don't agree with your decision. I want to speak to a supervisor.

- I am not receiving equal treatment. I want to file a grievance.
- As a last resort: I want an ethics consultation. (If you don't like the result, see what the appeal process is.)

Sample Letters to Providers

People often have a hard time communicating with medical providers or knowing what to say. Many feel the intense power imbalance, which can be even worse for Black and Indigenous people and people of colour; for fat, higher weight, and disabled people; for some LGBTQ2SIA people; or for any people or groups that face discrimination.

NoBodyIsDisposable has created the letters linked below to help give you some idea of what to say to health care providers. Or you can even show them to providers if that works best for you. Or you can also use these letters to write your own letter for your providers. In an emergency setting, remember it will be hard for providers to take the time to read, so keep your message short and focused. Making your letters as personal as possible is ideal.

Please choose the letter that applies best to your situation.[6]

- Letter for people who are higher weight and disabled: https://nobodyisdisposable.org/know-your-rights/covid-sample-letter-higher-weight-and-disabled/
- Letter for people who are higher weight: https://nobodyisdisposable.org/know-your-rights/covid-sample-letter-higher-weight/
- Letter for people who are disabled: https://nobodyisdisposable.org/know-your-rights/covid-sample-letter-disabled/
- Letter for people who are older (consider adding this language to one of the letters above if you need to): https://nobodyisdisposable.org/know-your-rights/covid-sample-letter-elder/

More Resources [7]

- Note on having your paperwork signed: In Ontario, you need two (2) witnesses to sign in person (no digital signatures). Your witnesses *cannot* be your guardian, spouse, partner, or child or be under your guardianship; the person you're naming your attorney (with power of attorney); the spouse, partner, or child of your attorney; or a person under the age of 18.
- Speak Up Ontario is an initiative of Hospice Palliative Care Ontario to improve awareness of health care consent and advance care planning. It provides many resources through Advance Care Planning Ontario (https://www.advancecareplanning.ca), including resources applicable to people hospitalized with COVID-19 and info on power of attorney:
    - Advance Care Planning Resource Guide: https://www.advancecareplanningontario.ca/resources-educational-support/resource-guide
    - Advance Care Planning Workbook: https://www.advancecareplanningontario.ca/acp/acp-workbook
- The Ontario Ministry of the Attorney General offers this online resource and a link to a free kit for creating a power of attorney yourself.
    - Ontario Ministry of the Attorney General: Make a Power of Attorney: https://www.ontario.ca/page/make-power-attorney
- ARCH Disability Law Centre is a specialty legal clinic that practices exclusively in disability rights law. ARCH is dedicated to defending and advancing the equality rights, entitlements, fundamental freedoms, and inclusion of persons with disabilities in Ontario.
    - ARCH's COVID-19 Resources: https://archdisabilitylaw.ca/covid/#
- #Pooran Law—Whole Life Planning Centre: https://pooranlaw.com. This legal firm is run by a lawyer who also teaches critical disability law at York University.[8]

- #NoBodyIsDisposable Campaign against Discrimination in Triage: https://nobodyisdisposable.org. Join our three-step action campaign to try to stop the discrimination being put in place.

COVID-19 vaccines have emerged as essential resources for some fat, disabled, and ill people in Ontario. Phase II of the province's vaccine roll out includes eligibility for people with BMI greater than 40 and other "high risk chronic conditions," which are detailed in the province's vaccination plan (Office of the Premier). This access has brought with it complicated community conversations and questions. What does it mean to be accounted for and protected by a structure that otherwise systemically harms us? What does it mean to be fat and or disabled and otherwise low-risk for COVID (either by ableist conceptions of health status and/or material working conditions) and claim access to vaccines early on in the vaccine roll out before many of our beloved community members who are at higher-risk? Does a diagnosis make a person high risk? What does it mean to accept a vaccine whose efficacy in fat bodies is not well documented? What does it mean to know that in a care-rationing triage scenario, BIPOC, fat, ill, disabled lives will be ransomed? We are fearful of COVID and of a lack of access to care, but we fight to live.

Conclusion

We spoke with a member of our community who contracted COVID-19 and reaffirmed that even when COVID-19 is not life-threatening, care for fat and racialized people is layered with multiple biases and complexity (Alberga et al.; Dryden and Nnorom; Levy et al.; Maynard; Rinaldi et al.; Thille; Williams et al.). Tavi identifies as a supersized, fat Black woman, and in our conversation, she expressed both gratitude for and disappointment with the medical treatment she received during her long and extreme illness. COVID-19 didn't lead her to hospitalization, but she was intensely ill at home, alone, and is now experiencing the long-term effects of COVID, or what some are calling long-COVID. Tavi described her experience of receiving quality care from the Toronto hospital COVID team when she tested positive. She was assigned a doctor who followed up with her by phone twice at the beginning of her illness. However, she felt she received inadequate treatment from her long-time general practitioner (GP). She repeatedly brought complaints of a secondary infection not related to COVID-19 to her GP, but her additional symptoms were completely dismissed. She asserted that this infection felt different than her experience of COVID-19, but she was ignored multiple times. Eventually, a family friend and physician did her a favour and performed an online clinical evaluation in which Tavi was properly diagnosed and prescribed the right course of treatment for the secondary infection. All the while she was dealing with ongoing COVID-19 symptoms including headaches, shortness of breath, body aches, aphasia (an impairment of language), dysgeusia (a distorted sense of taste), and significant and long-lasting brain fog. During the peak of her illness, Tavi would sleep restlessly for anywhere between 15 and 18 hours a day. She said that it felt like her body was betraying her.

Tavi recounted that her early complaints of shortness of breath were written off by her family members as fat-related breathing issues. But she declared, "I know fat-girl breathing, and this wasn't it." The dismissal of her intimate knowledge of her own body was effacing and felt like commentary about her size, as if they were saying, "You don't know your body—there is too much of it to know." We asked if she was ever afraid during this time, and she acknowledged she was. Her fears were rooted in being judged for contracting COVID-19 and interrogated for not taking better care of herself. She was afraid of fat stigma and fatmisia (fat hatred). Tavi described to us a powerful recurring dream in which she hears someone say, "There's no point in us treating you; you aren't going to live long anyway."

Tavi's experience isn't one that involved the ICU or any additional hospital visits beyond her initial visit to the testing site. The care she received from the hospital, as she described it, was "epic." And yet she's had disturbing dreams of being denied care because of her body. The knowledge she has of her body was denied twice during this time—once by family and the second time by her GP. She's afraid of the effects of long-COVID and the limited resources that may be available for treatment. She didn't use our guide, and she didn't need it. But she embodied some of the very fears that inspired our creation of the guide and has enacted some of the strategies for advocacy and survival within it.

We know the effects of COVID will be with us as a society for a long time. How we come to understand this time and what we learn from it as a collective will depend on whose experiences we reflect on. Fat, disabled, ill, and aging people's experiences of COVID-19, including the experiences of those who have not survived, must be a part of the reflective process as we consider the harms done and the mistakes made during COVID. In part, this chapter is an act of mutual support and a resource for survival. But it is also a way to reflect on how precarious our health care system is and how disposable certain lives become as a result. We offer it both as a record of events and as guidance for the future. We will continue to imagine and create other ways of being together and caring for ourselves and each other. And we will reflect on and learn from the deliberate racism embedded in the disproportionate risks and effects of COVID-19 on Black and Indigenous people and people of colour, as well as on the blatant eugenics ideology embedded in COVID-19 triage protocols that deem the lives of fat, disabled, ill, aging, and BIPOC people inconsequential. We are in awe of and uplift the power and capacity of the coalitional activism of fat, disabled, ill, and aging people and of BIPOC folks. We honour our embodied knowledge and experience; we value our differences and the space we take up.

Acknowledgments

The authors thank the #NoBodyIsDisposable Coalition, the Fat Legal Advocacy, Rights, & Education Project (FLARE), and Fat Rose for their activism and leadership throughout and beyond the COVID-19 triage care crises, and for supporting us through the adaptation of the #NoBodyIsDisposable Toolkit for the Ontario, Canada, context.

Notes

1 We finalized this paper in April 2021 at the height of the "third wave" of COVID-19 in Canada. The paper captures the intensity experienced during the early, pre-vaccine era of the pandemic.

2 We acknowledge that this account of events is mainly descriptive. In part, this chapter is an act of witnessing, a record for history. It is also an interpretive descriptive telling of how we came to produce a toolkit for fat, disabled, ill, and aging people for and with our diverse communities during the pandemic. Following Marcus et al., we place description at the "core" of analysis and evaluation (2). We anticipate that while our descriptions of these events are important for the here and now, their contributions may be most valuable in the future when we have more time and distance from them.

3 The "Know Your Rights" toolkit is only one of a number of community-created mutual aid resources. Also see, *Crips and Covid in Canada* (Ignagni et al.); Kay Hyatt's United Kingdom–based guide; *Fat-Assed Prepper Survival Tips for Preparing for a Coronavirus Quarantine* (Solovay et al.); *Half Assed Disabled Prepper Tips for Preparing for a Coronavirus* (Piepzna-Samarasinha); and *Pod Mapping for Mutual Aid* (Black).

4 There are several versions of the Clinical Frailty Scale, and with each new version, new levels have been added or the descriptors for each level have changed. The overall purpose and goal of the CFS, to determine quickly and efficiently a person's level of frailty, has not changed.

5 The anticipated revised protocol from the Ontario Government, which would have addressed community and legal criticisms of the biases embedded in the January 2021 protocol, never materialized.

6 You can find direct links to these letters for health care providers in the online version of the "Know Your Rights Guide" at www.nobodyisdisposable.org/know-your-rights/on-ca.

7 You can find direct links to these do-it-yourself resources in the online version of the "Know Your Rights Guide" at www.nobodyisdisposable.org/know-your-rights/on-ca. Note that some of these links have been updated in this chapter, as Speak Up Ontario is now part of the Advance Care Planning Ontario website.

8 We share Pooran Law as a possible resource, not as an endorsement. We have no connections to Pooran Law or its associates.

Works Cited

Ahmed, Sara. "The Organisation of Hate." *Law & Critique*, vol. 12, 2001, pp. 345–65.

Alberga, Angela, Iyoma Yvonne Edache, Mary Forhan, and Shelly Russel-Mayhew. "Weight Bias and Health Care Utilization: A Scoping Review." *Primary Health Care Research and Development*, vol. 20, no. e116, 2019, pp. 1–14. Cambridge University Press: https://doi.org/10.1017/s1463423619000227.

ARCH Disability Law Centre. "ARCH Submissions Detailing Its Position on the Inclusion of the Clinical Frailty Scale in Ontario's Triage Protocol." *ARCH Disability Law Centre*, 1 Sept. 2020, www.archdisabilitylaw.ca/resource/arch-submissions-detailing-its-position-on-the-inclusion-of-the-clinical-frailty-scale-in-ontarios-triage-protocol/. Accessed 27 Apr. 2021.

Berne, Patty, and Stacey Milbern. "No Body Is Disposable Series." *Barnard Center for Research on Women*, 9 May, 2017, https://bcrw.barnard.edu/no-body-is-disposable-series/. Accessed 20 Apr. 2021.

Black, Rebel Sidney. "Pod Mapping for Mutual Aid." *Google Documents*, 9 Mar. 2020, www.docs.google.com/document/d/1-QfMn1D-E6ymhKZMpXN1LQvD6Sy_HSnnCK6gTO7ZLFrE/edit?fbclid=I-wAR0VdECHUc0aUrYd8gp69359XPb8PpdmwJqjNAdDWEr-IfjkFPN4LlyHcRBU. Accessed 20 Apr. 2021.

Block, Sheila, and Grace-Edward Galabuzi. "Canada's Colour Coded Labour Market: The Gap for Racialized Workers." *Canadian Centre for Policy Alternatives*, 21 Mar. 2011, www.policyalternatives.ca/publications/reports/canadas-colour-coded-labour-market. Accessed 25 Mar. 2021.

Canada. Statistics Canada. "COVID-19 Mortality Rates in Canada's Ethno-Cultural Neighbourhoods." *StatCan COVID-19: Data to Insights for a Better Canada*, 28 Oct. 2020, www150.statcan.gc.ca/n1/pub/45–28–0001/2020001/article/00079-eng.htm. Accessed 20 Mar. 2021.

Canadian Broadcasting Company. "The Latest on the Coronavirus Outbreak for April 15." *CBC News Coronavirus Brief*, 15 Apr. 2021, www.cbc.ca/news/canada/coronavirus-newsletter-april-15–1.5989499. Accessed 15 Apr. 2021.

Casey, Liam. "Plans for 'Life-and-Death' ICU Triage Decisions Not Finalized, Ont. Health Minister Says." *CTV News*, 7 Apr. 2021, www.toronto.ctvnews.ca/plans-for-life-and-death-icu-triage-decisions-not-finalized-ont-health-minister-says-1.5378448. Accessed 7 Apr. 2021.

Chadha, Ena. "New Letter to Minister of Health on Critical Care Triage Protocol." *Ontario Human Rights Commission*, 1 Mar. 2021, www.ohrc.on.ca/en/news_centre/new-letter-minister-health-critical-care-triage-protocol. Accessed 16 Mar. 2021.

Cheung, Jessica. "Black People and Other People of Colour Make up 83% of Reported COVID-19 Cases in Toronto." *CBC News*, 30 July 2020, https://www.cbc.ca/news/canada/toronto/toronto-covid-19-data-1.5669091. Accessed 28 Mar. 2021.

Cooper, Charlotte. *Fat Activism: A Radical Social Movement*. E-book, Intellect Books, 2021.

Dryden, OmiSoore, and Onye Nnorom. "Time to Dismantle Systemic Anti-Black Racism in Medicine in Canada." *Canadian Medical Association Journal*, vol. 193, no. 2, 2021, pp. E55–E57. *CMAJ*: https://doi.org/10.1503/cmaj.201579.

Haney, Dawn, Max Airborne, and Charis Stiles. "Cultivating New Fat Liberation Movements: Growing a Movement Ecology with Fat Rose." *Fat Studies*, vol. 10, no. 3, 2021, pp. 312–27.

Harrison, Da'Shaun. "We Are Witnessing the CDC's Violent Eugenicist History in Real-Time." *Wear Your Voice*, 8 Apr. 2020, www.wearyourvoicemag.com/cdc-violent-eugenicist-history-obesity-covid-19/. Accessed 1 Apr. 2021.

Harrison, Da'Shaun. "Fatphobia (& Foodphobia) is Anti-Blackness." *Rebel Eaters Club* [S2 E1], 5 Jan. 2021, www.rebeleatersclub.com/episodes/dashaunharrison. Accessed 21 Feb. 2021.

Hauen, Jack. "Solicitor General Brushes off Disability Advocate Concerns about Triage Protocol." *QP Briefing*, 21 Apr. 2021, https://www.qpbriefing.com/2021/04/21/solicitor-general-brushes-off-disability-advocate-concerns-about-triage-protocol/. Accessed 21 Apr. 2021.

Ignagni, Esther, Eliza Chandler, and Loree Erikson. "Crips and COVID in Canada." *iHuman*, The University of Sheffield, www.sheffield.ac.uk/ihuman/covid-19-blog/disability-and-covid-19-global-impacts/crips-and-covid-canada. Accessed 2 Mar. 2021.

Johns Hopkins Bloomberg School of Public Health. "New Online COVID-19 Mortality Risk Calculator Could Help Determine Who Should Get Vaccines First." *Johns Hopkins Bloomberg School of Public Health News*, 11 Dec. 2020, www.jhsph.edu/news/news-releases/2020/new-online-covid-19-mortality-risk-calculator-could-help-determine-who-should-get-vaccines-first.html. Accessed 30 Apr. 2021.

Piepzna-Samarasinha, Leah Lakshmi. "Half Assed Disabled Prepper Tips for Preparing for a Coronavirus Quarantine." *Google Documents*, 10 Mar. 2020, www.docs.google.com/document/d/1rIdpKgXeBHbmM3KpB5NfjEBue8YN1MbXhQ7zTOLmSyo/edit?fbclid=IwAR-3h_0-bFJv8cuP-eP6QjmE3IcG7CTFZ5hQev8ln9HZmIVnoSEZeXi-Hda9g. Accessed 15 Mar. 2021.

LeBesco, Kathleen. *Revolting Bodies?: The Struggle to Redefine Fat Identity*. University of Massachusetts Press, 2003.

Levy, Jennifer, Donna Ansara, and Andi Stover. "Racialization and Health Inequities in Toronto." *Toronto Public Health*, Oct. 2013, www.toronto.ca/legdocs/mmis/2013/hl/bgrd/backgroundfile-62904.pdf.

Lind, Emma, et al. "Reconceptualizing Temporality in and through Multimedia Storytelling: Making Time with through Thick and Thin." *Fat Studies: An Interdisciplinary Journal of Body Weight and Society*, vol. 7, no. 2, 2017, pp. 181–92.

Lorde, Audre. "The Master's Tools Will Never Dismantle the Master's House." *This Bridge Called My Back: Writings by Radical Women of Color,* edited by Cherrie Moraga and Gloria Anzaldua, Kitchen Table Press, 1983, pp. 94–101.

Marcus, Sharon, Heather Love, and Stephen Best. "Building a Better Description." *Representations*, no. 135, 2016, pp. 1–21.

Maynard, Robyn. *Policing Black Lives: State Violence in Canada from Slavery to the Present*. E-book, Fernwood, 2017.

Mollow, Anna. "Unvictimizable: Toward a Fat Black Disability Studies." *African American Review*, vol. 50, no. 2, 2017, pp. 105–21, *Project Muse*: https://doi.org/10.1353/afa.2017.0016.

National Institute for Health and Care Excellence. "NICE Updates Rapid COVID-19 Guideline on Critical Care." *National Institute for* Health and Care Excellence News, 25 Mar. 2020, www.nice.org.uk/news/article/nice-updates-rapid-covid-19-guideline-on-critical-care. Accessed 5 Apr. 2021.

Noble, Safiya Umoja. *Algorithms of Oppression: How Search Engines Reinforce Racism*. E-book, New York, NYU Press, 2018.

NoBodyIsDisposable Coalition "Know Your Rights Guide to Surviving COVID-19 Triage Protocols." *NoBodyIsDisposable Coalition*, 28 July 2021, www.nobodyisdisposable.org/know-your-rights/. Accessed 2 Apr. 2021.

Office of the Premier (Ontario). "Backgrounder: Populations Eligible for Phase Two COVID-19 Vaccination." *Ontario Newsroom*, 5 Mar. 2021, https://news.ontario.ca/en/backgrounder/60570/populations-eligible-for-phase-two-covid-19-vaccination.

Ontario Health. *Clinical Triage Protocol for Major Surge in COVID Pandemic*. Ontario Health, 28 Mar. 2020, https://med.uottawa.ca/pathology/sites/med.uottawa.ca.pathology/files/clinical_triage_protocol_for_major_surge_in_covid_pandemic_-_march_28_20205.pdf. Accessed 20 Mar. 2021.

Rinaldi, Jen, et al. "Through Thick and Thin: Storying Queer Women's Experiences of Idealised Body Images and Expected Body Management Practices." *The British Psychological Society*, vol. 7, no. 2, 2016, pp. 63–77.

Schmidt, Harald, Dorothy E. Roberts, and Nwamaka D. Eneanya. "Rationing, Racism and Justice: Advancing the Debate Around 'Colourblind' COVID-19 Ventilator Allocation." *Journal of Medical Ethics*, vol. 48, no.2, 2022 pp.126–30. *BMJ Journals*: https://doi.org/10.1136/medethics-2020–106856.

Shackelford, Hunter Ashleigh. "When You Are Already Dead: Black Fat Being as Afrofuturism." *The Routledge International Handbook of Fat Studies*, edited by Cat Pausé and Sonya Renee Taylor, 1st ed., Routledge, Apr. 2021, pp. 253–57.

Sins Invalid. "Mission." *Sins Invalid*, www.sinsinvalid.org/mission. Accessed 21 Mar 2021.

Solovay, Sondra, et al. "Fat-Assed Prepper Survival Tips for Preparing for a Coronavirus Quarantine." *Google Documents*, www.docs.google.com/document/d/1Zz7EchIvq05wFDZ1EysJkGiMJTpzXxi998M2Ij2hYhg/edit?ts=5e69c961#heading=h.c7ae8c2fdudh. Accessed 2 Apr. 2021.

Tidgwell, Tracy, and Fady Shanouda. "Know Your Rights Guide to Surviving COVID-19 Triage Protocols. Ontario, Canada." *NoBodyIsDisposable Coalition*, 15 Jan 2021, www.nobodyisdisposable.org/know-your-rights/on-ca/. Accessed 2 Apr. 2021.

Tidgwell, Tracy, et al. "Introduction to the Special Issue: Fatness and Temporality." *Fat Studies*, vol. 7, no. 2, 2018, pp.115–23. *Taylor Francis Online*: https://doi.org/10.1080/21604851.2017.1375262.

Thille, Patty. "How Anti-fat Bias in Health Care Endangers Lives." *The Conversation*, 9 May, 2019, www.theconversation.com/how-anti-fat-bias-in-health-care-endangers-lives-115888.

Warner, Michael. "#COVID ICU Deaths of Those < 50 in Ontario Are Rising: Wave 1 (164 Days) = 27 or One Every 6d; Wave 2 (180 Days) = 36 or One Every 5d; Wave 3 (34 Days, so Far) = 12 or One Every 2.8d. The Variant Is a Different Disease. We Must Change Our Approach or More Young People Will Die." *Twitter*, 7 Apr. 2021, 8:55 a.m., twitter.com/drmwarner/status/1379779828170301445.

Williams, David R., Jourdyn A. Lawrence, and Brigette A. Davis. "Racism and Health: Evidence and Needed Research." *Annual Review of*

Public Health, no. 40, 2019, pp.105–25. *Annual Reviews*: https://doi.org/10.1146/annurev-publhealth-040218–043750.

Wong, Alice. *Disability Visibility: First Person Stories from the 21st Century.* E-book, Vintage Books, 2020.

Wong, Alice. "I'm Disabled and Need a Ventilator to Live. Am I Expendable during This Pandemic?" *Vox*, 4 Apr. 2020, www.vox.com/first-person/2020/4/4/21204261/coronavirus-covid-19-disabled-people-disabilities-triage. Accessed 1 Apr. 2021.

Diagnosis—Fat!

Derek Newman-Stille

Fat, Crip, Queer Poetics

I am a fat, femme, nonbinary, disabled person, which means that I spend a lot of time contemplating the ableism, fatphobia, and femmephobia I experience in medical encounters. These poems reflect encounters that I have had with medical doctors during which everything from mental health to syncopal episodes to a sinus infection has been attributed to my weight. Similarly, despite MRIs revealing significant damage to my spine, my doctor constantly told me that my spinal pain was due to my fatness and that there were no underlying conditions. The doctor would concede that I was right about my spine only after I brought in my own copies of my MRI. Ableism, fatphobia, and femmephobia intertwined in these encounters that ignored my bodily knowledge and the direct evidence of medical scans because of the belief that fatness was the root of these issues.

After being denied access to my doctor and described as being "non-compliant" because I did not accept that my sinus infection was due to being "overweight," I escalated my concerns to the College of Physicians and Surgeons of Ontario. I received a message back from the organization that my family doctor was correct in ascribing my sinus issue to being overweight, which reinforced the message that my fatness was a problem. I was told by the college that my weight alters "the risk of all infections, including those of the sinuses," and my concerns were rejected. With these words, the college reified the notion that fatness is antithetical to health.

My situation is not unique, and these types of dismissals are common for many fat femmes, especially for disabled fat femmes encountering the Canadian medical system. As an exercise with my Feminist Disability Studies students for the past three years, I have asked my students to reflect on their medical encounters, and the vast majority of female-identifying and femme students in the class identified that they have encountered both barriers to medical access and medical misdiagnoses. The number of misdiagnoses was much higher for students who were considered fat by their doctors, and these students were often told that they needed to lose weight before any other discussion about their health could take place.

Having these discussions with my students was a healing experience of unity and collectivity, allowing us to come together to critique and question the Canadian health system and fatphobic, ableist, femmephobic hegemonies of knowledge that are entrenched in that system. These poems are meant to continue that conversation with others and open up critical questions about the way that hegemonic systems of medical power situate "fat," "femme," and "disabled" as interwoven and oppressed body knowledges.

In my poem "Diagnosis—Fat!" specifically, I examine the dismissal that we encounter as fat people in the medical system. I examine the perception of medical science as objective and counter this by exploring the ways that medical systems and knowledges, like any other systemic knowledges, are shaped by other belief systems, including femmephobia, fatphobia, and ableism. I point out the way that body knowledges and experiences are dismissed and the way that, often, medical tests are dismissed unless those tests relate to fat.

"Diagnosis—Fat!" is a poem that examines the way that medicine, while pretending to be objective, is influenced by our fatphobic society the same way that any other cultural ideology is. The poem extends from a situation with my family doctor in which I was told first that my suicidal ideation was due to being overweight, and then that being overweight caused my sinus infections, and finally that fatness caused my ongoing migraines. Despite the lack of connection between body mass and any of these pathologies, my doctor could not see past my fat to any additional issues and actively ignored an MRI and nerve testing because of a belief that my fat was central to my experiences.

In this poem, I express the isolation of being unheard and erased because of my fat body. I bring up the medical perception that medicine and science are uninfluenced by societal beliefs such as fatphobia/sizeism and the assertion by my doctor that perceptions of my body are influenced only by unbiased, objective science. I hope to critique in this poem fatphobia and the pretension that medical experiences are not influenced by fatphobia. This poem is meant to be a dialogue between patient and doctor over the course of which the doctor takes over the narrative and provides no space for the patient to speak.

"A Deadly Plague, So I Am Told" shifts the focus from the idea that *fat* is a threat to the body to the notion that *fatphobia* is a threat to the body and that the rhetoric of fear and hate targeting fat harms people's well-being.

In "As Though My Body Isn't Mine," I explore the way that fat and disability are both considered spaces of public comment and the way that people feel the right to comment on our fat, disabled bodies. Encounters with a public, with people who believe they are informed enough to comment on our bodies, are common experiences for fat and disabled people and are magnified where fatness and disability intersect. Because of our marginalized status, public rhetoric about disability and fatness, and the way that fat is described as an epidemic and medicalized as a threat, people feel empowered to comment on our bodies and offer unsolicited "advice" about how to become "healthy." In this poem, I explore some of the comments that have been made towards me when people have seen me walking using my walker or my cane. I have been told that I could walk without my walker if only I lost weight and that I would "overcome" my disability if I weren't so heavy. I have even had people follow me for several blocks asking, "What's wrong with your body?" Because of our marginalized status, our bodies are perceived as public bodies and open to public parlance. "As Though My Body Isn't Mine" examines the fatphobic and ableist gaze as well as the perception that our bodies are made not only to be stared at but also to be publicly commented on. I examine the loss of self that comes with these encounters. These poems are meant to critically question rhetoric relating to the body and especially draw critical attention to the fatphobic, femmephobic, ableist rhetoric embedded in Canadian medical discourse. These poems are counter-textual, meant to stand in opposition to entrenched public discourse about our bodies and are an act of speaking back. They are acts of body-speak, allowing the body to speak back to the rhetoric that has been layered upon it.

Diagnosis—Fat!

What is the point of going to a doctor
	only to hear
you're fat
you're fat
you're fat.

Broken finger?
	Fat!
Flu?
	Fat!
Migraines?
	Fat!

No need for any other diagnosis
No need to listen

I think I know your body
	better than you.

I'm objective.

We need to deal with one thing at a time
and before we deal with anything
let's address your weight.

You are in danger.
No, not from misdiagnosis
just from your body
Your fat is coming to get you
It's right there
lurking
plotting

I don't need to look at your tests,
I can see your body
and the best diagnostic tool
is my discrimination
I *earned* it in medical school
learned it in medical school
scientifically,
objectively
uninfluenced by a fatphobic society
so I say what's wrong with you
is right here in your BMI
those letters and MD are all that matters.

No need for any other diagnosis.
No need to listen.

A Deadly Plague, So I Am Told

I'm told there is a plague
right here
right in my body

No, it's not viral
In fact, the hatred for this "disease" has gone viral
yet there's a fear it will spread
        that I will spread
        that my tissues will spread.

We're told it's an epidemic
        mostly because *they* consider it unsightly.

We're asked "what about the children"
        and campaigns tell them how to avoid this risky disease

We're told this disease is hungry
        that it keeps growing
        growing
        growing

This disease needs special clothing
        and no one carries it

This disease means doctors ignore everything else
        because they believe it is the most important crisis.

This disease is so horrifying that even its name strikes fear
        so it's called
                BMI
                BIG
                BIG BONED

EXTRA LARGE
CHUBBY
CHONKY
JOLLY
A GOOD PERSONALITY

They're afraid of my fat
You're afraid of my fat.
You're afraid to look at it.
It's an epidemic for your vision.

I'm terrifying
with every jiggle
every ample curve

Why be so afraid of my fat?
I promise I won't eat you...

As Though My Body Isn't Mine

"I bet if you lost weight
you wouldn't be disabled anymore"
random people say as they pass by

"If you were thinner
you'd be able to walk without that!"

"Obesity is your real disability"

As though I don't know my body
As though they know more at a glance
As though my body isn't mine

When did my body become public property?
When did I lose rights to it?
 to me?

Whose body is it?
How many of my pounds are mine?
How many of my pounds are theirs?

When they comment on my body
          strangers
 Does it become theirs?
 their responsibility?
                    theirs to own?

Weight-loss rhetoric
 cuts like knives
 carving into me
 but not cutting off the pounds

Are my pounds mine?
or public property:
          debated on
          criticized
          "a health care issue"

I'm told
I'm a health care crisis
 an epidemic
told I'm a drain on Canadian Medicare
told
told
told

Nothing I say back matters
it's all absorbed by my fat
consumed by their gaze
lost in rhetoric

"I'm crippled whether I'm fat
                              or thin"
I tell them.

"My fat cushions my spine"
I tell them

My body knowledge
                         is empty
 zero calories
 fat free
 reduced
Weighed against social rhetoric
 empty calories
 emptier words

My words lose weight as I say them
 thinning
 thinning
on the scale of public opinion.

"Excuse me"
they say, walking further around me
telling me I take up space
telling me I CAN'T take up space.

PCOS: A Journey of Fatphobia in the Medical Field

Kirthan Aujlay

THERE I WAS, SITTING IN A WHITE, brightly lit, minimalist office somewhere in North York. It was the spring of 2018 when I first sat across from Dr. G, an endocrinologist specializing in reproductive health. A few weeks before I had been sent for a battery of blood and urine tests, and the results were in. They showed that I had polycystic ovary syndrome (PCOS).

Dr. G was slow and precise with her words. She seemed understanding and warm as I wiped away tears from my eyes, and she explained how my lab work had shown that I had a certain number of markers for PCOS as well as insulin resistance. I was upset, but she seemed confident about being able to help me. It had been nearly a year since I had informed my family doctor that I had stopped getting my period, and now today marked the day that my PCOS journey would begin.

If I'm honest, the diagnosis wasn't exactly a surprise. In addition to my absent period, my body had been feeling increasingly out of sorts. It was hard to pin down, but something inside me felt off for reasons I couldn't figure out. For ten years, I had been slowly putting on weight. It seemed like new weight clung to me no matter what I did, and losing it was impossible. I had always been low energy, but I was even more tired than usual. At the time, I didn't know it, but my diagnosis would be the beginning of a long, strenuous battle against fatphobia in the medical field.

Each subsequent visit with my reproductive endocrinologist began the same way—the clerk would greet me with a cold hello and then begin to take my vitals. This was typically coded language for getting your weight and blood pressure taken.

For anyone who has ever had this done, getting weighed at the doctor's office is seldom a pleasant experience, and having your blood pressure taken is even worse.

Despite being seen for a medical issue known to cause weight gain, I was never given oversized cuffs to accommodate fat individuals getting their blood pressure readings when I visited Dr. G's office. Each time my blood pressure was taken, the cuff would squeeze my arm tightly and painfully, resulting in a reading that scored higher than the evaluations I typically had done at my family doctor's. These vitals check-ins had me starting off each doctor's visit on the wrong foot. Dr. G was convinced that my blood pressure was far higher than it actually was, confirming her assumptions that a high weight meant my health was at risk, although my weight generally stayed the same.

Each time my weight naturally fluctuated to be a few pounds lighter, my doctor seemed thrilled. When my weight went back up, she was disappointed. It felt like my parents were giving me the silent treatment, and I had failed the only task my mom had given to me.

My visits always ended with a prescription for metformin and advice to lose weight. As with most doctors, I wasn't given more than the usual platitudes: calories in, calories out, exercise more; it's all just a matter of caloric intake. At first, the most detailed advice I was given was "cut out sugar and excess carbohydrates." It all sounds so simple, and yet as anyone with PCOS can tell you, it's not.

PCOS bodies process things differently, often having difficulty with turning glucose into energy. PCOS bodies also often require a litany of extra nutritional supplements to help them work the way they are supposed to. But with zero nutritional guidance, I was left to navigate this strange new world alone, with little more than the help of friends and Facebook groups devoted to PCOS. I waded through message boards and Google search results, trying to find any information about improving my nutrition to treat my PCOS while facing an endless barrage of the same pro-diet messaging. I tried not to feel helpless, but everywhere I seemed to be told that going on an extreme diet was the only way I could begin to battle the effects of PCOS.

By my third appointment with Dr. G, I could tell she was getting frustrated. My weight seemed to stay in the same five-pound range, and I admitted that I was still eating sweets and drinking juice regularly. I wasn't consciously trying to undermine myself, but as someone with a lifelong sweet tooth, I knew that cutting these foods out cold turkey would most likely lead to a binge later on. I figured that at least I could slowly cut down on my consumption of sweets, but Dr. G was unimpressed. In one jarring moment, she suggested that my inability to cut out sugar altogether was psychological. She said she was happy to refer me to a psychologist who did "great work" with helping people lose weight. The implication seemed to be that my refusal to diet was a psychological problem. I declined to tell Dr. G that I was already in therapy.

As I sat there and processed my doctor's words, I noticed that she cavalierly unwrapped a small square of chocolate and popped it into her mouth. In that brief moment, everything became starkly apparent. There was Dr. G, thin, blonde, with photos of her own children on her desk (images that seemed like a trophy for someone working in a practice that specializes in fertility). Dr. G was the picture of everything Western women are supposed to be, and thus, she was allowed to have a small indulgence without judgment. I, on the other hand, embodied failure: fat, unmarried, unable to menstruate. Chocolate wasn't for me. Bodies like mine should know only deprivation until they are an acceptable size.

In subsequent visits, my doctor suggested that I try the keto diet or intermittent fasting because she had heard "*great things*" about these diets helping people shed even "the most stubborn of pounds." I tried my best to keep a poker face as I thought about all the negatives I had heard about the keto diet, from the bad breath to the headaches, brain fog, diarrhea, and foul vaginal odour—just to name a few. Oh, and don't get me started on intermittent fasting, which is simply disordered eating rebranded as health. Instead of focusing on my overall health, it felt as though my doctor was telling me one thing: lose weight at any cost.

I had been with Dr. G for over a year when a friend decided to recommend me to a US-based dietician, Julie D, who specializes in PCOS and has a firm anti-diet standpoint. I did some research and was immediately struck by how deep the dietician's knowledge ran. For the first time, it felt like I could talk to someone who would be able to explain what PCOS and insulin resistance were doing to my body, and the types of dietary changes I would need to make that didn't involve deprivation. Although I tried meeting with local dieticians, the advice always seemed to be the same—vague instructions to ensure that half of my plate was vegetables and examples of portion sizes. There was nothing to address what kinds of foods I could eat for more energy or what foods might help to lower my blood sugar. I decided to sign up for Julie's PCOS course.

During our first online session, I was shocked when Julie told me that I might not be eating enough. As a fat woman, I never thought that I would hear those words from a registered dietician. Julie also taught me that instead of feeling ashamed of my intense carb cravings (a common phenomenon for people with PCOS), I should pay attention to them and think of them as my body trying to communicate its needs. Most important, she firmly asserted that I did not need to diet and that dieting would ultimately do far more harm than good, even if I did lose weight. While I was grateful for Julie's guidance, I felt frustrated that I had to bypass the care offered to me as a Canadian and instead pay out of pocket for a private practitioner from the United States just so that I could get specialized help.

The more I learned about PCOS, the more it felt like the puzzle pieces that made up my life fell into place. In addition to her advice, Julie explained some of the lesser-known PCOS symptoms. She explained that people with PCOS are more likely to experience mental health issues such as depression and anxiety at the onset of puberty. Immediately, I thought back to my first experience with depression at age 12. I learned that heavy and painful periods (not just irregular or absent menstrual cycles) were also PCOS symptoms. Hearing that, I thought about the decades of heavy eight-day periods and painful cramping I suffered. I discovered that acanthosis nigricans, a skin condition that results in darkened skin on the armpits and around the neck, is highly associated with PCOS and insulin resistance. I recalled the dermatologist in my teens who brushed it off as just a benign cosmetic abnormality that "sometimes occurs in larger people."

Learning of these various, undiscussed symptoms left me in a state of both astonishment and dismay about my experiences with the medical field. As I reflected more on my experiences, I gained a greater realization of the fatphobia I faced from the medical field in Ontario from an early age. In particular, I reflected on the very sudden weight gain of 30 lbs I had at the age of 15. Instead of questioning why an otherwise healthy 15-year-old girl would rapidly put on 30 lbs with no changes in diet or exercise, my family doctor had simply told me to join Weight Watchers and lose the weight. I have to wonder how this doctor would have responded if I had rapidly lost 30 lbs for no apparent reason.

Another memory I revisited was when I went to my gynecologist in my early 20s. My doctor referred me to her to help me deal with my painful and heavy periods. She took one look at me and simply said, "Lose weight," with no explanation of how that was supposed to affect my period. With that, she left the room. I could feel my face get red as I tried to appear calm. I hadn't even had the opportunity to ask what weight had to do with my period. I didn't get to ask her why she refused to examine me or do a thorough intake. Instead, I left confused, wondering how weight loss was supposed to result in lighter, less painful periods. I felt shame and frustration with my large body but also anger at how quickly I was dismissed.

I know logically that a lot of these symptoms initially seemed to occur independently of each other. I know that my dermatologist, gynecologist, and family doctor were focusing on their specific areas of care instead of seeing how my symptoms interconnected and worked together. And yet, I can't help but wonder how I might have been treated if I weren't fat. I wonder how much earlier I could have been diagnosed if my family doctor had thought to send me for detailed blood and urine analyses instead of only advising me to lose weight. Perhaps I would have been able to get a better handle on my depression. Maybe I would have known how to better nourish my body to mitigate my experiences of such extreme fatigue and blood sugar crashes.

I can't change the past, but I *can change* my future.

While there is no known cure for PCOS, working with a dietician who focuses on a weight-neutral, intuitive eating approach has helped me ease some of my symptoms. Although I have been unable to find a replacement for Dr. G, I have found that focusing on Julie's teachings instead has helped me learn how to nourish myself. I eat food that makes me feel good. I move in ways that celebrate my body instead of punishing it. At times, diet culture is seductive. But perhaps instead of focusing on size, doctors could do some actual investigating when dealing with fat patients. Instead of giving "one size fits all" directions to simply lose weight, they could focus on genuine nutrition and each body's unique needs. And maybe, just maybe, they could learn that proper health is not found in the number on the scale but in eating and moving in ways that genuinely nurture the body.

I doubt I will ever satisfy Dr. G's demands to lose weight. But by eating intuitively, I have learned which foods make me feel nourished. I have discovered joyful movement, which is exercise that I do to feel good in my body instead of punishing it. I move with yoga, low-impact cardio, swimming, and walks. Most importantly, I have satisfied myself.

Behind Closed Doors: Navigating Fatphobia in Mental Health Spaces

Amanda Scriver

THE CHILLING AIR OF JANUARY blew against my face as I walked toward the nondescript office in Toronto's Forest Hill neighbourhood. Although this wasn't the first time I had sought therapy, it was my first time meeting with a highly specialized trauma therapist who offered eye movement desensitization and reprocessing (EMDR) therapy as a treatment option. In EMDR sessions, individuals are asked to safely reprocess traumatic information until it is no longer psychologically disruptive to their lives. After years of trying to treat my trauma and coming up empty-handed, I was willing to try anything.

In the waiting room, large knots formed in my stomach, reminding me of all those times I had prepared for a first date. While I knew it was totally normal to be this anxious, I still couldn't shake the feeling that there were so many things that I didn't know about EMDR. For many, this therapeutic approach is considered "unusual" as it asks patients to focus on past disturbing memories or adverse past events. I really had to think before going in: was I making the right choice? Would this therapist be a person I could trust? Would this person be someone I could connect with? But most of all, would this therapist be someone who could truly hold the space for me and all my baggage? As these thoughts started to swirl around my head, a door swung open. Knocked back into reality, I slowly shifted my eyes to the noise and gazed up.

"Amanda?" a voice called out. My eyes met with the therapist's as my nails dug in to the armrests of the deeply fatphobic chair. Although the chair held my body in place, it wasn't until that moment I felt it digging into my sides, causing discomfort and pain. My heart raced and my palms were sweaty. Fighting my body's own fight-or-flight responses, I hunkered down further into the chair and answered the therapist.

"Hi," I meekly squeaked out. The therapist waved a hand toward me, welcoming me from the cold waiting room and into the office. I got up, slowly stabilized myself, and walked through the door. I was a bit scared but ready for what was next.

***

When fat individuals, like myself, attempt to seek out mental health resources, there can be a mountain of barriers that prevent access to these services. From the sheer lack of fat-positive, body-positive, or even health-at-every-size resources available to them or the sheer lack of fat-identified therapists available to choose from, the landscape is, well—bleak. As if those barriers didn't already make accessing mental health care seem impossible, statistics have shown that Canadians in the lowest income group are three to four times more likely than those in the highest income group to not even bother seeking out the mental health care they need, while half of Canadians who are experiencing a major depressive episode are unable to access care due to geographical reasons (Centre for Addiction and Mental Health). These statistics suggest that people's unique social, cultural, and economic environments determine their access to spaces and places that can help them with their health and wellness.

From research papers (Alberga et al.) to activist work and media representations (Thorkelson), it has been well documented that Canada is rife with medical fatphobia. It's not that doctors are unaware of what fatphobia is; it's just that their own biases—according to the Canadian Medical Association's "Obesity in Adults" guidelines (Wharton et al.) and as discussed in various chapters throughout this volume—hold them back from treating patients with the dignity they deserve. This very same fat bias can appear when seeking out *mental health* treatment.

Fat individuals have spent most of their lives having their bodies vilified and dismissed; this can make taking the first step to meet with a mental health practitioner quite overwhelming. Many people will take years to find a therapist that they connect with, and it is incredibly difficult to find one who identifies as fat, which is often preferred as people believe a fat-identified therapist will understand and recognize some of their own lived experiences. However, even this step may not be enough. "Finding a fat therapist isn't necessarily going to mean having a fat-positive therapist," explains Carly Boyce, a registered social worker who identifies as a fat, genderqueer femme from Toronto, Ontario. Boyce further notes that for anyone seeking out mental health care, it's important to ask open and explicit questions about the potential caregiver's political and social beliefs, no matter that person's size, sharing that, "fatphobia is still considered socially acceptable because we (as a society) still believe people choose to be fat. That it is a moral failing, and those failings, especially in people coded as women, are pathologized." In a society that keeps telling fat people that their bodies need to be fixed or eliminated, by *living healthier* or *eating cleaner*, fat people are made to feel ashamed, as if they are morally lacking.

For fat individuals who are experiencing a range of symptoms that result in depression, disordered eating, anxiety, abuse, or any kind of mental illness, speaking to a professional can, therefore, seem out of reach. However, none of the shame, fear, or fat bias that comes along with seeking treatment should hold someone back from accessing the services they need. This is why we need to combat the stigma that patients who identify as fat experience when trying to access care. Because (and stick with me for a moment here), ***if*** experiencing stigma and discrimination negatively impacts our mental health just as much as our physical health, why have we not done more to fix the biases in our system to make it a safer space for fat folks to access?

***

As I followed the therapist down the dimly lit hallway to their office, they invited me to sit down. This time, the chair was, thankfully, slightly less fatphobic than the one in the waiting room. The room had beige walls and a withering plant on the desk. It felt stale and clinical: *I should have taken this as a sign.*

For one full hour, we sat across from one another as the therapist furiously scribbled notes and listened to me tell my life story. Occasionally, I would hear an enthusiastic "mm-hmm" letting me know they were still with me. At one point in our dialogue, I started talking about weight and how seeing a friend's sudden weight loss had activated a certain response in me. In a vulnerable moment, thinking it would be a safe space, the therapist asked me if there could be a psychological reason why I was having such an adverse reaction to this friend's weight loss. As I began to explain myself, noting my friend's right to their own bodily autonomy but how it could be triggering for those with eating disorders, the therapist sat up sharply in their chair and began to challenge me on my own body politic. For me (personally), fat liberation has always been about tearing down the systems that have denied fat folks full participation in society and life. However, the therapist suggested that I was perhaps projecting my own insecurities about my fat body onto this friend. Sitting across from this new therapist, I felt ashamed and almost gaslit, as their eyes penetrated through me. They weren't actually hearing me, but rather just seeing me, a fat person—a problem to be solved. A problem they could solve. All I could think to myself was, "This wasn't what I paid for." As I sat there further explaining to my therapist how deeply uncomfortable I was with the tone and direction of our session's conversation—specifically related to bodies and fat politics—they became increasingly defensive, shifting the blame back onto my "unhealthy relationship with my own body." I was shocked and dumbfounded. The session quietly wrapped up and my face flushed beet red.

What the fuck just happened?

***

Dr. Samantha Abel, PhD, MSW, RSW, interviewed several participants for her dissertation, *Let's Talk about Weight—How Fatphobia Manifests in Therapy.* In her study, participants stated that they had a hard time finding a therapist they could trust about weight and body issues due to previous negative experiences with therapists. Many of the individuals she interviewed experienced microaggressions such as unintentional negativity towards them (as a patient) or weight loss as a treatment plan.

Rather than receiving the immediate support they needed, Abel's participants instead felt powerless. Sadly, in my research for this piece, this feeling was significantly echoed. I had the opportunity to interview Jocelyn Tennant, a writer from Vancouver, British Columbia, who shared a similar experience as my and Abel's research participants. All her life, Tennant has experienced depression, recalling, "I've had a super supportive family and it wasn't that serious. I was on medication, and I saw a counsellor." But she recalls that when she left home for the first time in university, things took a turn. Living in the dorms, Tennant developed an anxiety disorder as well as insomnia. She explains, "I was regularly going to the walk-in clinics, the student clinic, and seeing sort of a rotating cast of doctors nearly every week just so I could survive."

When she first went to visit her on-site student clinic, the therapist asked if she had tried exercising more and suggested that if she "lost weight, she might feel better about herself." Tennant explained to me that while she was desperate for any kind of professional help, the experience left her paralyzed. "That sort of implication, that the root of all of my problems was my weight, and that we must deal with my weight before we deal with anything else, because surely that has to be the thing that is causing me so much emotional turmoil. Just wow." Tennant did not end up going back to class for a week afterward and even shared she was worried about whether she would pass her classes.

Fat bias and weight stigma are still things we're actively fighting against, even in spaces we consider to be fair minded and non-judgmental. Medical schools devote little attention to the subject of weight bias or do not provide any education to students on how physicians' bias and stigma can harm patients attempting to access care.

According to Obesity Canada (Taylor et al.), there are clear links between mental health and weight. For example, people with mental illnesses can experience many other risk factors, such as diabetes or high cholesterol levels (Canadian Mental Health Association Ontario), which may impact their weight.

Furthermore, antipsychotic medications have been shown to significantly impact weight gain.

For Tennant, the visit to her student clinic had a lasting effect on her. She explained that moving forward, she had a significant fear of going to the doctor and, eventually, renewing her medication, even though she knew she needed it. "I would sort of put myself into a situation where I was really struggling and then be in a crisis mode."

When I think about Canada and our health care system, I think about its mental health practitioners and how they can work with fat clients. What if we taught practitioners how to handle fat patients like myself or Tennant with more care? What if we had a future in which fat patients didn't have to worry about the potential harm their new therapist could cause them as they try to heal? Because—let's face it—we all know that therapy has a history of microaggressions and prejudices. What if the pervasive "fat is bad" rhetoric were erased, and we were able to just access care as needed?

When I ask Boyce what they think the future holds, they candidly share, "It's become so evident that the systems that we exist inside of are so broken, so as a therapist I just try to be really explicit about my own politics. I think there's a lot that can be done in the context of individual relationships and how we like to treat each other." They add, "I think there's not a lot of, like, political will to fight fatphobia. But I think if we could understand anti-fat bias as part of these interlocking systems to control certain kinds of people in certain kinds of bodies, there might be more solidarity inside of those movements." Boyce is right, blaming fatness and simply telling patients that they need to lose weight or uttering other fatphobic sentiments does nothing but cause shame and hurt, especially when weight loss may not be possible (due to a disability or medical and other factors) and won't make the individual feel mentally and emotionally any better.

By sharing my experience, I'm hoping that individuals like Jocelyn Tennant, myself, and every rad fattie in Canada (and, well, the world to be honest!) will no longer have to engage with mental health practitioners who don't think critically about the current fat liberation discourse. That one day we can meet with therapists who have a better awareness of our bodies and are open to our wellness journey, whatever that journey may be. At the end of the day, therapists must understand their patients' body politic as an issue of social justice and ethical concern and be willing to explore their own internalized fatphobia. I'm ready for a bigger, better fat future in mental health spaces in Canada. Now, where do we start?

Works Cited

Abel, Samantha. *"Let's Talk about Your Weight": How Fatphobia Manifests in Therapy.* 2020. York University, PhD Dissertation.

Alberga, Angela S., et al. "Examining Weight Bias among Practicing Canadian Family Physicians." *Obesity Facts,* vol. 12, no. 6, 2019, pp. 1–7.

Centre for Addiction and Mental Health. "Mental Illness and Addiction: Facts and Statistics." *CAMH,* https://www.camh.ca/en/driving-change/the-crisis-is-real/mental-health-statistics. Accessed 29 November 2021.

Canadian Mental Health Association Ontario. "The Relationship between Mental Health, Mental Illness and Chronic Physical Conditions." *CAMH Ontario,* https://ontario.cmha.ca/documents/the-relationship-between-mental-health-mental-illness-and-chronic-physical-conditions/. Accessed 4 February 2022.

Taylor, Valerie H., et al. "The Role of Mental Health in Obesity Management." *Canadian Adult Obesity Clinical Practice Guidelines,* Obesity Canada, 4 August 2020, https://obesitycanada.ca/wp-content/uploads/2021/05/7-The-Role-of-Mental-Health-v4-with-links.pdf. Accessed 29 November 2021.

Thorkelson, Erika. "Fat Shaming Shouldn't Be Part of Our 'New Normal.'" *The Walrus,* vol. 25, August 2020, https://thewalrus.ca/fat-shaming-shouldnt-be-part-of-our-new-normal/#. Accessed 7 February 2022.

Wharton, Sean, et al. "Obesity in Adults: A Clinical Practice Guideline." *CMAJ,* vol. 192, no. 31, 4 August 2020, pp. E875-E891, https://www.cmaj.ca/content/cmaj/192/31/E875.full.pdf. Accessed 29 November 2021.

DESIRING FATNESS

Sexy Fat

Leslie Walters

All bodies are good bodies. My personal journey into kink and the openness of that community has helped me to understand that no two bodies are alike. This image is about how all bodies are sensual if they choose to be so.

Punch(ing) My Paunch

Rohini Bannerjee

USING THE POETRY FORM OF A *GHAZAL*, [1] I present a collection of six (6) *ghazals* in English, spiked with Urdu-Hindi, honouring the five elements of a punch, the word and drink, originating from India (the colonized), via Hindi (*pāñć*), and brought to England (the colonizers). The typical five ingredients of a punch will serve as a theme for each of the *ghazals*: alcohol, sugar, lemon, water, and tea/spices. I will explore my experience of being a plus-size/fat/large Canadian woman of the Desi[2] diaspora using those five themes. Readers will meet a *maharani*/queen who enjoys her gin (alcohol), erotically licks her fingers after some *matai*[3] (sugar), has been accused of a tart (impolite) tongue (lemon) by the community Aunties, took adult swimming lessons in a bathing suit flaunting her curves (water), and can make a spicy cup of *chai* that would make any matchmaker cringe (tea). The closing *ghazal* poem is a moment of emancipation, an act of self-reflection moving away from the path of a Desi girl to a woman who speaks her full-size body and heart without hesitation.

Gin Royal

Goddess, nearly Natarajan herself, I'm a Devi, I say, pour me a gin.
Ice it down, now. Good brown girls never play, pour me a gin.

And when you're thick like me, Daddy Ji declares the white boys
Go à la galore, hands on my big, brown breasts do stay, pour me a gin.

Anything more than a handful is a waste, dude declared, you sure are
Bigger than Courtney and Jackie, I'm a wolf and you're my prey, pour me a gin.

You a Nova Scotian? You sure don't look like no McNally nor McGuire
More like a Krishna or Fatima, go on now, there's just no way, pour me a gin.

Hey White Boy! I only lie in bronze satin sheets, incense aroma alight, slow and steady
My Maharani Queen wide hips splay for display, don't need you to pour me a gin.

Savour

My sticky fingers go from deep inside of me to the buffet glass,
let me taste it
Is it my own cream desire I long for or thick rice *kheer* pudding
alas, let me taste it.

As if his rappie pie and tourtière acadienne won't widen my Desi
brown hips,
Auntie says stay on your diet 'cause *matai* will only widen your
ass, let me taste it.

From cardamom and cloves to cinnamon sticks and rosewater,
those desserts tempt me
Or is it that my soul longs for the sweet words you once offered
en masse, let me taste it.

Emotional eating is what my therapist calls when butter and
sugar clog my arteries
Let's hope the maple syrup and butter tart will break the impasse,
let me taste it.

I'll be sure to stay thick and full in all the right places for the good
brown boy you picked for me,
Perhaps until then I'll slow kiss Marc and Mark and pretend to
smoke grass, let me taste it.

Lemon à la mode

Where the Atlantic waves hit Peggy's Cove, oh my heart, let my lemon tongue be
I stood on the black edges, the salt forces would on me impart, let my lemon tongue be

Dangerous, untamed, unruly, Auntie says to the party guests, she's getting fat day by day
I know what I want to eat and how much; I eat like it's an art, let my lemon tongue be

Beti, don't talk back, Auntie says, eat small bits, just a taste of the samosa is enough
Oh, the waves tell me otherwise, engulf, swallow up, be smart, let my lemon tongue be

Auntie, worry about your own kids and their BMI, my belly rolls let loose as I exclaim
Who taught this old woman to be rude, generations we depart, let my lemon tongue be

Sensitive or is it sensible, like the Acadians say, maybe I just simply love food, that's all
Nibble or gnaw; I guess those salty snacks are just the start, let my lemon tongue be.

Floating Thighs

I nearly drowned once, kid pool party gone wrong, skinny girls
only to observe, my thick body
I sank, past depths of chlorine, my nostrils flaring for air, the light
did swerve, my thick body.

Fountain of fluid out of my thick chest, my bathing suit so tight,
my rolls all on display
Lifeguard was blonde and pretty, chastising me sayin' I had some
nerve, my thick body.

Never again I told myself and took on some adult swimming
lessons, he was some cute
Diver from Digby, Nova Scotia, military and all that, cradling my
hips' curve, my thick body.

He said just let go, float, let me hold your back and show you the
water is a haven for you
What if he sees my paunch now and my thighs that chafe are but
fat reserves, my thick body.

Do his Celtic freckles look past my Punjabi back spilling from my
tankini to see but a woman
Breaststroke, butterfly, this and that crawl; all an offering of life's
hors d'oeuvre, my thick body.

Steep

Uncle Ji says his son is ready to marry; he could consider chubby
me, yes, I'll brew some *chai*
Your Canadian sun has made you dark; oh, so fat too, I guarantee,
poor girl, go brew some *chai*

I have a boyfriend Uncle Ji, he's into my big breasts and thick
shoulders, says he likes thick girls
Thanks for the offer though; and for my man I will gladly fall to
my knee, and brew some *chai*

So lucky, *moti kuri,* fat girl, offers like my boy don't come every
day, such a burden, you know
Immigrant parents didn't come to Canada so I would end up a
devotee, yeah, I'll brew some *chai*

Too many books and so much freedom ruins our girls, and look
at that double chin, so sad
No need for pity, I butter my own parathas generously with ghee,
Uncle Ji, I'll brew some *chai*

He'll marry me or maybe he won't, my sari blouse will be made
to order, to fit my round arms
I could have a donair on my wedding night, let my heart fill with
glee, I'll just order some *chai*

Lick Shots

Looks like that Frooti punch is ready to pour; I feel your hard
horn by chance, time to lick shots
Bra straps dig under my sari blouse, *choli ke peeche*, I have you
in a trance, time to lick shots

Panties at ankles, my *bichwa* toe ring flickers under the caramel
satin sheets you laid out for us
Kalo mujhe, eat me, how he'd nibble my pussy *pakora* in the
south of France, time to lick shots

Why bother unpinning nine metres of silk? You once said I had
legs for days, calendar check
Why replace my hand with your pencil dick? I master my own
clitty dance, time to lick shots

Sure, I'll be your mocha treat, sweet and sour, *khati meeti*,
whatever wiggles your White tongue
My *pallu*, the loose end of my sari, grazes your neck; but to guard
your stance, time to lick shots

No *bindi* or *sindoor* needed, I'm no *dhulan*; I left my bridal nose
ring *nath* on a chair somewhere
Wipe your mouth now but keep your forked tongue away; get
your last glance, time to lick shots

Notes

[1] *Ghazal* (pronunciation "guzzle"): "Originally an Arabic verse form dealing with loss and romantic love, medieval Persian poets embraced the ghazal, eventually making it their own. Consisting of syntactically and grammatically complete couplets, the form also has an intricate rhyme scheme. Each couplet ends on the same word or phrase (the *radif*) and is preceded by the couplet's rhyming word (the *qafia,* which appears twice in the first couplet). The last couplet includes a proper name, often [that] of the poet ... In the Persian tradition, each couplet was of the same meter and length, and the subject matter included both erotic longing and religious belief or mysticism" (Poetry Foundation).

[2] Desi is a term for the people, cultures, and products of the Indian subcontinent or South Asia, and, increasingly, it also relates to their diaspora. Desi countries chiefly include North India and Pakistan and sometimes South India, Nepal, Bangladesh, and Maldives and Sri Lanka.

[3] Common word in Hindi for dessert or sweets.

Works Cited

Poetry Foundation. "Glossary of Poetic Terms—Ghazal." *Poetry Foundation*, https://www.poetryfoundation.org/learn/glossary-terms/ghazal. Accessed 15 March 2021.

Butch Bellies, Queer Desires

Karleen Pendleton Jiménez

for Julieta Fajardo

> i crave a lesbian who's fat and fleshy
> so big she can't fit through the door at starbucks
> and they set up an outdoor café just for her
> so fat she wears bangles on her fingers
> her belly is a boom box
> her stretch marks are hieroglyphic etchings
> she's so heavy, tectonic plates shift beneath her feet
> so huge, lake erie is her bathtub
> (de la tierra, "Ode to Unsavory Lesbians" 1)

San Diego, 1990

Me (short, solid 18-year-old butch): Mom, I'm worried that I only seem to get fat on my belly like a guy.

Mom (beautiful fat straight woman in her 50s): That's ridiculous. You're a woman, you'll get fat all over.

I write this as a tribute to butch bellies, starting with my own.

"Curves and Creases"

Laredo, 1991

At a Latina conference, I decide to be out publicly as a dyke for the first time in my life. I make the decision as I walk, balancing my lunch tray, from the cafeteria out to the aluminum picnic tables. I scan the tables. There are several straight women's tables. There is one visible lesbian table. There are several chubby butches sitting at the table. If I sit with them, everyone will know that I'm queer; there are at least a dozen women at the conference who go to the same school as me, and they will bring this news back to campus with them. Part of me thinks I am not like these dykes; I don't look so butch, I don't look so fat. The other part of me knows I am that butch, and that I will be that fat. I will look exactly like them sometime soon. They are my people. I sit beside them and stare down into my carnitas. They will become some of the most important community of my life.

In 1980, Adrienne Rich wrote of "compulsory heterosexuality," a concept consisting of both "physical force" and "control of consciousness" (20), which details with precision the combined pressures of heteronormativity, sexism, and homophobia, and how these pressures pulse anxiously and systematically, to keep us away from lesbians and from becoming lesbians. In 2016, Carla Rice documents a similar insidious and ubiquitous indoctrination, this time about the control of women's body weight. Through dozens of interviews with women of every kind, she shows how biopedagogies seek to prevent us from loving and accepting our bodies as they are. Fat bodies have been and continue to be particular targets of such biopedagogical practices.

Biopedagogies can be defined as "those disciplinary and regulatory strategies that enable the governing of bodies in the name of health and life. ... Biopedagogies can be understood as urging people to work on themselves" (Wright 14). Biopedagogies are every lesson taught from the media, from every institution our bodies have inhabited, from every friend, relative, enemy who insults the way our body looks, who questions its value and health. As Ivan Coyote outlines in their *Tomboy Survival Guide*, gleaned from a tomboy childhood in the Yukon, "the world will be full of messages telling you to be something other than what you are. Telling you that you are too skinny or too fat or too dark or too hairy. Too poor for pretty. Low fat hide your belly quick loss how to love less and find a man maps to time machines that only ever go backward" (159–60).

In other words, there were compounding forces at play to keep me away from the fat lesbian table. At 19, I had already received a comprehensive education to repel lesbianism and fatness; however, these weapons were not strong enough to overcome the "enormous potential counterforce" (Rich 20) within me. The harmful teachings did make my heart race, make me fear sitting beside those women, compel me to recognize their bodies as "unsavory" (de la tierra, "Ode to Unsavory Lesbians" 1) but they could not stop me from joining the marimachas.

I looked up from my plate and saw them with the same admiring eyes as a 14-year-old Leslie Feinberg in their first encounter with a lesbian butch at a bar:

> [Butch Al] was a big woman. I don't know how tall she really was; I was only a kid at the time. But she towered over me in height and stature.
>
> I immediately loved the strength in her face. The way her jaw set. The anger in her eyes. The way she carried her body.
>
> Her body emerged from her sport coat and was hidden. Curves and creases. Broad back, wide neck. Large breasts bound tight. Folds of white shirt and tie and jacket. Hips concealed. (83)

I wanted to find myself in their butch "curves and creases," at the picnic table, especially if it meant that I had somewhere safe to belong, especially if it meant I would be able to find a queer lover someday. The aluminum picnic table was our own "planet of women."

> Puede ser que nuestro planeta de mujeres sea no más que un sueño. Pero quién dice que las imagenes de las noches no son tan reales como las de los días. Nadie sabe cuaántas nos bañamos en los bosques ni quiénes volamos con el cuerpo abierto. Y no es para que lo sepan. Afortunadamente, el paraíso siempre lo soñamos, lo hacemos nuestro. Ahí nos encontramos y vivimos un recuerdo colectivo. [Our planet of women is nothing more than a dream. Who knows how many of us bathe

> in the woods or which ones of us have wings that let us fly with the flesh? It's not for anyone to know. Fortunately, we always dream paradise, we make it ours. There, we find each other and live in our collective memory]. (de la tierra, *For the Hard Ones* 15)

Panza Pedagogies

San Diego, 1996

My butch compadre explains to me how much she loves a woman's pancita, a full round tummy, that it's such an important part of her pleasure and attraction to a lover. Some guys like legs, some are ass men, others go for the boobs, but my buddy, she's a pancita butch. I had never considered the belly as a prominent focus of attraction, but seeing her smile and hearing her passion, the image stuck with me, and became part of my own desire as well.

To resist biopedagogies, I suggest instead "The Pedagogy of the Panza" (McMahon), a teaching of *The Panza Monologues*. Just to note, "*pancita*," in the above memory, is simply an endearing form of the word "*panza*," meaning a tummy or belly in English.

> Through well-crafted storytelling driven by humor, frankness, and realness to the nth degree, *The Panza Monologues* reframes our thinking about the body, the politics for food, matters of violence and trauma, and the necessity of self-love. As theatre, it documents a complex range of women's experiences by exploring how they come to perceive the body as a site of struggle and empowerment, particularly in direct relationship with the stomach as a gateway to emotional and physical health. ... [It shifts] consciousness about the female body as a personal storehouse of knowledge and a source of cultural memory. (López xi)

I offer this butch belly essay as one more panza monologue to the project of panza pedagogies.

"Rest on My Belly"

San Diego, 1997

Each night when we sleep, my girlfriend spoons me. She wraps her arm around me, clutching the bottom of my growing stomach with her long, slender fingers. "Mmmmmm," she says, sounding cozy and satisfied, "I'm in love with your boy belly."

In the previous two memories, the belly becomes more cherished through queer desire, through queer intimacy between two lovers. It's a queer woman's desire that Canadian singer-songwriter Ferron celebrates in her song "Belly Bowl."

> Babe you are my bellybowl
> My soft shoe shuffle
> I come behind
> I follow whole. (Ferron, "Belly Bowl")

Through these lyrics and driving rhythm, the listener can imagine Ferron coming up behind her lover, wrapping her arms sensually around her belly, and finding such comfort as to proclaim, "For me there is no other."

These moments make me think about the power of queer desire. In Ivan Coyote's description of their first queer lovemaking experience, it begins with a queer touch of their belly. In a West End Vancouver apartment, Ivan found themself in the loving hands of a jazz singer. "She slid a cool hand around my waist and let it rest on my belly. We stayed like that for a really long time, talking in the dark" (77–81). What does queer desire do? What does queer desire do to a butch belly? In my memories, it transformed a part of my body that at best I ignored, and at worst, detested. Queer desire changed it into a beloved object through touch. It transformed the butch belly into an important location to receive and experience joy from another person, at a time in my life when it was difficult to have the more "womanly" parts of me touched. The butch belly moved from being an object that brought shame to one that I came to associate with pleasure and happiness (Ahmed, "Happy Objects").

Language was part of the queer desire and of the resulting transformation. Lovers don't say stomach. A hard, abrupt word. What do all these consonants have to do with a soft belly? They renamed the object of desire. My compadre used the tender version of *panza*, her lover's "*pancita*," as the focus of her adoration. My girlfriend named her object of love a "boy belly," and I felt adored by her words as her hand cupped around it. Ferron named her lover's belly a "belly bowl"; a bowl is what holds the sustenance that feeds you.

The renaming of body parts by queer lovers has the potential to override biopedagogies and compulsory heterosexuality; by offering us new language, image, and/or meaning, it gives us a better chance at forming more caring relationships with our bodies. The decades of systemic shaming are shattered, even if only in the moment, or perhaps for years to come. In the early 2000s, Colombian-American poet, tatiana de la tierra travelled to Toronto to perform in the Toronto Fringe Festival (de la tierra, personal communication). She sang out the words of her poem, "big fat pussy girl,"

> she'd be exploring me with her questions and with her tongue and with her nose and with her fingertips and when her fingers finally got there, right there to my cunt, ahí, ahí, Margarita said, *Papayona, mira esta papaya tan sabrosa que tienes…Papayona.* Papayona. Big fat pussy. She said it. She named it. I didn't just have any pussy. I had a big fat pussy. And this was a good thing.

Belts

Tucson, 2002

"Yuck, I hate that," my friend exclaims.

"What?" I follow her gaze to a butch woman walking by us in a hotel lobby.

"She's wearing her belt below her belly," she shakes her head, "It looks terrible."

I shrug. While I love to wear a tie and try my best to look handsome, I'm no dandy. I'm mostly the kind of butch who's not very aware of what my clothing looks like or how one is supposed to wear it. I glance down quickly at my own belt snug beneath the bottom of my belly. I realize that I don't have any idea how I came to wear it that way. I just did what felt comfortable, especially as my tummy grew.

"But that's where I've got my belt," I offer.

"Just promise me you'll wear it across your tummy when you get fatter."

She is a femme straight woman with a round tummy of her own. She often schools me. I usually let her. I'm not sure this time.

Above the belly or below? The perennial question. Round flesh hanging over the belt. Round flesh held into place by the belt. Each with its pros and cons. I confess that I waiver between the two in the morning as I get dressed. But even when I commit to wearing my belt across my tummy, it falls to its comfortable place below. I don't notice when or where it falls, but it does.

Toronto, 2020

My girlfriend, out of the blue, questions me, "Don't you wear your jeans below the belly—in a manly way?" I answer by telling her about this piece that I am writing about butch bellies.

A cursory analysis of butch belt wearing as represented on the internet yields preliminary results: on Tumblr, butch bellies rest above, and flow over, belts, pants, and underwear. There are several adorable photos of butch bellies posted, for anyone who might have some affection for butch bellies (Dykesmith; Justashybutch; Lavenderlion; Phoenix). Lea DeLaria flashes her tummy on a video, and it also hangs over her pants ("Lea DeLaria Talks Type 2 Diabetes"). Canadian singer KD Lang wears an untucked shirt flowing over the belly and pants, so that the observer cannot tell which position she has taken (Buaya), and so does every model on the *Peau de Loup* ("We make clothing for bodies, not gender") website. But this move only brings up the other important decision: tucked or untucked?

Clothing Shapes

Chicago, 2012

A butch friend hangs out with me at a bar until closing, generously offering me company as I wait for an early morning flight. We don't know each other that well, so we share histories of family, coming out, relationships, gender, clothing.

I say, "I remember being a teenager, being forced to wear dresses, and how I would stand taller, my gut pulled in by control top nylons." I remember because the next day my men's jeans felt baggier, my tummy began to relax again, and filled them out until it slowly spilled over my belt once more.

She says, "Oh for sure." She takes a sip of her drink. "When I switched from women's to men's clothes, I noticed it immediately. Lots more room for my belly to grow."

"How much have our clothes shaped our bodies?" I wonder.

"I know, right," she answers.

We nod together in our epiphany.

Research has documented the numerous manipulations of women's bodies that succumb to the whim and will of male fashion designers (see for example Fillmer). Women's clothing and beauty standards can leave long-lasting deleterious effects on body size and health. I wonder what effects men's clothing have on butch bodies. Are our bellies rounder? Do we slouch more? Are they more relaxed in the loose clothing? Would our bodies even be recognizable to us had we instead spent the span of our lives in feminine clothing?

"Butches Are Fat"

Toronto, 2017

She is elegant and slim. She has short, silver hair and beautiful dark eyes and couldn't take a bad photo if her life depended on it. From the day I met her, I read her as another butch. But I don't say that out loud because a lot of people don't like the word butch. Maybe they hear it as derogatory, or ugly or base. She's fancy and came out during the women's movement when some lesbians saw butches as antithetical to feminism. So, I don't pry, but the word comes up during our dinner together, nevertheless. It's probably because I'm incapable of not bringing it up somehow, someway, a nervous tic when I'm around her.

She wrinkles her nose, "Ohhh, I hate the word, butch." She's in her 70s and getting crankier, more freely speaking her mind. It's generally why I like hanging out with older women. They're less polite, more unexpected.

"I never wanted to be one," she throws out her arms. "Butches are fat."

Whoa, I hadn't actually known the configuration of her distaste before. My eyes widen and I shift my big belly under my white men's dress shirt that suddenly feels too tight.

Sara Ahmed explains her need to return to lesbian feminism as a tool to fight against the structures that still block us. She returns to its valuing of "life as data collection; we gather information. And being a lesbian, gives us plenty of data. ... If living a lesbian life gives us data, lesbian feminism gives us the tools to interpret that data. And by data I am once again referring to walls" (*Living a Feminist Life* 214–15). She suggests "heterogender" as a wall, as well as sexism, homophobia, racism, any structures that block us in the course of our everyday lives.

I collect plenty of data from my lesbian life. I collect stories about the repulsion of my butch belly. Lesbian repulsion to butch fat is one such wall. Rich, Lorde, de la tierra, and Ahmed offer me lesbian feminist theory to analyse this wall, to recognize it, to feel it, to chip away at it, to climb over it.

Near Kingston, 2020

"Do you see me as fat?" I ask her.

We have a long drive and I have been discussing my ideas for this chapter. I ask because I'm still unsure whether I'm fat or not. I'm unsure how to write a chapter on dyke desire for fat butch bellies, when I don't know whether I have one.

"Hmm, I never thought of it before," she admits.

"Really?" I say, as I know I'm a lot bigger than her.

"I just don't look at butches with that lens. Butches are just butches." She worries, "I think I only see femmes as fat. That's terrible."

Are butches fat so often that it's become naturalized and therefore less visible? Do butches ride the same double-standard that men often benefit from, where fatness is not necessarily viewed as such on them as it would be on feminine women? As Canadian scholars McPhail and Bombak (paraphrasing Sykes) note, "fat butches take up the space typically only reserved for (dominant) men, and thus fatness becomes a positive reiteration of a certain type of butchness" (541). How does a butch come to know if they are fat or not? I've got no idea. Despite my scholarly/political position being enriched by hanging out with awesome critical fat studies scholars in Toronto for the past five years, it's apparent that clothing sizes and BMIs are the data I've unconsciously accepted. Numbers that have been regularly documenting my growing fatness for nearly 50 years. I have inadvertently squeezed my butch belly into numerical categories. These metrics are shoddy at the best of times, cruel at the worst, and apparently useless when it comes to butch bodies. I am not alone.

In a thoughtful post on an anonymous blog, "Butch Wonders," the author invites readers to share their experiences of butchness and body image. The following four responses comment on this recurring belief in a "natural" relationship between butchness and fatness.

> Alen: It's as if "masculinity" makes sense in a larger-bodied, strong-jawed woman—she's just "butch" in some way that is almost "natural" or beyond her control.
>
> Michelle: I could never imagine myself being "skinny" because I feel like it would take my masculinity/"butchness" away.
>
> Max: When I slim down, my body and presentation become more feminine, in a way that I'm still not comfortable with—I lose the veritable armor of

my hefty size. I would love that to come into the conversation, because I'm certain I'm not the only one who feels like being bigger = more butch.

Jess: I'm naturally thick and muscular and have never bulked up or worn baggy clothes as a way to hide my feminine shape. It's like there aren't any healthy images of what it's like to be a masculine presenting woman who isn't super heavy or super skinny.

Butch masculinity is aligned with "larger- bodied," "hefty size," "armor," "bigger," "bulked up," "baggy clothes," conditions that are "beyond her control." Butches who lose their size risk simultaneously losing "their masculinity/'butchness'" and becoming "feminine, in a way that I'm not comfortable with." Butches losing fat risk losing their very butchness. Butches that aren't "super heavy or super skinny" risk losing visibility entirely. As McPhail and Bombak explain, "fat embodiment sometimes creates a certain sense of legitimacy for butch women" (541). However, fatness is also perceived as a problem in need of elimination.

Working Out

Massachusetts, 2019

Walking together through a university campus.

Butch buddy one: (patting her round butch belly) I've gotta start working out again.

Butch buddy two: Well, then you better get going on it.

Me: (silence)

I am ashamed of my silence in that moment. While biopedagogies are generally described as the ubiquitous harmful messages about bodies around us, sometimes we also contribute to destructive biopedagogies by what we *don't* say. I wanted to protect chubby Butch buddy one from thin Butch buddy two but was unable to do so. My politics failed me when a close relationship was the context of the conversation. My misguided respect for Butch buddy two, combined with my inexperience discussing bodies amongst other butches, left me wordless. I propose the following dialogue instead.

Fantasy Redo of Massachusetts, 2019

Walking together through a university campus.

Butch buddy one: (patting her round butch belly) I've gotta start working out again.

Butch buddy two: Well, then you better get going on it.

Me (to Butch buddy one): Dude, you're looking as handsome as ever. Work out when you feel like it.

Butch buddy one: Aww, thanks, man.

Me (to Butch buddy two): Hey that wasn't cool.

Butch buddy two: What are you talking about?

Me (to Butch buddy two): We've got enough pressure on our bodies already.

Butch buddy two: What do you mean?

Me: The world already thinks we're not normal, or attractive, or healthy. The least we butches can do is to look out for each other.

Butch buddy two: Hadn't thought of it that way. (To Butch buddy one) Sorry, man.

How do we start learning how to talk about butch bodies working out?

These are especially impractical times for this discussion. I write this chapter in the midst of COVID chaos, where I sit at my desk in lockdown Toronto, conscious of my growing pandemic butch belly. It's a belly hidden by stay-at-home orders and social distancing. It's a belly omitted from my small black zoom window. It's a belly that has not been to the closed gym in nearly a year. It's a belly I've rarely spoken about.

Returning to the blog *Butch Wonders*, I see that both the themes of silence in relation to body image and the urge to exercise the body are raised in the post.

> There's a sense out there that it's just not "butch" to talk about being insecure about your physical appearance.
>
> Butches trying to lose weight may think they'll lose butch points if they admit to dieting. The diet industry paints monitoring food intake as something "feminine." I know *I* wouldn't feel comfortable telling a butch buddy that I'm on a diet. And when it comes to exercise, many of us want to look competent, because physical fitness is "butch," right? But what if we're wheezing after a half mile? What if we can't bench press as much as our femme friends can? Overall, it can be a lot easier to hide behind your butchness than to risk making yourself vulnerable... ("Butches and Body Image")

And from another edition of *Butch Wonders*:

> My Pretty calls me Jelly-Belly...She is a feeder and I love her food—so the combo works. Although I am forced to gym extra hard in order to keep my Jelly-Bellyness under control. ("Butch Pet Names")

On the other hand, another recent piece from the website *On Riding Mouths* is open and proud about the gym-working of the butch body, complete with sexy photos that feature a big strong butch belly.

> So one of my quarantine goals has been to get shredded so that I can share a body type with [another blogger] and I'm getting there, my core is SUPER thick and strong and ripped right now, please recognize. (Phoenix)

In this case, the author performs and requests queer desire of her butch belly.

Finally, in her video talk on type 2 diabetes, Lea DeLaria offers a glimpse and squeeze of her fat butch belly, lamenting how her older age has affected it.

> But because of my age, and this is natural, I lost 60 pounds
> quickly, I don't have the elasticity in my skin,
> so I've got like, this stomach that's hanging.
> I had my neck tightened because it was just weird.
> And I thought long and hard about it.
> I was like, am I gonna accept this, or...
> And I couldn't.
> I was like, I'm gonna get this tightened.
> I learned to love my body and myself, and who I am.

She describes a sense of practicality and disappointment over her flowing belly, followed quickly with the admission to the tightening of the skin on her neck, and finally to the learning of loving her body.

There are no conclusions offered through these examples of butch body management. Ambiguities are the only safe bet when considering the intersections (Friedman 246) between butchness and fatness. If there is any theme flowing throughout, it is the fragility of butchness, the threat to losing a claim to it, whether you talk about being fat, talk about dieting, are too fat, are not fat enough, or are not muscular enough. It's no wonder that the butch belly generally remains silent and invisible.

Belly Theory

Toronto, 2019

My lover traces fingers along the stretchmarks of my belly, whispers, "they're so beautiful," caresses the heavy curve of it, tells me, "I love the shape of it. You've got the most masculine belly I've ever seen on a butch."

Why does it feel so good to find out my belly is both beautiful and masculine? Why does it make me feel more proud and radical?

Audre Lorde instructs us that a woman's erotic is systematically suppressed (53). It is perceived as dangerous because it is powerful. She offers several definitions for the meaning of erotic, among them is, "...the power which comes from sharing deeply any pursuit with another person. The sharing of joy, whether physical, emotional, psychic, or intellectual, forms a bridge between the sharers..." (56). I experienced the erotic with my lover's touch of my forbidden butch belly. I feel joy and strength through that queer touch. Lorde continues, "recognizing the power of the erotic within our lives can give us the energy to pursue genuine change within our world..." (59).

If my belly were stroked, held at night, caressed, complimented, and I felt soothed and powerful and handsome, what change could I accomplish in the world? What revolution might I join? What revolution might you join if your belly were loved so tenderly?

I propose I start by making a theory of the butch belly. My theory is built from the memories I have shared of my life, from the words of dyke and trans authors, from the conceptualizing of lesbian feminists of colour, and from butch bloggers. My theory is composed of language and metaphor. It pushes toward a new "taxonomy" for the "unruly," "fat," "woman's body" (Gay).

The editors of *This Bridge Called My Back* turned to the backs of women of colour as the metaphor for the translation/strength/exhaustion of their lives (Rushin). tatiana de la tierra built a lesbian phenomenology through the naming of various aspects of our lives, including certain parts of our bodies: hands, looks, walks, dress, and fingers (*For the Hard Ones* 19). Finally, Ahmed turns to lesbian hands and arms as metaphors to break through the oppressive walls that block us:

> **... Intersectionality Is Army**
> We could think of lesbian feminism as willful carpentry: she builds with her own hands; she is handy. Maybe I am thinking too of your arms, your strong butch arms and what they can do, whom they can hold; of how they can hold me. If a feminist history is army ... that history is also a history of lesbian arms.
>
> **I think of being held by your arms.**
> **Yes, I do.** (*Living a Feminist Life* 232–33)

Ahmed describes intersectionality as army, as a history of lesbian arms, as an erotic image of herself being held by butch arms. It is not simply the butch arm but also her own queer desire to be held by that butch arm that makes it an image to cry over, in recognition and hope.

In my theory, an arm reaches in a queer caress of a butch belly. A butch dyke belly. A butch trans belly. A butch straight belly. And the arm that reaches is a woman's arm. A femme arm. A butch arm. A trans man's arm. A nonbinary arm. And all the names for queers that have yet to come. Their bellies and arms too.

The butch belly they find in their fingers is a soft part of a butch. The butch belly is a "panza pedagogy," resisting biopedagogies through the magic of queer desire. The butch belly hangs luxuriously. It takes up the space it needs. It's unselfconscious. It's comforting. It's vulnerable. It metabolizes (Friedman 243). It's not ugly. It's handsome and beautiful. It contracts. It stretches. It nourishes the two of them together.

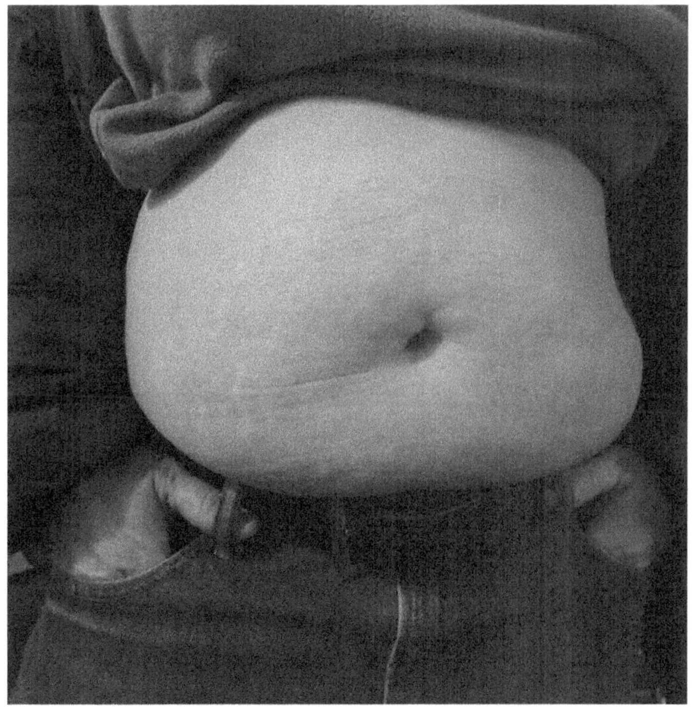

Figure 26.1 Author's Butch Belly
Photo by Hilary Cellini Cook

Works Cited

Ahmed, Sara. "Happy Objects." *Affect Theory Reader*, edited by Melissa Gregg and Gregory Seigworth, Duke University Press, 2010, pp. 29–51.

Ahmed, Sara. *Living a Feminist Life*. Duke University Press, 2017.

Buaya, Alisha. "Ready to Do Her Part! Canadian Singer KD Lang, 58, Keeps Cosy in a Coat as She Arrives in Sydney Ahead of Her Performance for Fire Fight Australia." *Daily Mail*, 15 Feb. 2020, https://www.dailymail.co.uk/tvshowbiz/article-8006929/KD-Lang-arrives-Sydney-ahead-performance-Fire-Fight-Australia.html. Accessed 31 January 2021.

"Butches and Body Image." *Butch Wonders*, 6 May 2013, https://www.butchwonders.com/blog/butches-and-body-image. Accessed 31 January 2021.

"Butch Pet Names." *Butch Wonders*, 30 May 2012, https://www.butchwonders.com/blog/butchpetnames. Accessed 31 January 2021.

Coyote, Ivan. *The Tomboy Survival Guide*. Arsenal Pulp Press, 2016.

de la tierra, tatiana. "Big Fat Pussy Girl." *tatiana de la tierra*, 12 August 2001, http://delatierra.net/?page_id=1037. Accessed 31 January 2021.

de la tierra, tatiana. *For the Hard Ones: A Lesbian Phenomenology*. Chibcha Press, 2002.

de la tierra, tatiana. "Ode to Unsavory Lesbians." *Lambda Literary*, 2016, https://www.lambdaliterary.org/wp-content/uploads/2016/08/15.-tatiana-de-la-tierra.pdf. Accessed 31 January 2021.

de la tierra, tatiana. Personal communication [She stayed in my home and practiced her singing of "Big Fat Pussy Girl" for the Toronto Fringe Festival performance]. 2000.

Dykesmith. "Butch Happy Trails." *Soft Flannel & Silk Sheets*, 4 Nov. 2020, https://blushedfemme.tumblr.com/post/633892731151859712/anyone-for-butch-tummy. Accessed 31 January 2021.

Feinberg, Leslie. "Butch to Butch: A Love Song." *The Persistent Desire: A Femme-Butch Reader*, edited by Joan Nestle, Alyson Publications, 1992, pp. 80–94.

Ferron. "Belly Bowl." *YouTube*, uploaded by CDBaby, 13 July 2015, https://www.youtube.com/watch?v=d7T6JLgaGfs. Accessed 30 April 2021.

Fillmer, Carel. *The Shaping of Women's Bodies: In Pursuit of the Fashion Silhouette*. 2010. James Cook University, Masters (Research) thesis. *ResearchOnline@JCU*: http://eprints.jcu.edu.au/29138/. Accessed 31 January 2021.

Friedman, May. "Dismantling the Empire: In Defence of Incoherence." *Thickening Fat: Fat Bodies, Intersectionality, and Social Justice*, edited by May Friedman, Carla Rice, and Jen Rinaldi, Routledge, 2019, pp. 243–53.

Gay, Roxane. *Hunger: A Memoir of (My) Body*. E-book, Harper, 2017.

Grise, Virginia, and Irma Mayorga. *The Panza Monologues*. E-book, University of Texas Press, 2014.

Justashybutch. "A Lil Butch Tummy for Your Tuesday." *Tumblr,* 13 Oct. 2020, https://babygirlfem.tumblr.com/post/631905107794067456. Accessed 31 January 2021.

Lavenderlion. "Butch Tummy for the Femmes." *It's Gay in Here*, 13 Apr. 2020, https://lavenderlion.tumblr.com/post/615265207435051008/butch-tummy-for-the-femmes. Accessed 31 January 2021.

"Lea DeLaria Talks Type 2 Diabetes, Hot Flashes, and Loving Your Body." *Self*, 2 Feb. 2018, https://www.self.com/video/watch/lea-delaria-talks-type-2-diabetes-hot-flashes-and-fat-suits. Accessed 31 January 2021.

López, Tiffany A. "Foreword." *The Panza Monologues*, edited by Virginia Grise and Irma Mayorga, E-book, University of Texas Press, 2014, pp. xi-xviii.

Lorde, Audre. *Sister Outsider*. The Crossing Press, 1984.

McMahon, Marci R. "Pedagogy of the Panza." *The Panza Monologues Blog*, 5 Jul. 2016, http://panzamonologues.blogspot.com/2016/. Accessed 31 January 2021.

McPhail, Deborah, and Andrea E. Bombak. "Fat, Queer and Sick? A Critical Analysis of 'Lesbian Obesity' in Public Health Discourse." *Critical Public Health*, vol. 25, no. 5, 2014, pp. 539–53. Accessed 30 April 2021. *Taylor & Francis Online:* https://doi.org/10.1080/09581596.2014.992391.

Peau de Loup, https://www.peaudeloup.com. Accessed [the tag line] 31 January 2021.

Phoenix. "On Riding Mouths." *Tumblr*, https://butchmare.tumblr.com/post/632815044058611712. Accessed 31 January 2021.

Rice, Carla. *Becoming Women: The Embodied Self in Image Culture.* University of Toronto Press, 2014.

Rich, Adrienne. "Compulsory Heterosexuality and Lesbian Existence." *Journal of Women's History*, vol. 15, no. 3, 2003, pp. 11–48. *Project Muse*: http://www.posgrado.unam.mx/musica/lecturas/Maus/viernes/AdrienneRichCompulsoryHeterosexuality.pdf. Accessed 31 January 2021.

Rushin, Kate. "The Bridge Poem." *This Bridge Called My Back: Writings by Radical Women of Color*, edited by Cherríe Moraga and Gloria Anzaldua, Kitchen Table: Women of Color Press, 1981, lvii-lviii.

Sykes, Heather. "The qBody Project: From Lesbians in Physical Education to Queer Bodies In/Out of School." *Journal of Lesbian Studies*, vol. 13, 2003, pp. 238–54. *Taylor & Francis Online*: https://doi.org/10.1080/10894160902876671.

Wright, Jan. "Biopower, Biopedagogies and the Obesity Epidemic." *University of Wollongong: Research Online*, 2009, https://ro.uow.edu.au/edupapers/708. Accessed 31 January 2021.

Let Us Taste

Susie Mensah

If I were to taste Pleasure, what form must I become?

May breath bring companionship, not transgression
May palms befriend the malleable mountains of body
Fiercely

Who calls Pleasure i   Who has She begotten

for some of us
only in hollow hushed voices
are we given praise for the vessel we are born into
in Her acres, admiration is given at the first streams of sunlight

there blooms fuck
the intertwining of brokenness
mine
and
yours
in a low lit room

the smaller girls swear by missionary
i tried
but my belly proved alive

will the dark rub of my inner thigh meet their eye
~~Pardon that~~

some of us have only known pressing together parts of ourselves
jars of new wine stored *somewhere*

missionary is
for a moment forgetting
that they are in full view of my fatty nakedness
is it so bad

the world is a big place
and we shrink it for ourselves
by shrinking the self

even before climax, i shy away from Her face
uncertain of entering another moment

I am descended from
world builders women with wide hips
shut thighs courage in their gaze
muted sighs
they have charged us to more
commitment to the beautiful
agony of want and again
not merely oohs and aahs
a holy inheritance
to inhabit the province
of all that we are

May She welcome all
Her own.

Artist Statement:

My creativity is connected to my willingness to tell the truth with reverence and awareness. I write to ensure that my ancestral longings are fulfilled, and so those who resonate with my experience can breathe a sigh of, "Yes." As the postmodern era cycles around the politics of desirability, societies have used fatphobia to gatekeep us from full participation in the erotic. "Let Us Taste" disregards a colonial understanding of sexuality as simply something to do, by retelling and reframing sexuality as an entity to know and a place to go (not outside ourselves). Mostly, it is a benediction for fat folks. Growing up in Canada, I saw that, in conjunction with ability, gender expression, and race, fatness is valued predominantly when being consumed as kink or inspiration porn. Being introduced to fat activism saved my life! My work occupies space (period) in a fatphobic and anti-Black society.

ALTERNATIVE FRAMEWORKS AND IMAGININGS

Fat and Mad Bodies: Out of, Under, and Beyond Control

Fady Shanouda

Introduction

My mom is in the kitchen with her back to the TV as my dad and I mindlessly scroll on our phones, ignoring the commercials waiting for our program to restart and snap us back into the living room. But we're brought about by my mom's exclamation, "*Aah, heyya sah la kidda*!"[1] she says in Arabic. This is a severe reprisal from a reserved woman who is often unaware of the television, always asking us to explain why we are laughing or scoffing or yelling at the TV. She is responding to a line in a Noom commercial. The client/actor says, "Once I understood why I was making those choices, it was easy for me to change those habits. And weight loss came naturally after that." The rebuke from my fat mom was sheer pleasure for me, her fat son. I remember smiling and thinking how awesome it was that she could see through the bullshit of this company and its claims. I remember recognizing this moment's significance but not fully comprehending its meaning. Now, thinking it through, I see that this moment was one filled with pain. It is a reminder of the many failed diets and fads she has tried over the years. Her retort was one of rebuke, for sure—a sort of "fuck off" (even though she would never use those words) to the claim that it had been her ignorance, all this time, that kept the weight on. It was also a reminder of her personal failure to meet the idealized bodily norms inculcated through decades of messaging about female beauty. My dad and I didn't say anything, and the moment passed as the program restarted. The energy in the room shifted again, and our attentions were back on the news.

When I think back on moments like the one above, I wonder how best to analyse and explain what is transpiring. As an interdisciplinary scholar, I'm overwhelmed by the theoretical possibilities one can apply to help elucidate moments like these in my life. It is obvious that fat studies will make an appearance and shine some light on the intricacies of this moment. Surely literature in women's and gender studies would help, as the moment reinforces gender dynamics with my mother in the kitchen and her male family members doing nothing in the living room—an image of domestic life almost as old as time. Even critical disability studies can help explain the dynamics in this vignette—although the effects of the moment seem to be more psychic than physical (not that I wish to relegate disability only to the physical). However, the collection of literature and the disciplinary area that might best attend to moments like these is mad studies.

Mad studies is an interdisciplinary field of study, with a long history of activism and scholarship in Toronto, Canada, that upends the conventions around mental health and illness (Burstow and Weitz; Church; Costa et al.; LeFrançois et al.; Reaume; Reville and Church). Mad studies centres the voices and experiences of those most impacted by psychiatry—mad people, psychiatric consumers, survivors, and ex-patients. Mad scholars and activists are critical of a particular regime of knowledge referred to as psy knowledge: psychology, psychiatry, psychoanalysis, and psychotherapies (McAvoy 1531). This critique, however, also extends more broadly and includes institutions and other social and cultural spaces that have taken on psy knowledges as their explanatory framework: education, rehabilitation sciences, and emerging and new technologies, to name a few. In addition to providing criticism that "unsettles the logics of mental illness schemas" (Snyder et al. 486), mad studies also contributes counternarratives that change and refine the meanings and understanding of madness (Voronka). The realm of thought/scholarship, in sharing the multiple stories of madness throughout history from the vantage point of mad people, provides an alternative, illuminating account of the oppression, survival, and pride of a group too often overlooked.

Together, fat and mad studies are disciplinary siblings that do the work of de-pathologizing difference. Their origins are different, but both stem from oppressed communities working on revealing their histories, reimagining the possibilities of their lives and body-minds (Clare xvi), and holding accountable institutions, disciplines, and individuals who exercise oppressive powers over them. Each field is named after reclaimed words that were once medical diagnoses and playground insults, now political identities/movements/studies. They critique the biological reductionism that purports to understand the origins of and treatment/cure for fat and mad bodies. They are also theoretically connected in their analyses of saneism and fatphobia— systems of oppression that operate alongside one another and that interconnect to re/produce social, cultural, and economic conditions that construct different body-minds as disposable. And both fields are guided by the political arms of the movement, mad pride and fat liberation. Despite all they have in common, scholars rarely put fat and mad studies into conversation with one another. So, while they may be siblings, they appear estranged.

One difficulty in writing about fields of study in this way is that you inevitably reduce their multiplicity, complexity, and richness—otherwise, their heterogeneity—into a homogenous blob. This is not my intention. These fields are incredibly diverse, with scholars, artists, activists, and community members engaging in theoretically and methodologically varied work. However, they are bounded by specific values, ethical principles, and most importantly, political commitments. These boundaries are an opportunity to discuss these fields together without reducing them to unrecognizable impressions.

The work presented here does not stem from any one study or project. This paper is a theoretical contribution to the areas of fat and mad studies and an invitation to future scholars to bring together work in these disciplinary fields. The stories I share throughout are from my personal life. They mark moments of pain and pleasure and are reflections that I hope will help the reader to more readily understand how fatphobia and saneism operate together to subjugate and oppress. These are vignettes, collected, edited, refined, and written with an audience in mind.

Following in the tradition of narrative and autoethnographic methodologies, these stories are adapted and rely on fiction techniques (Ellis). Like poets or novelists, autoethnographers strive to write beautiful, evocative prose, using language and words to appeal to the reader, even structuring their papers in ways that would otherwise be unacceptable in disciplines outside of creative writing (Ellis). Ellis argues:

> Autoethnographic writing goes hand in hand with fictional techniques such as dialogue, scene setting, and plot development. These strategies allow me to show rather than tell, present a feeling for how life flows, and display the autoethnographic process as I teach it (335).

Ellis describes the complexity and potential beauty of writing autoethnographically. The purpose, she argues, is to show a story. In fact, autoethnography is about constructing a consistent story that has the appearance of being possible and that is, most importantly, compelling and evocative (Ellis). Notions of objectivity or truth in storytelling are measured not against positivist conventions but rather against "literary criteria of coherence, verisimilitude, and interest" (Wells 156). Stories are measured by their consistency, authenticity, and significance. The stories I share with you in this chapter try to live up to this standard to convey the consequences of fatphobia and saneism, as well as to the thickened/cripped possibilities when our disabled and fat body-minds are not out of or under control, but quite far beyond it all.

Bodies Out of Control

The fat body is read as a body out of control—without a moral constitution, lacking self-management, and disordered to overeat and not exercise (Friedman, "Mother Blame" and "Mad/Fat/Diary"; LeBesco). This reading suggests that the fat body is discursively constituted as one that is also mad. The fat body is mad because it is outside of perceived conceptions of normalcy: normal eating and exercise habits, normal clothing sizes, normal ways of moving and interacting in the world, and the normal use of space. Defined through a variety of mechanisms, normal behaviour, emotions, and comportment are produced and reproduced through the psy knowledges that, in this example, define the fat body as physically unfit and mentally unstable. The logic undergirding these ideas sounds like this —"No sane person would ever allow themselves to get so out of shape, to lose that much control, to get so fat." Fat people hear these ideas expressed one way or another every day. Many of us have consciously or subconsciously internalized this logic and at times perpetuate the harmful discourses that marry being fat with being irrational.

The maddening part of *fat being* is not the conception of our bodies as out of control but that of dieting as a probable solution. Many fat people are expert dieters, and nearly all fat people have experienced the pressure to diet. Every. Single. God. Damn. One. Those who have dieted have tried (almost) all of them. Some of us have lost weight. Over my short lifetime, I've lost close to 200 pounds. I gained back every pound and more. Dieting has been more harmful and dangerous than *fat being* ever was or could be. But saneism and fatphobia work in tandem to construct *fat being* as the physical consequence of a psychic break. Participating in dieting, expecting a different outcome, is a maddening project—a cycle of abuse and self-hatred that can have long-lasting consequences.

Indeed, ideas about an out-of-control fat body have existed throughout history. Two of the seven deadly sins listed in the commandments are associated with fat bodies: gluttony and sloth. Giving in to these sins is as much a physical failure as a moral one. Consider Forth's historical material culture analysis of fats and oils in ancient Greek, Roman, and Hebrew texts. He argues that the description of oils and other fats are a precursor to ideas about the fat body-mind. From the both positive and negative descriptions of the fat body-mind through ancient times, Forth concludes that the modern West "inherited from antiquity a view of fat as a sign of vitality and fertility that, when present in excessive quantities or certain forms, was also capable of generating disgust" (143). Thus, descriptions of fat people as "sweaty, smelly or greasy, as if their very flesh is rotten or corrupt" (137) are not surprising or new. What is compelling about Forth's analysis, which he does not remark on, is the fat body-mind's depiction in ancient texts as wholly less than, as disabled/mad. The stereotypes attached to fat people as weak-willed and physically inferior, soft, and dense because of their fatness, also described their minds as foolish, stupid, and dim.

Forth describes one fourth-century idea that claimed ill-proportioned individuals, for whom "the distance from the navel to the chest is greater than the distance from the chest to the neck," have "diminished emotions" because their senses are "cramped" in too-small a space (147). Maybe the most revealing part of Forth's analysis and one that drives home my argument that fat and mad have always been in relation to one another is the origin of the word *fathead*. A thirteenth-century word used to describe the uncaring, stupid fat person, *fathead* was utilized in proverbs such as the following: "a belly full of gluttony will never study willingly"; "a gross belly does not produce a refined mind"; "fat bellies make empty skulls"; "fat bodies, lean brains" (Forth 148). What Forth's analysis suggests is that madness was a symptom of the fat body. These ancient ideas shape and reflect upon modern and contemporary discourses around fat body-minds. *Fathead* is still used as a pejorative to describe a whole host of characteristics, from over-inflated egos to lesser intelligence. Any analysis of current issues that impact and shape fat people's lives must consider how the fat body-mind is constituted as a mad body.

Beyond these discursive relations, fat people were treated as mad by a culture of surveillance and incarceration. Fat people have been institutionalized in child and adult fat camps, in weight-loss programs, in bariatric units in hospitals and clinics, and in eating disorder wards in psychiatric institutions. Anne Zbitnew, in her analysis of admissions forms to the Mimico Asylum in Toronto, Canada, in the early twentieth century (later named the Lakeshore Psychiatric Hospital), noted that one of the many reasons for institutionalization (including "wears strange clothing and jewelry" and "hears birds at night") was "the patient is fat." "Fat" continues, in effect, to be a psychiatric condition that merits incarceration.

Besides sharing these histories, fat and mad bodies also share similar pseudo-scientific explanations. Bad mothering was at one point a popular psychological explanation for both fat and autistic children. Rasmussen argues that psy knowledge rose to become an explanatory framework for "obesity" post-1940s, a framework that included Freudian psychoanalysis because of fears around the nation's mental state, especially the potential for the next generation to be fragile and careless (36). The psy knowledge replaced the endocrinological explanations for fatness, and soon scientists became overly concerned with the family structure and home, parenting techniques, anti-social behaviours, and, eventually, mothering styles. During this same time, psychologists were also linking autism to distant or "cold" mothers, whom they "cleverly" referred to as "refrigerator moms" (Douglas 95). As Friedman argues, these discourses have not disappeared and are ever-present in scholarly articles and print media focusing on the "obesity epidemic." Having both fat and mad/disabled/autistic bodies explained through the same psychological model of bad mothering further underscores these subject areas' interrelatedness.

Much like those for madness, explanations for fatness have swung between physiological and psychological. As each decade passes, the pendulum swings one way and then the other. We find ourselves at a time when the pendulum swings less wildly and when both explanatory models are pushed together to create a new framework—wellness. The type of wellness is far from Blank's idea of wellness in her discussion of fat sex or Harding and Kirby's wellness that calls for us to quit dieting. The new wellness framework takes up psychology and other psy knowledges to mask the promotion of weight-loss. Wellness combines the physiological and psychological. It frames fat and mad bodies as consequences of unregulated minds. The solution? Expensive self-intervention (yoga studio membership, personal coaching), biopedagogical surveillance (thousands of mental health and food tracking apps), and psychological reprogramming through, what Howell and Voronka (4) refer to as, the "increasingly authoritative techniques" of cognitive behavioural therapy (CBT). The new explanatory model is complimentary. It feeds the fat body into a cycle of recovery that defines fatness as a consequence of poor psychology that can be rehabilitated only through physiological changes (weight loss) that then heals psychological trauma. The inevitable failure of dieting restarts the cycle—the body-mind more damaged each time.

The wellness framework I am referring to here shares some characteristics with healthism, especially in that they both reduce complex health issues to the level of the individual and develop solutions at that same level (Crawford). The goal of healthism, Chandler and Rice maintain, is a neoliberal one, "to put individuals in charge ... rather than to promote the rights of disabled and fat people and to combat the pervasive culture of ableism/healthism" (236). While healthism can help us to articulate clearly the ableism and fatphobia that are organizing the abjection of fat/disabled bodies in the weight-loss industry, it is less helpful in analysing how saneism, as an equally important belief structure, permeates our collective understanding of weight loss. Wellness, as an organizing framework, is a marriage of saneism/fatphobia that, over and above healthism, codes fatness as not *of* the body but rather, the body-mind. Through this framework, the failure to lose weight is conceived as ultimately a consequence of poor mental capacity.

Bodies Under Control

The recovery model espoused by these new wellness frameworks is not new to mad studies scholars who have been critical of the co-option of recovery and resiliency by the psy industrial complex in its increasing efforts to mandate individual responsibility for socially produced issues (see Harper and Speed; Howell and Voronka; McWade; Morrow). There are differences between recovery, resiliency, and wellness. Howell and Voronka define recovery as "the ability of subjects to recover from an illness" (4). Their definition for resiliency is "the innate capacities of people to 'bounce back' in the face of ... distress" (Howell and Voronka 4). Wellness, like resiliency, promotes the individual capacity of each of us do this work, but rather than focus on distress alone, wellness is about "promoting a state of well-being to develop adequate levels of physical, mental, and social activity" (Miller and Foster 5). What and who defines what is deemed *adequate* seems to be changing continually. Still, from my vantage point, it appears that the expectations grow each year with every new wellness trend and promise for a healthier and happier tomorrow.

Undergirding these ideas is the cultural and economic project of neoliberalism that eschews social responsibilities, transferring them to the individual while simultaneously slashing and cutting public support (Howell and Voronka; Morrow; Ward). Fat and mad became individual responsibilities to be corrected and cured. Before demonstrating how fat studies scholars can employ the criticisms mad scholars and activists have developed against the wellness, recovery, and resiliency industry, it might be best to illustrate how psy knowledges through wellness discourses shape contemporary fatness interventions.

Fat bodies have become increasingly steeped in contemporary psy knowledges through massive changes to the diet industry that saw giants like Weight Watchers and Noom employ the language of wellness and behaviour change. As the fallacy around dieting becomes mainstream, companies have resorted to adopting wellness language (Wischhover). Weight Watchers changed its name to "WW"—a lazy effort to move away from the word "weight" in its name. The company's new tagline is "Wellness that works." Little else has changed (Weiner). Noom is, in my opinion, more forthcoming about its efforts to imbue weight loss with psy knowledge as the corporation combines the language of psychology with that of big data, thus underscoring the possibilities of weight loss through CBT (Conason). Noom is not shy in advertising its use of psychology to promote weight loss. It boasts of using 4 billion data points of behaviour patterns from 45 million users to learn and understand clients' eating and moving habits (Noom). It certainly appears that one might be more successful given the massive quantitative data behind Noom's psy-informed weight-loss model, but there is no evidence that the program works. In fact, one study of Noom's approach, which followed customers for only 6 to 12 months after their weight-loss, failed to show any long-term "success." Conason argues that this study, in only tracking those who lost weight, ignores those customers who tried the app, failed to lose the weight, and abandoned it early. I like to think that my mom, in her response to the Noom ad, was expressing a similar analysis, albeit from her lived experience with similar claims made by other companies in the past.

Noom is also making another move that suggests the company is using the same recovery and resiliency playbook as the psy industry. As advertised, Noom's focus is now on chronic and pre-chronic issues (e.g., obesity, diabetes, and hypertension). Thus, Noom is both a weight-loss and illness-prevention company. I can only explain this as a sort of *minority report of health*. Here, of course, I'm referencing the 2002 Tom Cruise film set in a land where crimes are prevented before they take place. Here, one is sick and in need of treatment before actually getting ill. Howell and Voronka argue that combining intervention with prevention has expanded medicine's boundaries to every part of life. They argue that this has reduced alternative approaches to interventions outside of the medical system for psychiatric survivors (Howell and Voronka 2). The consequences for mad people are ongoing psychiatric interventions that self-responsiblize care while limiting individual capacity and decision-making. Joining Noom is still a choice for fat people, but with this move to prevention, the company has all but claimed *all* bodies—fat or otherwise—as potential clients. Every individual is a pre-chronic customer. This is reminiscent of a friend's words spoken to me while I was shopping one day, after I had lost 100 pounds in six months, an alarming amount of weight to lose in such a short time. While I was trying on a new winter coat to fit my "new" body, she remarked, "Why buy a new coat now, if you're going to lose more weight?" Sadly, I hadn't planned on dieting anymore, but her remark confirmed to me that my body, at any weight above the average, would always be unacceptable. I would always be "sick" until—well—I disappeared entirely. The interconnections of saneism, ableism, and fatphobia are layered and pierce through these examples as they set the stage for a conditioning of different body-minds as unacceptable, and of health as attainable only through market-backed corporate rationales.

Maybe the most illuminating example of the psychiatrization of fat bodies comes from the companies HealthyWage and

DietBet. On these platforms, individuals, friends, or corporate groups can bet on their weight-loss efforts. Lose the weight in the agreed-upon time, and you can receive the wager back—minus, of course, state and federal taxes and an administrative fee that can cost you 25 per cent of the original wager (Lexell). Lose more than agreed upon, and you may get a payout. If you fail to lose the weight, you lose the wager. There are no refunds—ever. Individuals report being denied a refund even after notifying the company of a new diagnosis that would make further weight loss dangerous (Lexell). HealthyWage and DietBet use the same psychology that draws individuals into casinos, creating addicts from causal gamblers. Now, in addition to winning money, there is the ultimate promise of a healthy life. Weight-loss wagers can have devastating health impacts since I imagine the only way one can lose weight so quickly is by engaging in disordered eating and over-exercising. These platforms employ addiction psychology and fatphobia to make a profit. Like Noom and WW, they advertise these efforts under the banner of wellness. HealthyWage's corporate challenges are named "workplace wellness challenges." The company's current spokesperson Sherri Shephard posts regularly on HealthyWage's Instagram page about mindful eating and body and mind connections to weight loss. HealthyWage is less interested in covering up its focus on weight loss, but like the other companies I have discussed, it continues to employ the discourses of wellness, recovery, and resiliency.

I want to make one final argument to underscore the similarities between the psy and weight-loss industries and the latter's increased psychiatrization. In the first decade of the century, pharmaceutical companies began researching childhood depression and subsequently advertising and selling antidepressants for children (Fraad). Fat children have always been under surveillance, but the weight-loss industry had not yet tried to convert fat children into fat customers. That is until 2018 when Weight Watchers announced free memberships for children premised on its newfound direction in promoting wellness and healthy habits to "everyone." The criticism was loud and swift (Weiner). Finding new markets is essential for shareholder satisfaction, hence the inclusion of children in new marketing campaigns (Fraad). However, more importantly, the benefit of targeting and procuring children to participate in these industries is to create life-long patients, users, and customers in these cycles of recovery.

Therefore, in much the same way that recovery and resilience has been co-opted by psychiatry, further limiting the alternatives to medical intervention available for psychiatric survivors, the weight-loss industry has appropriated wellness to propagate weight loss as healthy living—while simultaneously psychiatrizing fatness. Mad studies scholars are keenly aware that recovery and resiliency have been, as McWade argues, "politically neutralized" and "used to negative effect in service user's lives" (64). Fat studies scholars must push back against wellness—especially when it is wrapped in the discourse of psychology and sold as scientifically rigorous.

Bodies Beyond Control

The most exciting prospect of putting fat and mad studies scholars in conversation is the innovative theorizing that each may spark in the other. As categories of bodies that change over time and space, fat and mad bodies can be read together as intertwined throughout history and in our contemporary cultural and social spheres. Such analyses can generate new and compelling ideas about the experiences of living, being, and becoming fat and mad. Some fat scholars have already made these connections (Friedman; Kurowicka and Usiekniewicz) as have some mad scholars (Spandler and Poursanidou). I hope this chapter adds to these discussions and encourages further collaborations between the two fields.

We can already draw on many similarities to examine the elements that make up fat and mad bodies' experiences. Longhurst argues, fat occupies "a borderline state that disturbs order by not respecting proper boundaries" (256). Interestingly, Longhurst's claim could just as easily be a definition of madness. Words like *borderline* and *disturb* hold different meanings in mad communities. Still, desires to push beyond boundaries of respectability and definitions of human capacity are recognizable among psychiatric survivors. *Fat being* is one way to understand the body beyond its established limits, borders, and capacities, extending, growing, and exceeding possibilities. Similarly, madness reframes the body-mind's capacity—to hear and see what others cannot and experience and think and imagine more than what was thought possible or considered acceptable. The fat and mad body pushes beyond current definitions of the human and, indeed, of human variation. In seeking to open up what it means to be human, these fields may be asking similar questions about the limitations of an anthropocentric worldview, essentialism, binaries, and the boundaries of the material body-mind. Colls argues, "Fat is positioned on the body below the skin ... It is ambiguous; placed simultaneously under the skin yet materialised as a substance in and of itself" (358). Fat is both an adjective and a noun; thus, fat, as Forth argues, is "within bodies as well as outside of them" (136). Indeed, there have been those who have speculated madness's origins in nearly every organ in the body throughout time. However, mad studies scholars and psychiatric survivors have fought to constitute madness as also outside the body. Take Gorman's definition of madness "as a name for an assemblage of an individual's engagements with sedimented formations of social/cultural relations" (310). Madness, according to Gorman, is defined through relations with the material world. The theoretical similarities in being both inside and outside the body indicate another analytic space that may draw new insights.

We can get stuck in the visibility politics schism that may separate experiences of fatness and madness—but this would be a mistake. The schism is real, and visibility is experienced very differently by each group, even differently amongst members of each group. As a non-visible disabled, fat person of colour, I am keenly aware that my fat, racialized body is what people see first. It may be months, years—never—before people learn that the DSM shaped my early life, segregated me from my peers for years, led to experiences of assault and violence, and left me with an inferior education. Coming out is so hard, emotionally exhausting, psychologically straining, and at times physically dangerous, but my disability is not invisible in and of itself. Instead, as Titchkosky argues, disability is *made* invisible by "the multivarious but taken-for-granted appearance of normalcy" (134) that masks reality to ensure conceptions of normalcy persist—that the illusion of the normate body-mind is maintained. Fat people do not get the opportunity to come out in the same way—although there are exceptions (Saguy and Ward)—but the invisibility and hypervisibility that fat people can experience are a result of the same mechanism that Titchkosky describes, a mechanism working to ensure the status quo and to reinforce established borderlines or normative personhood. Fat bodies become invisible through their relations and interactions within the world, in not finding a seat or clothing that fits, in our absence in cultural and social spaces—because those spaces do not accommodate us. Fat people are hypervisible when we eat, walk, and take up space in public. We become the objects that parents point to and warn their kids against if they "don't eat their veggies." Visibility does not divide mad from fat. The experiences may differ, but the underlying logic that sustains the schism is as much a construction as anything. We have much to learn from each other. There is so much we can pass along to further strengthen our shared political values in resisting the medicalizing/psychiatrizing of fat and mad bodies and in seeking access, social justice, and cultural recognition for our diverse body-minds.

Conclusion

I read the opening piece to my mom in the car as we wait in the underground parking garage for my dad. He's having emergency dental surgery, and since this is taking place during the COVID-19 pandemic, we have been asked to stay in the car. I finish reading the piece. She's beaming. I'm thrilled and relieved. I wondered how she would feel to be called fat. To have the word "failed" ascribed to her actions; to have this moment analysed as one filled with pain. She agreed with my analysis. There was pain behind those words. There were feelings of frustration and failure. With every new weight-loss attempt, there is a tension between physiological and psychological that ends with her body-mind feeling less whole—fractured and exhausted with the pain of not meeting the expected goals. My mother's rebuke was also a moment of resistance—one that reflects a desire to reject fatphobic discourse yet simultaneously demonstrates their psychic effects. A lingering quality sits in and shapes our body-minds, in different, unknown ways. Our bodies (my mom and me) have always been ones that we've tried to control. We blamed our fatness on our lack of willpower, poor choices, and inability to resist meals after 7:00 pm. We wondered if we were psychologically inferior or if we just had not *yet* found the right approach—the right diet. We understand calls for moderation, but these still remind us of diets—the counting, the measuring, the points, and the weighting—and of the unending balancing and self-management. We are done dieting. We have abandoned trends and fads. Food has been for too long the enemy, our body-minds too long hated, rejected—worse—unloved. We see through wellness for what it is—another trend. We now know that you cannot rest the "problem" of fatness at our feet, or at the base of our minds. Our bodies are meant to be overflowing, round, curved, smooth, soft, and sumptuous.

We sit in the car and talk about our bodies in positive ways. If a psy professional were sitting in the back seat, I am confident they would have jotted down "bad mothering; co-dependence; recommend CBT; encourage wellness and weight-loss." But it is in these conversations that mad and fat bodies find alternative paradigms to conceptualize and live in bodies that are otherwise socially and culturally rejected. Our bodies grow bigger as we sit there and speak of our body-minds as spaces we love and cherish, as we are filled with joy knowing that we are beyond control.

Notes

1 The English translation: "Ya right. It's just that easy!"

Works Cited

Blank, Hanne. *Big Big Love: A Sourcebook on Sex for People of Size and Those Who Love Them*. Oakland, Greenery Press, 2000.

Burstow, Bonnie, and Don Weitz. *Shrink Resistant: The Struggle against Psychiatry in Canada*. New Star Books, 1988.

Chandler, Eliza, and Carla Rice. "Alterity In/Of Happiness: Reflecting on the Radical Possibilities of Unruly Bodies." *Health, Culture and Society*, vol. 5, no. 1, 2013, pp. 230–48.

Church, Kathryn. *Breaking Down/Breaking Through: Multi-voiced Narratives on Psychiatric Survivor Participation in Ontario's Community Mental Health System*. Ontario Institute for Studies in Education, University of Toronto, 1993.

Clare, Eli. *Brilliant Imperfection: Grappling with Cure*. Duke University Press, 2017.

Colls, Rachel. "Materialising Bodily Matter: Intra-action and the Embodiment of "Fat."" *Geoforum*, vol. 38, no. 2, 2007, pp. 353–65.

Conason, Alexis. "Is Noom a Diet? Spoiler Alert: Most Definitely." *Psychology Today*, 5 May 2020, https://www.psychologytoday.com/ca/blog/eating-mindfully/202005/is-noom-diet.

Costa, Lucy, et al. "Recovering Our Stories: A Small Act of Resistance." *Studies in Social Justice*, vol. 6, no. 1, 2012, pp. 85–101.

Crawford, Robert. "Healthism and the Medicalization of Everyday Life." *International Journal of Health Services*, vol. 10, no. 3, 1980, pp. 365–88.

Douglas, Patty. "Refrigerator Mothers." *Journal of the Motherhood Initiative for Research and Community Involvement*, vol. 5, no. 1, 2014, pp. 94–114.

Ellis, Carolyn. *The Ethnographic I: A Methodological Novel about Autoethnography*. E-book, Rowman Altamira, 2004.

Fraad, Harriet. "Profiting from Mental Ill-Health." *The Guardian*, 15 March 2011, https://www.theguardian.com/commentisfree/cifamerica/2011/mar/15/psychology-healthcare.

Forth, Christopher E. "The Qualities of Fat: Bodies, History, and Materiality." *Journal of Material Culture*, vol. 18, no. 2, 2013, pp. 135–54.

Friedman, May. "Mad/Fat/Diary: Exploring Contemporary Feminist Thought through My Mad Fat Diary." *Feminist Media Studies*, vol. 17, no. 6, 2017, pp. 1073–87.

Friedman, May. "Mother Blame, Fat Shame, and Moral Panic: 'Obesity' and Child Welfare." *Fat Studies*, vol. 4, no. 1, 2015, pp. 14–27.

Gorman, Rachel. "Quagmires of Affect: Madness, Labor, Whiteness, and Ideological Disavowal." *American Quarterly,* vol. 69, no. 2, 2017, pp. 309–13.

Harding, Kate, and Marianne Kirby. *Lessons from the Fat-o-sphere: Quit Dieting and Declare a Truce with Your Body.* E-book, Penguin, 2009.

Harper, David, and Ewen Speed. "Uncovering Recovery: The Resistible Rise of Recovery and Resilience." *De-medicalizing Misery II*, edited by Ewen Speed, Joanna Moncrieff, and Mark Rapley, Palgrave Macmillan, London, 2014, pp. 40–57.

Howell, Alison, and Jijian Voronka. "Introduction: The Politics of Resilience and Recovery in Mental Health Care." *Studies in Social Justice*, vol. 6, no. 1, 2012, pp. 1–7.

Kurowicka, Anna, and Marta Usiekniewicz. "Fat Girl's Wet Dream: Girl Sexuality, Fatness, and Mental Disability in My Mad Fat Diary." *Fat Studies*, vol. 10, no. 1, 2021, pp. 7–20.

LeBesco, Kathleen. *Revolting Bodies?: The Struggle to Redefine Fat Identity.* University of Massachusetts Press, 2004.

LeFrançois, Brenda A., Robert Menzies, and Geoffrey Reaume, editors. *Mad Matters: A Critical Reader in Canadian Mad Studies.* Canadian Scholars' Press, 2013.

Lexell, Olga. "Weight-Loss Wagering Apps Are a Game You Can't Win." *The Future*, 5 December 2019, https://theoutline.com/post/8392/weight-loss-wagering-healthywage-dietbet.

Longhurst, Robyn. "Fat Bodies: Developing Geographical Research Agendas." *Progress in Human Geography,* vol. 29, no. 3, 2005, pp. 247–59.

McAvoy, Jean. "Psy Disciplines." *Encyclopedia of Critical Psychology*, edited by Thomas Teo, Springer New York, 2014, pp. 1527–29. *Springer Link*: https://doi.org/10.1007/978-1-4614-5583-7_611.

McWade, Brigit. "Recovery-as-Policy as a Form of Neoliberal State Making." *Intersectionalities: A Global Journal of Social Work Analysis, Research, Polity, and Practice*, vol. 5, no. 3, Dec. 2016, pp. 62–81.

Miller, Gord, and Leslie T. Foster. *Critical Synthesis of Wellness Literature.* University of Victoria, 2010.

Morrow, Marina. "Recovery: Progressive Paradigm or Neoliberal Smokescreen?" *Mad Matters: A Critical Reader in Canadian Mad Studies*, edited by Brenda. A. LeFrançois, Robert Menzies, and Geoffrey Reaume, Canadian Scholars' Press, 2013, pp. 323–33.

Noom. "Noom Reveals Behavior Patterns of Consumers Who Succeed with Weight Loss Resolutions." *Cision PR Newswire,* 2 January 2018, https://www.prnewswire.com/news-releases/noom-reveals-behavior-patterns-of-consumers-who-succeed-with-weight-loss-resolutions-300576263.html.

Rasmussen, Nicolas. *Fat in the Fifties: America's First Obesity Crisis.* E-book, JHU Press, 2019.

Reaume, Geoffrey. *Remembrance of Patients Past.* University of Toronto Press, 2000.

Reville, David, and Kathryn Church. "Mad Activism Enters its Fifth Decade: Psychiatric Survivor Organizing in Toronto." *Organize!: Building from the Local for Global Justice*, edited by Aziz Choudry, Jill Hanley, and Eric Shragge, PM Press, 2012, pp. 189–201.

Saguy, Abigail C., and Anna Ward. "Coming Out as Fat: Rethinking Stigma." *Social Psychology Quarterly*, vol. 74, no. 1, 2011, pp. 53–75.

Snyder, Sarah N., et al. "Unlearning through Mad Studies: Disruptive Pedagogical Praxis." *Curriculum Inquiry*, vol. 49, no. 4, 2019, pp. 485–502.

Spandler, Helen, and Dina Poursanidou. "Who Is Included in the Mad Studies Project?" *The Journal of Ethics in Mental Health*, vol. 10, 2019, pp. 1–20.

Titchkosky, Tanya. "From the Field—Coming Out Disabled: The Politics of Understanding." *Disability Studies Quarterly*, vol. 21, no. 4, 2001, pp. 131–39.

Voronka, Jijian. "The Mental Health Peer Worker as Informant: Performing Authenticity and the Paradoxes of Passing." *Disability & Society*, vol. 34, no. 4, 2019, pp. 564–82.

Ward, Lizzie. "Caring for Ourselves? Self-Care and Neoliberalism." *Ethics of Care: Critical Advances in International Perspective*, edited by Marian Barnes and Tula Brannelly, Policy Press, 2015, pp. 45–56.

Weiner, Jennifer. "Take Your Daughter to the Movies, Not to Weight Watchers." *New York Times*, 3 Mar. 2018, https://www.nytimes.com/2018/03/03/opinion/sunday/oprah-winfrey-teens-weight-watchers.html.

Wells, Sarah. "An Autoethnography on Learning about Autoethnography." *International Journal of Qualitative Methods*, vol. 5, no. 2, 2006, pp. 146–60.

Wischhover, Cheryl. "As 'Dieting' Becomes More Taboo, Weight Watchers Is Changing Its Name." *Vox*, 24 Sept. 2018, https://www.vox.com/the-goods/2018/9/24/17897114/weight-watchers-ww-wellness-rebranding.

Hefty Harm-Reduction: Body Liberation and/as Anti-Violence Work

Sookie Bardwell

Introduction

I do not believe in hiding from hard truths, and so I'm going to be honest with you. For much of my life, I hated myself. More specifically, I hated my fat body. But really, what's the difference? My body and me, we are one and the same: my body/self.[1] My self-hatred did not spring up out of nowhere; like all hatred, it is something that I learned. I came to understand my body/self as worthy of hatred because I learned that my fatness was bad and wrong. In being fat, it/I failed to meet the minimum requirements of respectability and worthiness of care. I learned that I deserved the anti-fat violence that I was experiencing, and I came to accept it as punishment for the failure of my fatness. According to the logic of white supremacy, patriarchy, and capitalism on which the violent colonial project of (so-called) Canada is built and continues to operate, my body/self is simultaneously "too much" and "not enough" to fit into the limited/ing mythical norm of "appropriate" embodiment. These systems made my body the enemy, weaponizing it against me and doing violence to and through it/me.[2]

Growing up in Ontario in the 1990s and early 2000s, I was taught these lessons of (self)hatred through the anti-fat messages that bombarded me. They were inescapable: embedded in and reinforced through my relationships with my peers, my family, the Canadian institutions of public education, medicine, and the national media, all of which scaffolded the development of my sense of self and my place in the world. Through anti-fat messaging, I learned to hate my fat body/self, and the messaging was abundant, such as the *BodyBreak*[3] PSAs broadcast into my living room on the limited Canadian national television channels that we could pick up on the aerial in my childhood home or my doctor's fixation on my growing body's "too high" BMI[4] and the need to get this "under control" by any means necessary, with no notice of or concern about the disordered eating this fixation blossomed into. This same fixation was reinforced by similarly minded teachers in their delivery of the Ontario Health and Physical Education curriculum in publicly funded school gymnasiums and by the way my peers came to understand bodies like mine as a liability through this curriculum. My peers communicated this understanding in picking teams for the sports and movement activities that the curriculum centred, and that my disconnected/ing body was too awkward to excel at or enjoy. My peers mocked it/me when I tried to move my "too much" and "not enough" body/self, and even more so when I did not. I heard similar things from my family members in their putting down and making fun of the fatness of their own and one another's bodies. No matter where I looked, listened, or went, there was no moment of peace or respite. There was no way of avoiding these lessons in (self)hatred.

Recognizing my experiences of/with anti-fatness as violence, and starting to heal from these experiences, has taken a lot of time, effort, and support. I owe my understanding of anti-fat violence and the Body Liberation–centred tools and frameworks that allow me to resist, prevent, and intervene in this violence to the generosity of my fat friends, loved ones, and community members;[5] collaborators and fellow-educators; and countless authors, theorists, creatives, and media makers who have shared their brilliance. They have taught me so much about refusal, resistance, and resilience, called me out/in, and informed the ongoing reflexive practice that is central to my work and to the way in which I aspire to move through the world. I feel very fortunate to now have the opportunity to share the Body Liberation lessons that I have learned through my relational coaching work, through providing support to folks seeking healing from distressed and disordered eating, and through facilitating wellness promotion and anti-violence programming on elementary, secondary, and post-secondary school campuses and in a variety of community spaces between 2018 and 2021 (Bardwell, "A Space at the Table" and "In the Thick"; Bardwell and Hsu, "Body Buddies" and "Robust"; Bardwell and JDP, "In the Thick" and "Loving Large" and "Robust"; Bardwell et al.). In the Body Liberation–centred conversations that I have in all these spaces, I often hear that anti-fat violence is something that folks have not heard about or considered before.

In the following pages, I will discuss my approach to addressing anti-fat violence through Body Liberation–centred harm-reduction work. I begin with an exploration of my foundational understanding of anti-fat violence as relational violence that is rooted in, connected with, and supporting of multiple other systems of oppression—and that can be understood and must be addressed as we would any form of relational violence. I will also reflect on Body Liberation as a useful approach in addressing anti-fat relational violence, and the ways in which this approach is informed by and must simultaneously address other systems of oppression/domination to be effective. Finally, I will provide an overview of the four "Sturdy Trunks" that structure my Body Liberation–centred coaching, support, wellness-promotion, and anti-violence work, and that aim to support individual and collective capacity to refuse and resist anti-fat violence alongside all other interconnected forms of body terrorism[6] and increase access to resilience and healing from them.

Anti-Fat Violence

> *You don't think the whole world isn't constantly telling me that I'm a fat piece of shit that doesn't try hard? Every fucking magazine, and commercial, and weird targeted ads telling me to freeze my fat off or to drink a tea so that I'll shit my brain out my ass? And at this point I could be a licensed fucking nutritionist, because I've literally been training for it since the fourth grade, which is the first time that my mom said that I should just eat a bowl of Special K and not the dinner that she made for everyone*

> *else so that I might be a little bit smaller, and so that ... I could have boys like me. Honestly, I don't even blame her because it's a fucking mind prison, you know? ... I've wasted so much time and energy and money [and I wish that someone had said this to me when I was younger] because it would have saved me so much time and pain.*
> —Annie Easton [Aidy Bryant], *Shrill* ("Pool")

I want to briefly return here to my self-hatred with a specific focus on how that self-hatred developed. Making fat people hate ourselves is something that capitalism, patriarchy, and white supremacy do *on purpose*, as doing so is not only lucrative but essential for their continued existence. The anti-fatness of these oppressive systems makes it unsafe to move through the world in a fat body, and the experience of that constant unsafety makes an enemy of our bodies/selves. I hated myself because (as reflected in the above quotation from *Shrill*) everything and everyone, everywhere, all the time, told me that by being fat, I was failing. Failing by being simultaneously both "too much" and "not enough." The deep self-hatred that this sense of failure engendered in me impacted every aspect of my life. It poisoned my relationships with a nagging, ever-present feeling of inadequacy that obscured any sense of my own boundaries, made me feel unworthy of care, and in so doing limited the choices that I felt empowered to make in relation to others. Moving through the world in a fat body is an experience of constant violence (and especially so when that fat body is also "out of bounds" in other ways, like my queer, nonbinary, dis/abled, working-class, femme body is). This violence is something that those of us in bodies out of bounds (Evans Braziel and LeBesco) are encouraged to accept and expect, as deserved punishment for having a body wrong. Worse, it is violence that we often learn to do to ourselves.

It is important that anti-fat violence be understood as rooted in and upholding ongoing colonial violence and anti-Black and anti-Indigenous racism (Bodirsky and Johnson; Harrison; Strings). Anti-fatness has been leveraged throughout the colonial project as it persists into the present day in order to define, assert, and police boundaries around the category of whiteness, positioning slender white bodies as morally, aesthetically, an superior to fat Black, Indigenous, and other bo (Strings). This violence plays out in a variety of sett through the metrics most commonly used to measu "health" such as the (ineffectual though still commo scale[7] and Canada's Food Guide,[8] both of which have significant histories of racism in their development, implementation, and usage (Jackson-Gibson; Tennant; Vansintjan). This anti-fat racialized violence coexists alongside and is amplified by anti-fat gender-based violence, e.g., rape culture (Bear; Dawson Women's Shelter; Gailey and Prohaska); dis/ableism; and other forms of embodiment-centred oppression (Deerwater)—with disastrous impacts on the individual and collective psychosocial and physical health and well-being of fat and straight-sized[9] folks alike (Jackson-Gibson).

Despite the fact of ubiquitous anti-fat sentiment in contemporary Canadian culture,[10] I'm unsurprised by how frequently I hear that people have not thought much about anti-fatness as a form of violence. Part of the reason for this is that our collective understanding of violence and what it looks/sounds/feels like is intentionally obscured by the oppressive systems behind it. As the legendary psychosocial educator Mr. Rogers so wisely reminds us, "anything that is mentionable can be more manageable" ("What Is Mentionable"). If we do not know how to mention something, or worse, if we do not even know how to recognize that it is there, it becomes very difficult to manage.

Cultural and structural anti-fat violence is normalized and thus rendered invisible. Because anti-fatness is everywhere, all the time, as illustrated in the quotation from *Shrill*, it becomes difficult to recognize that it should not be. As Johan Galtung explains in his work on peace and violence, cultural and structural violence often exist outside of the conscious awareness of those not targeted by these forms (see figure 29.1). The idea that fatness is evidence of personal and social failure is widely accepted and continually reinforced through a cycle of social domination/oppression.

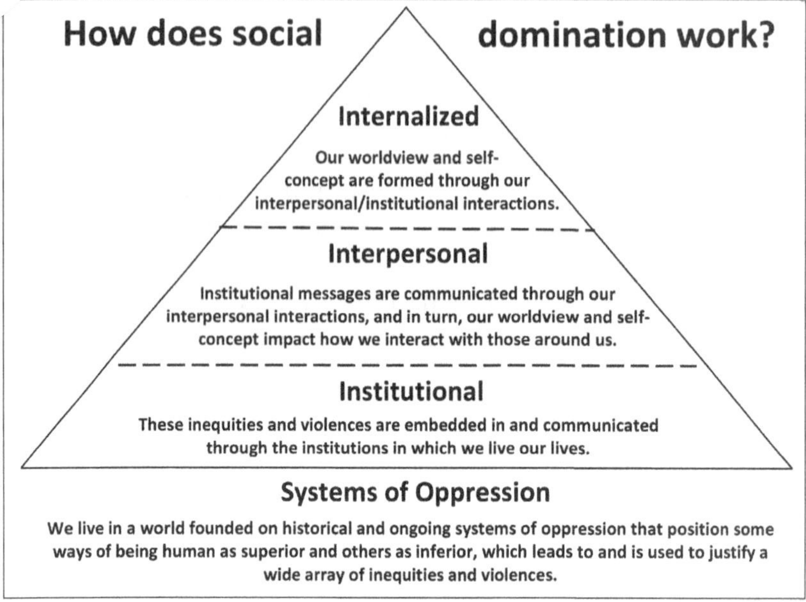

Figure 29.1 Pyramid of Social Domination/Oppression, Adapted from Johan Galtung's "Violence Triangle"

Source: Galtung, "Cultural Violence"

We learn that fat bodies are less valid and valuable than other bodies through almost every possible institution: through anti-fat health promotion programs in school, through representations of fat bodies in the media that position fat people as undesirable and worthy of disrespect, through the anti-fat bias and medicalized fatphobia pervasive in the medical system (Hawkins), and through teachings in communities of faith that position fat bodies as morally suspect or failures. These messages are communicated to us through our interpersonal relationships, such as the para-social relationships we have with the characters we encounter in media, the relationships we have with our families and friends, and the equally though perhaps differently intimate relationships we have with trusted professionals (such as doctors, teachers, and clergy), in which we may rightly expect to receive care and affirmation. We internalize these messages, and they can impact how we think about ourselves, our bodies, and those of others. In coming to believe this anti-fat rhetoric, we develop a fear of becoming fat, if we are not already, and if we are, we are encouraged to devalue ourselves and do anything and everything we can, no matter how self-harming, in order to shrink our fat bodies out of existence or to expect and accept violence if we fail to do so (Bordo; Hesse-Biber). I don't know about you, but I can't think of anything more violent than an imperative to cease to exist.

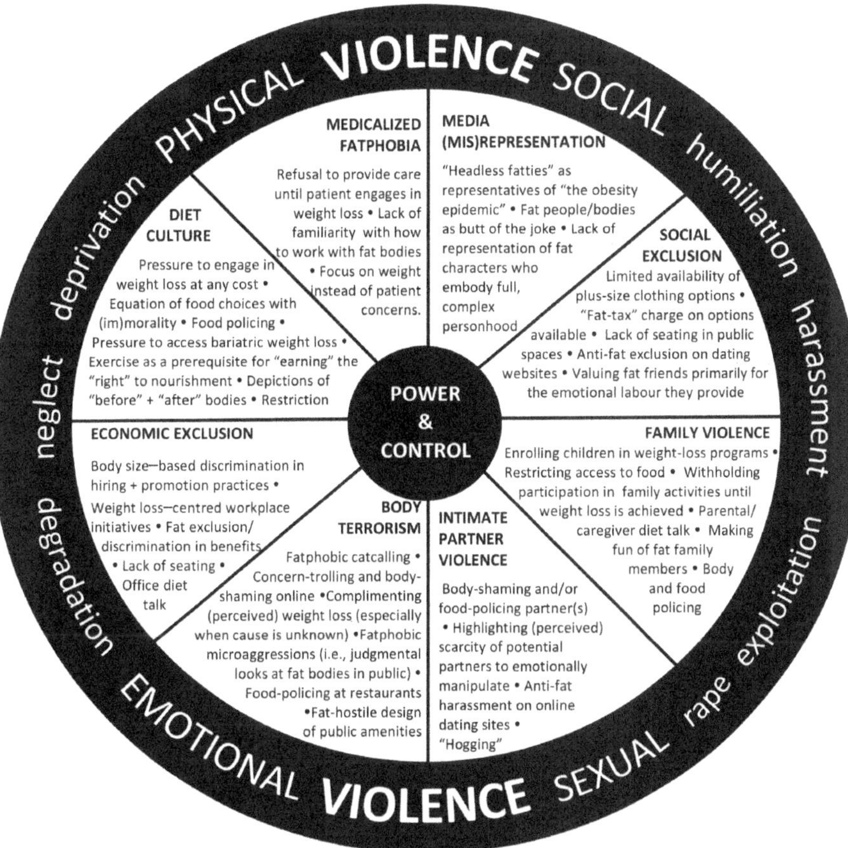

Figure 29.2 Anti-Fat, Violence-Specific Adaptation of the Duluth Model

Source: "Duluth Model" adapted by Sookie Bardwell 2020

The adapted "Duluth Model" (see figure 29.2.) is often used to elucidate common ways in which intimate partner violence takes place. An adaptation of this model may be similarly useful in clarifying some of the specific ways in which anti-fat violence manifests in interpersonal relationships and in interactions with institutions. While the examples that are included herein can provide a useful starting place, it should be noted that this is by no means an exhaustive list of the myriad instances of anti-fat violence that people of size face daily. It is also important to note that both the type and severity of the violence that individuals experience are also impacted by their specific social location, and that those of us living multiply marginalized lives are especially hard hit, as we may be experiencing sizeism simultaneously and alongside other types of oppression such as racism, classism, ableism, and/or (cis/hetero)sexism, to name just a few. Further, it is important to note that the experience of anti-fat violence that folks who move through the world in super fat/infinifat[11] bodies is likely to be much greater than that of small or medium fats (FluffyKittenParty).

Experiences of anti-fat violence (or the threat of anti-fat violence, if it is not experienced directly, as is often the case even for those moving through the world in smaller bodies) start to function as an internal "panopticon"[12] (Foucault), fostering a continuous sense of malaise in one's own body. What emerges from these experiences is a feeling of both constant surveillance and deprivation of autonomy, which separates us from ourselves and obscures our sense of our physical needs. This disconnection makes it hard to access safety and to care for ourselves, fostering a "Vicious Cycle of Body Distrust" (as seen in figure 29.3) similar to the "Cycle of Violence" that is used to illustrate the cyclical way in which intimate partner violence often takes place (Burton; "Cycle of Body Distrust").

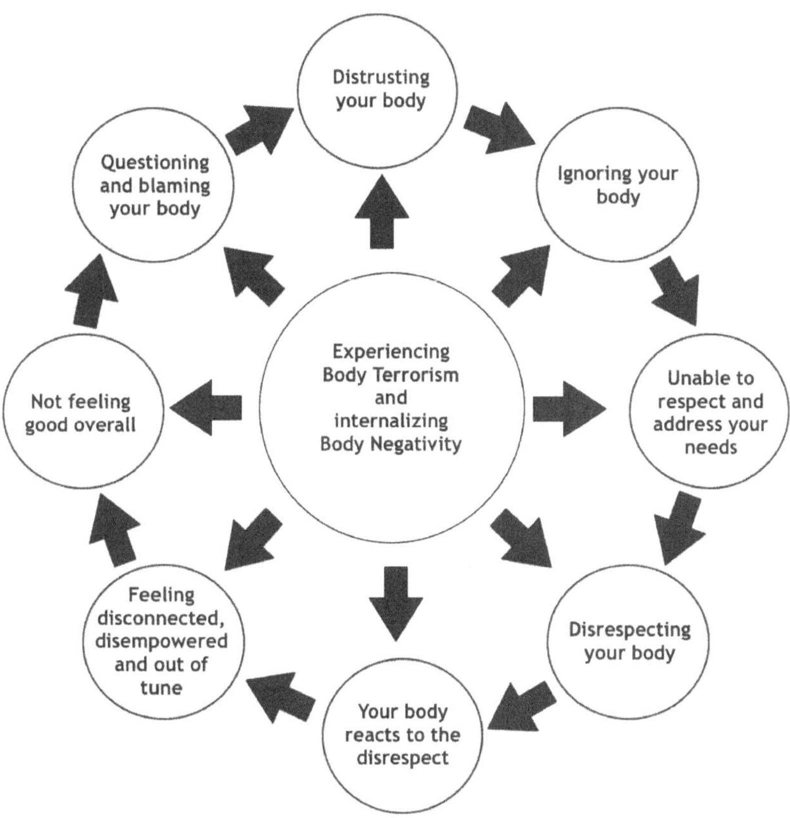

Figure 29.3 The Vicious Cycle of Body Distrust
Source: Adapted from "Cycle of Body Distrust" found online at yourhappyhealthy.com

An anti-fat worldview that positions having a fat body as something to be avoided at all costs demands disconnection from the material reality of embodiment and encourages bodily distrust. This distrust can lead to ignoring the messages that your body communicates (e.g., hunger and satiety cues, pain from overexertion, demands for rest) leading to an inability to provide what it needs (e.g., appropriate nourishment, care and rest) and to treating it in a neglectful, disrespectful, and self-harming way. Understandably, the body reacts to this disrespectful treatment, making a plea for the care it needs through experiences of suboptimal functioning, pain, and illness. This bodily reaction leads to further feelings of disconnection and disempowerment, and a profound sense of failure. The overarching physical malaise that results from this process then engenders a whole new round of questioning the inherent wisdom of your body and blaming self for not measuring up. The resulting thought process that emerges for me and that I've heard from others is something along these lines: "I feel bad because I'm 'having a body wrong.' If I could just make my body different, I wouldn't feel bad." Escaping this cycle is difficult and is further complicated by the trauma responses triggered by experiences of ongoing anti-fat violence in interpersonal and institutional interactions. These responses—such as increased vigilance (fight), avoidance (flight), freezing (invisibility), submission (appeasement), or unhealthy attachment, based on a desire to connect and find affirmation (Ali citing Fisher; van der Hart)—impact the way in which we then engage in our interpersonal relationships, and the cycle of anti-fat violence continues, as the anti-fat sentiment that we have internalized is then directed outwards towards others and, in turn, reinforces the institutional violence from which it originates.

The Four "Sturdy Trunks" of Body Liberation

So, how can the impacts of pervasive anti-fat violence be addressed? Trees provide some excellent lessons that can be integrated into a Body Liberation–centred approach to addressing this violence. They give one another space to grow ("crown shyness" is a phenomenon in which gaps remain between the canopies of full-grown trees of the same species so that access to sunlight isn't hindered), they communicate with one another, and they even share nutrients through complex connections between their root systems and mycelial networks (Wohlleben).

My own anti-violence and wellness promotion work is supported by four "Sturdy Trunks" of Body Liberation: "Autonomy," "Non-Judgment," "Body Neutrality," and "Validation + Celebration."

Autonomy

Autonomy is in equal parts about an empowered relationship with boundaries and access to the resources needed to attain one's best possible outcomes, not just to survive, but to thrive. At their heart, boundaries are about the way we are able to relate to our own needs and limitations. This can be significantly complicated by experiences of violence and marginalization, as when you have never been permitted to have edges, it is difficult to figure out where yours are.

Fat folks are often encouraged from a very young age to distrust one of our most fundamental needs; we are encouraged to disregard or downplay our internal hunger and satiety cues, as though nourishing ourselves is undeserved by virtue of existing in our unruly bodies. Many of us have also experienced social rejection because we fail to adequately conform to the rigorous demands of the amatonormative politics[13] of desirability or have been valued by our peers exclusively for the emotional labour that we provide. This is especially true for fat femmes, and even more so for fat femmes of colour (Luna, "On Being" and "Treating My Friends"). Humans are social creatures, and our drive to connect with and be valued by one another is no less integral to our survival than any other biological need, and so the threat of loneliness and social isolation is something we experience as viscerally as hunger or thirst (Kurzgesagt). After a lifetime of experiences like these, we fatties often have an incredibly tenuous relationship with our own needs and limitations. Paired with the ever-present spectre of anti-fat violence, this disempowered relationship with our own boundaries puts us at risk—and all the more so if we're living multiply marginalized lives.

Marginalization also drastically limits access to the basic resources required for survival. The anti-fat violence of weight bias, weight stigma, and weight discrimination limit fat people's access to employment and opportunities for advancement in the workplace (Ruggs et al.) and detrimentally impact our access, both to equitable and effective health care (Phelan et al.) and to loving relationships in which we are treated with value and care (Luna "On Being" and "Treating My Friends"). These limitations make it very difficult for fat people to thrive.

Through the "Sturdy Trunk" of Autonomy, Body Liberation supports a culture of consent and care. It asserts that we are all the captains of our own underpants, and that we are unilaterally in charge of what happens to and for the body inside of those underpants. It holds as true that all bodies and all people deserve to be treated with respect and that we all deserve to access the resources, both material (e.g., employment, health care, education) and immaterial (e.g., care, connection, safety), that we need to be our best selves and live our best lives.

Non-Judgment

Judgment itself is not inherently negative; in the absence of social inequality, judgments can also be neutral or even positive. Unfortunately, the rampant anti-fatness of diet culture often means that fat bodies are judged through a negative lens, found lacking, and subsequently subjected to high levels of body terrorism. For this reason, Body Liberation encourages a non-judgmental approach to bodies, our own and those of others. The "Sturdy Trunk" of Non-Judgment urges us to resist body-negative messaging, to refuse to accept the idea that any body is any less valuable or valid than any other, to oppose all forms of body terrorism, and to treat every body with the respect and care that each of us deserves simply by virtue of being alive.

Body Neutrality

Non-Judgment is also an essential part of the "Sturdy Trunk" of Body Neutrality. Experiences of body terrorism, including body negativity and body policing, make it very difficult to feel neutral about our bodies given that this violence renders the experience of being embodied "incorrectly" fundamentally unsafe. In an ideal world, body positivity would provide an excellent tool to resist this violence and to reclaim safety within ourselves. Unfortunately, this world, configured as it is around myriad systems of social domination/oppression, is far from ideal, and feeling positively about our bodies is therefore a very difficult (if not impossible) task for many of us. This difficulty is worsened by the presence of toxic positivity, which asserts that we "ought to feel good about ourselves" without affirming the barriers to doing so. What's more, contrary to its radical roots in fat liberation, body positivity has become caught up in capitalism and is increasingly being appropriated by corporate culture in order to market goods under the guise of supporting consumers in "feeling good about ourselves" through engaging in commodified and depoliticized acts of "self-care" disguised as resistance while reinforcing the very systems that make us feel bad in the first place.

Body Neutrality provides a space of resistance that does not demand our positivity. It simply requires a refusal to accept that we ought to feel negatively about our bodies, even if feeling positively about them seems out of reach, as so often it does when we are subjected to ongoing anti-fat violence and other forms of body terrorism including racism, classism, (dis)ableism, healthism, ageism, heterosexism, and cissexism.

Validation + Celebration

Finding spaces in which our experiences of embodied violence are validated can make it easier to access Body Neutrality, since having the validity of these experiences affirmed by others who share them or are able to find solidarity within them through related experiences can help assure us that the pain we feel as a result of body negativity is real. Body Liberation–centred spaces like NOLOSE and Fat Awesome and Queer—spaces by and for fat, queer, and trans people grounded in a commitment to intersectional fat acceptance and liberation—have been foundational in my own process of healing from and being able to refuse and resist anti-fat body terrorism and violence. Surrounded by the robust love and support of other empowered, politicized fats, in all of these spaces I am reminded that I am far from alone, and I am emboldened to fight back alongside my fat community for the Body Liberation we *all* deserve.

Both refusing to accept that we deserve the violence to which we are subjected and celebrating our bodies when they have been positioned as bad, wrong, and unworthy of respect and care are acts of resistance. Celebrating ourselves and one another supports our collective resistance to the body terrorism to which many (especially the multiply marginalized) among us continue to be subjected. It emboldens us to affirm one another in our inherent validity and value; it provides a possibility model for the world, which we strive to create for one another and everyone else; and it empowers us to work collectively to realize this dream of Body Liberation for all.

Body Liberation and/as Anti-Violence Work

At its heart, Body Liberation *is* anti-violence work. It is rooted in and seeks to support multiple other movements for social justice, including but not limited to those for Indigenous self-governance and decolonization, racial justice, gender justice, reproductive justice, disability justice, and fat acceptance and liberation. All these movements seek to address the violence done to bodies that are devalued under the colonial systems of capitalism, patriarchy, and white supremacy. The application of a Body Liberation framework has much to offer supportive, anti-violence, and wellness programming—especially that which seeks to take a robust, intersectional approach to interrupting cycles of relational violence through prevention and intervention and to supporting recovery and healing.

The body terrorism directed at fat bodies is often stochastic terrorism in that it is "violence motivated by [an] ideology" of anti-fatness (Dictionary.com). In stochastic terrorism, rhetoric directed against a group of people motivates violence indirectly by creating a feeling of threat without explicitly telling someone to engage in violent acts. Not only is fatness framed as an existential and moral threat through the rhetoric of the "obesity epidemic," but in a fatphobic society, becoming fat is perceived as threatening because doing so opens one up to the devaluation and constant violence to which fat bodies/people are subjected. Individuals (both fat and non-fat) are motivated to participate in and enact that violence as a mechanism by which they can disavow and distance themselves from fatness. This impulse to avoid violence by creating a distinction between (non-fat) self and (fat) Other is often a motivating factor in interpersonal violence, even within otherwise caring relationships. Anti-fat violence is also frequently enacted under the guise of care through concern-trolling loved ones in our intimate friendships, family, and other "supportive" relationships (i.e., "I'm worried about your health;" "I just want you to find love;" etc.) Perhaps worst of all—having internalized the fatphobic messages we receive through our interactions with institutions and through our interpersonal relationships and then directing that violence back at ourselves—as the brilliant Mia Mingus states in her transformative piece *Dreaming Accountability*, "most of us are in an abusive relationship with ourselves."

Body Liberation provides a mechanism through which the anti-fat violence we do to ourselves and others can be interrupted by encouraging an understanding that everybody's bodily autonomy ought to be respected, that all bodies are inherently valid and valuable, that no one deserves to experience violence, and that all people deserve to be treated with respect and kindness—regardless of their embodiment.

Conclusion

The "Sturdy Trunk" of Autonomy reminds us to cultivate an awareness of and respect for one another's boundaries and our own and to work to ensure that we can all access the resources that we need to collectively thrive—rejecting the uncaring ethic and false scarcity of capitalism, patriarchy, and white supremacy. The "Sturdy Trunk" of Non-Judgment provides an opportunity to give ourselves and one another a break and empowers us to refuse to perceive any bodies through a negative lens, so we can work towards Body Neutrality. And from this place of Body Neutrality, we can validate one another in the harms we (have) suffer(ed) through our experiences of anti-fat and other embodiment-centred violence and affirm one another in our right to move through the world without experiencing violence of any kind. Finally, we can resist all forms of body terrorism and support one another in recovering and healing from these violences by *celebrating* the beautiful diversity of every single one of our majestic, very much enough and never "too much" bodies.

Notes

1 I have used the language of body/self here in recognition of the false body-mind distinction, which is one aspect of the colonial violence taking place in the (so-called) Canadian context. My understanding of this distinction as violent is also informed by Eli Clare's exploration of the role of the body-mind distinction in ableist violence inherent in the idea of "cure" as an assumed aspiration for dis/abled folks (Clare). This connection has been central to the way in which I understand my own dis/abled, fat, queer, nonbinary, femme, working-class body and the way I have been encouraged to understand my body/self as in need of "fixing" and to pursue a "cure" for my inappropriate/inadequate embodiment in order to be worthy of respect and care.

2 Within the logic of white supremacy, patriarchy, and capitalism, which underly the colonial context of (so-called) Canada, the mythical norm of "appropriate" embodiment is defined as a white, settler, (presently) able-bodied, neurotypical, cisgender, heterosexual body able and willing to participate in the (re)production, maintenance, and advancement of an ongoing colonial project of erasure, extraction, and exploitation.

3 In the late '80s and early '90s *BodyBreak* public service announcements (PSAs)—produced through the Canadian National Participation initiative—regularly aired on Canadian television channels. Hal Johnson and Joanne McLeod hosted these short, fitness and wellness-focused segments, which encouraged Canadians to get moving and pursue a healthy lifestyle (BodyBreak). While I cannot pinpoint a specific instance in which I heard the hosts make fatphobic statements, I do remember never seeing fat bodies like mine represented or spoken about as bodies with access to fitness, health, or wellness, and that weight management was represented as a desirable outcome.

4 The Vox-produced video "What BMI Doesn't Tell You about Your Health" presents an excellent and expedient (under five minutes) overview of why BMI should not be held up as a useful measure of health and well-being (Vox).

5 Deepest, fattest gratitude to my fat best-femme, JDP, to all the Fat, Awesome and Queer (FAQ) and NOLOSE babes, and to rad fatties far and wide for existing, resisting, and enveloping me in your big, fat love! Fat, Awesome and Queer is a social and activist group founded by JDP and a group of fat, awesome queers in Toronto in 2013; the group continues to exist on Facebook (https://www.facebook.com/

groups/faqtoronto/). NOLOSE is a volunteer-run organization based in the United States that hosts a bi-yearly conference for queer and trans fat folks and our allies and funds regional, community-run programming. It was founded as the National Organization of Lesbians of Size Everywhere by Dot Nelson-Turnier and has since become an organization "by and for people of all genders" (NOLOSE). I attended the NOLOSE conference in Portland, Oregon, in 2013, and it changed my life forever. It was the first time that I had the opportunity to be in a fat-centred space, and the support I received and revolutionary frameworks to which I was introduced there continue to deeply impact my sense of self-worth and to inform my Body Liberation work.

6 Body terrorism encompasses the many forms of body-centred violence that target individuals and groups who experience marginalization in relation to their embodiment, namely, those of us with fat bodies, racialized bodies, queer and trans bodies, dis/abled bodies, and other marginalized or rejected bodies (Taylor). Body terrorism encompasses body negativity, body policing, and body shaming, along with other forms of direct and indirect violence, which are intended to maintain and reinforce the mythical norm of "appropriate" embodiment by punishing failure to conform to this narrowly defined standard.

7 In developing the BMI scale, Belgian statistician Lambert Adolphe Jacques Quetelet (who was neither a doctor nor a health expert of any kind) was primarily interested in determining a benchmark for "the average man," whom he considered representative of a type of "perfection" (Jackson-Gibson). In developing the scale, he considered the weight to height ratio of a survey sample consisting of only the bodies of white European men, as he had no intention that the resulting index would be used to measure health or wellness at all (Jackson-Gibson). The use of the BMI scale for these purposes not only fails to account for social determinants of health, such as the chronic stress of marginalization resulting from things like ongoing experiences of racialized, gender-based, ableist and sizeist violence, but also *creates* dangerous disparities in health care access because of medicalized fatphobia (further amplified by other forms of medicalized oppression/violence), with catastrophic impacts on health outcomes for fat people (Jackson-Gibson).

8 The development of Canada's Food Guide was fundamentally informed by nutritional experiments done without consent in Indigenous communities and residential schools in the 1930s and 40s in the

context of widespread (and intentional) malnourishment resulting from violent colonial policies that forcibly removed Indigenous people from their lands, placed limits on their livelihoods, and disrupted traditional foodways (Tennant). The impact of disrupted traditional food systems and the (intergenerational) trauma of both food scarcity and these non-consensual nutrition experiments continues to result in an increased incidence of health challenges in Indigenous communities (Tennant). Further, the ongoing presentation of the Food Guide continues to be rife with food racism by centring the dominant (white) culture's idea of "good" food and vilifying or not including foods that are culturally important/relevant while simultaneously ignoring the higher rates of food insecurity in BIPOC communities (Vansintjan).

9 The term *straight-sized* refers to folks who are not fat and would not be included on the "fat spectrum." Similar to the language of the fat spectrum, this term refers to clothing sizes and includes any body able to fit into clothing available at most online and brick-and-mortar retail outlets (i.e., up to a US women's size 16).

10 According to stats published by the unfortunately named and highly problematic organization Obesity Canada regarding Canadian's experiences of/with weight bias, stigma, and discrimination, fat elementary school-aged children are 63 per cent more likely to be bullied than their straight-sized peers; 54 per cent of fat adults reported being stigmatized by co-workers; 64 per cent of fat adults reported experiences of weight bias from health care professionals; and 72 per cent of images and 77 per cent of videos featured stigmatized depictions of fat bodies/people (Obesity Canada).

11 FluffyKittenParty provides an explanation of the fat spectrum on their website (fluffykittenparty.com), along with definitions of the range of sizes included in each of the categories of fatness and information about the origin of these pieces of terminology. The boundaries of each category are related to dress sizes, as this is a metric that resonates with many given that we live in a world that insists we must wear clothing to enter the public sphere. This spectrum includes small fat (US women's 18, or sizes 1x–2x), mid fat (US women's 20–24, or sizes 2x–3x), large fat (US women's 26–32, or sizes 4x–5x), superfat/infinifat (a term attributed to Ash, a superfat activist, referring to women larger than US size 32), and death fat (a term coined by fat activist and writer Lesley Kinzel in 2008, which is not related to a specific size range but is instead intended to be used by fatties of any size who want to reclaim "morbid" fatness as an act of resistance.

[12] The concept of the panopticon as a means of social control was introduced by English philosopher Jeremy Bentham who proposed a prison design with a central guard tower surrounded by cells backlit by an external window. Those in the cells would never know when they were or weren't being observed by guards in the tower. Foucault discusses this concept as facilitating the functioning of power since, by internalizing the idea that we're being surveilled and monitored, we no longer need to be because we end up policing ourselves (Foucault). This idea is particularly important when considering anti-fat violence, as through constant subjection to toxic diet culture, repeated encounters with body negativity, and ongoing experiences of body terrorism, we begin to shame and police ourselves in relation to every (perceived) instance of deviation from the "mythical norm."

[13] *Amatonormativity* is a term coined by Elizabeth Brake. It refers to the dominant social expectations around experiences of attraction and the configuration of intimate relationships. Amatonormativity positions heterosexual attraction and monogamous relationships between cisgender, able/bodied, neurotypical, same-race, same-age, same-sized non-fat bodies as normative and understands attraction and relationships that fail to conform to this norm as deviant and less valid. Amatonormativity impacts our internal concepts of desirability, the way in which we navigate relationships, and how relationships are or are not recognized, understood, and represented within/by institutions, e.g., state, church, medicine, and the media (Brake).

Works Cited

Ali, Ronnie. "How We Respond to Threats." Document shared directly by colleague. Accessed 3 Feb. 2021.

Ash. "Beyond Superfat: Rethinking the Farthest End of the Fat Spectrum." *The Fat Lip*, 20 Dec. 2016, http://thefatlip.com/2016/12/20/beyond-superfat-rethinking-the-farthest-end-of-the-fat-spectrum/.

Bardwell, Sookie. "A Space at the Table: Unpacking the Social and Cultural Underpinnings of Disordered Eating." Radical Wellness Week, 18 Mar. 2019, Centre for Student Equity, Diversity and Inclusion, Wilfrid Laurier University, Waterloo, Ontario. Presentation. Information available at Chub Love for Wilfrid Laurier University, www.facebook.com/events/centre-for-student-equity-diversity-and-inclusion-laurier-waterloo/radical-wellness-week/532233510635799/. Accessed 1 Jan. 2021.

Bardwell, Sookie. "In the Thick of It: Challenging Weight Stigma for Everyone's Wellbeing." Radical Wellness Week, 18 Mar. 2019, Centre for Student Equity, Diversity and Inclusion, Wilfrid Laurier University, Waterloo, Ontario. Presentation. Information available at Chub Love for Wilfrid Laurier University, www.facebook.com/events/centre-for-student-equity-diversity-and-inclusion-laurier-waterloo/radical-wellness-week/532233510635799/. Accessed 1 Jan. 2021.

Bardwell, Sookie, and Christine Hsu. "Body Buddies Movement Group: Building A Body-Liberation-Centred Movement Practice." Sheena's Place, Toronto, Ontario, June–Aug. 2020. Course. Information available at sheenasplace.org/wp-content/uploads/2020/06/Sheenas-Place-Calendar-SUMMER-2020-v.3.pdf. Accessed 1 Jan. 2021.

Bardwell, Sookie, and Christine Hsu. "Robust Relationships: Building a Body-Liberation-Centred Approach to Being Humans Together." Sheena's Place, Toronto, Ontario, Jan.–Mar. 2021. Course. Information available at sheenasplace.org/wp-content/uploads/2020/11/Sheenas-Place-Calendar-Winter 2021.pdf. Accessed 1 Jan 2021.

Bardwell, Sookie, and JDP. "In the Thick of It: Challenging Weight Stigma for Everyone's Wellbeing." RE:SHAPE: Reshaping Our Approach to Gender Based Violence, 26 Feb. 2020, Western University, London, Ontario. Presentation.

Bardwell, Sookie, and JDP. "Loving Large: Creating a Size-Inclusive Practice." Fortieth Annual Guelph Sexuality Conference (June 13–15, 2018), 14 Jun. 2018. Workshop. Information available at www.guelphsexualityconference.ca/past-conference-schedule/gsc_program_2018.pdf. Accessed 1 Jan. 2021.

Bardwell, Sookie, and JDP. "Robust Relationships: Unpacking Fatphobia and Sizeism for Heartier Connections." RE:SHAPE: Reshaping Our Approach to Gender Based Violence, 26 Feb. 2020, Western University, London, Ontario. Presentation.

Bardwell, Sookie, Ronnie Ali, Rebecca Benson, Christine Hsu, and JDP. "Sidelining Sizeism: Healing from Fatphobia, Together." Sheena's Place, Toronto, Ontario, Sept.–Nov. 2019. Course. Information available at sheenasplace.org/wp-content/uploads/2019/08/Sheenas-Place-Calendar-FALL-2019-v.3-digital.pdf. Accessed 1 Jan. 2021.

Bear, Sarah. "Should You Be Wearing That?: Fatphobia's Connection to Rape Culture." *Prevent Connect*, 30 Jul. 2019, http://www.preventconnect.org/2019/07/should-you-be-wearing-that-fatphobias-connection-to-rape-culture/. Accessed 1 Jan. 2021.

Bodirsky, Monica, and Jon Johnson. "Decolonizing Diet: Healing by Reclaiming Traditional Indigenous Foodways." *Cuizine: The Jour-*

nal of Canadian Food Cultures, vol. 1, no. 1, 2008, www.erudit.org/en/journals/cuizine/1900-v1-n1-cuizine2503/019373ar/. Accessed 1 Jan. 2021.

BodyBreak. "About BodyBreak," *BodyBreak*, 2013, https://bodybreak.com/about/bb-story/. Accessed 14 May 2021.

Bordo, Susan. *Unbearable Weight: Feminism, Western Culture, and the Body.* University of California Press, 2004.

Brake, Elizabeth. "Amatonormativity," *Elizabeth Brake.com*, 2012, https://elizabethbrake.com/amatonormativity/. Accessed 14 May 2021.

Burton-Hughes, Liz. "Understanding the Cycle of Violence in Domestic Abuse." *hub from High Speed Training,* 6 Mar. 2015, www.highspeedtraining.co.uk/hub/domestic-abuse-facts/. Accessed 1 Jan. 2021.

Clare, Eli. *Brilliant Imperfection: Grappling with Cure.* Duke University Press, 2017.

"Cycle of Body Distrust." *yourhappyhealthy.org*. Accessed 5 Sept. 2019.

Dawson Women's Shelter. "Ending Fatphobia to End Violence." *Dawson Women's Shelter Blog,* 9 Dec. 2020, www.dawsonwomensshelter.com/blog/16-days-reading-list-2020-zyyjj-4g5ab. Accessed 1 Jan. 2021.

Deerwater, Jen. "Dear Thin People: On Ableism, Fatphobia & Other Intersections of Oppression." *Rest for Resistance*, 24 Aug. 2017, www.restforresistance.com/zine/dear-thin-people-on-fatphobia-ableism-other-oppressions. Accessed 1 Jan. 2021.

Dictionary.com. "What Is 'Stochastic Terrorism,' and Why Is It Trending?" *Dictionary.com,* 4 Aug. 2019, www.dictionary.com/e/what-is-stochastic-terrorism/. Accessed 1 Jan. 2021.

Duluth Model. "Power and Control Wheel (Thorne Harbour Health Adaptation)." *Domestic Abuse Intervention Programs,* 2019, https://www.theduluthmodel.org/wp-content/uploads/2019/08/Power-and-Control-Thorne-Harbour-Health.pdf. Accessed 1 Jan. 2021.

Evans Braziel, Jana, and Kathleen LeBesco. "Editors' Introduction." *Bodies Out of Bounds: Fatness and Transgression*, edited by Jana Evans Braziel and Kathleen LeBesco, University of California Press, 2001 , pp. 1–18.

Fisher, J. *Psychoeducational Aids for Working with Psychological Trauma.* Centre for Integrative Healing, 2009.

FluffyKittenParty. "Fategories—Understanding 'Smallfat Fragility' & the Fat Spectrum." *FlufflyKittenParty.com*, 5 Oct. 2019, fluffykittenparty.com/2019/10/05/fategories-understanding-smallfat-fragility-the-fat-spectrum/. Accessed 1 Jan. 2021.

Foucault, Michel. *Discipline and Punish: The Birth of the Prison.* Pantheon Books, 1977.

Gailey, Jeannine A., and Ariane Prohaska. "'Knocking off a fat girl': An Exploration of Hogging, Male Sexuality, and Neutralizations." *Deviant Behaviour*, vol. 27, 2006, pp. 31–49.

Galtung, Johan. "Cultural Violence." *Journal of Peace Research*, vol. 27, no. 3, 1990, pp. 291–305.

Harrison, Da'Shaun L. *Belly of the Beast: The Politics of Anti-Fatness as Anti-Blackness*. North Atlantic Books, 2021.

Hawkins, Hannah. *Do No Harm: Fatphobia & the Medical Industry*. New Degree Press, 2020.

Hesse-Biber, Sharlene. *The Cult of Thinness*. Oxford University Press, 2006.

Jackson-Gibson, Adele. "The Racist and Problematic History of the Body Mass Index" *Good Housekeeping*, 23 Feb. 2021, https://www.goodhousekeeping.com/health/diet-nutrition/a35047103/bmi-racist-history/. Accessed 5 Mar. 2022.

Kurzgesagt. "Loneliness." *YouTube*, uploaded by Kurzgesagt—In a Nutshell, 17 Feb. 2019, www.youtube.com/watch?v=n3Xv_g3g-mA&vl=ru. Accessed 1 Jan. 2021.

Luna, Caleb. "On Being Fat, Brown, Femme, Ugly, and Unloveable." *BGD*. 21 July 2014, www.bgdblog.org/2014/07/fat-brown-femme-ugly-unloveable/. Accessed 1 Jan. 2021.

Luna, Caleb. "Treating My Friends Like Lovers: The Politics of Desirability." *The Body Is Not an Apology*, 17 Mar. 2018, www.thebodyisnotanapology.com/magazine/how-to-be-fat-caleb-luna-sub/. Accessed 1 Jan. 2021.

Mingus, Mia. "Dreaming Accountability." *Leaving Evidence*, 5 May 2019, leavingevidence. wordpress.com/2019/05/05/dreaming-accountability-dreaming-a-returning-to-ourselves-and-each-other/. Accessed 1 Jan. 2021.

NOLOSE. "About NOLOSE." *NOLOSE: The Revolution Just Got Bigger*, 2021, http://nolose.org/about/ Accessed May 14, 2021.

Obesity Canada. "Weight Bias." *Obesity Canada*, https://obesitycanada.ca/weight-bias/. Accessed 1 Jan. 2021.

Phelan, S. M., D. J. Burgess, M. W. Yeazel, W. L. Hellerstedt, J. M. Griffin, and M. van Ryn. "Impact of Weight Bias and Stigma on Quality of Care and Outcomes for Patients with Obesity." *Obesity Reviews*, vol. 16, no. 4, 2015, pp. 319–26.

"Pool." *Shrill,* developed by Aidy Bryant, Ali Rushfield, and Lindy West, performance by Aidy Bryant, season 1, episode 4, Broadway Video, 2019.

Ruggs, Enrica N., Eden B. King, and Mikki R. Hebl. "The Opportunity Costs of Weight Bias at Work." *MIT Sloan Management Review*, 8 Oct. 2020, sloanreview.mit.edu/article/the-opportunity-costs-of-weight-bias-at-work/. Accessed 1 Jan. 2021.

Strings, Sabrina. *Fearing the Black Body: The Racial Origins of Fat Phobia*. NYU Press, 2019.

Taylor, Sonya Renee. "What Is Body Terrorism?" *The Body Is Not an Apology*, https://thebodyisnotanapology.com/about-tbinaa/what-is-body-terrorism/. Accessed 14 May 2021.

Tennant, Zoe. "The Dark History of Canada's Food Guide: How Experiments on Indigenous Children Shaped Nutrition Policy." *CBC Radio: Unreserved*, 19 Apr. 2021, https://www.cbc.ca/radio/unreserved/how-food-in-canada-is-tied-to-land-language-community-and-colonization-1.5989764/the-dark-history-of-canada-s-food-guide-how-experiments-on-indigenous-children-shaped-nutrition-policy-1.5989785. Accessed 5 Mar. 2022.

van der Hart, Onno, Elbert R. S. Nijenhuis, and Kathy Steele. *The Haunted Self: Structural Dissociation and the Treatment of Chronic Traumatization*. W. W. Norton & Co., 2006.

Vansintjan, Aaron. "The Racism in Healthy Food." *McGill Daily*, 17 Oct. 2013, https://www.mcgilldaily.com/2013/10/the-racism-in-healthy-food/. Accessed 5 Mar. 2022.

Vox. "What BMI Doesn't Tell You about Your Health." *YouTube*, uploaded by *Vox*, 1 Feb. 2018, https://www.youtube.com/watch?v=z_3S2_41_FE. Accessed 14 May 2021.

"What Is Mentionable Is Manageable: Mister Rogers." *PBS Learning Video*, WUCF Corporation for Public Broadcasting, https://www.pbslearningmedia.org/resource/mentionable-manageable-mister-rogers-video/meet-the-helpers/. Accessed 13 Oct. 2022.

Wohlleben, Peter. *The Hidden Life of Trees: What They Feel, How They Communicate*. Greystone Books, 2016.

The Affective State of Fat-Beingness within Debility Politics

Ramanpreet A. Bahra

Introduction: Juggling Two Worlds—Life and Death

The concepts of "personhood," "the human," or the "personal register" may seem irrelevant, as we hold ever so tightly to the presumptions of liberalism, equality, and multiculturalism in contemporary Canadian society. It is as if there is this sigh of relief in the air that we have moved past our imperial-colonialist history. However, this is far from the truth, seeing that our current political and "public health" climate (encompassing both the COVID-19 pandemic and the "obesity epidemic") reify a paradox of belonging, where bodies continue to be constituted by the very idea of the personal register that enables the operationalization of inclusionary-exclusionary politics. Across disciplines like fat studies, critical disability studies, and postcolonial and Black studies, we witness the multiple ways that body politics come to life, reminiscent of earlier colonial, racist, and sexist discourses of the West that point to what bodies belong, are to live, and are to die, in this settler nation we call home—Canada. This form of body politics outlines the constructions and restrictions of bodily containment and productivity, concluding in the question of what bodies are in fact "politic" and/or "incapable of forming or fully entering into a body politics" (Puwar 21). James Overboe's notion of the personal register is taken up to speak on how the discourses of race, disability, and fatness are structurally interdependent, mutually productive, and constantly illuminating the genre of "Man" and its "racializing assemblages," as they map out the stages of "being human" from the fully human to the not-quite to the non-person (Overboe, "Theory"; Weheliye).

Language, culture, the medical industrial complex, and carceral geographies have all established and legitimated the criterion of the personal register (the white, elite, nondisabled, heterosexual, cisgender, thin/muscled man) and its racializing assemblages that position bodies into what Achille Mbembe has conceptualized as lifeworlds and deathworlds. Under the banner of the "obesity epidemic" and the broader violent policing of racialized, fat, disabled or mad bodies by the state, we usually see deathworlds become a reality for those construed as the "transgressive," "dangerous," "burdensome" entities of society, those who are not deemed worthy of being called *a life*. The discourse of the personal register is riddled with this concept of "normalcy" and its exclusionary practices that continue to divide the "good" and "bad" versions of bodies. The resulting dichotomy of this constructed knowledge of "what a body can do" and its method of ranking bodies via racializing assemblages has underpinned much of my relationship with my body, as I found myself on the lower echelon of the scale of humanity. The social construction of the registry of humanness and its constant examination, re-evaluation, and discipline produce a myriad of social inequalities that are practiced, felt, and lived within and through bodies. In the mapping of racialized fat bodies, we are exposed to the colonial-imperial systems that discipline and regulate us, particularly the ways in which our fat-beingness is positioned as a zone of non-being in the status of life and death across social systems (e.g., family, health care, education, law). This takes us to the crux of this chapter: the application of Jasbir Kaur Puar's theorization of the triangulation of disability, debility, and capacity to explore fat-beingness as debilitated. Her advancement of disability politics through the concepts of affect, capacity, and debility may enable us to consider fat racialized bodies as always in a debilitated state. Debility politics, as a result, may enable us to better understand what it means to be at the intersections of fatness, racialization, disability, and madness in the overall body politics, and the ways in which marginalized bodies are put onto a path of both slow and/or accelerated death based on the "personal register."

Methodology

For this chapter, I weave together stories of my experiences—both of learning about the personal registry through language, interactions, and spaces and of taking up the position of the "phobogenic object," the not-quite human or sometimes non-human person ascribed to me due to the way in which my brownness, femmeness, and fatness signify a failed embodiment (Overboe, "Theory"; Fanon; Weheliye). As a second-generation Punjabi migrant, I have seen fatphobia play a large role in my family's story, particularly mine and my mother's as we become the fat object in the home-space, medical-space, etc. My fatness has always been under the scrutiny of structures of oppression and their parameters of the full versus lacking body (Bahra), resulting in the disciplining of my tongue (i.e., speech, caloric intake) or bulges (i.e., BMI, body fat calibre). The materialization of my body can be better understood as sets of complex relations articulated through the territorializing structures grounded in white supremacy, heteropatriarchy, thinness (and the hourglass shape), and ableism (Weheliye 49). As I reflect upon my fat, cisgender, femme, Punjabi body, it is apparent that the discourse of "the human" and "the Other" has initiated these cycles of racism, ableism, and sizeism/shapeism at an ideological and systemic level in society, which has subsequently impacted the way I have learnt and performed—and been excluded on the basis my brownness, fatness, and femmeness as the non-human.[1] These intersecting experiences and their ongoing process of marking, categorizing, and disciplining difference based on labels of "normalcy" or "superiority" legitimate the standardized corporeality, while marking mine and my mother's as "pathological," "unintelligible," and in need of rehabilitation. To unpack these relations, over the last few years I have taken on a journey of affirming the very aspects of myself that have been problematized. For instance, in being critical of skin bleaching products or yo-yo diets, I have worked on mending and celebrating my relationship to my body by asking, "What can my body do?"—rather than wondering "what a body is" (Bahra and Overboe; Hickey-Moody and Page). This has enabled me to reflect on how I hold subjugated knowledges and have the potential to reconfigure micropolitical relations and bring about social change (Hickey-Moody and Page). My own body-project and research are rooted in using storytelling, art creation, and autoethnographic methodologies to present my own intersectional "episteme" influenced by the works of critical disability scholars, fat activists/scholars, and Black feminist scholars, while also challenging normative ideologies through rethinking "the human." This methodological process allows me to begin imagining a future that includes the desiring of flesh and its materiality even in the spaces, like the deathworlds, where I may be devoid of "life" under neoliberal regimes.

The Personal Registry and Exiting the Lifeworld

The personal registry is underlined with many complex layers of ideological, political, and economic connotations, all linking back to this question of what it means to be human and who can enter the national body politic (Overboe "Affirming"; Overboe "Theory"). In an earlier piece, I and Overboe argue that the personal register "determine[s] who is human enough through its established attributes and preoccupation with identity, representation, and ranking of bodies," and this produces the larger debility, disposability, and death of those who fall outside of the ranks of being human enough (200). Within critical race and critical disability scholarship, we often see these questions arise to demonstrate how both racialized and disabled bodies have always been subsumed by the structure and processes of a historical system that produces this essentialist concept of the universal human and establishes the alien Other. According to Alexander G. Weheliye, the registry is largely rooted in the genre of human as "Man," representing the "modern incantations of the human" and the masculinist, imperial, colonial, and racist histories upon which they come out of and depend (21). He further claims that, in being defined against the "genres of Man"—established with the heterosexual, elite, nondisabled, thin or muscular, cisgender man as the privileged body—racialized, disabled, and fat bodies come to be the bearers of ontological and biological lack. The centralization of the "genre of Man" in the discourse of the body takes a deeper hold through its "racializing assemblages" of social forces that continuously grant the status of complete human to a select few, while mapping out the not-quite human or non-human form. Within the works of both Weheliye and Achille Mbembe in particular, we see the ways in which racializing assemblages are deployed to determine who enters lifeworlds and who is pushed into deathworlds. This bifurcation of bodies is set alongside the aforementioned histories, and language, legal policies, science, the medical industrial complex, and neoliberal culture further legitimate the criteria of the registry, while contextualizing racialized, disabled, and fat bodies as aliens or potential "space invaders" within society, ultimately categorizing them as lacking and putting them into a stream of life-in-death (i.e., deathworlds). The label of "human" continues to "make people" and shape a white, ableist, sizeist, and shapeist perception of what constitutes a state of complete humanity and, of course, of what constitutes "the bad taste" that is the non-human.

As we explore what fatness means in the Canadian context, we must expose how such perceptions persist. The processes of these racialized or fat-assemblages based on the genres of "Man" are always being created, co-constituted, and reified at all levels, leaving fat bodies questioning their sense of humanity due to state and interpersonal interactions that tend to label and police their fat as Otherness. What can be offered in this application of racializing assemblages is that the oppressive regimes preserve the white, nondisabled, thin body as the authentic state of being, while continuing to name, differentiate, and interpret the racialized, disabled, and fat body as the template of the failed non-human that is made into a spectacle, "tolerated," and "never accommodated" (Overboe "Theory"; Bahra and Overboe; Bannerji 37). The construction of these very different bodies reflects not just the discourses of whiteness and ableism as separate axes; together, they co-constitute and mutually shape the concept of fatness to subjugate the physicalities of the "human" form much more intensely. Janell Hobson suggests that the "perceptions of 'visual' difference based on spectacle and surveillance are assigned social and cultural values that are mapped onto the body and given political meaning. Thus, the spectacle of Black bodies exists as a 'deviation' in comparison with the 'normative' white body" (10). Sabrina Strings builds on Hobson's analysis by illustrating how a racial element has always undercut the politics of the body and concept of subjectivity. The logics of racial grammar, specifically underlined with the discourse of anti-Blackness combined with anti-fat narratives deepens the boundaries between the fat racialized 'Other' and the normative aesthetic of whiteness, with the added layer of thinness and/or the hourglass figure in contrast to the "gluttonous nature" associated with the "abnormal" fat racialized body (149).The personal registry, its two very different worlds, and its entailing life experiences have manifested and continue to manifest as heavy waves in my family. Some of the more explicit tides have been the poverty and racism experienced by my paternal family in the Canadian Punjabi diaspora for the last 50 years. Sizeism, however, has had both an implicit and explicit presence in my family. At the age of 24, my mother arrived from Punjab, India, to Toronto, Canada, in 1990 on the Canadian equivalent of a K-1 fiancé visa. She had no one with her but her own mother, for a span of two weeks, and distant relatives she met for the first time, as she prepared herself for the next chapter of her life: the fat bride from Punjab. As she exited one family and nation to enter the next family in *vadesh* (a foreign country), one aspect of her life remained: the fatphobic narratives linked to her body. She went from being the fat sister in Punjab to the fat wife, fat *bhabi* (brothers' wife), and later fat mother. The same year as her migration and marriage, my mother became pregnant with me. She recalls being told by family members that she used to resemble Bollywood actress Hema Malini, but with the pregnancy-related weight gain, she was far from that doe-eyed beauty icon. She also shares memories of the crude comments associated with her fatness and a particular emphasis on her being lazy and gluttonous, with little consideration of the changes occurring during pregnancy and postpartum. Fatphobia was always present in her formative teenage years, but in this *vadesh* and new family, anti-fat narratives took on a new life, and weight loss became her objective at all costs. What does this have to do with the personal registry, you ask? These are examples of the dialogues that shape my family's collective experience. Amongst the trauma of fatphobia within and outside of the family, racism within the workplace (i.e., factories, personal support worker jobs), or belonging to the working class and the struggle to make ends meet, my parent's immigrant story, in particular my mother's, has always gone back to her body and the access she had to the lifeworld in front of her. Throughout my life, I have witnessed her metaphorically and literally be en route to death because of racism and fatphobia. My mother's experience has created a cartography of its own, which I now find myself sprouting from. Our mutual experiences of sizeism, or as I like to call it, intergenerational sizeism, and the overall personal registry have stamped us with this state of ambivalence located in between life and deathworlds as the "non-human."

The racist, sizeist/shapeist, and ableist dialogues of the registry fold into the fat-assemblages shared between my mother and I, wherein we find ourselves in a triple bind. The coding of our fat-, brown-, female-beingness renders us as lacking and pathological, yet excessive and threatening, thus not considered worthy of being invited into the realm of the not-quite human, let alone the full human. Growing up, I came to learn of this personal registry and its figure of the so-called universal full human through being assigned various labels, such as "Paki," *sabla raang* (wheatish colour), *madjj* (buffalo), *saand* (pig), or "fatty" within conversations with my peers and family members, or as I moved through different spaces, like schools, hospitals, and home (Bahra). I cannot recall my mother being called similar names in front of me, but the *boliyan* (Punjabi folk songs) we sang, talk of her fat tummy needing to be sliced away, and the policing of her food intake by family members and medical practitioners has always left this affective residue of the personal register. In our mother-daughter assemblage, the individual and conjoined experience of the sizeist and shapeist discourses manifested in the form of the docile body in order to gain access to the lifeworld's personal registry and its privileges from the onset. We share with one another how the fatphobic attitude did not end with her but worsened in our home-space as I began to hear the words *madjj* (cow) and *mautti* (fatty) now attach to me as I got fatter.

Similar to my mother sitting in as the symbol of the pathology and excessiveness in spaces, like the medical office or the rooms of our family gatherings, I too became that symbol as the fat cousin to the younger kids in my family. I still hear the echo of a statement my 11-year-old cousin made referencing my fatness and shape: "I can't eat this [referencing roti], because then I'll look like you and *bhua* [paternal aunt]. I want to look like my mum," gesturing to her mother's thin and appropriately curvy body. Here we witness how both my mother and I became spectacles of "gluttonous nature" and how the hourglass shape my cousin desires maintains this dichotomy between thin but curvy and fat and gluttonous. Under the racializing assemblage, the pervasive notion of the personal registry surfaced in multiple ways, and collectively, we found ourselves received as the phobogenic fat-assemblage that needed disciplining because of the characterization of fatness as lacking and a form of life-in-death. We preserve not only systems of sex and gender, caste, colour, and race within Punjabi communities but also ideals of size and shape informed by anti-fat discourses. I simply am and continue to be the bad taste of my Punjabi-Canadian family that exits lifeworlds to enter deathworlds alongside my mother.

The Capacity and Debility of Fat-Beingness: Entering Deathworlds

In looking at the notion of the personal register in the affective realm, we can possibly approach an even greater understanding of fatness and the various experiences that arise across the intersections. When we think through the body as "affectus," there is potential to "validate emergent epistemologies, or subjugated knowledges" (Hickey-Moody and Page 6). This Deleuzoguattarian thought, which centres the affective body in its analysis, pushes for a new understanding of the body as a process and product of multiple knowledge systems from which we can approach alternative knowledges surrounding bodies and their movements within the larger dominant system (Hickey-Moody and Page 18). As such, the "affective intensities" of non-normative bodies "challenge heteronormative understandings of [queer] intimacy," disability, racialization, and even fatness

(Chen 207). Informed by affect studies and critical disability studies, Puar advances a discussion that positions disability politics as shifting to debility politics. She attempts to reframe disability as existing "in relation to assemblages of capacity and debility, modulated across historical time, geopolitical spaces, institutional mandates, and discursive regimes" (*The Right to Maim* xv). I take on Puar's conceptualization of the triangulation of disability, debility, and capacity and apply a fat studies lens to ask, "Can we think of fat or fatness as debility?"

In *The Right to Maim: Debility, Capacity, Disability*, Puar brings to light the interdependent relationship between bodily capacity and bodily debility, which reproduces neoliberalism's demand for what we can label a discourse of "bodily capacity." This is where we find Puar's initial argument: if debility is defined as a lack or loss of certain bodily abilities, there is a need to consider how the market, globalization, and the overall ongoingness of structural inequality and suffering implicate debilitated bodies, specifically, how social injustices mark populations for wearing out, therefore putting and leaving them in the state of debility. Debility then encompasses the systemic production of disability in relation to bodily capacity and the various experiences of bodily difference that may conclude in limited access to adequate health care, nutrition, income, and other societal "goods" (Puar, *The Right to Maim*). Consequently, debility exists at a higher rate in racialized communities, particularly those at the intersections of disability and madness, as they are denied basic necessities and life overall largely as a function of white supremacy (Koivisto). In taking up fat as debility, we can look at the ways in which "practices of global domination and social injustice" create debilitated fat bodies through exclusionary practices (Puar, *The Right to Maim* 92). As in her analysis of disability and race as debility, in our consideration of fat as debility, we can see the linkages between power-knowledge structures and the social, economic, political, and environmental conditions that cause oppression—fat oppression in our case. We can also consider the affective state of fat-beingness as debility to interrogate how sizeism and shapeism latently manifest to create the conditions for fat embodiment and for fat populations to become even more precarious as settler colonialism, racism, ableism, and sizeism—all together—become central to producing and unleashing violence onto bodies that do not fit the narrative, making that violence seem to be "a normal consequence" (Puar, *The Right to Maim* xvi).

In what Patricia T. Clough calls the "biopolitics of an affect economy," race, disability, and now fatness, as "phobogenic" entities prompt us to think of how our relation to our differences is marked through the personal registry. In the national biopolitical landscape, any interactions with the "normative" full racialized assemblage concludes in this sense of "non"belonging and overall "non"citizenship. According to Puar, "neoliberal mandates" regarding productivity and capacitated bodies "recreate an abled body not only in terms of gender and sexuality"—here I would also add both race and fatness—"but also in terms of economic productivity and the economic development of national economy" (Puar, "Bodies with New Organs" 47). This produces a generalized transformation of capacitated bodies into worthwhile neoliberal subjects. Capacity, therefore, becomes a site of discipline within a normalized society, in which productivity is attached to the personal registry and internalized by the non-normative body. What this means is that under neoliberal mandates, bodies are always being evaluated in relation to their input into the market, as well as "their success or failure in terms of health, progressive productivity, upward mobility, enhanced capacity" (Puar, "Coda" 155). This continues the claims of "it gets better" as disability and fatness are put into these tropes of rehabilitation—as the figure of the disabled or once-fat hero. Critical disability theorist Dan Goodley takes up debility politics to argue that "neoliberal capitalist regimes of biocapital produce bodies that are never healthy enough, and thus always in a 'debilitated state in relation to what one's bodily capacity is imagined to be'" (94). What this indicates is that the prognosis of the personal register is always measured against this aspiration of what one's bodily capacity could be. It becomes a fantasy of full capacity, and the attached sense of security and futurity that comes with this celebrated corporeality is one that is beyond reach.

There is a sense of achievement circulating within this nexus of personal registry and fatness. Often practices associated with passing as normal, such as weight loss via dieting or cosmetic surgery, have been heavily practiced due to the idolization of the thin and/or muscular body (Bahra and Overboe). Furthermore, in the "trend" of body positivity within social media and in the burgeoning field of biomedicine, self-help literature or programs geared towards weight loss or rehabilitation creep into these moments of accommodation and place the fat body in a site of active entrepreneurship, a market in which the exchange, production, and consumption of fatness remains problematic as a state of pathology that fails self-management and its containment (Goodley; Shildrick). So, this idea of progress and its underlining tone of "it gets better" reflects a desire for the reinstatement of white, nondisabled, thin privilege that was lost by being fat. When looking at debility and capacity, Puar suggests that although they seem to be contradictory concepts, the heightened demands for bodily capacity and neoliberal formulations of health or what she calls a "liberal eugenics of lifestyle programming" produce biotechnologies and population aggregates in which health is turned into a side effect of successful normativity (Puar, "Coda" 153; Puar, "The Cost"). Recapacitation in this affective politics generally functions like rehabilitation, reinforcing the hierarchy and allowing the medical industrial complex to profit from acts of normalization. In this assemblage of capacity and debility, "health" in itself has become a fantastical commodity; affect here operates as a form of sociality and temporality that regulates this objective of normalcy and happiness (Bahra). All in all, while some bodies are deemed to be more precarious, what is important to realize is that fat bodies are always debilitated in and by globalization.

Dying Slowly

On the affective register, the racializing fat-assemblages of fatphobia and racism disseminate in a rhizomatic manner as the states of capacitation and debilitation are diminished and augmented in various ways. As fat and racialized bodies are pushed into these deathworlds, we witness the impact of the biopolitics of an affective economy as it comes to designate a position to those capacitated and debilitated following the quality of life outlined by the institution of health care and the state overall. In many ways, the production of the personal registry and its association with quality of life become linked with work, productivity, illness, disease, the environment, and more, resulting in this ambivalent state of slowly dying (Puar, "Prognosis Time" 162). We now approach the question of how the politics of size, shape, disability, and race continue to push marginalized bodies onto certain trajectories of discipline in accordance with the personal registry, to the point that they are in the process of dying slowly.

Debility politics, as proposed by Puar, identifies the debilitated state as being in the process of what Lauren Berlant calls "slow death" during which those on the marginalizing ends of racializing assemblages are in a temporal and spatial zone that forces the constructed non-normative bodies to survive a life-in-death (Berlant; Shildrick; Koivisto). There is a recognition here of the social barriers constituted by the social and economic spheres that create debilitated bodies that come to slowly die in these "deathworlds." Slow death, for Berlant, accounts for "the physical wearing out of a population in a way that points to its deterioration as a defining condition of its experience and historical existence" (95). At the centre of the medical-industrial complex, we witness the wearing out of fat bodies through anti-fat discourses and the need for rehabilitation, circulating under the banner of the "obesity epidemic." With slow death in this debility politics, we shift from the social fixation on pathologizing fat bodies to fully comprehending how structures and social relations create and maintain fat oppression. In the affective residues of slow death and what counts as a living body, the intergenerational traumas of both racism and sizeism can also be located in racialized- and fat-beingness, as these generational experiences of "excess," "grotesque," "gluttonous," or "*madjj*" and their alignment with death have been deeply felt temporally and affectively. Temporality in this nexus of slow death and fatness entails a form of living that may follow the pathway of "it gets better." The precarious reality of "it gets better" for fat-beingness illustrates the direct activity of the state, the community (i.e., kin), and the individual upon fat bodies to optimize their life-in-death through rehabilitative practices, such as weight-loss surgeries and dieting, so as to move them to the assemblage of the full human (Berlant; Puar, *The Right to Maim* 12). Additionally, slow death as a form of temporality sheds light on the temporal nature of compulsory ableism, racism, and sizeism/shapeism and their sites of discipline and regulation that displace marginalized communities. Both Berlant and Puar utilize a temporal analysis of slow death to deconstruct day-to-day events that may seem ordinary but present a dialogue on capital, nationhood, and the fantasy of futurity.

To examine what is considered missing in both fat studies and critical disability studies, Marta Usiekniewicz and Anna Mollow, in their individual pieces, write of the insidious role of racism, ableism, and sizeism in creating debilitated bodies through food deserts, limited access to housing and medicine, and police brutality, which they regard as exemplars of events that lead to the exhaustion of fat, racialized, disabled bodies within the American context. Mollow argues that policing, medicine, and environmental policy are "deeply embedded cultural constructions of Blackness, fatness and disability" that "operate together to legitimize the maintenance of a social terrain in which Black people are regarded as unvictimizable and their lives are treated as expendable" (106). Within settler colonial Canada, the added layer of "healthism" to the banner of the "obesity epidemic" and the co-operationalization of ableism and saneism pose an ongoing threat to the mental, physical, and overall health of fat, racialized people and populations due to the lack of access that subjugates fat, racialized bodies to this experience of life-in-death. This theme of dying slowly in the debilitated state demonstrates how the structures of injustice that promote the bodily injuries, exclusionary practices, and rehabilitative practices are readily enacted by neoliberalism. Stories of fatphobia within the medical field among racialized women have been widely discussed across fat studies literature. For instance, Black fat women have a harder time seeking or attaining adequate medical assistance due to societal and medical discrimination against both fat and Black people. In addition, the lack of assistance perpetuates this "catchall source of blame for every death of every large person"—it is "claimed that fatness rather than violence was responsible for injuries or deaths suffered by fat," Black, and/or other racialized people (Mollow 110). This vulnerability to violence in a state of debilitation becomes a part of the daily lived experience of fat, racialized, disabled persons, and comes to define their existence in terms of these institutionally created deathworlds.

In my collective family, I saw debility manifest in multiple ways: the colonial violence of the 1947 Partition and Sikh genocide in 1980s India; the racism faced in settler colonial Canada, where my dad at the age of 16 was repeatedly called Paki and beaten for wearing his turban during his first week of high school in Calgary; and the uneven distribution of income through piecework, factory work, or the complete denial of employment. Fat-beingness as a debilitated state surfaced in the multiple ways discussed earlier in this chapter, but it has intensified over the years, as I witnessed slow death become a reality in our mother-daughter assemblage at home. As a caregiver for my mother for her sick periods between 2015 to 2018 for various illnesses, I witnessed how our interactions with the medical-industrial complex touched on Puar's concept of debility and capacity in relation to this idea of progress and futurity. Throughout the process of seeking access to health care, of my mother being denied care, and of her being admitted into the emergency triage or other wards of our local hospital in Brampton, Ontario, when she was granted access, I witnessed unethical care being provided to fat bodies. The affective residue of the fatphobia we experienced was overwhelming. From the hallway care my mother received to the (semi)private rooms where the lack of care remained persistent, the "circulation of hatred" evident in the words and body language of both medical professionals and thin people seeking medical assistance, who read both of our fat, brown bodies as incapacitated (Rinaldi et al., "Mapping the Circulation"). As we manoeuvred our way through the medical system, we often experienced being fat-blamed for the health issues my mother was experiencing, as well as the withholding of medical intervention, because her fatness would be the cause of her death, a statement we heard on multiple occasions as she was denied certain procedures. The medical and lay language used by medical providers often brought upon us this feeling of being constructed into fat-spectacles and fat-shamed because our fat, racialized bodies did not embody "futurity itself"; all they embodied was a lacking state of being or, as the doctor put it, "early death" unless my mother lost more than half her weight to prolong her life. Thus, in such events, "living increasingly becomes a scene of the administration, discipline, and recalibration of what constitutes health" (Berlant 97). Fat as debility surfaces to pave the way for a logic of cure not just for the individual but also for collective society (Berlant).

Dying Quickly

In considering the role of the language of spectacle, progress, and productive capacity, one sees that fat bodies continue to be disciplined into the status of burdens that must be rehabilitated to be productive members of society. In this process of demarcating bodies in accordance with compulsory able-bodiedness, whiteness, and thinness, we come to see how the medical-industrial complex determines and utilizes bodily capacity and debility to map out and organize fat, disabled, and racialized bodies. Berlant in their discussion of the "obesity epidemic" claims that the topic of fatness as an epidemic comes to be about "the destruction of life, bodies, imaginaries, and environments by and under contemporary regimes of capital" (Berlant 104). This aspect of debility as slow death paints a reality of how the white, nondisabled, and thin body as a state of normative bodily capacity is constantly used to reinforce the framing of oppositional bodies as unproductive, burdensome, and debilitated. Overboe and I argue that under this neoliberal model that pathologizes disabled and fat bodies as burdens upon the progression of society, the personal registry comes to enact a shelf of normalcy in which disabled and fat people must alter themselves through cosmetics, diets, exercise, and/or surgery to fit its prescriptive notion in order to remain on that shelf. These different bodies, as a result, become fixations of medicalization and "unnatural" or "abnormal" states of being under the neoliberal mandates of progress. Jen

Rinaldi and her colleagues suggest that the framing of fatness as an "obesity epidemic" not only removes the fat person from the national body but also subsequently results in the reification of the discourses of compulsory thinness and heteronormativity, as fat bodies come to be assessed, medically categorized, and situated as a threat to public health standards and a drain on health care services ("Fatness and Failing" 220–21). Generally speaking, those in these debilitated states will always be mapped into this relation of living and dying, where fat bodies will never be thought "healthy" enough but will be considered as being on an accelerated road to death.

Fatphobia and ableism together function as a device of anti-Black and anti-Indigenous violence. In thinking through debility, we come to truly understand the displacement experienced by vulnerable bodies. As both Usiekniewicz and Mollow emphasize, fatness (size and/or shape) has always been used to justify the murdering of Black, Indigenous, otherly racialized, disabled, mad, and/or queer people. For example, fat Black men regardless of their age are interpreted as "scary bigness" and "dangerous" (Usiekniewicz). The attributes of "big," "scary," "dangerous," and "violent" attached to their fatness and Blackness are used to justify the use of violence against them by law enforcement, putting them on a path of "accelerated death" rather than "slow death" (Usiekniewicz 40, 42). Within the United States, fatness has been used to remove accountability for the police murder of Black people. We in Canada share a similar reality of the displacement and, to the extreme, murder of racialized communities that is rarely acknowledged. Desmond Cole outlines the affective residues of Black death at the hands of state violence in Canada, arguing "'Black lives have no borders. We exist everywhere regardless of the fact that they may not want us to" (2). While reviewing literature for this chapter, I could not help but think of all the people who have been targeted and killed by state institutions, such as the police or health care, because of their doubly or multiply marginalizing positions—how racialization, fatness, and disability as debility have been narrated in a wholly different manner. While watching the media footage of the deaths (in process and afterwards) of both George

Floyd in the United States and Ejaz Ahmed Choudry in Ontario, Canada, by the hands of the police in 2020, I questioned how long it would take for their size to be read as "dangerous" in the public narrative. Their debilitated bodies, which were in their own way subjected to the surveillance of police, were interpreted as dangerous *for* the police, rather than the police being another hazardous part of Floyd's and Choudry's debilitated states of being. Within 20 seconds of the police arriving via the patio entrance of Choudry's apartment, for what was a non-urgent 9-1-1 call for help by a family dealing with a mental health crisis, Choudry's madness, brownness, age, and fatness came to experience not just metaphorical death but literal death, as the police failed to handle the situation (Lamoureux). Choudry is one of multiple people who come from populations that have been marked not only for slow death, due to their experiences of trauma, inadequate access to mental health care, and, of course, police violence, but also for a form of accelerated death.

In discussing this slow and accelerated death, we are prompted to consider how fat bodies are continuously labelled life-in-death and ignored to the point of literal death. In conjunction with debility and slow death, fat futurity appears to be unrealistic in this disciplinary world of fatphobia and its encompassing racializing assemblages; thus, dying fat and quickly has always come across as a "normal" future for fat bodies unless they work towards recapacitating themselves. During this global pandemic of COVID-19, organizations such as Obesity Canada have outlined fat bodies as more susceptible to and on a faster route for disease progression. Under this oppressive narrative, fat bodies come to encounter the same or possibly a more aggressive experience when trying to access health care, which is triaged, or other medical treatment (whether it be for a COVID-19 test or general concerns). Seeing that the most common COVID-19 symptoms reported are fatigue, shortness of breath, and/or fever, a concern of mine is how a superfat, disabled person, like my mother, would be received when those symptoms have become a daily part of her life due to the path of slow death she has been on.

We return to my assemblage with my mother in present day, six months into her recovery from COVID-19, as I continue to see fatphobic and ableist discourses travel the medical and vibrational spaces in which she and I exist. As an "essential" worker in the Peel Region, a coronavirus hotspot, my mother worked the entire pandemic at high risk for exposure to COVID-19. In January 2021, my mother was infected with COVID-19 and wound up in the intensive care unit (ICU) at our local hospital, with low oxygen levels, loss of breathing, and pneumonia. On January 13, we received a call from the physician letting us know that she would be put on a ventilator and to prepare ourselves for the worst. I remember asking him, "Why do you keep telling us to do that? I have faith she'll come home soon." His response was to mention her "pre-COVID" health conditions, hinting that her fatness might prevent her from surviving the treatment, as the virus was so invasive. With every Telehealth call we received the first few days of her being on that route of "getting better," I felt as if the callers were asking me to give up on her, to think of my fat mother's body as not worthy of living or not worth saving, especially in this COVID-19 version of a deathworld. Reminded of the fat, Black, Indigenous, and otherly racialized women who have been ignored by medical professionals, I wondered if my mother would come out of this with the medical support needed or if she would be another statistic of the pandemic deathworld.

Upon being transferred from our local hospital in Brampton, Ontario, to one in Hamilton, Ontario, my mother was even more at risk: steps like placing her in a prone position on abdomen or side, which significantly improves oxygen levels and prevents pressure ulcers from forming, were stopped. I thought the hydraulic lift installed in her room would be utilized to move her body between a prone and supine position, but that was not the case. There was little to no communication shared with me by the medical team of the ICU unit as to why she remained in a supine position, lying flat on her back with central lines all around her. Due to our limited access to the ICU floor, contact continued through only my daily call with the nurses, who simply told me, "She's comfortable as is." When allowed visitation, I viewed her deconditioned body lying there, and once again I asked if she were being rotated into prone position, since the facility had the lift available as a tool for the medical team. The response I received was that she was not, because her fatness causes the ventilator pipe to crinkle. Keeping her on her back was the best thing to do, since ulcers due to her comatose state appeared to be a small issue compared to the larger diagnosis of COVID-pneumonia.

Four weeks out, she was off the ventilator and slowly gaining consciousness, and during my initial visit in her room, I saw how her fat body was treated. As I stood there in personal protective equipment (COVID-19 PPE) recording our first glance, all I felt was a sense of gratitude for her surviving death. But then I sensed her cry of neglect through her nonverbal communication, as she tried to share her discomfort: tears ran down her cheeks, and she attempted to move her hands to direct my eyes while sliding her bottom down. All she could whisper was "*hai hai*" (a painful "ohh"). During my second visit, my five senses kicked in. I smelt and saw the neglect of her fat body: she had pressure ulcers in many places, like her head, fat bottom, chest, and foot, and blood and bacteria leaked away from her fatty skin cells through her hospital robe. Her madness, impairment, and fatness all echoed a trauma she had previously felt at the hands of the medical-industrial complex and its members, the so-called saviours of thinness. She cried to me that they ignored her basic needs and spoke of how she felt that fat hatred in her hospital bedroom, particularly from the first few nurses in acute care. One of the nurses called it a "mere hallucination" she was having. But to some extent, I think this entire event was rooted in her ongoing state of debilitation over the years. Yes, it may have been the trauma of being on a ventilator, on heavy sedatives, with no recollection of how she got to that hospital; however, I believe that her statements that the doctors and nurses were going to kill her were rooted in a life-long fear and experience of fatphobia in the medical realm. Her homecare wound care specialist and nurses spoke of their shock at seeing her in such a condition—with gaping wounds that received no care whatsoever. Six months into her recovery, the long-term effects of COVID-19 remain, but the larger impact is the unethical medical practice that is imprinted on her fat body through a 16-centimetre-deep tunnel on her bottom that has finally shrunk to 4 centimetres through various interventions. My mom's health care service providers continue to be perplexed that she, a personal support worker, did not get the support she needed while she was literally in a state of life-in-death. We started this journey on January 8, 2021, and now, as we hit her "first COVID-19 anniversary," we continue to see the long-term effects the virus has had on her fat body and the way in which her fatness continues to stand in as the potential "risk" to her "health"—rather than the known and unknown effects of COVID-19 itself. As we approach her second year "almost-death" anniversary, we sit here today with a large box containing documents of the communication that has occurred so far between the WSIB, the employer, and my mother, which shows the push for her to return to work. Her fatness remains front and centre in the multiple reports medicalizing her fatness, rather than any consideration of the impact of the virus or of the numbness and pain it has caused throughout her body.

Concluding Thoughts

As the operator of what I called "the Bahra hotline," I answered calls of concern from family and friends while my mother suffered from COVID-19. After the initial worried comments asking after my mother's and our family's welfare, the calls turned to optimistic proclamations that, with the help of medical professionals, she was probably "sleeping off" the weight while comatose since she was no longer being gluttonous! It got to the point that relatives were suggesting that the moment she returned home, she would need to "control her diet" as she must have lost so much weight and should maintain that. My mother was once again the spectacle that was rehabilitated from not only COVID-19 but also her fatness. She continues to be positioned as the spectacle at home where, instead of medical professionals, I am the lead hand for curing her of her fatness. As her caregiver, I must police her body in every way, including her eating habits, to make sure my superfat mum sheds her fatness and goes from being a "bad fatty" to a "good fatty." But it does not end there, as I am expected also to police my body to move towards the fully human assemblage. As Ontario's COVID restrictions lift, we have family members visiting, and, right after praising my mother's exit from the hospital, they turn to us to say, "I thought you lost weight, but you look the same," or "You gained weight." Thus, not only do these conversations differentiate between the thinness-fatness dichotomy of the registry, but they also issue a regulatory and disciplinary script following its genres that takes on affective residues across time and space.

The personal registry and its claims subjugate fat, racialized, and disabled bodies in accordance to racializing assemblages that are marked as space invaders in the national body in both the literal and metaphorical way (Overboe, "Theory"). Fat racialized people across the intersections will always fail to meet the demand to become, or to achieve the status of, the full human in the racializing assemblages that dictate this politics of life and death (Bahra; Bahra and Overboe; Weheliye; Mbembe). Within debility politics, we find ourselves at a similar theoretical crossroads. In reconfiguring fatness as debility, we may be able to present a narrative that critiques our institutions and interpersonal relations, as well as reclaims our fat bodies without the declaration of bodily incapacity. The various examples shared throughout this chapter are moments that exemplify how systemic racism, ableism, and sizeism trap us in a slow death and the further debilitation of our fat bodies, as such logics of the personal registry continue to designate bodies like ours to be eradicated, maimed, or slowly killed off. Racism, ableism, and fatphobia overall function as a weapon of globalization that places personal responsibility on fat, racialized, and/or disabled bodies, instead of pinning down how social inequality and intergenerational suffering are experienced by marginalized communities here in Canada. Within Canada and globally, these Othered populations are marked and pushed into a state of both slow and accelerated death under the relationship between debility and capacity; hence, these oppressive systems put Black, Indigenous, and otherly racialized, fat, disabled people at a greater risk of institutional violence. To think of racialized and/or disabled people as both debilitated and disposable truly shows how the temporality of slow death may actually speed up to a form of accelerated death based on the question of what lives are considered worth saving in accordance with the racialized assemblages that have dictated these two different worlds for so long (Mollow; Puar; Usiekniewicz). Although not discussed in this chapter, debility politics, in a way, enables us to imagine multiple futures where race as debility, disability as debility, and fat as debility are no longer anchored in these systems of oppression, in the logics of cure, or in an "it gets better" future (Puar, *The Right to Maim* xxiv). Debility politics can open doors to giving presence to the expressions of life in this "life-in-death" of deathworlds and, therefore, no longer keep us yearning for this sense of happiness or for a position as a full human in a lifeworld that was never built for us.

Notes

1 Caste should be included in this list, as I have experienced caste oppression within the Greater Toronto Area, but this axis of oppression falls outside of the scope of the current chapter. As members of the Sikh faith, we are to hold an abolitionist lens and follow egalitarianism; however, the casteist practices of India continue to be practiced in the South Asian Sikh diaspora located in Canada and the United States. Casteism is rooted in Brahmin- and Jatt-supremacy, very much akin to white supremacy. Caste oppression establishes its own set of power/knowledge relations and subjugates individuals who do not fit the elite caste to extreme violence. Within Canada and the United States, the hierarchies and exclusionary practices of casteism are utilized within the Sikh-Punjabi community to gatekeep the Sikh faith from queer Sikhs. As Manmit S. Chahal and Manu Kaur share "cisheterosexual oppressor caste men continue to restrict Sikh liberation on the grounds of caste, gender, and sexuality in ways that maintain these power dynamics to benefit these men." They argue that casteism and its interlocking systems of queerphobia, transphobia, and anti-Blackness need to be prioritized and addressed for us to be in solidarity with caste oppressed, queer, and trans communities in the diaspora and elsewhere. See Manmit S. Chahal's and Manu Kaur's series of pieces as an entry point to this dialogue: https://kaurlife.org/2021/01/22/when-will-caste-oppressed-and-queer-and-trans-folks-find-liberation-in-sikh-spaces/.

Works Cited

Bahra, Ramanpreet A. "'You Can Only Be Happy If You're Thin!' Normalcy, Happiness, and the Lacking Body." *Fat Studies: An Interdisciplinary Journal of Body Weight and Society*, vol. 7, no. 2, 2017, pp. 193–202.

Bahra, Ramanpreet A., and James Overboe. "Working Towards the Affirmation of Fatness and Impairment." *Thickening Fat: Fat Bodies, Intersectionality and Social Justice*, edited by May Friedman, Carla Rice, and Jen Rinaldi, Routledge, 2019, pp. 197–207.

Bannerji, Himani. *The Dark Side of the Nation: Essays on Multiculturalism, Nationalism and Gender*. Canadian Scholars' Press, 2000.

Berlant, Lauren. *Cruel Optimism*. Duke University Press, 2011.

Chen, Mel Y. *Animacies: Biopolitics, Racial Mattering, and Queer Affect*. Duke University Press, 2012.

Clough, Patricia T. "The Affective Turn: Political Economy, Biomedia, and Bodies." *The Affect Theory Reader*, edited by Melissa Gregg and Gregory J. Seigworth, Duke University Press, 2010, pp. 206–28.

Cole, Desmond. *The Skin We're In: A Year of Black Resistance and Power*. Doubleday Canada, 2020.

Fanon, Frantz. *Black Skin, White Masks*. Grove Press, 1952.

Goodley, Dan. *Dis/Ability Studies: Theorising Disableism and Ableism*. Routledge, 2014.

Hickey-Moody, Anna, and Tara Page. "Introduction: Making, Matter and Pedagogy." *Arts, Pedagogy and Cultural Resistance: New Materialisms*, edited by Anna Hickey-Moody and Tara Page, Rowman & Littlefield International, 2016, pp. 1–20.

Hobson, Janell. *Venus in the Dark: Blackness and Beauty in Popular Culture*. Routledge, 2005.

Koivisto, Mikko O. "(Live!) The Post-Traumatic Futurities of Black Debility." *Disability Studies Quarterly*, vol. 39, no. 3, 2019, https://dsq-sds.org/article/view/6614/5411. Accessed 15 October 2022.

Lamoureux, Mack. "Canadian Cops Keep Killing People During Wellness and Mental Health Calls." *Vice,* https://www.vice.com/en/article/ep4vzj/canadian-police-killed-chantel-moore-ejaz-choudry-during-wellness-and-mental-health-calls. Accessed 15 February 2021.

Mbembe, Achille. *Necro-politics*. Duke University Press, 2019.

Mollow, Anna. "Unvictimizable: Toward a Fat Black Disability Studies." *African American Review*, vol. 50, no. 2, 2017, pp. 105–21.

Overboe, James. "Affirming an Impersonal Life: A Different Register for Disability Studies." *Journal of Literacy & Cultural Disability Studies*, vol. 1, no. 3, 2009, pp. 241–56.

———. "Theory, impairment and impersonal singularities: Deleuze, Guattari and Agamben." Disability and Social Theory. Palgrave Macmillan, London, 2012, pp. 112–26.

Puar, Jasbir K. "Bodies with New Organs: Becoming Trans, Becoming Disabled." *Social Text*, vol. 33, no. 3, 2015, pp. 45–73.

———. "Coda: The Cost of Getting Better, Suicide, Sensation, Switchpoints." *GLQ: A Journal of Lesbian and Gay Studies*, vol. 18, no. 1, 2012, pp. 149–58.

———. "The Cost of Getting Better: Ability and Debility." *The Disability Studies Reader*, 4th ed., edited by Lennard J. Davis, Routledge, 2013, pp. 177–84.

———."Prognosis Time: Towards a Geopolitics of Affect, Debility and Capacity." *Women & Performance: A Journal of Feminist Theory*, vol. 19, no. 2, 2009, pp. 161–72.

———. *The Right to Maim: Debility, Capacity, Disability*. Duke University Press, 2017.

Puwar, Nirmal. *Space Invaders: Race, Gender and Bodies Out of Place*. Berg Publishers, 2004.

Rinaldi, Jen, Carla Rice, Crystal Kotow, and Emma Lind. "Mapping the Circulation of Fat Hatred." *Fat Studies: An Interdisciplinary Journal of Body Weight and Society*, vol. 9, no.1, 2020, pp. 37–50.

Rinaldi, Jen, Carla Rice, Andrea LaMarre, Deborah McPhail, and Elisabeth Harrison. "Fatness and Failing Citizenship." *Somatechnics*, vol. 7, no. 2, 2017, pp. 218–33.

Shildrick, Margrit. "Death, Debility and Disability." *Feminism & Psychology*, vol. 25, no. 1, 2015, pp. 155–60.

Strings, Sabrina. *Fearing the Black Body: The Racial Origins of Fat Phobia*. New York University Press, 2019.

Usiekniewicz, Marta. "Dangerous Bodies: Blackness, Fatness, and the Masculinity Dividend." *A Journal of Queer Studies*, vol. 11, 2016, pp. 19–45.

Weheliye, Alexander G. *Habeas Viscus: Racializing Assemblages, Biopolitics, and Black Feminist Theories of the Human*. Duke University Press, 2014.

Fat Trans Bodies in Motion: Hazards of Space-Taking

Gin Marshall

Introduction

In 2015, as she lay on her deathbed, her body wracked with cancer, in a moment of clarity, my mother called me to her side: "Darling," she said, lifting the waistband of her pants. "Just look at how much weight I have lost." She had accepted both cancer and death but fought with her weight even until the very end of her life. In her hospice room, which was consumed with the process of dying, fatphobia was very much alive and well-fed, unlike those of us affected by it. My mother's experience, even while in active death, speaks to the deep hold the cis-heteropatriarchal and fatphobic discourses attached to the body have, to the point that fatness will always be considered the "killing factor" rather than disease, cancer in her case, or the structural inequalities that set out intersectional experiences of oppression.

The cis-heteropatriarchal machine has been designed so that the bodies of those people who are assigned female at birth must be curated within the confines of thinness and attractiveness to suit and please the male gaze that remains afloat in different spaces. This "beauty standard" is indoctrinated into us via multiple forms of media (e.g., magazines, film, social media) and the people we interact with. From the moment we are born, we perform this standard resulting in what Cecilia Hartley describes as "large chunks of time and energy that could be channeled into making real, substantive changes in society being spent pursuing the ideal body image. ... Women in particular are literally terrified of getting fat" (Hartley 64). This requirement to be thin and attractive is strictly regulated throughout our lifetimes as it maps out celebratory timelines for thinness. When fat bodies fail to meet such timelines and continue this curse of fatness, they are then framed as too big to fit into the cis-heteropatriarchal machine and are assigned to an exclusionary space where they are deemed in breach of contract. Thus, fat bodies are constantly left in a state of starvation, craving a return to the spatiality and temporality of thin acceptance, even on our deathbed. In taking up fat studies literature to explore the deeply personal, yet political, contexts that shape fat queer experiences, this chapter aims to demonstrate how fatphobia is enacted and is consequently a controlling and discriminatory factor in the surveillance of many queer or "different" bodies. The nature of fatphobic discourses entails this power of shaming and carrying out discriminatory practices that are rooted in questions of gender, though the discrimination remains invisible despite its powerful impact on us all. Lastly, I draw on fat studies literature to emphasize that, far from being unique to my own experience with fatphobia, there remains an inherent power to the shaming and invisibility experienced in this very gendered discriminatory process.

Methodology

In this chapter, I blend autoethnography and critical and institutional ethnography to examine how fatphobia works in a range of deeply personal contexts. A range of spaces are taken up in this chapter to grapple with my gender expectations and perceptions, such as on the aeroplane, at the sports outfitters, on the hiking trail, and at the surgeon's office.

Institutional ethnography was first mentioned by Canadian sociologist Dorothy Smith in her 1987 book *The Everyday World as Problematic: A Feminist Sociology*. Smith described institutional ethnography as being a Marxist feminist methodology that "proposes an inquiry intended to disclose how activities are organized and how they are articulated to the social relations of the larger social and economic process" (Smith 152). As this methodology evolved to include critical ethnography and autoethnography, Angelina Castagno pointed out the methodological aspirations to "shift attention away from individuals as problematic to structures as problematic" (Castagno 374). While autoethnography does take a personal stance, as a form of standpoint, it is used to illuminate the need for attention and resistance to the institutional problems that exist (e.g., see Kotow). These methodologies that centre a problem as residing within structures, systems, and institutions are appropriate for interrogating sites where fat bodies in particular are policed, surveilled, and contested.

Notes on Positionality

As this chapter uses a blended methodology, I believe it is important to make note of my own positionality, considering that this collection speaks to the various fat experiences located in Canada. Standpoint epistemology becomes most effective, then, when we engage in critical reflection by not only acknowledging our social location but also wrestling with the role of power in the process of knowledge production (Davis and Khonach 104; Pausé). I am a white, fat, trans settler with invisible disabilities, and much of this chapter considers fatness in the context of class-privileged, two-income partnership activities. Although this is no longer my financial and personal reality, I am aware that there is a lot of class privilege reflected in the vignettes shared later in the chapter. The structures that privilege whiteness are rarely introspective or self-critical, preferring instead a naïve positionality of innocence that reinforces whiteness without accountability. These systems are further cemented by "cultural and social structures [that] privilege the thin, or at least what has been deemed a 'normal'-sized body" (Kwan 146). My white positionality cannot include, but acknowledges, the important perspectives brought forth by Black, Indigenous, and otherly racialized communities on experiences of racism and white supremacy that they are subjected to on a daily basis, in addition to the anti-fat discourses that police their body size. As white allies, we must be aware that the world "can certainly be hostile to other parts of our identities as many white women and most LGBTQIA and disabled and poor and working-class and fat whites can attest. But our society is *not* hostile to our whiteness" (Larbalestier).

Fat and queer scholars have often engaged in discussing the parallel but different paths that fat folks take while participating in everyday life experiences. Many thin and/or straight-sized people often take for granted the access they have to spaces and experiences involving travel and outdoor activities. They also tend to have access to health care, well-aware that their ailment or complaint will most likely be seen and addressed by medical professionals. For fat folks, both travel and health care are not equally accessible as their bodies are seen as too disorderly for airline seats or not quite alive enough for health care professionals to intervene in any way other than to address their fatness as a "disease" to be treated. Additionally, a disability studies lens has often been applied to examine the intersections of fat embodiment and disability to map out a radical politics speaking to the social structures that unleash violence upon fat and/or disabled bodies. This approach can be helpful for many; however, "[w]hile the language of disability opens up a protocol for accommodating non-normative bodies and travel needs, the functional need of an 'obese' body is to sit in a seat that fits" (Rinaldi et al. 148). Within the medical-industrial complex, this "functional need" translates to the requirement for health care providers to provide health care that fits our fat bodies and needs, something that is rarely provided without tremendous personal cost.

Air Travel: Flying While Fat

Prior to the coronavirus (COVID-19) pandemic, many people in the Global North took access to travel for granted, despite its expense. For fat people, this expense also often includes hefty emotional costs. In preparing for a trip to Eastern Canada, I had researched seats for the flight and set my phone timer for the exact time that the extra-space seats were released. I had felt so lucky to get the bulkhead seat since I travel with a physical disability and thought of the comfort that came from being able to stretch my legs. I was left with relief that all would be well on the day of departure.

On the day of the flight, due to long lineups, I ran through Toronto Pearson International Airport, sweating, while clinging to this optimistic vision that, once I got past the gates, there would be a pleasant, comfortable seat waiting for me on the plane with plenty of legroom. When I finally reached the gate all out of breath, I ran up to the check-in desk, still holding on to the vision of my seat, thinking "I'm almost there," ready to take up space. I had purchased 1A, the most comfortable bulkhead seat at the front, which gave me the space I needed for my legs. As I burst onto the already entirely boarded aircraft, the flight attendant met me at the front entrance, blocking the aisle, and asked if I knew where I was sitting. I looked at 1A, thinking "Aha, right there" but was left in disarray as I saw a woman sprawled in my seat. The very seat I had made sure to book in time. The seat that would accommodate my fatness.

Pointing in the seat's direction, I said, "I am sitting right there." But at that moment, the presence of thinness took hold of that aircraft as I saw the non-fat intruder lounging comfortably in my seat, making her declaration for my seat. She asked the flight attendant, "Could I please sit in hers?" while still occupying my seat. As I stood there quite visible in the aisle with my sweaty fat body, listening to her verbally misgender me, I was excluded from the decision-making and any possibility of speaking up. I looked to where she pointed, and my eyes followed her finger to see her actual seat, three rows back and significantly more cramped. I was left wondering as my eyes returned to 1A—"That's my seat though"—while the flight attendant and the woman's husband looked at me, with their gazes pleading her case to me. I remained standing with my fatness and bags close to me, left feeling too exhausted to plead my case for the seat I had purchased. Yet one thing was clear to me: in the aircraft with my presence as the only hypervisible passenger, my fatness, transness, and disability made me invisible. As Jennifer Gailey states "fat presents an apparent paradox because it is visible and dissected publicly; in this respect, it is hypervisible. Fat is also marginalized and erased; in this respect, it is hyperinvisible" (7). The flight attendant continued to block the aisle withholding from me any form of advocacy, well aware that the seat was listed on my boarding pass. All the while the woman in my seat made zero attempts to get up and move to her spot, as she was adamant about keeping me from my seat for her own security. Feeling like I had no choice and nowhere to go but to the back of the aircraft, I exclaimed, "Fine!" to get away from the gaze of those judging eyes. The flight attendant made no comment for me or to me, but did respond to the non-fat intruder: "See—that is karma for you."

So, I shuffled down the aisle and took my seat three rows back, a seat that was never mine to begin with. As I moved in that space, disgruntled and upset upon hearing that statement, I thought, "What about *my* karma?" In fact, the scenario had nothing to do with destiny, but with the larger structures of labour and cis-heteropatriarchy. Upon seeing me—a visibly trans and fat solo traveller—together, the flight attendant, seat thief, and her husband utilized their wealthy thin-privileged cis-heteronormativity to put me on display, while honing their power to rob me of the seat I had paid for in advance to avoid the inaccessibility to seats for fat people. I also could not help but think how this interaction was rooted in fatphobia. In this instance of flying while fat and trans, I came to feel that I was seen as not good enough and less deserving to take up that seat—that space—compared to my counterpart. This experience was nothing different from past ones, which left me feeling this way and rarely gave me the opportunity to say no. This experience of the shame that comes from being fat and fat shamed in public silenced me, prevented me from saying to the woman, the flight attendant, and the whole planeload of passengers the following: "NO, I want my seat, I worked hard to get that particular seat, ask someone else or work to get that seat yourself!" This shame prevented me from speaking up for my fatness to resist this thin-centric space that was the airline.

After this event took place, I drafted a letter to the airline and did receive an apology and a flight coupon for what had taken place. However, this does not remove the shame that I was forced to feel in that moment. A sense of manipulative shame that I have lived in and with for a very long time. This sense of shame was felt as a body failing to fit in, in both the literal and metaphorical sense, with the "normal" bodies of flyers surrounding me. Overall, my body was not permitted to move until I consented to these folks' plan—a consent that was forced by cornering me with their pleas of thinness. The public shame and spectacle rendered my queer and fatness "sick" in the Foucauldian sense in this space that was peopled by an audience of entitled "normal" bodies. The flight crew allowed the woman to occupy my seat, similarly to the multiple ways in which other professionals (i.e., medical) have come to occupy my fatness through the initial process of the thin-cis-heteronormative gaze's act of shaming. In the Foucauldian sense, this polarity between "sick" and "normal" bodies is heavily present in the airline space, as bodies such as mine come to be manipulated under the discourse of thinness and cis-hetero-ableism.

As airlines continue to maximize seats in planes, travel becomes a complicated business for any fat person. Non-fat people scrutinize the fat body in the airport waiting area with particular contemptuous hostility as they stare down the "bad fatty." Their thin gaze quietly asks, "Will the fatty get the seat beside me and spill over into my tiny seat?" A representative "claimed that ... nine out of 10 customer complaints are from passengers who get squeezed in their seats by obese neighbours" (Huff 177). Airlines such as Southwest in the United States have been in the news about their seat policies, maintaining such fatphobic discourses. People who are not fat complain about the size of airplane seats and legroom, so it stands to reason that fat people find these restrictions doubly uncomfortable. In Canada, the policy for what the Canadian Transportation Agency refers to as "obese" fliers was amended: "for domestic services, these carriers may not charge more than one fare for persons with disabilities who ... require additional seating for themselves, including those determined to be functionally disabled by obesity" (Canadian Transportation Agency). In practice, this policy requires the fat person to persuade their doctor to report them as so "obese" that it constitutes a disability, thus making them eligible for the additional seating. In order to pass this sizeist and ableist test to gain access to space, we fat people must find a doctor to take our measurements and determine them to be sufficiently outside the "norm." Within Canada, subsequently, the declaration of fatness as disability resulted in some Canadian airlines needing to provide the fat person an extra seat free of charge for domestic flights on the major carriers. But, of course, in many non-Canadian airlines, the extra seat is offered at full or only partially discounted rates, once again sustaining fatphobia and its capitalist nature. All in all, the fat body is seen as being outside this image of the "ideal" thin traveller, making the charge for the extra seat plausible, along with the shame and ridicule. And the cost of the humiliation and "extra" seat? We get all this for the same price as the "normal-sized" person's ticket, thereby paying far more than double. Thus, when a fat person must fly, there are a series of worries taken aboard alongside; fitting in an airplane seat these days is a painful and restrictive space for any fat and trans body.

A Fat Person Hiking

The destination of the airplane trip described above was Newfoundland, where I was meeting my partner for a hiking holiday. I write this, sitting in the Gros Morne National Park Visitor Centre, while I watch folks wander in and out of this beautiful facility, enjoying the panoramic view of this "Canadian" landscape located on the lands traditionally inhabited by the Beothuk and Mi'kmaq peoples since time immemorial (Gros Morne National Park, paras. 9, 11). Gros Morne National Park is considered a place for serious hiking, so the hiking gear is taken just as seriously. For instance, it would be best if you had rugged clothes to withstand the elements, keep warm enough or cool enough, and stay in sync with Newfoundland's ever-changing weather and surfaces. However, no sizes of those rugged clothes were available to me as a fat masculine-presenting trans person. The people who wander in and out of the Visitor Centre and those we meet on hikes and beaches and in coffee shops have many things in common. For one, they dress the same, wearing clothes and boots from sporting goods stores that offer sizes for the thin and narrow. Their shoes and drip dry or zip-off pants and shirts are seen as practical and comfortable, and they all look the same. Most of the hikers carry considerably less body fat and have more congruent gender presentations than I do. Many of them are also white able-bodied people who can walk, sit, and inhabit ordinary places without fear of feeling like a "space invader" or out of the "norm." Once again, Foucault echoes this felt experience: those hiking in this beautiful space are mapped as "normal" bodies, while my fat trans body remains excluded. This surveillance from my fellow travellers for moving around while being a fat and trans white settler is unsettling.

To fit into this persona of the hiker, my partner wanted to go to Mountain Equipment Company (MEC) in Toronto, Ontario, to get outfitted for this hiking trip. We both identify as trans persons, though, as he is male and thin-passing and I identify as fat, our shopping experiences differ in many ways. When he asked me to come to MEC with him, he said, "Maybe you will be surprised and find something that fits you." My fat shame prevented me from answering back angrily about the absolute truth of the experience of shopping as a fat person: my past experience of MEC had informed me that it was no place for fatties. All I would find myself doing is moving around the store window shopping, so that thin people would not get to keep their judging eyes on me for too long. What their gaze stated was that I should be thinner and more active, conflating these notions of thinness, "healthism," and active lifestyles for those participating in such outdoor activities. Afterall, I was at MEC in the first place to fulfil this expectation of being a hiker with the goal to become more active. (The goal of being thinner is a more complicated one of course.) As my partner carried the many choices of pants in his size into the waiting room, I tried as hard as I could to make myself small, inconspicuous, and nonchalant as I wandered through the aisles looking at the men's clothing. The largest size they had was an extra-large, and, well, that would not come close to fitting someone like me. So, I continued to pace, so the judging eyes would not rest too long on my "abomination" of a body. I walked so that no gaze would fall too long upon my body and the many parts that did not fit: my chest, beard, belly, or my bigness. The thing is—I want to wear hiking pants from MEC. I want to be part of the conversation of the hiking world that consists of clothing, fabric, and shorts that don't ride up. I would like to talk about shirts that keep the sun out and let the sweat out. That cannot happen at MEC for me, because once again the looks and judgment about my fatness and transness (together with only straight-sized clothing options) exclude me before I can even enter such spaces, let alone conversations.

I calmed myself and managed to find some courage outside this fat shame and entered the shoe section, hoping that the lack of fat fashion would not continue to erase me here. My feet fall within a "normal" range, and I felt some marginal confidence to ask for what I needed and wanted in the shoe department. As soon as I saw the benches, however, my enthusiasm dissipated. The benches were flimsy. I knew they would collapse under my weight. This basic need for safety in seating is so extraordinarily invisible and becomes such an impactful way to exclude fat people! So I perched instead of sitting and desperately waited for this entire experience to end.

For the fat person, there is no accommodating environment, nor any truly accessible space. We constantly witness a form of spatial discrimination unleashed onto fat bodies. Lesleigh Owen illuminates this lack of accessible space for fat people:

> From the moment a fat person awakens in the morning, s/he is reminded of living fatly in a thin-centric world. Shower stalls in which we have to stand sideways (baths are rarely an option); towels that won't fasten around our waists or chests; disproportionately expensive or ill-fitting jewelry, belts, shoes, and clothing; narrow doorways, hallways, aisles, and bathrooms; too-tiny and/or molded plastic seats in buses and on subway trains; narrow, flimsy, or armed office, lawn, theater, airplane, restaurant, and dining room seating; weight limits on exercise equipment; hospital gowns, blood pressure cuffs, MRIs, life jackets, seatbelts, and other health or safety devices that simply don't fit: all are constant reminders that fat persons don't fit, that our most basic needs, desires, and safety therefore matter less. (294)

As I move around in MEC, I am reminded of a conference I attended and how I felt my trans fat body navigate itself within thin and able-centric space. The issue of seating and accommodating in general is less thought of; strikingly, even small groups of people working against spatial discrimination often miss this fundamental issue of seating when organizing. For example, at the annual Congress of the Humanities and Social Sciences in Canada held at Toronto Metropolitan University (formerly Ryerson University), Toronto, in 2017, an all-too-brief fat studies mini-conference was arranged. The room assigned had the flimsiest chairs and the seating had to be changed at the last moment to accommodate the fat bodies that were presenting. This issue reoccurred not long after at the book launch for a significant publication in the field of disability studies, once again reminding presenters and the audience that they are outside the "norm." What a painful place to be made invisible and excluded again, especially at two association conferences that advocate a social justice framework for marginalized communities! While academic and shopping spaces are very different, as our bodies search for access to space and fashion, the undercurrents of the discourse of cis-heteronormativity, ableism, and sizeism continue to shape the Canadian fat experience.

I return to the present reflecting on the ways things have not changed even as we take on the agenda of fat liberation across institutions in Canada. Instead of shopping at the fat-exclusionary store MEC, I found the rest of what I needed for our trip online, which of course was just as complicated as in-person shopping. A thorough search let me know that hiking pants for a body like mine exist, but at a high price and with a significant delay in delivery timelines. I thought to myself, if only I had started this search earlier! So, I went to my old standby clothing store, Mr. Big and Tall, hoping to find options. I have been going in there for so long that I forget that my understanding of my gender and that of the Mr. Big and Tall salespersons are very different. They take a look at my body with their cis-heterosexual gaze and come to ignore my facial hair or low voice; rather they hyperfocus on my fatness and determine I am a female, misgendering me at that moment. Bear Bergman describes this experience: "I am just barely fat enough to shop at what I call the Big Fat Tall Guy Store and can sometimes find my size in your usual boy-upholstery emporia. Major clothing labels, like Levi Strauss, make nice things in my size" (141). My gender is not perceived as authentic there, but the salespeople help me get the sizes I need. Despite the store's clothes not being what I wanted, I settled upon two pairs of shorts from Mr. Big and Tall. As a result, on the long hikes, without the fancy microfibre moisture-wicking pants, I fought the shorts bunching all through the paths of Gros Morne National Park. All I wanted was the pants that everyone wears to hike, but that was not an easy task: trying to achieve this goal always contained hints of fat shame and a sense of "lack." The pants signify insiderhood, that you are a part of the conversation and being indoctrinated into this active hiking lifestyle, therefore stepping close to the "ideal" body seen hiking the trails of Gros Morne National Park.

Transgender Reflections on the BMI and Fat-Shaming in Health Care

I often feel that I am the fattest person in the room. It was interesting that once I started looking around at the people who were assigned male at birth, there was a significant discrepancy in their body sizes and the ways that their fatness was read. It was interesting to me to realize that these bodies assigned male at birth had been invisible to me when I was observing bodies in the room, car, bus, subway, park and restaurant, sidewalk. Male-assigned bodies of size were merely a variation on a socially acceptable theme, and I did not grow up hearing a story of how these bodies needed to be corrected. My childhood conditioning had served to erase the assessment of fatness in masculine bodies and enhance the evaluation of all female bodies.

The qBody Project is a qualitative research project led by Ontario Institute for Studies in Education Professor Dr. Heather Sykes that "aims to understand how students with 'queer bodies' are impacted by heterosexism, transphobia, ableism, and fat phobia in Canadian physical education" (238). In the study, one of the participants named Johnathon (per Sykes quotation below) spoke about the gendering of fatness:

> Johnathon, who self-identified as straight, suggested that "men can have certain amounts of baggage in a kind of simplistic sense and not be viewed as being fat or whatever." This point echoes Susan Bordo's ... insight that men can have fat without being fat whereas women cannot. (Sykes 250)

Sykes's reference to "having fat without being fat" was a phenomenon I began to experience as I identified and dressed in more traditionally masculine garb. Although I was not a participant in the study, I related to this general experience. When I was gendered as a woman, I was seen as not only fat but extraordinarily and repugnantly so. As I identified more trans-masculinely, my fatness was received by folks who understood my transness as neither extraordinary nor repugnant, merely sizeable.

In his article "Part-Time Fatso," Bear Bergman tackles the experience of walking in the gender juncture between masculine and feminine presentation and the resulting impact on perception. Bergman shares, "[A]s a man, I'm a big dude, but not outside the norm for such things. As a woman, I am revolting. I am not only unattractively mannish but also grossly fat" (Bergman 141). Fatness is a significant factor in gender presentation. As a masculine-presenting individual needing gender-affirming top surgery, my fatness was discussed, analysed, and presented as a potentially severe obstacle to gender-affirming surgery. For trans people, the body mass index (BMI) is utilized to map out which bodies are accepted for medical procedures. One year ago, I had knee surgery, and the process entailed a weighing in before the surgery. But despite my knee being one of the two pins on which my body rests, the medical professionals involved at no time determined that surgery was not possible due to risk from my BMI. However, when it came to the case of seeking gender-affirming surgery, the BMI became a tool used to shame me and dictate my existence as one not deserving of medical care *or* my gendered experience.

The entire process of accessing care for gender-affirming top surgery was dehumanizing. As a fat person, I would prefer not to enter a cosmetic surgeon's office under any circumstance due to its ideological nature that constantly broadcasts the discourse of thinness and attractiveness. However, as they are the only medical professionals that perform chest surgery, it becomes a necessity to seek a form of health care in such a space.

When I exited the elevator and entered the very gendered space of this doctor's suburban clinic, with its own princess chair in the waiting room, it was made clear that I was the before picture plastered on the walls. My fat, old, hairy, gender-transgressive body was apparently a woman's nightmare. With every before picture of a person came an advertisement that spoke of how to cut the fat out of your body in one place, inject it into your ass, your lips, or your cheeks in order to make you more youthful. As I looked around, I also saw other adverts on fat freezing or the removal of unsightly body hair, along with a little mannequin of a doll in a dress holding business cards. The key words that continue to stand out and speak to this negation of fat embodiment were *youthful*, *beautiful*, *little*, *female*. As Bahra and Overboe argue, "The personal register is one that determines who is human enough through its established attributes and preoccupation with identity, representation, and ranking of bodies" (200). All these words remind us how "monstrous," "unattractive," "grotesque," or unhappy fatness is constructed under the medical-industrial complex (Bahra). I asked myself, "Is this the place, one determined on and by a thin-centric culture, where I must be and trust the doctor to slice off my chest tissue and form my chest?"

After an interminable amount of time in the waiting room, the doctor's assistant took us to another similarly gendered waiting room. While a cardboard cut-out of what a female body SHOULD look like beckoned from behind the examining chair, I was facing a mirror of myself. The assistant sat beside me and explained to me that she had just had "her eyes done." I nodded as if that meant something to me. I was left baffled by the gender politics in that room, especially considering the gender politics that I had come to challenge in that very space for my own story to unfold. The assistant proceeded with some preliminary questions, and in awe and shock, I too asked some of my own. For instance, I wondered what percentage of the clinic's business consisted of trans or nonbinary people like me looking for gender-affirming chest surgery, as I considered the impact this space has in relation to the discourse of anti-fatness. The assistant responded stating, "It is our most popular procedure." I almost fell off my chair as I heard those words exit her mouth. Why would this place that depended on people who look somewhat like me have a waiting room that looked like that?

Perhaps the business does not reflect the needs of people who look like me because our participation is guaranteed as mandatory in the Canadian capitalist medical-industrial complex—in that queer people, especially fat queer people, need to navigate medical discrimination in order to access *any* health care. The clinic I reference is one of the few places people can access top surgery; its waitlist is longer than two years, and appointments are booked solid six months in advance. I ask again. Why are the adverts about "beauty" and cosmetic procedures made the focus of such spaces, when the ads could instead convey positive narratives centred on trans lives? Well, trans folks are not the clients these companies have to honour, service, or chase using such false adverts. Such a clinic will always have our business, despite the waiting room that makes us invisible. Although we visit this clinic to access gender-affirming surgery, it requires us to walk through the portals of heteronormative female body shaping. And due to our need for gender-affirming surgery, we will continue to come to such clinics even if our fat, trans bodies are symbolic of the before pictures posted on the walls. Particularly in this business, trans-masculine folks are a "one-off." We know what we need; we get referred and fill in forms; we come into the office for a consultation for this one procedure that will align us to our bodies. With extensive research to get to this point, we realize the troubles in accessing this service. There simply are no other medical offices to go to for a second opinion or a better price. For those that do not have unlimited funds, and no other place to get gender-affirming surgery, this clinic remains the only option. These medical practitioners are actively participating in the medical-industrial complex that dehumanizes our bodies while also exploiting them for financial gain, all because they know that we are so happy to have made it this far. They are aware that the trans person in their waiting room is delighted to have reached the point of accessing this life-altering surgery and thus will be obedient and passive and do many things to get the surgery, even if it means facing the portals of fat shame and cis-heteronormativity. They have the power, and we have none. In fact, in the extensive medical-industrial complex, we are nothing more than a means to an income and perhaps to pride among surgeons. In this relationship between OHIP and medical practitioners, we are both the currency and commodity they need for this capitalist medical system to thrive.

The next stage of the visit to the plastic surgeon was the dreaded fat talk. Friends of mine who had been here had forewarned me about it, and I had steeled myself for this. From the moment the cisgender male surgeon walked into the examining room with his inhumanly high and full cheekbones, I was no longer a patient. I was an "obese" patient that became an object of an anti-fat examination. He began by discussing the surgery and then went ahead to look at my chest and measure it. As he measured me, he commented to me that I was sweaty. This comment added to the feeling occasioned by all the biopolitcal apparatuses at work in the space, each piece of me part of the equation that always equals unacceptable fatness. He turned to me with a very stern look, only to state, "I see your weight here—you are pretty heavy. That is a problem. We are going to need that BMI down before the surgery. I'm sure you will be able to get it down, and we will need it down." I mustered up all my courage and asked the surgeon, why does the BMI matter for this procedure? He informed me that it is riskier to perform surgery on "obese" people and that the post-op results will not be as good compared to those for someone much thinner. He continued to suggest that, due to my fatness, the wound would end up with what Loh et al. call a "dog ear ... a term used to describe the raised mound of tissue resulting from the closure of wound surfaces of unequal length" (341). Francis Ray White and other fat trans scholars question the relationship of top surgery to fat activism. White ponders whether "[t]he 'flat chest' so desired by ... transmasculine people, myself included, is as much a slender bodily ideal as it is a non-feminine one" (96). This question would be one I would continue to mull over as, after the appointment when I was exiting the office space, I was yet again reminded of these top surgery dog ears.

Before leaving the surgeon's office, I asked the assistant who had written down my name on the waitlist whether top surgery was possible for me. She responded with a "yes" but continued to state that my post-op results just would not be as great as those of my thin trans counterparts. Once again, I tried to read between the lines. Are staff making this statement for insurance reasons? Is it maybe to hint at possible death on the table due to the supposedly "high risks" that come with my fatness? Or maybe they're just suggesting that fat trans people cannot have good-looking chests because the "dog ears" look so terrible? All in all, with each question and answer, my fatness was interrogated and made into this object that would, supposedly, severely influence the surgeon's ability to do his job. As unsure as I felt in that space that catered to cisgender women, I held hope that he would be able to do my surgery. A sense of hope remained that even if my BMI were the same, my participation in the hiking lifestyle and in other fitness activities, plus physiotherapy, would help the surgeon make the decision to accept me as the "fitter patient."

Concluding Thoughts

I'm writing this in May of 2021. The world is still in the throes of the global coronavirus pandemic. As variants continue to spread, so does the anti-fat discourse that comes to take on a virality of its own. The pandemic had been raging for almost a year when, on December 14, 2020, in Toronto, Ontario, frontline worker Anita Quidangen received the first shot of the Pfizer coronavirus vaccine—marking a change for the better, so we thought (Tsekouras). As the vaccine rollout was occurring, the Ontario government vaccinated fat folks in the second phase of the plan (Ontario Ministry of Health); the word spread through social media that people with a BMI score of over 40 would be able to book a vaccine earlier than others in their age group due to their medicalized fatness. I asked myself, who was this really protecting? Did the Ministry of Health really want to protect us fatties, or was this a trial run selling "Pfizer for Pfatties"? In the end, we flocked to the vaccine centres and received our jabs, most of us viewing this as a complicated yet welcome privilege (Milligan). Was this a kind gesture realizing the right of fat folks to live and prosper even during a pandemic? Was this policy an empathetic understanding that fat folks were more susceptible to the rages of the coronavirus and more likely to have serious outcomes? Or, more possibly, was this a reaction to our susceptibility, to the fear that we would be a drain on the system?

The multiple vignettes shared in this piece help to crystallize how spaces (airplanes, stores, clinics, conference rooms) and activities (travelling, hiking, accessing health care and vaccines) are not designed with fat folks in mind, and how those places and pursuits abnormalize fat bodily experiences. This autoethnographic piece also demonstrates the ways in which fatness and transness have always been located at the margins, especially when considering the spatial politics at hand. Fat and trans people are always made into this image of the "space invader," whether it be in cis-heteronormative or thin spaces that continue to map out what and whose bodies are to be protected and valued.

My mother died in 2015, five years before the start of the pandemic. Once she had slipped into a coma, I sat beside her and told her all about my gender journey and what it all meant for me. Part of me was grateful that this woman who had dropped me off alone at Weight Watchers when I was 10 years old would hear my story without asking intrusive questions about how my fatness would impact the surgery. As I spoke with her, I imagined that a part of her was grateful that I was going to physically become the person I had always been. In seeking this oneness with the self, I choose delight. No disapproving surgeon armed with reasons to disqualify me, no unwelcoming office, no mandatory dieting can truly dim the joy that this life-affirming procedure will offer me. Medical attempts to mandate the shape of my body will affect, upset, and annoy me, but in no way do they deter me from accessing gender-affirming care. I hope this gender-affirming care will mean that when I defend my right to a seat in an airplane, my two feet are planted beneath a body that fits me. I aspire to one day being ableto ask for a seatbelt extender without a whiff of shame.

The differently abled parts of me are proud that this body held together and worked hard to complete the hikes over the rough ground and sand and hills that challenged us in Gros Morne National Park, Newfoundland, even in the wrong clothes. My fat self is proud that I held my head high and experienced the gorgeous vistas and sweaty challenges of this lovely time outdoors. After that trip, I was inspired to search for and find some activewear for body sizes like mine. I am conflictedly grateful for access to the coronavirus vaccine that increases the odds that I may have another opportunity to spend a hiking trip in nature. My trans self is grateful that next year or maybe the year after that, my fat body will more distinctly match my soul's gender. I will continue to place myself in all the spaces I choose, regardless of whether or not the place has made space for people like me. Clear the sidewalks, widen the chairs, I'm on my way.

Works Cited

Bahra, Ramanpreet A. "'You Can Only Be Happy If You're Thin!' Normalcy, Happiness, and the Lacking Body." *Fat Studies: An Interdisciplinary Journal of Body Weight and Society*, vol. 7, no. 2, 2017, pp. 193–202.

Bahra, Ramanpreet A., and James Overboe. "Working Towards the Affirmation of Fatness and Impairment." *Thickening Fat: Fat Bodies, Intersectionality and Social Justice*, edited by May Friedman, Carla Rice, and Jen Rinaldi, Routledge, 2019, pp. 197–207.

Bergman, Bear S. "Part Time Fatso." *The Fat Studies Reader*, edited by Esther D. Rothblum and Sondra Solovay, NYU Press, 2009, pp. 139–42.

Canadian Transportation Agency. "Highlights of One-Person-One-Fare Policy Decision." *Canadian Transportation Agency: Accessible Transportation*, 6 August 2019, https://otc-cta.gc.ca/eng/highlights-one-person-one-fare-policy-decision. Accessed 10 November 2021.

Castagno, Angelina E. "What Makes Critical Ethnography 'Critical'?" *Qualitative Research: An Introduction to Methods and Designs*, ed ited by Stephan D. Lapan, MaryLynn T. Quartaroli, and Frances J. Riemer, Jossey-Bass/Wiley, 2011, pp. 373–90.

Foucault, Michel. "Troisième entretien—'Je suis un artificier.'" *Michel Foucault, entretiens*, edited by Roger-Pol Droit, Odile Jacob Publishers, 2004, pp. 89–136.

Gailey, Jeannine A. *The Hyper(in)Visible Fat Woman: Weight and Gender Difference in Contemporary Society*. Palgrave Macmillan, 2014.

Gros Morne National Park. "Indigenous Programs," *Parks Canada*, https://www.pc.gc.ca/en/pn-np/nl/grosmorne/activ/decouverte-tours/ab. Accessed 24 June 2021.

Hartley, Cecilia. "Letting Ourselves Go, Making Room for the Fat Body in Feminist Scholarship." *Bodies Out of Bounds: Fatness and Transgression*, edited by Jana Evans Braziel and Kathleen LeBesco, University of California Press, 2001, pp. 60–73.

Huff, Joyce L. "Access to the Sky." *The Fat Studies Reader*, edited by Esther Rothblum and Sondra Solovay, NYU Press, 2009, pp. 176–86.

Kotow, Crystal Lee Marie. *Big, Beautiful Affect: Exploring the Emotional Environment of BBW Social Events and Its Relationship to Fat Women's Embodiment*. 2020. York University, PhD dissertation. https://yorkspace.library.yorku.ca/xmlui/handle/10315/37938.

Kwan, Samantha. "Navigating Public Spaces: Gender, Race, and Body Privilege in Everyday Life." *Feminist Formations*, vol. 22, no. 2, 2010, pp. 144–66.

Larbalestier, Justine. "How to Write Protagonists of Colour When You're White," *Justine Larbalestier*, 20 June 2016, https://justinelarbalestier.com/blog/2016/06/20/how-to-write-protagonists-of-colour-when-youre-white/. Accessed 28 March 2022.

Loh, Charles Y. Y., Alex Y. H. Loh, and Syed Abuzar Mashhadi. "A Novel Method for Repairing the Dog Ear." *Journal of Plastic, Reconstructive & Aesthetic Surgery*, vol. 66, no. 11, 2013, pp. 341–42.

Milligan, Susan. "Dropping the Weight: Obese People See Rare Advantage in Coronavirus Vaccination Priority." *US News & World Report*, 5 March 2021, https://www.usnews.com/news/the-report/articles/2021-03-05/obese-people-see-rare-advantage-in-coronavirus-vaccination-priority. Accessed 7 May 2021.

Ontario Ministry of Health. "COVID-19 Vaccines." *Government of Ontario COVID-19 (Coronavirus) Information*, https://covid-19.ontario.ca/covid-19-vaccines-ontario Accessed 13 May 2021.

Owen, Lesleigh. "Living Fat in a Thin-Centric World: Effects of Spatial Discrimination on Fat Bodies and Selves." *Feminism & Psychology*, vol. 22, no. 3, 2012, pp. 290–306.

Pausé, Cat. "Ray of Light: Standpoint Theory, Fat Studies, and a New Fat Ethics." *Fat Studies*, vol. 9, no. 2, 2020, pp. 175–87.

Rinaldi, Jen, Carla Rice, and Emily Lind. "Failure to Launch: One-Person-One-Fare Airline Policy and the Drawbacks to the Disabled-By-Obesity Legal Argument." *Fat Studies*, vol. 10, no. 2, 2021, pp. 144–59.

Sykes, Heather. "The qBody Project: From Lesbians in Queer Education to Queer Bodies In/Out of School." *Journal of Lesbian Studies,* vol. 13, no. 3, 2009, pp. 238–54

Smith, Dorothy E. *The Everyday World as Problematic: A Feminist Sociology.* University of Toronto Press, 1987.

Tsekouras, Phil. "Ontario Administers First Doses of COVID-19 Vaccine in Toronto." *CTV News*, 14 December 2020, https://toronto.ctvnews.ca/ontario-administers-first-doses-of-covid-19-vaccine-in-toronto-1.5230004.

White, Francis Ray. "Fat/Trans: Queering the Activist Body." *Fat Studies*, vol. 3, no. 2, 2014, pp. 86–100.

Please Come and Be Fat

S. Bear Bergman

"Hey, um," he says, obviously trying to hide some urgency, "can I ask you for kind of a weird favour?"[1]

I'm standing behind the Flamingo Rampant book table at this trans conference in Seattle, 3,000 miles from my home in Toronto, where I have been standing for two days. I've been visiting with friends, greeting acquaintances, and answering questions for parent after parent after anxious parent of trans and nonbinary kids looking for reflections of themselves. I'm a little tired and a little hoarse, a little dry-mouthed and a little hungry, and I feel, standing here, like I have been in service all day but also I like this young fellow and I love to be helpful, so I nod: yes.

He pours it out: "We're doing top surgery show and tell across the hall. It's pretty packed, but everyone who came to show their results is, like, me-sized. But a bunch of the guys who are looking to check out results are more... you-sized. So I was wondering, if I watched the books and all for a few minutes, could you maybe... "

"Go in there and be fat?" I ask.

He laughs nervously, all 5'5" and 115 pounds of himself, compact and sleek as an otter, and nods. "Basically."

And so I do.

I walk across the hall, into a remarkably large ballroom in which trans men and nonbinary folks are spaced evenly around the room along the walls, shirtless. Some of them are flexing and posing, some just standing, but indeed all of them are the approximate size of my young acquaintance—skinny, lean, trim, athletic, like the collegiate swim team for a small, liberal arts university with an unusual number of tattoos. A fair number of them seem to have waists the circumference of my thigh. I don't pause, because I know if I stop I will quail, and so: I take a deep breath and walk directly to an empty spot, drape my shirt over a nearby chair and attempt to look relaxed.

I can't, of course, but it doesn't matter—in short order there's a wave of rearrangement around the room, as though someone passed a magnet under the floor and drew all the bigger boys to me like one of those games where you use iron filings to put hair and a beard on the outline of a face. I take slow breaths, I try to find a place of comfort in being shirtless and hairy and more than a little sweaty here in the hotel conference room, and soon I am answering questions, different questions. How much do I weigh? Do I weigh the same as I did when I had surgery? Who did the work? Did they make me lose weight beforehand? Do I like my chest? Did I have a revision? Am I happy with my results?

Several of the guys are there with a lover or parents. One woman, whom I suppose to be a mother, reaches up reflexively to touch my scar line and then stops short, embarrassed, and laughs a brittle little laugh. "Sorry!" she says, obviously abashed, "It's just...I've never seen this before." She takes a step back and focuses on me, taking me in from head to foot, noting my beard and my wedding ring, the fur on my shoulders, and the lop of my ample belly that eclipses my belt buckle. She looks from me to her son, who is also fat, probably not older than twenty and standing with the hunched, shoulders-rolled-in stance I know so well from years of binding. His shirt is a size too big; his binder is doing heroic work but doesn't erase the telltale swell of his chest that he is obviously more than done with. She smiles at me and says to him, "I could see this. I could see you like this."

I just stand there and take more deep breaths. I concentrate on my posture, on rolling my shoulders back and keeping my chest up and out. I don't think about being fat and half-naked in a roomful of strangers; I answer questions and shift my weight minutely from foot to foot and try not to think about the failure of my right nipple, about the soft, rumpled patch in the centre of my chest that looks like an unmade bed. I named it, after a while. I decided it was the guest bed of my heart, but that hasn't made me like it much better so far. Oh, well.

It's complicated to be doing this, and I don't like it at all, and in the same hand, I'm grateful for the small-framed acquaintance who rabbited out of the room and came to get me. I'm glad he saw what was happening and found a way to solve the problem. I don't want to be standing here as a model of fat transness but I am glad to be because nobody else is.

In the thirty minutes I stand there, a number of people come by to look and ask questions. Most often, they want to know if I'm happy with it. I make jokes: "Well, I was never going to be Channing Tatum, so... " "It's not much, but it's all mine!" and so on.

The truth is, I am happy with it, most of the time, even though there are days I would be happier to look like any of the guys arrayed around the room than like I do now. I am happy to be free of my binder, sticky and sweaty and always hot and itchy, even on a cool day. I'm happy to stand up straight most of the time. I'm happy to be able to wear swim trunks and take my kids to the pool and throw them around, even though that too brings questions (there's a non-zero number of "What happened to you!?" comments that crop up, even considering the fabled Canadian politeness). I'm happy to sweat and not be stuck in my cooling sweat for the rest of the day inside my sausage casing. I'm happy that my shirts, even the most disreputable falling-apart T-shirts, look right on me when I look in the mirror.

And so, when my nervousness starts to pass, when my sense that I am way out on a creaky and overburdened limb starts to ease, I stop joking and start telling the truth: yes, I am happy with it. I'm more in my body now than I ever have been, though that's not saying much. This is okay for me. It took a lot of doing, but it was worth it.

The half hour during which I have agreed to do this extremely peculiar community service passes very, very slowly. I try to decide if it's more obvious to blot the sweat off with my shirt (ew) or just let the droplets roll down the dunes and rolls of my sides and fall to the floor (also ew). At length, someone else handsome and muscular with a great tan and fanciful body art gets back up on the small raised podium and thanks all of us who modelled (!) and says we can get dressed again and come up for Q&A, but

I don't. I bid the last of the lookers goodbye and put my shirt on and slip out and back to my work, making picture books that show kids who don't usually see themselves getting to have adventures and solve problems and be loved. I get it, there's a metaphor here.

Later, the same guy who asked me to come join the skin parade stops back at my table and asks if he can come around and give me a hug, to which I agree with good cheer. That's when he says, quietly, that he's been doing this show-and-tell situation for several years, and that there's never anyone fat, and that he keeps noticing and he's glad for once he was able to do something about it. He thanks me until I order him to cut it out, and we have the promised hug and he heads off to do whatever-and-then-some with the other twenty-five-year-olds while I sell more children's books to more concerned straight moms of trans kids, who are still so hungry for any way to imagine their children into a real future, and not a sensationalized one.

Sometimes I feel overwhelmed, or even aggravated, at how much there still is to do and how many times a day being a possibility model, to use the brilliant Laverne Cox's phrase for it, is demanded of us all. Sometimes I really and truly do not want it. And even still, fat and sweaty behind my table, in that moment I'm glad he asked. There is a lot of possibility yet to model, and honestly: the more of us the better.

Notes

1 This chapter first appeared as a post on medium.com.

Slender Trouble: From Berlant's Cruel Figuring of Figure to Sedgwick's Fat Presence

Lucas Crawford

Foreword[1]

This article is about fat feeling, temporality, and their relation to queer theory—most notably, to the work of American theorists Eve Kosofsky Sedgwick and Lauren Berlant—but the story of the article's genesis can illustrate its derivation from and relevance to Canadian contexts. I wrote this article while living in Vancouver and working as the Ruth Wynn Woodward Lecturer in Gender, Sexuality, and Women's Studies at Simon Fraser University, during which time my mandate was "Fat Matters." It did, and it does, and this was perhaps never so plain to me as when my then-partner and I—both superfat at the time (2013)—glided through the Vancouver International Airport via moving sidewalks on an initial visit to the city. We shared a sense not only that we were creating a spectacle but also that our audience was thinner, richer, and more taken aback than the Edmontonian ones to which we had grown accustomed. It was in Vancouver that I committed in earnest to "never read the comment section" when I appeared in media. "I almost had pity for this guy, but I lost it in one of his fat, sweaty rolls" was one of dozens that rushed in under a *Georgia Straight* (alt-weekly) article announcing our first Fat Matters event, and it's clearly not one I've forgotten.

That first event was probably our best-attended one: a screening of *My Big Fat Diet*, a 2008 CBC documentary that tracked the low-carb weight loss efforts of residents of Alert Bay, BC, who were guided for one year by Dr. Jay Wortman, a Métis physician from Fort Vermilion, AB, who is now based in

Vancouver. The documentary underlines prohibitive food costs in small Northern communities such as this one, and champions a return to Indigenous foodways as a way to avoid diabetes. Weeks later, one of the panellists who spoke after the screening, himself a First Nations anthropologist of food, posted a series of tweets arguing that fat people should not be eligible for political office. To paraphrase: *if they can't control their bodies, how can they control anything else?* Now that we have heard years of fatphobia as evidence of Donald Trump's ineptitude, this argument has only become more popular. Remembering this event reminds me that intersectional approaches to fatness are neither as easy nor as obvious as we might like them to be. People we look to for worthy accounts of colonialism may also openly promote fatphobia, and people who organize queer fat events are also people who have lots to learn—don't I know it! To me, it's difficult but wonderful that people and oppressions are not reducible to equations, that none of us is worth more or less than both respect and scrutiny.

During the three years we lived in Vancouver, I can say with confidence that I was the fattest person in every room I entered—a fact I didn't realize fully until I moved, in 2016, to Fredericton, NB. Very few people stared at me; I saw superfat people frequently; I was rarely the only superfat person in the room. (To flesh out the travel story somewhat: flying from Vancouver to Fredericton required accommodation. To apply for this, we decided on WestJet's process of having a physician measure one's maximum diameter, versus Air Canada's requirement that a doctor trace one's ass imprint onto paper and mail it in.) Having lived in rural Nova Scotia for the first twenty-two years of my life, I was not shocked by the relative size of Maritimers but was somewhat surprised by the effect that New Brunswick's far less moneyed aesthetic and larger body norms had on me. At least in this way (if not others), Fredericton felt more familiar, and again, the point that social class and body size are tightly related felt immediate and obvious.

As Sander Gilman points out, fat's relationship to other discretely defined bodily traits or experiences—such as social class—varies across time and space. While fatness "in the Americas is often equated with poverty," it was instead "a problem of the nobility in prerevolutionary France, where the rallying cry was 'the people against the fat'" (*Fat Boys*, 2–3). A tangential point made in my article is that fat people are subjected to a no-win situation regarding notions of class: though fatness in the American and Canadian contexts are linked more closely to poverty or working-class life than to wealth, we still live in representational economies and bitter public discourses that equate our bodies to "bad" and ostensibly aristocratic morals of resource-hoarding, greed, and excess. If you have ever walked through Vancouver's Downtown Eastside and then through Kitsilano—the birthplace of Lululemon—you know as well as I do that certain modes of slenderness are, generally, a more compelling index of social class privilege than is fatness (though an index is only as useful as, well, an index). The different racial make-ups of those neighbourhoods tell a similarly complex story of fat's current relationship to oppression.

Through an equal measure of pandemic disasters and happy accidents, I find myself again in Vancouver as I write this addendum to the article. I'm living on Carrall Street, where West Hastings becomes East. I am working my New Brunswick job online until my resignation date of July 1, 2021, awaiting vaccination in a province with better health care resources and higher rates of COVID-19 than New Brunswick. Despite its relative wealth, BC, unlike neighbouring Alberta, has *not* listed "obesity" as a condition of high risk for severe outcomes of COVID-19, and so it does not make one eligible for early vaccination; make of this discrepancy what you will.

One constant across the provincial moves described above is my own fat trans body's interpellation by others as working class. While this is my origin and not a vector of shame for me, it interests me the frequency with which members of the public assume I'm working when I'm simply walking by, sitting on a bench, or shopping at a drugstore. In the past two years, this includes being mistaken for a driver (twice), security guard (twice), salesperson (many times), and janitor. If this survey stretched to 2007, I could tell you about the taxi driver who saw my unfortunate ensemble of sporty brown, orange, and yellow, and took me directly to A&W and wished me a good shift, instead of to the nearby address I'd given.

This is all to say: this article was written by someone whose bodily experiences of various Canadian cities and provinces (notably but not exclusively Edmonton, Vancouver, and Fredericton) bear out the thorny and ambiguous visceral realities of upward academic mobility as a fat, white, disabled, genderqueer person. Yet, the article resists (my) identity as a resting place or an unassailable source of knowledge. Instead, it traces out new affective possibilities for fat that escape identitarian models and may be gleaned from poetry, theory, and pop culture.

Nation is a crucial part of this tracing, especially in the analyses of magazine covers that comprise the article's first substantial section. On the cover of *The Atlantic*, a fat Statue of Liberty mocks and chides large bodies (with considerable side-eye towards immigrants) as failures of the nation. What is the Canadian corollary to this cover? I think it lives suspended in tensions: between Vancouver and Fredericton, between Lululemon and weight-loss reality TV, and between Canadians' smugness for being less fat than Americans and the speed with which our ostensible politeness often fails non-normative bodies. Inconsistency is not necessarily a vice, and pointing it out is not automatically a moral position. But it is because of these tensions—the immediate need to survive them, the ongoing challenge of permitting ambiguity and pain, and the future need to create better tensions—that I wrote this article that forwards affective alternatives to the binary of fatphobia and fat pride. "Fat presence" is what I called this alternative. Inasmuch as no subject ever attains full presence, and inasmuch as I am still engaged daily in learning how to live and "be present," it remains an idea that animates and perplexes me. I wish the same for the readers of this collection.

Introduction

Scarcely a minute passes that a faceless fat body—cropped so as to narrow the focus to guts and butts—does not sashay across the screens of Western newscasts, asking viewers to misrecognize ourselves as or against these non-human images. Few moments go by that the funhouse mirrors of myriads do not reflect back fatter faces to those who fret about the caloric content of a morning omelette. Fat occupies. Still, who has *time* for fat?

Fat has partly replaced queer as the figure of decadent desire through which narratives of degeneracy and epidemic are filtered; as Sander Gilman suggests, "The 'moral panic,' which was associated in the 1980s with HIV/AIDS as a potentially global disease, [has been] transferred to obesity" (*Fat Boys* 14). Crucially, this attribution of devolution to fat locates fat's time as always already past or even as pushing us back toward it. Likewise, fat does not live in represented futures. As Francis Ray White argues in "Fat, Queer, Dead: 'Obesity' and the Death Drive," it may even be the case that fat people now occupy the role of the death drive in the cultural symbolic of the West. By reading for tropes of degeneracy in the UK's Change4Life anti-obesity campaign, White shows that "the bleak future foretold by dominant 'obesity' discourse is born in part from fears of social disintegration or regression that are frequently manifested in the idea of a death drive" ("Fat, Queer, Dead" 2). As happens with queers in the face of HIV/AIDS, the concept of the obesity epidemic has been framed as an "evolutionary inevitability"—as a plague that has arrived to return the human race to a purportedly natural moral order (9). With a similar desire to close the narrative of the fat body, our reality programs stage the spectacle of dieting with all the pain and predictability of repetition compulsion, installing again and again a sense of finality to the "after" of weight loss that just cannot keep its promises.

Following Lee Edelman's lead, White does not combat the equation of fat with death but instead breathes new life into the insult by refiguring it as a queer ethics of the body ("Fat/Trans"). However, not all queer theorists would condone White's manoeuvre; Lauren Berlant, for example, dismisses fat and eating as matters that exercise only a "lateral" or weak form of agency that is "not a projection toward a future" (*Cruel* 117), a figuration to which the present article returns. A preliminary question, however: isn't "eating right" generally held aloft as the golden ticket—or is it a dangling carrot?—that is supposed to lead fat people to locate our truest selves *only* in the future, following one's weight-loss-to-come? If anything, fat people are mandated to live in the future exclusively, all the while being denied access to any cultural fantasies of such a future. At a time when fat people are increasingly forced to live out the temporal paradox of simultaneously inhabiting such ever-deferred futures and traumatic pasts—to carve out a plus-sized seat in the interstices of "before" and "after"—it is fair to say that, discursively, we are on borrowed time. Or, are we timeless? As Gilman points out, the notion that the world is decaying because of excessive girth was a popular idea for the ancient Romans and many who have come after, even though fat people have not yet succeeded in eating/ending the world. What is at stake in this discourse is not actual life expectancy but instead a fever to rhetorically starve fatness out of any tenable position in discourse.

This article acknowledges that despite and because of all the time spent on fat in the past two decades, there is, rhetorically, no such thing as a fat present—or, therefore, fat presence. When fat bodies can be permitted only if they can "pass as on-the-way-to-thin," it is not even possible to say that anyone *is* fat; fat people are launched into the future anterior tense in which we "will have been" fat (LeBesco 95).[2] To move against this temporal conundrum, this fat queer author will, in what follows, develop a theory of fat presence that lingers on immediate scenes of fat bodily contact. By so doing, I also show that queer theory's scarce interest in fat has led us to underestimate the vital ideas about fat produced by Eve Kosofsky Sedgwick. Primary among her works that address fat is her poetry book, *Fat Art, Thin Art*, which contains a short poem, "The Use of Being Fat." In this piece, the famous theorist remembers hugging a cherished body. I argue that this poem figures fatness as a folding and folded space in which XXX and XXXL come together or, moreover, are shown to have always come from the same (stretchy) cloth. Against Berlant's work and the other slender-normative approaches detailed below, this desire to imagine fat presence/presents demands of queer theory that we develop both a new three-dimensional approach to bodies that eschews the spatial binary of surface and depth and also a new way to figure "figure."

To clarify: "exclusion" of fat people is not what is at stake; while neoliberal activism might have a fat person fight one's way into the present through evocations of one's happy usefulness, neither Sedgwick nor the present article takes such an unambiguously affirmative approach, opting instead for a recurring fat scene imbued with pain and sorrow as much as possibility and sexuality.[3] To practice or even notice the fat temporalities of Sedgwick's fat text means at least three hermeneutical and figural shifts are necessary: (1) a refusal to rush to the causes and consequences of fat whenever such bodies emerge—in other words, to refuse to allow the Western medical model of the body to sneak back into queer theory via fat; (2) a development of one's capacity to read as though fat bodies were affectively *present* and perhaps even sustaining/sustainable to the degree that other bodies may be; and (3) a remaking of the slippage between bodily "figure" and literary "figure"—in other words, the development of a new metaphorical language of the body that does not lazily make fat into a catchall metaphor for all bad things and for the limits of language. This is not an argument about fat people not deserving the violence of figuration, as if an unfigured life were somehow possible. Indeed, as I show, Sedgwick herself traffics in metaphors of fat. Rather, this article pries back open the affective and interpretive capacities that have been shut down by particularly expedient figurations of fat in queer theory and elsewhere. An underlying question emerges: what possibilities for queer reading and relations does such figural expediency conceal? Certainly, if fat becomes present *as death* when our language fails, this attests less to the marginalization of fat than to the centrality of its role as figure—as the deficiency or large empty space from which the presumably slender text, writer, and reader speak.

No Time for Fat

Before proceeding to Sedgwick and fat presence, it is useful to illustrate the constraining fat temporalities from which this article emerges.

Exhibit A: an August 2003 cover of *Newsweek* features the profile of a fat white man, from the moustache down, framed by the headline "Fat World" and a pronouncement that "obesity is the globe's newest epidemic." The background is outer space, and, over the perfect sphere of the fat man's white-undershirted belly, a round photograph of the Earth has been photoshopped. In this particular cosmos of fatness, a fat man seems to be pregnant with the whole world—a world that he is thought, nonetheless, to be killing. In this representational economy, a fat man becomes a bad mother who has already "miscarried" his weight-cum-world, even though it is normative culture that "orbits" the fat body, circulating it (and around it) with pioneer spirit. The whiteness and attire of this body suggest it is a distinctly "American" body/politic that will deliver this future fat world by virtue of having the power to spread even its problems around the world or universe. This new American space program, like the real one, imagines extending itself into unfamiliar lands.[4] That this imagery routes its fat panic through both the language of epidemic and the symbolism of pregnancy means that it is routed equally through sexual reproduction, gender, and the phantom of a recent and ongoing history of HIV/AIDS as the "epidemic" associated with deviant forms of sex. Here fatness can make even pregnancy signify not the future of the world but its death; fat people practice, apparently, the wrong kind of "delivery."

Exhibit B: the award-winning May 2010 cover of *The Atlantic* morphs the Statue of Liberty into an extremely fat woman. Under the title "FAT NATION," the plus-size green giant becomes America's fatness personified. While Exhibit A shows America's fatness taking over the world, here it is the United States' avatar of immigration that appears bloated. In this fantasy, she who would welcome the hungry or wounded becomes an icon of the idea that one's body is national property. "Hungry" citizens are welcomed, the statue's text reads, but this magazine cover suggests that nobody take that word too far; a responsible American will not let the nation greet the world with fat. However, the humour of the image relies on something equally disturbing: a juxtaposition of fatness with the statue's association with freedom. What is "liberty," many might ask, if not a thin body?[5] Liberty becomes the liberty to choose exacting norms of slenderness. What usually stands as a proud sign of the nation's openness to *arrivals*, that is, the *new*, becomes a self-flagellating call to *return* to non-prodigal diets, a reinstatement of normalcy that shall be celebrated with anything but a fatted calf—perhaps with yogurt, which, as the *New York Times* reports, is now the official snack of New York State. On this magazine cover, it is not the queerly gendered fat man who will miscarry the world but the queerly evoked immigrant and nation who have perhaps desired "wrongly" in the land of plenty. Again, anxiety about misdirected *desire* is the underbelly of what may appear to many as just another fat joke.

Exhibit C: Michelle Obama appreciates a good apple. The fruit replaces the letter "O" in the visual identity of her "Let's Move!" campaign. Apples have also featured in at least two magazine covers featuring this First Lady whose mission it was to lead us back to the garden of clearly defined good and evil eats. On the cover of a March 2010 *Newsweek*, Obama sits, teacher-like, behind an apple that sits atop a desk. The apple occupies the centre of the photo, lending that all important "balance" that mythically keeps the doctor away. The headline, which describes Obama's authored article, takes the odd form of a lesson: "FEED YOUR CHILDREN WELL." Looking down at the camera slightly, Obama's posed body and its setting return the adult readers who "need" her lesson to the status of child by sitting them in a remedial classroom. (To be clear, while parents certainly have some agency while living within economic and racialized conditions not of their choosing, the headline overestimates this agency. This is not to mention just how narrowly many of us tend to define the quest to eat "well.") At a time when questions of childhood fatness are tainted by accusations of child abuse (Doyle), this image tells us that fat children need help not because they are treated horribly or live with injustice but because the people feeding them have yet to grow up.[6] A lesson in proper parenting delivered by a governmental figure contains an inherent lesson in heterosexual relationality, where such relationality becomes tantamount to citizenship. Viewers of this cover get a glimpse into the rapidly cohering cultural truth that what it means to be a fit parent is to be a "fit" parent. Not "fitting in" to the family form is or used to be a queer story; here it is relocated, equally sexualized and gender charged, to the fat body.

Obviously, judgments about time underlie specifically hetero- and gender-normative ideas about fat bodies, where fat bodies can stand in for now unacceptable explicit homophobia. In Exhibit A, readers see fat people as simultaneously pregnant with the future and as threatening that future. In Exhibit B, the very icon of the better futures of American fantasy threatens to block all ports while the magazine's instructions on "how to beat obesity" promise a better path forward. The imagery and tone of Exhibit C return readers to the classroom and to the historically but not gastronomically rich symbol of the apple and its seeds. Though the stories behind these covers deserve analysis of their own, I insist that magazine stories about fat must, in a sense, be judged by their cover: to read these covers in isolation is to read them in the manner of the browsing customer for whom a picture of fat must be worth a thousand words. (This is not to mention that the most common way in which fat people encounter others is for several seconds on a sidewalk or other public space; thus, this *is* the speed at which fat bodies are often read.) When faced with these vivid images in which fat bodies become the new icon for inappropriate desire, miscarriages of the future, and "unfit" parenting, we would do well to demand of queer theory a hearty response, one that turns work on queer temporality toward the fatphobia and implicit queerphobia of such images. We would do well to demand that queer theoretical work on fat both understand the heterosexism of quotidian fat panic and also undertake the hard work of asking just how queer affect and queer temporality exist when such projects are, as they always are, involved with fat bodies, with fat foods, and fat fantasy of so many harmful or exciting or mysterious kinds.

Yet, as I show here with Exhibit D, the heaviest hitter on fatness in queer theory is an author who employs fat in a manner that jars with queer theory's ethos of fighting the normalization and disciplining of bodies. Namely, I turn to Lauren Berlant's much-lauded *Cruel Optimism* (2011), which imbues fat with tremendously weighty metaphorical power in three ways. First, Berlant associates fat with "slow death": "the physical wearing out of a population ... the mass physical attenuation under global-national regimes of capitalist structural subordination" (95); second, she describes fat as "the congealed form of history that hurts" (142); and, finally, Berlant regards fat and pleasure-eating as forms of "lateral agency" (95), a figure that mistakes the literal spreading of fat for one's unacknowledged or falsely conscious temporal divestment from the future. This lack of "presence," as I then suggest with reference to Berlant and Edelman's *Sex, or the Unbearable* (2013), leads to Berlant's incapacity to be present to fat.

Fat Nachträglichkeit

One of Berlant's essays, "Two Girls, Fat and Thin," defines fat as, in a tidy phrase worth repeating, "the congealed form of history that hurts" (*Cruel* 142).[7] In this model, fat is the bodily trace of eating that one pursued during or in the wake of traumatic pasts. In other words, fat experience resembles what Sigmund Freud calls *Nachträglichkeit*; a fat body is a body onto and as which trauma has returned, belatedly. Berlant's equation presumes a sequence: trauma makes one eat more; eating more is what "causes" fatness; fatness is therefore a manifestation of that trauma. As a first response to this model of fat as *Nachträglichkeit*, it is useful to point out that all sorts of body modification regimes may be understood as responses to trauma, loss, and one's inevitably scarring confrontations with life. Dieting, exercise regimens, television marathons, junk food binges, daily eyebrow plucking, and the promotion of vegan ethics can all be understood as such responses, since all are bodily practices to which one has formed an attachment. While Berlant may not disagree with that, readers should perhaps be, therefore, all the more taken aback that Berlant makes example of eating and fatness with such frequency. The enjoyment of the labour of self-denial and discipline goes missing in Berlant's account, despite the fact that fat people are not the sole owners, or even the most obvious owners, of relationships to hurt that are managed via eating and exercise regimens. This is a difficult point to accept because "comfort eating" is such a highly recognizable trope, while "comfort dieting" seems conveniently imperceptible as an emotional project or a response to injury. Likewise, because talking about one's traumatic past is required of those participating in the weight-loss genre, these very few permitted narratives of fatness also guide fat subjects to narrate themselves in excessively retrospective fashion.

However, because fat pasts are not the only traumatic or complex ones, and because no fat body has as direct a relation to trauma as Berlant's metaphor suggests, a question is necessary: what upholds this inclination to regard fat bodies in particular as the belated effect of trauma? The answer, I argue, is a simple decision to attribute *causality* and linear temporalities far more casually to fat bodies than to normative ones. In this model, fat must be regarded as primarily a *result*, rather than a state of being or becoming with phenomenological characteristics that are not wholly self-evident. As Gilman shows, even the etymology of our current vocabulary for fat bodies—"obesity"—betrays this colloquial sense of fat's (re)turn to the past (*Fat Boys* 9). As he puts it, "The word *obesity* has an odd double meaning. The Latin *obesus* refers to a body that is eaten away and lean as well as one that has eaten itself fat. It is the past participle of *obedere*, to devour. ... A slippage between 'medical' labels for the fat body and popular, pejorative ones is ... evident" (9). The most important thing to note here with regard to fat temporality is that even the most widely recognized word for fatness defines the fat present as a past act precisely by laying claim to medicine's constructed objectivity about "obesity," despite the word's origin in the pejorative. This is a simple equation but one that is extraordinarily difficult to live with or to refuse: fat only "is" what one "has done." This is not to argue that fat has no relation to the past; it is to suggest that we need to query how it happens that some bodies are interpreted as a moving set of devolutionary symptoms and others are invited to fantasize their bodies as being entirely in the present, without history, and as deserving of futures. Berlant too acknowledges this etymology: "For insurance purposes obesity had been deemed an illness, the rest of the literature call it something like a chronic condition, *etymologically a disease of time*, and vernacularly a condition that can never be cured, only managed" (*Cruel* 143).

Cruel Optimism is interestingly inconsistent when it comes to diagnosing the temporal conditions of this "disease." Berlant's adoption of the model of *Nachträglichkeit*, in which fat is the belated congealment of loss, clashes with her other argument that disordered eating is "a condition different from that of melancholia" (*Cruel* 24). This suggestion has at its heart a judgment about temporality in particular: the melancholic subject, she suggests, "desire[s] to temporize and experience the loss of an object," while it is possible to say of an eater engaged in an attachment of "cruel optimism" that "whatever the *content* of the attachment is, the continuity of its form provides something of the continuity of the subject's sense of what it means to keep on living on and to look forward to being in the world" (24). Here, attached eaters alone are configured as temporally stupid, requiring and prioritizing stability above the content of their attachments. Might not an eater with strict discipline and routine have made an equally or even more appropriate avatar of this temporality? When all bodies are archives that do not just remember their pasts but are built of these pasts, why are fat bodies given nearly mythical powers to signify traumatic experience? What dissimulated archives of eating, trauma, and construction lie behind the privileged position of the slender-normative body that is interpreted as inhabiting the present, unfettered by history? For Berlant, as discussed below, part of the way this is accomplished is through an overinvestment in excessively literal readings of the fat body.

Lateral Fat: Fat Is Stuck in the Present

Elsewhere in *Cruel Optimism*, Berlant departs from this theory of eating as a haunted way to deal with hurt in order to instead describe fat as a form of "lateral agency" that does not extend into a future. To repeat her words: "Eating adds up to something, many things: maybe the good life, but usually a well-being that spreads out for a moment, not a projection toward a future" (117). This figure of "lateral agency"—the "spreading out for a moment" that she distinguishes from "upright" agency that extends up into the future—capitalizes on the literal spreading of fat matter and uses this physiological characteristic to stand in for conceptions of weakness with regard to agency, action, and futurity. Even at a phenomenological level, this is incorrect in its presumptions about how "eating affects" or "food feelings" work; eating not only stokes the future becomings of the body but also, as a bodily, social, aesthetic, and perceptive experience, leaves the body with an archive of knowledge and feeling, just as music listened to solely for enjoyment, or sex undertaken solely for pleasure, also affect us in ways that we cannot presume to know fully. This figural "lateral" move requires readers to switch from literal fatness to metaphorical and back again, bringing along a judgment that has been accomplished by diction. Berlant may well believe that fat bodies or fat people do not extend anything useful into the future, but the fact that fat matter sometimes *spreads* is not an argument for it. (And, later in the present article, Sedgwick is seen to take apart any such simple conception of "use.") It is just as easy to say that the spread of fat matter shows that fat people's bodies extend farther into space than others or that fat moves one toward the other, both of which are interpretations loaded with "projection[s] toward a future" (Berlant, *Cruel* 117). It would be equally easy to say that slender bodies *starve* themselves of queer affect, *emaciate* the possibilities of becoming, or *narrow* the horizons of their futures, but none of these are necessarily true. The narrative manoeuvring from literal to metaphorical fat and back is itself a lateral move. It is tempting in this moment, at which Berlant has foreclosed fat futures in almost apocalyptic fashion in favour of temporal binaries that obscure fat life, to quote *Sex, or the Unbearable*. As she writes there, "Part of my resistance to apocalyptic crescendos is that they can well blot out the delicacies that got us there" (19). Indeed, gestures toward the inevitability of fat disaster or even of the fat apocalypse do "blot out" the "delicacies"—a term as loaded as a baked potato—that got us to these bodies and to this point in the history of fatness. Given the way in which Berlant discusses food and eating in the rest of her oeuvre, it is not hard to understand this use of the word *delicacies* as wholly figural, as emptied of any literal connotation of food. Is actual eating simply not "delicate" enough a matter to enter into these food-based figurations?

Conveniently, as if to show that Berlant's reading is indeed steeped in a slender-troubled abjection of fat possibility, another queer theorist has already interpreted the literally "lateral" or "sideways" spread of fat in a very different way: Kathryn Bond

Stockton, in *The Queer Child, or Growing Sideways in the Twentieth Century* (2009). For Stockton, it is precisely the queer and/or fat child's propensity for "sideways growth," his/her/their capacity to grow away from "the stature of straightness," that allows that child to grow into a different future (20). This is an unsurprising idea for those of us whose fatness disqualified us from heteronormative gazes early in life, which is a mode of childhood queerness less acknowledged than many others. In turn, we seldom understand the drive to pathologize and normativize fat children's bodies as a new mode of forcing queer bodies extinct.

While Berlant discusses fat as a ghost of trauma that manifests belatedly, Stockton analyses representations of fat ghosts: the actual body of a fat teen hanging from a noose in *The Hanging Garden*. As I show with Sedgwick, Stockton reads the fat ghost as a node of queer affect and temporality; in her words, the image of the fat teen hanging gives the audience "a moving suspension at the crossroads of adulthood" (21). Berlant's fat ghost is fat itself, coming to get a heretofore slender person, while Stockton's ghost is the visible effect of a fat past and the violence that that particular fat past endured, or not. In any case, by finding much to admire in "sideways growth," Stockton shows that fat's "spread" can indeed be co-opted for purposes besides attaching to a future.

A 2014 advertisement produced by Change4Life (a collaboration between the UK Department of Health, Cancer Research UK, Diabetes UK, and the British Heart Foundation) summarizes the stakes of this temporal mode of lateral agency: a young white boy sits lifelessly playing video games, with large bold letters above him: "RISK AN EARLY DEATH, JUST DO NOTHING." Another ad shows a small white girl contemplating a cupcake. As in Berlant, intertwined conceptions of agency and temporality are routed through images of laziness and eating: eating and its pleasures, as well as those of video gaming, are regarded as "doing nothing." This may sound sensible, but consider the following: the ad would certainly not work if it were to feature an equally sedentary activity that better aligns with normative family values, such as a "family games night," a "girls' night in," or a marathon of football viewing. This is not to say anything in favour of or against sedentary lives; rather, it is to point out that the strong sense of action and agency attributed to normative modes of health depends on a juxtaposition with eating and fat as "doing nothing," as only a "lateral" agency. In this rhetoric, fat people do not just have a weak ability to do "healthy" things; we have only a weak ability *to do*.

In Berlant's portions of *Sex, or the Unbearable*, this simple notion of fat being unable to *do* much becomes a trend of interpreting fat as not able to *signify* much. In the book's analysis of Miranda July's 2005 film, *Me and You and Everyone We Know*, the "gestures of feeling" and unsettled relations that Berlant champions rely specifically on images of fat and of fatty foods (22), a crucial factor that she elides. In the film, two young boys of colour have a cyber-flirtation with a white adult woman (an art curator), which ends up focusing on the boys' anal-erotic image of "poop" being passed between "butts" forever. While much is made of the poop in Berlant and Edelman's dialogic text, the same cannot be said for the following food and fat moments. As Berlant writes, "Before there is a relation durable enough to become event there are the gestures of feeling that are never fully absent from intimacy's long middle. Robby gets curious. He wants to know if the woman likes bologna; Peter asks her if she's got big bosoms" (22). Perhaps the "middle" of this intimacy is not "long" but instead round, or gelatinous, or chubby! In any case, the "gestures of feeling" of which Berlant speaks are, precisely, intimate questions about the curator's tastes in food and about her sexualized fat flesh ("bosoms"). That such exploratory affective gestures are expressed as desires for food and fat signifies that eating and being composed of fat are the matters through which relations could be made differently; in other words, food and fat are the unique figures (of figure) through which gestures of feeling are made, "without a mutually agreed-on idiom of optimistic misrecognition like identity or love" (21). It is fat that makes the queer affect of the scene possible, just as it is food that makes poop (whether passed between butts or not) possible.

More important, as the scene continues to unfold, it is on the precise possibility of the fat body that the excitement and unsettledness of the scene's queer relations depend. That is, as Berlant puts it, the young boys "do not even know that the writer is a 'she' because, as Peter points out, 'she's probably a man ... a fat guy with a little wiener,' or something else, as 'everyone just makes stuff up on these things,' these chat rooms" (21). To maintain the fantastical element of their online encounter, the boys summon spectres of fat gender-liars (where "little wiener" seems to go naturally with "fat guy"). The spectre of fat gender-crossing does not pose risk or create fear for the boys; it does not cause them to give up on the connection; on the contrary, the attractive tenuousness of the connection they have made remains exciting *because* a fat man might be writing to them. Here the small "wiener," which is a short step from the "bologna" about which Robby is curious, operates as yet another fatty connector to the unknown, this time to literal fat embodiment. Berlant praises the "nonknowledge" of the conversation's participants, and she suggests that this "nonknowledge" means that they share no illusions about truly knowing the other to whom they speak; nonknowledge is part of "becom[ing] non-sovereign in a different way" (21). In this scene, the nonknowledge pivots meaningfully between fat man or bosomed woman, or between wiener and bologna. These mechanically separated meats and the technologically (dis)connected bodies that they signify are the unnamed material figures through which Berlant's reading flows.

When her fat temporalities and elisions are taken together, it is clear that Berlant's fat is both a ghost from the past and an effect to be experienced in the future, even though it also lacks the signifying capacity to project toward a future or to constitute the unsettled relations Berlant imagines in *Sex, or the Unbearable*. Fat is not "present" to Berlant, or might we suggest instead that Berlant is not able to be present to fat? What feelings and habits does this performed and repeated denial of fat presence and futurity both validate and reinforce for what queer theory must finally name and recognize as the *form* of the slender-normative subject? In the absence of slender-normative desires and anxieties, in the absence of the need to abject fat matter and fat bodies, in the absence of the compulsion to play a never-ending game of *fort/da* on the scale, what affective room becomes available to fat, and what will we do with it?

Refuse, Reuse, Recycle: "The Use of Being Fat"

In contrast to the cultural texts exhibited above, Sedgwick's "The Use of Being Fat" invests heavily in fat presents and fat presence. In this poem, readers witness a recursive fat moment into which we ourselves are folded as readers. I suggest that this fat-enfolding of the reader could be a model for future considerations of how to build fat encounters between text and reader, where "fat" may refer more to affect than to body size. After all, most of us "feel fat" these days; why not put this affective experience to better use than public self-flagellation? In addition to developing a theory of the fat present, then, an underlying methodological question here is this: how can a reader become involved with a queer-fat reading encounter? To begin, here is the poem in its entirety:

> I used to have a superstition that
> there was this use to being fat:
> no one I loved could come to harm enfolded in my touch—
> that lot of me would blot it up,
> the rattling chill, night sweat or terror.
> I've learned that I was wrong.
> Held, even held
> they withdraw to the secret
> scenes of their unmaking.
> But then I think
> it is true they turn away inside.
> It feels so like refusal
> maybe still there is something to my superstition. (*Fat Art* 15)

With a poem this succinct, it is necessary to dispense with the common-sense interpretation it may invite. This reading might proceed like this: "I *used* to think there was some *point* to being fat. I thought fat could protect my cherished others when they were sick. But fat can't protect them; they still die. But, well—

when they turn away, *I* feel rejected. So maybe my fat protects *me*. Maybe there is some point of fat—to protect me from feeling refused." This reading is possible only if the reader consents to normative ideas about fat; Sedgwick, as I show, does not. For this common-sense reading to cohere, fat must be seen as a failed protector of *others* and of oneself. This interpretation therefore relies on the well-trod belief, one that Berlant echoes, that fat may be understood as a way to pack on protection from a society in favour of one's social withdrawal—a pre-emptive strike against an inevitably hurtful society, accomplished via backward-appearing desires to "cushion" such blows. Indeed, as Berlant describes one of her primary text's protagonists, "Obesity and ugliness create a force field around her, seeming to neutralize what, in those 'gatherings of the normally proportioned,' might come from others—curiosity or attachment" (*Cruel* 28). One immediate response: as many readers may know, fat neither shields nor hides oneself, neither dulls one's senses nor makes one invisible or impervious to connection, disappointment, and other feelings. As Gilman points out, this notion that fat is a protector that dulls feeling is a relic of nineteenth-century Anglophone equations of fat with "coarseness of feeling," "insensitivity of emotional response," and with a general affective "impairment," which are all equations that Gilman argues have their basis in the age-old idea that "fat people are stupid" and are therefore less responsive or, in other words, less capable of feeling—of, in other words, being present or projecting presence (*Fat* 45–46). Given that Sedgwick's poem is so thick with emotion, and given that her work on theoretical fatness focuses on feeling in particular, that hermeneutic makes little sense as an approach to Sedgwick's poem.

Reading this poem as a theory of fat presence, temporality, and feeling is far more in line with Sedgwick's abiding interests and with the poem's subtext. Sedgwick's temporalities, culled by critics from other texts, can be witnessed here. Stephen Barber and David Clark, for instance, argue in their introduction to *Regarding Sedgwick* that a "persistent present" underlies the "queer temporality" of Sedgwick's work (8). By this, they mean that "queer" becomes a "continuing moment" that constantly disrupts regular linear temporality while also troubling the body's felt habits or tendencies. As they put it, Sedgwick's "queer temporality ... is at once indefinite and virtual but also forceful, resilient, undeniable ... a crossing of temporality with force" (8). We can understand this to mean, in part, that Sedgwick's work generates in the reader a felt disorientation from linear time.[8] "The Use of Being Fat" is a textbook case of this "persistent present," with its affect-loaded and dizzying temporal mode. In these folds of time, the speaker "used to have a superstition" "but then ... think[s]" otherwise, only to end by reasserting the original thought, but provisionally and with a different feeling: "maybe still there is something to my superstition." The persistent present of fat feeling keeps remaking itself here by returning with difference to condition a new moment. Instead of being read into a traumatic past or deathlike future, fat keeps reinstating itself by repeating with a twist: fat is not a "chronic" condition here but is instead a chronic interruption to any stable sense of feeling. It is anything but a layer of protection that makes one not present to feeling or the world.

A careful reading of the poem's tenses reveals at least six folds of time, italicized here: it is a *turn* to refusal that is a *retrospective reclaiming* of a *memory* of a *superstition*. Layers of temporal distance are enfolded in the immediate presence of a hug; folds of time become actual folds of fat that both perform the singular event of each hug and also contain the bodily memories that make these hugs into a chronicle. This translation of words into fat is very much in keeping with Sedgwick's own understanding of her writing as sustenance and as fat; as Jason Edwards points out, when "discussing her long, incomplete, narrative poem, 'The Warm Decembers,' Sedgwick pondered the text's 'swollen proportions'" while "she also appetisingly described her haikus as 'fat, buttery condensation[s]'" (99–100). This last figuration is another example of how one might understand the contingency of the figuration of fat in ways other than Berlant's sense of "congealed" hurt. As Sedgwick already thinks of her poetic works in particular *as fat*, a reading of this poem as performatively fat has delicious precedent; the temporally folded body *of* the poem enfolds the reader just as the body *in* the poem enfolds the other to whom it is attached affectively. To remake a familiar fat insult: even the folds of this poem have folds! While Sedgwick's fatty metaphors here rely on similar slippages between bodily figure and literary figure, some crucial offerings she makes in her "figurings of figure" are to link ostensibly temporary fat to the permanence of text; to use metaphor in such a way that guides the reader to view fattiness as luscious and present; and to make fat into a performative matter that requires the participation, via enfolding, of the reader.

To extend this last point: in the form of a folded fat poem, the reader is not delivered to any synthesized next step because distinctions such as forward or backward and inside or outside are suspended. As such, the reader hangs out in a present that nonetheless keeps happening. It is necessary to remember that one of Berlant's overarching moves in *Cruel Optimism* is to critique what she calls the "stretched-out present" of constant-crisis culture. Sedgwick, however, shows that rather than a stretched-out present in which nothing ever arrives, we might instead live in a "persistent present" in which immediacy and contact are possible, and in which the ever-deferment of futurity is best represented not by the chronic condition of "obesity" but instead by the persistence of fat to survive, to grow, to occur, to fold, or, in other words, to be present (Barber and Clark 8). For Barber and Clark, Sedgwick's "persistent present" is best characterized as a queer temporality; we can add that it is literal fat that is the occasion for and generator of this persistence, despite opposing "figures of figure" from Berlant.

In contrast to Berlant's sense of fat as an unfeeling protective layer, then, the main event of Sedgwick's poem is a fat feeling that recurs and changes. The event of the poem is an immediate, embracing assemblage of bodies that, when becoming something new together, produce the feeling and direction of "refusal." As the poem reads, the friends or lovers or others being hugged "turn away inside. / It feels so like refusal." Such "turns" and the "refusal" they make are complex temporal figures, as Heather Love shows in *Feeling Backward* (2007). There she argues that a *turn* in literature may be most usefully understood as a literal and metaphorical refusal to face forward by prioritizing futurity above all. For Sedgwick, this goes a step farther: the fat of this queerly turning temporality blurs or even breaks down the boundaries of the human subject. Indeed, in addition to the multiply folded bodies and times of the poem (which, to repeat myself, already muddy spatiotemporal binaries such as past or present and inside or outside), the subjectivities of the huggers are made ambiguous. Instead of "he" or "she," Sedgwick uses the nongendered plural pronoun "they," a choice that suggests that the poem's scene, seemingly a highly unique and intimate one, has already been repeated before its story *of chronicity itself* is told here; "they," the speaker's partners in hugging, become an indeterminate and indeterminately gendered series, rather than one or many unique bodies or people. (Although "they" could indeed refer to just one person in 2017, this was not the case in 1994.) This implication of recurrence, and its attendant impossibility of definitively pinning down any subject in the poem, is vital to the poem's openness and persistence. It leaves the attentive reader with many questions: does the subject turn away from the speaker despite the hug, from the illness because of the hug's strength, or toward the illness despite the hug? Does the turn "inside" refer to inside the hug, inside the illness, inside oneself, or into a privileged interior that excludes the speaker? If so, doesn't the entanglement of fat and temporal folds confound this architecture? Is the speaker's hug refused, her fatness, her protection, or her superstition? In these enfolded ambiguities, a "turn" to "refusal" occurs, but the agency of any such turn—a subjective location for feeling—is not clearly situated. In this sense, fat in this poem becomes a matter of connection and assemblage rather than a matter of attempted withdrawal from society; fat becomes a connective tissue through which queer acts of refusal are generated together, even if painfully. But let us presume for a moment that Sedgwick's own life of witnessing is implicated in the poem; here fat becomes the matter through which her attachments to AIDS and death *are felt*; fat connects her to, rather than withdraws her from, the pain and memory of death, and connects her to the possibility of persisting, which, in a poem about recurrence, is not the same as "moving on." If readers can fairly imagine the speaker hugging friends or lovers who may die of AIDS, then the poem's contradictory movements are especially novel and poignant: fat and AIDS are finally connected *not* through a hyperbolic juxtaposition of greed versus illness or fat versus very thin but instead through fat envelopment, persistence, and the painful refusal of all bodies to persist infinitely.

Given the sense of pain the reader finds in this poem, it is necessary to ask about the qualities of this feeling of "refusal." This is a quintessentially temporal question and a queer question; Love calls refusal "a form ... of queer negativity ... that we have yet to consider because [its] connection to any recognizable form of politics is too tenuous" (137). What is at stake here, then, is the question of whether refusal has any use for the future. This is Sedgwick's question as well; recall the title of the poem! Love goes on to suggest that the imperative to "alchemize queer suffering" into something *useful* is to, by adopting a too utilitarian approach, make suffering into happiness prematurely (137). Sedgwick also refuses the imperative to be positive and productive, but a key difference between these thinkers exists in their respective spatial figurings of refusal as a possible use. Sedgwick's turn is not around or backward; as the line reads, "they turn away inside." While, for Love, these turns away from the future are nostalgic and are mired in loss and trauma, my reading of Sedgwick's turn configures a fat turn or refusal as a turn toward undoing and remaking, what readers of Gilles Deleuze and Félix Guattari might understand as an involutionary turn.[9] This is an enfolding turn inward, a creative turn, and a continuous, repetitive turn that is the very opposite of the marches forward or backward presupposed by narratives of evolution or by the narratives of degeneration and decay that are attributed to fatness. The refusal created in the recurring fat assemblage of this poem can therefore be recast as acts of re-fusing, as repeatedly interrupted and reconnecting flesh and feeling. The persistence of fat re-fusing across the boundaries of fat, queer, and AIDS becomes for the speaker a not-painless collaborative refuge not *from* but *in* a world that regards many of us as so much refuse, bodies as good as quickly or slowly dead.

This emphasis on refusal may well sound excessively negative or reactionary rather than generative. Berlant and Edelman, however, view negativity as "the relentless force that unsettle[s] the fantasy of sovereignty" (vii). I agree with this view but find it troubling that Berlant does not apply the following statement to her considerations of fat: negativity's "effects ... are not just negative, since negativity unleashes the energy that allows for the possibility of change" (vii-viii). While fat, read by Berlant as negative, does unleash energy, it is unclear why she offers no ideas about how this negativity could "allow ... for the possibility of change." Surely there are other changes, other ways that fatness (even if one is determined to define it as wholly negative) can and does generate change in ways that override the subject's feigned sovereignty. Inasmuch as uncontrollable appetites for food are one of the key images, if not *the* key image, of an "encounter with non-sovereignty" in our cultural imagination, it is indeed curious that Berlant shrinks from food and fat as an exemplar of this ethic (vii).

In the above paragraphs, as in the title of Sedgwick's poem itself, it is clear that "use" value is often the unchecked mode of assessment when it comes to discussing fat people and our stake in the future. For Berlant, fat is more useful when it can figure as a tidy antithesis to thriving, not when it may question the modes of heroic agency implicit in the fat figurations she uses so often. By this, I mean that while Berlant seeks alternatives to heroic agency, her fat figurations derive from common-sense notions about fat that are underpinned by the idea that there is nothing more heroic, personal, or agential than losing weight. Being fat is now treated as one of the most serious failures of will or agency that a person can commit, yet Berlant's figurations leave that bodily project unmarked while piling figural weight onto weighty bodies. Fat is indeed very "useful" to Berlant, but only in particular ways.

Even though queer people are accustomed to critiquing the reduction of bodies to economic signs, such rhetoric and the "value" judgments on which it is based do survive in queer theory. For instance, Barber and Clark state correctly that Berlant, in "Two Girls, Fat and Thin," understands the hunger of a fat person as an "allegory of insatiability" and as a figure for "maddening absence" (32). This figuring leaves a fat person wondering why it is fat people and fat hunger in particular that carry such metaphorical weight with regard to the constitutive lack of the human subject. Again, might not the cruelly optimistic and insatiable desire for interminable weight *loss* with its always brand-new magic bullets, new clothes, new foods, and new exercise regimens make an even more compelling figuration of lack? In a reading that presumes normative notions of "use" and "economies" of the body, bodies, fat and otherwise, can only be simple symptoms of ideologies rather than ambiguous refusers of the very symptoms they may show. It is in this way that Berlant's "slow death" focuses on "the destruction of bodies by capital" while configuring as false consciousness the ways that eaters, among others, attempt to keep living within and during destruction (*Cruel* 108).[10] This is not to say that bodies are sovereign and capable of living outside destructive systems, or to valorize any sense of pure agency or self-determination; rather, it is to show that *how* we choose to see ambiguous flashes of agency within capitalism matters. Unlike Berlant's more unilateral sense of destruction and the false consciousness of cruelly optimistic attachments, Sedgwick's ambiguous bodies act together and separately in inscrutable ways that defy normative conceptions of sovereignty and agency, but still persist and refuse, even with pain and with life conditions not of their choosing. Sedgwick's poem, then, announces itself as one about "use" that ends with an act of "refuse," which my reading rearticulates as re-fuse, or fusing with others again. Bodies are undergoing "destruction" in Sedgwick's poem, but her reparative mode leads her to experiment with what can be made, "used" and "re-fused," in the fat present, with the willingness of the reader to read fat in a similarly reparative mode.

Elsewhere in her oeuvre, Sedgwick laments the reduction of fat to use value and economic rhetoric in a way that encourages us to further rethink "use" in this poem. For example, as she writes in *A Dialogue on Love*, "the issue was never fat or not fat, but—given fat—worth something or worth nothing?" (68). Even at this moment in which Sedgwick is affirming that she "did identify with that sense of myself [as fat]," it is the question of worth and value that defines her self-conception. Her dialogue with Michael Moon, "Divinity: A Dossier, a Performance Piece, a Little-Understood Emotion," is the work that most forcefully complicates the way in which fat bodies are put to "work" as economic metaphor. In language that echoes my doubling of re*fuse* with *re*fuse, Moon suggests there that "the fat woman's work of emblematizing the circulatory embolisms of a culture might be said to fall into the economic category not of either production or reproduction but rather of waste management" (30). In such a culture, waste management and waist management become the same thing. The labour and capital that one invests in one's slender body are not just signs of personal mastery but of economic responsibility; as Sedgwick puts it when discussing Dickens's loathing of fat women, "not her bodily opulence but her bodily meagerness comes to be the guarantee of the woman of substance" (30). This moralizing of bodily traits is the result, Sedgwick suggests, of reading the fat body "phobogenically," as the "literal image of exploitative accumulation" (30). By invoking "phobogenics," Sedgwick traces the purportedly neutral figuration of fatness as capitalist accumulation par excellence to a suspect and dissimulated affect, to a *fear* or "phobia" of fatness.

Ironically, however, fat people are often excluded from the capitalist economy as which we are so often figured. As Sedgwick and Moon suggest, the most serious insult one can deliver in a capitalist culture is to say to a would-be consumer that "there's nothing here for you to spend your money on" (14). When we consider that many or most fat people have great difficulty finding clothes to wear, we see the true strength of phobic fat affect; after all, when are capitalist marketplaces not flexible enough to find a way to profit from such a large market? Fat people are treated to "the primal denial ... of a stake in the symbolic order"; you cannot accumulate because you *are* accumulation; or "who and what you are means that there's nothing here for you" (14). Again, fat people are made to inhabit a paradox; as Sedgwick and Moon put it, we are both "a disruptive embolism in the flow of economic circulation" and the "very emblem of that circulation" (15–16). These paradoxical conceptions of "use" and circulation hinge, once again, on fraught fantasies about fat temporality; fat bodies are interpreted as having unfairly stockpiled resources, as having planned for the wrong future. This is an ironic state of discourse given that fat people are also barred from investing in fat futures and from accumulations in terms of clothes and access to other money-spending projects. (This is not to worship at the slender feet of consumer goods, to be sure, but clothes, for instance, are definitely something required to maintain the semblance of a subjectivity!) The literal denial of access to the marketplace of subjectivity cannot help but confirm for the fat subject that she or he or they cannot access cultural fantasies of futurity.

It is in both (1) this highly charged discourse about use, accumulation, and capital and (2) Sedgwick's long-standing urge to refuse the contours of this discourse that the poem's use of the word *lot* can be best understood. Why, in a poem that queers the idea of fat "use" and temporality, might Sedgwick describe her fat body as "that lot of me"? By talking about fat as "a lot," Sedgwick translates the economic rhetoric of fat-as-excess into one of fat-as-abundance. By using a word that captures the general ethos of capitalist accumulation—that is, having a lot—Sedgwick opens to the fat reader the possibility that our discursive position vis-à-vis accumulation could be rewritten. In a generous reading, *lot* could remind us of the now-obsolete European unit of weight measurement that, until last century, was equal to the literal mass of one unit of the local currency. Here the double meaning of *pound* assumes its full meaning; mass and wealth were truly transposable. However, since the poem features a "turn" and a "refusal," this "lot" of fatness might well remind us of one of Love's main examples of the queer turn from futurity: the biblical Lot, whose wife disobeyed divine advice, turned to look back on Sodom, and was transformed into a pillar of *salt*, the representative "sin" of which has now shifted from greedy sodomy to greedy gluttony and cholesterol. This "Lot" lives with the staid outcomes of a rule-breaking woman who turns toward *the* locale of queerness and punishment, and must also live with the fact that he offers his daughters to Sodomites to prevent his male house guests from being raped. Reciprocally, Sedgwick's "lot" is also an archive of gendered unruliness, of involutionary turns, and of her celebration of anal pleasures. Most significant, given that the biblical Lot also reminds us of Sedgwick's penchant for connecting queer and Jewish thought, it should be emphasized that the Hebrew etymology of Lot's name is the verb *lut*, "to wrap closely or to envelope."[11] *Lot* queers the economic rhetoric of fatness, connects us to queerness and Jewish history, and, yes, even captures the recurring enfolding/enveloping hug of Sedgwick's poem. One derivative of *lut*, the masculine noun *lat*, takes us directly to Sedgwick's ongoing theorization of what it means to *know* a fat body; the word also carries resonances of secrecy. It is no coincidence, then, that when discussing the "closet of size," Sedgwick and Moon ask a question that retains this definition of fat-as-lots: "What kind of secret can the body of the fat woman keep?" (26–27). People tend to receive fat bodies in public as ones that cannot help but give up the truth of their habits and morals, but via Sedgwick and Moon's theories, it becomes clear that in Sedgwick's poem, being a "lot" of person can create new secret worlds into which to turn recursively. Being a lot can mean new folds of fat assemblage to inhabit, ones that may not be perceived by those who expect to be able to read the bodies of others at a distance. The poem's fat folds, which we can think of as the poem's "lots," or its "hugs-as-secrets," eschew any two-dimensional understanding of the body as a matter of surface or depth, a binary that persists in queer theory, to instead demand that a queer reader feel out the less determinate matter of shape when involving oneself with a text. The root of *lot* in *lat* also brings us to a radical revision of Berlant's "lateral agency." The lat of the fat body's secrets is the same lat of *lateral*. The difference between Berlant and Sedgwick becomes clear: Berlant's "lat" moves fatness to the periphery, taking it sideways out of futurity, while Sedgwick's "lat" makes the fat body a "lot" and sees potential, pain, and ambiguous relations in the fat present and its envelopments.

Conclusion: Slender Trouble

This article has developed a queer theory of fat presents/presence in three ways. First, fat presence was defined as a mode of temporality that refuses to be pulled between traumatic pasts and slender futures; second, Sedgwick's particular fat temporality was seen to function in the mode of recursion or involution rather than of evolution or degeneration, which are temporal terms often used to validate treatment of both queers and fat people; and, finally, in this "refusal" to "face" or be ruled by a deferred and ever-slenderer future, fat presence was imbued with the possibility of casting off the economic rhetorics of personal investment and accumulation in favour of being a "lot." These fat temporal modes refuse, in turn, the popular fat temporalities with which the article began: fat *Nachträglichkeit*, fat as temporally lateral, future anterior fat, and fat as slow death. Queer theory cares about temporality; this alone is an argument for the relevance of disturbing the temporalities attributed to body size, in general, and to attend to the fat temporalities of an emblematic queer theorist, in particular.[12] However, I conclude by bringing this article's ideas to bear on three matters.

First, I return to the reproductive futurist magazine covers with which I began: it is indeed possible, even necessary and queer, to find ways to experience and to address fat children as something other than symptoms of their own negated futures. Indeed, fat moves the child's body outside heteronormative desirability, which can give a child the appealing if difficult opportunity to craft affective habits with other materials, in other directions, and perhaps on different timelines. This possibility, long known to be an exciting one to many fat queers, is even recognized indirectly by those who wish to fight unambiguously against the very existence of fat children. For instance, a group called Children's Healthcare of Atlanta launched a campaign called "Strong4Life," in which black-and-white photos of sad fat children are emblazoned with warnings, a form that gently recalls the aesthetic of cigarette packets. One young white girl, arms crossed, is labelled with the following line: "It's hard to be a little girl / if you're not." This warning is laced with the threat of fat's possible interruption to the heteronormative life trajectory. As such, it gets to the heart of Stockton's proposal that fat children may queer the body; not being a "little" girl does indeed break the form of the "little girl" as a particularly heteronormative avatar of childhood. The genders and desires of fat children have a special possibility of growing "sideways" as well.[13] Queer theory's ongoing work on temporality, often routed through considerations of children, must take up fatness if it is to be attentive to what is probably now the most frequent bodily trait through which children are made heterosexually legible tokens of a normative future.

Second: how, in the clearest terms, does this article provide an alternative to Berlant's *Cruel Optimism*? If we were to accept that we live in a cruelly optimistic world in which affective attachment is antagonistic to one's flourishing, the question would remain: how do we, as attaching bodies, develop modes of attachment that are neither cruel nor optimistic, that work against the capitalist and falsely conscious modes of which Berlant writes, and that view attachment as both inevitable and, sometimes, as a tool for flourishing? Sedgwick's response is to let a painful fat embrace fold and unfold in chronic fashion, with neither optimism about cure (and certainly not weight loss) nor pessimism about the usefulness of a hug between pained and limited bodies. Put differently, the alternative Sedgwick offers is one that eschews cruel pessimism without falling into myths of neoliberal fat dignity or of restored agency or of any form of self-presence being complete; indeed, the poem's hug persists; it is a pained attachment that nonetheless does something else, too. Earlier, I suggested that Sedgwick's reparative mode is enacted between reader, author, and text; still earlier, I argued that readers are drawn by the text into an enfolded and folding world of fat affect. Now, if it is possible to rethink the word *repair*, another step is added to this fat hermeneutic. *Repair*, in addition to being a noun of cure, is also a verb of persistent action; the "repairs" of this persistent hug, while they do not repair anyone in the sense of protection or cure, are indeed the scene of collaborative repairing, which also becomes recursive re-pairing. A homonym of *repair* gives us another sense: when one "repairs to the kitchen" or "repairs to the boudoir," one imagines an old place to which one intends to return anew, after an event. This hug, then, is reparative—but without cure, cruelty, or even optimism. The poem's pained attachments do not ascend or aspire to any *telos* but their own failure, a failure to protect that becomes a success as an assemblage of bodies and readers, a success that may depart from the will of the acts' doers.

In *Sex, or the Unbearable*, Berlant links repair and temporality in a useful way, something she does not do throughout her works on fat:

> Most fantasies of repairing what's broken ... are ways of staying bound to the possibility of staying bound to a world whose terms of reciprocity—whether in intimate personal or political idioms—are not entirely in anyone's control and which yet can be changed by a radical collective refusal of normative causality, of the normative relation of event to effect. (20)

While I agree with this, the present article shows that it is quite necessary to refuse (via Sedgwick's "refusal") the "normative causality" of Berlant's fat-focused oeuvre, the causality in which certain traumas cause certain congealed bodies. This refusal is also a refusal of Berlant's "normative relation of event to effect," in which she traps fat in past events and future effects (20). This is all to underline the following: while Berlant certainly does exploit fat via the promulgation of normative figurations of it, any such "misrepresentation" of fat bodies is not the main event here. Rather, it is Berlant's failure to imagine how bodies, big and small, can attach and flourish—even while dying—via routes other than falsely conscious optimistic models of pure subjectivity or the accumulation of capital, via routes that do not remain stuck exclusively in traumatic pasts or impossible futures.

Third, how might the development of a fat present/presence influence considerations of queer hermeneutics and queer method, which are receiving renewed energy at the moment? I suggest that one overarching change is especially significant in light of this article. As Sedgwick and Butler shifted critical focus from gay and lesbian inclusion to an affective architectonics of heteronormative subjectivities, we too must move from questions of the inclusion, dignity, and mis/representation of fat subjectivities to instead notice and refuse to settle for the styles, tendencies, and melancholies of the normative and heretofore unmarked category with regard to fatness: the slender. We must trace out the form and structure of the slender-normative subject and its reading practices. Many questions come to mind as next steps. What are slender hermeneutics and by what affective debilities are they motivated? Do the affective habits of the slender-normative subject conflict with queer flourishing? Does a thin hermeneutic produce "flat" affect? If Sedgwick is correct to trace suspicious interpretations of fat bodies back to "phobogenic" origins, then what is the quality of the fat fear of the slender-normative subject? What injuries are concealed by one's abjection of fat through figuration? (Here we can remember the digestive and edible scenes of Butler's other becoming shit, and of Kristeva's gagging at the skin that grows atop milk; abjection is already about wrong kinds of eating and indigestion.) If queer theory has encouraged us to see man-woman sexual partnerships as potentially queer in their cultural meanings and outcomes, and to see many same-sex relationships as homonormative, then when and how shall we know if our readings and bodies are "fat" or "slender"? Sedgwick insists that fat bodily contact, persistence, being a "lot," rethinking the "usefulness" of bodies, a willingness to involve oneself with fat matter, and developing reparative modes of reading and feeling are key questions in any such determination. "Fat" and "thin" do not, then, become floating signifiers or simply a new spin on queer/heteronormative; indeed, the fat body, even in its figurations, remains present for Sedgwick and for the shift in queer theoretical reading that I propose here by way of conclusion. What other interpretive and affective possibilities may proliferate, right now, in the encroaching depths of our labouring and sweaty folds of flesh? Let such a question become the material of our fat future-to-come. Can the gift of that fat future be received, in due time?

Notes

1 This chapter first appeared as Lucas Crawford, "'Slender Trouble': From Berlant's Cruel Figuring of Figure to Sedgwick's Fat Presence,"

GLQ: A Journal of Lesbian and Gay Studies, 23, no. 4 (2017): 447–72. Reprinted with permission. The author has added the foreword for this collection. When this article was published in *GLQ*, Lauren Berlant used she/her pronouns in both personal and professional realms. As many learned after their death in 2021, Berlant had begun to use they/them pronouns in the latter realm.

2 Readers of Jacques Derrida will recognize the "future anterior" from *Of Grammatology*. Here Derrida shows the troubling way in which we project ourselves into the future and see our present as merely a future past.

3 After all, in "Divinity," Sedgwick identifies, with "abjection and defiance," "as a gay man," while her (his?) co-author Michael Moon refers to himself (herself?) "as a fat woman" (215).

4 Gilman's chapter "Chinese Obesity" in *Fat: A Cultural History of Obesity* shows the nuanced way in which it has become almost a point of national pride to adopt Western models of public health and disease, especially if the disease itself may be represented as Western in origin. As he suggests, "China, like America, is suffering from a new epidemic, but one that documents its modernity; no model of oriental, primitive infectious diseases here. Rather, a claim of 'invasion from the West.' However, the negative aspects of the new economy can be confronted through the importation of models of obesity from Western public health. Obesity and its treatment may both be understood as parts of a system of modernization, with all the pitfalls recognized and the 'cure' in sight" (163).

5 As an anonymous peer reviewer pointed out, the "liberty" to be slender (i.e., the liberty to choose something culturally obligatory) is so much easier for many people to understand as liberty than, say, the liberty to eat to excess, the liberty to look and grow as one wants, etc. This all brings into focus the compromised and incomplete version of agency with which we must work when discussing any kind of "liberty."

6 Doyle reports in the *Daily Mail* that between 2009 and February 2014, seventy-four fat children were forcibly removed from their families and placed in state care in the UK. Panic about fatness and its threat to Western fantasies of childhood has created a situation in which being placed in state-run institutions is regarded as a better life than a fat one. It is possible that public distrust in fat has outgrown even our most conservative trust in the family form.

7 Though Berlant's essay appears in an earlier form (Barber and Clark), I use the pagination of *Cruel Optimism* for simplicity.

[8] Ironically, Barber and Clark's description of this "persistent present" is not so different from the "chronic" temporality that Berlant mentions.

[9] Deleuze and Guattari use the term involution to refer to "evolution between heterogenous terms" (238). This word allows them to reject the sense of progress or degeneration presupposed by vocabularies of evolution or devolution. It also suggests the manner by which such changes occur; involution is not the natural march of progress but is instead the action of "involving." As they say, "Becoming is involutionary, involution is creative" (238–39). I have suggested that the bodies of Sedgwick's poem are "involved." This kind of assemblage implies a very different temporality than do common understandings of fatness because the bodies and their involvement eschew any sense of progression or regression.

[10] To witness Berlant demarcating cruelly optimistic people as a case study in false consciousness, see the following passage especially: "One more thing: sometimes, the cruelty of an optimistic attachment is more easily perceived by an analyst who observes the cost of someone's or some group's attachment to x, since often persons and communities focus on some aspects of their relation to an object/world while disregarding others" (24). While it is true that no person notices or cares about every aspect of every attachment that he, she, or they sustain, perhaps it could be said, more generously, that people prioritize the aspects of their attachments that are important to them. We may critique how people prioritize these aspects—and in this article I certainly take issue with the way that Berlant cannot perceive the affective investments of slenderness as a project—but to say that an "analyst" (Berlant?) is better suited to perceive a situation because he, she, or they are uninvested is both unfair and inaccurate. Queers know too well what happens when only voices beyond an affected group are trusted; moreover, if one sees fit to interpret and publicly comment on a topic (as Berlant does very often with regard to fat), one is likely not uninvested personally. Queer theory has shown us that heteronormative people have a great deal at stake in representations of queerness; concomitantly, the slender subject requires certain fantasies and abjections of fat. Berlant is "attached" to fat too.

[11] Any Hebrew dictionary of Hebraic names contains this description. On this occasion, I have consulted the online *Biblical Name Vault* ("The Name Lot").

[12] For works on queer temporality, see, e.g., Freeman, McCallum and Tuhkanen, and Halberstam.

[13] Ironically, the image of a parent "making" a child fat is cause for great panic and concern in Western culture, while the image of "making" a child normatively gendered and heteronormative is seen as the pinnacle of good parenting. A queer understanding of public health discourse might lead us to ask, which is more detrimental to a child's "health"? And, can we imagine that not being a "little girl"—i.e., being written out of the fantasy of innocent childhood that Edelman and others critique—might be a good queer thing indeed?

Works Cited

The Atlantic. "Fat Nation." Cover image. May, 2010.

Barber, Stephen M., and David L. Clark. "Introduction." *Regarding Sedgwick: Essays on Queer Culture and Critical Theory*, edited by Stephen M. Barber and David L. Clark, Taylor & Francis, 2002, pp. 1–45.

Berlant, Lauren. *Cruel Optimism*. Duke UP, 2011.

Berlant, Lauren, and Lee Edelman. *Sex, or the Unbearable*. Duke UP, 2013.

Butler, Judith. *Gender Trouble: Feminism and the Subversion of Identity*. Routledge, 1990.

Change4Life. "Risk An Early Death, Just Do Nothing." UK Department of Health, 2014. Original post removed. Information available at *The Guardian*, Keith Stuart, "Ban THIS sick filth?" *The Guardian*, 9 March 2009, http://www.theguardian.com/technology/gamesblog/2009/mar/09/gameculture-controversy. Accessed 15 June 2014.

Children's Healthcare of Atlanta. "It's Hard to Be a Little Girl When You're Not." 2011. Original post removed. Information available at *Huffington Post*: Emma Gray, "Georgia Anti-Obesity Ads Say 'Stop Sugarcoating" Childhood Obesity," *Huffington Post*, 3 January 2012, www.huffingtonpost.com/2012/01/03/ georgia-anti-obesity-ads-stop-sugarcoatingn1182023.html. Accessed 10 April 2013.

Deleuze, Gilles, and Félix Guattari. *A Thousand Plateaus: Capitalism and Schizophrenia*, translated by Brian Massumi. 1980. Continuum, 2004.

Derrida, Jacques. *Of Grammatology*, translated by Gayatri Chakravorty Spivak. 1976. Johns Hopkins UP, 1997.

Doyle, Jack. "More Than Seventy Morbidly Obese Children Taken into Care Due to Concerns over Their Health." *Daily Mail Online*, 28 February 2014, www.dailymail.co.uk/news/article-2569922/More-70–morbidly-obese-children-overfed-parents-taken-care.html.

Edelman, Lee. *No Future: Queer Theory and the Death Drive.* Duke UP, 2004.

Edwards, Jason. *Eve Kosofsky Sedgwick*. Routledge, 2009.

Freeman, Elizabeth. *Time Binds: Queer Temporalities, Queer Histories.* Duke UP, 2010.

Freud, Sigmund. "From the History of an Infantile Neurosis." *The Freud Reader*, edited by Peter Gay, Vintage, 1995, pp. 400–26.

Gilman, Sander L. *Fat: A Cultural History of Obesity*. Polity, 2008.

———. *Fat Boys: A Slim Volume*. Nebraska UP, 2004.

Halberstam, Judith. *In a Queer Time and Place: Transgender Bodies, Subcultural Lives*. New York UP, 2005.

Kristeva, Julia. *Powers of Horror: An Essay on Abjection*, translated by Leon Roudiez. Columbia UP, 2005.

LeBesco, Kathleen. *Revolting Bodies? The Struggle to Redefine Fat Identity*. Massachusetts UP, 2004.

Love, Heather. *Feeling Backward: Loss and the Politics of Queer History*. Harvard UP, 2007.

McCallum, E. L., and Mikko Tuhkanen, editors. *Queer Times, Queer Becomings*. State University of New York Press, 2011.

"The Name Lot in the Bible." *Biblical Name Vault*, www.abarim-publications.com/Meaning/Lot.html#.VIoxsDHF98E. Accessed 4 July 2014.

New York Times. "Animated Debate in New York State Capital? It's about Yogurt." 6 May 2014. nyti.ms/1jbqlpD.

Newsweek. "Fat World." Cover image. 2 August 2003.

Newsweek. "Feed Your Children Well." Cover image. 13 March 2010.

Sedgwick, Eve Kosofsky. *A Dialogue on Love*. Beacon, 1994.

———. *Fat Art, Thin Art*. Duke UP, 1994.

Sedgwick, Eve Kosofsky, and Michael Moon. "Divinity: A Dossier, a Performance Piece, a Little Understood Emotion." *Discourse*, vol. 13, no. 1, 1990–1991, pp. 12–39. *JSTOR*: www.jstor.org/stable/41389168.

Stockton, Kathryn Bond. *The Queer Child, or Growing Sideways in the Twentieth Century*. Duke UP, 2009.

White, Francis Ray. "Fat, Queer, Dead: 'Obesity' and the Death Drive." *Somatechnics*, vol. 2, no. 1, 2012–2013, pp. 1–17. *Edinburgh University Press Journals*: dx.doi.org/10.3366/soma.2012.0035.

———. "Fat/Trans: Queering the Activist Body." *Fat Studies*, vol. 3, no. 2, 2014, pp. 86–100. *Taylor & Francis Online*: dx.doi.org/10.1080/21604851.2014.889489.

Fat Magic: On Fatness as a Magic Show

Ameema Saeed

THERE ARE MANY SIMILARITIES between fat people and magic shows—and not just because magicians and fat people both likely had a harder time getting laid in college... There's a certain element of mystery and intrigue, with people wondering how someone fatter than them can also be more flexible than them. There's also the drama—for magic shows, it's confined to a stage, but for fat people the whole world is a stage, and the drama is a collective anti-fat bias that has started a whole *war* against obesity. Both fat people and magic shows also see their fair share of unnecessarily bedazzled outfits (have you *ever* shopped in a plus-size store?). Lastly, of course, magicians and fat people—we both have our tricks.

Even the word *fat* is magic. While *technically*, *fat* is a neutral descriptor—a word like *short*, or *blue*, or *generous*—when people say "fat," they usually mean "lazy" or "ugly" or "disgusting" or "something to be feared or hated."

Fat is a weapon: It is the swords skewering the box we're standing in; The saw that cuts us in half; The bullet we catch.

Sure, there are fewer pyrotechnics and rabbits in our lives than in a *traditional* magic show, but if you get down to it—there are a lot more similarities than you'd think.

Misdirection

Magicians are *known* for misdirection, and doctors seem to think that fat people are experts in misdirection as well. Fat people are never given the benefit of the doubt—we are seen first and foremost as fat, and that means everything else is just dramatic flair, meant to distract and misdirect. We come in for a sprained wrist or a rash, and, somehow, we always seem to leave with the thing we never knew we needed all along—*weight loss advice*.

Dating apps and online dating are two other minefields for misdirection. Fat people like us, especially fat women, have to find ways to come across as attractive and simultaneously make sure potential partners realize we're fat—lest we be accused of "catfishing." So, we feature photos that show our whole body, reference our fatness in our bios, or find ways to bring it up in conversation before we meet a potential partner for the first time. It often feels like we have to do everything in our power to disclose our fatness ahead of time, so we are not accused of misdirection. Society tells us over and over again that we need to fit into a specific mould of Eurocentric beauty standards—and none of us is exempt from this messaging, or its potentially harmful consequences. Many of us take steps to try to meet or fit into these expectations by changing aspects of the way we look, or who we are entirely. But those changes often feel loaded. Where is the line between a harmless misdirection, such as Spanx, contouring, or A-line silhouettes, and a misdirection that other people will view as more sinister?

Time and time again we're told to become something different, but how do we decide where a harmless magic trick ends, and where the lies begin?

Sleight of Hand

Sleight of hand is a term often used while performing tricks. It means a skillful deception. And like any good magician, fat people are masters of it.

My best trick as a fat person? Finding ways to take up less space—physically, socially, and visibly. On transit or planes, in the middle seat of a car, on an elevator—I somehow manage to contort and conceal myself so I can take up less space than I need to. Sometimes, even less space than the straight-sized people around me.

Fat people are already on the margins; however disabled, queer, trans, and nonbinary fat people, as well as superfat and infinitfat people (Scott) and fat Black and Indigenous people and people of colour have been taught to hide [ourselves] from an early age. Every day, our bodies seek permission just to exist, and every day, we continue to make ourselves smaller and smaller to fit into the world around us, rather than the world expanding to fit us.

Unfortunately, even that contortion, and invisibilization isn't enough for some people.

Shock and Awe

Fat people, like magicians, are very often met with surprise and incredulousness—whether from medical professionals, loved ones, or society at large. There's something about us that makes people view us through a shroud of shock and disbelief.

People view fat people as monoliths—injecting their fear of fatness, their disgust, and their hatred into hypotheses about what it means to be fat. Society views us as lazy, undesirable slobs—so when we challenge that, people lose their minds.

Society has a really hard time accepting it when fat people go against its anti-fat and reductive expectations. Fat athletes and fat people who engage in and are proficient in fitness activities, like yoga or dance, are frequently met with disbelief or shock. From thin people offering unsolicited explanations on how to use gym equipment to subtly (or unsubtly) competing with you by increasing their weights, incline, or resistance levels until they match or surpass yours—people *refuse* to accept that a fat person could be as fit as or even more fit than them, as that challenges their narrow perspectives on what it means to be fit...Leaving them wondering "what is this sorcery?"

Straight-sized people also have a hard time accepting fat people as objects of desire. With the exception of the fetishization of fat bodies—especially fat women's bodies, fat people are rarely seen as sensual, sexy, or desirable. Fat women often play a background role in the "show" that is their romance. On multiple occasions, fat women have shared their stories with me, about their thinner partners having been hit on by thin women, even right in front of them, these thinner women simply refusing to accept that a thin person would date a fat woman. Our fatphobic society has continuously told us that fat people don't deserve respect, dignity, or love. So much so, that when straight-sized people see fat folks respected, desired, or valued, they react with shock, disbelief, or outright hostility. It goes against their perceptions of ***us***.

Audience Participation

Like most magic shows, being fat involves an element of audience participation. The key difference is that for fat people, ours is unsolicited.

Something about fat bodies ***entitles*** people to comment on or police them into thinness. Fat people are marginalized not just systemically but socially as well—often through practices of dehumanization and demonization. Under the guise of "concern for [our] health"—strangers, acquaintances, and loved ones alike will find it acceptable and sometimes even their ***duty*** to give us unsolicited weight-loss or exercise advice, to comment on our eating habits or our weight, to remove things from our grocery basket or plate, or even to touch us without consent.

It's like—when you're fat, you no longer belong to yourself. You are the magician's assistant, and society is the magician, directing you, controlling you, and putting you into a box so you can change or disappear entirely. *Presto Chango!* You become a scapegoat for society—its fears, its disgust, and its failures all projected on you. You are serving as a prop, to be poked and prodded and manoeuvred and, most especially, *belittled.*

There's something heartbreaking, but also terrifying, in the way the audience comes together against us. Stomping feet, frothing at the mouth, clamouring, chanting as our fat bodies are displayed on stage: *"Cut her in half!"*

Transformation

Magicians can turn a red handkerchief green, or a rabbit into a dove, but the most impressive kind of transformation is the kind that fat people have done. We've transformed from regular people into something to be hated. There are whole systems that have made us fat. Among Canadian women, low socio-economic status has been shown to be correlated with "obesity" (Hajizadeh et al.); corporate food lobbies often hinder or prevent policies or initiatives related to increasing the amount of information about the nutritional values of foods (Crowe). Many Canadians, especially those from Black and Indigenous populations, experience food insecurity due to a lack of affordable access to nutritious food and/or other basic necessities (Tarasuk and Mitchell). However, despite all of these collective societal failings—we have somehow transformed fat people into the real villains, the failing bodies in our society.

Fatness is seen as a moral failure. We view fat bodies as a disease—something to be demonized, and "fixed." Within society, fatness is seen as our great shame. Whenever fat people are discussed, we are labelled society's most pressing health crisis, and the conversation is dominated by rhetoric on how we can (and should) lose weight.

It's like every conversation we have with our doctors, our families, our friends is centred on how to change ourselves: how to lose weight, what not to eat, whether or not we've thought any more about weight-loss surgery. We are an object, a moral failure, a body to be "cut in half."

Fat people are always the problem. The solution is always to shrink ourselves. To harm ourselves. To cut inside our soft flesh and remove parts of ourselves. We are somehow exempt from being treated as human...And that's *quite* a trick, if I do say so myself.

Invisibility

For my next trick, I will make fat people disappear!

Despite being *larger than life*, fat people embody something that makes us and our needs invisible. We are so often talked *about*, and so rarely spoken *to*. As if we're manic pixie dream girls, it feels like people are more consumed by the *idea* of us than the reality.

The "war on obesity" is framed as a question of health, yet it often seems to neglect the many social and systemic barriers that have led to weight gain or poor nutrition, and only focuses on addressing the results (fat people). You would think, if people actually cared about the health of others, there would be more of a fight against the systems that have made us (or kept us) fat. There has been a slight cultural shift as of late, with Canada's new obesity guidelines focusing on the root causes more than judgment-based weight-loss advice (Wharton et al.). While this is a start, there is a great deal of cultural unlearning and social change that still needs to occur: for example, an increased push to raise the minimum wage and increased access to affordable nutritious foods, as well as increased access to medical care by professionals who treat fat people fairly and respectfully. Maybe *then* people will stop talking *about* fat people and start talking *to* us instead, so as to better understand and address our needs and our concerns.

Navigating the health care system as a fat person is a lesson in resilience. Doctors and nurses often treat you poorly or talk about you and your weight (even when they know you can hear them), displaying harmful but normalized anti-fat bias. You are diagnosed "fat" before anything else. Even though fatness does not automatically equal being "unhealthy," doctors frequently dismiss the concerns of fat people, often attributing medical issues to weight without further testing. Even if medical professionals wanted to do more testing, many diagnostic tools aren't built with fat bodies in mind. Additionally, fat people are often refused care or medical procedures ***until*** they lose a certain amount of weight. There are even multiple medications that don't work on people over a certain weight. I can't help but feel that fat people are an afterthought. When we look behind the curtain of the show we call our health care system, the dismissal of fat people's health and our needs is merely another trick of the trade.

Fat Magic

We fat people are a magic show, but we are so rarely seen as *magic.*

Our bodies are weaponized against us. When we dare to be

joyful in our fatness and we have the audacity to love ourselves, we are told we are glorifying sickness. That our fat bodies are a problem to be fixed.

We often find ourselves caught in complicated feats of balance. If we want to lose weight, we worry we're betraying the fat and body-positivity communities. If we *don't* want to lose weight, we're worried we're propagating the notion that fat is synonymous with unhealthy. There is no middle ground. We are so rarely given the breathing room to simply ***be***.

Just like magic, we aren't allowed to exist outside of the confines the world has approved for us.

But there *is* magic in fat people, especially in the face of the constant pressure of other people's judgments. Despite being told, over and over again, that we are both too much and not enough—despite living in a world that was designed without us in mind, and sometimes even *in spite of us*—***we are here***. We are resilient, we are multi-dimensional, we are beautiful, we are flawed, we are something extraordinary to behold. We are magicians, and we are also the magic.

Fat is not a bad word. Fat people are not a disease. We are escaping from the shackles of judgment and oppression before your very eyes. We are the rabbits pulled out of a hat. We are the dramatic flourishes of the magician's capes. We are the beautiful assistant sawed in half and then magically put back together again, still whole, still fat. We are *exactly* the card you were thinking of.

Despite being told over and over, by everyone around us, that we are not deserving of respect, or care, or protection, or love, so many of us are realizing the same thing—*Abraca-DAMN, it's such sweet magic being fat.*

Works Cited

Crowe, Kelly. "Are Food Politics Defeating Canada's Healthy Eating Strategy?" *CBC News*, 20 July 2019, https://www.cbc.ca/news/health/front-of-package-label-marketing-unhealthy-food-kids-health-canada-lobby-food-industry-1.5218783.

Hajizadeh Mohammad, M. Karen Campbell, and Sisira Sarma. "Socioeconomic Inequalities in Adult Obesity Risk in Canada: Trends and Decomposition Analyses." *European Journal of Health Economics*, vol. 15, no. 2, 2014, pp. 203–21.

Scott, Michelle V. "Fat Privilege: Revelations of a Medium Fat Regarding the Fat Spectrum." *Medium*, 14 August 2019, https://medium.com/@michellevscott/fat-privilege-revelations-of-a-medium-fat-regarding-the-fat-spectrum-ec70dc908336. Accessed 9 May 2021.

Tarasuk Valerie, and Andy Mitchell. *Household Food Insecurity in Canada, 2017–2018*. Research to Identify Policy Options to Reduce Food Insecurity (PROOF), 2020.

Wharton, Sean, et al. "Obesity in Adults: A Clinical Practice Guideline." *Canadian Medical Association Journal*, vol. 192, no. 31, 2020, pp. E875-E891, https://www.cmaj.ca/content/cmaj/192/31/E875.full.pdf. Accessed 5 May 2021.

Yummy Body Types

Leslie Walters

Bodies are often compared to food or objects to describe their shapes. This image offers samples of the "Ice Cream Cone" shape that I feel describes my body. The possibilities are endless!

Afterword

May Friedman

Introduction

It's a strange time to be fat in Canada. The world is increasingly burning, fuelled by ecological disasters. We live, for those of us who are settlers, on stolen land, complicit in the pillage of Indigenous territory. As I write, the pandemic rages, fuelled by impotent policy makers and a denial of the impacts of poverty, racism, and other disenfranchisements that lead to heightened diagnoses and deaths. We live in a Canada that is held in the grip of the obesity witch hunt, which demonizes large bodies and, in the context of socialized medicine, views them as both social and economic threats. All of this occurs against the backdrop of heightened violence against Black and Indigenous people and people of colour, many of whom are especially villainized by obesity discourses. These struggles are structural, political, but they also feel deeply, uniquely personal.

> *My body is weary. My "soft office,"*[1] *while deliciously nest-like, is letting my body down, letting everything droop and sag. My spine sinks into the pillows, bending from the weight of my head and my heavy thoughts. Many days I do not leave the house, despite berating my children to get outside. My life has become lean, stripped down to required tasks—working, eating, cleaning, child and elder care. On the one hand, I feel like I've never done less; at the same time, I've never been more exhausted and besieged. I find myself in the grip of both virus and virulence—pinned down by both the pandemic*

> *and its pernicious side effects of judgment, racism, fatphobia. When I escape my house to walk around my neighbourhood, I am not sure whether eyebrows are raised in response to my large body or my large family, both seemingly in violation of "appropriate" size. I amble around the block, try to find hope in the newest blooming things or the weak spring sunshine, and return back to my nest of pillows.*

It's a strange time to write about being fat in Canada. Even as our fat bodies are reviled, there is a burgeoning fat studies movement, a growing fat activism. Rooted in the weird bifurcations of Canadian culture, *Fat Studies in Canada* lives in the margins of an imperfect and uncertain Canadianness. This book cannot possibly engage with the breadth of Canadian fat experiences. The settler project now known as Canada spans enormous geographic and cultural variation; likewise, our experiences of corpulence are entangled with enormous variegation. Nonetheless, the authors of this volume begin to explore some of the nuances that come with particular experiences of living large in this space.

Strong? and Free?

The colonial nation that we have come to know as "Canada" is vast. Its landscapes span oceans and mountains, prairies and arctic tundra. Under the care of Indigenous peoples, this land flourished and now, in its (post?) colonial manifestations, it labours under the impacts of capitalism, corporatization, environmental degradation, and other ugliness that speak to the tensions between the land, in its purity, and the overwhelming soiling of that land. Canada's inhabitants experience a similar tension, between the beautiful innocence of the bodies we are born with, in all their diverse manifestations, and the toxic messaging that is overlaid on those bodies. This book explores the intersections between the land, the people, and the messaging, using a range of approaches to investigate the unique experiences of fat in Canada.

Of course, this grandiose claim cannot possibly be truly fulfilled; fat is an experience with infinite intersections and complexities. Comparing the experiences of a fat person in Nunavut with that of someone in southern Ontario might be deeply inconsistent; the variations of sexual and gender identities, age, race, family status, and dis/ability, as well as the infinite multiplicities of other experiences, inform and alter fat experiences. While this book aims to encapsulate some of the unique tensions borne of fatness in the Canadian landscape, it does so through an imperfect and incomplete triangulation of experiences. This collection doesn't claim to convey the full range of fat Canadian experiences; rather, *Fat Studies in Canada* hopes to begin to dissect some of the key themes and congruities of fat in the northern half of Turtle Island. As we close this volume, I want to consider what we mean by these key terms: What and who do we mean by "fat"? And what can we really say or understand about "Canada"?

What Do We Mean by Fat? What Do We Mean by "Canada"?

As this book amply displays, we mean lots of different things when we talk about fat. We use *fat* to escape from the tyranny of *obesity* and *overweight*, to reclaim a reviled word and use it for our own purposes. We mean the viscous substance under our skin, in our chubby rolls, but also our complicated fat thinking. Thinking and writing about fat lets us expose indignities, question common sense, confront oppression and marginalization.

Talking about fatness in Canada exposes a different and unique challenge, borne of the extent to which "Canadianness" itself is profoundly difficult to circumscribe. Canadian culture is an amalgam, an alchemy of different influences and experiences. While the "multiculturalism" for which Canada is often renowned in the global imaginary is often simply a thin veneer of gentility over pernicious racism, Canada is the product of many different waves of immigration and conquest, from a range of different places of origin. Conquest is a deep part of this nation's story, the story of violence and greed against the land's original peoples and the quashing of Indigenous cultures, the primacy of particular European settler cultures, and the overwhelming cultural impact of the United States. All of these different pieces play into an uneasy and difficult description of Canadianness. If we understand Canada as a country of conquest, perhaps the specific degradations aimed at fat bodies become easier to understand, part of the framing of our "glowing hearts"?

When it comes to fat scholarship, as a discipline, fat studies is popularly understood to have launched with the inception of two 2009 collections: *The Fat Studies Reader*, published in the United States, and *Fat Studies in the UK*. These two specific collections as a fat studies origin story are deeply relevant to the present volume. US and UK approaches to fat architect an orientation to fat studies that draws on specific cultural influences that are deeply embedded in Canadian nation making. While "Canada" and "Canadianness" are dynamic and messy concepts, there's no question that the dual influences of commonwealth Britain and the cultural onslaught of the United States have huge impacts on the Canadian nation. How can we reconsider fat studies in the uniquely Canadian context outside of the waves of culture that come from the UK and the US, and in a context responding to many other influences beyond? In part, we cannot—we are an intersectional nation, in part, in our engagement with popular culture from outside our (settler) borders. Many chapters in this collection thus take up cultural artifacts that are not especially Canadian but that engage themes relevant to Canadians. Such analyses reveal the porousness of our colonial borders, the ways that our experiences of being in and on this land are not easily contained by the project of statehood.

How Do We Think about Fat in Canada?

While the Canadian imaginary is not easily defined, we are often understood in the context of *less:* smaller, blander, quieter. As Mordechai Richler famously noted, "The sour truth is that just about everybody outside of Canada finds us boring. Immensely boring" (quoted in Hart 202). Despite our standing as an immense nation, we are a country of people who are implicitly expected to be small. How then, can we contextualize the impact of living large in a muted country, one that views excess as dangerous and disgusting? How do we explain the impacts of our multiple, intersected, collaborative, and messy experiences of living fat in Canada?

Many of the constraints to fatness are uniquely bound up with the value systems of this settler nation. A neoliberal focus on independence and self-reliance bolsters the Canadian project and is deployed against our unruly bodies. The bizarre celebration of "multiculturalism" repackaged as a new form of monoculture (think Barbies in slightly different hues) upholds the normativity of the Canadian project. The foregrounding of nice and bland Canadian behaviours is at odds with the flamboyant excesses of fat. Simply put, there are fundamental tensions between fat and Canada.

Charlene Elliot writes that "obese individuals are implicitly and explicitly framed as 'less equal' citizens, and the conspicuous body is read as not merely the sign of moral failure, but the failure of personal responsibility as well" (135). She adds: "This is the body of the lesser citizen, the one that explicitly cries out to be controlled because it has shown that autonomy has led to poor choices" (140). To be fat in Canada is to fail at colonization, to fail at success, to fail at whiteness and the type of bootstrapping rhetoric that characterized neoliberal modernist capitalism. Who are our default Canadians? Mounties, slim men on muscular horses with tall hats accentuating their long leanness, the poison of their role in policing hidden in a cute costume? Anne of Green Gables, eternally thin, set up (as explored in this volume) in perpetual contrast to her less intelligent and less regulated buxom best friend? Cartoon Indigeneity, represented in the trope of the noble savage, wiry and sly, living off the land?

Of course, these caricatures do not resemble the actual body of the nation. Our population is overwhelmingly rotund, with over a third falling into the poorly defined BMI category of overweight and a further third of us stoutly tipping into the absurd category of "obesity." In body, as in so many things, there is a radical disconnect between Canada as it is imagined and "Canadians" as we are. Despite considerable whitewashing, we come in a range of hues. Despite the excessive political attention paid toward our dual "founding" languages and cultures, we speak an endless array of languages and dialects. Our excessive nation is inadequate to contain our multitudes, our intersections.

Where Do We Go from Here?

As the pandemic numbers rise and we hunker down at home, fat bodies are being treated with increased virulence. The COVID-19 pandemic has led to the abuse and intolerance of fat, between memes bemoaning the weight increase of sedentary life, to proto-eugenic discourses that want to ensure fat bodies are kept off of ventilators in dire circumstances. Our bodies are positioned as threats, as bombs waiting to go off. Once again, the political becomes acutely personal:

> *Ironically, the amplification of obesity as disease has led to vaccinations for fatties. It's a peculiar moment to lean into the demonization of fatness—to choose to uphold the myth of fat failure in order to break free of COVID prison.*
>
> *This morning I biked to the hospital to get my vaccine. In the midst of a wretchedly slow vaccine rollout, I received multiple emails from fat community folks letting me know that my fat body could be eligible because I am perceived as living at high risk. I found myself in the grip of a strange introspective loop: Am I fat enough? In the absence of the scale, I am guessing at my BMI—and it feels like a strange betrayal to even enter the numbers that yield that calculation, knowing, as I do, how flawed and oppressive a measure it is. Am I perpetuating myths of fat failure by agreeing that my body is broken? Is my getting the vaccine for the "reason" of obesity just upholding an oppressive medical system? Am I getting away with something? Am I supporting injustice? Am I taking up space to which I am not entitled?*
>
> *As I found myself asking that last question, the source of my discomfort came into focus: as a fat, racialized woman, I find it extremely uncomfortable to take up space. Surrounded by critiques of the ways that my body is both socially and economically threatening, choosing to lean into fatness and show up for my needle feels like the equivalent of stretching out on the subway. For all my*

> *fat politics, I am only permitted to exist if I minimize the impact of my existence.*

This psychic discomfort is even more prevalent in the Canadian context, where genteel, unremarkable, and white existence is exalted. This book stands in opposition to this context; it seeks instead to resist normative tropes and populate uncertain and complex spaces. Taking up themes of policy and process, such as in analyses of Obesity Canada guidelines, looking at the particular impacts of fat on Indigenous and racialized folks, and thinking through the complicated alchemy of culture and bodies swirling through space, this book avoids comprehensive conclusions and tidy endings. Most of all, this book seeks, like our bumpy bodies, to disrupt the sleek lines of certainty.

The neoliberal contract asks us to be self-reliant and sleek. Especially in these plague-ridden times, personal responsibility is increasingly valorized with institutional and structural support oddly minimized. This trope is epitomized in discussions of ventilator priorities that make clear that fat people, impaired by their own perceived poor choices, will be lowest on the list. It's impossible to ignore that the same logic that allows me faster access to a vaccine, by pointing to my body as simultaneously excessive and inadequate, is also going to deny my care, potentially contribute to my death, in the event that I do fall ill. If the Canadian state demands that I look out for myself, how on earth could I be expected to avoid a vaccine at the earliest moment it's offered, even if in getting vaccinated early I am contributing to the same rhetoric that I seek, in word and deed, to abolish?

Conclusions (for Now)

This book explores fat in Canada from myriad perspectives. Eva Mackey writes, "The project of Canadian nation-building is an extremely contradictory, conflicted, contested and incomplete process" (18). We draw upon this ambiguous and contested Canada to ask how our policies and practices tip toward the presumed default Canadian, erasing and abusing our lived realities through punishing and judgmental tropes and practices.

Importantly, this volume seeks to prioritize new ways of seeing and understanding, not only by shifting the gaze toward a more nuanced and compassionate exploration of fat in Canada but also by allowing for engagements that truly allow us to see with different eyes. Drawing from a range of personal experiences and including academic writing, poetry and prose, and other radical engagements, this book presents a collective story of a multiplicity of experience found in the fat north.

Thinking through fat Canada from many angles, including poetry, prose, and art, deepens and twists our understandings beyond the skinny limits of what is considered scholarship, the thin tip of what is popularly considered to be research. In so doing, we aim to destabilize knowledge itself by considering what more we might know if we opened ourselves up to our not-knowing, to a refreshed and constantly evolving experience of truth and story. Fat in Canada asks us to swim in the many seas of our understanding, to take our saltwater flesh and wrap it in our honeyed words as an antidote to the despair that plagues us. Sick of being misunderstood, abused, mythologized, or maligned, we aim instead just to exist, to live in our capacious flesh without debate.

Notes

1 "Soft office," as explained in a personal communication with disability scholar Kayla Besse, refers to the way we may shift our understandings of professional environments. We work in a range of spaces, and our productivity isn't contingent on our sleek contained spaces—rather, like our bodies themselves, our "offices" may need a range of adaptations and arrangements to support our optimal functioning. In my case, my workspace is my living room sofa, with pillows added or deleted depending on the task and my embodied experiences from day to day.

Works Cited

Besse, Kayla. "Soft Office." Personal communication, 26 April 2021.

Elliot, Charlene D. "Big Persons, Small Voices: On Governance, Obesity, and the Narrative of the Failed Citizen." *Journal of Canadian Studies,* vol. 41, no. 3, 2007, pp. 134–49.

Hart, Michael. "Of Friends, Interests, Crowbars, and Marriage Vows in Canada-United States Trade Relations." *Images of Canadianness: Visions on Canada's Politics, Culture, Economics*, edited by Leon d'Haenens, University of Ottawa Press, 1998, pp. 199–220.

Mackey, Eva. *The House of Difference: Cultural Politics and National Identity in Canada,* University of Toronto Press, 2002.

Contributors

Faith Adodo is a PhD candidate in the gender, feminist, and women's studies program at York University. She also holds a BA (honours) in law and society, a double major in sociology, a BA in political science, and MA in critical disability studies. Her research focuses on the controlling and policing of women's bodies to maintain mail dominance, using women from the Benin Kingdom as a case study to expose the complex construction of gender and its impact on women. She is also interested in highlighting the association of fatness with wealth in the Nigerian context.

Emily Allan is a creative non-fiction writer whose work poetically explores fat liberation as an intersection of feminist politics. Born and raised on a little island off of Vancouver, she is now based in Toronto where she runs a small writing group, affectionately named Snack Club. Her writing has appeared in *Understorey Magazine, The Fat Zine* blog, and Caitlin Press's *BIG: Stories about Life in Plus Sized Bodies*, a spring 2020 BC bestseller. You can find her on Twitter at @emilynallan.

Jill Andrew, PhD (she/her), is a Black feminist fat activist among many things. She is a child and youth worker, educator, equity advisor, and a body justice advocate. Her PhD dissertation, *"Put Together" Black Women's Body Stories in Toronto: (Ad)dressing Identity and the Threads that Bind*, explored the "trifecta" of anti-Black racism, sexism, and fat hatred experienced by Black women and their accommodation and resistance of dominant body ideals through fashion and dress, activism, self-valuation, and social interactions. Jill is co-editor of both *Body Stories: In and Out and With and Through Fat* and *Black Sisterhoods: Paradigms and Praxis*, co-founder of Body Confidence Canada, and the Ontario NDP member of provincial Parliament (MPP) for Toronto—St. Paul's. She was recently featured in the documentary *Body Politics*, part of Hot Docs *Citizen Minutes* series. @JillsLastWord

Kirthan Aujlay is a death doula and grief educator living in downtown Toronto. She runs the death education account @that_goodnight on Instagram. As a biracial and bisexual fat femme, Kirthan often enjoys exploring the intersection of sexuality and pop culture in her writing. Her work has appeared on the platform *Refinery29*, in *Autostraddle*, and in the blog *shedoesthecity*.

Ramanpreet A. Bahra is a PhD student in the sociology department at York University, Ontario, Canada. Her research concentrates on social theory, fat studies, and disability studies. Following new materialism and affect studies, her research interrogates the intersections of fatness, race, disability, and gender to offer alternative perspectives on the notion of the body and embodiment. In particular, the nexus of affect and fatness is interrogated to better understand how fat, racialized bodies experience this paradoxical state of life-in-death through the operationalization of the discourse of personhood and its inclusionary-exclusionary politics. Additionally, she is exploring the ways in which a feminist pedagogical practice rooted in social justice principles, research-creation, and emotionality can challenge the neoliberal mandates of post-secondary education, and thus offer new mappings and methods for learning in and through the collective body.

Rohini Bannerjee (she/her) born and raised in Dartmouth, Nova Scotia, Canada, daughter of immigrants from Himachal Pradesh, India, is Associate Vice-President, Diversity Excellence, and a professor of French and francophone studies in the Department of Languages and Cultures at Saint Mary's University, Halifax, Canada.

Sookie Bardwell (she/her/hers + they/them/theirs) is far too fat, far too loud, and far too fed up with all the ways that this colonial nightmare insists that most of us are "far too" and "not enough" of whoever or whatever we are to be safe in our own bodies. They are a "formally credentialled" (MA, gender studies and feminist research, McMaster; OCT Certified Teacher; Opt BC Certified Sex + Relationship Educator) white settler citizen invested in the work of decolonization, racial justice, radical education for social change, and other intersecting efforts to challenge and dismantle all the institutions that seek to separate us from ourselves, one another, and the rest of the living things on this planet. She is also a working-class, fat, queer, genderqueer, casual/lumberjane femme living with invisible disability. Their work is informed by all of these ways in which they move through the world. She believes that everyone deserves to be treated like a person (a.k.a. with respect) and that everyBODY is valid and valuable by virtue of being an alive creature here in the world. They are honoured to work in service of this belief as founder of shamefree.ca; co-founder of Challenge Accepted Learning Collective and chublove.ca; co-editor of the Far Too Fat zine (@fartoofatzine); and in providing Body Liberation-centred support and psychoeducation for other folks navigating the impaces of anti-fat violence in their body/minds and lives.

S. Bear Bergman is the author of nine books (*Special Topics in Being Human*, most recently, from Arsenal Pulp Press in 2021), founder of Flamingo Rampant press, and frequent consultant in equity and inclusion to business and government. Bear began his work in equity at the age of 15, as a founding member of the first ever Gay/Straight Alliance, and has continued to help organizations and institutions move further along the pathways to justice ever since. These days, Bear spends his time making trans cultural competency interventions however he can and trying to avoid stepping on his children's Lego.

Yolanda Bonnell (she/they) is a bi/queer 2 Spirit Anishinaabe-Ojibwe, South Asian mixed performer, playwright, and multidisciplinary creator/educator. Her play *bug* was nominated for four Dora awards, while the published version was shortlisted for a Governor General Literary Award. Yolanda was also the first Indigenous artist recipient of the Jayu Arts for Human Rights Award for her work and won the PGC Tom Hendry Drama Award for her play *My Sister's Rage*. Yolanda has taught/facilitated at schools like York University and Sheridan College and proudly bases her practice in land-based creation, drawing on energy and inspiration from the earth and her ancestors.

Emily Bruusgaard (she/they) is a sessional instructor in the department of English at Trent University, currently at work on a larger project on the relationship between Canadian women's writing, domestic needlework, and the construction of white, middle-class femininity. When not teaching or writing, they are out hiking along Lake Ontario with their two dogs, usually with tea in hand.

Joanna Carson studied creative writing at Dalhousie University and now works as a content operations manager at Rakuten Kobo Inc. While she mostly writes poetry, since 2018, she has also been working on a YA novel about two fat best friends. She lives in Toronto where she spends her time hyper-fixating on new hobbies and cuddling her two cats.

Jinwen Chen is a social geographer and a current PhD candidate at the Flinders University. She is interested in social research with an applied and critical focus. Alongside academic publications, she has published a number of collaborative reports on food insecurity, international volunteering, and philanthropy.

Katie Cook (they/them) holds a PhD in community psychology from Wilfrid Laurier University in Waterloo, Ontario. Katie's work uses feminist affect theory to examine how marginalized—e.g., disabled, racialized, fat, queer—bodies are constructed and Othered in various social contexts.

Lucas Crawford is Canada Research Chair of Transgender Creativity and Mental Health at the University of Alberta

(Augustana Faculty). Crawford is the author of *Transgender Architectonics: The Shape of Change in Modern Space* (Routledge 2016), as well as four books of poetry. Crawford's latest, *Muster Points*, is forthcoming with University of Calgary Press.

Francine Cunningham is an award-winning Indigenous writer, artist, and educator. Her debut book of poems *On/Me* (Caitlin Press) was nominated for a 2020 BC and Yukon Book Prize, a 2020 Indigenous Voices Award, and the 2020 Vancouver Book Award. You can find out more about her at www.francinecunningham.ca.

Calla Evans (she/her) is a fat, queer, disabled, white settler living on the stolen lands of the xʷməθkwəy̓əm (Musqueam), Skwxwú7mesh (Squamish), and səl̓ilwətaʔɬ/Selilwitulh (Tsleil-Waututh) peoples, colonially known as Vancouver, BC. She is an image-maker, visual storyteller, digital problem solver, fat activist, and ex-academic. Much of her practice explores the material conditions of fatness in so called "Canada" as well as digital fat identity construction and performance. Calla currently works as a digital storytelling facilitator at Re•Vision: The Centre for Art & Social Justice. She is also the general manager of the Open Access Foundation for Art & Culture, a disability-justice-situated organization that centres agency, self-determination, and disability-informed futures.

May Friedman works as a faculty member at Toronto Metropolitan University. May's research looks at unstable identities, including bodies that do not conform to normative tropes of race, ethnicity, ability, size, beauty, and health. Most recently, much of May's research has focused on intersectional approaches to fat studies considering the multiple and fluid experiences of both fat oppression and fat activism. Drawing on a range of arts-based methods, including digital storytelling as well as analyses of treasured garments, May has explored meaning making and representation in relation to embodiment and experience.

Jacqui Gingras, PhD is an associate professor in the Department of Sociology at Toronto Metropolitan University in T'karonto,

Ontario, Canada. Her research explores social health movements, fat studies, radical democratic pedagogies, and the decolonization of health professions within the entanglements of colonial neoliberal economics and intersectional feminisms. She has published in the *Fat Studies Journal*, the *Journal of Sociology*, and *Critical Public Health*. She is an associate member of the communication and culture graduate program, a joint program between Toronto Metropolitan and York University, where she and colleague May Friedman are teaching a graduate course on fat studies. She is the founding editor of the *Journal of Critical Dietetics*, an open-access, peer-reviewed journal.

Kelsey Ioannoni, PhD, is a fat solo mom and sociologist based out of Toronto, Canada. Her research focuses on the power dynamics between primary care physicians and patients (fat women), and how their conceptualizations of health—based on the BMI—negatively affects the lives of fat Canadian women. Further, she is interested in exploring the way fat women navigate fertility and reproductive care in Ontario.

Karleen Pendleton Jiménez is a mixed Chicana/white writer, professor, and butch who teaches education, gender, and social justice at Trent University. She focuses on creative writing, queer feminisms, and scandal in education. Other selected butch writings include "A Beautiful Creature" (*Persistence*, 2011), "The Weight of Queerness: Reflections on a Digital Storytelling Project" (*Studies in Canadian Literature*, 2021), her memoir *How to Get a Girl Pregnant*, and the short film *The Butch and the Baby Daddy*.

Audrey Laurin is an art history PhD student at Université du Québec à Montréal. Her thesis explores critical and aesthetics discourses on women's art practice interrogating feminine beauty representations since the 1990s. She published "Le capital érotique et les plaisirs de la chair : Le cas des nus monumentaux de Jenny Saville" in *Recherches féminites* in 2019 and an essay called "Le génie au féminin: Le personnage public de Tracey Emin et la critique d'art" in *Loin des yeux, près du corps: Femmes, théorie, creation*, edited by Thérèse St-Gelais, in 2012.

Mars, a nonbinary, fat, queer, disabled, Latinx creator, works with mixed media arts and dabbles in creative writing. For this collection, they have chosen a group of personal poems and illustrations that represent some of their experiences as a fat person growing up in Ontario. The illustrations are mixed traditional and digital media.

Gin Marshall (they/he) is a Toronto-based PhD student in the social work program at York University, studying queer and trans cultural histories through an anti-racist, decolonial, and feminist lens. Gin's work draws on their activist background and is also grounded in twenty years of experience in information and database technology. Gin is student co-chair of the Sex Gen Committee and represents Sex Gen on the President's Advisory Council on Equity, Diversity & Inclusion. After organizing the Canadian Professional Association for Transgender Health (CPATH) National Conference in 2019, Gin served on the CPATH Board of Directors as treasurer from 2020 to 2022. In their spare time, Gin can be found creating mosaics, playing tennis, writing, and enjoying hiking and exploring with beloveds and their daughter Kate and son-in-love Mark.

Deborah McPhail is an associate professor in community health sciences at the University of Manitoba. Her research focuses on the lived realities of social oppressions and fatness, particularly within clinical spaces and institutional health care systems.

Born in Osu, Ghana, **Susie Mensah** has been fat her whole life. She adamantly believes that she is in this body for a reason and has found ways to rejoice and be glad in it. She is invested in creating and reliving memories of being and emotion. As a writer, model, social worker, and artist of unlimited thought, Susie is passionate about the physic and spiritual aspects of human experience.

Lauren Munro is a PhD candidate in the community psychology program at Wilfrid Laurier University, whose personal and professional life is driven by a commitment to social justice. She is a fat activist, artist, and writer who strongly believes in the importance of integrating academia and grassroots activism to create projects that push boundaries and challenge the status quo. Lauren has been involved in projects that cut across a variety of disciplines including fat studies, mad studies, 2SLGBTQ+ health, sexual health and reproductive justice, and disability justice. At the time of publication, she is a limited-term faculty member in the School of Disability Studies at Toronto Metropolitan University and also holds an adjunct appointment at the Institute for Disability and Rehabilitation Research in the Faculty of Social Science and Humanities at Ontario Tech University.

Derek Newman-Stille MA, PhD ABD (they/them) is a disabled, queer, nonbinary writer, editor, academic, activist, and artist. They are completing their PhD at the Frost Centre for Canadian Studies, examining the representation of disability in Canadian speculative fiction. Derek is the eight-time Prix Aurora Award–winning creator of the digital humanities hub Speculating Canada (www.speculatingcanada.ca) and the associated radio show. They are the editor of three recently published collections: *Whispers Between Fairies* (Renaissance Press, 2020), *We Shall Be Monsters* (Renaissance Press, 2019), and *Over the Rainbow: Folk and Fairy Tales from the Margins* (Exile, 2019).

Jake Pyne is an assistant professor in the School of Social Work at York University. His current work focuses on the intersection of autistic and trans communities.

Jen Rinaldi is an associate professor in legal studies at Ontario Tech University. Her last project involved working in partnership with Rainbow Health Ontario to create digital stories about queer (cis and trans) women's experiences of weight stigma.

Bidushy Sadika is a PhD candidate in social psychology with a specialization in migration and ethnic relations at Western University, Canada. Her research interests include intersectionality and feminist theories, gender roles and stereotypes, body image, and the lived experiences of racialized women, immigrants, newcomers, and refugees. She has published peer-reviewed articles on the experiences and media representations of women, LGBTQ2S+ individuals, and persons with disabilities. Currently, she conducts research and is involved in community- and government-based projects on immigration and settlement and the intersections between immigration status, gender, race, ethnicity, and culture. Bidushy can be contacted at bsadika@uwo.ca.

Ameema Saeed (@ameemabackwards) is a storyteller, an avid bookworm, and a curator of very specific playlists, customized book recommendations, and cool earrings. She's currently the books editor for *shedoesthecity*. She writes about books, unruly bodies, and her lived experiences, and she hopes to write your next favourite book one day. When she's not reading books, she likes to talk about books (especially diverse books, and books by diverse authors) on her bookstagram: @readwithmeemz

Amanda (Ama) Scriver (@amascriver) is a freelance journalist and social media strategist best known for being fat, loud, and shouty on the internet. Ama's writing has appeared in *Refinery 29* as well as the *Toronto Star*, *THIS*, *Healthline*, and *Xtra*. They recently launched *High Low Brow*, their podcast dedicated to providing high-brow takes on low-brow culture, including pop culture and beyond. Ama lives in Toronto with their partner, River, and their adorable dog, Ocean.

Fady Shanouda (he/him) is a critical disability studies scholar whose contributions lie at the theoretical and pedagogical intersections of disability, mad, and fat studies and include socio-historical examinations that surface the interconnections of colonialism, racism, ableism, saneism, and fatphobia. He is an assistant professor at the Feminist Institute of Social Transformation at Carleton University, where he conducts his work diversely positioned as a queer, disabled, fat, POC immigrant and settler, living, working, and creating on the ancestral and traditional territories of the Algonquin nation.

j wallace skelton is an assistant professor of queer studies in education at the University of Regina. j is committed to a practice of community ethics, of researching within communities j is a part of, in ways that serve communities rather than extract from them. Much of j's research explores co-research and supporting gender independent and nonbinary and trans (GIANT) children and youth.

John-James Stranz graduated from Toronto Metropolitan University with a BA in sociology and is currently completing his master's degree in sociology and legal studies at the University of Waterloo. His master's research on social policy involves a critical focus on harm reduction and the social determinants of health in Ontario.

Allison Taylor (she/her) is a SSHRC Postdoctoral Fellow at Re•Vision: The Centre for Art and Social Justice at the University of Guelph. She holds a PhD in gender, feminist, and women's studies from York University. Her current research uses arts-based methods to examine how intersecting ableism and anti-fatness constitute barriers to public resources, services, and spaces for people of marginalized genders in Ontario. Allison is also working on creating a digital archive and a pedagogical module for Re•Vision on the subject of fat activist art. Her work can be found in many places, including *Fat Studies: An Interdisciplinary Journal of Body Weight and Society*, the *Journal of Lesbian Studies*, *Psychology & Sexuality*, and the *Routledge International Handbook of Fat Studies*.

Tracy Tidgwell works in the folds of process and connection to explore everyday experience, the body, knowledge, and their mysteries. She draws on ritual, land epistemologies, movement(s), collaboration, hospitality, queerness, and accessibility to listen, learn, and relate, and works in performance, sound, writing, facilitation, curation, film, clay, and video. Tracy is co-editor of *The Future Is Fat*, a book of scholarly and artistic interventions that reimagine understandings of time to allow for new expressions of fat experience; co-creator of the *Fat Liberation Peoples History*, a community oral history project; a member of Fat Rose, an art and activism incubator; a member of the Visioning Connective with

FAR Feminist Art Retreat; and serves on the Board of Directors at Tangled Art + Disability Gallery. Until their retirement in 2004, she was a member of the fat art and performance collective Pretty Porky and Pissed Off. Tracy also works as the producer and project manager for *Hemispheric Encounters: Developing Transborder Research-Creation Practices* in the School of the Arts, Media, Performance & Design at York University.

Leslie Walters (she/her/they/them) has a specialized BFA in painting and drawing from York University. Leslie has curated and participated in art shows, contributed to zines and websites, published a colouring book, been a DJ and radio host, and made music in bands. Leslie is currently a freelance illustrator, graphic designer, and enjoys face painting. She is the creator, blogger, and owner of Learning-curvy.com. Other interests include autism acceptance, unschooling, food forests, and guerrilla gardening.

Fardosa Warsame is a PhD candidate in the gender, feminist, and women's studies program at York University. She also holds a BA (honours) in psychology and MA in critical disability studies. Her research focuses on the association between mental health and immigration/refugee policies, how fatness is perceived in the Somali community, and anti-Black racism in union spaces.